CORNERSTONE
BIBLICAL
COMMENTARY

CORNERSTONE BIBLICAL COMMENTARY

Ezekiel

David L. Thompson

Daniel

Eugene Carpenter

GENERAL EDITOR
Philip W. Comfort

featuring the text of the
NEW LIVING TRANSLATION

TYNDALE HOUSE PUBLISHERS CAROL STREAM, ILLINOIS

Cornerstone Biblical Commentary, Volume 9

Visit Tyndale online at tyndale.com and newlivingtranslation.com.

Designed by Luke Daab and Timothy R. Botts.

Library of Congress Cataloging-in-Publication Data

Cornerstone biblical commentary.
p. cm.
Includes bibliographical references and index.
ISBN-13: 978-0-8423-3435-8 (hc : alk. paper)
1. Bible—Commentaries. I. Thompson, David L. II. Carpenter, Eugene
BS491.3.C67 2006
220.7′7—dc22 2005026928

Printed in the United States of America

30 29 28 27 26 25 24
8 7 6 5 4 3 2

CONTENTS

CONTRIBUTORS TO VOLUME 9

Ezekiel: David L. Thompson
AB, Indiana Wesleyan University;
BD, ThM, Asbury Theological Seminary;
PhD, The Johns Hopkins University;
F. M. and Ada Thompson Professor of Biblical Studies, Asbury Seminary.

Daniel: Eugene Carpenter
BA, Bethel College;
MDiv, Associated Mennonite Biblical Seminary;
PhD, Fuller Theological Seminary;
Scholar in Residence and Professor of Old Testament, Hebrew, and Biblical Theology, Bethel College, IN.

GENERAL EDITOR'S PREFACE

The *Cornerstone Biblical Commentary* is based on the second edition of the New Living Translation (2007). Nearly 100 scholars from various church backgrounds and from several countries (United States, Canada, England, and Australia) participated in the creation of the NLT. Many of these same scholars are contributors to this commentary series. All the commentators, whether participants in the NLT or not, believe that the Bible is God's inspired word and have a desire to make God's word clear and accessible to his people.

This Bible commentary is the natural extension of our vision for the New Living Translation, which we believe is both exegetically accurate and idiomatically powerful. The NLT attempts to communicate God's inspired word in a lucid English translation of the original languages so that English readers can understand and appreciate the thought of the original writers. In the same way, the *Cornerstone Biblical Commentary* aims at helping teachers, pastors, students, and laypeople understand every thought contained in the Bible. As such, the commentary focuses first on the words of Scripture, then on the theological truths of Scripture—inasmuch as the words express the truths.

The commentary itself has been structured in such a way as to help readers get at the meaning of Scripture, passage by passage, through the entire Bible. Each Bible book is prefaced by a substantial book introduction that gives general historical background important for understanding. Then the reader is taken through the Bible text, passage by passage, starting with the New Living Translation text printed in full. This is followed by a section called "Notes," wherein the commentator helps the reader understand the Hebrew or Greek behind the English of the NLT, interacts with other scholars on important interpretive issues, and points the reader to significant textual and contextual matters. The "Notes" are followed by the "Commentary," wherein each scholar presents a lucid interpretation of the passage, giving special attention to context and major theological themes.

The commentators represent a wide spectrum of theological positions within the evangelical community. We believe this is good because it reflects the rich variety in Christ's church. All the commentators uphold the authority of God's word and believe it is essential to heed the old adage: "Wholly apply yourself to the Scriptures and apply them wholly to you." May this commentary help you know the truths of Scripture, and may this knowledge help you "grow in your knowledge of God and Jesus our Lord" (2 Pet 1:2, NLT).

Philip W. Comfort
General Editor

ABBREVIATIONS

GENERAL ABBREVIATIONS

b.	Babylonian Gemara
bar.	baraita
c.	*circa*, around, approximately
cf.	*confer*, compare
ch, chs	chapter, chapters
contra	in contrast to
DSS	Dead Sea Scrolls
ed.	edition, editor
e.g.	*exempli gratia*, for example
et al.	*et alli*, and others
fem.	feminine
ff	following (verses, pages)
fl.	flourished
Gr.	Greek
Heb.	Hebrew
ibid.	*ibidem*, in the same place
i.e.	*id est*, the same
in loc.	*in loco*, in the place cited
lit.	literally
LXX	Septuagint
M	Majority Text
m.	Mishnah
masc.	masculine
mg	margin
ms	manuscript
mss	manuscripts
MT	Masoretic Text
n.d.	no date
neut.	neuter
no.	number
NT	New Testament
OL	Old Latin
OS	Old Syriac
OT	Old Testament
p., pp.	page, pages
pl.	plural
Q	Quelle ("Sayings" as Gospel source)
rev.	revision
sg.	singular
t.	Tosefta
TR	Textus Receptus
v., vv.	verse, verses
vid.	*videtur*, it seems
viz.	*videlicet*, namely
vol.	volume
y.	Jerusalem Gemara

ABBREVIATIONS FOR BIBLE TRANSLATIONS

ASV	American Standard Version
CEV	Contemporary English Version
ESV	English Standard Version
GW	God's Word
HCSB	Holman Christian Standard Bible
JB	Jerusalem Bible
KJV	King James Version
NAB	New American Bible
NASB	New American Standard Bible
NCV	New Century Version
NEB	New English Bible
NET	The NET Bible
NIV	New International Version
NIrV	New International Reader's Version
NJB	New Jerusalem Bible
NJPS	The New Jewish Publication Society Translation (*Tanakh*)
NKJV	New King James Version
NRSV	New Revised Standard Version
NLT	New Living Translation
REB	Revised English Bible
RSV	Revised Standard Version
TEV	Today's English Version
TLB	The Living Bible

ABBREVIATIONS FOR DICTIONARIES, LEXICONS, COLLECTIONS OF TEXTS, ORIGINAL LANGUAGE EDITIONS

ABD *Anchor Bible Dictionary* (6 vols., Freedman) [1992]

ANEP *The Ancient Near East in Pictures* (Pritchard) [1965]

ANET *Ancient Near Eastern Texts Relating to the Old Testament* (Pritchard) [1969]

BAGD *Greek-English Lexicon of the New Testament and Other Early Christian Literature*, 2nd ed. (Bauer, Arndt, Gingrich, Danker) [1979]

BDAG *Greek-English Lexicon of the New Testament and Other Early Christian Literature*, 3rd ed. (Bauer, Danker, Arndt, Gingrich) [2000]

BDB *A Hebrew and English Lexicon of the Old Testament* (Brown, Driver, Briggs) [1907]

BDF *A Greek Grammar of the New Testament and Other Early Christian Literature* (Blass, Debrunner, Funk) [1961]

BHS *Biblia Hebraica Stuttgartensia* (Elliger and Rudolph) [1983]

CAD *Assyrian Dictionary of the Oriental Institute of the University of Chicago* [1956]

COS *The Context of Scripture* (3 vols., Hallo and Younger) [1997–2002]

DBI *Dictionary of Biblical Imagery* (Ryken, Wilhoit, Longman) [1998]

DBT *Dictionary of Biblical Theology* (2nd ed., Leon-Dufour) [1972]

DCH *Dictionary of Classical Hebrew* (5 vols., D. Clines) [2000]

DLNTD *Dictionary of the Later New Testament and Its Development* (R. Martin, P. Davids) [1997]

DJD *Discoveries in the Judean Desert* [1955–]

DJG *Dictionary of Jesus and the Gospels* (Green, McKnight, Marshall) [1992]

DOTP *Dictionary of the Old Testament: Pentateuch* (T. Alexander, D.W. Baker) [2003]

DPL *Dictionary of Paul and His Letters* (Hawthorne, Martin, Reid) [1993]

DTIB *Dictionary of Theological Interpretation of the Bible* (Vanhoozer) [2005]

EDNT *Exegetical Dictionary of the New Testament* (3 vols., H. Balz, G. Schneider. ET) [1990–1993]

GKC *Gesenius' Hebrew Grammar* (Gesenius, Kautzsch, trans. Cowley) [1910]

HALOT *The Hebrew and Aramaic Lexicon of the Old Testament* (L. Koehler, W. Baumgartner, J. Stamm; trans. M. Richardson) [1994–1999]

IBD *Illustrated Bible Dictionary* (3 vols., Douglas, Wiseman) [1980]

IDB *The Interpreter's Dictionary of the Bible* (4 vols., Buttrick) [1962]

ISBE *International Standard Bible Encyclopedia* (4 vols., Bromiley) [1979–1988]

KBL *Lexicon in Veteris Testamenti libros* (Koehler, Baumgartner) [1958]

LCL Loeb Classical Library

L&N *Greek-English Lexicon of the New Testament: Based on Semantic Domains* (Louw and Nida) [1989]

LSJ *A Greek-English Lexicon* (9th ed., Liddell, Scott, Jones) [1996]

MM *The Vocabulary of the Greek New Testament* (Moulton and Milligan) [1930; 1997]

NA[26] *Novum Testamentum Graece* (26th ed., Nestle-Aland) [1979]

NA[27] *Novum Testamentum Graece* (27th ed., Nestle-Aland) [1993]

NBD *New Bible Dictionary* (2nd ed., Douglas, Hillyer) [1982]

NIDB *New International Dictionary of the Bible* (Douglas, Tenney) [1987]

NIDBA *New International Dictionary of Biblical Archaeology* (Blaiklock and Harrison) [1983]

NIDNTT *New International Dictionary of New Testament Theology* (4 vols., C. Brown) [1975–1985]

NIDOTTE *New International Dictionary of Old Testament Theology and Exegesis* (5 vols., W. A. VanGemeren) [1997]

PGM *Papyri graecae magicae: Die griechischen Zauberpapyri.* (Preisendanz) [1928]

PG *Patrologia Graecae* (J. P. Migne) [1857–1886]

TBD *Tyndale Bible Dictionary* (Elwell, Comfort) [2001]

TDNT *Theological Dictionary of the New Testament* (10 vols., Kittel, Friedrich; trans. Bromiley) [1964–1976]

TDOT *Theological Dictionary of the Old Testament* (15 vols., Botterweck, Ringgren; trans. Willis, Bromiley, Green) [1974–]

TLNT *Theological Lexicon of the New Testament* (3 vols., C. Spicq) [1994]

TLOT *Theological Lexicon of the Old Testament* (3 vols., E. Jenni) [1997]

TWOT *Theological Wordbook of the Old Testament* (2 vols., Harris, Archer) [1980]

UBS[3] *United Bible Societies' Greek New Testament* (3rd ed., Metzger et al.) [1975]

UBS[4] *United Bible Societies' Greek New Testament* (4th corrected ed., Metzger et al.) [1993]

WH *The New Testament in the Original Greek* (Westcott and Hort) [1882]

ABBREVIATIONS FOR BOOKS OF THE BIBLE

Old Testament

Gen	Genesis	Deut	Deuteronomy	1 Sam	1 Samuel
Exod	Exodus	Josh	Joshua	2 Sam	2 Samuel
Lev	Leviticus	Judg	Judges	1 Kgs	1 Kings
Num	Numbers	Ruth	Ruth	2 Kgs	2 Kings

1 Chr	1 Chronicles	Song	Song of Songs	Obad	Obadiah
2 Chr	2 Chronicles	Isa	Isaiah	Jonah	Jonah
Ezra	Ezra	Jer	Jeremiah	Mic	Micah
Neh	Nehemiah	Lam	Lamentations	Nah	Nahum
Esth	Esther	Ezek	Ezekiel	Hab	Habakkuk
Job	Job	Dan	Daniel	Zeph	Zephaniah
Ps, Pss	Psalm, Psalms	Hos	Hosea	Hag	Haggai
Prov	Proverbs	Joel	Joel	Zech	Zechariah
Eccl	Ecclesiastes	Amos	Amos	Mal	Malachi

New Testament

Matt	Matthew	Eph	Ephesians	Heb	Hebrews
Mark	Mark	Phil	Philippians	Jas	James
Luke	Luke	Col	Colossians	1 Pet	1 Peter
John	John	1 Thess	1 Thessalonians	2 Pet	2 Peter
Acts	Acts	2 Thess	2 Thessalonians	1 John	1 John
Rom	Romans	1 Tim	1 Timothy	2 John	2 John
1 Cor	1 Corinthians	2 Tim	2 Timothy	3 John	3 John
2 Cor	2 Corinthians	Titus	Titus	Jude	Jude
Gal	Galatians	Phlm	Philemon	Rev	Revelation

Deuterocanonical

Bar	Baruch	1–2 Esdr	1–2 Esdras	Ps 151	Psalm 151
Add Dan	Additions to Daniel	Add Esth	Additions to Esther	Sir	Sirach
Pr Azar	Prayer of Azariah	Ep Jer	Epistle of Jeremiah	Tob	Tobit
Bel	Bel and the Dragon	Jdt	Judith	Wis	Wisdom of Solomon
Sg Three	Song of the Three Children	1–2 Macc	1–2 Maccabees		
		3–4 Macc	3–4 Maccabees		
Sus	Susanna	Pr Man	Prayer of Manasseh		

MANUSCRIPTS AND LITERATURE FROM QUMRAN

Initial numerals followed by "Q" indicate particular caves at Qumran. For example, the notation 4Q267 indicates text 267 from cave 4 at Qumran. Further, 1QS 4:9-10 indicates column 4, lines 9-10 of the *Rule of the Community*; and 4Q166 1 ii 2 indicates fragment 1, column ii, line 2 of text 166 from cave 4. More examples of common abbreviations are listed below.

CD	Cairo Geniza copy of the *Damascus Document*	1QIsa^{b}	Isaiah copy ^{b}	4QLam^{a}	Lamentations
1QH	*Thanksgiving Hymns*	1QM	*War Scroll*	11QPs^{a}	Psalms
1QIsa^{a}	Isaiah copy ^{a}	1QpHab	*Pesher Habakkuk*	11QTemple^{a,b}	*Temple Scroll*
		1QS	*Rule of the Community*	11QtgJob	*Targum of Job*

IMPORTANT NEW TESTAMENT MANUSCRIPTS

(all dates given are AD; ordinal numbers refer to centuries)

Significant Papyri (𝔓 = Papyrus)

𝔓1 Matt 1; early 3rd
𝔓4+𝔓64+𝔓67 Matt 3, 5, 26; Luke 1–6; late 2nd
𝔓5 John 1, 16, 20; early 3rd
𝔓13 Heb 2–5, 10–12; early 3rd
𝔓15+𝔓16 (probably part of same codex) 1 Cor 7–8, Phil 3–4; late 3rd
𝔓20 Jas 2–3; 3rd
𝔓22 John 15–16; mid 3rd
𝔓23 Jas 1; c. 200
𝔓27 Rom 8–9; 3rd
𝔓30 1 Thess 4–5; 2 Thess 1; early 3rd
𝔓32 Titus 1–2; late 2nd
𝔓37 Matt 26; late 3rd
𝔓39 John 8; first half of 3rd
𝔓40 Rom 1–4, 6, 9; 3rd

𝔓45 Gospels and Acts; early 3rd
𝔓46 Paul's Major Epistles (less Pastorals); late 2nd
𝔓47 Rev 9–17; 3rd
𝔓49+𝔓65 Eph 4–5; 1 Thess 1–2; 3rd
𝔓52 John 18; c. 125
𝔓53 Matt 26, Acts 9–10; middle 3rd
𝔓66 John; late 2nd
𝔓70 Matt 2–3, 11–12, 24; 3rd
𝔓72 1–2 Peter, Jude; c. 300
𝔓74 Acts, General Epistles; 7th
𝔓75 Luke and John; c. 200
𝔓77+𝔓103 (probably part of same codex) Matt 13–14, 23; late 2nd
𝔓87 Philemon; late 2nd
𝔓90 John 18–19; late 2nd
𝔓91 Acts 2–3; 3rd
𝔓92 Eph 1, 2 Thess 1; c. 300
𝔓98 Rev 1:13-20; late 2nd
𝔓100 Jas 3–5; c. 300
𝔓101 Matt 3–4; 3rd
𝔓104 Matt 21; 2nd
𝔓106 John 1; 3rd
𝔓115 Rev 2–3, 5–6, 8–15; 3rd

Significant Uncials

ℵ (Sinaiticus) most of NT; 4th
A (Alexandrinus) most of NT; 5th
B (Vaticanus) most of NT; 4th
C (Ephraemi Rescriptus) most of NT with many lacunae; 5th
D (Bezae) Gospels, Acts; 5th
D (Claromontanus), Paul's Epistles; 6th (different MS than Bezae)
E (Laudianus 35) Acts; 6th
F (Augensis) Paul's Epistles; 9th
G (Boernerianus) Paul's Epistles; 9th
H (Coislinianus) Paul's Epistles; 6th
I (Freerianus or Washington) Paul's Epistles; 5th
L (Regius) Gospels; 8th
Q (Guelferbytanus B) Luke, John; 5th
P (Porphyrianus) Acts—Revelation; 9th
T (Borgianus) Luke, John; 5th
W (Washingtonianus or the Freer Gospels) Gospels; 5th
Z (Dublinensis) Matthew; 6th
037 (Δ; Sangallensis) Gospels; 9th
038 (Θ; Koridethi) Gospels; 9th
040 (Ξ; Zacynthius) Luke; 6th
043 (Φ; Beratinus) Matthew, Mark; 6th
044 (Ψ; Athous Laurae) Gospels, Acts, Paul's Epistles; 9th
048 Acts, Paul's Epistles, General Epistles; 5th
0171 Matt 10, Luke 22; c. 300
0189 Acts 5; c. 200

Significant Minuscules

1 Gospels, Acts, Paul's Epistles; 12th
33 All NT except Rev; 9th
81 Acts, Paul's Epistles, General Epistles; 1044
565 Gospels; 9th
700 Gospels; 11th
1424 (or Family 1424—a group of 29 manuscripts sharing nearly the same text) most of NT; 9th-10th
1739 Acts, Paul's Epistles; 10th
2053 Rev; 13th
2344 Rev; 11th
f^1 (a family of manuscripts including 1, 118, 131, 209) Gospels; 12th-14th
f^{13} (a family of manuscripts including 13, 69, 124, 174, 230, 346, 543, 788, 826, 828, 983, 1689, 1709—known as the Ferrar group) Gospels; 11th-15th

Significant Ancient Versions

SYRIAC (SYR)

syr^c (Syriac Curetonian) Gospels; 5th
syr^s (Syriac Sinaiticus) Gospels; 4th
syr^h (Syriac Harklensis) Entire NT; 616

OLD LATIN (IT)

it^a (Vercellenis) Gospels; 4th
it^b (Veronensis) Gospels; 5th
it^d (Cantabrigiensis—the Latin text of Bezae) Gospels, Acts, 3 John; 5th
it^e (Palantinus) Gospels; 5th
it^k (Bobiensis) Matthew, Mark; c. 400

COPTIC (COP)

cop^{bo} (Boharic—north Egypt)
cop^{fay} (Fayyumic—central Egypt)
cop^{sa} (Sahidic—southern Egypt)

OTHER VERSIONS

arm (Armenian)
eth (Ethiopic)
geo (Georgian)

TRANSLITERATION AND NUMBERING SYSTEM

Note: For words and roots from nonbiblical languages (e.g., Arabic, Ugaritic), only approximate transliterations are given.

HEBREW/ARAMAIC

Consonants

א	*aleph*	= *'*	מ, ם	*mem*	= *m*
בּ, ב	*beth*	= *b*	נ, ן	*nun*	= *n*
גּ, ג	*gimel*	= *g*	ס	*samekh*	= *s*
דּ, ד	*daleth*	= *d*	ע	*ayin*	= *'*
ה	*he*	= *h*	פּ, פ, ף	*pe*	= *p*
ו	*waw*	= *w*	צ, ץ	*tsadhe*	= *ts*
ז	*zayin*	= *z*	ק	*qoph*	= *q*
ח	*heth*	= *kh*	ר	*resh*	= *r*
ט	*teth*	= *t*	שׁ	*shin*	= *sh*
י	*yodh*	= *y*	שׂ	*sin*	= *s*
כּ, כ, ך	*kaph*	= *k*	תּ, ת	*taw*	= *t, th* (spirant)
ל	*lamedh*	= *l*			

Vowels

ַ	*patakh*	= *a*	ָ	*qamets khatuf*	= *o*
חַ	*furtive patakh*	= *a*	ֹ	*holem*	= *o*
ָ	*qamets*	= *a*	וֹ	*full holem*	= *o*
ָה	*final qamets he*	= *ah*	ֻ	*short qibbuts*	= *u*
ֶ	*segol*	= *e*	ֻ	*long qibbuts*	= *u*
ֵ	*tsere*	= *e*	וּ	*shureq*	= *u*
ֵי	*tsere yod*	= *e*	ֲ	*khatef patakh*	= *a*
ִ	*short hireq*	= *i*	ֳ	*khatef qamets*	= *o*
ִ	*long hireq*	= *i*	ְ	*vocalic shewa*	= *e*
ִי	*hireq yod*	= *i*	ַי	*patakh yodh*	= *a*

GREEK

α	*alpha*	= *a*	ι	*iota*	= *i*
β	*beta*	= *b*	κ	*kappa*	= *k*
γ	*gamma*	= *g, n (before* γ, κ, ξ, χ)	λ	*lamda*	= *l*
			μ	*mu*	= *m*
δ	*delta*	= *d*	ν	*nu*	= *n*
ε	*epsilon*	= *e*	ξ	*ksi*	= *x*
ζ	*zeta*	= *z*	ο	*omicron*	= *o*
η	*eta*	= *ē*	π	*pi*	= *p*
θ	*theta*	= *th*	ρ	*rho*	= *r* (ῥ = *rh)*

σ, ς	*sigma*	= *s*	ψ	*psi*	= *ps*
τ	*tau*	= *t*	ω	*omega*	= *ō*
υ	*upsilon*	= *u*	ʽ	*rough breathing mark*	= *h (with vowel or diphthong)*
φ	*phi*	= *ph*			
χ	*chi*	= *ch*			

THE TYNDALE-STRONG'S NUMBERING SYSTEM

The Cornerstone Biblical Commentary series uses a word-study numbering system to give both newer and more advanced Bible students alike quicker, more convenient access to helpful original-language tools (e.g., concordances, lexicons, and theological dictionaries). Those who are unfamiliar with the ancient Hebrew, Aramaic, and Greek alphabets can quickly find information on a given word by looking up the appropriate index number. Advanced students will find the system helpful because it allows them to quickly find the lexical form of obscure conjugations and inflections.

There are two main numbering systems used for biblical words today. The one familiar to most people is the Strong's numbering system (made popular by the *Strong's Exhaustive Concordance to the Bible*). Although the original Strong's system is still quite useful, the most up-to-date research has shed new light on the biblical languages and allows for more precision than is found in the original Strong's system. The Cornerstone Biblical Commentary series, therefore, features a newly revised version of the Strong's system, the Tyndale-Strong's numbering system. The Tyndale-Strong's system brings together the familiarity of the Strong's system and the best of modern scholarship. In most cases, the original Strong's numbers are preserved. In places where new research dictates, new or related numbers have been added.[1]

The second major numbering system today is the Goodrick-Kohlenberger system used in a number of study tools published by Zondervan. In order to give students broad access to a number of helpful tools, the Commentary provides index numbers for the Zondervan system as well.

The different index systems are designated as follows:

TG	Tyndale-Strong's Greek number	ZH	Zondervan Hebrew number
ZG	Zondervan Greek number	TA/ZA	Tyndale/Zondervan Aramaic number
TH	Tyndale-Strong's Hebrew number	S	Strong's Aramaic number

So in the example, "love" *agapē* [TG26, ZG27], the first number is the one to use with Greek tools keyed to the Tyndale-Strong's system, and the second applies to tools that use the Zondervan system.

The indexing of Aramaic terms differs slightly from that of Greek and Hebrew. Strong's original system mixed the Aramaic terms in with the Hebrew, but the Tyndale-Strong's system indexes Aramaic with a new set of numbers starting at 10,000. Since Tyndale's system for Aramaic diverges completely from original Strong's, the original Strong's number is listed separately so that those using tools keyed to Strong's can locate the information. This number is designated with an S, as in the example, "son" *bar* [TA/ZA10120, S1247].

1. Generally, one may simply use the original four-digit Strong's number to identify words in tools using Strong's system. If a Tyndale-Strong's number is followed by a capital letter (e.g., TG1692A), it generally indicates an added subdivision of meaning for the given term. Whenever a Tyndale-Strong's number has a number following a decimal point (e.g., TG2013.1), it reflects an instance where new research has yielded a separate, new classification of use for a biblical word. Forthcoming tools from Tyndale House Publishers will include these entries, which were not part of the original Strong's system.

Ezekiel

David L. Thompson

INTRODUCTION TO *Ezekiel*

IN THE BOOK OF EZEKIEL readers encounter perhaps the most striking and eccentric (some have said deranged!)[1] figure among Israel's prophets. He is also among the most theologically daring and creative of the prophets. Ezekiel survived spiritual, social, and national upheaval, as well as personal trauma. In the midst of it all he heard and saw the God of Israel in unprecedented ways. He then expressed these visions in extraordinary passages, many of which are difficult to understand.

In spite of the difficulties confronting interpreters, the book of Ezekiel addresses God's people powerfully and uniquely. Generations trying to come to terms with their role and stake in human tragedy have found instruction here. Persons seeking to contextualize the ancient faith in their own worlds have found caution and guidance. People of God struggling to make sense of the loss of everything that gave meaning and structure to their lives, and others groping for hope in their apparently dead-end situations, have heard a life-giving word here.

AUTHOR

If we identify the prophet Ezekiel as the author of this book, as has traditionally been done, we have some information about him. Ezekiel was a Zadokite priest, the son of a certain Buzi (1:3),[2] living in Judah during the decades leading up to the first conquest of Jerusalem by the Babylonian king Nebuchadnezzar (2 Kgs 24). From his youth, Ezekiel followed priestly Torah and imbibed priestly convictions (4:14); he had become passionately committed to Israel's whole Torah and her historic covenant faith. Along with other intelligentsia, artisans, leaders of Judah, and King Jehoiachin, he had been deported by Nebuchadnezzar to Babylon and settled in a community at Tel-abib on the Kebar River near Nippur (1:1-3). In his thirtieth year—the fifth year of King Jehoiachin's exile (593 BC)—the Lord commissioned him as a prophet to the rebellious nation of Israel, especially to the exiled community (2:1-5; 3:15). Four and a half years later his beloved wife died (24:1, 15-18). Ezekiel continued his prophetic ministry at least through April 571 BC, the time of his last dated oracle (29:17-21). We have no information regarding the close of his ministry or the end of his life or the precise relationship between him and "his" book as it now stands, beyond what may be inferred from the book itself. The book itself does, however, offer extensive information about Ezekiel's passions, convictions, theology, and ministry.

The dominantly autobiographical character of the book of Ezekiel suggests that the prophet himself wrote substantial portions of the work (by his own hand or through a scribe, as Jeremiah did through Baruch).[3] Repeated connection of Ezekiel with the message reception formula[4] ties massive amounts of the book directly to him, with no evidence in these oracles preventing a written connection. This remains true, even though the dates (e.g., 8:1) most likely locate the oracles that immediately follow them rather than entire segments or sections they introduce. Association of the prophet with the actual recording of at least some of what he heard and saw tends in the same direction (24:2; 43:11).

The book's pervasive first-person stance could also suggest that Ezekiel himself was responsible not simply for recording various oracles but for shaping and structuring the present book. The unusual attention to precise dating of oracles and Ezekiel's explicit connection to the chronological matters in the book could support this (24:2). Some other exilic/postexilic prophets give precise attention to dates (e.g., Hag 1:1; Zech 1:1), but the number of chronological references in Ezekiel (14), the import of this chronological flow to the unfolding structure of the book, and the interrelationships between this chronology and the prophet's experience as spokesman for the Lord are striking. The prophet's apparent connection with extensive portions of the book has also led many to attribute the whole to him, precisely because they perceived throughout the work the pervasive influence of the same person. Further, nothing in the book points necessarily to a writer and readers after the fall of the Neo-Babylonians or beyond any significant return of exiles to Judah. These and other factors allowed S. R. Driver to summarize critical opinion at the opening of the twentieth century by declaring "No critical question arises in connection with the authorship of the book [of Ezekiel], the whole from beginning to end bearing unmistakably the stamp of a single mind" (1909:279; similarly Cornill 1907:315-316).[5]

Various Views of Authorship. Identification of the prophet as the author, however, is not a foregone conclusion. Among the church fathers, Jerome questioned the link between Ezekiel and the book. Like all the prophetic books and many other biblical works, the book of Ezekiel comes to us anonymously. The book names no author or editor(s). The Talmud notes that "the men of the Great Synagogue wrote Ezekiel" (*b. Hagigah* 14b); this probably refers, however, to their work of copying (perhaps editing) rather than authorship. Specifically how much, then, of the material in the book of Ezekiel can be traced to Ezekiel's hand, and to what extent does Ezekiel's hand figure in the literary structure and logic of the book we now have?

As early as 1756, Oeder questioned the literary integrity of the book, regarding chapters 40–48 as a spurious addition to Ezekiel's work of chapters 1–39 (Pfeiffer 1941:525-526). In 1792, Corrodi reckoned that chapters 33–39 did not come from the prophet either (Pfeiffer 1941:526). Against the majority opinion in nineteenth-century critical scholarship, already in the 1830s, Zunz (followed by Seinecke in the 1880s) concluded that the book of Ezekiel was actually pseudepigraphic, composed by an unknown writer centuries after Ezekiel.[6] Convinced of the structural and stylistic unity of the book, once they had separated it from Ezekiel on other grounds, they found it necessary to attribute the whole to later, unknown hands. Still, the majority of scholars were not persuaded to set aside the book's apparent connection of the prophet with substantial materials in the book, if not with the book as a whole. Again in the 1930s C. C. Torrey championed a "Pseudo-Ezekiel," with its core written around 230 BC, but he failed to convince many (Eissfeldt 1965:366, 369).

Kraetzschmar introduced the idea of multiple recensions as a key to the book's composition (1900). Focusing on parallel texts and doublets found in the book, Kraetzschmar thought two recensions by Ezekiel himself, one in the first person and a shorter recension in the third person, were later joined by a redactor. Many credit G. Hölscher's 1924 work, *Hesechiel: Der Dichter und das Buch* (*Ezekiel: The Poet and the Book*), with providing the main impetus for opening these questions to critical study (Childs 1979:357). Analyzing the book's style, Hölscher assigned to Ezekiel only those portions of the book he regarded as poetic—170 of 1,273 verses—leaving the rest to a fourth-century-BC writer who completely reshaped the prophet's work. By 1943, Irwin could lament the fact that the "newer commentaries" he read[7] on these questions could agree on little more than that the book was composite (it had not been written as a whole by Ezekiel) and that the editorial and redactional process of producing the work as we have it began with Ezekiel (Irwin 1943:23). Irwin noted the highly tentative nature of conclusions drawn and claimed the failure to reach consensus was due to the lack of "clear criteria of originality" for distinguishing the prophet's words in the present text (1943:24).[8]

Kraetzschmar, Hölscher, and others modifying and extending their research turned scholarly attention to the *process* by which the book arose, from earliest materials by the prophet or another person through successive handlings by other readers and on to the book as we have it. Study of this compositional process, eventually known as redaction criticism, entailed close examination of the history of the traditions taken up in the book and the ways in which persons handling Ezekiel's text modified it with glosses, explanations, modifications, extensions, insertions, and rearrangement of related materials (the foci of redaction criticism). Materials that an earlier generation discarded as "secondary" accretions in order to uncover the "authentic" or "genuine" words of Ezekiel were now viewed as clues to the literary journey from the prophet's writings to the book as we have it (cf. contrasting approaches of Torrey 1930:71 and Eichrodt 1970:18-22).

Walther Eichrodt and Walther Zimmerli present the best recent examples of a form- and redaction-critical approach to Ezekiel. Both writers seek to discern the original text of the prophet and to explain the relationship of every other word in the text to those original writings of the prophet, aiming in the end to interpret the book as we have it. Zimmerli's commentary is widely regarded as the pinnacle of scholarly work on Ezekiel from the tradition-historical, redaction-critical perspective. Both Zimmerli and Eichrodt offer rich theological interpretations of the book. At the same time, both scholars invest major effort and space in enterprises that remain highly speculative.

In spite of his immense respect and sympathy for Zimmerli's work, Brevard Childs lodges theological and exegetical critiques against it. His objections highlight difficulties in the tradition-historical, redactional-critical approach to biblical texts. Childs retains more confidence than many in our present ability to distinguish the prophet's original writings from later additions to and alterations of the text leading to the book as we have it. Even so, he makes the general point that Zimmerli (1979:369) makes the "original 'Grundttext'" (foundational or basic text) to which his traditio-historical work leads him the primary text for the work of exegesis. Thus, a reconstructed "original" text, not the canonical text, becomes the main text to be interpreted (1979:369). More specifically, Childs claims Zimmerli has "missed the significance of the canonical process," which not only shaped the text (as Zimmerli has seen) but brought that process to a definitive end when it fixed the canonical text. A "pre-canonical stage" in the text's development is substituted for the "normative canonical text" as the target of interpretation. Consequently, Zimmerli "runs the danger of losing the inner dynamic of the full canonical passage," reducing attention to the literary entity of the book of Ezekiel with its own integrity, not to be identified with the sum of its parts. Finally, Childs challenges the assumption that introducing the historical work of tracing the redactional-canonical process actually enhances illumination of the text in every case. Sometimes helpful, often "hypothetical and fragile," the value of the observations seems overestimated (1979:370).

Critiques of this sort have produced significant responses in the most recent interpreters of Ezekiel. Moshe Greenberg has developed what he calls a "holistic" approach to interpretation, seen in his Anchor Bible Commentary on Ezekiel (1983 and 1997). First, Greenberg begins with the Masoretic Text as the "least shaky foundation" for the study of the book of Ezekiel that we possess (1983:20). In one way or another, it must ultimately go back to the prophet himself. Removed at least eight centuries from the prophet himself, the Masoretic Text cannot be regarded as a "verbatim record" of Ezekiel's publication, Greenberg reasons, because of the changes known to occur in the course of extended scribal transmission. Nevertheless, it serves as our primary source for the study of this prophetic book "until proved unreliable by anachronism (linguistic, historical, or ideational), or indubitable [textual] corruption, or intolerable variations in style or texture" (1983:19). In the case of Ezekiel, the ancient versions provide only limited access to stages preceding the Masoretic Text, and help from Qumran texts is sparse. Second, Greenberg is thoroughly skeptical of scholarly attempts to reconstruct an "original" Ezekiel and track the development of the present book from that reconstruction. He considers such endeavors often flawed by the imposition of modern and often unexamined assumptions regarding composition and style that fail to hear the ancient text on its own terms (1983:20-21). Even where the Septuagint presents sufficient divergence as to raise the question of another layer in the literary development of the book, Greenberg is inclined to suggest Ezekiel as his own first editor, leading to such a *Vorlage* for the Septuagint (1997:396). Finally, Greenberg tries to immerse himself in the text of Ezekiel as a piece of ancient literature with its own compositional conventions, shaping, and patterning often quite at odds with modern intuitions. He proceeds with the working assumption that "the present book of Ezekiel is the product of art and intelligent design," the product of "an individual mind of powerful and passionate proclivities." In the book "a coherent world of vision" emerges, "contemporary with the sixth-century prophet and decisively shaped by him, if not the very words of Ezekiel himself" (1983:26-27).

Leslie Allen sees his work on Ezekiel in the Word Biblical Commentary as something of a "rapprochement" between Zimmerli and Greenberg, between a mainly historical-critical inquiry and a primarily literary approach (1994:xxiv). Allen finds no reason to deny substantial tracts of the book and much of its design to Ezekiel. The prophet had plenty of time to commit his prophetic reports to writing, and the messenger formula consistently ties Ezekiel to the oracles that inaugurate literary units. Working with "redaction criticism of a moderate kind" (1994:xxiii), Allen also sees indication that others have amplified the prophet's own work, "equally partaking of prophetic authority by continued use of Ezekiel's messenger formula." Regularly throughout the text Allen sees literary units composed of "three layers: (1) a basic oracle, (2) a continuation or updating that stays relatively close to the basic oracle, and (3) a closing oracle that stands apart from the earlier two pieces." He concludes that the first two layers belong to Ezekiel, while the third comes from "heirs of his work . . . concerned to preserve it and adapt it to the needs of a succeeding generation" (1994:xxv). All of this has happened by perhaps the early 540s BC, for the book shows no signs either of the fall of the Neo-Babylonian empire nor of a return of exiles to Judah (1994:xxv-xxvi; so also Greenberg 1983:15). Allen avoids Zimmerli's pitfall of making a reconstructed text the basis of his reading by reversing Zimmerli's reading strategy. Zimmerli stands beside the Ezekiel he has reconstructed and reads looking forward through the trail of redactional commentary to the book as a whole. Allen proposes to read from the present text back to Ezekiel, with the emphasis on reading the edited text (i.e., the canonical text) as an early "re-reading" of the prophetic record "from a later standpoint" (1994:xxvi).

Daniel Block argues that very little of the scribal, compositional, and editorial work entailed in producing the book of Ezekiel need be removed from the prophet's own hand (1997:17-23). Conceding some "editorial clarifications by later hands" such as 1:2-3, he nevertheless sees no evidence to demand extending the "chronological, geographic, and temperamental distance between prophet and book" common in the history of the critical study of Ezekiel (1997:23). This commentary will proceed mainly along the lines of Greenberg and Block. Theologically and theoretically I have no serious quarrel with Allen's moderate redaction criticism. But I lack confidence in our ability (especially my own!) to consistently delineate various layers of redaction in documents like Ezekiel. Where editorial and redactional work seems clearly present, I will use it to illuminate the reading of the Masoretic Text as it now stands. For convenience, I will refer to Ezekiel as the author, without reentering debate about the precise stages of the composition of the book.

The Author Himself: The Priest and Prophet. Having tied the prophet Ezekiel closely to the composition of the book of Ezekiel, we may return once more to the brief notes about his identity. Ezekiel was clearly a prophet, this "sentinel" status emphasized by including the prophet's commission and instruction among introductory theological concerns. But the first vocational designation of Ezekiel in the book is as a priest. The Masoretic Text and the New Living Translation are ambiguous as to whether the title "priest" (1:3) modifies Ezekiel or his father. The Septuagint takes it to describe Ezekiel (*Iezekiēl huion Bouzi ton hierea;* "priest" is marked by accusative case, agreeing with "Ezekiel" and "son"), which is the perspective I take in this commentary. Whether Ezekiel had officially been consecrated a priest we do not know. Biblical tradition varies without easy harmonization on the age from which priests may perform their duties: age 20 in 1 Chronicles 23:24 and Ezra 3:8; age 25 in Numbers 8:24; age 30 in Numbers 4:3 (Wenham 1981:97-98, note 2). Interestingly enough, two of these ages figure significantly in Ezekiel the priest. In his 25th year he was deported along with Jehoiachin to Babylon; in his 30th year he saw the visions opening his prophetic ministry (1:1). Even if Buzi were "the priest" of 1:1, Ezekiel, as his son, would have been well on his way toward priestly office and steeped in priestly instruction. A faithful priest's heart animates this book through and through. (See "Major Themes and Theological Concerns" below.)

The Sanity of Ezekiel. As was mentioned at the outset, Ezekiel's radical and highly unusual behavior has brought his mental health into question. This man thinks himself spiritually transported to distant places, lies motionless and speechless for months at a time, refuses to mourn the death of his beloved wife, seems to relish the grotesque (bordering on the pornographic), has a fascination for blood and excrement, and more. As early as 1877, critical scholars looked to mental pathology as providing the most promising explanation (Zimmerli 1979:17). While the majority of Ezekiel students have not followed this tack, interest has continued. E. C. Broome's "Ezekiel's Abnormal Personality" probably takes the prize for abuse of the text and misunderstanding of prophetic and religious experience. He concluded that Ezekiel exhibited symptoms of paranoid schizophrenia. Here, he thought, "we are dealing with a true psychotic," Ezekiel's flashes of spiritual insight notwithstanding (1946:291). Unfortunately, periodic interest persists in this approach as Halperin's recent work shows (1993).

Should it be concluded that Ezekiel did indeed serve with mental disabilities, it would not in itself remove him from the honored roll of Yahweh's servants or remove his book from the Canon. At the same time, many scholars across a wide theological spectrum have rightly pointed out the dubious nature of psychoanalytical diagnoses across the huge cultural chasm and 2,500-year distance that separate us from this man. Perhaps more to the point, analyses like Broome's and Halperin's frequently do not share a worldview in which the creator God actually does address prophets, communicate to them in dreams and visions, and provide them access to "channels of communication not normally available to others" (Howie 1950:84). Sign-acts bizarre to us, including public nudity, were not unique to Ezekiel among ancient prophets (e.g., Isa 20:1-4). Spiritual transport to places familiar in detail to Ezekiel prior to his exile and now in the context of his ministry seems more the mark of a mystic than of one mentally impaired. "Fascination" with feces has nothing to do with feces and everything to do with Ezekiel's polemic against idolatry. His favorite name (used 39 times) for idols was *gillulim* [TH1544, ZH1658], perhaps meaning "droppings" (HALOT 1.192; NIDOTTE 1.864-865). The vulgar "turd balls" might catch the utter disdain, not only of Ezekiel, but of other Old Testament writers who used the slanderous term.

Impaired or not, some of the experiences Ezekiel reports immersed him in physical and mental trauma. Ezekiel was a suffering servant. The prophet and his word of judgment become united in these experiences. Eichrodt concludes, "Ezekiel's solidarity with human misery is shown . . . by the bodily suffering imposed upon him . . . a prophetic symbol of his people even in his bodily life, as it were submerged in their dying, overwhelmed by the destructive power of the divine wrath which he himself proclaimed" (1970:33).

Ezekiel's View of Women. In Ezekiel's elaboration of "female imagery of earlier prophets," says Katheryn Pfisterer Darr, he produced "some of the Bible's most misogynistic texts" (1998:192). She has chapters 16 and 23 especially in mind. (Renta J. Weems also brings several of the core issues together in the title of her 1995 book, *Battered Love: Marriage, Sex, and Violence in the Hebrew Prophets.*) According to Darr, Ezekiel "depicts female sexuality as the object of male possession and control, presents physical abuse as a way to reclaim such control, and then suggests that violence can be a means toward *healing* a broken relationship"—all behaviors offensive to Christian conscience (1998:198).

This commentary approaches these issues as follows. First, I recognize that Ezekiel and other Old Testament writers reflect in their works the deplorable plight of women in the ancient Near East in their several contexts. They spoke from this world and to it. Darr accurately states that plight in the quote above. With some exceptions, women lived as the property of men, with less human value, less social standing and rights, and with more restricted behavior than men. Scripture itself presents this plight as a result of human sin and in the end makes it part of the Old Testament's redemption agendas (Gen 2–3).

Second, I side with Ezekiel in the viewpoint that harlotry and adultery are particularly appropriate metaphors for depicting Israel's unfaithfulness to covenant (cf. Ortlund 1996:182-183). At the same time I remain aware that the same imagery could not have been constructed around an unfaithful husband, because of the cultural biases present. The practice of polygamy and Israel's understanding of adultery as an offense committed by wives against their husbands, not the reverse, precluded use of this image in a way unflattering of husbands. Third, I acknowledge that there are texts with sufficiently explicit sexual language and sufficient hazard for misappropriation that special pastoral care is warranted for their public reading and use (chs 16 and 23 among them). Fourth, I urge people to read the text as accurately as possible, especially in these contested passages. To contend, for example, that the central *women* in chapters 16 and 23 are gang-raped, mutilated, hacked up, and have their children killed fails to follow Ezekiel's shifts from his extended metaphor to the language of war interpreting that metaphor as a city under military attack. Ezekiel accurately describes the atrocities of war. Assimilating these interpretive lines into the metaphor itself transforms them into misogynist speech. Moreover, Ezekiel's choice of imagery may simply be intentionally shocking. A picture of God as an abusive husband (if that were to be granted) does not exonerate abusive husbands any more than a portrayal of God as a drunken soldier (Ps 78:65) condones drunkenness.

Fifth, I consider a hermeneutic of suspicion inappropriate for interpreting Scripture in the church. Thus, we will not defend the women weeping for Tammuz in 8:14-15 and the false prophetesses in 13:17-19 if the biblical presentation rejects them—which it does. Darr (1998:196-197) rightly notes Ezekiel's outrage at what he considers an idolatrous abomination in the Jerusalem women's mourning for

Tammuz. Then, however, Darr comments sympathetically that quite possibly others in Jerusalem did not share Ezekiel's view but saw the Tammuz liturgy as consistent with Yahweh worship. Further, she thinks we cannot be sure the prophet accurately characterizes the women's activity because he seeks to discredit methods and messages at odds with his own. In my judgment, this approach to reading the prophet reduces Ezekiel's view simply to one among many.

There certainly *were* such persons with "alternative" Yahweh theologies in the Jerusalem Temple. And there certainly were "alternative" approaches to prophecy in Judah. That's what chapters 8 and 13 are about! But all of the canonical prophets who addressed issues like this matter of weeping for Tammuz, including Ezekiel, condemned them. And the church has historically privileged the canonical prophets' views, thinking itself theologically compelled to agree with these prophets in their rejection of all such "alternative" approaches to Yahweh faith. To set that canonical stance aside, as though it has no privilege in the church, seems to me a grave mistake. A canonical approach calls upon the reader to agree with Ezekiel's viewpoint rather than to critique it as suspect. See Corrine Patton's work (2000) for a particularly trenchant critique of contemporary feminist readings of Ezekiel, especially at the points of reading the text in its historical context and reading with an eye toward the text's theological point as a prelude to any worthy appropriation of it.

Finally, I will avoid anachronistic and patronizing attitudes toward the prophet, as though I could personally take credit for developing a conscience superior to Ezekiel's and as though Ezekiel should be expected to write with a highly developed Christian conscience. I recall that the moral sensitivities leading to women's suffrage and later to legitimate feminist concerns did not rise out of the Enlightenment. Instead, along with the abolition of slavery (and by a parallel hermeneutic), feminist insights arose from the scriptural convictions of orthodox Christians in the nineteenth and early twentieth centuries (Swartley 1983; Thompson 1996). The same Bible that reports Ezekiel's metaphor with its problems also carries the streams of revelation that eventually provide insight with which to critique Ezekiel and the culture out of which he wrote. Ezekiel himself actually contributed to those streams. One is reminded of Childs's musings in a related context as to "whether the problem lies with the imagery, or with a generation which no longer possesses the needed 'reader competence' to render the Bible as scripture for the church" (1986:40).

DATE AND OCCASION OF WRITING

Ezekiel's prophetic ministry largely took place from 593 to 571 BC. As discussed above under "Various Views of Authorship," some scholars have asserted that the book of Ezekiel was not completed until centuries after Ezekiel. But the book as it now stands shows no awareness of the fall of the Neo-Babylonian Empire to Cyrus the Persian (539 BC), nor of the return of exiles to Jerusalem. Thus, Allen's judgment that the book essentially as we have it had been produced by the 540s BC seems sound (1994:xxv-xxvi). The occasion for the book stems from a larger sequence of historical events, outlined below.

Although Ezekiel does refer to Israel's early and pre-monarchic history (16:3, 8, 45; 20:1-17; 36:35), the nearer historical background for his book is best understood beginning with Judah's King Manasseh (687/6–642 BC),[9] under whom Judah's fate in judgment was sealed (2 Kgs 21:10-15; 23:26; 24:3). It was the Assyrians who dominated Manasseh's world—and indeed the whole ancient Near East at that time. From that era, several critical streams flow almost directly into the life of Ezekiel and his contemporaries and through Ezekiel to his book.

The Legacy of Manasseh and the Assyrians. By the time young Manasseh came to the throne in Judah, the Assyrians held effective control from the Persian Gulf and the Zagros Mountains in the far east to the border of Egypt in the southwest, and on up the Mediterranean coast to Cilicia in the north. Although God had saved Hezekiah from destruction at the hands of Sennacherib (2 Kgs 18–19), the Assyrians had plundered Jerusalem's treasures and placed Hezekiah under heavy tribute. And, for the short term at least, the Assyrians put an end to Egypt's inveterate meddling in the politics of ancient Palestine. His whole life, Manasseh had witnessed Assyria's ability to march at will through Judah either to conquer or brutalize Judah herself or make other imperial exploits farther to the south and west. Assyrian troops were garrisoned throughout the territories. Their advanced technology and enviable culture presented themselves to any who had eyes to see their weapons, their attire, and the other artifacts that their troops and officials brought with them.

Manasseh seems unfortunately to have accommodated himself extensively to this state of affairs. Politically, life under Assyrian domination was most undesirable for any head of state,[10] and Manasseh appears to have become entangled at some point in real or suspected rebellion against Assyria (cf. 2 Chr 33:11-13). But culturally and spiritually, his "cosmopolitan" tastes led him to reverse every reform his father Hezekiah had instituted and to direct the kingdom of Judah down a path from which it never recovered (2 Kgs 23:26; 24:3).

Manasseh restored altars and sacred symbols associated with Canaanite idolatries around the kingdom. He even installed a carved Asherah pole for the consort of the Canaanite high god, El, in the Jerusalem Temple of Yahweh, providing royal sponsorship again to fertility faith[11] in Judah.[12] He also introduced into Yahweh's Temple an altar to astral deities (at least the stars, if not the sun also) and took up the practices of sorcery, divination, witchcraft, and consultation with mediums and psychics. He even sacrificed his own sons by fire in the valley of the Son of Hinnom just south of Jerusalem (2 Kgs 21:1-9; 2 Chr 33:1-11).

This absolute low point in Judah's spiritual decline is emphasized in Kings by comparison to the evils with which the house of Ahab degraded the northern kingdom of Israel and its capital Samaria (2 Kgs 21:3, 13). Kings and Chronicles describe these evils with clear reference to Deuteronomy 4:15-19 and 5:8-9, which expressly forbid such activities as rebellion against Yahweh.

These evils were not in the main innovations, but a convergence of pressures made this a period of incredible danger in Judah for historic faith in Yahweh. The idolatries and practices themselves were mostly native to the Canaanite culture with which keepers of Yahweh's covenant had battled since Israel's entry into the land. The danger here was not so much that Judahites would outright reject their historic god, Yahweh. The threat was that God's people had become so theologically confused that they would finally and thoroughly incorporate the worship of various Canaanite gods (Baal, Asherah, Molech, and others) into the worship of Yahweh. Yahweh's worship would include sexual and sacrificial practices indigenous to fertility faith but completely incompatible with covenant theology and morality. Discerning Yahweh's mind would include magical and spiritual means at odds with Israel's sovereign and self-revealing God. (See 2 Chr 33:17 for something of this confusion, even during a time of relative reform.) Assyria's domination and apparent invincibility compounded this threat. Its conquest of nation after nation implied to some the superiority of Assyria's god Asshur to the gods of the nations they subdued.

In the generation following Manasseh, the prophet Zephaniah denounced the royal family and Jerusalem elites for their infatuation with things foreign, quite likely including things Assyrian, and by that time, Babylonian (Zeph 1:8). Ezekiel himself ridiculed Israel's attraction to the Assyrians' handsome appearance (23:6). Some would also argue that the importation of astral deities into the Temple reflects an obligation to show deference to the Assyrians' deities, and that reversion to divination and magic includes taking up practices popular in Assyria.[13] Hence, not only was covenant faith threatened by syncretism with Canaanite religion, Yahweh's superiority among the gods was called into question by his apparent ineffectiveness against the forces of Asshur. Syncretism with Assyrian religion or outright capitulation to Assyrian deities was a potent temptation. By Ezekiel's time some cynics had even concluded that Yahweh was not only inferior but also irrelevant (Zeph 1:12).

Over against this love for "things Assyrian" (and later "Babylonian"), a "Zionist" stance had emerged. Sennacherib (704–681 BC) forced Manasseh's father, Hezekiah (715–687/6 BC), into costly submission. But he did not conquer Jerusalem and desecrate Yahweh's Temple, as he tacitly admits in his royal annals.[14] Instead, as Isaiah had promised, Yahweh dramatically delivered Jerusalem. When his army was decimated by the angel of the Lord, Sennacherib lifted the siege and returned to Nineveh (2 Kgs 18:13–19:37; 2 Chr 32:1-22).

For many this astounding deliverance of Jerusalem confirmed their confidence in the inviolability of Zion. These persons interpreted the apparently unconditional nature of Yahweh's historic promise to David of an everlasting dynasty (2 Sam 7:8-16; see also 2 Sam 7:17-29) to mean that Jerusalem itself and the Temple would never be conquered. The theological confusions described above provided no safeguard against this delusion that ignored both the precise content of the promise and the conditionality integral to prophetic promise. This skewing of authentic Zion theology carried a strong voice right up to the fall of Jerusalem at the hands of Nebuchadnezzar (24:21, 25-27; Jer 7:4-15).

The Chronicler celebrated Manasseh's repentance during an imprisonment and exile by the Assyrians (2 Chr 33:10-13). Upon Manasseh's return to the throne in Judah, he expressed his newfound allegiance to Yahweh by destroying much of the paraphernalia of the idolatries he had sponsored (2 Chr 33:14-17). Strangely the writer of Kings does not mention this. Instead, he records in some detail a landmark reform by Manasseh's grandson, Josiah (640–609 BC). Perhaps we are to assume a wholesale return to Manasseh's policies during his son Amon's reign (642–640). What remains clear is that there was a far-reaching reform led by King Josiah, prompted by the discovery of the Book of the Law (2 Kgs 22:8-13), most likely Deuteronomy or portions thereof. Josiah restored the national observance of Passover, renewed the covenant with Yahweh, and, as we just noted, removed the abominations Manasseh and kings before him had endorsed (2 Kgs 22:8–23:27; 2 Chr 34–35; cf. 2 Chr 33:14-19 on Manasseh's own Temple reforms). Only of Josiah was it said, "Never before had there been a king like Josiah, who turned to the LORD with all his heart and soul and strength, obeying all the laws of Moses. And there has never been a king like him since" (2 Kgs 23:25).

Josiah, the Collapse of Judah, and the Call of Ezekiel. Josiah's reforms came to a dramatic halt in 609 BC when he died in battle against the Egyptian king Neco II (610–594) at Megiddo. Neco was en route to reinforce the remnants of Assyria's army in the upper Euphrates region, where the Babylonians were advancing under Nabopolassar (626–605; cf. 2 Kgs 23:29-30). Josiah's son and immediate successor, Jehoahaz (609), quickly demonstrated that he did not intend to perpetuate his father's reforms (2 Kgs 23:32) and reigned only briefly before Neco replaced him with Jehoiakim (609–598). Jehoiakim proved no better (2 Kgs 23:37)—he brazenly cut up and burned Jeremiah's scroll of Yahweh's judgments against Judah that had been read at the Temple (Jer 36:1-26)! The royal house itself clearly was divided regarding the soul of Judah and the nature of covenant faith, as Zephaniah claimed (Zeph 1:8-9). Ezekiel was about 14 years old in 609, and was most likely living in Jerusalem at the time Josiah was slain and when these radical shifts in national faith and ethos occurred.

Although Neco defeated Josiah, his campaign to bolster the Assyrians failed at Haran, thereby forcing his troops to regroup at Carchemish. Babylonian involvement elsewhere allowed some time for Neco to strengthen his grip on Judah and other land taken en route to the north. It was Neco himself who removed the "people's choice," Jehoahaz, sent him as prisoner to Egypt, and installed his brother Jehoiakim in his place (2 Kgs 23:31-37).[15] But in 605 BC Nabopolassar's vigorous son, Nebuchadnezzar (605/4–562), routed the Egyptians at Carchemish and set out to expel them from the lands between the Euphrates and the Nile rivers. Delayed briefly by the death of his father, Nebuchadnezzar and his army were in Palestine by late 604, imposing his rule on the Philistine cities to the Brook of Egypt. He had begun a reign that would last over 40 years, nine years beyond the last dated oracle of Ezekiel.[16]

With the Babylonians marching at will in Palestine, King Jehoiakim wisely transferred loyalties to Nebuchadnezzar, becoming a vassal under tribute (2 Kgs 24:1). But limited Babylonian success in dealing decisively with Egypt led Jehoiakim and the Jerusalem establishment once again to think their hopes lay with Egypt. Jehoiakim withheld tribute from Nebuchadnezzar, counting on Egyptian support. By December 598 BC Nebuchadnezzar and his army were again in Judah. Jerusalem surrendered on March 16, 597. Fortunately for Jehoiakim[17] he died before falling into the hands of the Babylonians. His son Jehoiachin became king and ruled for three months before surrendering to the Babylonians. Second Kings summarizes the events:

> *In the eighth year of Nebuchadnezzar's reign, he took Jehoiachin prisoner. As the LORD had said beforehand, Nebuchadnezzar carried away all the treasures from the LORD's Temple and the royal palace. He stripped away all the gold objects that King Solomon of Israel had placed in the Temple. King Nebuchadnezzar took all of Jerusalem captive, including all the commanders and the best of the soldiers, craftsmen, and artisans—10,000 in all. Only the poorest people were left in the land. Nebuchadnezzar led King Jehoiachin away as a captive to Babylon, along with the queen mother, his wives and officials, and all Jerusalem's elite. (2 Kgs 24:12b-15)*

Nebuchadnezzar appointed as king a fourth son of Josiah, Mattaniah, whom he renamed Zedekiah (597–587 BC). It would be yet another decade before the Babylonians actually destroyed Jerusalem. But this date—that of Jehoiachin's capture and exile by Nebuchadnezzar—became the chronological starting point for Ezekiel's mission. The dates and Babylonian setting of Ezekiel's earliest prophetic experiences and his references to "our captivity" (33:21; 40:1) imply that Ezekiel himself was among those deported with Jehoiachin. This would surely have been the most traumatic experience of his life up to that point. He was 25 years of age at the time, a junior member of the Jehoiakim–Jehoiachin generation.

Few if any left in Jerusalem were capable of governing the kingdom at all, let alone dealing with the enormous challenges facing Judah. Persons of wisdom and competence had been killed by Jehoiakim or deported. National character had hopelessly eroded. If Ezekiel's vision of the Jerusalem Temple in chapter 8 reports actual conditions there, as it probably does (cf. 2 Chr 36:14), the situation was beyond deplorable. By 589 BC, perhaps with hopes kindled by the ascent to the throne of a new king in Egypt (Apries, 589–570) and the distraction of Babylon elsewhere, Zedekiah allowed his advisors to talk him into striking for independence from Babylon. The biblical narrative cuts to the chase and focuses directly on the siege of Jerusalem (2 Kgs 25), though Nebuchadnezzar actually marched throughout Judah, destroying her strongholds one by one, totally isolating the capital. By Zedekiah's ninth year (January 588), Nebuchadnezzar had laid siege to the city, holding it in lockdown for two years, with one brief reprieve. On July 18, which was Zedekiah's eleventh year (586), the conditions in the city were deplorable due to severe famine followed by the breaching of its fortified walls. Zedekiah was captured in an attempt to escape and taken 200 miles north to Riblah in Syria for judgment before Nebuchadnezzar himself. "They made Zedekiah watch as they slaughtered his sons. Then they gouged out Zedekiah's eyes, bound him in bronze chains, and led him away to Babylon" (2 Kgs 25:7). One month later (August 14), after extracting all the remaining treasures of the Temple, Nebuzaradan, an official of Nebuchadnezzar, supervised the burning and dismantling of the city, all its major buildings, and its walls. Everyone left who had sworn allegiance to Nebuchadnezzar was put under guard and marched off to Babylon. Officials of the Temple and army and selected citizens identified as anti-Babylonian voices in the city were taken to Riblah and executed. "So the people of Judah were sent into exile from their land" (2 Kgs 25:21), reads the incredibly sad concluding statement in the narrative of the fall of Jerusalem (2 Kgs 25:1-21).

Nebuchadnezzar had appointed Gedaliah, a nobleman of reputable family, as governor of a newly created province. But royalists, some of whom had escaped to

Ammon, still held out for resistance against the Babylonians. In short order they assassinated Gedaliah. Many fled the land for fear of reprisals from Nebuchadnezzar. It was this group of refugees that took Jeremiah, under protest, to Egypt (2 Kgs 25:22-26; Jer 40:5–43:13). Yet a third deportation in 582 BC may have been associated with this foolishness. It marked the last we know of Nebuchadnezzar's dealings with Judah as such.

Midway between Ezekiel's deportation with King Jehoiachin and the fall of Jerusalem, the spiritual earthquake of his life occurred. On July 31, 593, the fifth year of Jehoiachin's deportation, while Ezekiel was with the Judean exiles by the Kebar River, "the heavens were opened" to him and he saw "visions of God." Then "the LORD gave [a] message" to him, and he "felt the hand of the LORD take hold of him" (1:1-3). Before it was over, he had been called and "sent" as a prophet to rebellious Israel and commissioned as a sentry for them (2:1–3:22). A brief rebellion in Babylon and renewed hopes of Egyptian aid caused stirrings for independence that unsettled Nebuchadnezzar's western holdings (17:15-18). Zedekiah (Jer 27:2-8) and even prophets among the exile community whom Nebuchadnezzar slew (cf. Jer 29:20-22) were involved. The Lord's initiative with Ezekiel may at least in part have come in response to these events. Whatever the causes—and they are surely more complex than a response to this single disquiet—neither Ezekiel, nor Israel, nor the world would be the same after this.

Nebuchadnezzar directly impacted the world of Ezekiel in two other important ways. First, he determined Ezekiel's Babylonian home address. The Babylonians appear to have primarily relocated the Judean exiles to seven villages along the Kebar River (a major canal) near Nippur and Babylon. Exactly where Ezekiel came to live in exile is not clear, though his commissioning as a sentry for Israel occurred near the colony of Judean exiles in Tel-abib, one of these seven enclaves (3:15).[18] From start nearly to finish, the Kebar River furnished a geographic point of reference for significant experiences of Ezekiel (from 1:1 to 43:3).

Second, Ezekiel found himself repeatedly interacting with Babylonian political affairs. For example, in about 585 Nebuchadnezzar laid siege to the city of Tyre, perhaps in reprisal for Tyre's support of Judah's final break from Babylon. Ezekiel foresaw this massive effort of Nebuchadnezzar (26:7–28:19), which turned out to be a marathon siege lasting 13 years.[19] Nebuchadnezzar forced Tyre to accept Babylonian suzerainty, removed the offending king, Ittobaal II, and appointed a governor of Tyre. But the outcome was not the wholesale destruction of the island fortress, which both Nebuchadnezzar and Ezekiel had anticipated. To this state of affairs Ezekiel responded in his last dated oracle, promising the plunder of Egypt in lieu of Babylon's sparse compensation for its labors at Tyre (29:17-20, dated April 571, not long after the end of the siege). The string of 15 dates preserved, strategically placed, and basic to the structure of the book cannot be seen *simply* as evidence that Ezekiel kept a journal. Placed and used as they are, the dates show the author's concern to relate his prophecies to the flow of events in Jerusalem and also among the exiles. The author provides the explicit historical contexts for his oracles, in good part to provide a basis for validating the fact that Israel had "had a prophet among them" (2:5).

Ezekiel's Chronological Notes

DATE (BC) YYY/MM/DD	EZEKIEL REFERENCE	DATE IN MT* YY/MM/DD	EZEKIEL'S APPROXIMATE AGE**	OCCASION
593/7/31	1:1	30/4/5	30	Heavens opened
593/7/31	1:2	05/--/5	30	Correlation with Jehoiachin
593/8/7	3:16	05/4/12?	30	Appointed sentry
592/9/17	8:1	06/6/5	31	Temple vision
591/8/14	20:1	07/5/10	32	Leaders request message
588/1/15	24:1	09/10/10	35	Siege of Jerusalem begins
585/2/3	26:1	11/--/1	36	Oracles against Tyre
587/1/7	29:1	10/10/12	35	Oracles against Pharaoh
571/4/26	29:17	27/1/1	51	Tyre reconsidered
587/4/29	30:20	11/1/7	35	Oracle against Pharaoh
587/6/21	31:1	11/3/1	35	Oracles against Pharaoh
586/7/18	2 Kgs 25:3	By Zedekiah's reign	36	Jerusalem's wall breached
586/8/14	2 Kgs 25:8	By Zedekiah's reign	36	Jerusalem and Temple razed, burned
585/3/3	32:1	12/12/1	36	Oracles against Pharaoh
585/3/17	32:17	12/1/15	36	Oracle against Egypt and others
585/1/8	33:21	12/10/5	36	Refugee from fallen Jerusalem arrives
573/4/28	40:1	25/1/10	49	Temple vision, 14 years after conquest of Jerusalem

*The Masoretic Text uses the Hebrew calendar.
**Arbitrarily regarding July 31, the day of the opened heavens, as his birthday.

AUDIENCE

The audience for Ezekiel's book is best assessed by discerning the readers assumed by the book itself. What reader identity, situation, needs, and concerns can be inferred from the book, considered in the light of data concerning the biblical world from the sixth and fifth centuries BC? (As mentioned, Ezekiel delivered his last dated oracle in April, 571 BC, and the book appears not to point to readers who lived after the fall of Babylon to Cyrus the Persian in 539 BC.) The primary target audiences for the book, one suspects, would have been those of the prophet's actual ministry: the twin audiences of the deportees taken with Jehoiachin and then with Zedekiah, and the people left in the land. Secondarily, the book may also have the communities of the larger Diaspora in view.

The questions of the audience for Ezekiel's prophetic ministry and that of the book are intertwined. Regarding the immediate audience and location of Ezekiel's ministry, there has been long disagreement. Because of Ezekiel's intense interest in Judah and Jerusalem, some have insisted that the prophet either was a prophet primarily or only in Judah (Brownlee 1986:xxiii-xxxiii),[20] or that he must have prophesied in Jerusalem at least for some time prior to a ministry in Babylon (May 1952). Positing a Palestinian location creates more problems than it solves, especially with regard to understanding the compositional history of the book as it is (Soggin 1989:355-356).

Several points help us understand Ezekiel's audience. First, the group to whom Ezekiel was sent was the whole "nation of Israel," the "people of Israel" (2:3; 3:4). He addressed Jerusalemites, Judeans, and exiles, separately and together. Second, though travel was much slower then, we must not think of these communities and others of the Diaspora as hermetically isolated. Jeremiah 29:24-32 indicates a lively interaction between communities by correspondence. Ezra later made the trip in about 100 days, encumbered with a large group (Ezra 7:9; 8:31). A courier intent on travel could cut that time significantly. Third, the whole Israelite community, though geographically separated, shared a rebellious character and a failed relationship with Yahweh (2:3-5, 7; 3:7). Indictment for breach of covenant with Yahweh, analysis of the plight and future of Jerusalem and the nation before and after its fall, perspective from Israel's history, calls to repentance and promise of restoration—all of these topics related to the whole "house of Israel." Exiles remained interested in the Temple and Jerusalem in part because of family left behind and the personal impact upon them of events "back home" (24:20-21).

The fall of Jerusalem demonstrated dramatically that prophets like Ezekiel, Jeremiah, and Zephaniah had been correct on at least one point—Jerusalem and the Temple were going to be destroyed! *How to interpret that destruction* remained the critical question. Even after exiles began to return, debate on this continued. Based on the Sinai covenant and priestly teaching, Ezekiel interpreted the destruction of Jerusalem and the Temple as judgment for the sins of Judah. He pressed this repeatedly in oracles and reports of visions now scattered through chapters 2–24. The content and design of the book of Ezekiel assured that Ezekiel's covenantal interpretation of these events would continue to be heard in the Judean, Jerusalemite, and Israelite communities of the mid- and late-exile period. The condition of the text itself and the early versions attest to continuing, intense interest in the book of Ezekiel's message.

What lay ahead for these communities apparently loomed just as large in their minds as did understanding their past misfortune. What was to become of them now? God promised through Ezekiel that against all odds—including their persistent rebelliousness and the political insignificance of the tattered remains of God's people—he himself would restore his people to their land. After bringing them back to his land, he would make them face their sins (36:31) and would also give them a new heart and his own Spirit to do his will (chs 36–37). He would even grant limited restoration to Egypt (29:13-15). By himself he would cause the nations to acknowledge him (the statement "know that I am the LORD" is repeated through chs 25–35, 38–39).

CANONICITY AND TEXTUAL HISTORY

Canonicity. A discussion of canonicity treats the inclusion and place of a given book in the sacred, authoritative Scriptures of the Christian community, among its "canon" or "canonical writings." The Greek term for "canon" designated a straight rod; it was used metaphorically for a criterion of excellence. Christian writers of the late fourth century AD began to apply the term to the collection of books regarded as authoritative Scripture and to lists of them.

Neither the Jewish community nor the earliest Christian community used the term "canon" to designate the content and boundaries of their sacred Scriptures. Even so, among the Jews the "canonical" concept was indicated in at least three ways: (1) by designation of certain books as those which "render the hands unclean" (*m. Yadayim* 3.5); (2) by including the book in "Bible translation" projects; and (3) by formal quotation or reference with the specific rubric, "(as/for) it is written (in)" or its equivalent. The last two also functioned in the Christian community well before official canonical lists.

The forces that led to the book's inclusion in the Hebrew Scriptures and then in the Christian canon were present from the day it left Ezekiel's hand. Some group of persons received it as truly significant, perhaps even authoritative, and heard God speaking through it. They preserved it and deemed it worthy of editing and transmission for other places and times. Already in the late pre-Christian centuries and the apostolic period, evidence from multiple sources shows wide acceptance of the book of Ezekiel as a part of Israel's sacred Scripture. The earliest attestation to the canonicity of Ezekiel is its appearance in the Septuagint. Work on this oldest of the ancient translations of the Hebrew Scriptures appears to have begun with the law of Moses in the late third century BC in Alexandria, Egypt, continuing on into the second century with the translation of the prophets and other Old Testament books. Ezekiel's inclusion in the Septuagint shows broad acceptance as a "canonical" prophetic book (Klein 1974:1-5; Würtwein 1979:51-53).[21] In the latter third of the first century AD, Josephus counted 13 biblical, prophetic works without naming any but apparently assuming the inclusion of Ezekiel (*Against Apion* 1.38-40).[22] Arguing the superiority of Israel's "histories" (i.e., their sacred books), Josephus refers to Ezekiel in tandem with Jeremiah as equally credible prophets of the fate of Zedekiah at the hands of Nebuchadnezzar (*Antiquities* 10.140-141). He notes differences between the two prophets that were used by Zedekiah to evade the divine word (Ezek 12:13 versus Jer 34:3; cf. *Antiquities* 10.106-107), and says Ezekiel prophesied from Babylon, wrote his prophecies down, and sent them to Jerusalem (*Antiquities* 10.104-106).

The earliest citation of the book of Ezekiel is in Sirach, a work written in Hebrew early in the second century BC and translated into Greek by the author's grandson later in that century. The translator's prologue assumes a tripartite collection of treasured Hebrew writings, referring in its first line to "the law and the prophets and the other books of our fathers" (the first such reference to the Hebrew Scriptures). Then in Sirach 49:8 the writer claims "it was Ezekiel who saw the vision of glory, which God showed him above" (NRSV), referring to 1:28. Beyond Sirach, 4 Maccabees (c. 63 BC–AD 120), in a list of scriptural references, quotes 37:3, "shall these dry bones live?" as the "word of Ezekiel" (4 Macc 18:17), presumably regarding it as Scripture.

Two major sources preserve Jewish rabbinical teaching from the second through the fifth centuries AD. The Mishnah was composed from the work of rabbis in Jewish academies of Galilee. It reached its present form around AD 200 under the editorial hand of Yehudah HaNasi. The second source, the Talmud, contains extensive commentary on the Mishnah and follows the order of the Mishnah's text. The Jerusalem Talmud (Talmud Yerushalmi) is thought to have been completed around 450, the Babylonian Talmud (Talmud Bavli) about 500. All of these Jewish sources incorporate traditional material reaching back long before their "closings," but certainty eludes us as to age of specific sections.

The Mishnah not only states a "canonical" criterion (*m. Yadayim* 3.5, see above), it cites the book of Ezekiel frequently with the rubric of canonical recognition ("as it is written in . . .": *m. Sotah* 1.6 on 23:48; *m. Yoma* 8.9 on 36:25; *m. Avot* 3.3 on 41:22; and *m. Middot* 4.1 on 41:23). See also *m. Middot* 4.2 (on 44:2) ≈ *m. Tamid* 3.7, as well as references in *m. Sukkah* 5.4 and *m. Middot* 3.1. Parallel to references to Genesis, the Mishnah stipulates that "the chapter of the Chariot" (i.e., the difficult and controversial ch 1) is not to be "expounded before one, unless he is a sage" (*m. Hagigah* 2.1), nor is this chapter to be read as "a reading from the Prophets" [as one would otherwise expect from a "canonical" prophetic book] (*m. Megillah* 4.10). In the context of discussing the "writing" of the Hebrew Bible, the Talmud notes the writing (copying?) of Ezekiel by the men of the Great Assembly (*b. Bava Batra* 15a). Earlier it considers the correct order of the scrolls of Scripture, defending the order Jeremiah, Ezekiel, Isaiah and the Twelve—clearly a discussion regarding "canonical" writings (*b. Bava Batra* 14a). Ezekiel's deviations from Leviticus are treated in *b. Menahot* 45a.

Indirect evidence of Christian acceptance of Ezekiel as canonical begins already in the New Testament, as its writers reflect the Jewish traditions out of which they wrote, including those regarding the boundaries of sacred Scripture. The New Testament contains nearly 200 references of various sorts to the book of Ezekiel, treating it as it does other sacred texts (see NA^{27} 914-915 and UBS^{2} 795-796).[23] The Old Latin, the church's earliest translation(s) of the Old Testament (late second century), also included Ezekiel, attesting to this presumed canonical status (Würtwein 1979:87-90). This early inclusion of the book of Ezekiel in Christian Scripture has never, to my knowledge, been challenged in any branch of the church.

Textual History. The book of Ezekiel was most likely written in Hebrew sometime in the mid- to late sixth century BC. Drawing a continuous line from the Hebrew text used by modern translators back to the text produced by Ezekiel and his definitive editors is the task of writing Ezekiel's "textual history." Most modern translations work primarily from the *Biblia Hebraica Stuttgartensia* (BHS), the common text of present scholarly research. The Stuttgart text is a text-critical edition of the Codex Leningradensis (also called "Leningrad B19^{A}" or "L"). Dating from AD 1008, Codex Leningradensis is the oldest complete manuscript of the Hebrew Bible, a product of the highly regarded Ben Asher family of Masoretic scribal scholars from Tiberias. It is the best single witness to the Masoretic Text.

Until the discovery of the Qumran manuscripts ("Dead Sea Scrolls"), beginning in 1947, the question hounding students of the text of Ezekiel was the relationship between this eleventh-century Ben Asher manuscript and the composition produced by Ezekiel 14 centuries earlier. Confidence in the Ben Asher text rose dramatically with the recovery of the Qumran manuscripts. Numerous biblical scrolls and fragments proved to be almost identical to Codex Leningradensis. These scrolls dated from the second century BC to the mid-first century AD. Clearly the Masoretic Ben Asher text preserved with astounding accuracy an ancient textual tradition. Evidence of five Hebrew Ezekiel scrolls, preserving 4 to 5 percent of the text of Ezekiel, has been found at Qumran (1QEzek; 3QEzek; 4QEzek[a]; 4QEzek[b]; 4QEzek[c]; and 11QEzek; García Martínez 1992:466-519). They reflect closely the Masoretic Text of Codex Leningradensis (Lust 1986a:90-101). In a single stroke the line running from the *Biblia Hebraica Stuttgartensia* to Ben Asher was extended back nine to eleven centuries to the apostolic period and before! This is about as far as we can firmly "connect the dots" in the history of the Hebrew text, working back from the Bible now in our hands. Four to five centuries of textual transmission of a proto-Masoretic text still remain largely unaccounted for between Qumran and the hand of Ezekiel.

Discovery of the Qumran scrolls, however, did not just push our horizon on the Old Testament text back a millennium; it also revealed a textual environment much more complex than imagined. In the period between the first edition of Ezekiel and the text forms in existence by the time of the Septuagint and the first Christian century, we are presented with several different Hebrew textual traditions, the proto-Masoretic Text being but one of them (Cross and Talmon 1975:177-195, 306-320). This means that if we begin from Ezekiel's end of the history and attempt to draw the historical line on through to the *Biblia Hebraica Stuttgartensia* of our day, we quickly run out of secure "dots" to connect. By the third century BC, various Hebrew textual traditions of the Torah and other biblical books were in use in Egypt, Palestine, and Babylon. Almost certainly the books of the prophets, including Ezekiel, were similarly disseminated, though explicit evidence for Ezekiel is not yet available (Cross and Talmon 1975:190-195, 306-320). We do not know precisely which text form best represents the first edition of the book of Ezekiel. But we have enough evidence to conclude that we have a strong and reliable text of Ezekiel with which to work. The astounding discoveries at Qumran have shown us how quickly the landscape of the Bible's textual history can be illuminated and radically redrawn, and how ill-advised skepticism regarding the Bible's textual validity is.

The Masoretic Text of Ezekiel itself perhaps carries hints about the text's history *prior to* production of the book. Some passages, e.g., chapters 3, 6, 18, 20:1-31, and 28:1-10 are "largely free from textual difficulties," as Zimmerli describes them, whereas others, chapters 7, 21, 28:11-19, "appear badly disturbed" (1979:75). Zimmerli thinks this evidence raises the question of the circulation of individual sections in "differing qualities of preservation" (1979:75).

LITERARY STYLE

The book's pervasive autobiographical stance presents the most obvious aspect of Ezekiel's literary style. This autobiographical stance is evident at the very beginning of the book (1:1-3) where we read the first person singular (i.e., "I," "me," "my") with reference to Ezekiel himself as he provides his age, his geopolitical-social situation, his family identification, professional heritage, and his visual and verbal encounter with Yahweh.[24] Other prophets carry similar, introductory lines, but none of those editorial introductions are autobiographical. (The third person references in 1:3 appear to be intrusive and are probably editorial notes intended to emphasize Ezekiel's family and professional connections. See the notes on 1:1-3.) This first person stance does appear elsewhere among the biblical prophets, but the extent to which it pervades the book of Ezekiel is unique, appearing repeatedly from 1:1 to the final set of oracles in 47:8. Interestingly, Ezekiel's name itself occurs only twice in the book (1:3; 24:24). In many places where we would ordinarily expect a third person report naming Ezekiel, the report comes instead in the first person.[25]

Consequently, the book of Ezekiel calls dramatic attention to the prophet as inextricably bound up with the word from God. The book also invites the reader to see through Ezekiel's eyes and listen through Ezekiel's ears. At the same time, paradoxically, the primary focus of the book of Ezekiel is not on the prophet himself. Instead, center stage belongs to the glorious God of Israel, then secondarily to God's people, and finally to other nations to whom God directs Ezekiel. The words of God comprise almost the entirety of the book's content, introduced by first person rubrics. Also, the Lord's common address of Ezekiel as "son of man"[26] repeatedly underscores the chasm between this human being (and by inference all humankind) and the exalted one who speaks, cloaked in brilliant splendor, from the heavenly throne. And the book closes and reaches its climax with the new city's name, "Yahweh Is There!" (48:35).

As for its general literary type, which is an elementary aspect of style, the majority of the book of Ezekiel is Hebrew prose. There are some poetic sections, as well. For example, while editing the Masoretic Text for the *Biblia Hebraica Stuttgartensia,* Eilliger formatted several longer passages as poetry: 7:2-27; 17:2-10; 19:2-14; 21:13-22; 27:3-10, 25-26, 28-32, 34-36; 30:2-5; 31:2-9; 32:2-8, 12-15 and 18-28, along with a number of shorter stretches of poetry, e.g., 18:2; 23:32-34; 24:3-5; 26:17-18; 29:3, 5-7; and 35:3-4, 9. The NLT not only formats all of these as poetry but also sets some other portions as poetry.[27] This disparity in literary judgment may reflect the fact that it is often difficult to tell whether we have "elevated prose," sharing substantially the cadence and parallelism of Hebrew poetry, or less-than-stellar poetry. Harrison (1969:839) cites Lowth's 1835 *Lectures on the Sacred Story of the Hebrews,* equating Ezekiel's poetic abilities with Aeschylus, but Harrison also notes J. A. Brewer's contrary estimate that Ezekiel proved "prosaic even when writing poetry" (citing *The Literature of the Old Testament with Historical Development,* 1922). As a poet, Ezekiel is no match for Job or Isaiah, but his lines can nevertheless be forceful. The writer at least once uses poetic genre to underscore the conclusion of a literary unit (7:2-27).

"Halving," as Greenberg calls it, is probably the most prominent stylistic feature of the book of Ezekiel. In this artistic device, the writer propounds an initial theme in an opening oracle. Following this a second theme is developed, more briefly, often with a concluding "coda" intermingling elements from the first two oracles (Greenberg 1983:25; Block 1997:23). This stylistic signature also, of course, deals with structure. "Halving" provides the organizing principle for the oracles in chapters 6; 7; 13; 16; 17; 18; 21; 22; 24:1-14; 24:15-27; 26:1-21; 28; 30; 31; and perhaps others, according to Greenberg (1983:25-26).

Style and structure interface again in Ezekiel's habit of "resumptive exposition" (Block 1997:24-25, following Greenberg). Two approaches surface here: (1) The writer frequently reuses themes already treated (e.g., the sentinel theme; 3:16-21; 33:1-9); (2) he at times gives preliminary treatment to a theme expounded at length elsewhere, as in the exposition of the throne chariot and the divine glory first in 1:1-28 and then at length in 8:1–11:25. This dimension is distinctive of Ezekiel's style. Block notes that extended narrative presentations, like the massive vision reports in chapters 8–11 and 40–48, are parade examples. Block further notes that chapter 16 alone, with its 830 words, is longer than six of the twelve Minor Prophets (1997:39)!

One can easily confuse *prophetic* style with *literary* style. As a prophet, Ezekiel used at least 22 different forms of prophetic speech, such as formulaic utterances, vision reports, laments for the dead, work songs, and disputations (Zimmerli 1979:vii). He also did astounding "sign-acts," such as devouring a scroll (2:9–3:3), laying siege to a brick city he had made (4:1-3), and not mourning the death of his beloved wife (24:15-18). These varied forms and amazing deeds surely made Ezekiel an engaging communicator, as God noted (33:32).

Some matters of prophetic style, however, have left their mark on Ezekiel's literary style. First, the use of *formulaic prophetic introductions*, familiar from other prophetic works, abound in Ezekiel and generate what one might call a basic prophetic style: "The LORD gave me a message" (1:3; 3:16), "This message came to me from the LORD" (over 40 times), and related expressions.[28] The style itself says, "This is a *prophetic* book!" Second, the prophet's frequent use of "metaphorical discourses," as Zimmerli terms them (1979:30), gives the work a sapiential flavor, full of analogy, sometimes moving all the way to allegory. The figure of the vine (ch 15), the foundling child (ch 16), the two eagles, the cedar, and the vine (ch 17), the two lions and a vine (ch 19), the two sisters (ch 23), and the great ship Tyre (ch 27) are most important. Third, the underscoring of message with a particularly fitting literary form marks Ezekiel's style. He couches his allegorical depiction of Judah's final days and destruction (ch 19) metrically in a funeral song and concludes by announcing the funeral implied in the lament! Fourth, his frequent dating of oracles with a standard year/month/day formula reminds one of the Aramaic papyri from the fifth-century-BC Jewish garrison communities in upper Egypt at Aswan (ancient Syene) and Elephantine. These predominantly administrative letters, pertaining to both local and international matters, commonly open with a day/month/year formula. Ezekiel's habit introduces an administrative, chronicling ambiance to a document that is clearly neither administrative nor a chronicle. Finally, Ezekiel's frequent reports of his vision experiences (chs 1, 3, 8–11, 37, 40–48) take the reader *visually*, almost tangibly, into the world God and the prophet share, at times guided by God himself or his representative. This visionary perspective opens, closes, and logically propels the book.

Ezekiel's language itself figures in his style. He writes in a Hebrew form that stands between classical, biblical Hebrew and postbiblical, late Hebrew, perhaps heading toward "late biblical Hebrew." His extensive use of preverbal elements is an example of this style/syntax. The book bears the marks of a speaker or writer immersed in Babylonian culture and its Aramaic lingua franca for at least 30 years. He carried within him 30 years of Jerusalem Hebrew and ancient Hebrew tradition, now making its home in Babylon. Over a dozen Aramaic expressions found in the Hebrew Bible appear only in Ezekiel; lexical and grammatical Aramaisms appear in Ezekiel's book at twice the rate of his contemporary Jeremiah's back in Jerusalem (Block 1997:40, citing M. Wagner, *Die lexikalischen und grammatikalilschen Aramäismen im altestmentlichen Hebräisch.* Pp. 140-141 in *Beihefte zur Zeitschrift für die alttestamentliche Wissenschaft* 96. Berlin: Töpelmann, 1966). Ezekiel also contains around 40 percent more hapax legomena (words occurring only once in biblical Hebrew) than Jeremiah does, even though Jeremiah is 16 percent longer than Ezekiel; this fact is another possible clue to Ezekiel's distance from "ordinary Jerusalem speech" (Block 1997:40, citing *Theologisches Handwörterbuch zum Alten Testament* 2.541). Akkadianisms in the book also show influence from the Babylonian setting itself (Block 1997:40, citing S. P. Garfinkel, *Studies in Akkadian Influences in the Book of Ezekiel* [Ann Arbor: University Microfilms, 1983]).

MAJOR THEMES AND THEOLOGICAL CONCERNS

The Integrity of Ezekiel's Prophetic Mission and the Fate of Jerusalem. Early on in the book we confront the conflict over the future of Jerusalem as debated by Judeans at home and in exile in the years just before its fall in 586 BC. Was the city safe when it was on the verge of independence from a distracted Babylon? Or was it doomed, as prophets like Jeremiah, Zephaniah, and Ezekiel had said? Some public officials called for home-building, implying the long-term stability of Jerusalem and the country (11:2-3), rejecting these prophets' predictions. Conventional wisdom had it that time made a liar of every prophet—"Time passes, and prophecies come to nothing" was the proverb (12:22).

Having raised the topic, the writer addressed the debate head-on, blaming the malaise on "false prophets" (12:24–13:23). Their character and behavior were reprehensible, he charged. Joining a long line of such "prophets," they told people what they wanted to hear (13:10-12, 16) and used prophetic language about the source of their message to give authority to their deceptions (13:6). In particular, one thinks of Jeremiah's nemesis, Hananiah (cf. Jer 28:1-2 with Jer 29:4-11). Whether they were sincere but deceived or outright charlatans, they were liars according to God (13:6, 8, 10; cf. 22:25, 28).

But even more to the point, a theological and existential watershed divided these false prophets from Ezekiel. Their "prophetic" pronouncements were not only audience driven, they were self-generated (13:3). They brought no revelation from outside their deluded world; they replaced the true word of God with inventions. Yahweh (1) had not sent them (13:6); (2) he had not spoken to them (13:7; 22:28); (3) he had shown them nothing in visions (13:3, 7, 8); and (4) these prophets brought no real help to God's people (13:10-15). The whole enterprise of seeking and giving a prophetic word had become so corrupted that Yahweh himself used the process to judge the participants (14:9).[29] Each of these indictments against the false prophets reflected a fundamental requirement of true prophets. In the book of Ezekiel, the writer at the outset establishes his credentials as an authentic prophet of Yahweh. The God of Israel *had* spoken to this man from outside his normal world (1:4-28); God *had* actually "fed him" his word (2:9–3:3). Yahweh *had* commissioned ("sent") Ezekiel (2:1–3:21). And the visions he had seen *were* from God (e.g., 1:1-3).

Of old Yahweh had established criteria by which Israel could separate false prophets from persons truly speaking for him. Anyone who enticed Israel to serve other gods was known to be a false prophet, no matter what other exploits or signs they might accomplish (Deut 13:1-5). Anyone who discerned the will of Yahweh through divination, soothsaying, sorcery, necromancy, wizardry, or other such means was also discredited as a false prophet (Deut 18:9-14). Persons who practiced child sacrifice could in no case be accredited as a prophet of Yahweh (Deut 18:10). And prophets whose threats or promises failed to materialize (i.e., did not "come true") were known not to be from Yahweh (Deut 18:21-22). On all of these counts Ezekiel was accredited as a true prophet of God.

Ezekiel carried the prophetic debate further, addressing women whose prophecies shared the same fatal flaw of being essentially self-generated and culture bound (13:17). He focused on three major evils in their approach to prophecy: First and most often mentioned, they ensnared God's people in magical practices (13:18, 20, 21, 23), betraying a worldview alien to authentic covenant faith. Little in historic revelation led Israel to believe that the God of covenant was open to manipulation by magic. Instead, Yahweh invited persons to trust him and obey his word, relating in modes essentially "personal," not magical. Second, Ezekiel chided them for their "prophecy for hire" approach (13:19; cf. Amos 7:12-15; Mic 3:5). Finally, they either ignored, confused, or reversed the relationship between covenant faithfulness and life-consequences found in Israel's historic covenant with Yahweh (13:19-23; cf. Lev 26; Deut 27:1–30:20). The behaviors of these women betrayed a fundamental confusion of and perhaps outright abandonment of authentic Yahweh faith. At best, they lived a syncretistic faith, worshiping and "serving" Yahweh as though he were another of the gods of the nations—at best, a first-among-equals deity. Quite likely, the prophets addressed in 13:1-16 would have shared their malaise.

This confusion involved conflicting worldviews, which (as we have seen in considering Manasseh) manifested streams of theological corruption present in Judah's (and Israel's) religious establishment running back to the beginning. From early on there had been a fierce battle over these matters. The conflict persisted in Ezekiel's day and, more important for reading the book, apparently figured significantly in the lives of persons for whom the book was designed. The claims inherent in Ezekiel's call refuted these practices as well, for the call he received and the God he saw came from a world not reached by magical charms but revealed by the gracious Sovereign of Israel's covenant. Ezekiel's interest in dating his oracles that warned Jerusalem of her eminent doom pertained to this question (8:1; 20:1; 24:1). The gainsayers and mockers notwithstanding, and the official line from palace and Temple notwithstanding, Ezekiel had been hearing from and speaking for the God of Israel all along.

Ezekiel's Priestly Convictions. In the book of Ezekiel, the whole world divides into what is clean and unclean, holy and profane, which are bedrock priestly concerns. Indeed, the priesthood's failure in its leadership role to distinguish between "what is holy and what is not . . . . what is ceremonially clean and unclean" provides major cause for Jerusalem's threatened destruction (22:26). This is a particularly priestly way of putting Jerusalem's problem. These two key, opposing word-pairs—"holy" versus "unholy/profane," "clean" versus "unclean," (*ben-qodesh* [TH6944, ZH7731] *lekhol* [TH2455, ZH2687] . . . *uben-hattame'* [TH2931, ZH3238] *letahor* [TH2889, ZH3196])—appear elsewhere only in Leviticus 10:10 and in Ezekiel's hope (44:23). Although hope for an end to defilement marks Ezekiel's view of restoration (44:23), the prior question of Jerusalem's judgment and the fate of Yahweh's Temple occupied him first.

Priestly language and concerns permeate the book of Ezekiel. Scattered across the book, from 4:4 to 48:22 in all but nine chapters, over 200 of Ezekiel's 1,273 verses contain one or more references to Leviticus, the Old Testament's priestly book par excellence. In the process, over 147 verses in Leviticus (from Lev 3:17 to 27:28) are touched in some way (quotation, allusion, borrowed language or terminology).[30] These numbers increase significantly if we include in the survey not just the book of Leviticus but passages throughout the books of Moses widely identified by scholars with the priests thought to have produced Leviticus as it now stands (the so-called "P" materials). Ezekiel did not simply pass on priestly tradition contained in Torah, although he was a faithful expositor of Torah. At points Ezekiel departed significantly from priestly teaching as we have it in the books of Moses. For example, Ezekiel's restriction of priestly presentation of sacrifices at the altar to Zadokite priests stood at odds with Moses's restriction of these duties to the Aaronide priests (44:15-16; cf. Lev 8:6-7; Num 3:1-3; 18:2-6). These "contradictions" with Moses posed a significant enough problem for early rabbis to seek resolutions (*b. Menahot* 45a; *b. Hagigah* 13a).[31]

Already in chapter 4, Ezekiel's revulsion at personal defilement over dietary matters surfaces (4:12-14; cf. 44:31). He protested his lifelong avoidance of being "defiled" (*metumma'ah* [TH2930, ZH3237]) by food, in terms unique to Leviticus and Ezekiel (4:14; cf. Lev 7:24; 17:15; 22:8). He concluded with a priestly technical term for forbidden meat (*piggul* [TH6292, ZH7002], only here and Lev 7:18; 19:7). In context, this sign-act regarding unclean food was headed toward the message that Israel would eat their bread unclean (*lakhmam tame'* [TH3899/2931, ZH4312/3238]) "in the Gentile lands" where God was going to "banish them" (4:13). Clearly, to God and the prophet, this defilement itself was part of the catastrophe.

Defilement by contact with dead bodies also figures early and repeatedly in the book.[32] This issue magnifies the judgment involved in threats that Yahweh will strew Israel's "slain" (*khalal* [TH2491, ZH2728]) before her idols (6:4, 6-7, 13), throughout the Temple (9:7), and in Jerusalem itself (11:6-7).[33] Ezekiel's visionary encounter of a valley littered with dry bones (37:1-4) adds defilement to death and thereby compounds the odds against restoration of this wretched army.

But most important to Ezekiel, idolatry defiles peoples and their lands (20:7, 18, 31; 22:3-4; 23:7, 30; 36:18). This defilement by idolatry presents the major sin that has ensured Jerusalem's end. Ezekiel's hope includes the land rid of this defilement

(37:23). But preceding that hope, no ritual expiation for the land is available, "and, hence, the expulsion of its inhabitants is inexorable (Lev 18:24-29; 20:2)" (ABD 5.457). In 6:4-6, emphasizing judgment itself as involving defilement with corpses, the prophet brings together three terms—incense stand (*khamman* [TH2553, ZH2802]), corpse (*peger* [TH6297, ZH7007]), and lifeless idol (*gillulim* [TH1544, ZH1658])—which appear together in Old Testament literature in only one other place, the covenant curses of Leviticus 26:30: "I will destroy your pagan shrines and knock down your [incense altars] (*khammanekem*). I will leave your lifeless corpses (*pigrekem*) piled on top of your lifeless idols (*gillulekem*)."[34]

Leviticus 26 catalogs the blessings promised to those who live by Yahweh's commands (Lev 26:3-13) and the curses Yahweh will bring upon those who do not keep covenant with him (Lev 26:14-43).[35] Forty-four verses in Ezekiel 4:14–39:27 share significant language with 19 verses from this single chapter, Leviticus 26, repeatedly evoking from a priestly perspective covenant logic and the consequences of breaking covenant.[36]

The Debate over the Fate of Solomon's Temple. After introductory passages (1:1–3:27), debate over the fate of Jerusalem dominates the next 21 chapters of the book. While the writer gives extensive attention to Israel's sins, the accent falls continually on the fact that *because* of these sins the land, the city, and its Temple are doomed (e.g., 2:2-7; 4:1-8; 5:1-13; 6:10; 7:1-5; 12:25, 28; 14:12-23; 16:15-18; 21:1-17; 22:4). Frequently the indictments themselves are implicit in the announcement of impending judgment (e.g., 6:1-7). The burden falls not simply on the identification of Israel's sins but on the consequences of those sins in Israel's doom.

The book ties this fate of Jerusalem and Israel directly to priestly matters just as it does to prophetic debates (see above). First, Ezekiel focuses his indictments on priestly concerns such as defilement and purity, sacred and profane, idols, altars, shrines, worship utensils, and gods other than Yahweh. Second, Ezekiel devotes significant space to Temple visions (chs 8–11 of the Solomonic Temple; chs 40–47 of the future Temple), along with repeated attention to the integrity of the Temple functions.

We lack sufficient information to reconstruct precisely the historical development of Israel's faith in Yahweh so as to make proper sense of the information we do have. The topic continues to generate scholarly debate.[37] Nevertheless, some important claims carry wide agreement. The biblical record itself traces the Israelite priesthood to Aaron, established through Moses, and the founding of Israel at Sinai. It also traces to those same Mosaic roots a theology of Yahweh being Israel's only God, perhaps even *the* only God, creator of heavens and earth and of all the other "gods." With Moses rose a radical, new alternative to the gods and power of Pharaoh and the entire fallen world.[38] Biblical and extrabiblical data also seem to indicate from the outset competing understandings of Yahweh's place among the gods and consequently also competing views of the priesthood and the identity of "legitimate" priests in Israel. Ezekiel himself traced idolatry in Israel back beyond Sinai to Egypt (20:4-8).

The Temple visions draw the reader directly into the center of this fray. These visions reveal the complex world of political and theological turmoil exhibited in the Jerusalem Temple of Ezekiel's own day. In the first Temple vision (chs 8–11) Ezekiel's visual collection of abominations, with a certain air of unreality, may present for the reader a "montage" of hallmark breaches of Yahweh faith that had plagued the Jerusalem Temple over the period of the monarchy (Greenberg 1983:201-202). But just as likely in view of the illicit materials cleared from the Temple under Josiah (2 Kgs 23:4-14) or Manasseh (2 Chr 33:15) and the reversals of reform sponsored by Josiah's successors, the scene may have pictured the confusion in Yahweh's Temple in the summer of 592 BC (Smith 1990:116, 120).

One suspects that these various idolatries were generally thought of as aspects of Yahweh worship sponsored by the crown, priesthood, and civic leadership of the last years of the kingdom of Judah. They almost surely involved either outright incorporation of alien worship into the Jerusalem Temple or a Yahweh theology positioning Israel's national deity Yahweh in a pantheon "enriched" by other deities, who were part of Israel's own past as well as that of Israel's Canaanite neighbors and the imperial cultures to which Israel had been subject (Egypt, Assyria, Babylon; cf. 11:12).

However these idolatrous practices are understood, the Yahweh of the book of Ezekiel shows no sympathy whatsoever for any of them. Yahweh regarded these "innovations" and historic deviations alike as "detestable sins" (8:6), and the idols as "vile images and detestable idols" (11:18, 21). Persons involved in these practices—priests and laypersons alike—would be slain (9:1-6; 11:8-12, 21), receiving the full force of Yahweh's judgment. When exile was over, Yahweh's people who returned to the land would "remove every trace" of these abominations (11:18).

The book of Ezekiel (like many other OT documents) is unabashedly "sectarian" and polemical on these points. It stands intentionally against all priestly traditions participating in and contributing to the theological chaos in the Jerusalem Temple. The collage of "detestable" worship in the Jerusalem Temple required at least some cadre of Jerusalem priests, presumably Yahweh priests, hospitable to their presence in the Temple or at least willing to tolerate them. The book of Ezekiel could scarcely be more forceful in its rejection of these accommodations. In reality, the reader repeatedly hears that these compromises sealed the destruction of Solomon's Temple. The prominence and extent of this priestly debate shows the conviction that the fundamental issues were pertinent not only to Ezekiel's historical audience but also to future readers to whom the book would come.

The Future Temple. The book of Ezekiel returns fully to the issue of the Temple in a vision of the future Temple (loosely chs 40–48). In spite of the fact that this vision is dated almost 13 years after the Temple of chapters 8–11 had been razed by the Babylonians, the book returns to earlier issues of idolatrous worship. God specifically rejects "adulterous worship of other gods" (43:7) such as plagued Solomon's Temple. The vision singles out the entanglement of Judah's kings with the Temple as partly responsible for its tragic history, and it strictly forbids those entanglements in the new Temple (43:7-9).

Moving beyond the defiling idolatry that doomed the first Temple, the vision engages ancient controversy regarding legitimate priestly leadership in Israel. As with the history of Israel's Yahweh faith, sufficient evidence does not exist to reconstruct precisely the history of the development of the priesthood in Israel

(Milgrom 1991; Rehm 1992). The large, canonical picture in Scripture is relatively clear (Childs 1986:150ff). God established Israel's worship and priesthood at Sinai through Moses and exclusively from the tribe of Levi (Exod 6:14-25; 28–29; Lev 8–10; Deut 33:8). Integral to the covenant, priests were ordained both to enable sacrifice and to instruct God's people in his ways (Exod 19; 24; 28; 33:7-11).

As Israel's first consecrated priests (Exod 28; Lev 8–10), Aaron and his sons had preeminence. God distinguished priests and Levites, appointing the Levites subordinate to Aaron and his sons to minister by caring for the Tabernacle and its furnishings (Num 1:47-54; 3:5-10; 18:1-24) and to serve as guardians of the covenant (Deut 33:8-11). The Levites were also noted historically for their zeal for Yahweh and zeal against idolatry, especially remembered over against Aaron's leading the people astray already at Sinai with the golden calf (Exod 32). On the other hand, the book of Deuteronomy appears to speak of Levites with full priestly duty (Deut 18:1-8; 33:8-11). This stands in tension with the traditions cited above and complicates attempts to outline the history of Israel's priesthood without appeal to compositional processes of which we are ill informed.

The period of the Judges saw a decline from Mosaic priestly ideals (Judg 17; 1 Sam 2:22-25). Under David and Solomon, critical developments in the priesthood occurred. Although Abiathar served as David's priest and brought him the ephod early in David's reign (1 Sam 22:20; 23:6), after the capture of Jerusalem Abiathar and Zadok appear to have shared the high priesthood under David (2 Sam 15). Following Abiathar's support of Adonijah as successor to David, Solomon exiled him to Anathoth and made Zadok the sole high priest (1 Kgs 1:5–2:35). Two centuries later, Hezekiah's chief priest was of the house of Zadok (2 Chr 31:10), and a century beyond that, Zadokites still dominated the Jerusalem Temple during the reign of Josiah. The fact that some priests supported—or at least protected—Jeremiah (Jer 29:24-32) while others opposed him (Jer 20:1; 26; 38) may show the complex state of affairs concerning the priesthood.

By the time of Josiah's reforms, Levites could be found among paganized priests and priests of the Lord, serving at local shrines where they had been installed over the years by Israel's kings![39] Josiah killed paganized priests and brought other priests of the Lord (who also had served at the compromised shrines!) to Jerusalem. These either chose not or were not allowed (by the Jerusalem Zadokites?) to function as priests at the Jerusalem Temple (2 Kgs 23:5-9; see NLT mg). Meanwhile, the Zadokites presided over or at least participated significantly in a Temple highly conflicted in its theological loyalties (ch 8).

God gave Ezekiel a vision of the future Temple addressing the confusions in this history (40:1–46:24). Not only the architecture of the envisioned Temple but also new Torah, couched within the vision, spoke to this point, turning on the issue of holiness (43:7-12, 18-27; 44:2-31; 45:1–46:18). Foreigners who were not even sworn participants in covenant with the Lord ("uncircumcised"; 44:6-9) had long served as Temple guards and entered far too much in Temple affairs. The Lord excluded these people entirely from the future Temple. Instead, Levites, not of the family of Zadok, would serve as Temple guards and gatekeepers. And proselyte foreigners who *were* sworn participants in the covenant would now enter the sanctuary

(44:9). These Levites would also slaughter animals for sacrifice (cf. Lev 1:5, 11) and assist in cooking portions. They would have charge of maintenance and general duties in the Temple. But, because of their complicity in Israel's defilement in idolatry, they would be barred from actually serving as priests at the altar (44:10-14). Only Levitical priests of the family of Zadok would serve as the Lord's ministers, standing in his presence, offering the fat and blood of sacrifices on the altar, entering the Lord's sanctuary, and approaching his table, exemplars of faithfulness in the face of Israel's idolatry (44:15-16).

How Ezekiel saw the Zadokites as faithful priests, in light of the condition of the Jerusalem Temple over which they presided (chs 8–11), is unclear. Perhaps there were Zadokite factions of varying orthodoxy at odds in the Temple itself. What *is* clear is the anticipation of a Temple free from all its historic pollutions and governed by the basic law of "absolute holiness" (43:12). In the Temple as elsewhere, God's people would keep covenant with him (44:7).[40] Authentic worshipers would populate the new land and the new Temple. Whether foreigners or born Israelites, they would bear the mark of the covenant (circumcision) and live surrendered to the Lord, having a "heart for God" (lit., "circumcised in heart"; 44:7-9).

Moral Accountability and the Lord's Sovereign Grace. The book of Ezekiel shows major concern regarding both of these topics—individual moral accountability and Yahweh's sovereign grace. It shows little if any concern to reconcile tensions others have felt between the two.

The accountability issue surfaced especially regarding responsibility for the threatened doom of Jerusalem. It receives extended treatment in chapter 18 and again in 33:12-20 (cf. 14:1-23). Ezekiel propounds a concept of authentic, dynamic moral accountability. Tradition had it (2 Kgs 21:10-15; 23:26; 24:3) that Jerusalem's doom was already sealed. Manasseh's sins had been so grievous that, although the Lord would delay her destruction for the sake of Josiah, the city would nevertheless fall to a foreign power. When Ezekiel warned the exiles that their sins and those of the present leadership of Judah would bring the Temple and city to ruin, they deflected blame to their ancestors with a proverb: "The parents have eaten sour grapes, but their children's mouths pucker at the taste" (18:2). Ezekiel rejected the proverb as an invalid and inadequate approach to understanding their part in Jerusalem's destiny (18:3). He countered instead with this claim from God: "The person who sins is the one who will die"—not that person's offspring. This emphasizes not the sin but the identity of the one to die (18:4). Then 18:5-32 expounds his claim.

First, Ezekiel explores the intergenerational consequences of sin. He claims that individual righteous persons will live (18:5-9). They are considered righteous because they act righteously. Ezekiel draws no dichotomy between their being and doing. A righteous life issues in the promised destiny of the righteous—they live. Children of such persons who reject justice and righteousness and do evil will die as they should (18:10-13)! Their parents' righteousness does not save them. Their own character determines their fate. Ezekiel emphasizes this by moving to a third generation, the child of the hypothetical wicked person (18:14-18). If children reject their parents' wickedness and instead live righteously, the children will live! And they will do so not because of the righteousness of their grandparents and without reference to the destiny of their parents. God sees and judges them on the basis of their own character and behaviors. Against protests of alleged unfairness on God's part, Ezekiel repeatedly insists on the principle with which he began: The person who sins—not another—will die (18:19-22).

Second, Ezekiel moves to intragenerational accountability for sin (18:21-24; cf. 33:12-20). Not only does the God of Israel "track" accurately the moral identity of each generation, he judges persons as they are at any given point in their lives, within their generation. Wicked persons who turn from their disobedience and embrace God's way will live. Sadly, when righteous persons take up the way of sin, leaving their righteous behavior behind, they will die (18:21-24). Contrary to protests against the teaching, Ezekiel emphasizes the authentic and dynamic nature of God's interest in human character and behavior, not only intergenerationally, but also intragenerationally (18:25-30).

Ezekiel's concept of moral accountability can be described as "authentic" in that God sees persons precisely as they are, evaluating their character on the basis of their persistent behaviors and assigning them appropriate consequences. It is dynamic, in that the character of persons and their consequent destiny is not locked-in or static, but capable of movement and dramatic change. Individuals can "turn" from one way of life to another, a "conversion," involving "a decisive redirection" of life. This is one of Ezekiel's most important insights (Blenkinsopp 1990:173). Ezekiel speaks of actual, dominant, life patterns, not hour-to-hour vacillation in a person's life. He assumes people reveal developed and identifiable character over their lives, including trust in God or the lack thereof. Even these developed patterns can change, sadly for the worse or happily for the better.

The change argued for here constitutes real change. It is not that they really were not wicked or righteous and simply manifested what they had actually been all along. They actually chose and exhibited a different moral identity and way of life. God does not arbitrarily hem persons in to a certain destiny, claims Ezekiel—not by his knowledge of their parents' or grandparents' ways, and not by their own earlier character. It is not where people came from or how they began the journey that concerns God, but who they themselves are morally now and how they end the race.

Ezekiel stresses here the fairness of God (18:19, 25, 29; 33:17). God has not denied the reality of intergenerational or lifelong consequences of sin and righteousness. He has rebutted the misuse of traditions like Exodus 34:7b ("I lay the sins of the parents upon their children and grandchildren; the entire family is affected—even children in the third and fourth generations") and pulled the rug out from under Israel's attempts to dismiss the preaching of the prophet. Ezekiel also emphasizes the compassionate disposition of God. God is eager to hear Israel's prayers (36:37). His threats notwithstanding, God emphatically desires life for the wicked. He takes no delight in judging or destroying them. The Lord pleads for Israel to repent and live, saying, "Why should you die, O people of Israel?" (18:23, 30-32; 33:11).

Yahweh's Sovereign Grace to Redeem. From the first lines of Ezekiel's book, Yahweh's sovereign grace leaps from the pages. God's initiative in disclosing himself and calling the prophet leads the presentation. The glorious one moves and speaks again, as on Sinai! God's indictments of Israel and the nations great and small assume a Sovereign with character and capacity to hold human beings and their cultures accountable. Threats of judgment and promises of redemption stand on the presumption that Israel's God will have his way in the history of the world. The prophetic span of centuries and horizons reaching clear to Eden tie this Sovereign One to the creation of the world as well. Only Yahweh is God; the prophet mocks all divine pretenders as pollutants the Lord will destroy (e.g., 30:13). These theological assumptions undergird the entire book. The expression, "Sovereign LORD," ubiquitous in Ezekiel, drives home this perspective.[41]

The most dramatic and most extensively pursued expression of Yahweh's sovereign grace centers in his promise to restore his people (chs 33–48). Ezekiel concluded that if God's people are ever to live again in the land and are ever to live at peace with him, it will be God's doing, not theirs! And it will be for God's own purposes, not in response to the repentance of his people. This is so, in spite of the pleas for repentance, for life, for getting a new heart and new spirit. Early on, at the conclusion of the first Temple vision and the frightful departure of God's glory from it, most facets of the program are announced. (1) Yahweh, who will scatter Israel among the nations, will gather them and give them the land once again (11:17). (2) God will give his people a "tender, responsive," obedient heart in place of their stubborn, rebellious heart (11:19). (3) God and his people will live in authentic covenant relationship (11:20). In the process the returned people will do away with their detestable idols (11:18).

Two other major concerns surface in God's sovereign restoration of his people—the reputation of the land of Israel and of God himself. Deserted, ruined, and in waste, the mountains of Israel became the brunt of humiliating claims and the target of plunder by the surrounding nations (36:1-5, 13). Because God "cares" about the land, he promised that an increased population would carefully tend the land. Even animals would abound! The mountains of Israel would once more be the territory of the people of God (36:8-12, 14-15).

As for God's own name, the scattering of Israel among the nations was two-edged. Israel reaped the consequences of her betrayal of covenant. Yahweh, however, appeared unable to protect his people. Now Yahweh's name was shamed among the nations (36:16-20). Not the quality or deserts of the people but concern for his own reputation would prompt Yahweh to bring his people back, to transform their character, giving them a new heart and new spirit to serve him. They would enjoy a lavish harvest and never again become the laughingstock of the nations. Then, after God had brought them back, they would acknowledge their sins. They would "repent" after, not prior to, God's sovereign act to clear his name among the nations (36:21-36; cf. 16:60-63; 20:39-44). Repeatedly through these promises, the purpose is that Israel and especially the nations will acknowledge that Yahweh, God of Israel, has acted before their eyes (30:26; 36:23, 36; 37:28; 38:16, 23; 39:7, 23).

New Covenant, New Heart. Judah and Jerusalem's plight lay in breaking covenant with God. The covenant at Sinai (Exod 20–24) positioned Yahweh as the Great King, after the analogy of treaties between suzerains and conquered vassals. In a surprising twist, however, Israel's "Great King" had not conquered them and imposed terms but had rescued them from bondage in Egypt and offered a way to life. In response, they agreed to keep all the terms of the covenant (Exod 19:3-8). Ezekiel repeatedly accused Israel of breaking that covenant and threatened the coming consequences, with both Levitical and Deuteronomic language. The curses of the broken covenant were upon Israel. The covenant relationship yielded well also to a marital analogy (chs 16 and 23; Jer 2:2, 23-35; 31:32; Hos 1:2–2:13).

Pursuing the marriage metaphor, Hosea had envisioned a "new covenant" without explicit use of that language (Hos 2:14-23 [16-25]). Against the backdrop of the Sinai covenant, Ezekiel's older contemporary Jeremiah promised a "new covenant" (Jer 31:31-33). The "new covenant" provided theological structure for God's restoration of Judah and Jerusalem, about to be destroyed under the curses rightly to fall on those who would not keep covenant (Lev 26; Deut 27–29). Yahweh's promise of a new covenant spoke of abounding mercy. The Great King had no continuing obligations to Judah. As Hosea had seen it, they were no longer his people. Apart from love, he had no obligation to them (Hos 1:8-11 [1:8–2:2]).

Jeremiah's "new covenant" (Jer 31:31-34) and "everlasting covenant" (Jer 32:36-44) feature the distinctive promise of character transformation. Together with promises of gathering his people again to the land and blessing them there with bounty, God declared: "I will put my instructions deep within them, and I will write them on their hearts" (Jer 31:33). He would give them "one heart and one purpose: to worship me forever" (Jer 32:39). One day, after God's destruction of Babylon, Israel and Judah would join together, "weeping and seeking the LORD their God" and would reciprocally "bind themselves to the LORD with an eternal covenant," never to be broken (Jer 50:4-5). He would enable them to do from the heart all that he required, truly a miracle of grace.

Without repeating Jeremiah's "new covenant" language, Ezekiel carried forward his theological claim and advanced it, explaining *how* the promised transformation would occur. The book diagnoses Israel's fundamental problem as a character flaw described in terms of the heart (the human faculty of thinking, judging, committing, feeling, reflecting, deciding) and spirit (one's sense or mind). Israel's heart was "stubborn [hard]" (2:4; 3:7), a wanton and adulterous heart (6:9), stony and unresponsive (11:19; 36:26), obsessed with detestable abominations (11:21; 20:16), preoccupied with idols (14:3-7), proud (28:2, 17), and set on violent gain (33:31). Israel's record of disobedience and response to the prophets substantiated these accusations. Ezekiel found himself urging his audience and readers to "find yourselves a new heart and a new spirit" as the answer to the sin that was leading to national destruction (18:30-31).

Integral to literary contexts carrying the promises of full restoration is the promise of moral and spiritual renovation that repeatedly appears. This necessarily accompanied the promises to gather his scattered people home to resettle and till the land, to repopulate the villages and cities, and to cause his people to live in bounty and harmony with each other and the world around them in a kingdom once again united. God would take away his people's stony heart (11:19; 36:26), "cleanse" them from their idols (36:25-26; 37:23), and instead give them "singleness of heart" and "a new spirit" (11:19; 36:26). He would give them new, responsive hearts (36:26). Ezekiel explained the core dynamic enacting these transformations with the claim that God would *put his own Spirit in his people* (36:27; 37:14; 39:29), enabling them to do his will. In these contexts, Ezekiel holds out the promise of God's people actually living God's way (11:20; 20:39-41; 36:27; 37:23-24). In this process, God's people become aware of the fulfillment of the ancient covenantal idea that they truly *are* his people and that he indeed *is* their God (11:20; 34:24, 30; 36:28; 37:27-28) and that God is with them (34:30; 37:28).

This awareness itself, this knowledge of and acknowledgment of God, constitutes a major, integrating theme of the book. It is repeatedly given as the purpose of Yahweh's disclosure and Ezekiel's ministry. It also holds the key to Ezekiel's understanding of Israel's moral identity. Not finally out of innate moral capacities but out of a transforming knowledge of God and of themselves, Israel has the hope of being empowered to choose actions pleasing to God. This knowing of God includes but exceeds cognitive awareness. It involves Israel's "full attention" to her relationship with Yahweh (Lapsley 2000:125).

Ezekiel applies the concept of "salvation" or "rescue" to this whole business (36:28-29; 37:23). While he talks of "renewing" covenant as part of these hopes (16:60, 62), his favorite concept for this bundle of blessed realities is the everlasting "covenant of peace" (34:25; 37:26). This "covenant of *shalom*" [TH7965, ZH8934] envisions God's provision of life in full and complete harmony—with him, with other persons, with the land, and with all creation. Twice this reality appears with the promise of an unending Davidic kingship as an answer to Israel's repeated leadership crises—crises not just of leadership skill but especially of leadership character (34:22-31; 37:21, 24-28). The overarching point of this extensive display of God's capacity to bless would be the global acknowledgment of Yahweh as the real and vindicated God of Israel (20:41-42; 36:16-23, 36; 37:11-13; 39:27).

Ezekiel and the New Testament. Just as Ezekiel had done with "biblical" and traditional material that he handled, so later readers of Ezekiel interpreted and adapted his words to hear and speak a word from God for their own times. I will focus briefly on three of the many important points of impact by the book of Ezekiel upon the New Testament.

The first is the Davidic hope. The New Testament clearly understands Jesus as the fulfillment of the Old Testament's messianic hopes regarding a son of David whom the Lord would send to fully redeem his people. (See the bundle of blessings listed above.) Ezekiel stands among the voices from which pious Jews of the decades surrounding Jesus' birth drew their expectations (34:20-31; 37:21-28). Luke 1 provides a clear picture of these expectations upon which the entire New Testament builds.

The second is the new covenant and a new heart. Jesus claimed his blood was ratifying the promised new covenant, which would be fulfilled through him in the messianic community (Luke 22:20), a tradition passed on by Paul (1 Cor 11:23-26). This claim provides one of the major hermeneutical grids through which early Christians understood Jesus and interpreted their own situation. For example, Paul combines language from Jeremiah and Ezekiel to understand (1) his own apostleship—he is minister of a new covenant (2 Cor 3:6); (2) the pastoral situation at Corinth—the Corinthians themselves are a letter of recommendation written by the Spirit on "human hearts" (lit., "fleshy hearts"; *kardiais sarkinais* [TG2588/4560,

ZG2840/4921]; 2 Cor 3:3; cf. Ezek 36:26); and (3) the secret of spiritual transformation and victorious life now—gazing upon the "glory of the LORD" (recall chs 1–3), living in the liberating Spirit, seeing human weakness and finitude as arenas best suited for life to the glory of God (2 Cor 3:12-18; 4:7-11).

The third pertains to the throne of God and the eschaton. John the Revelator draws heavily on Ezekiel for narrating his own "visions of God." His early vision of the heavenly throne adapts Ezekiel's language extensively to describe the scene around the throne of the "Lord God Almighty" (1:4-28; Rev 4). He appropriated Ezekiel's "Gog and Magog" (chs 38–39) to describe God's final, decisive victory over evil from the ends of the earth (Rev 20:7-10). His vision of "a new heaven and a new earth" not only echoes and borrows language and concepts from Ezekiel but also forms a narrative commentary upon Ezekiel's own vision of the new Temple, the new land, the new city, and the river of life (chs 40–48; Rev 21–22).

LITERARY STRUCTURE AND OUTLINE

The book of Ezekiel divides clearly into four major sections, five when 1:1-3 is regarded as a discrete unit:

I. Introduction to the Visions and Book of Ezekiel (1:1-3)
II. The Prophet's Commission to the House of Israel (1:4–3:27)
III. Enactments, Visions, and Oracles of Jerusalem's Coming Doom (4:1–24:27)
IV. Oracles against Israel's Neighbors (25:1–32:32)
V. Oracles and Visions of Israel's Restoration (33:1–48:35)

These units are discernable from their topical coherence, the same coherence that governs smaller units in the book. Discussing the correct order of the prophetic books as a whole, *b. Bava Batra* 14a lists Jeremiah, Ezekiel, Isaiah as the order of the larger prophetic compositions. The rabbis explain:

> *Since the end of the book of Kings is about the destruction, and Jeremiah is wholly devoted to destruction, and Ezekiel starts off with destruction but ends up with consolation, while Isaiah is wholly consolation, we locate destruction adjacent to destruction, consolation to consolation.*

While this data is often dismissed, its testimony to the early use of topical coherence as a principle for ordering literary units (here books) may well support the same approach to the ordering of prophetic oracles within a book.

Several literary logics that overlay one another knit the book together and propel its movement. A surface, "narrative" movement is evident. In spite of the fact that the narrated location of the prophet from the outset is Babylon, attention soon shifts to Jerusalem and its plight as well as that of the whole land of Judah (chs 4–24). Jerusalem and its Temple dominate the oracles in this unit, though other related concerns find their place as well. In chapters 25–32, focus turns from Judah to the nations, near and far. These oracles are also (even if not primarily) for the people of Israel, though the unit focuses elsewhere. Finally, the writer returns to the people of God with major attention again to the holy city and Temple (chs 33–48).

A substantial theological logic parallels these topical shifts. Chapters 4–24 declare unrelenting indictment and threat of doom, with significant but scant anticipation of hope and restoration. Chapters 33–48 offer a parade of striking oracles and visions of hope and restoration. The intervening oracles against the nations theologically integrate judgment and restoration; judgment of the nations in prophetic works usually involves the blessing of Israel. Here it is explicitly the case (28:25-26). The movement after the introductory paragraphs is judgment, then judgment-restoration, and finally restoration, with the last section standing in stark but marvelous contrast to the opening chapters.

A visual-theological logic regarding the presence of the Lord dramatizes these movements. The book opens with Ezekiel's sight of God's glory in Babylon (chs 1–3). In spite of its important presence, this Babylonian setting recedes literarily because of the focus on Judah and Jerusalem. But early on, the Temple vision in chapters 8–11 picks up this literary reality. Here Ezekiel and the reader watch the glory of the Lord spectacularly depart the Jerusalem Temple and the city to travel east toward Babylon and the nations. In the book's grand, concluding vision, the glory of the Lord returns from the east, moving step-by-step into the Temple, filling it (43:1–44:4).

A semantic and rhetorical (artistic) structural scaffolding governs the book, relating its parts (see Cotterell and Turner 1989:221-248 for a treatment of this sort of structural reading). After the introduction and commissioning, the first and last major units (4:1–24:27 and 33:1–48:35) stand in direct contrast to one another, judgment versus salvation, while at the same time echoing each other with repetition of the sentinel vocation and the matter of individual accountability introduced in 3:17-21 (e.g., 18:1-32 is taken up again in 33:1-20). The middle section (25:1–32:32), directed against the nations, partakes both of judgment and salvation as previously noted; it both contrasts and coheres with the large units on either side. The writer signals this complex relationship of the oracles against the nations with surrounding materials by the insertion of 28:25-26, an oracle of blessing with explicit reference to the relationship of the people of Israel to the surrounding nations. This word to Israel stands almost exactly at the halfway point in the oracles against the nations, with 98 verses preceding, 97 verses following it in the oracles against the nations (Block 1998:4-5).[42] Thus, a more complex chiastic structure emerges following the introduction and commissioning (1:1–3:27):

A. Jerusalem-Temple-Land Focus; Judgment (4:1–24:27)
  B. Nations Focus; Judgment and Blessing (25:1–28:24)
    C. Promised Gathering of Israel; Blessing (28:25-26)
  B'. Nations Focus; Judgment and Blessing (29:1–32:32)
A'. Jerusalem-Temple-Land Focus; Blessing (33:1–48:35)

Finally, the movement of the Shekinah,[43] which dramatizes the semantic and rhetorical structure of the book, having gone full circle, reaches its thematic climax in the very last words of the book in the restored city's name: *yhwh shammah* [TH3068/8033, ZH3378/9004], "The LORD is There" (48:35).

OUTLINE

I. Introduction to the Visions and Book of Ezekiel (1:1-3)

II. The Prophet's Commission to the House of Israel (1:4–3:27)
   A. Visions of God: The Speaking Glory (1:4-28)
   B. Ezekiel Sent as a Sentinel Prophet to Rebels (2:1-3:15)
   C. Ezekiel, a Watchman for Israel (3:16-27)

III. Enactments, Visions, and Oracles of Jerusalem's Coming Doom (4:1–24:27)
   A. Watchman's Warning of Israel's End (4:1–7:27)
      1. Enactments of Jerusalem's destruction and exile (4:1–5:4)
      2. Wrath and reproach for Jerusalem's abominations (5:5-17)
      3. Sword, famine, and plague for Jerusalem (6:1-14)
      4. "The end has come!" (7:1-27)
   B. The Glory of the God of Israel Driven from Temple and City (8:1–11:25)[44]
      1. Vision of abominations in the Temple (8:1-18)
      2. Marked foreheads spared (9:1-11)
      3. The Lord's glory at the Temple's east gate (10:1-22)
      4. The Lord's glory leaves doomed Jerusalem (11:1-25)
   C. False Hopes Demolished (12:1–14:23)
      1. The certainty of Israel's deportation (12:1-20)
      2. Refutation and rejection of false prophets (12:21–13:23)
      3. No righteous hero could save Israel (14:1-23)
   D. Pictures of Jerusalem's Doom (15:1–19:14)[45]
      1. Allegory of the useless vine (15:1-8)
      2. Allegory of Jerusalem, the orphan harlot (16:1-63)
      3. Allegories of eagles and a vine (17:1-24)
      4. The one who sins dies (18:1-32)
      5. Lamentation riddles: the lioness and the vine (19:1-14)
   E. The Lord Draws His Sword (20:1–24:27)
      1. The Lord rejects an inquiry from the elders of Israel (20:1-44)
      2. The Lord's sword drawn and polished (20:45–21:32 [21:1-37])
      3. Jerusalem's abominations cataloged and requited (22:1-31)
      4. The harlots Samaria and Jerusalem punished (23:1-49)
      5. The delightful one's death not mourned (24:1-27)

IV. Oracles against Israel's Neighbors (25:1–32:32)
   A. Oracles against Immediate Neighbors (25:1-17)
      1. Oracle against Ammon, who celebrated the Temple's defilement (25:1-7)
      2. Oracle against Moab, who ridiculed Judah's distinction (25:8-11)
      3. Oracle against Edom, who acted vengefully against Judah (25:12-14)
      4. Oracle against Philistia, who perpetuated animosity (25:15-17)

B. Oracles against Tyre and Her King (26:1–28:24)
  1. Unthinkable responses to Tyre's taunt (26:1-21)
  2. Lamentation over the shipwreck of Tyre (27:1-36)
  3. The destiny of Tyre and her proud prince (28:1-19)
  4. The judgment of scornful Sidon (28:20-24)
C. Israel Gathered to Dwell Safely (28:25-26)
D. Oracles against Egypt and Her King (29:1–32:32)
  1. The arrogant king of Egypt to be brought low (29:1-21)
  2. The Day of the Lord for Egypt and allies (30:1-19)
  3. The Lord breaks Pharaoh's arms (30:20-26)
  4. Egypt's "towering cedar" plummets to the pit (31:1-18)
  5. An international lament over Pharaoh (32:1-16)
  6. Egypt consigned to the pit (32:17-32)

V. Oracles and Visions of Israel's Restoration (33:1–48:35)
A. Israel's New Heart; Yahweh's New Name (33:1–37:28)
  1. Ezekiel: watchman or singer of love songs? (33:1-33)
  2. The Lord himself to shepherd Israel (34:1-31)
  3. Mount Seir, mountains of Israel: a question of possession (35:1–36:15)
  4. The house of Israel's new heart (36:16-38)
  5. Can dry bones live again? (37:1-14)
  6. Reunion of Israel and Judah (37:15-28)
B. Destruction of Gog from Magog (38:1–39:29)
  1. The Lord marshals and destroys Gog's forces (38:1-23)
  2. Gog's destruction reveals the Lord's ways (39:1-29)
C. Vision of the Lord's New Temple (40:1–42:20)
  1. Temple tour (40:1–41:26)
  2. Rooms for the priests (42:1-20)
D. Vision of the Lord's New Worship (43:1–46:24)
  1. Glory returns to the Temple, Torah, and the altar (43:1-27)
  2. The priesthood (44:1-31)
  3. Land allotment (45:1-25)
  4. Duties of the prince (46:1-24)
E. Vision of the Lord's New Land (47:1–48:35)
  1. Life-giving stream from the Temple (47:1-12)
  2. Borders and division of the land (47:13–48:35)

ENDNOTES

1. As Weiser bluntly puts it, "His numerous visions . . . his states of ecstasy and trance . . . and his symbolic actions show an inclination to the bizarre which is expressed in grotesque and in part repulsive forms bordering on the pathological" (1961:223).
2. Ezekiel's father, Buzi, is known only from 1:3.
3. Only two passages in the book as we have it refer to Ezekiel in the third person, 1:2-3 and 24:24. Jeremiah 36:4-18 tells of Baruch writing down Jeremiah's oracles under his

dictation and even composing a book (scroll) of them. The precise relationship of that book to the canonical book of Jeremiah remains unknown.

4. "Then a message came to me from the LORD: 'Son of man' . . ." and variations thereof; see 3:16; 6:1; 7:1; 11:14; and so on through 38:1.
5. Lange (n.d.:21) put it this way: "The book which bears Ezekiel's name is *pervaded throughout by one and the same spirit alike of God and of man.* In all its separate parts there meets us, as respects contents and form, mode of representation and language, the same very peculiar stamp of this prophet." Even De Wette claimed, "There is no doubt that Ezekiel, who commonly speaks of himself in the first person, wrote the whole book" (1858:432).
6. Otto Eissfeldt (1965:366-369) cites Zunz's article in *Zeitschrift der deutschen morgenlandischen Gesellschaft* 27 (1873):676-689 and Seinecke's article in *Geschichte des Volkes Israel II* (1884):1-20. Zunz had published his views in 1832, *Gottesdienstliche Vorträge der Juden*, 157-162 (Cornill 1907:316).
7. Harford 1935, Cooke 1936, Bertholet 1937, and Berry 1939.
8. Irwin himself illustrates the lack of clear criteria and the overconfidence often seen in earlier critical scholarship in conclusions drawn from highly speculative bases. Criticizing Herntrich's rejection of Hölscher, Irwin proceeds: "His [Herntrich's] treatment of chapter 6 will serve to show the inadequacy of his methods. He divides the chapter, quite properly, into the sections 1-7, 8-10, and 11-14. The first is original, the second is a 'later, exilic addition,' and the third is dismissed as 'giving the impression of a later imitation.' At only one point will this course commend itself under careful examination; verses 8-10 are certainly spurious. But to accept 1-7 without further analysis is an undiscriminating judgment that argues a complete blurring of the critical faculty. And 11-14, while in part 'later,' yet contain a passage that cannot by any reasonable criticism be relegated to the class of imitation: it is genuine beyond any doubt" (1943:21). All of this Irwin claims without evidence of his own.
9. Miller and Hayes (1986:262-266). The best resources we have for entry to this world are the Assyrian Royal Annals, various chronicles of Neo-Babylonian kings, especially along with the biblical books of 2 Kings, 2 Chronicles, Jeremiah and Ezekiel, and also Lamentations, Nahum, Habakkuk, and Zephaniah.
10. See ANET 291 and 294 for texts of Esarhaddon and Ashurbanipal listing Manasseh of Judah among kings that they forced to contribute to Assyrian building projects and military campaigns.
11. The term "fertility faith" rather than "fertility cult" is used to describe the primary theological option open to the ancient Israelites other than monotheistic, covenant faith. For an interesting account of the Canaanite stream of this unfortunately robust, ancient faith, see Lawrence E. Toombs, "Baal, Lord of the Earth," in Meyers and O'Connor (1983:613-623).
12. See "Asherah," ABD 1.483-487 for the role of the high god El's consort in Canaanite and Israelite religion.
13. Bright (2000:312). Cf. Weinfeld (1991:206).
14. ANET 287-288. Sennacherib's now-famous line reads: "[Hezekiah] I made a prisoner in Jerusalem, in his royal residence, like a bird in a cage." But there is no word of actual capture or conquest.
15. Changing his name to Jehoiakim (a Yahweh [Yeho-] name) from Eliakim (a generic "God/god" ['el-] name). The irony of these royal names is that all the final kings of Judah—Josiah, Jehoahaz, Jehoiakim, and Zedekiah—are theophoric names built on some form of the divine name Yahweh. Their parents situated themselves sufficiently within the stream of Yahweh faith to name their sons after this god, as persons devoted to Baal did with their children (e.g., Ittobaal). But the confused nature of this "Yahweh faith" may well express itself in the character of these men's lives.
16. For Nebuchadnezzar's own account of his dealings with Judah and the Palestinian west, see Wiseman 1956 and 1983.
17. Judging by the ghastly treatment the rebel Zedekiah received 10 years later (2 Kgs 25:7).

18. Aharoni and Avi-Yonah name Tel-abib, Tel-melah, Tel-harsha, Cherub, Addan, Immer, and Casiphia as the seven villages housing exiles (1968:105). See further Hoshitaka Kobayashi, "Tel-abib," ABD 6.344, for textual bases for these identifications.
19. Josephus *Antiquities* 10.228 [10.11.1].
20. Brownlee (1986) gives an extensive review of proponents of a Palestinian location for Ezekiel.
21. Unfortunately, no Targum (Aramaic translation) of Ezekiel is attested among the Qumran finds, even though one is present later in the full Targums known from the sixth century AD (Würtwein 1979:75-79).
22. Josephus includes in the 13 the "former prophets" (Joshua, Judges, Samuel, and Kings, apparently also combining Judges with Ruth, Jeremiah with Lamentations, and Ezra with Nehemiah). Cf. H. St. J. Thackeray's note b on Josephus *Contra Apionem* I.39-40, in the Loeb Classical Library.
23. The list of "quotations" from the 1968 *Greek New Testament* and the catalog of "citations" from the 1993 *Novum Testamentum Graece* include a wide variety of references to the OT in the NT. These include explicit quotations, paraphrases, allusions, and echoes of various sorts.
24. The MT and LXX leave "year thirty" undefined regarding its referent, and also have third person references throughout 1:3, picking up the first person again in 1:4, as do many versions (e.g., NIV, RSV, NRSV, NKJV, NASB, ESV, REB, NAB [with 1:3b in first person]).
25. Even the rather autobiographical Jeremiah still has the prophet's name 129 times in that book.
26. *Ben-adam,* a total of 93 times from 2:1 through 47:6. The idiom is the conventional way of describing offspring of a particular creature, in this case a human. Cf. Chris C. Caragounis, "*ben,*" NIDOTTE 1.674-675 and especially H. Haag, "*ben adam,*" TDOT 2.163.
27. NLT scans the following poems and poetic lines: 7:1-13, 14-27; 17:2-10; 19:2-14; 21:9-17, 26-27, 28-32; 23:32-34; 24:3-13; 26:17-18; 27:3-9, 26-36; 28:2-10, 12-19, 22-24; and 35:3-4.
28. Compare RSV, "the word of the LORD came to me," and "Say to _______, thus says the LORD."
29. Moshe Greenberg's comment is especially apt on 14:9, noting that Ezekiel went beyond Deut 13:2ff, and 1 Kgs 22:20ff, in actually ascribing the false prophets' error to "divine misguidance": "The obtuseness of the Israelites, including prophets, is culpable, and God punishes it by corrupting the spring of inspiration, leading inquirer and respondent alike to destruction" (1983:254).
30. From materials in Driver (1909:46-51, 130-135, 141-159).
31. According to Talmudic teaching, Hanina ben Hezekiah, head of the school of Shammai, took 300 barrels of lamp oil to an upper room for the endeavor that reconciled the differences sufficiently to preserve Ezekiel's place in the canon (*b. Hagigah* 13a).
32. See Lev 5:2; 7:24; 11:8, 11, 24-28, 35-40; 17:15; and 22:8 for defilement by contact of various sorts with the dead bodies of insects, animals, and human beings.
33. The presence of "the slain" appears also in the judgment of the nations (28:23 for Sidon; 30:4, 11 for Egypt; 35:8 for Mount Seir).
34. Cf. "sword" (*khereb* [TH2719, ZH2995]) and "pestilence" (*deber* [TH1698, ZH1822]) in Lev 26:25 and also in 5:12; 6:11, 12; 7:15; 12:16.
35. That keeping Yahweh's commands and obeying his laws (Lev 26:3ff) is specifically a matter of covenant-keeping is clear from Lev 26:15.
36. 4:14, 16, 17; 5:2, 12, 16, 17; 7:24; 11:8, 20; 12:14; 13:10; 14:11, 13, 15, 17; 16:60, 62; 20:9, 14, 16, 22, 41; 22:16; 24:21, 23; 28:25; 29:8; 30:6, 18; 33:10, 28; 34:25, 26, 27, 28; 36:3, 11; 37:26, 27; 38:23; and 39:27. Leviticus 26 references are Lev 26:3, 4, 5, 6, 9, 11, 12, 13, 19, 20, 22, 25, 26, 30, 33, 36, 39, 43, and 45. References to eight of these are loaded into Ezek 5:2-17.
37. See Smith (1990:144-157) for a recent bibliography and a discussion that isolates key problems involved.

38. Cf. Walter Brueggemann's exposition of this radical alternative (Brueggemann 2001, chs 1 and 2).
39. Perhaps reflected in Deuteronomy's view of "Levitical priests."
40. The covenant mentioned in this verse is perhaps the so-called covenant with Levi; Num 25:10-12; Deut 33:8-11; Zech 3:7; Mal 2:4-5.
41. "Sovereign LORD" translates *'adonay yhwh* [TH136/3068, ZH151/3378], lit., "Lord Yahweh." This name for God appears 217 times in Ezekiel, only 14 times in Jeremiah, 25 in Isaiah, and 25 in the book of the Twelve Prophets as well.
42. If one includes 28:24 in the word to Israel, as Block does, exactly 97 verses stand on either side of the 28:24-26 passage within this section. The exact center of the book by Masoretic word count is the verse now numbered 26:1—not far from our passage.
43. The "Shekinah" is one of several postbiblical circumlocutions for the divine name. It designates especially the royal presence of God and its movement. Cf. Moore 1927:1.434-438 and Jastrow 1927:1573.
44. The word "driven" is based on 8:6—*lerakhoqah* [TH7368, ZH8178] *me'al miqdashi* [TH4720, ZH5219]—"to be far off from my sanctuary."
45. Placement of 15:1-8 is problematic. It could go with chs 16–19, making the "vine" metaphors in chs 15 and 19 brackets for the unit. It would go well with an entire unit of symbols/metaphors/allegories. However, it can also logically be seen to underscore (substantiate) the conclusion reached in 14:12-23 of the certainty of Israel's doom. Its recognition formula, which announces Yahweh's "face set against" Jerusalem and the uselessness of the vine, can also be seen to support this connection with what precedes.

COMMENTARY ON

Ezekiel

◆ I. Introduction to the Visions and Book of Ezekiel (1:1-3)

On July 31* of my thirtieth year,* while I was with the Judean exiles beside the Kebar River in Babylon, the heavens were opened and I saw visions of God. [2]This happened during the fifth year of King Jehoiachin's captivity. [3](The LORD gave this message to Ezekiel son of Buzi, a priest, beside the Kebar River in the land of the Babylonians,* and he felt the hand of the LORD take hold of him.)

1:1a Hebrew *On the fifth day of the fourth month,* of the ancient Hebrew lunar calendar. A number of dates in Ezekiel can be cross-checked with dates in surviving Babylonian records and related accurately to our modern calendar. This event occurred on July 31, 593 B.C. 1:1b Or *in the thirtieth year.* 1:3 Or *Chaldeans.*

NOTES

1:1 *July 31 of my thirtieth year.* The NLT understands the MT's "in the thirtieth" year as referring to the prophet's age, as Origen first suggested (so also Allen 1994:21; Blenkinsopp 1990:16; Block 1997:82). Undefined as it is, the reference has occasioned diverse interpretations. Some have taken the "thirtieth" to refer to: (1) the reign of a king—Nabopolassar, Jehoiachin, or even Manasseh (see Allen 1994:20-21, for details and bibliography); (2) the time since Hilkiah's discovery of the Book of the Law (2 Kgs 22:8; so the Targum, Jerome); (3) a year in a Jubilee chronology, making the year of Jehoiachin's deportation the midpoint in a 50-year cycle, or the deportation of Jehoiachin the start of a symbolic Jubilee cycle, either one related to the "twenty-fifth year" date in 40:1 (Kimchi, Hitzig, in Zimmerli 1979:113), or a garbled editorial dating related originally to 1:2-3 (Zimmerli 1979:114, citing Fohrer 1952). The NLT reading requires the fewest extratextual assumptions and does justice to the text as we have it. This date and others throughout the book reference the ancient Hebrew lunar calendar (see NLT mg; see Freedy and Redford 1970, and Kutsch 1985, for definitive treatments).

while I was with. Whereas most prophetic books begin with title-like superscriptions (cf. MT in Isa 1:1; Jer 1:1-2; Hos 1:1; Joel 1:1; Amos 1:1; Mic 1:1; Nah 1:1; Hab 1:1; Zeph 1:1; and Mal 1:1), Ezekiel begins with a first-person narrative report, which is characteristic of the entire book (similar to Jonah 1:1; Hag 1:1; and Zech 1:1).

the Judean exiles. Heb., *haggolah* [TH1473, ZH1583]. In Ezekiel, *haggolah* refers either to the community of deportees from Jerusalem and Judah, as it does here, or to the experience of being exiled (as in 12:3-4, 11; 25:3). It can refer to the entire exilic community in Babylon (1:1; 3:11) or to the specific enclave of exiles at Tel-abib (3:15; 11:24-25).

the Kebar River in Babylon. The NLT adds "in Babylon" (i.e., modern-day Iraq) to make the location explicit. Cuneiform evidence links the Kebar River with a canal, *nar Kabari,* in the vicinity of Nippur, not the more important artery, Shatt en-Nil, as was once thought (Greenberg 1983:40).

1:2 ***This happened during the fifth year of King Jehoiachin's captivity.*** This note synchronizes 1:1 and 1:3, tying the unspecified 30th year of 1:1 to a specific time in the Exile assumed by 1:3. Verse 2 should perhaps be included in the parenthesis with 1:3, parallel to the syntax of Hag 1:1 and Zech 1:1. See also the Introduction on "Date and Occasion of Writing."

1:3 ***The LORD gave this message to Ezekiel.*** Lit., "the word of the LORD was/came unto Ezekiel." This standard rubric frequently introduces prophetic oracles. It occurs 48 times beyond this occurrence in Ezekiel, all of them in the first person ("This message came to me from the LORD"; cf. 3:1, 16; 6:1; 7:1). The NLT places all of 1:3 in parenthesis, recognizing the way this normally introductory rubric seems to interrupt the flow of the opening lines of the book as we now have it. The third-person reference may indicate that it is an editorial note intended to bring the book's opening lines more into conformity with the superscriptions of other prophetic books (cf. Jer 1:3; Jonah 1:1; Zech 1:1).

a priest. Although Ezekiel's father was also a priest if Ezekiel was (and vice versa), the parallel syntax in Zech 1:1 supports taking "a priest" to refer to Ezekiel (Zimmerli 1979:111). That is, the text flags the priestly identity of Ezekiel, not of his father.

he felt the hand of the LORD take hold of him. Six times Ezekiel uses this rubric to describe the Lord's apprehension of him in a major spiritual transport or direction (also 3:14, 22; 8:1; 37:1; 40:1-2). "Take hold of" translates MT's "was upon," conveying the potent divine engagement involved in the expression. Because the other five occurrences of this rubric are all first-person references, some, with support of the LXX, Syriac, and some Hebrew mss, emend to a first-person reading here (Allen 1994:3-4). (The third-person reference here may depend on the other notes for its language.) In the occurrence of this phrase at 1:3, the MT includes "there," locating the event emphatically in Babylon, outside the sacred precincts of Jerusalem (cf. 8:1) and forming an inclusio with the final word of the book, naming the city *yhwh shammah* [TH3068/8033, ZH3378/9004], "Yahweh Is There!"

COMMENTARY

Strictly speaking, the opening three verses as they now stand introduce not the book as a whole but the first vision of the enthroned glory of the Lord (1:4–3:15). This vision presents the call and commission of Ezekiel as a prophet to the nation of Israel. It locates this vision temporally in the year that Ezekiel would have become a priest, and geographically and socially in south Babylon among Judean exiles, who had been carried away from Jerusalem with King Jehoiachin five years earlier (March 597 BC). They had been settled along one of the small irrigational and navigational canals lacing the Tigris and Euphrates rivers' floodplain (see notes on 1:1).

At the same time, because of its location, the paragraph serves practically as an introduction to the book as a whole. These lines emphasize God's sovereign and gracious initiative in opening the divine theater and granting Ezekiel sight of realities totally beyond his normal purview. They place one immediately in a visionary experience, visions intended as "message"—that is, being and containing "message" content. They couch the presentation in Ezekiel's distinctively autobiographical stance. Paradoxically, here as through the book, they focus primary attention on God himself as the subject of the disclosures. They introduce "the hand of the LORD [taking] hold" of Ezekiel as the hallmark metaphorical description of God's seizure of Ezekiel in powerful spiritual experiences of transport and revelation. All of these prepare the reader, not only for chapter 1, but also for the book.

◆ II. The Prophet's Commission to the House of Israel (1:4–3:27)

A. Visions of God: The Speaking Glory (1:4-28)

4As I looked, I saw a great storm coming from the north, driving before it a huge cloud that flashed with lightning and shone with brilliant light. There was fire inside the cloud, and in the middle of the fire glowed something like gleaming amber.* 5From the center of the cloud came four living beings that looked human, 6except that each had four faces and four wings. 7Their legs were straight, and their feet had hooves like those of a calf and shone like burnished bronze. 8Under each of their four wings I could see human hands. So each of the four beings had four faces and four wings. 9The wings of each living being touched the wings of the beings beside it. Each one moved straight forward in any direction without turning around.

10Each had a human face in the front, the face of a lion on the right side, the face of an ox on the left side, and the face of an eagle at the back. 11Each had two pairs of outstretched wings—one pair stretched out to touch the wings of the living beings on either side of it, and the other pair covered its body. 12They went in whatever direction the spirit chose, and they moved straight forward in any direction without turning around.

13The living beings looked like bright coals of fire or brilliant torches, and lightning seemed to flash back and forth among them. 14And the living beings darted to and fro like flashes of lightning.

15As I looked at these beings, I saw four wheels touching the ground beside them, one wheel belonging to each. 16The wheels sparkled as if made of beryl. All four wheels looked alike and were made the same; each wheel had a second wheel turning crosswise within it. 17The beings could move in any of the four directions they faced, without turning as they moved. 18The rims of the four wheels were tall and frightening, and they were covered with eyes all around.

19When the living beings moved, the wheels moved with them. When they flew upward, the wheels went up, too. 20The spirit of the living beings was in the wheels. So wherever the spirit went, the wheels and the living beings also went. 21When the beings moved, the wheels moved. When the beings stopped, the wheels stopped. When the beings flew upward, the wheels rose up, for the spirit of the living beings was in the wheels.

22Spread out above them was a surface like the sky, glittering like crystal. 23Beneath this surface the wings of each living being stretched out to touch the others' wings, and each had two wings covering its body. 24As they flew, their wings sounded to me like waves crashing against the shore or like the voice of the Almighty* or like the shouting of a mighty army. When they stopped, they let down their wings. 25As they stood with wings lowered, a voice spoke from beyond the crystal surface above them.

26Above this surface was something that looked like a throne made of blue lapis lazuli. And on this throne high above was a figure whose appearance resembled a man. 27From what appeared to be his waist up, he looked like gleaming amber, flickering like a fire. And from his waist down, he looked like a burning flame, shining with splendor. 28All around him was a glowing halo, like a rainbow shining in the clouds on a rainy day. This is what the glory of the LORD looked like to me. When I saw it, I fell face down on the ground, and I heard someone's voice speaking to me.

1:4 Or *like burnished metal;* also in 1:27. **1:24** Hebrew *Shaddai.*

NOTES

1:4 ***gleaming amber.*** Precise identification of the MT's *khashmal* [TH2830, ZH3133], translated "amber," is uncertain (also 1:27; 8:2; HALOT 1.362). The LXX and Vulgate understand it as an alloy of gold and silver. This and "amber," with its brownish gold beauty, fit the fiery context. Among possible cognates Greenberg favors Akkadian *elmeshu,* found in mythical contexts, associated at least once with a deity's face, flashing "like lightning," and argued by Landsberger to mean "amber" (1983:43; cf. NIDOTTE 2.316-317). The color and brilliance of this radiant material glowed from the heart of the flashing storm.

1:5-9 ***four living beings that looked human, except.*** These four composite figures emerged from the storm. Though predominantly humanoid, each had four different faces, only one of them human. Each of the living beings had four wings, human hands, straight (i.e., standing) legs and feet with hooves like a calf. No precise analogues are known from the ancient Near East, but such composite figures commonly appear in Mesopotamian and Syrian art representing deities or figures bearing deities or the sky. In Scripture, the Lord mounts a cherub and soars on the wings of the wind (Ps 18:10 [11]; cf. Ps 104:3), is "enthroned between the cherubim" (1 Sam 4:4; 2 Sam 6:2; Ps 99:1) and speaks from there (Exod 25:22). For photos of similar figures from Israel's environment, consult ANEP (and supplement), pictures 472-474, 486, 500, 501, 531, 534, 537, 830, and 835. Though the elements are "traditional," this portrayal is uniquely Ezekiel's. The four figures are arrayed in a square ready to go in any direction without turning (Greenberg 1983:54).

1:10 ***human face in the front, the face of a lion on the right side, the face of an ox on the left side, and the face of an eagle at the back.*** Rather than presenting four figures, each with a different face (so Calvin 1948:65), the text is best understood as describing each of the four figures having four different faces, probably representing the major realms of creation (humankind, wild creatures, domesticated animals, and birds).

1:15-16 ***four wheels . . . one wheel belonging to each. . . . a second wheel turning crosswise within it.*** Each of the four living beings stands in a chariot. Throughout the chapter various aspects of their association with chariot imagery become known, and attention shifts from their amazing mobility to their function as a throne-bearing chariot or to creatures in a chariot whose function is to carry the enthroned deity. The NLT renders the MT and LXX phrase "a wheel within a wheel" as a complex with the inner wheel oriented perpendicular to the outer wheel, stressing the figure's ability to move straight ahead in any direction. Others understand the phrase as indicating wheels with hubs or rims in concentric circles, reminiscent of a throne chariot known from Assyrian art (Brownlee 1986:12-13; Greenberg 1983:57 and bibliography there).

1:16 ***beryl.*** This is a lustrous crystal, aquamarine or yellow, likely golden topaz, known from its ancient association with Spain—in the MT known as *tarshish* [TH8658, ZH9577] (HALOT 4.1798; NIDOTTE 4.33-34).

1:22 ***a surface like the sky, glittering like crystal.*** The MT's *raqia'* [TH7549, ZH8385], as in Gen 1:6, names the sky, in its appearance from earth, as a bowl-shaped canopy in which and above which beings and objects could be found.

crystal. The MT's *qerakh* [TH7140, ZH7943] can also mean "ice" (Job 6:16; 37:10), or "frost" (Gen 31:40, KJV), but the NLT, like the LXX *krustallos* [TG2930, ZG3223] (crystal), has captured the writer's predilection for images of precious stones. This and other features of the entire vision provide inspiration for John the Revelator's first vision of the heavenly throne room (Rev 4, summarized well in Brownlee 1986:17).

1:26 ***blue lapis lazuli.*** The MT has the loan word *sappir* [TH5601, ZH6209], derived from the Greek word *sappheiros* [TG4552, ZG4913] (sapphire). Ugaritic evidence suggests the Heb. *sappir* may name the precious stone lapis lazuli. A brilliant blue, and more easily worked than true sapphire because of its softness, it was prized throughout the ancient Near East as a jewel often used for decorating sacred or precious objects (as in the heavenly throne room, Exod 24:10; the high priest's breastplate, Exod 28:18; 39:11; the king of Tyre's vestment, 28:13). The Hebrew association of the word with *tahor* [TH2889, ZH3196] ("clear"; see Exod 24:10), however, makes one suspect Heb. *sappir* could also mean "sapphire," since lapis lazuli is not "clear" (see HALOT 2.764; NIDOTTE 3.281).

a figure whose appearance resembled a man. Lit., "a thing like (*demuth* [TH1823, ZH1952]) resembling (*ke*-[TH3509.1, ZH3869]) the appearance of (*mar'eh* [TH4758, ZH5260]) a human." Here we have the penultimate culmination of a series of emphatic comparative expressions (1:4-28), which five times also includes *ke'en* [TH5869, ZH6524] (lit., "like the eye of"), meaning "like the appearance of." The noun *demuth*, "a likeness," and the particle *ke*, "like, resembling," preceding the noun *mar'eh*, "appearance," underscore by repetition and redundancy the distance between the things seen by Ezekiel and their actual substances or realities. The ultimate climax of this visionary distancing occurs in 1:27-28 with seven occurrences of *mar'eh*, together with *ke'eyn*, "like the appearance of," and ending with *demuth* and *mar'eh* occurring in construct, lit., "the appearance of the likeness of the glory of the LORD" (1:28).

1:28 *the glory of the* LORD. This is "the divine Majesty," as Greenberg puts it (1983:80), the Shekinah of postbiblical piety, manifesting radiantly the very presence of the "God of Israel" (10:20). Cf. Introduction, endnote 43.

I heard someone's voice speaking to me. The NLT follows the MT's *setumah* (a reading break), as do most versions. Some make the unit break at 1:28b, resuming with "Then I heard the voice of one speaking [2:1] and he said . . ." (Block 1997:115; Greenberg 1983:61; Zimmerli 1979:89). Others even place it before Ezekiel's fall to the ground in 1:28 (REB). Following the traditional break seems wise in view of the lack of criteria upon which to interrupt the series of consecutively linked verbs that span the chapter break here. The NLT, the majority of versions, and modern interpreters follow the LXX in discerning the syntax of the clause (versus JB, NAB, NASB, in forms of "I heard a voice speaking."). The "someone" must be identified from context as the figure, the Majesty himself (2:1; cf. 10:20).

COMMENTARY

In this section Ezekiel reports his inaugural vision, moving from a huge storm cloud on the distant, north horizon to a spectacular view of the enthroned Glory. The account moves from general to specific throughout, as though from the view of a distant storm to a 360-degree close-up, filling the whole sky and drawing the readers' gaze upward to the splendor now looming overhead. Ezekiel's[1] language here is repetitive and disjointed at points. Textual evidence suggests this may have come in part from repeated attempts to edit and clarify the text. It may also stem from powerful disruptions of Ezekiel's thoughts during his encounter with the God of Israel.

Israelite tradition and Canaanite culture alike held appearances from the north to be of special portent (Block 1997:92 versus Greenberg 1983:42). Whether Ezekiel thought in these terms or simply saw another storm coming from the north, the cloud quickly mushroomed into a dazzling and fiery display. Already amidst brilliant flashes of lightning, there shone in this cloud an amber-colored gleam that, upon closer view, proved to be the radiance of the glory of the God of Israel (1:4, 27).

Four composite creatures emerged from the cloud. The living beings (1:5-14), something like humans but with hooved feet, four wings, human hands, and four faces, "look" strange to moderns. But Ezekiel almost surely would have recognized them either as deities or as the bearers of a god. Each being had four faces, perhaps representing the four major realms of creation over which the God of Israel sat enthroned. Jewish midrash captured this in *Exodus Rabbah*: "Four kinds of proud beings were created in the world: the proudest of all—man; of birds—the eagle; of domestic animals—the ox; of wild animals—the lion; and all of them are stationed beneath the chariot of the Holy One" (*Exodus Rabbah* 23:13, cited by Block 1997:96 and Greenberg 1983:56).

Arrayed in a square, with wings touching at the corners, a human face looked outward on each side, ready to move "ahead." Wheels set to the four points of the compass could move the Lord's throne chariot in any direction without need to reorient (1:15-17, 19-21). The connection between the movement of the living beings and their wheels is perfectly synchronized due to the presence of the beings' spirit in the wheels (1:20-21). Not only the wheels, but the creatures themselves, move at the behest of the spirit in them (1:12). Ezekiel's report of the vision plays on the Hebrew word *ruakh* [TH7307, ZH8120], meaning both "wind," as in 1:4 (NLT, "storm"), and "spirit" (1:12, 20-21), preparing for the following chapters (2, 3, 36, 37). Their wheels filled with eyes (1:18), the creatures have full awareness for action anywhere. They speed throughout the vision's landscape at will (1:14).

Ezekiel's vision of these creatures—later identified as cherubim (10:20-22)—trades in tradition in which cherubim sit atop the Ark of the Covenant at either end of the cover and guard the place where the God of Israel dwells, the place from which he speaks (Exod 25:17-22; Num 7:89). Solomon carried this architectural design into the Yahweh Temple in Jerusalem, where almost certainly the Ark was seen as the throne of the God of Israel, guarded by the cherubim (1 Kgs 6:23-35; 8:6-7; 2 Kgs 19:15, assuming Ezekiel's view in 43:3-7 reflects earlier interpretations of the Solomonic Temple). While Ezekiel reflects this earlier iconography, he also adapts it. The earlier cherubim have one face, not four, so far as we know, and they are not associated with wheels or chariots; at these points Ezekiel reflects his Mesopotamian setting. As the vision unfolds, we discover these heavenly beings actually carry above them the throne of the Glorious One (1:26-28). They ride in a chariot throne, transporting God's glory.

The vision engages Ezekiel with a startling sensory experience. Awareness of the grip of the Lord in an unsolicited divine vision frames the whole. The storm flashes with lightning and a brilliant glow (1:4), ablaze inside with the look of gleaming amber (1:4). From the cloud come beings shining like burning coals or blazing torches (1:13). Darting around, they themselves look like lightning (1:14). Their wheels sparkle with fiery colors like beryl (1:16), while the sky above glitters like crystal (1:22). Deafening noise as though from a shouting army or breakers crashing on a rocky shore, or like the voice of the Almighty himself (i.e., like thunder; 1:24), presages movement to the climax of the vision. The barrage of sound emphasizes by contrast the silence of the creatures when their wings come to rest (1:24-25). There at the apex, a throne of gorgeous, blue lapis lazuli or sapphire carries one who himself seems ablaze (1:27). He stands wrapped about with splendor refracted in dazzling colors of a rainbow (1:28) and speaks from the stunning silence.

A triad of events climaxes the vision to this point: Ezekiel's sight of the Glorious One, his prostration before that sight, and the sound of the Majesty speaking. At the founding of the people Israel, Yahweh's glory appeared in a cloud (Exod 16:7, 10). Moses ascended Sinai into the cloud of God's glory (Exod 24:15-18), but he did not see Yahweh's "face" (Exod 33:20, 23). Isaiah saw the Lord enthroned but only *heard* of the glory of the Lord via the song of the seraphim (Isa 6:1-4). Jeremiah implies he saw the Lord (Jer 1:9). Ezekiel sees the glory of Yahweh, sees the enthroned figure, though in semblance, and hears its voice speaking. The speaking voice in 2:1 becomes a commissioning voice, moving almost seamlessly to the call and commission, with which the opening visions of God "form an indissoluble unity" (Rendtorff 2005:234). Not only is the God of Israel present in the land of captivity, but he is prepared to speak new realities into existence there. And yet the mystery of the God of Israel is preserved, for throughout we are told of images that "resemble" realities, revealing—while at the same time concealing—the God who eludes full comprehension.

This vision of God enthroned upon the cherubim opens a theme that structures the entire book by providing a visual movement parallel to the logical movement of Ezekiel's message. In this inaugural vision, Ezekiel sees the Lord gloriously present in the land of his people's exile. In chapters 8–11 Ezekiel sees this same Glorious One back in the Jerusalem Temple (8:3) and then watches its dramatic departure toward the east (9:3; 10:1-5, 20-22; 11:22-24). The Lord no longer inhabits his house! Its ruin cannot be far away. Then, at the conclusion of the book, Ezekiel, having been directed to proclaim hope to despairing exiles, is given a vision of the Shekinah returning to the new Temple (43:1-5; 44:1-4). God takes up his residence and rule again among his people (cf. 37:24-28).

John the Revelator adapts this imagery to interpret life under Roman rule to believers at the end of the first Christian century when he sees the divine throne (Rev 4). The one seated on it and the whole scene sparkles with the beauty of brilliant gemstones, flashing with lightning and resounding with thunder, all reminiscent of the theophany in chapter 1 (Rev 4:1-6a). On each side of the divine throne in heaven, John sees "living beings" (*ta zoa* [TG2226, ZG2442], as in LXX of Ezek 1) standing, the first having the form of a lion, the second the form of an ox, the third that of a human, and the fourth that of an eagle (Rev 4:6b-7). Each has six wings, covered with eyes (Rev 4:8). Throughout the book of Revelation, these creatures attend the throne of God and of the Lamb (Rev 7:11; 14:3; 15:7; 19:4). John draws a nearly straight line from Ezekiel's vision of the enthroned Glory of God to the God and Father of Jesus, gloriously enthroned in the heavens and sovereign in the affairs of this earth, even in the face of imperial Rome.

ENDNOTE

1. I will refer throughout to Ezekiel as the writer for convenience, without intending to beg questions of editorial or recensional activity, treating editorial, redactional, and recensional matters only when germane to the interpretation of the text as it now stands. See the Introduction on "Author."

◆ B. Ezekiel Sent as a Sentinel Prophet to Rebels (2:1–3:15)

"Stand up, son of man," said the voice. "I want to speak with you." 2The Spirit came into me as he spoke, and he set me on my feet. I listened carefully to his words. 3"Son of man," he said, "I am sending you to the nation of Israel, a rebellious nation that has rebelled against me. They and their ancestors have been rebelling against me to this very day. 4They are a stubborn and hard-hearted people. But I am sending you to say to them, 'This is what the Sovereign LORD says!' 5And whether they listen or refuse to listen—for remember, they are rebels—at least they will know they have had a prophet among them.

6"Son of man, do not fear them or their words. Don't be afraid even though their threats surround you like nettles and briers and stinging scorpions. Do not be dismayed by their dark scowls, even though they are rebels. 7You must give them my messages whether they listen or not. But they won't listen, for they are completely rebellious! 8Son of man, listen to what I say to you. Do not join them in their rebellion. Open your mouth, and eat what I give you."

9Then I looked and saw a hand reaching out to me. It held a scroll, 10which he unrolled. And I saw that both sides were covered with funeral songs, words of sorrow, and pronouncements of doom.

CHAPTER 3

The voice said to me, "Son of man, eat what I am giving you—eat this scroll! Then go and give its message to the people of Israel." 2So I opened my mouth, and he fed me the scroll. 3"Fill your stomach with this," he said. And when I ate it, it tasted as sweet as honey in my mouth.

4Then he said, "Son of man, go to the people of Israel and give them my messages. 5I am not sending you to a foreign people whose language you cannot understand. 6No, I am not sending you to people with strange and difficult speech. If I did, they would listen! 7But the people of Israel won't listen to you any more than they listen to me! For the whole lot of them are hard-hearted and stubborn. 8But look, I have made you as obstinate and hard-hearted as they are. 9I have made your forehead as hard as the hardest rock! So don't be afraid of them or fear their angry looks, even though they are rebels."

10Then he added, "Son of man, let all my words sink deep into your own heart first. Listen to them carefully for yourself. 11Then go to your people in exile and say to them, 'This is what the Sovereign LORD says!' Do this whether they listen to you or not."

12Then the Spirit lifted me up, and I heard a loud rumbling sound behind me. (May the glory of the LORD be praised in his place!)* 13It was the sound of the wings of the living beings as they brushed against each other and the rumbling of their wheels beneath them.

14The Spirit lifted me up and took me away. I went in bitterness and turmoil, but the LORD's hold on me was strong. 15Then I came to the colony of Judean exiles in Tel-abib, beside the Kebar River. I was overwhelmed and sat among them for seven days.

3:12 A possible reading for this verse is *Then the Spirit lifted me up, and as the glory of the LORD rose from its place, I heard a loud rumbling sound behind me.*

NOTES

2:1 ***son of man.*** "Human" or "man," in the sense of a human being, best translates this expression, the only name or title by which the Lord addresses Ezekiel in the book. Of the OT's 107 occurrences of this expression, 93 appear in 38 of Ezekiel's 48 chapters (it is omitted only in chs 1, 9, 10, 18, 19, 41, 42, 45, 46, 48). Translations that isolate mortality (NJPS and NRSV read "mortal"; Goodspeed reads "mortal man") as the defining aspect of being human connoted by this expression narrow the semantic field of the title, which should convey all that it means to be human. In Dan 7:13, the Aramaic equivalent of "son of man" describes the one who receives universal dominion from the Ancient of Days. In Ezekiel, it carries none of the messianic overtones seen in some NT uses, in which "Son of Man" (as used by Jesus) is a Messianic title carried over from Dan 7:13. Throughout the book of Ezekiel "son of man" underscores the relative impotence of Ezekiel and captures the immense difference between human beings and the glorious God of Israel, especially here in contrast to the awesome one in 1:28.

2:2 ***The Spirit came into me.*** The translation of *ruakh* [TH7307, ZH8120] here and elsewhere in Ezekiel presents several challenges. One must render it in such a way as to preserve the wordplays of the divine visions (begun in 1:4) between *ruakh* as "wind" and *ruakh* as "spirit," and further between "spirit" as a general energizing reality and the divine Spirit, without imposing NT and Trinitarian doctrine upon Ezekiel. "The Spirit" (ESV, NASB, NIV, NKJV) emphasizes most forcefully the movement from storm wind in early ch 1 to energizing divine spirit here. Others translate simply "Spirit entered" (Eichrodt 1970:59; Greenberg 1983:60), perhaps guarding against doctrinal imposition, and following the MT, which lacks a definite article, as do LXX and Targum. The renderings "the spirit" (JB; Allen 1994:3; Zimmerli 1979:89), "a spirit" (NRSV, REB), "spirit" (NAB), with small "s," emphasize the ambiguity of the term and separate it further from later theological constructs, while also reflecting the anarthrous *ruakh*. In 3:12 and 14 Block translates it as "wind" ("divine spirit/wind" in comments), carrying on the storm vision and the picture of being blown about effortlessly by the wind, albeit a divine wind. In 8:3 he translates "the Spirit," linking "wind" with transport and "Spirit" with levitation (Block 1997:132, 140, 227). Whether or not the latter distinctions can be maintained, they illustrate the ambiguity inherent in *ruakh*.

2:3 ***I am sending you.*** "Send" (*shalakh* [TH7971, ZH8938]) is a technical term when used in the divine commissioning of prophets. It comes from the administrative world of the official sending of royal or other designated messengers (cf. 17:15). An unusual word order here [verb participle + subject pronoun] raises the possibility of a precative, urging force: "Let me send you!" (Andersen 1970:38, see 474, 494; cf. Waltke and O'Connor 1990:§8.4a). The 11 such occurrences in Ezekiel, however, show no tendency toward precative force. The reference is an announcement, not a request. The participle highlights that the process has begun, which is well reflected in NLT's wording ("I am sending"). This concept of the prophet as the Lord's officially designated messenger is often tied to the ubiquitous messenger formula, "this is what Yahweh says" (see next verse and note).

2:4 ***This is what the Sovereign Lord says!*** With these words the NLT translates "thus says the Lord Yahweh" (*koh 'amar 'adonay yhwh* [TH136/3068, ZH151/3378]), a familiar expression (with variants in the divine name) in the prophetic books (e.g., Isa 43:1; Jer 2:2; Amos 1:3). The rubric appears 123 times as it is here, 3 times with "LORD/Yahweh" (*yhwh*) alone (11:5; 21:8; 30:6), and once with "Lord" (*'adonay*) alone (21:9 [14]).

This introductory claim is known as the "messenger formula." Its functional-equivalent rendering, "this is the message of [sender's name]," was the standard introductory line in official letters carried by accredited messengers for centuries across the ancient Near East. The couriers carried tablets with these words introducing the sender's message, read them to the recipient, and then delivered the hard copy as well. See Gen 32:4 (Jacob to Esau), Num 20:14 (Moses to the king of Edom), and especially 1 Kgs 20:2 (Syrian king Ben-hadad to Ahab) for interesting biblical samples from official correspondence. The messenger delivered the very words given him by the sender and spoke *as* the sender, *in the place of* the sender. Serving as something like ambassadors, these messengers were to have diplomatic immunity. Political repercussions resulted from mistreatment of them. God and his prophets brought this world of language, form, and social expectations to divine communication when they used the "messenger formula" to introduce a proclamation of Yahweh's word to their listeners. See Arnold and Beyer 2002:166-170 for interesting examples from the ancient Near East.

the Sovereign Lord. Heb., *'adonay yhwh* [TH136/3068, ZH151/3378], lit., "my Lord Yahweh." The ancient pronunciation of the Tetragrammaton, "Yahweh," the God of Israel's "personal" name, has not been preserved. Jewish piety since the late OT period forbade pronouncing the name, using in its place *'elohim* [TH430, ZH466] (God) or *'adonay* (my Lord) or simply *hashem* [TH8034, ZH9005] (the Name). The MT pointing and marginal note customarily, as here, instruct one to read *'adonay 'elohim* (Lord God), instead of "Lord Yahweh" (or however *yhwh* was actually vocalized). Jerome followed this reading convention in translating *Dominum Deus,* "Lord God." The LXX conventionally rendered Yahweh with *kurios* [TG2962, ZG3261] (Lord) and also regularly in Ezekiel collapsed *'adonay yhwh* to *kurios.* The use of "LORD" with capital letters in modern translations indicates translation of the Tetragrammaton, thereby following LXX's *kurios* (lord) precedent, while adding the printing convention of the small capitals to distinguish Yahweh's name from other Hebrew words that actually do mean "lord" (*'adon* [TH113, ZH123] and *ba'al* [TH1167, ZH1251]). The NLT's "Sovereign" then translates the appellative *'adon* (lord). Universally in Ezekiel the word appears in this divine name as *'adonay.* It is perhaps best understood as a singular noun with a substantival afformative of emphasis, well translated "Lord of all" or "Lord par excellence" (Waltke and O'Connor 1990:§7.4.3).

2:6 *surround you like nettles and briers.* This biting description of Ezekiel's audience, "nettles and briers," is alliterative and assonant in Hebrew (*sarabim wesallonim*) to catch the ear. The first of the plant names, *sarabim* [TH5621, ZH6235] (nettles), occurs only once in the OT and once in Sir 41:2; its meaning is uncertain. Ancient versions read it as *sobebim* [TH5439, ZH6017] (surrounding) or took *sarabim* as having to do with "inciting, provoking." The Ben Sira occurrence is associated with pits (hence translated "pitfalls and thorns" by Brownlee 1986:28). The NLT sticks with the association of *sarabim* with the better-known *sallonim* [TH5544, ZH6141] (briers).

2:8; 3:2 *Open your mouth, and eat what I give you. . . . So I opened my mouth, and he fed me the scroll.* Did Ezekiel actually eat a scroll? Opinion is divided here. The rather porous line between Ezekiel's visionary experiences and "real time" events, especially in the text as it is now composed, complicates the issue. Some interpreters, emphasizing this, take the eating as an "actual event" in which "even his [Ezekiel's] corporeality is over mastered by the all-embracing claim of God" (Eichrodt 1970:64; similarly Block 1997:125-126; Greenberg 1983:77-78). Others emphasize the location of the ingesting of the scroll *within* Ezekiel's vision experience, signaled by the continuing language of seeing (1:27, 28; 2:9) and hearing (3:12-13), and conclude the eating is a "visionary, symbolic event" (Allen 1994:40; cf. Brownlee 1986:29-32).

2:10 *pronouncements of doom.* The NLT follows the MT reading (*hi* [TH1958, ZH2113]), understanding it either as a by-form or corruption of *hoy* [TH1945, ZH2098] or *nehi* [TH5092, ZH5631], both meaning "lamentation."

3:12, 14 *the Spirit lifted me up . . . and took me away.* A similar question arises here as with the eating of the scroll. Are we dealing with spiritual or physical transport? Allen (1994:43-45) and Block (1997:133-135) see here Ezekiel's actual "translation" to his place of ministry, akin to Elijah's transport to heaven (1 Kgs 18:12; 2 Kgs 2:16) and Philip's experience in Acts 8:39. Most recent interpreters have taken Ezekiel's "transport" here, along with those in chs 8, 11, 37, and 43, to be part and parcel of his visionary experience, a subjective reality described with objective language (Brownlee 1986:40-41; Eichrodt 1970:66-67; Greenberg 1983:70-74; Taylor 1969:66-67; Zimmerli 1979:138-139). I am inclined to agree with these latter interpreters of Ezekiel because of the similar language in the incidents of chs 8, 11, 37, and 43, and the clear emphasis on the visionary, mystical, or spiritual context. This seems especially clear in 11:24, where the Spirit has "lifted" and "brought" Ezekiel, in this case, from Jerusalem to Babylon, literally, "in the vision, in/by the divine Spirit. Then the vision which I had seen went up from me." Greenberg notes that in 3:14 we actually have the transition from vision ("The Spirit lifted me up and took me away") to Ezekiel's actual travel to Tel-abib ("I went . . . then I came to the colony") (1983:70). We do not know the distance covered in this spiritual and physical travel because we do not know precisely where by the Kebar River (i.e., how far from Tel-abib) the opening visions of God occurred. We are not told whether coming "to the colony . . . in Tel-abib" covered a few steps or several miles.

3:12 ***(May the glory of the Lord be praised in his place!)*** The NLT with LXX, Targum, and Latin Vulgate translates the MT without emendation, although this is not entirely successful. The MT's *mimmeqomo* [TH4725, ZH5226] is not as well served by "in this place," as it would be by "*from* this [or its] place." Also, the spontaneous doxology, though possible, lacks obvious contact with its immediate context. The difficulties are severe enough that the NLT textual note on 3:12 offers another reading, "as the glory of the Lord rose from its place." The note follows the emendation of the word *baruk* [TH1288A, ZH1385] to the phrase *berom* [TH871.2/7311, ZH928/8123], positing an easy scribal confusion between paleo-Hebrew *m* and *k* in the consonantal text, suggested long ago by Hitzig (1847:24).

3:15 ***Tel-abib.*** This is one of the sites at which Nebuchadnezzar located deportees from Judea; its exact location remains unknown. According to Ezekiel, it was situated along the Kebar River, one of the canals that brought water from the Tigris and Euphrates Rivers to the surrounding floodplain near Nippur. Scholars have frequently identified it with the large, now dry Shatt en-Nil, the "Euphrates of Nippur," which ran directly through that city. A reference in the Murashu correspondence to the *nar Kabari* (the Kebar) as being "near Nippur," seems to negate that identification, leading us to locate Tel-abib by one of the smaller canals of the area (Greenberg 1983:40). Akkadian *Til-abubi* would have meant "mound of ruins from the [great] flood." Hebraized as Tel-abib, the settlement's name means "Hill of Spring Fruit" or "Hill of Fresh Barley" (see ABD 6.344; Aharoni and Avi-Yonah 1968:105).

I was overwhelmed. The MT's *mashmim* [TH8074, ZH9037] is an active verb: "overwhelming," "causing distress," or the like. Most versions, ancient and modern, repoint the text as a Polel, giving an intransitive meaning: "distraught," "overwhelmed," "stunned," or the like. This seems best suited to the immediate context.

COMMENTARY

Both ends of this literary unit (2:1–3:27) prove difficult to mark with certainty. Both the precise point of transition from the vision of the glory of the Lord (1:4-28) to Ezekiel's commissioning (2:1-4) and the point at which the commission concludes remain debatable. Some draw the division at 3:15, making the charge as sentinel (3:16-21) the introduction of the materials that follow it and seeing the binding with ropes as the first of the sign-acts introducing chapter 4 (Allen 1994:14-20; Blenkinsopp 1990:81-82; Eichrodt 1970:59, 74; Greenberg 1983:72-81). Some see 3:22-27 as introducing Ezekiel as "the suffering servant" (Brownlee 1986:v).

This commentary stands on the fact that 3:16-27 focuses on the clarification of the prophet's role and the mode of prophetic utterance to which he will submit, at least at the start. Important rhetorically also are the parallel climactic structures marked by the words, "I fell face down on the ground" (1:28; 3:23), and the repeated "the Spirit came into me . . . and he set me on my feet" (2:2; 3:24) tying the foregoing materials together (cf. Block 1997:77-79).

The narrative of Ezekiel's vision flows seamlessly from 1:28 into 2:1 and beyond, knit together by a connected series of verbs in the Hebrew text. The chapter break marks a change in focus, but not in visionary experience. The glorious one now unveils a critical facet of his character: He is the self-disclosing, speaking God. Unforced, unbidden, he has invaded Ezekiel's world and shown him marvels. Now this one encircled in the fiery rainbow addresses Ezekiel. The emphasis falls first on the commission of Ezekiel as a prophet to Israel, then on the character of the audience to which he is sent, and then on the preparation of Ezekiel to carry out this mission. The first paragraph (2:1-5) puts before the reader most of the agendas covered at greater length in 2:6–3:27. In rapid succession come the address, a command, and Ezekiel's commission.

The divine voice does not address Ezekiel by his name here, or ever in the book, but instead uses the descriptor, "son of man." The words underscore the creatureliness and human neediness of Ezekiel and the stark contrast between him, a human, and the one speaking. The enthroned figure may have looked something like a human, as divine representations in the ancient world did. But this figure was of a totally different genre of being than the man, Ezekiel. The speech begins with a command for Ezekiel, still prostrate before the overwhelming vision, to "stand up" (1:28–2:1). Simultaneous with the command to stand, the Spirit of the one speaking enters Ezekiel and brings him to his feet (2:2). Whether we should see reluctance in Ezekiel's lack of action apart from the Spirit's initiative is unclear. Immediate urgings for him *not* to join in the nation's rebellion could point that way (2:6-8). I am inclined, however, to understand here a continuation of the theme already begun in 1:4-28—namely, the capacity and necessity of the Spirit of a being to enable action in concert with that being (1:20-21). Similarly now in the vision, Ezekiel senses God's Spirit enabling him to do what the voice has asked. Ezekiel repeatedly brings the reader back to the fact that God's Spirit moves God's prophet in accord with his will, and also enables God's people to do his will (3:12, 14, 24; 8:3; 11:1, 5, 19, 24; 36:26-27; 37:1, 5-10, 14).

The "commission" is an announcement—"I am sending you" (2:3), as God had sent Moses (Exod 3:10) and Jeremiah (Jer 1:7)—not a quest for volunteers (Isa 6:8) or a negotiation. The technical language itself of being "sent" as a messenger tells Ezekiel that he will speak and act on behalf of King Yahweh (see note on 2:3). This commissioning language appears repeatedly throughout this unit (2:3-4; 3:5-6), in reference to Ezekiel's vocation. The text emphatically calls the reader to see Ezekiel as God's duly accredited prophet.

The commission includes the identity and character of Ezekiel's "target audience," again moving from general to specific through the section. The "nation of Israel" (2:3) is Ezekiel's "constituency" under its broadest designation. It includes the Judean exiles now in Babylon, but also encompasses the inhabitants of Jerusalem and Judea still in the land, and even remnants of the northern kingdom of Israel (e.g., 37:16-22).

The wording of 2:3 makes it clear that the people are rebels—the whole lot of them (cf. 3:7). Of all the traits that might have come under consideration, Israel's character proves most germane to Ezekiel's commission, judging by the order and breadth of its coverage here. The Lord used metaphorical language related to political intrigue, language especially appropriate in view of Israel's historic covenant (i.e., "treaty") with Yahweh. The Israelites were rebels, people in revolt against their King (*marad* [TH4775, ZH5277]; cf. Gen 14:4; Neh 6:6). Contentiousness and recalcitrance colored their rebellion (*meri* [TH4805, ZH5308]; 2:5, 6, 7, 8; 3:9, 26, 27). They have proved to be disloyal, guilty of criminal behavior (cf. *pasha'* [TH6586, ZH7321]; 2:3) in breaking with and breaking away from the God of the covenant. Their very demeanor, the look on their faces, betrays their wicked resolve. They are "stone-faced," "brazen," impassive, and thoroughly unimpressed with matters that should move them deeply (Greenberg 1983:63-64). This was their history from earliest days to the present, Josiah's reforms notwithstanding (cf. 20:8; 23:3, 8, 19, 27).

These behaviors and expressions signal a perverse inner resolve, which exposes the root of the problem. They are stubborn—literally, "tough-hearted" (*khizqe-leb* [TH2389/3820, ZH2617/4213]; 2:4) and "tough-foreheaded" (*khizqe-metsakh* [TH4696, ZH5195]; 3:7)—calling to mind vocabulary applied to Pharaoh in Exodus 7 (Greenberg 1983:64). Israel is "hard-hearted" (*qeshe-leb* [TH7186/3820, ZH7997/4213]; 3:7) and "hard-faced" (*qeshe panim* [TH6440, ZH7156]; 2:4). The heart is the faculty where they should render moral judgments and make steadfast commitments, but that heart has become impervious to impression, perhaps beyond being moved. In the final analysis, they are simply not willing to hear and do the will of God (twice in 3:7). Throughout this section Israel's rebellious character is mentioned to explain the likelihood that they will not listen to Ezekiel (2:7; cf. 3:7, 9, 27). It shows why, in part, the prophet should not fear their threats (2:6) and why Ezekiel will not serve as an "arbiter" or "reprover" for these people (3:26). Two metaphors drive home the fact that such an audience poses a threat to the prophet: Their hostile words will surround him like "nettles and briers" and like "stinging scorpions" (2:6).

The goal of Ezekiel's ministry is that this rebellious people will "know they have had a prophet among them" (2:5). Here we encounter the first entry in a theme pervading the book of Ezekiel: The purpose of prophetic and divine action is that the people will know the Lord has been among them in the presence of a prophet. That they know this is more important even than whether they heed the prophet's words! This is *not* because Yahweh and the prophet seek no behavioral change among the listeners (or readers). Instead, this represents Ezekiel's breakthrough understanding that reformed behavior comes not simply from response to exhortation but instead flows from the knowledge of God. "Ultimately this kind of knowledge points to Yahweh, and it is the knowledge of *Yahweh* that is at stake" (Lapsley 2000:113). For the people to enter into the future of hope Yahweh and Ezekiel will ultimately offer them they "must embrace a new way of thinking about themselves as moral selves, a way of thinking that puts the knowledge of Yahweh at the center of that new self" (Lapsley 2000:113).

Regarding the prophetic word, Ezekiel was to proclaim "this is what the Sovereign LORD says" (2:4; cf. 3:11, 27). The messenger formula implied that Ezekiel would speak a message specifically given to him by the one sending him. He would not be left to his own imagination to know what to say. However his gifts and creativity might be engaged, the message he delivered would be the Lord's. He would speak with the authority of Israel's God and would stand in a line of similar speakers—Hosea, Amos, Micah—whose reputations had dramatically increased when the Assyrians conquered Samaria, as they had promised (Jer 26:18). More emphatically for Ezekiel, he will speak *with* (or *in*) Yahweh's very words (3:4). God narrowed Ezekiel's ministry more strictly than what he had done previously with prophets. Ezekiel will *only* be a messenger. He will not be a mediator or an intercessor (cf. 3:26; 14:3, 7; 20:3; Gen 20:7). He will become united with God's message (as is shown by the eating of the scroll) and will proclaim it.

What the messenger formula implies, the visionary experience of eating the scroll unambiguously dramatizes, whether or not Ezekiel physically ate a scroll (2:8–3:3; see note on 2:8). In the vision, the hand that reaches out must be the hand of the enthroned one, though Ezekiel makes no identification of the source of the hand (2:9). The hand offers and opens the scroll (2:9-10). The voice urges eating (2:8; 3:1, 3), and presumably God's hand feeds Ezekiel the scroll (3:2). Clearly, God will provide Ezekiel's message, will even press his message upon Ezekiel. Consequently, the message has a certain autonomy, a life of its own beyond the prophet's control. The scroll contains writing on both sides, symbolizing a full and extensive word. The emphasis of Ezekiel's message is clear: "funeral songs, words of sorrow, and pronouncements of doom" (2:10). A promise of restoration will be possible only after the people have received these sober and unwelcome communiqués. His task is "to make known to Israel the author of judgment and the just grounds for its execution" (Davis 1989:56), as the ubiquitous "recognition formula" shows ("you shall know that I am Yahweh"). Moreover, Ezekiel will not serve as a disinterested conduit for divine data. In his vision, he must and he does ingest and digest the entire scroll. Only when he has internalized and embodies the words God gives him will he go speak, claiming "this is what the Sovereign LORD says."

Whether physical or mystic, the eating of the scroll amounts to an ordeal in which Ezekiel proves full obedience to the divine urging. Sending him into a spiritually and physically threatening environment, God urged Ezekiel four times not to fear the people or their threats (2:6; 3:9). He warned Ezekiel not to be rebellious but, in contrast to his countrymen, actually to "listen to" (i.e., "obey") what God was telling him (2:8). Ezekiel's obedience here is a key signal of compliance with this difficult and potentially intimidating call. Even after his obedience, another exhortation comes: "Let all my words sink deep into your own heart first. Listen to them carefully for yourself. Then go" (3:10-11). The prophet must first open his own heart to the message—all of it. It must shape his assessment of everything; it must guide and inform his commitments. He must reflectively receive God's word before he is fully qualified to speak as God's emissary.

After these warnings comes encouragement, sandwiched between God's final words of sending (3:4, 11). The language and culture of the audience will be no barrier (3:5-6)—his listeners are no foreigners. Things might be easier if they were! Wholesale lack of receptivity by inveterate covenant breakers will pose the problem (3:7). Using language precisely parallel to the description of Israel's obstinacy, God claims he has already fortified Ezekiel for the challenge (3:8-9). Ezekiel's adamant, resilient delivery and God's living message will more than match Israel's stubbornness in rejecting and evading Ezekiel's message.

God identified and focused the purpose of Ezekiel's efforts, further preparing him for his mission. A single focus would guide him: to demonstrate that a true prophet of God had appeared among the people of Israel (2:5 and again also strategically at 33:33). He would not have the responsibility of ensuring a particular response. Ezekiel must be obedient and speak the Lord's word faithfully and persuasively, but the response was theirs to make (2:5; 3:7, 27, and the analysis of this in 3:16-21 and 33:2-9). This was true of every prophetic messenger of Yahweh. The emphasis on it here is striking, however. Ezekiel would not mimic the prophets then in vogue in Israel. Prophets and prophetesses who had not been sent by God appeared both among the exiles and back home (ch 13; cf. Jer 28). He must speak and act a message so securely tied to God's word and God's continuing revelation to him that, grudgingly or not, Israel would have to acknowledge Ezekiel as an authentic prophet of God. The series of dates regarding the threats of Jerusalem's destruction, to the very day of the promised fall, and those regarding post-deportation issues (cf. chart on p. 16), serve partly to demonstrate the credibility of Ezekiel as a prophet. Like the God who sent him, what he threatened came to pass. What he claimed God would do, his dated oracles showed God had done (cf. Ezekiel's extensive interest in this, as stated in 12:25, 28; 17:24; 22:14; 24:14; 33:33; 36:36; 37:14).

In the final section (3:10-15), Ezekiel returns again to the question of the purpose and approach God has mandated. The report on the vision begun in 1:4 comes to a close, though talk of Ezekiel's mystical experience continues (3:12, 14, 24). Commissioned, filled with God's word, and committed to God's message, he experiences the Spirit launching his actual engagement with the exiles (3:12). Just as the experience of spiritual transport began, the departure of the living beings with their throne chariot and its wheels sends up a rumble like an earthquake, emphasizing one last time the force of that inaugural vision (3:12-13; see notes on these verses).

Ezekiel describes the transition from vision to Spirit-impelled reality in 3:14-15. The Spirit lifted him and took him to the colony, where he sat overwhelmed among them.

Ezekiel's call and commission produced mixed feelings that left him overwhelmed (3:15). Warnings to not be afraid probably indicated he had feelings of foreboding (2:6; 3:9). The ordeal of eating the scroll ended with the taste of honey in his mouth (3:3). Not the taste of the scroll itself but the ingestion of God's word gave him the taste of sweetness (cf. Ps 19:10). Yet as he felt himself driven by the Spirit and pressed into service by God to engage the exiles at Tel-abib, he expressed bitter anger (3:14-15). Having swallowed God's word, Ezekiel had perhaps begun to identify with the anger of God, becoming convinced of the appropriateness of the message of doom he had been called to proclaim. Or we may be seeing an unwilling prophet in turmoil, struggling to come to terms with a most undesirable call (Block 1997:136-138). Or perhaps he was sitting fully spent, disoriented by the whole set of events that just occurred (Allen 1994:43-45). I find it difficult to decide, though other recorded prophetic experience, especially Jeremiah's, and the repeated urgings to Ezekiel incline me to the second option or some complex combination of them.

◆ C. Ezekiel, a Watchman for Israel (3:16-27)

16After seven days the LORD gave me a
message. He said, 17"Son of man, I have
appointed you as a watchman for Israel.
Whenever you receive a message from me,
warn people immediately. 18If I warn the
wicked, saying, 'You are under the pen-
alty of death,' but you fail to deliver the
warning, they will die in their sins. And I
will hold you responsible for their deaths.
19If you warn them and they refuse to re-
pent and keep on sinning, they will die in
their sins. But you will have saved yourself
because you obeyed me.

20"If righteous people turn away from
their righteous behavior and ignore the
obstacles I put in their way, they will die.
And if you do not warn them, they will die
in their sins. None of their righteous acts
will be remembered, and I will hold you
responsible for their deaths. 21But if you
warn righteous people not to sin and they
listen to you and do not sin, they will live,
and you will have saved yourself, too."

22Then the LORD took hold of me and
said, "Get up and go out into the valley,
and I will speak to you there." 23So I got
up and went, and there I saw the glory of
the LORD, just as I had seen in my first
vision by the Kebar River. And I fell face
down on the ground.

24Then the Spirit came into me and set
me on my feet. He spoke to me and said,
"Go to your house and shut yourself in.
25There, son of man, you will be tied with
ropes so you cannot go out among the
people. 26And I will make your tongue
stick to the roof of your mouth so that
you will be speechless and unable to re-
buke them, for they are rebels. 27But when
I give you a message, I will loosen your
tongue and let you speak. Then you will
say to them, 'This is what the Sovereign
LORD says!' Those who choose to listen will
listen, but those who refuse will refuse,
for they are rebels.

NOTES

3:17 *watchman.* The sentry was literally "the one who keeps a look out, who stands watch" (Heb., *tsopeh* [TH6822A, ZH7595]), generally from atop the city wall. See 1 Sam 14:16; 2 Sam 18:25-26; 2 Kgs 9:17-20 for informative passages on the city sentinels. See also ANET 321-322 (especially Ostracon IV), for the sorts of letters generated by watchmen who were contemporaries of Jeremiah and Ezekiel. See also ANEP, illustrations 366, 369, and 373 for pictures of city towers used for defense and for positioning watchmen.

3:26 *you will be speechless.* Some have regarded the paragraph 3:22-27 as a literary extrapolation from the brief, symbolic "dumbness" expressed in 24:26-27 and 33:22, centering on the fall of Jerusalem. They see it positioned here because of its import as a characteristic of Ezekiel's ministry (Eichrodt 1970:76; Zimmerli 1979:160). But this view does not account for the chronological connections set up by the present text, and has no textual support. This view also depends on the assumption that a prolonged muteness for the prophet is "improbable." Brownlee concludes, incorrectly I think, that the present text has Ezekiel mute the entire time from 593 to 587 BC, from near his call to the fall of Jerusalem, without interruption (1986:57), a situation so "bizarre" as to need resolution by textual reconstruction. Pathological explanations of clinical aphasia (Blenkinsopp 1990:32) suffer from the failures of the psychoanalytical approach to Ezekiel in general and do not account well for the text (Friebel 1999:373-374). Allen sees "no compelling objections" to understanding the passage "in terms of [a literal dumbness with] the intermittent delivery of judgment oracles till the city fell seven years later" (1994:64). This may seem excessively long but is not out of character with the book. Taking the same stance on the nature and length of the prophet's dumbness, Block points out that taking his return to speech as a sign in 24:27 requires a literal understanding of his lack of speech (1997:152). The dumbness could have been self-imposed (Friebel 1999:373-374), but seems more directly attributed to the action of God.

unable to rebuke them. Lit., "you will not be a *mokiakh* man for them." The frequently attested meaning of the verb upon which the participle *mokiakh* [TH3198, ZH3519] is built leads one to expect it to designate a person who "reproves," "accuses," or the like. But the context makes it clear that Ezekiel *would* indeed continue to function in a reproving or rebuking role. Prohibition of that accusatory role seems contradictory here. Hence we conclude with Block (1997:157) that *mokiakh* in this passage means "an arbitrator" or "a mediator," as it does in Job 9:33 (against Allen 1994:62, and Hartley 1992:443; cf. Isa 2:4; Mic 4:3). The time for mediation is past. Ezekiel will speak indictments and threats of judgment when he is authorized to speak.

3:16-21, 22-27 Scholars debate whether these paragraphs should be read (1) as a separate section between 1:1–3:15 and 4:1–5:17 (Greenberg 1983, linking 3:22-27 with 4:1–5:17; Zimmerli 1979, with modifications); (2) as the introduction to the series of sign-acts and their interpretation in chs 4ff (Allen 1994, Brownlee 1986, linking 3:16-21 with the preceding); or (3) as the conclusion of the sections dealing with Ezekiel's commission in 1:1–3:27 (Blenkinsopp 1990; Block 1997). Mesopotamian literary parallels to the binding and the opening of the mouth add support to 3:22-27 as an aspect of the prophet's commission, not the first of his sign-acts (Block 1997:158). It is hard to be certain, though. The vision experience (3:22-23) and the absence of a standard introductory line in 4:1 make the connection of 3:22-27 with ch 4 an attractive possibility. Nonetheless, in my view, the plethora of linguistic ties of 3:16-27 with the preceding materials, tips the balance in favor of the third option. Note the recurrence of (1) "seeing" a vision or "appearance" (1:1, 4, 5, 13, 14, 15, 16, 26, 27, 28; 2:9; 3:23 and then not until ch 8); (2) "living beings" (1:1-5, 13 [twice], 14, 15 [twice], 19 [twice], 20, 21, 22; 3:13, and then the verb "to live" in the Hebrew of 3:18, 21); (3) the "Kebar River" (1:1, 3; 3:15, 23); (4) the "hand" (Yahweh's or Ezekiel's) (1:3, 8; 2:9; 3:14, 20, 22 and then not until 6:14); (5) the Spirit/wind (1:4, 12, 20, 21; 2:2; 3:12, 14, 24 and then 5:2, 10, 12); (6) the Spirit entering Ezekiel, setting him on his feet (2:2; 3:24); (7) the word of Yahweh (1:3; 3:16; not again until 6:1); (8) "the exiles" (1:1; 3:11, 15; then not until 12:3); (9) to fall face down (1:28b; 3:23); (10) the "glory of the LORD" (1:28; 3:12, 23 [twice]); (11) listening and refusing (2:5, 7; 3:11, 27). Many of these form brackets, joining 3:16-27 to 1:28–2:5 by inclusio.

COMMENTARY

Two more clarifications of Ezekiel's call remain in this introductory unit of the book. Both are words of God addressed to Ezekiel. Thus, the very first oracular message in the entire book ("The LORD gave me a message," 3:16) is for the prophet himself. His appointment as a watchman (3:16-21) emphasizes the nature of the prophet's task and the differing accountabilities involved in the God-prophet-people triangle. The sequestering of Ezekiel in his own house defined the unusual mode of address the prophet would have (3:24-27).

The "watchman" metaphor comes from common ancient experience: Watchmen or sentinels had two defining tasks. First, they scanned the horizon from towers atop the city wall, gathering intelligence pertinent to the city's welfare. Second, they informed those in the city who posted them of what they saw. Especially, they warned of approaching danger, shouting news down to the city or blowing the warning signal. Without watchmen those inside city walls were cut off from critical information. Failure or incompetence (cf. Isa 56:10) here could be a life-and-death matter.

In the sentry image, God underscores Ezekiel's warning task (3:17, 18 [twice], 19, 20, 21). God adapts the *watchman's lookout* task to the *prophet's listening* role. When God speaks to the prophet, warning the house of Israel, the prophetic watchman *must* sound the alarm and pass the message on. God belabors the obvious—the benefits of dependable, competent warning and the hazards of failure in transmitting the warning. The responsibilities are clear. The prophet must deliver God's words of warning. The task of heeding the warning belongs to the people. They are accountable for their own response to the prophetic word. For both prophet and people these responsibilities hold life-and-death import. (See the Introduction, "Major Themes and Theological Concerns: Moral Accountability and the Lord's Sovereign Grace," and also the commentary on ch 18 for further reflection on the responsibilities of the listener.)

The watchman appointment (3:17-21) picks up the earlier emphasis that separates the prophet's faithfulness from whether or not the audience heeds his word (2:5, 7; 3:11; and then again in the final line, 3:27). In addition, it provides a literary anchor for the introduction to the oracles and visions of Jerusalem's doom (chs 4–24). In this function, it stands parallel to the slightly revised and extended treatment of this topic in 33:1-9, which anchors the oracles and visions of Israel's restoration (chs 33–48).

On the surface, an apparent discontinuity stands between the emphases of the introduction up to this point (1:1–3:15) and implications of the sentry appointment. Up to this point Ezekiel has primarily set forth the negative content of the message he was to carry and his primary purpose of demonstrating God's sending of an authentic prophet, no matter what the response of rebel Israel. The sentry role, however, implies that the judge who has passed the death sentence "is loath to order the execution" (Allen 1994:58). It raises the possibility of repentance and hope if there is a proper response to the warning, and it means a reconsideration of the nature of Ezekiel's mission itself. This has led some to see the sentry appointment as foreign to Ezekiel's initial call, interrupting the flow from 3:16a to 3:22ff and dependent upon 33:1-9.

Whatever the redactional relationship between 3:16-21 and 33:1-9, these sections clearly serve to anchor the units carrying primarily warning and indictment, on the one hand, and promise and hope, on the other. The sentry role applies with equal force to both aspects of prophetic ministry. The placement here anticipates briefly a feature of Ezekiel's mission to be taken up again repeatedly and finally at length in the book (11:16-17; 28:25-26; chs 33–48). Some of the disjunction stems from presuming a uniformly negative content to the messenger formula in 2:1–3:27. Ezekiel was called to proclaim, "This is what the Sovereign LORD says!" (2:4; 3:11,

27). Emphasis falls here, however, on *whose words* he will speak, *not* strictly on *what words*. In the book as a whole, the messenger formula introduces key positive messages (11:16-17; 28:25; 36:4; 37:5, 9, 12, 19, 21) and therefore should not be prematurely restricted. Ezekiel was to be a sentry. Whatever the precise mixture of the messages in Ezekiel's "real life," the book gives major attention first to the sentry's stern warnings.

Finally, Ezekiel concludes his introductory considerations by disclosing the unprecedented and supremely ironic approach to the prophetic task given him (3:24-27). He had been commissioned to speak. His warning role has just been underscored. He learns now, however, that he is to be sequestered in his own house, cut off from his audience, *and* mute except when released to speak what the Lord says. This concluding aspect of his commission came in the context of a vision of the glory of the Lord (3:22-23), as did the initial ones (2:1ff). Seized by the Lord, he obeyed fully the command to leave the riverside where he had sat dismayed for a week (3:15-16) and made his way into the wide plain of the Tigris-Euphrates Valley, expressly to hear the word of the Lord. Again he fell prostrate at the sight of the Glory, and again the Spirit entered and positioned him to receive the word of God (3:23-24, parallel to 1:28–2:2).

He was to shut himself up in his house (3:24). Two startling developments would occur there. First, he would be literally bound with cords, under a sort of house arrest (3:24-25), accosted by unnamed persons, presumably exiles already opposed to his message. (One thinks of the similar treatment of Jeremiah; Jer 20:2; 37:16; 38:6-13.) Perhaps he spoke at Tel-abib during his seven days of anger and dismay (3:14-16). Second, God would render him unable to speak, except when God spoke to him and released him to function as the messenger he had been commissioned to be (3:26-27; cf. 2:4; 3:11). Although possibly self-imposed (Friebel 1999:373-374), this dumbness seems more likely a result of the action of God.

But why? Perhaps the dumbness constitutes a punishment for his seven days of rebellion at Tel-abib, with one year of mute ministry for each day of rebellion (Block 1997:150-151). It would be seven years until his dumbness was lifted at the announcement of the fall of Jerusalem (24:27; 33:21-22). This seems to exaggerate the resistance of the prophet and underemphasize the role of the people's own rebellion (3:27). Mental pathology does not account for the text well either (see notes on 3:26). More likely the muteness constitutes God's response to the rebellion of Israel, stressed throughout the unit (Allen 1994:61). Ezekiel will not be able to function as a mediator for them or exercise the intercessory role so important to historic prophecy (Gen 20:7; Jer 9:1; Amos 7:2-3, 5-6). The time for mediation has passed, at least for Ezekiel, for now. People will not get "answers" upon request from Ezekiel; he will speak when God enables him and only then. His silence represents the silence of God (Allen 1994:61). The binding and the silence also make suffering a constitutive part of Ezekiel's prophetic identity.

Ezekiel, bound and mute, functioned as a sign to the people, a function directly related to the goal of knowing God (cf. 12:6, 11; 24:24). As a sign, Ezekiel conveys "a complicated, holistic kind of knowledge, involving the identity of Yahweh and the people's relation to him," knowledge that is to "be absorbed in such a way that the self is transformed by this new knowledge" (Lapsley 2000:115). Beyond his role as an informing sign, Ezekiel will also be a model. He acted out of knowledge not native to himself but given to him by God. As such he embodied who the people are themselves to be, a community living out of new knowledge of God and of themselves (Lapsley 2000:116-117).

With these lines, filled with language repeated from earlier in the unit, the introduction of the book of Ezekiel draws to a close and transitions to the sign-acts that provide the foundation for his next unit (see note on 3:16-21, 22-27). The introduction has stressed the authenticity and distinctive character of Ezekiel as a prophet of God. Let the reader know: Ezekiel was a true prophet of the God of Israel. He had ingested God's word, submitted himself fully to God's word, and had spoken with God's words. The proclamation will bring suffering to the prophet. But Israel, not God or the prophet, bears responsibility for the response to the warnings and promises.

◆ III. Enactments, Visions, and Oracles of Jerusalem's Coming Doom (4:1–24:27)

In this section the writer plunges the reader into 20 chapters of nearly unrelenting announcement of coming destruction for Judah and Jerusalem (4:1–24:27). He walks the reader through frightful visions of accusation and judgment. Exploiting allegory, parable, and straightforward oracles, Ezekiel declares, substantiates, and elaborates on the coming destruction of God's people and land, God's city, and God's Temple. Carried out through the imperial goals and policies of Nebuchadnezzar and the Babylonians, the destruction actually constitutes God's judgment for Israel's long-standing breach of covenant. Periodic glimpses of hope beyond the catastrophe appear, presaging wider coverage later (11:14-21; 16:59-63; 18:23-32)—but glimpses they are. Before we read much of restoration, we will have to go through the destruction.

This section of the book of Ezekiel concludes with oracles dated to the day Nebuchadnezzar laid siege to Jerusalem (January 15, 588 BC), a year and a half before the fall of the city. By the time we read Ezekiel, the threats had come to pass. The city was burnt to ashes; thousands had been deported to Babylon. Both the deportees and those left behind struggled to make sense of it all. Before any extended talk of restoration and hope could occur, readers must understand what actually happened and why. They needed to know whose sword it was that Nebuchadnezzar held. Therefore, chapters 4–24 explain theologically the fall of the kingdom of Judah and everything it entailed.

These chapters serve another major purpose in the book. The oracles were dated in order to establish the fact that Ezekiel was correct about the fate of Israel, though he spoke years before its realization. He accurately anticipated Jerusalem's fate. Because he was a true prophet of Yahweh, he got it right, and these oracles prove it. They establish his "prophetic capital" and commend the second half of the book as worthy of the readers' full consideration. Ezekiel's success as a prophet of doom commends him also as a prophet of hope.

A. Watchman's Warning of Israel's End (4:1–7:27)

1. Enactments of Jerusalem's destruction and exile (4:1–5:4)

"And now, son of man, take a large clay
brick and set it down in front of you. Then
draw a map of the city of Jerusalem on it.
2Show the city under siege. Build a wall
around it so no one can escape. Set up the
enemy camp, and surround the city with
siege ramps and battering rams. 3Then
take an iron griddle and place it between
you and the city. Turn toward the city and
demonstrate how harsh the siege will be
against Jerusalem. This will be a warning
to the people of Israel.
4"Now lie on your left side and place the
sins of Israel on yourself. You are to bear
their sins for the number of days you lie
there on your side. 5I am requiring you to
bear Israel's sins for 390 days—one day for
each year of their sin. 6After that, turn
over and lie on your right side for 40 days—
one day for each year of Judah's sin.
7"Meanwhile, keep staring at the siege
of Jerusalem. Lie there with your arm
bared and prophesy her destruction. 8I
will tie you up with ropes so you won't be
able to turn from side to side until the
days of your siege have been completed.
9"Now go and get some wheat, barley,
beans, lentils, millet, and emmer wheat,
and mix them together in a storage jar.
Use them to make bread for yourself dur-
ing the 390 days you will be lying on your
side. 10Ration this out to yourself, eight
ounces* of food for each day, and eat it at
set times. 11Then measure out a jar* of wa-
ter for each day, and drink it at set times.
12Prepare and eat this food as you would
barley cakes. While all the people are
watching, bake it over a fire using dried
human dung as fuel and then eat the
bread." 13Then the LORD said, "This is how
Israel will eat defiled bread in the Gentile
lands to which I will banish them!"
14Then I said, "O Sovereign LORD, must I
be defiled by using human dung? For I
have never been defiled before. From the
time I was a child until now I have never
eaten any animal that died of sickness or
was killed by other animals. I have never
eaten any meat forbidden by the law."
15"All right," the LORD said. "You may
bake your bread with cow dung instead
of human dung." 16Then he told me, "Son
of man, I will make food very scarce in
Jerusalem. It will be weighed out with
great care and eaten fearfully. The water
will be rationed out drop by drop, and the
people will drink it with dismay. 17Lacking
food and water, people will look at one
another in terror, and they will waste
away under their punishment.

CHAPTER 5

"Son of man, take a sharp sword and use it
as a razor to shave your head and beard.
Use a scale to weigh the hair into three
equal parts. 2Place a third of it at the center
of your map of Jerusalem. After acting out
the siege, burn it there. Scatter another
third across your map and chop it with a
sword. Scatter the last third to the wind, for
I will scatter my people with the sword.
3Keep just a bit of the hair and tie it up in
your robe. 4Then take some of these hairs
out and throw them into the fire, burning
them up. A fire will then spread from this
remnant and destroy all of Israel.

4:10 Hebrew *20 shekels* [228 grams]. 4:11 Hebrew 1/6 *of a hin* [about 1 pint or 0.6 liters].

NOTES

4:1–5:4 ***And now, son of man.*** Lit., "And you, son of man." This call to attention is repeated in 5:1 and echoed in "Now lie" (4:4), "Now go and get" (4:9), as reflected in NLT's use of "now" in these instances. Notice how the shorter addresses at 4:4 and 4:9 link them to the foundational scene in 4:1-4, whereas that in 5:1, which includes "son of man" as in 4:1, places it in parallel with 4:1.

4:1 ***draw a map of the city of Jerusalem on it.*** Allen cites a similar map of the city of Nippur (1994:64; ANEP, picture 260).

4:2 ***siege ramps and battering rams.*** See ANEP, illustrations 368 and 373, for pictures of these war machines.

4:3 ***warning.*** Lit., "sign."

4:16 ***I will make food very scarce in Jerusalem.*** Lit., "I will break the staff of bread"—i.e., the sticks that held round or perhaps ring-shaped loaves of bread off the ground and away from rodents. The phrase "staff of bread" occurs elsewhere only in 5:16; 14:13; Lev 26:26; Ps 105:16.

be weighed out. The Hebrew conveying this rationing (*lekhem bemishqal* [TH3899/4948, ZH4312/5486]) closely parallels the phrase *lakhmekem bammishqal* in Lev 26:26.

5:1 ***sword.*** Heb., *khereb* [TH2719, ZH2995]. This word constitutes a lexical thread with which Ezekiel will stitch this whole section together (5:1, 2 [twice], 12 [twice], 17; 6:3, 8, 11, 12; 7:15 [twice]), and then not use again until ch 11.

COMMENTARY

Ezekiel 4:1–7:27 focuses primary attention on the destruction and exile of Jerusalem. In one way or another it all revolves around the claim in chapter 7 that "the end" has come (7:2, 6). Indictments abound in the unit but do not stand on their own. Instead, the accusations appear in the logic behind the coming doom, which remains in the foreground. This section opens with two sign-acts that dramatize Jerusalem's end and exile: the "brick city" under siege (4:1-17) and Ezekiel's shaved head and weighed hair (5:1-4). Both are introduced with the address "son of man." The first sign-act itself divides into three scenes: the "brick city" siege (4:1-3); the prone positions for punishment (4:4-8); and the measured diet (4:9-17).

These enactments (4:1–5:4) place before the reader in general terms the judgment to be particularized and substantiated in some detail in 5:5–7:27 (Boadt 1986:188-193). This elaboration concludes in the climatic and repetitive poem on Israel's end in chapter 7. The shift in literary genre, from prose to poetry, accentuates the theme and signals the conclusion of the unit. The sign-act section (4:1–5:4) and the following commentary on it (5:5–7:27) are bound together by an extensive catalog of common vocabulary. While chapter 7 functions as the climax of this section, it functions also as a "hinge" segment, with lexical ties opening onto the following chapters, as well. ("[My eye will not spare . . .] and show no pity," translated variously by the NLT in 7:4, 9; 8:18; 9:5, 10.) The sign-acts themselves are extensively intertwined (Friebel 1999:195-202).

Whether we are to understand a close historical connection between these acts and Ezekiel's confinement at his house (3:24-27) is unclear, but if so, these behaviors qualify in some ways the constraints imposed there. *Literarily* the two are related, perhaps informing our understanding of the bonds God places upon Ezekiel. It would appear Ezekiel could not do these acts tied hand and foot. This might lead us to view God's "binding with cords" as an expression analogous to God's "hand taking hold of" Ezekiel, as suggested by the Akkadian parallels cited by Block (1997:158-160).

The actions Ezekiel describes here by their very character would not be routine behavior. Yahweh specifically designates the first act (and by implication similar acts) as a "warning" to the people (cf. Jer 44:29). In addition, prophetic behaviors of this sort carried particular rhetorical power in Ezekiel's world. Babylonian culture and significant portions of the exiles managed life—illness, enemies, the gods, and the future—by magic. Covenant faith undermined magic by providing entirely different structures for human relationships with God, with others, and with one's environment. We know something of Ezekiel's disdain for magical charms (13:17-23). Nevertheless, in such a culture dramatically orchestrated acts of this sort would have been potent events. Their intent, however, has been shown to be rhetorical, not magical (Friebel 1999:42-50). In the book and quite likely in Ezekiel's ministry, these acts and their interpretation by God himself are closely related.

The first sign portrays Jerusalem under siege, using in its opening scene a medium native to Babylon—a mud brick or mud tablet (4:1-3). He was either to build a model Jerusalem or, more likely, to score a map of Jerusalem on the brick while it was soft. Then Ezekiel was to add features to show the city under siege. The wall that protects the city hems it in under full siege. He would model an enemy camp, siege ramps for approaching the wall at strategic points, and battering rams (4:2). He was to place an iron griddle between himself and the model city, turn his face toward the city, bare his arm, and "demonstrate" by the scowl and rage on his face "how harsh the siege will be." Ezekiel's position places him in some ways in the position of God, miming God's wrath toward the city and God's role in bringing the siege. The griddle, as a wall, could bring Isaiah 59:2 to mind (i.e., the people's sin has separated them from God). This, of course, would be true, but here the wall does not represent the sins of God's people but instead the nature of God's relationship with the city. God has raised an impenetrable barrier between himself and his people. He has set himself with implacable resolve to a course of action (Keil and Delitzsch 1989:70; Eichrodt 1970:83; Greenberg 1983:83, 104). Separating verse 4 from verses 1-3 as a separate sign-act does not bring greater clarity or meaning to the fore (against Brownlee 1986:64-65). The sign-act in 5:1-4 also places Ezekiel in the role of God, not simply pressing the siege but pursuing Jerusalem's inhabitants inside the city and beyond it.

The second scene (4:4-8) was to be an ordeal. God compelled Ezekiel to lie on his left side for 390 days and then on his right side for 40 days (4:4-6), "bearing" the sins of Israel and Judah. The formula at work is "one day for each year" of the guilt of Israel and Judah respectively. How the 390 days and 40 days are to be calculated remains a puzzle. The Deuteronomic history calculated 433 years for the monarchy itself (2 Samuel—2 Kings), counting to the end of Zedekiah's rule. Ezekiel's customary use of "Israel" to designate the whole people of God, *not* the northern kingdom, favors the opinion that the 390 days for Israel refers in round numbers to the life of Solomon's Temple, and the 40 days for Judah to the coming exile (Friebel 1999:212-220). Ezekiel's later reference to the Exile as being in the wilderness of the nations (20:23) could suggest the 40 days/years here may intend to evoke Israel's wilderness wandering as a picture of the Exile more than to account precisely for the length of the Exile. (See Block 1997:175-179 for a review of the possible approaches.) The Temple, which should have been an instrument of relief from sin, had become a site of incurring guilt.

"Bear their sins" (4:4) translates the Hebrew expression, "to carry [the responsibility or consequences for] someone's iniquity (or sin)" (*nasa' 'awon* [TH5375/5771, ZH5951/6411] or *khatta'th* [TH2403A, ZH2633]; cf. Exod 32:32). Used positively *nasa' 'awon* conveys forgiveness—carrying the account for *another's* iniquity, mainly of God's forgiving ways (Exod 34:7; Mic 7:18). More often it conveys bearing the consequences of one's own sin (e.g., Lev 5:1). Forgiveness seems clearly not in the picture here. Instead, God symbolically puts upon Ezekiel the consequences of his people's sin, not for redemption, but as a drama of consequence. Ezekiel suffers here *not on behalf of* but *because of* the sin of the people. This second warning act (4:4-8) assumes the first. While he lies in a prone position, he maintains his threatening stare at the modeled city, with the length of the siege tied to the days lying prone (4:7-8).

The third scene of the city under siege enacts the catastrophic food shortage the Jerusalemites could anticipate as the siege wore on (4:9-17). The NLT understands God's directions to mean Ezekiel will bake bread periodically during the 390 days (4:9; also Allen 1994:69). In view of the fact that the directions have to do with eating instead of making, and the fact that the food, not the ingredients, is weighed (4:10), another view may commend itself. At the outset Ezekiel was to make enough hardscrabble bread to last all the days he lies burdened with Israel and Judah's iniquity (4:9). Ingredients that would normally be separated, prepared, and served in various dishes were to be mixed together in a storage jar and used to make bread. (Perhaps "bread" means more generally "food." The picture stays the same either way.) At a set time daily, he was to ration this out by weight, 8 ounces a day, and wash it down with a pint of water, also dramatically measured out for all to see. The bread will get more and more tasteless as the siege wears on, and the supply, meager as it is, will dwindle before their eyes. To top it all off, Ezekiel was to bake these cakes over a fire fueled with human excrement, adding another feature to the sign (4:12).

Ezekiel's strict priestly convictions, nurtured since his youth, surface in his immediate protest. No Levitical law forbids eating food prepared over dung, human or animal, although instructions for burying human excrement outside the camp imply its uncleanness (Deut 23:12-14). If the bread was baked directly on hot stones instead of a griddle (cf. 1 Kgs 19:6), the food would be defiled by contact with the fuel. The Torah's emphasis on defilement by human bodily emissions (Lev 15) may have also led Ezekiel to this scruple (cf. Deut 23:12-14 [13-15]). He argued his point by claiming long abstinence from eating sick animals or those killed by predators and thus being defiled. His habit had been stricter than the instruction in Leviticus (Lev 7:24; 17:15; 22:8). Whatever its source, he was loath to break his conviction, so God conceded some ground, permitting cow excrement in place of human excrement (4:15).

In any case, God articulates the messages that the act itself would have signaled. Israel would "eat defiled bread" in the foreign lands to which God would soon "banish them" (4:13). Perhaps just eating in Gentile territory itself would have been defiling (cf. Josh 22:19; Amos 7:17). Perhaps reference is to siege conditions when cultic sensitivities could not have been observed. And God was going to "make food very scarce" in Jerusalem (4:16). It would be a terrifying, draining experience (4:17).

Covenant curse language drives home the seriousness and theological framework of Ezekiel's mission. The statement "I will make food very scarce in Jerusalem" is carefully worded. This famine would not be a mere occurrence. God would bring it upon his people as judgment. The writer accomplishes two things with this statement. He ties this sign-act of chapter 4 to the exposition in chapter 5, and he evokes the lengthy, eloquent, priestly version of the Sinai covenant's blessings and curses (Lev 26:3-45). Readers who had heard Temple teaching from faithful priests would have recognized these connections.

The final sign-act of this unit (5:1-4) pictures Ezekiel shaving his head, then handling his shaved hair in strange ways in another miming of Jerusalem's fate. This sign also assumes and builds on the brick city siege model (5:2), and again has Ezekiel acting for God in the drama. Shaving with a weapon, not a razor (5:1), would be a foreboding sign from the start. War and slaughter will dominate (cf. Isa 7:20). Another shock: According to Leviticus 21:5, a priest was never to shave his head. The hairs represent the Jerusalemites and are divided into thirds, again dramatically and precisely with a scale (5:1). The first third Ezekiel is to put in the heart of the brick city; acting out the siege, he is to burn them in the conflagration that ends a siege to the death (5:2). Another third gets strewn across his map and hacked with the razor-sharp sword (5:2). The point will be obvious. The last third gets tossed to the wind, save a little bit he is to keep back (5:3). But even the "saved" remnant winds up ablaze, spreading the fire from the city to all Israel (5:4).

◆ 2. Wrath and reproach for Jerusalem's abominations (5:5-17)

5"This is what the Sovereign LORD says: This is an illustration of what will happen to Jerusalem. I placed her at the center of the nations, 6but she has rebelled against my regulations and decrees and has been even more wicked than the surrounding nations. She has refused to obey the regulations and decrees I gave her to follow.

7"Therefore, this is what the Sovereign LORD says: You people have behaved worse than your neighbors and have refused to obey my decrees and regulations. You have not even lived up to the standards of the nations around you. 8Therefore, I myself, the Sovereign LORD, am now your enemy. I will punish you publicly while all the nations watch. 9Because of your detestable idols, I will punish you like I have never punished anyone before or ever will again. 10Parents will eat their own children, and children will eat their parents. I will punish you and scatter to the winds the few who survive.

11"As surely as I live, says the Sovereign LORD, I will cut you off completely. I will show you no pity at all because you have defiled my Temple with your vile images and detestable sins. 12A third of your people will die in the city from disease and famine. A third of them will be slaughtered by the enemy outside the city walls. And I will scatter a third to the winds, chasing them with my sword. 13Then at last my anger will be spent, and I will be satisfied. And when my fury against them has subsided, all Israel will know that I, the LORD, have spoken to them in my jealous anger.

14"So I will turn you into a ruin, a mockery in the eyes of the surrounding nations and to all who pass by. 15You will become an object of mockery and taunting and horror. You will be a warning to all the nations around you. They will see what happens when the LORD punishes a nation in anger and rebukes it, says the LORD.

16"I will shower you with the deadly arrows of famine to destroy you. The famine will become more and more severe until every crumb of food is gone.
17And along with the famine, wild animals will attack you and rob you of your children. Disease and war will stalk your land, and I will bring the sword of the enemy against you. I, the LORD, have spoken!"

NOTES

5:5 *This is an illustration of what will happen to Jerusalem.* Lit., "This is Jerusalem!" The singular "this" probably refers to the immediately preceding sign-act (5:1-4). Placed as it is, however, it gathers up all the material from 4:1 to 5:4, introducing the expository section to follow (5:5–7:27).

5:7-10 *Therefore . . . Therefore . . . Because.* Each verse begins with a causal conjunction providing a chain of reasons for God's judgment. Verse 10 also begins with a causal in the Hebrew text. But abrupt changes in person, gender, and number jar the reader (third person fem. sg. references in vv. 5a-6a; third person masc. pl. in 6b; second person masc. pl. in v. 7; second person fem. sg. in vv. 8-9, and third person masc. pl. in v. 10). These likely reflect intertexual allusions and quotations and interpretive expansions (from Lev 26:3, 15, 29) in which the pronominal adjustments one might desire have gone lacking (Allen 1994:72-77).

5:7 *the standards of the nations.* "Standards" translates *mishpatim* [TH4941, ZH5477], used most often to describe specific regulations, criteria for life, and judgments revealed by God in covenant law. The indictment is searing. The NLT rendering helps one see also how this word functions when used not of the nations' standards, but of God's (as in 5:6-7, translated "regulations").

5:8 *punish.* Ezekiel plays on the preceding lines, tying the accusation and judgment together lexically. Israel rejected God's *mishpatim* [TH4941, ZH5477] (prescribed standards); God in response will enact *mishpatim* ("judgments"; NLT, "punish") (5:8, 10).

5:9 *detestable idols.* Lit., "abominations" (*to'aboth* [TH8441, ZH9359]). Ezekiel does not objectively refer to idols—they are abominable. In 7:20 he uses the neutral word *tselamim* [TH6754, ZH7512] (images), but qualifies it immediately by the same descriptor used in 5:9, *to'aboth* (abominable, detestable). *Semel* [TH5566, ZH6166], meaning "an image, a statue" or "sculpture" appears in 8:3 and 5, and would be a neutral term, but is qualified with the phrase "that has made the LORD very jealous." In 5:11 and 7:20 Ezekiel refers to Israel's idols as *shiqqutsim* [TH8251, ZH9199], meaning "an object to abhor" (HALOT 4.1640). Ezekiel's preferred label for idols (used 39 times in the book), and the most vulgar, is *gillulim* [TH1544, ZH1658], meaning "round things" (e.g., 6:4; see NLT mg). The "round things" probably denote dung, or as suggested in the introduction to pick up the slander intended, "turd balls" or "turd idols" (the related forms *galal* [TH1556, ZH1670] and *gel* [TH1561, ZH1645] designate human excrement). Alternatively, *gillulim* could simply refer to idols as shapeless (heaps of) stones (Baudissin 1876:95). This does not seem sufficiently uncomplimentary, however, if the word has been intentionally vocalized, either by Ezekiel himself or by the Masoretes later, to match *shiqqutsim,* "vile things/images." Either meaning was intended as slander (Allen 1994:82; TDOT 3.1).

COMMENTARY

This section begins with the statement, "This is an illustration of what will happen to Jerusalem" (5:5). This is a separate oracle in which Ezekiel expounds and substantiates the message implicit in the sign-acts, the "warnings," addressing not only Jerusalem but all Israel. Prior to specific treatment of the sign-acts (5:11–7:27), several lines

(5:5-10) lay out redundantly and emphatically the core logic of the section, as well as the logic of the first half of the book. First, Ezekiel levels the Lord's basic accusation (5:6). Then, in a chain of explicit reasoning, he repeats the accusation and draws God's conclusion (see note on 5:7). From the outset in 5:5, we learn that Jerusalem had a privileged place "at the center of the nations," as celebrated by Zion theology (e.g., Pss 46, 48, 76, 87, 122). But she had forsaken God's law. In this passage, Ezekiel employs vocabulary foundational to the book. Israel had "rebelled" (Heb., *marah* [TH4784, ZH5286]; 5:6), a verb picking up the "rebellious" character (*meri* [TH4805, ZH5308]) exposed in chapters 2–3 (2:5, 6, 7, 8; 3:9, 26, 27). To put it more specifically, she had "rejected" God's "regulations and decrees" (5:6), deliberately refusing to live faithful to her covenant with him. God's "regulations" (*mishpatim* [TH4941, ZH5477], "prescribed judgments for living") and "decrees" (*khuqqoth* [TH2706, ZH2976]) express the specifics of his covenant will. These terms appear in tandem repeatedly in Leviticus and Deuteronomy. Ezekiel employs them together more than any other Old Testament writer outside of those covenant books of Moses, indicating the covenant base and traditional ties on which he built his case. Not only had Israel rejected God's ways, but she had behaved worse than the nations (5:6-7).

Based on Israel's behavior and in accord with the covenant's provisions, God would "punish" Israel (see note on 5:8). Thus in 5:5-10, Ezekiel anticipates a central theme he will later take up repeatedly. Her "detestable idols," with their defilement of Temple and the land, present the hallmark symptom of her unfaithfulness (5:9), the chief cause of her coming doom. The word translated "detestable idols" (*to'aboth;* see note on 5:9) is the lead term in a rich vocabulary Ezekiel employs to describe the paraphernalia of idolatry he so despised. He also anticipates his exposition of the sign-acts by describing one of the unspeakable "necessities" forced on those in protracted siege—cannibalism—and by reference to scattering survivors to the wind (5:10). (Recall the dwindling, measured food and drink in 4:9-17 and tossing the shaved hair to the wind, 5:1-4, to which these refer.)

In 5:11-17, God explains the coming catastrophe, and he further interprets the sign-acts built around the brick city under siege (4:1–5:4). He begins with commentary on the "thirds" in the shaved and divided hair act of 5:1-4. Then, underscored by an oath sworn upon his own being, the sovereign Lord promises he will cut Israel off completely and without pity. This will be an expression of his holy anger and will not stop until that anger has been assuaged (5:13, 15). The Great King of the covenant was rightly enraged at the breach of promise in the face of repeated warnings and extension of grace. The sign-acts had pictured conditions of "disease and famine" (5:12), "deadly arrows of famine" (5:16), "disease and war," and the enemy's "sword," which in some sense is God's own sword (5:13, 17). Nebuchadnezzar would wield his sword on God's behalf.

"Disease," "famine," and "sword" do not present random vocabulary. These three words in close proximity appear throughout this unit (5:12, 17; 6:11, 12; and climactically in 7:15, with *khereb* [TH2719, ZH2995] [sword] translated "war" in 6:12 and 7:15). Two agendas are present. *Literarily,* these words are a thread tying chapters 5–7 together. *Theologically,* they invoke the covenant curses once again; this collection of vocabulary appears elsewhere in the two classic catalogs of covenant curses (cf. Lev 26:25, 33, 36, 37 and Deut 28:21-22, 48).

These blows to Jerusalem entailed an additional feature of judgment—loss of face in a world heavily governed by shame and honor (5:14-15). Brought to ruin, Jerusalem would become the laughingstock of the surrounding nations, who would mock and taunt them and be utterly aghast at what they had been put through. The nations might think that this judgment came for several reasons: (1) Jerusalem was such a wicked city that their God brought catastrophe upon them. (2) Jerusalem was not wicked, but her God abandoned her for reasons of his own. (3) Or perhaps he did not abandon her, but struggled vainly against the Babylonians' gods and was defeated. From any one of several angles the Jerusalemites would lose face. In the first scenario, they stand shamed by their own character; in the latter two, by the inadequacy of their god in character or power.

At this very point Ezekiel engages another major concern of the book—namely, theodicy (justifying the ways of God to men). As just noted, not only the Jerusalemites but also God himself stood to lose face in the destruction of Judah. Thus, the purposes of the threatened destruction focus here on the vindication of God and his word (a concern already hinted at in 2:5). When these events occurred, God's people (and in some cases the nations) would realize that when Ezekiel spoke, the Lord had spoken and had done so in his anger (5:13). Neither God nor his prophet on earth was speaking without warrant. On God's part, he had the will and resources to follow through (6:10, 13). They would know that the only God bringing this judgment was the Lord, Israel's covenant God (6:7, 10)—not the god in whose name the deceived prophets of peace spoke (ch 13). In sum, they would know that the God active in Ezekiel, in their lives, and in the destiny of the city and nation was Yahweh (6:14; 7:4, 27). The fulfillment of these promised events would "prove" the Lord *to be* the Lord and to be in the right (see note on 6:14).

◆ 3. Sword, famine, and plague for Jerusalem (6:1-14)

**Again a message came to me from the
LORD: 2"Son of man, turn and face the
mountains of Israel and prophesy against
them. 3Proclaim this message from the
Sovereign LORD against the mountains of
Israel. This is what the Sovereign LORD
says to the mountains and hills and to the
ravines and valleys: I am about to bring
war upon you, and I will smash your pa-
gan shrines. 4All your altars will be demol-
ished, and your places of worship will be
destroyed. I will kill your people in front
of your idols.* 5I will lay your corpses in
front of your idols and scatter your bones
around your altars. 6Wherever you live
there will be desolation, and I will destroy
your pagan shrines. Your altars will be de-
molished, your idols will be smashed, your
places of worship will be torn down, and
all the religious objects you have made
will be destroyed. 7The place will be lit-
tered with corpses, and you will know that
I alone am the LORD.**

**8"But I will let a few of my people es-
cape destruction, and they will be scat-
tered among the nations of the world.
9Then when they are exiled among the
nations, they will remember me. They will
recognize how hurt I am by their unfaith-
ful hearts and lustful eyes that long for
their idols. Then at last they will hate
themselves for all their detestable sins.
10They will know that I alone am the LORD
and that I was serious when I said I would
bring this calamity on them.**

**11"This is what the Sovereign LORD says:
Clap your hands in horror, and stamp your
feet. Cry out because of all the detestable**

**sins the people of Israel have committed.
Now they are going to die from war and
famine and disease. 12 Disease will strike
down those who are far away in exile. War
will destroy those who are nearby. And any-
one who survives will be killed by famine.
So at last I will spend my fury on them.
13 They will know that I am the LORD when
their dead lie scattered among their idols
and altars on every hill and mountain and
under every green tree and every great
shade tree—the places where they offered
sacrifices to their idols. 14 I will crush them
and make their cities desolate from the wil-
derness in the south to Riblah* in the north.
Then they will know that I am the LORD."**

6:4 The Hebrew term (literally *round things*) probably alludes to dung; also in 6:5, 6, 9, 13. 6:14 As in some Hebrew manuscripts; most Hebrew manuscripts read *Diblah*.

NOTES

6:9 ***detestable sins.*** Heb., *to'eboth* [TH8441, ZH9359] (abominations). The paraphernalia of Israel's abominations were "pagan shrines" (*bamoth* [TH1116, ZH1195], 6:3, 6), unauthorized or pagan "altars" (*mizbekhoth* [TH4196, ZH4640], 6:4-6), "idols" (*gillulim* [TH1544, ZH1658], 6:4, 5, 6, 9, 13), forbidden "places of worship" (*khammanim* [TH2553, ZH2802], 6:6—sometimes also translated "incense altars"; cf. ANEP, illustration 575), and "religious objects" (6:6) made by the people (*ma'asim* [TH4639, ZH5126]).

6:14 ***Riblah.*** The NLT follows a reading in some Hebrew mss; most Hebrew mss read "Diblah" (with LXX, Targum, Vulgate). Diblah is the more difficult reading and would thus generally be preferred. If it is a place name, as seems indicated by the context, we know nothing of it beyond this occurrence, which is the main difficulty with it. Riblah would be the place in the north to which Nebuchadnezzar later summoned Zedekiah for punishment (2 Kgs 25:6). Situated near the northern borders of Israel's historic and anticipated greatness (47:16; 1 Kgs 8:65), it would contrast with the southern border, the wilderness of south Judah, something like "from Dan to Beersheba" (e.g., Judg 20:1). In the context of ch 6, it marks out the reach of the coming destruction.

Then they will know that I am the LORD. Such statements have become known as "proof sayings," in which a prophetic prediction or announcement serves the larger goal of showing "Yahweh's historical self-manifestation" (Zimmerli 1982:100-103). Eight times in this section (4:1–7:27), Ezekiel addresses this purpose of vindicating God, his word, and (by implication) his prophet's word (5:13; 6:7, 10, 13, 14; 7:4, 9, 27). The formula does not appear again until 11:10 (67 times in the book as a whole, with some variations).

COMMENTARY

In chapter 6, Ezekiel turns first to detailing Israel's idolatry and God's judgment of it (mentioned briefly in 5:9). The message from the Lord is addressed to and against "the mountains of Israel" (6:2-3, 13), to every nook and cranny of them (6:3). A similar, complementary address of restoration to the mountains of Israel meets the reader in chapter 36. The Lord addresses the mountains as though speaking to Israel, but maintains the address to the mountains through the two oracles here by keeping reference to the people in the third person ("they," "them") in 6:8-11. At one level this is simply a literary device called metonymy, referring to a particular thing by naming another thing closely associated with it—in this case addressing the people living *on* the mountains by speaking to the mountains. The metonymy also has theological implications. From Ezekiel's perspective, the land and the people were more inextricably bound together than we might assume. Levitical teaching had it that if Israel adopted the ways of the Canaanites, they would defile the land, God would visit *the land's* iniquity upon it, and the land would vomit them out (Lev 18:25-28). Ezekiel picks this up again in 7:22: The invading marauders will defile the land when they come plundering. Thus, God threatens to bring sword, famine, and disease upon the land (6:4, 11-12).

Ezekiel pronounces the judgment in such a way that attention is drawn primarily to the *causes* of the coming judgment—namely, the pagan shrines, altars, and idols that were forbidden to the Israelites (see note on 6:9). They were scattered everywhere in the land, especially on hills and under trees thought to provide a special point of contact with the divine (6:13). There they offered to their idols the sacrificial fragrance that should have been given to Yahweh (6:13; cf. Lev 1:9, 13, 17). They and the cities and shrines that housed them would all be torn down, smashed, brought to an end. As earlier (2:4; 3:7), Ezekiel penetrates to the character defect behind the covenant-breaking behaviors: "unfaithful hearts and lustful eyes," longing for their idols (6:9). Persons "in their totality" had turned from God in their "inner being" (hearts) by looking at (eyes) and lusting for things in the physical world (Zimmerli 1979:189).

A judgment particularly odious to priests and to persons taught from the Temple gets repeated mention. The corpses (Heb., *khalalim* [TH2491, ZH2728] and *pegarim* [TH6297, ZH7007]) of those slain in the coming siege would be strewn around these "sacred" sites, piled around altars like debris (6:4, 5, 7, 13). Their bones would be strewn around their altars (6:5). These people would perhaps be cut down in the very act of worship at the shrines, or in the course of trying to defend the shrines, or dragged there as a particular travesty. Levitical tradition taught that corpses and bones defiled the places where they lay. So not only were the sites and trappings destroyed, the sacred places were also made unfit for use by their defilement (Lev 5:2; 21:1-4).

Meanwhile, the lexical connections with the covenant curses in Leviticus 26 continue. Leviticus 26:30-31 reads, "I will destroy your pagan shrines (*bamoth* [TH1116, ZH1195]) and knock down your places of worship (*khammanim* [TH2553, ZH2802]). I will leave your lifeless corpses (*pegarim* [TH6297, ZH7007]) piled on top of your lifeless idols (*gillulim* [TH1544, ZH1658]), and I will despise you. I will make your cities desolate and destroy your places of pagan worship (*miqdashim* [TH4720, ZH5219]). I will take no pleasure in your offerings that should be a pleasing aroma to me." The vocabulary of chapter 6 aligns with that of Leviticus 26 in line after line (Allen 1994:92-96).

In 6:9 Ezekiel returns to the topic of 5:11 with talk of a few escapees scattered among the nations. God anticipates that after the catastrophic siege, the traumatized survivors in exile will in some ways come to their senses. They will remember God. As Zimmerli (1979:189) comments, "remember" here and generally in the Old Testament does not signify any "romantic turning back to what once was." Instead, it describes "a genuine grasping of a reality which then becomes a new living and present fact"—the recalling of God's acts in such a way as to transform present reality. From the scale of destruction they will judge the measure of God's profound "hurt" from their betrayal. They will see their detestable sins for what they were, loathe themselves for those sins, and acknowledge God's relentless integrity in keeping covenant and speaking through commissioned prophets like Ezekiel (6:10).

Ezekiel 6:11-14 summarizes the commentary in 6:1-10 with hyperbole. Ezekiel reaches back to 5:4, which speaks of the fire spreading from the remnant, destroying all of Israel. In 6:11 even those in exile will be struck down. The siege of Jerusalem (the "brick city" of ch 4) will end up engulfing the entire land, from south to north (6:14). The flourish in this closing paragraph of chapter 6 prepares the reader for the shift in genre—from prose to poetry in chapter 7.

4. "The end has come!" (7:1-27)

Then this message came to me from the
LORD: 2"Son of man, this is what the Sov-
ereign LORD says to Israel:

"The end is here!
Wherever you look—
east, west, north, or south—
your land is finished.
3 No hope remains,
for I will unleash my anger
against you.
I will call you to account
for all your detestable sins.
4 I will turn my eyes away and show
no pity.
I will repay you for all your
detestable sins.
Then you will know that I am the LORD.

5 "This is what the Sovereign LORD says:
Disaster after disaster
is coming your way!
6 The end has come.
It has finally arrived.
Your final doom is waiting!
7 O people of Israel, the day of your
destruction is dawning.
The time has come; the day of
trouble is near.
Shouts of anguish will be heard
on the mountains,
not shouts of joy.
8 Soon I will pour out my fury on you
and unleash my anger against you.
I will call you to account
for all your detestable sins.
9 I will turn my eyes away and show
no pity.
I will repay you for all your
detestable sins.
Then you will know that it is I,
the LORD,
who is striking the blow.

10 "The day of judgment is here;
your destruction awaits!
The people's wickedness and pride
have blossomed to full flower.
11 Their violence has grown into a rod
that will beat them for their
wickedness.
None of these proud and wicked
people will survive.
All their wealth and prestige
will be swept away.
12 Yes, the time has come;
the day is here!
Buyers should not rejoice over
bargains,
nor sellers grieve over losses,
for all of them will fall
under my terrible anger.
13 Even if the merchants survive,
they will never return to their
business.
For what God has said applies to
everyone—
it will not be changed!
Not one person whose life is
twisted by sin
will ever recover.

14 "The trumpet calls Israel's army
to mobilize,
but no one listens,
for my fury is against them all.
15 There is war outside the city

and disease and famine within.
Those outside the city walls
will be killed by enemy swords.
Those inside the city
will die of famine and disease.
16 The survivors who escape to the mountains
will moan like doves, weeping for their sins.
17 Their hands will hang limp,
their knees will be weak as water.
18 They will dress themselves in burlap;
horror and shame will cover them.
They will shave their heads
in sorrow and remorse.

19 "They will throw their money in the streets,
tossing it out like worthless trash.
Their silver and gold won't save them
on that day of the LORD's anger.
It will neither satisfy nor feed them,
for their greed can only trip them up.
20 They were proud of their beautiful jewelry
and used it to make detestable idols and vile images.
Therefore, I will make all their wealth
disgusting to them.
21 I will give it as plunder to foreigners,
to the most wicked of nations,
and they will defile it.
22 I will turn my eyes from them
as these robbers invade and defile my treasured land.

23 "Prepare chains for my people,
for the land is bloodied by terrible crimes.
Jerusalem is filled with violence.
24 I will bring the most ruthless of nations
to occupy their homes.
I will break down their proud fortresses
and defile their sanctuaries.
25 Terror and trembling will overcome my people.
They will look for peace but not find it.
26 Calamity will follow calamity;
rumor will follow rumor.
They will look in vain
for a vision from the prophets.
They will receive no teaching from the priests
and no counsel from the leaders.
27 The king and the prince will stand helpless,
weeping in despair,
and the people's hands
will tremble with fear.
I will bring on them
the evil they have done to others,
and they will receive the punishment
they so richly deserve.
Then they will know that I am the LORD."

NOTES

7:1-27 There are several textual and compositional difficulties in this chapter. Hebrew poetry, with its expanded vocabulary and less explicit syntax, invited scribal commentary (glosses and additions) aimed at clarifying the text, but more often than not, these eventually contributed to further complications of the text. Particular difficulties are found in 7:5, 10-11, 13, 16, and 27. See Allen 1994:99-103, Block 1997:247-269, and Zimmerli 1979:193-200, for detailed text-critical and redaction-critical notes. The widely divergent translations in, e.g., ESV, REB, NIV, NRSV, and NLT at these points mark the underlying textual disturbance. The LXX diverges strikingly from the MT in this chapter, pointing to early interpretive and textual difficulties. Attempts to reconstruct the compositional history also suffer from the difficulties in the text and the LXX's striking divergence and brevity. See Zimmerli (1979:193-194) for his summary of the poem's development.

7:2 *Israel . . . your land is finished.* God addresses his message to "the land of Israel" (*'admath yisra'el* [TH127/3478, ZH141/3776]) 17 times in Ezekiel, but nowhere else in Scripture.

7:3 *No hope remains.* This translates well the MT's "now the end is upon you."

7:7, 10 *your destruction is dawning. . . . your destruction awaits!* "Destruction" represents *tsepirah* [TH6843, ZH7619], a word of uncertain meaning in this chapter, which has remained "unexplained" (HALOT 3.1048). Block's attempt to understand the word based on its only other OT occurrence, Isa 28:5, and its possible contextual "answering" with "chain" (*rattoq* [TH7569, ZH8408]) in 7:23 seems more plausible to me than other attempts (1997:251-252; cf. review of other attempts in Greenberg 1983:148). Block understands *tsepirah* to be a "garland" of shame, a "leash." "The leash has come upon you."

7:19-20 *tossing it out like worthless trash. . . . I will make all their wealth disgusting to them.* Behind the expressions "worthless trash" and "make disgusting" stand Hebrew expressions using the word *niddah* [TH5079, ZH5614]. According to TDOT 9.232-234, the word has three uses: (1) "menstrual impurity," (2) "impurity" in general, i.e., "abomination," and (3) "lustration" for purification from the menstrual uncleanness. The third meaning does not work in this passage. The first meaning is cultic and refers primarily to the period of sacral impurity associated with menstruation, rather than the menstruation itself, as in 18:6; 22:10. The "impurity" carried something of the potency associated with the mystery and import of blood, life, and its loss in Levitical Torah (Lev 17:10-16). But 7:19-20, as the NLT attempts to show, seems to convey not simply cultic or general defilement, but something especially odious or repugnant, recognizable even by Gentiles (as in Lam 1:17). One wonders if the reference may even be to the menstrual discharge itself or to menstrual cloths thrown out (elsewhere called *beged 'iddim* [TH899A/5708, ZH955/6340], Isa 64:6 [5]).

COMMENTARY

Chapter 7 contains two poetic oracles that together punctuate the conclusion of this section (chs 4–7). The first poem (7:2-4) introduces themes expanded in the second oracle (7:5-27) in two stanzas, 7:5-9 and 7:10-27. The address reverberates with ancient promise regarding all the people of God and the land he was to give them (Exod 20:12; Lev 20:24; Deut 4:40; 11:9).

"The end is here! . . . No hope remains" (7:2-3). This states the core message. If the reader has not seen it yet, the poet will drive it home line after line in chapter 7. "The end" meets the Hebrew reader five times in the first six verses. This is the definitive end—no more chances, no more negotiation, no more time—no more hope! It uses traditional prophetic language already known from Amos's vision (Amos 8:1-3). While Amos's words addressed Samaria and Jeroboam's chapel at Bethel, Ezekiel aims his warning at Jerusalem and the Lord's Temple. The message calls up the "Day of the Lord" expectations of eschatological judgment from Amos (Amos 5:18-20) and other earlier prophets, turning public expectation on its head.

After stating "the end is here," Ezekiel introduces the other themes of 7:2-27, which are as follows: The end expresses God's anger (7:3b); God in the end calls Israel to account for "detestable sins" (7:3c, d) and repays Israel for these detestable sins (7:4b); the Lord will show no pity (7:4a); the result: Israel will acknowledge the Lord (7:4c). These latter expressions form a refrain tying the two oracles together (7:3c-4c and 7:8-9), with the poem concluding with a reworking of the refrain and final statement: "Then they will know that I am the LORD" (7:27). A sense of foreboding pervades. The end, destruction, and judgment are *coming.* Indeed, the Hebrew root *bw'* (cf. *ba'* [TH935, ZH995]), with its meaning of "arriving," "entering," "coming," ties this chapter together from beginning to end (appearing 13 times from 7:2 to 7:26). We read, for example, "Disaster is coming. . . . Doom is waiting. . . . Destruction is dawning. . . . Trouble is near. . . . The time has come" (7:5-7, 12).

"The end" as a revelation of God's fury and an expression of his anger in action surfaces repeatedly. God will "unleash" his anger (7:8). It is under his "terrible anger" that the people will fall (7:12). The people's refusal to listen to this warning will provoke God's "fury" against them (7:14). Clearly the God of Israel is quite different from the Greek notion that the divine is "impassible" (i.e., without passion, unfeeling).

Ezekiel elaborates the "detestable sins" for which he called Israel to account and for which they would be repaid. General descriptions or behavior appear: "wickedness" (7:10-11); "terrible [bloody] crimes" (7:23); and "evil" (7:27). He also lists specific accusations: "pride" (7:10); "violence" (7:11, 23); "detestable idols and vile images" (7:20); they defiled the land with violence (7:23); they are wicked (7:11), "twisted by sin" (7:13), and they live in "greed" (7:19).

This poetic exposition focuses first largely on the pitiless destruction itself (7:5-9). Then Ezekiel emphasizes the causal connection between the coming destruction and the people's own wickedness. Their iniquity and violence bring the end (7:10-13). No way out will be found (7:14-22). In a supreme irony, the city will experience in the invasion their failure to heed the prophetic watchman's warning (3:16-17). The sentinel sounds the alarm ("the trumpet") to mobilize defense—but no one heeds the warning (7:14). Inside the besieged city and even beyond it, no one will escape (7:15). When this realization dawns on the people, it will leave everyone in remorse and a state of shock (7:16-18). Life will be turned on end. Money and holdings that leveraged so much before the siege will be worse than worthless in the end (7:19-20). The vile Babylonians will plunder the money and jewelry, defiling God's land with their behavior and their very presence. It will be so revolting that God will avert his gaze to keep from seeing it (7:22).

The concluding stanza (7:23-27) draws together several of the poem's (and the larger unit's) themes, while elaborating the helpless, hopeless plight of those caught in the siege. The rattle of chains anticipates the exiles led off as prisoners (7:23; cf. Jer 40:1; Amos 4:2; cf. bound captives; ANEP, illustrations 1, 311, 326, 332, 357). Along with the frightful specter of the invaders, foreign robbers are to come (7:21-22), famously ruthless plunderers (7:24a). They will tear down supposedly impregnable fortresses like Lachish and Arad (7:24b). Ezekiel pictures people overwhelmed, leaders totally incapacitated, paralyzed by the horrors accumulating around them (7:25-27). God has subverted the whole range of institutional resources upon which the nation has depended for guidance and leadership. Prophets, priests, leaders, king, prince—none of them would prove able to render the "services" in their charge when the people need them most. All of this is the work of Yahweh. Through the Babylonians he will bring richly deserved punishment upon his people (7:27). Then one last time, the concluding refrain underscores a facet of God's purpose that is distinctively important to Ezekiel: acknowledgment that the hand at work in all of this belongs to the Lord God of the ancestors and of the covenants with Israel.

The announcement that God is bringing "the end" on Jerusalem and Judah brings with it the major theological claims of chapters 4–7. The Sovereign Lord of Israel works through political and social realities of history to accomplish his will, in this case the judgment of his people. For Ezekiel, history has a moral hinge, and the Sinai covenant outlines that "hinge." God's people (and by implication all persons) stand accountable to God for their inner and outer life. They cannot fill their culture with greed, violence, and filth, without reaping the consequences. Particularly reprehensible to God is their betrayal of their covenant with him in the worship of other gods. The way of the other gods cannot sustain life and *shalom* [TH7965, ZH8934]—all creation being and doing as the Creator intended. The prophet's task in this situation is to sound the alarm clearly and forcefully. And the prophet sounds the alarm as a citizen of the city. God brought the prophet himself into the suffering of the people whose demise he announced.

These sober realities might imply more positive notes, which Ezekiel will in due time pursue. One suggests this not because a good story should have a happy ending, but because Yahweh, God of the covenant, more often than not brings judgment with salvation eventually in view. Ezekiel would have known this from Leviticus 26 (among other sources), an extended treatment of the very issue to which the prophet has repeatedly made reference over the last few chapters. For the time being, however, the book hammers home the threat of impending judgment. For now, the reader wrestles with the bad news.

◆ B. The Glory of the God of Israel Driven from Temple and City (8:1–11:25)

1. Vision of abominations in the Temple (8:1-18)

Then on September 17,* during the sixth
year of King Jehoiachin's captivity, while
the leaders of Judah were in my home, the
Sovereign LORD took hold of me. 2I saw a
figure that appeared to be a man. From
what appeared to be his waist down, he
looked like a burning flame. From the
waist up he looked like gleaming amber.*
3He reached out what seemed to be a
hand and took me by the hair. Then the
Spirit lifted me up into the sky and trans-
ported me to Jerusalem in a vision from
God. I was taken to the north gate of the
inner courtyard of the Temple, where
there is a large idol that has made the
LORD very jealous. 4Suddenly, the glory of
the God of Israel was there, just as I had
seen it before in the valley.

5Then the LORD said to me, "Son of man,
look toward the north." So I looked, and
there to the north, beside the entrance to
the gate near the altar, stood the idol that
had made the LORD so jealous.

6"Son of man," he said, "do you see what
they are doing? Do you see the detestable
sins the people of Israel are committing to
drive me from my Temple? But come, and
you will see even more detestable sins than
these!" 7Then he brought me to the door of
the Temple courtyard, where I could see a
hole in the wall. 8He said to me, "Now, son
of man, dig into the wall." So I dug into the
wall and found a hidden doorway.

9"Go in," he said, "and see the wicked
and detestable sins they are committing
in there!" 10So I went in and saw the walls
engraved with all kinds of crawling ani-
mals and detestable creatures. I also saw
the various idols* worshiped by the people
of Israel. 11Seventy leaders of Israel were
standing there with Jaazaniah son of
Shaphan in the center. Each of them held

an incense burner, from which a cloud of incense rose above their heads.

12 Then the LORD said to me, "Son of man, have you seen what the leaders of Israel are doing with their idols in dark rooms? They are saying, 'The LORD doesn't see us; he has deserted our land!'" 13 Then the LORD added, "Come, and I will show you even more detestable sins than these!"

14 He brought me to the north gate of the LORD's Temple, and some women were sitting there, weeping for the god Tammuz. 15 "Have you seen this?" he asked. "But I will show you even more detestable sins than these!"

16 Then he brought me into the inner courtyard of the LORD's Temple. At the entrance to the sanctuary, between the entry room and the bronze altar, there were about twenty-five men with their backs to the sanctuary of the LORD. They were facing east, bowing low to the ground, worshiping the sun!

17 "Have you seen this, son of man?" he asked. "Is it nothing to the people of Judah that they commit these detestable sins, leading the whole nation into violence, thumbing their noses at me, and provoking my anger? 18 Therefore, I will respond in fury. I will neither pity nor spare them. And though they cry for mercy, I will not listen."

8:1 Hebrew *on the fifth day of the sixth month,* of the ancient Hebrew lunar calendar. This event occurred on September 17, 592 B.C.; also see note on 1:1. **8:2** Or *like burnished metal.* **8:10** The Hebrew term (literally *round things*) probably alludes to dung.

NOTES

8:1 *on September 17.* Lit., "on the fifth day of the sixth month," of the ancient Hebrew lunar calendar. This event occurred on September 17, 592 BC— i.e., 414 days since Ezekiel's call on July 31, 593 (1:1) and just beyond the 390 days mentioned in 4:5. (See note on 1:1.)

the Sovereign LORD took hold of me. Lit., "the hand of the Sovereign LORD fell upon me there." (See note on 1:3.)

8:2 *a figure that appeared to be a man.* The MT has "that appeared like fire" (*'esh* [TH784, ZH836]), which is not impossible. The LXX, however, read *'ish* [TH376, ZH408], "man" for MT's *'esh,* relying perhaps on references in 1:26 and 40:3. This supplies a referent to a following pronoun and avoids fire in the upper half of the figure, in keeping with the immediate context. The NLT follows the LXX.

8:3 *He reached out. . . . Then the Spirit lifted me up . . . in a vision.* See note on 3:12 concerning spiritual, visionary transport.

in a vision from God. Lit., "in visions of God," and so translated in 1:1. The NLT calls attention to the content of the vision of the glory of God that follows 1:1, and to the source of the vision in 8:3 and 40:2 where the expression reoccurs. The Hebrew syntax involved allows equally for either translation, so translation depends (as always) on context.

to the north gate of the inner courtyard of the Temple. Lit., "to the *entrance/door* of the inner gate [or 'the gate of the inner courtyard'] that faces north" (emphasis added). The route of Ezekiel's movement through the Temple is not entirely clear. But in view of the route taken in chs 40–48 and the consistent use of the Hebrew verbs involved in describing the conduct of the tour here and in chs 40–48, it seems more likely that Ezekiel was guided from the far north side of the Temple in something of a straight line into increasingly sacred space, culminating between the altar and the Temple building itself. This is the interpretation in Allen 1994:138-141, countering exegetes (e.g., Block 1997:277; Greenberg 1983:166-173) who trace something of a "zigzag" route (cf. Allen 1994:129). (Zimmerli 1979:236-243, following the Old Greek, omits MT's *penimith* [TH6442, ZH7164] (inner) in 8:3 and starts the tour at the north city gate, also resulting in a linear movement.) If the MT's "inner" is retained (as in NLT), it is possible that it is not Ezekiel's visual movement, but his points of visual interest that move in a "straight line." But it is difficult to visualize accurately, and perhaps best not to be overly eager to trace the precise line of movement (Greenberg 1983:166-173).

where there is a large idol. The MT has "where there is the seat (*moshab* [TH4186, ZH4632]) of the idol." This indicates a throne, cultic pedestal, or other prominent place marker. The NLT perhaps reflects this in translating "a *large* idol" (emphasis added), since no explicit note of size appears in the MT.

8:5 ***the idol that had made the* L*ORD* *so jealous.*** The NLT understands *semel haqqin'ah* [TH5566, ZH6166] to refer to an actual idol, not simply an orthostat (i.e., a freestanding stone, often uncarved; cf. Albright 1968:166) or a guardian figure common in Mesopotamian gates (Zimmerli 1979:239). The two best candidates for this idol are both goddesses—(1) Astarte (OT Ashtoreth), the Queen of Heaven, consort of Baal, or (2) Asherah, consort of the Canaanite high god, El.

Old Testament readers know the Queen of Heaven, Ashtoreth, especially from Jeremiah (Jer 7:18; 44:15-19; see also Judg 2:13; 10:6; 1 Sam 7:4; 12:10; 1 Kgs 11:5; 2 Kgs 23:13). Asherah or the plural, Asheroth, is also widely attested in the OT, though it is difficult in many cases to know whether the reference is to the goddess, to her symbol, a pole or tree, or to representation of some more "feminine" aspect of Yahweh. Eichrodt (1970:122) equates these two deities, thinking the Queen of Heaven was Asherah. Dever (2005:230-235), however, reviews a wide range of archaeological, especially iconographic, evidence and recent interpretive literature. He convincingly argues two points germane to our paragraph. First, though occasionally identified with each other, the two goddesses were distinct deities, both with wide appeal in popular (and at times "official") religion in Israel, and both with deep roots in Canaan and beyond. Second, Jeremiah's "Queen of Heaven" was "Astarte" (or "Ishtar," as she was known in the East), with her crown, astral iconography, and the connection with baking cake figurines of her (Jer 7:18; 44:19; cf. Hos 3:1) especially important to her identification.

Lady Asherah probably makes the best candidate for the goddess represented in the outrageous idol mentioned by Ezekiel, the *semel haqqin'ah* (so also Allen 1994:142; Greenberg 1983:168; against Zimmerli 1979:239). King Manasseh actually placed a *semel 'asherah* into the Temple (2 Kgs 21:7; cf. 2 Chr 33:7). Later he or Josiah removed the idol, chopping it up and burning it (2 Kgs 23:4; 2 Chr 33:15). Asherah figurines are ubiquitous in Canaan from the Late Bronze Age into the Iron Age. In Judah, especially in the eighth and seventh centuries they are found in household contexts. Her figurines in late preexilic Judah, lacking genitalia and proffering ponderous breasts, appear to have gravitated from representations of Asherah as "lascivious courtesan of the gods" to Asherah as a "nursing mother," "the Great Mother," without forfeiting interests in "earthy" religion and fecundity concerns (Dever 2005:185). Block, who does not actually identify the idol, is surely correct in his judgment: "It is clear that the image is not simply an ornament or a symbolic temple guard. It is overtly idolatrous and poses a direct challenge to Yahweh" (1997:282). See also Keel and Uehlinger (1998:177-281, especially 198-204, 210-248, 277-281).

8:10 ***all kinds of crawling animals.*** This phrase is reminiscent of Egyptian deities. The multitude of "theriomorphic [animal forms] deities" in Egyptian religious iconography was stunning even in the ancient world (Greenberg 1983:169-170; see ANEP, illustrations 548-573).

various idols. Heb., *gillulim* [TH1544, ZH1658] (lit., "round things") probably alludes to dung. (See note on 5:9.)

8:14 *weeping for the god Tammuz.* Block has suggested that the expression refers not to weeping *for* Tammuz, but weeping "*the* Tammuz," indicating the specific lament genre or possibly a specific lament. He finds support for this in the article and the Hebrew direct object indicator (*'eth* [TH853, ZH906]) here attached to the divine name (1997:282). This is possible, in view of the fact that the verb root, *b-k-h,* occurs only here in the D-stem (i.e., Piel) with the direct object indicator. But the lack of syntactic parallels with *b-k-h* makes a firm conclusion difficult. More importantly, in the G-stem (i.e., Qal) this root occurs several times with the direct object indicator clearly with the sense of "weep *for* X" (e.g., Gen 37:35; 50:3; Deut 34:8; Jer 9:10). Brownlee argues that the direct article perhaps refers to Yahweh as "*the* Tammuz *par excellence*" (1986:136). In either case, the women are lamenting the demise of Tammuz, with weeping "*the* Tammuz" being more vivid. We especially know Tammuz from materials about his courtship and marriage with the goddess Inanna/Ishtar. (See ANET §§ 52, 84, 101, 109 for sample texts in which Tammuz surfaces.)

8:16 *twenty-five men.* Speculation as to the significance of the number of men has reached no satisfactory conclusion. Perhaps they were representatives of the 24 priestly classes plus the high priest (Hitzig, Lightfoot, cited by Zimmerli 1979:243). Perhaps, following LXX, the correct number is 20, the number of the sun-god, Shamash, in Babylonian theology (Greenberg 1983:172). But in light of LXX and the MT at 11:1, where Ezekiel sees 25 men, the reading 20 seems less likely. Perhaps another meaning is to be sought.

8:17 *thumbing their noses at me.* It is difficult to know what the Hebrew here actually means; it reads literally "they even stick the branch (?) to their nose." Whatever it meant, it was highly offensive and is thought originally to have referred to God's nose, reading *'appi* instead of *'appam* [TH639, ZH678]. Early scribes numbered this change among the *tiqqune sopherim,* perpetual scribal corrections removing offensive references to God from the text. The fact that the expression (actually threatening to touch God's real, physical nose with "the branch") involves such a blatant anthropomorphism could support a scribal move to resist such readings. Some have ventured explanations by analogy to Persian or other ancient Near Eastern cultic practices or a phallic cult. These do not really seem sufficiently repugnant to account for the scribal reaction and the weight the expression needs to bear in this context. Greenberg cites a rabbinic "scatological" interpretation of 8:16 in which those bowing to Shamash actually *exposed* their buttocks. This reading suggested to some medieval commentators that 8:17 had to do with "breaking wind" in Yahweh's face, referring to the stench of idolatrous worship (Greenberg 1983:172-173).

COMMENTARY

The dramatic movement of the glory of God departing the Temple and then the city of Jerusalem provides the dominant coherence for chapters 8–11 (8:4; 9:3; 10:4, 18-19; 11:22-23). This departure has its reverse image in Ezekiel's vision of the return of that Shekinah glory to the city and its Temple in chapters 40–48 as part of the book's chiastic structure. (For details see "Literary Structure and Outline" in the Introduction.) This literary section is also designed chiastically, with matching items arranged concentrically at the beginning and the end of the unit (A, B, C, D, C′, B′, A′). Ezekiel's ministry context appears in 8:1a and 11:25 (A, A′). The descent of Yahweh's hand marks the "onset" of the vision in 8:1b, with the vision ascending from the prophet in 11:24b (B, B′). The Spirit transports the prophet to Jerusalem in 8:3b and back to Babylon in 11:24a (C, C′). The core of the vision itself, 8:4–11:23, forms the main body of the composition (D) (cf. Allen 1994:129-130). Thus, the compositional design of chapters 8–11 makes this section foundational to the movement of the book as a whole. The unit's setting *within a vision experience* also brings coherence to these chapters. The "vision from God" opens in 8:1b and closes in 11:24. Chapters 8–11 cohere as a vision report. The report reaches its climax in the movement of the glory of God out of the city to the mountain to the east (11:23).

Beyond recurring vocabulary that knits the unit together thematically, a multileveled causal logic governs chapters 8–11. The general reasoning of chapters 4–7 is reversed. There, indictments follow announcements of judgment, providing reasons for the threats. In chapter 8, indictments open the unit and lead causally to the judgment response, summarized in 8:18 and pictured in chapters 9–11, with a similar causal logic present within chapters 9 and 11.

By comparison of 8:1 and 1:1-4, Ezekiel was 414 days into the sign-act of lying on his sides as instructed in 4:4-6 (presuming he did the acts) when the Lord apprehended him, transporting him via a vision to the Temple in Jerusalem. (On spiritual and visionary transport, see note on 3:12, 14.) Exiled Judean leaders (Heb., "elders") were with him, perhaps waiting for an oracle or trying to inquire of him, when he saw himself being carried to Jerusalem.

Ezekiel first saw a humanlike figure who took hold of him and who would be his guide (8:2) on this visionary tour of the Temple. The description, though reversed, parallels that of the enthroned figure in 1:27-28. This figure is the one who called and commissioned him, even though the picture is veiled in layers of "appearance" and simile. This description, the Spirit as the agent of transport, and the appearance of the glory of God, all take the reader back to the inaugural vision. The striking similarities between 8:1-3 and 3:22-24 lead one to think that Ezekiel himself no doubt remembered encountering the same glory of God in the valley (3:22). He sees none other than the glory of the God of Israel (8:4; 9:3; 11:22), the glory of the Lord, Yahweh himself (10:4). As in 1:26-28 and 3:22-24, the apprehension by Yahweh, the sight of the Shekinah, and the presence of the Spirit introduce the divine one speaking to Ezekiel. The Lord speaks (8:5, 12) as he conducts Ezekiel through the desecrations of his own Temple (8:6, 14, 16; 10:19; 11:1).

The tour unfolds in four stops, perhaps moving into increasingly sacred space: (1) the outrageous idol at the north (outer?) gate (8:5-6); (2) the leaders' "secret" idolatry in a chamber in the inner courtyard wall (8:9-13); (3) the women weeping for Tammuz inside the inner north gate (8:14-15); and finally (4) the 25 men worshiping the sun in the inner court, between the altar and the Temple itself, immediately in front of the Temple porch and steps (8:16). Yahweh claims that each one is more detestable than the previous, the first three concluding with the refrain urging the narrative forward, "you will see" or "I will show you even more detestable sins than these" (8:6, 13, 15). (See the Introduction, "Date and Occasion of Writing," for information on the developments leading to the theological crisis exposed in this tour of Yahweh's Temple.)

Set down in the Temple's (outer?) court (see note on 8:3), directed to look north (toward, and probably through, the north gate of the Temple compound), Ezekiel saw "the [outrageous image] that had made the LORD so jealous" (8:5). Defined simply by the article, Ezekiel clearly assumed readers would know *the* image to which he referred. Scholarly debate over the identity of the image shows that "obvious" identification has been lost (see note on 8:5). If Ezekiel referred to images of an actual alien deity, and not simply a representation of some aspect of Yahweh, two major candidates emerge: (1) "the Queen of Heaven" (most likely West Semitic Ashtoreth/Astarte, Mesopotamian Ishtar) and (2) Asherah, consort of the Canaanite high-god, El.

Archaeological and textual evidence contemporary with Ezekiel indicates that the Queen of Heaven was widely worshiped in Judah prior to and after the fall of Jerusalem, even enjoying royal sponsorship at some periods going back to Solomon (1 Kgs 11:5). She was a widely revered Canaanite goddess, the consort of Baal (god of the storm and fertility), especially beloved by women and connected with concerns of fertility in home and flock (cf. Deut 7:13; 28:4, 18, 51). In Egypt she was connected with war and military patronage. She was the favorite goddess of Tyre, Sidon, and the Phoenician world in the first millennium BC. Devotion to her had been disrupted during King Josiah's reform. Judean refugees in Egypt, however, flatly blamed their troubles and the fall of Jerusalem itself on the reform that stopped the worship of Astarte, which had included offering her cakes, libations, and burning incense (Jer 44:15-19).

More likely, however, Asherah was the deity represented by the "large idol" (*semel* [TH5566, ZH6166]) that made the Lord jealous (8:3, 5). King Manasseh had introduced a *semel* of Asherah into Yahweh's Temple at the low point of Judah's theological confusion (2 Kgs 21:7; cf. 2 Chr 33:7). Josiah, and perhaps also Manasseh before him, removed and burned the idol (2 Kgs 23:4-5; 2 Chr 33:15), along with paraphernalia associated with Baal, astral deities in general, and especially Shamash the Sun. These abominations were apparently reintroduced by King Josiah's ungodly successors, especially Jehoiakim. (For wider context, see "The Legacy of Manasseh and the Assyrians" in the Introduction.)

Periodically, as under Manasseh and apparently again later, Asherah enjoyed official sponsorship. But she was especially and widely beloved in folk religion of Israel and Judah. She was "The Great Mother," worshiped across the ancient Near East under various names; she was the patroness especially of women and family concerns of fecundity and lactation. Her presence in the Temple indicated serious distortion of historic, Mosaic faith. Her presence at the head of this chapter's tour signals a context of theological compromise and confusion for all that follows. It involved obtaining the blessing of Yahweh upon home and field and nation by magic-laden liturgies at odds with the Sinai covenant's structure of trust and obedience as the means by which covenant blessings are experienced (Lev 26; Deut 27–29). As consort of the Canaanite high-god, El, some may well have seen Asherah as Yahweh's consort, with Yahweh claiming El's place as high-god. If so, Asherah may have served as a divine Temple guard, prominently situated at the gate entrance, mediating Yahweh's will and blessing to worshipers.

At the site of the second abomination, Ezekiel found himself in a dark chamber, with 70 leaders worshiping Israel's various idols (8:7-11). Because of the cryptic nature of the site's description no scholarly consensus exists regarding its precise location (Block 1997:288-294; Eichrodt 1970:124-125; Greenberg 1983:169-170).

Apparently Ezekiel had moved to the north gate of the inner court, into either a chamber in the wall (a casemate wall?) or one of the storage or service rooms connected to the wall. Why Ezekiel dug through a hole instead of using a door is perhaps to be chalked up to visionary experience more than architectural realities. It remains a mystery (Block 1997:289).

Ezekiel first notices two things about the site: (1) "all kinds of crawling animals and detestable creatures" carved on the walls and (2) Israel's "various idols," none specifically identified (8:10). Vocabulary links evoke Leviticus 11:10-42 and Deuteronomy 4:16-24 as the background against which this paragraph is to be read (cf. also Lev 26:1; Num 33:52). The setting reeks with idolatrous flouting of historic priestly concerns for cultic purity and with utter disregard of the covenant ban on the making and worshiping of images of any sort (e.g., Exod 20:4-5). Emphasis on the variety of creatures carved on the walls suggests a possible Egyptian influence (see note on 8:10). The "various idols" could include Canaanite and Mesopotamian themes found in folk and official Israelite religion alike at various periods.

"Seventy leaders of Israel" (8:11) were in the chamber, each at an image carrel, with censors wafting the smoke and aroma of incense toward their images. This use of incense was an important liturgical function and a potent feature of religious practice in Israel and beyond. Incense figured in appeasing God's wrath (Num 16:46-47), was in some circumstances comparable to whole offerings (Deut 33:10), and was associated also with idolatrous private cults (Isa 65:3; Jer 19:13). For these lay leaders to use censors at all was a breach of Yahweh worship practice, trespassing on a prerogative reserved for priests (cf. Num 16:1-40).

Some indication of the level of leadership gathered here may be seen in the central figure identified as Jaazaniah son of Shaphan, most likely identical with Shaphan ben Azaliah, state secretary under Josiah (2 Kgs 22:3-14) and father of two other sons associated with Jeremiah (Jer 26:24; 29:3; not Jaazaniah son of Azzur, 11:1). Jaazaniah had clearly marked out a different spiritual course for himself, far from the convictions of King Josiah and the prophet Jeremiah. It is quite possible that this cultic activity involved a religious expression of Jaazaniah's political agenda, indicating a party intrigued with things Egyptian and open to the temptation to lean on Egypt for support against Nebuchadnezzar and the Babylonians (17:15; cf. Jer 37:7). The elders rationalized their deviant practice with claims that "the LORD doesn't see us; he has deserted our land!" (8:12). Perhaps they echo the contemptuous and cynical view among Jerusalem elites of roughly the same time, spoken of by Zephaniah—Yahweh is irrelevant because he is either unwilling or unable to enter national affairs in significant ways (Zeph 1:12)! The claim of desertion seems to indicate that they concluded from Neco's victory over Josiah and Nebuchadnezzar's subjugation of the land that Yahweh had left the land defenseless. In their mind, Yahweh had rejected the land for some unknown reason—they did not accept the explanations of these events by Jeremiah (Jer 5:19; 9:13), Zephaniah (Zeph 1:2-18), and Ezekiel (e.g., Ezek 5:5-10). Thus, they concluded that God has an undependable character and inadequate power. They decided to turn to other theological options. God called these options "detestable sins" (8:13).

The third sinful scene, "even more detestable" than the leaders' secretive cult, consisted of women at the north gate, "sitting there, weeping for the god Tammuz" (8:14-15). They were apparently just inside or just outside the gate entering the north side of the inner court. The women are anonymous, and only two verses are devoted to this abomination. Still, it apparently carried significant weight for Yahweh. Tammuz was a Mesopotamian deity whose cult was known already in ancient Sumer, almost two millennia before Ezekiel (Sumerian *Dumuzi*). Some have regarded Tammuz as a classic "dying and rising" god revered later by both Assyrians and Babylonians (Dever 2005:234-235; Eichrodt 1970:106). Others have cautioned that the various traditions through which we know of Tammuz do not cohere in as clear an identity as one might wish (Oppenheim 1964:196; ABD 6.316-318). His delivery to the underworld by Ishtar and his subsequent descent into the realm of the dead was associated with the withering of vegetation and lamented with full mourning. Dever (2005:234-235) compares Tammuz to Baal as a god dying in the early summer when the rains ceased, and then descending into the underworld as though dead. Ishtar mourned his passing, but in the fall she helped to bring him back to life, finally consummating their sexual reunion. "Thus," says Dever, "nature was fructified in an unending cycle of love, death, and reunion," a Mesopotamian version of a "pan-Mediterranean seasonal myth" featuring Baal and Anat, Tammuz and Ishtar, Osiris and Isis in Egypt, Adonis in Syria, and Dionysius in Greece (cf. Brownlee 1986:136).

What is secure in the materials is the death of Tammuz and the mourning mandated for it in the fourth month, named after him in Babylon. Weeping here in the sixth month may be weeping over his being dead so long (Brownlee 1986:136). It could be just a cultural variant on the Tammuz cult or a caricature of Judean religious syncretism (Block 1997:295). Interestingly, this month name is still used today on Jewish calendars: 17 Tammuz is the fast for the destruction of the Second Temple, and 9 Tammuz was a fast for the breach of Jerusalem's walls in 586 (Zech 8:19; cf. Jer 52:6-7). Though widely popular in Mesopotamia (especially among women), Tammuz was not an important god in the political structures of the Mesopotamian pantheon and not a national deity like Asshur or Marduk. It is unlikely, therefore, that either the Assyrians or the Babylonians would have imposed his cult on Judeans for political purposes. More likely we have here evidence of Judean syncretism and "willful" adaptation of Yahweh worship to the worldview of neighbors near and far. These women may well have seen Yahweh's blessings of fertile field, flock, and family mediated in some way through Tammuz. This sacrilege near the Temple symbolically exposes how extreme Israel's apostasy had become.

The fourth and most grievous scene of the detestable sins (8:16-17) finds 25 men between the great altar and the vestibule of the Temple building itself, prostrating themselves to the sun, Shamash. They face east toward the rising sun, thus turning their backs to the Temple and to Yahweh himself, enthroned within it upon the cherubim. They simultaneously submit themselves to Shamash and reject their covenant god, Yahweh. This site, between the great altar and the vestibule, is the most sacred space in the Temple complex besides the interior of the Temple building itself. An alien deity could be elevated no further without actually having his likeness inside the Temple.

Sun worship had royal sponsorship in late Neo-Assyrian times under Manasseh, with horses and chariots for the sun, along with altars for the entire host of heaven (sun, moon, and stars) introduced into the Temple and purged later by Josiah or Manasseh (2 Kgs 21:5; 23:11). As with Asherah, this cult was likely reintroduced by King Josiah's successors. There is perhaps a chance that some pressure from Babylon was involved, but more likely we have here the resurgence, or coming to full flower, of the solarization of Yahweh, which had roots in Israel reaching back to Solomon. This Yahweh theology had Canaanite and more ancient Near Eastern background in language expressing "theophanic luminosity," as Smith puts it (1990:114-124). It also arose under the influence of ancient royal titles exploiting solar imagery to describe the king and to narrate the king's audience before the sun as part of his credentials for kingship. The 25 men may have been worshiping Yahweh as king manifest in the sun. Ezekiel rejected these "alternate" Yahweh theologies and joined the polemic that insisted that the sun is not a manifestation of Yahweh, but a creature of Yahweh, attesting to God and providing order in the created cosmos (Ps 19; Smith 1990:120-121).

The final "scene" of the Temple tour actually leaps the bounds of the Temple itself and calls Ezekiel's attention to the whole land, seen through the lens of the Temple. The question in 8:17, "Have you seen this, son of man?" (as in 8:6, 12, 15), marks this as a related but separate point of interest. The question is rhetorical, calling attention to the scene: "*Look* at this despicable sight, son of man!" Interestingly enough, the final indictment in the Temple tour switches categories abruptly: The concern moves from the profaning of sacred space and the exhibition of theological chaos to wholesale moral failure, "leading the whole nation into violence" (8:17b). This presents the crowning abomination! This is the cultural fruit of introducing the unholy in the holy, of disdaining matters of cultic purity and sacredness. Ezekiel's priestly concerns clearly must not be understood as arcane preoccupation with cultic regulations. Here and elsewhere in the book, Ezekiel shows Yahweh's profound concern with human behavior, particularly with the security and integrity of the community under the covenant of the Torah. Ezekiel follows up this general indictment in 9:9, speaking of a land full of murder, a city filled with injustice (cf. "wicked counsel," 11:2; endless murder, 11:6; adultery and sexual sin, robbing and abusing the poor, living unjustly and dishonestly and more, 18:5-18; 22:1-16). Liturgy and life, as well as theology and communal well-being, are inextricably bound together in Ezekiel's mind. Israel's wholesale breach of covenant life is the last straw, a veritable "thumbing their noses" at Yahweh (8:17, see note).

The parties indicted in this chapter may surprise us. The Jerusalem priesthood carries some blame, but Ezekiel reserved his most scathing indictments for the laity of Judah. Family and clan leaders ("elders," *zeqenim* [TH2205, ZH2418], e.g., 8:11, 12), selected "officials" (*sarim* [TH8269, ZH8569], 11:1-3), and undesignated laypersons receive the brunt of Ezekiel's criticism. The final verse of the chapter (8:18) draws the horrific conclusion from this parade of detestable sins: Yahweh's response in fury, without pity, sparing none, with no hope for reversing this verdict. These brief lines tie the reader back to the refrain of chapter 7's announcement of "the end," and open the way for chapter 9's elaboration of this judgment (cf. 9:5, 10).

◆ 2. Marked foreheads spared (9:1-11)

Then the LORD thundered, "Bring on the men appointed to punish the city! Tell them to bring their weapons with them!" 2Six men soon appeared from the upper gate that faces north, each carrying a deadly weapon in his hand. With them was a man dressed in linen, who carried a writer's case at his side. They all went into the Temple courtyard and stood beside the bronze altar.

3Then the glory of the God of Israel rose up from between the cherubim, where it had rested, and moved to the entrance of the Temple. And the LORD called to the man dressed in linen who was carrying the writer's case. 4He said to him, "Walk through the streets of Jerusalem and put a mark on the foreheads of all who weep and sigh because of the detestable sins being committed in their city."

5Then I heard the LORD say to the other men, "Follow him through the city and kill everyone whose forehead is not marked. Show no mercy; have no pity! 6Kill them all—old and young, girls and women and little children. But do not touch anyone with the mark. Begin right here at the Temple." So they began by killing the seventy leaders.

7"Defile the Temple!" the LORD commanded. "Fill its courtyards with corpses. Go!" So they went and began killing throughout the city.

8While they were out killing, I was all alone. I fell face down on the ground and cried out, "O Sovereign LORD! Will your fury against Jerusalem wipe out everyone left in Israel?"

9Then he said to me, "The sins of the people of Israel and Judah are very, very great. The entire land is full of murder; the city is filled with injustice. They are saying, 'The LORD doesn't see it! The LORD has abandoned the land!' 10So I will not spare them or have any pity on them. I will fully repay them for all they have done."

11Then the man in linen clothing, who carried the writer's case, reported back and said, "I have done as you commanded."

NOTES

9:2 ***Six men . . . each carrying a deadly weapon. . . . With them was a man . . . who carried a writer's case.*** Six executioners and a scribe make seven. Seven is the number of completeness. In this case it is a full expression of the wrath and mercy of Yahweh, several times achieved in a 6 + 1 pattern, as done here (46:1, 4, 6). For more information, see Marvin Pope's interesting article, "Seven, Seventh, Seventy," regarding the symbolic and liturgical importance of these numbers (IDB 4.294-295).

9:4 ***a mark on the foreheads.*** The scribe is to mark these persons with the Hebrew letter Taw, which was shaped like an "X" in Ezekiel's day.

9:6 ***they began by killing the seventy leaders.*** The NLT starts the judgment with the 70 leaders—as the vision moves away from the bronze altar to the hidden chamber where the 70 had been wafting their incense to their idols (8:9-12). But the MT (with the Targum and Vulgate) contains no number (70 or 20) but simply begins the slaughter with the elderly men "before the Temple" (so REB, NKJV, JPS, NIV, ESV)—this would imply they began with those elderly men among the 25 who had been bowing to Shamash in front of the Temple building, between the altar and the vestibule. The JB probably has it best: "so they began [the killing] with the old men in front of the Temple." This is where the executioners had stationed themselves (9:2) and seems most likely. The LXX lacks "old/elder" and has them "within the Temple [complex]," probably emphasizing their interior location. The NLT does not account well for the MT's "in front of the Temple" and probably takes the repetition of the Hebrew word for "old man, elder" in both 8:11 and 9:6 as its cue in adding the number 70 here. The MT, however, doesn't specify here that these elders were "of Israel" as it did in 8:11.

COMMENTARY

Ezekiel's vision (9:1-2) continues with Yahweh's thundering call for heavenly executioners to carry out the judgment pronounced in 8:18. Seven angelic figures respond to the call and appear at the upper north gate. Six have brought deadly weapons, as commanded. One, dressed in linen, has the tool of a scribe, "a writer's case." The fact that the scribe wears linen could indicate he is a *priestly* scribe (cf. Exod 28:42; 39:28; 1 Sam 2:18; 22:18). If so, here a priest has leadership in avenging the Temple desecration (cf. ch 44). But it is more likely that the linen garb signals angelic status (cf. Dan 10:5; 12:6-7).

The executioners take up position beside the great bronze altar (1 Kgs 8:64), within sight of the men bowing to Shamash (9:1-2). Simultaneously the glory of the God of Israel rose from between the cherubim in the Most Holy Place and moved to the Temple threshold (9:3). This move ominously recalls 8:6 and anticipates steps in the larger story of the Shekinah's departure from Jerusalem.

Yahweh issued three sets of orders. First, the scribe is to go throughout the city marking the foreheads of "all who weep and sigh because of the detestable sins being committed in their city" (9:4). Second, the six executioners are to follow, killing without mercy every man, woman, and child not carrying the mark. But they are not even to touch those with the mark on their foreheads (9:5-6). The seven are to begin their work of marking and slaying in the Temple itself, with the result that the leaders bowing to the sun between the altar and the vestibule of the Temple (8:16) are the first to fall (rather than the leaders in the hidden room as in the NLT; see note on 9:6). Apparently, judgment will trace in reverse the route of Ezekiel's tour of detestable sins in the Temple (9:6). Finally, Yahweh urged the grim team to litter the Temple courts with the bodies of those slain in the very act of their apostasy (9:7), thus defiling the sacred place. These had desecrated the Temple by their idolatrous worship. Yahweh would desecrate his own precincts as an act of judgment. Ezekiel's vision anticipates the reality to befall the Temple at the hands of the Babylonians (6:4, 7; 24:21).

Ezekiel responded to this ghastly scene with a passionate question for the sovereign Lord of Israel: "Will your fury against Jerusalem wipe out everyone left in Israel?" (9:8). Ezekiel was probably the only living person left in a Temple now filled with worshipers cut down by the executioners in the vision. He prostrated himself in an attempt at prophetic intercession (cf. Gen 20:7; Amos 7:1-6). He asked whether the remnant of Yahweh's people left in the land would survive Yahweh's fury. Yahweh offered no direct answer; instead, he reiterated the incredible sinfulness of his people (9:9). Murder and injustice permeated the land (8:17). Furthermore, the elders believed that Yahweh had deserted the land and didn't see what they were doing (8:12). Forcefully setting divine reality over against these charges, Yahweh sarcastically warned that his "eye" (9:10, NASB), which allegedly could not see, would not spare them the consequences of their sin (8:18).

This portion of Ezekiel's vision report concludes with the scribe's report of mission accomplished (9:11). His statement "I have done as you commanded" echoes words famous because of their presence in the account of Moses assembling the Tabernacle in obedience to the Lord's commands (Exod 40:19, 21, 23, 25, 27, 32). In Exodus, following this obedience, the glory of the Lord fills the Tabernacle (Exod 40:34-35). Here in Ezekiel, the glory is seen departing the Temple.

◆ 3. The Lord's glory at the Temple's east gate (10:1-22)

In my vision I saw what appeared to be a throne of blue lapis lazuli above the crystal surface over the heads of the cherubim. [2]Then the LORD spoke to the man in linen clothing and said, "Go between the whirling wheels beneath the cherubim, and take a handful of burning coals and scatter them over the city." He did this as I watched.

[3]The cherubim were standing at the south end of the Temple when the man went in, and the cloud of glory filled the inner courtyard. [4]Then the glory of the LORD rose up from above the cherubim and went over to the door of the Temple. The Temple was filled with this cloud of glory, and the courtyard glowed brightly with the glory of the LORD. [5]The moving wings of the cherubim sounded like the voice of God Almighty* and could be heard even in the outer courtyard.

[6]The LORD said to the man in linen clothing, "Go between the cherubim and take some burning coals from between the wheels." So the man went in and stood beside one of the wheels. [7]Then one of the cherubim reached out his hand and took some live coals from the fire burning among them. He put the coals into the hands of the man in linen clothing, and the man took them and went out. [8](All the cherubim had what looked like human hands under their wings.)

[9]I looked, and each of the four cherubim had a wheel beside him, and the wheels sparkled like beryl. [10]All four wheels looked alike and were made the same; each wheel had a second wheel turning crosswise within it. [11]The cherubim could move in any of the four directions they faced, without turning as they moved. They went straight in the direction they faced, never turning aside. [12]Both the cherubim and the wheels were covered with eyes. The cherubim had eyes all over their bodies, including their hands, their backs, and their wings. [13]I heard someone refer to the wheels as "the whirling wheels." [14]Each of the four cherubim had four faces: the first was the face of an ox,* the second was a human face, the third was the face of a lion, and the fourth was the face of an eagle.

[15]Then the cherubim rose upward. These were the same living beings I had seen beside the Kebar River. [16]When the cherubim moved, the wheels moved with them. When they lifted their wings to fly, the wheels stayed beside them. [17]When the cherubim stopped, the wheels stopped. When they flew upward, the wheels rose up, for the spirit of the living beings was in the wheels.

[18]Then the glory of the LORD moved out from the door of the Temple and hovered above the cherubim. [19]And as I watched, the cherubim flew with their wheels to the east gate of the LORD's Temple. And the glory of the God of Israel hovered above them.

[20]These were the same living beings I had seen beneath the God of Israel when I was by the Kebar River. I knew they were cherubim, [21]for each had four faces and four wings and what looked like human hands under their wings. [22]And their faces were just like the faces of the beings I had seen at the Kebar, and they traveled straight ahead, just as the others had.

10:5 Hebrew *El-Shaddai.* 10:14 Hebrew *the face of a cherub;* compare 1:10.

NOTES

10:1 ***throne of blue lapis lazuli.*** See note on 1:26.

10:2 ***whirling wheels beneath the cherubim.*** Here and in 10:6 and 13, the MT calls the wheels of the cherubim *galgal* [TH1534, ZH1649]; elsewhere they are *'opan* [TH212, ZH236]. The NLT differentiates the two by translating *galgal* as "whirling wheels" (similarly in ESV, NIV). The LXX translates them all with *trochos* [TG5164, ZG5580], but in 10:13 transliterates as *Gelgel,* perhaps as a technical term where Ezekiel equates the two. Thus NAB translates, "I heard the wheels given the name 'wheelwork.'" See note on 1:15-16.

cherubim. For the most part, "cherubim" (i.e., cherubs) in ch 10 names the "living beings" of ch 1. The MT appears to use the plural to refer to these living beings, and to use the singular (10:4a; also 9:3a), also translated "cherubim" by the NLT, to refer to the pair of cherubs in the Holy of Holies since the time of Solomon. The singular also appears when reference is to "one of the cherubim" (living beings), as in 10:7.

10:5 *God Almighty.* Heb., *'el-shadday* [TH410A/446, ZH7706/8724]. Cf. 1:24 and NLT mg note. This term occurs only twice in Ezekiel, here echoing the vision of ch 1.

COMMENTARY

Three major concerns occupy the writer in this unit. First, continuing the narrative of the angelic executioners, the scribe of chapter 9 becomes an "incendiary" to set Jerusalem ablaze (Allen 1994:151). Second, Yahweh's glory moves closer to the abandonment of his Temple and city. Third, the writer elaborates connections between the present vision and the inaugural vision of chapter 1. These three items jostle for coherence in the chapter in a way that has resulted in scholarly appeals to redaction (Zimmerli 1979:231-235, 253-256) or textual emendation (Allen 1994:151; Greenberg 1983:181).

Chapter 10 starts as chapter 1 ended, with the sight of the heavenly throne followed by the voice of the enthroned one (10:1). Yahweh commands "the man in linen clothing" to scatter burning coals taken from among the wheels beneath the cherubim across the city (10:2, 5). These sacred coals from the presence of the God of Israel deliver unrelenting judgment. The narrative of the angelic executioners concludes abruptly. The writer chooses not to narrate the carrying out of the act, but tells us Ezekiel watched as the man did as he was told (10:2).

The link with the "visions of God" in chapter 1 begins and ends the unit (10:1 and 20-22). "Cherubs" here designate the "living beings" of chapter 1 (10:15, 20, 22). These were the living beings Ezekiel had seen by the river Kebar (1:3-28; 10:20-22). Together with the movement of the glory of the God of Israel, the references back to chapter 1 dominate the unit. Ezekiel's vision of the divine throne scene (1:22-27) is the backdrop for this chapter, as well. The following lines in chapter 10 recollect the inaugural vision in chapter 1: the sound of the cherubs' wings like "the voice of the Almighty" (10:5; cf. 1:24); the apparently human hands beneath the cherubs' wings (10:8; cf. 1:8); the wheel assemblages (10:9-13; cf. 1:15-18); the four faces (10:14; cf. 1:10); the covering with eyes (10:12; cf. 1:18); the brilliance of the scene (10:4; cf. 1:27, 28); and the motion of the cherubs and the wheels in unison (10:16-17; cf. 1:19-21). Along with these clear recollections of chapter 1, puzzling differences appear as well, regarding the area covered with eyes and regarding the order of the four faces of each cherub's head. This state of the text may argue for a redactional history now beyond our ability to retrieve. In any case, these textual oddities should instruct us regarding the freedom involved in the thematic adaptation of texts.

Ezekiel intends the reader to relate this present vision of the cherubim in chapter 10 to the other sectors of the Temple vision (8:3-4) and to the more distant theophany in chapter 1. Development in terminology (from "living creatures" to "cherubim") and alteration of details (in the order of the faces and the location of the eyes) should not block the reader's instinct to bring these together, to allow each to inform the reading of the other.

Ezekiel's vision of these creatures—identified as cherubim (21 times in ch 10!)—taps into the tradition in which creatures called cherubim sit atop the Ark of the Covenant and guard the place where the God of Israel dwells, the place from which he speaks (Exod 25:17-22; Num 7:89). Solomon evoked this tradition in the architectural design of the Yahweh Temple in Jerusalem, where almost certainly the Ark was seen as the throne or the footstool of the God of Israel, guarded by the cherubim (1 Kgs 6:23-35; 8:6-7; 2 Kgs 19:15, assuming Ezekiel's view in 43:3-7 reflects earlier interpretations of the Solomonic Temple). While Ezekiel reflects this earlier iconography, he also adapts it. The earlier cherubim have one face, not four (so far as we know), and they are not associated with wheels or chariots. At these points Ezekiel reflects his Mesopotamian setting (see note on 1:5-9). As the vision unfolds in chapter 1 we discover these heavenly beings actually carry above them the throne of the glorious one (1:26-28), a task only implied in earlier tradition (cf. Exod 25:17-22; Num 7:89; 1 Sam 4:4). They comprise a chariot throne, transporting God's glory.

This vision of the Glory of God enthroned upon the cherubim continues a theme that structures the entire book by providing a visual movement parallel to the logical movement of Ezekiel's message. In Ezekiel's inaugural vision he sees the Lord gloriously present in the land of his people's exile. Here in chapters 8–11 Ezekiel sees this same glorious one back in the Jerusalem Temple (8:4) and then watches his dramatic departure toward the east (9:3; 10:1-5, 20-22; 11:22-24). If the Lord no longer inhabits his house, its ruin cannot be far away! Then, at the conclusion of the book, having been directed to proclaim hope to despairing exiles, Ezekiel is given a vision of the Shekinah glory returning to the new Temple (43:1-5; 44:1-4). God takes up his residence and rule again among his people (cf. 37:24-28).

Why does chapter 10 use such extensive ties back to chapter 1? The theological claims of that earlier vision are deliberately brought forward with this reappearance. The enthroned one who called and commissioned Ezekiel now executes judgment on his Temple and city. The God alleged not to see actually rules an entourage covered with eyes. The one thought to have deserted the city has actually appeared dramatically to those with eyes to see. He will indeed depart, but not in flight before the enemy. He will leave in response to the defilement of his Temple and land (8:6), in a far more deliberate, destructive, and complex manner than anticipated.

The movement of the glory of the God of Israel provides dramatic literary progression to the unit. Twice we are told that the glory of God had risen from between the cherubim in the Most Holy Place and moved to the "entrance" (9:3) or "door" (10:4; Heb., *miptan* [TH4670, ZH5159] both places) of the Temple between the nave and the porch. The Shekinah glory left the place where it had rested since the dedication of the Temple (1 Kgs 8:1-11). Meanwhile, the four cherubs stood at the south end of the Temple (10:3), opposite the scenes of apostasy in chapter 8 and of execution in chapter 9. The "cloud of glory" filled the inner courtyard (10:3), perhaps eventually the whole courtyard (10:4), while the fluttering of the cherubs' wings could be heard "even in the outer courtyard" (10:5). As the cherubs began to rise, the glory of the Lord moved from the Temple door to hover above them (10:15) on a new, mobile throne. Then the whole assemblage moved in synchrony to the east gate of the Temple (10:18). Departure was imminent but delayed.

◆ 4. The Lord's glory leaves doomed Jerusalem (11:1-25)

Then the Spirit lifted me and brought me to the east gateway of the LORD's Temple, where I saw twenty-five prominent men of the city. Among them were Jaazaniah son of Azzur and Pelatiah son of Benaiah, who were leaders among the people.

2The Spirit said to me, "Son of man, these are the men who are planning evil and giving wicked counsel in this city. 3They say to the people, 'Is it not a good time to build houses? This city is like an iron pot. We are safe inside it like meat in a pot.*' 4Therefore, son of man, prophesy against them loudly and clearly."

5Then the Spirit of the LORD came upon me, and he told me to say, "This is what the LORD says to the people of Israel: I know what you are saying, for I know every thought that comes into your minds. 6You have murdered many in this city and filled its streets with the dead.

7"Therefore, this is what the Sovereign LORD says: This city is an iron pot all right, but the pieces of meat are the victims of your injustice. As for you, I will soon drag you from this pot. 8I will bring on you the sword of war you so greatly fear, says the Sovereign LORD. 9I will drive you out of Jerusalem and hand you over to foreigners, who will carry out my judgments against you. 10You will be slaughtered all the way to the borders of Israel. I will execute judgment on you, and you will know that I am the LORD. 11No, this city will not be an iron pot for you, and you will not be like meat safe inside it. I will judge you even to the borders of Israel, 12and you will know that I am the LORD. For you have refused to obey my decrees and regulations; instead, you have copied the standards of the nations around you."

13While I was still prophesying, Pelatiah son of Benaiah suddenly died. Then I fell face down on the ground and cried out, "O Sovereign LORD, are you going to kill everyone in Israel?"

14Then this message came to me from the LORD: 15"Son of man, the people still left in Jerusalem are talking about you and your relatives and all the people of Israel who are in exile. They are saying, 'Those people are far away from the LORD, so now he has given their land to us!'

16"Therefore, tell the exiles, 'This is what the Sovereign LORD says: Although I have scattered you in the countries of the world, I will be a sanctuary to you during your time in exile. 17I, the Sovereign LORD, will gather you back from the nations where you have been scattered, and I will give you the land of Israel once again.'

18"When the people return to their homeland, they will remove every trace of their vile images and detestable idols. 19And I will give them singleness of heart and put a new spirit within them. I will take away their stony, stubborn heart and give them a tender, responsive heart,* 20so they will obey my decrees and regulations. Then they will truly be my people, and I will be their God. 21But as for those who long for vile images and detestable idols, I will repay them fully for their sins. I, the Sovereign LORD, have spoken!"

22Then the cherubim lifted their wings and rose into the air with their wheels beside them, and the glory of the God of Israel hovered above them. 23Then the glory of the LORD went up from the city and stopped above the mountain to the east.

24Afterward the Spirit of God carried me back again to Babylonia,* to the people in exile there. And so ended the vision of my visit to Jerusalem. 25And I told the exiles everything the LORD had shown me.

11:3 Hebrew *This city is the pot, and we are the meat.* 11:19 Hebrew *a heart of flesh.* 11:24 Or *Chaldea.*

NOTES

11:1 ***The Spirit lifted me and brought me . . . where I saw twenty-five prominent men of the city.*** Parallels with 8:1-3 raise the question as to whether we have here a continuation of the earlier Temple vision or a second vision. The number of men (25) encountered here at the east gateway (11:1) prompts one to think of the 25 leaders Ezekiel saw worshiping the sun between the sanctuary and the altar (8:16). But if the report involves an intelligible narrative sequence, the account seems to assume the sun worshipers of ch 8 have already been dispatched (9:6). These men in 11:1 would also be different persons than the 70 encountered with Jaazaniah ben Shaphan (8:11).

Allen resolves the problem by taking 11:1-13 as a second vision, not intended as a sequel to the 8:16 event (1994:159-162). Zimmerli appeals to a complex history of editorial work layered over much more abbreviated, authentic Ezekiel material and responsible for narrative confusions of this sort in the text (1979:256-260). Greenberg acknowledges some disruption in the text (especially in ch 10) but resolves most of them through careful analysis of literary devices of compositional design (1983:192-205).

Jaazaniah son of Azzur. One of four men in the OT carrying the name "Jaazaniah" and differentiated by their fathers' names (i.e., son of Maacah in 2 Kgs 25:23, son of Jeremiah in Jer 35:3, son of Shaphan in Ezek 8:11). It is possible, though perhaps not likely, that a finely crafted cylinder seal from the sixth century BC inscribed with the words "belonging to Jaazaniah, the king's servant," belongs to our Jaazaniah, described here as a "leader among the people." "Pelatiah son of Benaiah" is also one of four persons in the OT carrying the name Pelatiah. Three are differentiated by their patronymics (Hananiah's son in 1 Chr 3:21, Ishi's son in 1 Chr 4:42, and Benaiah's son here in Ezek 11:1). Pelatiah in Neh 10:22 carries no patronymic, but all four men are differentiated by historical setting. We know nothing of Pelatiah ben Beniah beyond the information in Ezekiel.

11:19 See the Introduction ("New Covenant, New Heart") and the commentary on chs 36 and 37 for fuller treatment of these matters.

singleness of heart. The NLT (cf. NIV, NASB, REB, RSV, ESV) follows the MT (*leb 'ekhad*) with the support of Jer 32:39; 1 Chr 12:38; and 2 Chr 30:12. Here and in Jer 32:39 (LXX 39:39) LXX reads *leb 'ekhar*, "another/a different heart," the Hebrew Resh at times being almost indistinguishable from the Daleth. BHS suggests following some Syriac and Targum manuscripts by reading "a new heart," *leb khadash*, parallel to "a new spirit" and citing 18:31 and 36:26.

within them. The NLT, like the LXX, NASB, NIV, and most modern versions, reads a third-person pl. masc. pronoun against the MT's second-person pl. masc. pronoun here: "within you."

responsive heart. The Hebrew is lit., "heart of flesh" (cf. NLT mg).

11:23 ***the mountain to the east.*** Most likely a reference to the Mount of Olives, though Ezekiel does not name the mountain. The narrative appears to assume the glory of God can be seen on the mount from Ezekiel's station inside the Temple. It carries symbolic meaning, dramatizing the departure of the Glory from not only the Temple but the city as well. But the symbolism rests on an identifiable location outside of the city and within sight of it. The fact that it is within sight of Ezekiel in the Temple rules out reference to a Babylonian ziggurat.

11:24 ***Babylonia.*** Lit., "Chaldea" (NLT mg). See note on 1:3. Here the reference is to the land of the Chaldeans, a West Semitic people whose tribes gained control of southern

Mesopotamia, territory to that point ruled by native Babylonians (Kassites). See Arnold 2004:87-105 on the Chaldeans, Babylonians, and the rise of the Neo-Babylonian Empire.

COMMENTARY

Chapter 11 continues the movement in the Temple vision begun in the narrative of chapters 8–10. At the outset, the Spirit transports Ezekiel to the Temple's (outer?) east gate, where he encounters "twenty-five prominent men of the city" (11:1). At the conclusion, the cherubim with the glory of God depart the city for "the mountain to the east" (11:22-23), and the Spirit transports Ezekiel back to Babylon (11:24).

Response to two false claims about the city and the exiles occupies the majority of the unit. First (11:2-13), Ezekiel rebuts influential opinion shapers in the city who had rejected Ezekiel's claim that Jerusalem faced doom, in particular Jaazaniah son of Azzur and Pelatiah son of Benaiah. Ezekiel had just seen the city engulfed in a firestorm (10:2). They saw it as prime real estate for development, perhaps appropriating the property of people they had killed (11:6) along with the homes and land of the exiles (11:15). They pictured Jerusalem as an iron pot and themselves as choice chunks of stew meat, safe inside the pot (11:3). As we shall see, the statement is quite ironic.

This claim and behavior triggers a prophetic response (11:5-12). Whatever his mysterious relationship with the city, the Lord knew the murderous schemes and deeds of these leaders. He held them accountable for the social decay of Jerusalem, now awash in violence (11:5-6). Then, turning their "iron pot" metaphor against them, the Lord says the only "safe" ones in the city are those slain by these misguided leaders. The slain are the "stew meat." The leaders will die at the hands of foreigners, chased down all the way to the borders of Israel (11:7-11). As a consequence, they will realize (and perhaps acknowledge) the Lord as the one active in these events and as the one whose will they have rejected (11:10, 12).

Two startling responses occur. With Ezekiel's prophecy yet in progress, Benaiah unexpectedly dies! Taking this to be the work of God, Ezekiel falls on his face and once again attempts intercession in the form of a question of protest (11:13), as he had done in 9:8. Neither event draws comment in the text. The prophetic word had smitten both receiver and bearer of the message. But note that all of this transpires in a vision that Ezekiel will recount, not in "real time" events being narrated.

The second response in this unit reveals a misunderstanding of the relationship of the exiles to the Lord and to the land (11:14-21). Jerusalemites left behind after the deportation of 597 BC claimed that those exiled were "far away from the LORD" (geographically and probably spiritually) and then erroneously concluded that God had given the exiles' land to them (11:14-15). Although some in Jerusalem thought that the Lord had abandoned the city and was ignorant of events there (8:12), this group claimed that the Lord, who was actually in the process of withdrawing his presence from the city, was resident in the city—thus the exiles, not they, were far away from God.

God directed the prophetic response to the exiles by addressing his present relationship to them and the relationship to the land he planned for them (11:16-21).

First, his dispersion of them in judgment did not imply their absence from him or his from them. On the contrary, he himself would be their sanctuary during their exile (11:16-17). Without Temple or sacrifice they would still have his presence. He would be with them in exile, making the lands of their dispersion holy ground. And yet he would be acting in Jerusalem as well. The vision of the Lord's movement out of the Temple and city addresses God's covenant relationship with his people, not the geographic "location" of the God of Israel. Second, God had not given their land away—he planned to gather them back and give the land of Israel once again *to them* (11:17)!

This planned return coupled with God's promise of a monumental character transformation is briefly elaborated in 11:18-21. This paragraph is bounded by reference to "vile images and detestable idols" (11:18, 21). God would inspire them and enable them to "remove every trace" of these idolatrous betrayals from the land (11:18) and to obey his covenant law (11:20). This would happen because he would give them a "tender, responsive heart," undivided in its loyalty to him (11:19-20). God promised to create an authentic covenant relationship between his people and himself ("truly . . . my people, and I . . . their God"). At the same time, God would fully repay those unswervingly loyal to their "vile images and detestable idols" (11:21).

This subunit (11:1-25) concludes the extended account of Ezekiel's visit to Jerusalem via a supernatural vision (chs 8–11) with notes chiastically mirroring key features that open the account in 8:1-4: The removal of the glory of the God of Israel closes this part of the vision (11:22-23). We are reminded that this has all transpired in a vision and by spiritual transport (11:24). Finally, the vision proves to be not primarily or only for the benefit of the prophet; Ezekiel returns to speak to the exiles about all the Lord had shown him (11:24-25).

◆ C. False Hopes Demolished (12:1–14:23)

1. The certainty of Israel's deportation (12:1-20)

Again a message came to me from the
LORD: 2"Son of man, you live among rebels
who have eyes but refuse to see. They
have ears but refuse to hear. For they are
a rebellious people.

3"So now, son of man, pretend you are
being sent into exile. Pack the few items
an exile could carry, and leave your home
to go somewhere else. Do this right in
front of the people so they can see you.
For perhaps they will pay attention to
this, even though they are such rebels.
4Bring your baggage outside during the
day so they can watch you. Then in the
evening, as they are watching, leave your
house as captives do when they begin a
long march to distant lands. 5Dig a hole
through the wall while they are watching
and go out through it. 6As they watch, lift
your pack to your shoulders and walk
away into the night. Cover your face so
you cannot see the land you are leaving.
For I have made you a sign for the people
of Israel."

7So I did as I was told. In broad day-
light I brought my pack outside, filled
with the things I might carry into exile.
Then in the evening while the people
looked on, I dug through the wall with my
hands and went out into the night with
my pack on my shoulder.

8The next morning this message came

to me from the LORD: 9 "Son of man, these
rebels, the people of Israel, have asked
you what all this means. 10 Say to them,
'This is what the Sovereign LORD says:
These actions contain a message for King
Zedekiah in Jerusalem* and for all the
people of Israel.' 11 Explain that your ac-
tions are a sign to show what will soon
happen to them, for they will be driven
into exile as captives.

12 "Even Zedekiah will leave Jerusalem at
night through a hole in the wall, taking
only what he can carry with him. He will
cover his face, and his eyes will not see
the land he is leaving. 13 Then I will throw
my net over him and capture him in my
snare. I will bring him to Babylon, the land
of the Babylonians,* though he will never
see it, and he will die there. 14 I will scatter
his servants and warriors to the four
winds and send the sword after them.
15 And when I scatter them among the na-
tions, they will know that I am the LORD.
16 But I will spare a few of them from
death by war, famine, or disease, so they
can confess all their detestable sins to
their captors. Then they will know that I
am the LORD."

17 Then this message came to me from
the LORD: 18 "Son of man, tremble as you
eat your food. Shake with fear as you
drink your water. 19 Tell the people, 'This is
what the Sovereign LORD says concerning
those living in Israel and Jerusalem: They
will eat their food with trembling and sip
their water in despair, for their land will
be stripped bare because of their violence.
20 The cities will be destroyed and the
farmland made desolate. Then you will
know that I am the LORD.'"

12:10 Hebrew *the prince in Jerusalem;* similarly in 12:12. **12:13** Or *Chaldeans.*

NOTES

12:2 ***who have eyes but refuse to see.*** Ezekiel will return repeatedly in this chapter to the topics of spiritual perception with the vocabulary of "seeing," "perceiving" (*ra'ah* [TH7200, ZH8011], 12:2, 3, 6, 12, 13; 13:3; 14:22, 23), and "seeing visions" (*khazah* [TH2372, ZH2600], *khazon* [TH2377, ZH2606], 12:22, 23, 24, 27; 13:6, 7, 8, 9, 16, 23).

12:5 ***Dig a hole through the wall.*** Block (1997:370) thinks the view that Ezekiel digs through his house wall from the inside out and thus represents refugees fleeing the city is "problematic." He points out that "wall" (*qir* [TH7023, ZH7815]) designates a mud wall or house wall rather than a *khomah* [TH2346, ZH2570], a defensive city wall, and he points to the difference between the behavior of refugees fleeing through breaches in a city wall and exiles preparing for a long, forced march. He proposes that Ezekiel digs from the outside in, representing invading Babylonians. The main problem with Block's view is the explicit application of Ezekiel's symbolic act to Zedekiah, the prince of that time (12:10-14), and the designation of the (presumably) city wall through which Zedekiah digs also as a *qir* (12:12). In addition, it was the city wall that the Babylonians breached, so Block's suggestion does not really solve the problem he raises.

12:6 ***into the night.*** Heb., *'alatah* [TH5939, ZH6602] refers not to the nighttime, which would be *laylah* [TH3915A, ZH4326], but to the darkness of night. The NLT's "into the night" subtly conveys this.

12:10 ***These actions contain a message.*** Ezekiel does not elsewhere use *massa'* [TH4853, ZH5362], literally "burden," in its common sense of a prophetic oracle. Even so, that meaning, reflected in the NLT and most translations, remains less problematic than suggestions that make Zedekiah himself (Block 1997:373) or the sign-act of carrying (Friebel 1999:626) the referent of *massa'*.

King Zedekiah in Jerusalem. Lit., "the prince in Jerusalem"; similarly in 12:12. Ezekiel never mentions Zedekiah by name, perhaps an indication of his lack of respect for Judah's last king. Although Ezekiel uses the Hebrew words *melek* [TH4428, ZH4889] (king) and *nasi'* [TH5387, ZH5954] (prince) almost interchangeably for Israelite kings, his preferred term is *nasi'*. As here, in some cases *nasi'* may well carry an implicit critique of the person(s) named (Duguid 1994:31-33). Note in contrast that Ezekiel called Jehoiachin *hammelek* and recall that Ezekiel had sufficient regard for Jehoiachin as to derive the dates for his ministry from this king's deportation. None of this implies that Ezekiel held any of Judah's last kings (after Josiah) in high regard.

12:19 ***the people.*** Lit., "the people of the land" (*'am* [TH5971A, ZH6638] *ha'arets*). Quite likely, Ezekiel speaks not to a general population of "people," but to clan and family heads, who, throughout the kingdom period, influenced royal policy and were active, for example, in the overthrow of Queen Athaliah and the installation of Josiah (2 Kgs 11:14-20; 21:24). They would have been among the representative leaders Nebuchadnezzar exiled with Jehoiachin (Schniedewind 2004:106-113, 150).

COMMENTARY

Chapters 8 through 11 explore various causes justifying Jerusalem's impending destruction. In chapters 12 through 14 the writer emphasizes again the certainty and imminence of that "end" (as in ch 7). Thematic and lexical ties with chapters 4 through 7 abound. Two sign-acts dramatize the coming exile (12:1-20). Two sayings dismissing prophetic warnings are rejected (12:21-28). Ezekiel undercut false prophets and prophetesses that perpetuated the illusion of peace (13:1-23). Yahweh promised judgment as his response to idolatrous inquirers (14:1-5). The brief call for the house of Israel to repent (14:6-8) and the note on salutary aspects of the coming judgment (14:9-11) *might* be the points to which the preceding, dire messages were leading the reader. Nonetheless, these calls would be rejected, and the destruction of Judah and Jerusalem could not be averted (14:12-23).

The obstinate character of Ezekiel's constituency (12:2) provides the backdrop against which the entire unit (12:1-20) should be read. The house of Israel in exile and back in Jerusalem has been noted as rebellious (cf. 2:5, 6, 7, 8; 3:9, 26, 27; 5:6). Yahweh says they are spiritually deaf (12:2; cf. 2:5, 7; 3:6, 7, 11) and blind (12:2, see note). Perhaps these rebels, unmoved by the prophetic word, would respond to the rhetoric of prophetic drama, the so-called "sign-acts." Ezekiel related two such dramatizations that forced the observers to look exile square in the face.

In plain view of all onlookers, Ezekiel was to pretend he was going into exile (12:3-7). In broad daylight he was to prepare a bundle of the things exiles would desperately salvage to carry with them (12:3-4). This was to evoke thoughts of siege survivors preparing for a long, forced march into exile. Then in early evening, he was to dig through the wall of his house, and finally, at dusk he was to go out through that hole and walk off into or perhaps under the cover of the deepening darkness (NLT, "night"), his head covered so he could not see the land he was leaving (12:5-6). Art celebrating Assyrian victories and deportations includes sad scenes of such baggage-toting exiles (ANEP, illustrations 366, 373). Ezekiel did all this because God had made him a *mopeth* [TH4159, ZH4603]—a "portent," a sign of impending doom. Yahweh used Ezekiel not simply as a conduit of spoken word; he used his very person as a persuasive instrument with its own dramatic rhetoric (12:6, 11).

The meaning of the entire act, with apparently shifting referents, is not crystal clear. Perhaps the *mopeth* didn't convey exactly the same message to each observer. Perhaps, like a spoken parable, this sign-act was designed to prompt a range of images, all of them in opposition to the idea that things would be well back home in Jerusalem. Whatever the case, the interpretation focuses mostly on King Zedekiah and Israel, as his fate indicated theirs (12:8-16).

Some interpreters (e.g., Blenkinsopp 1990:65; Brownlee 1986:173-174) have felt compelled to view the Zedekiah oracle (12:8-16) as a *vaticinium ex eventu*—a "prophecy" after the event—because of parallels with the account of Zedekiah's attempt to flee Jerusalem and escape capture by the Babylonians (2 Kgs 25:1-7). But more notable than its parallels are its striking *differences* with the horrific account in 2 Kings, if indeed the prophet worked from actual accounts of the event. Time would tell how ghastly Zedekiah's inability to see the land would be. (Nebuchadnezzar slew Zedekiah's sons before him and then gouged out the king's own eyes.) All of it spoke directly and indirectly of the spiritual blindness of the royal house, and of Israel in Jerusalem and in exile.

The Zedekiah oracle emphasizes the Lord's direct role in the coming events. "I will throw my net . . . and capture him. . . . I will bring him to Babylon. . . . I will scatter his servants. . . . When I scatter . . . I will spare" (12:13-16). Other paragraphs will acknowledge the role of Nebuchadnezzar, the Babylonians, palace intrigue, treaty breaking, and other geopolitical realities driving Jerusalem toward destruction. Whatever Nebuchadnezzar's motives, the sovereign Lord of Israel was accomplishing his purposes through him. Zedekiah and Jerusalem's fate were in God's hands, not Nebuchadnezzar's.

In spite of the upheaval of his judgment, God would also be at work saving some. As he frequently does, Ezekiel introduces a theme briefly that receives further attention later: A single line here announces God will "spare a few" (12:16). Emphasis rests not so much on the sparing as on the purpose—"so they can confess all their detestable sins to their captors" (12:16). This will involve a "conversion" of sorts, a different assessment of their behavior than contemporary wisdom was applauding. Saying God will spare some "by *war, famine,* or *disease*" (emphasis added), Ezekiel cited specific covenant curses (Lev 26:25, 33, 36-37; Deut 28:21-22, 48; 32:24; see commentary on 5:11-17). This vocabulary brings readers back to the covenantal theological base from which both his priestly and prophetic ministries work. He will cite this trilogy of curses again in 14:21, bracketing the material in chapters 12–14.

The second sign-act, sparsely described in 12:17-20, recalls the "measured diet" in 4:9-17. There Ezekiel's behavior mimed the hardships of the coming siege. Here he portrays the terrors of captives trying to eat on forced march. They would be traumatized when they saw how the Babylonians ravaged the land during the siege (12:19; cf. 7:11, 23; 8:17).

The deportation, capture, and accompanying horror presented in the sign-acts would issue in profound, new acknowledgments by the participants in those events (12:15, 16, 20). They would discern that the God of Israel is the one who brings these traumatic events to pass according to his word. The God they had thought either absent or misguided was very much alive and true to his word. For interpretation of Ezekiel's book, the insights of the anticipated readers would be more important than those of the participants in the events (though early on these groups could well overlap). By the time readers picked up Ezekiel's book, the events would have unfolded just as he warned. His prophetic credibility would be underscored. Readers therefore could see the historic indictments as moral direction and continued warning. And the credibility of Ezekiel's warnings would then warrant the credibility of his vision for the restored people and their land.

◆ 2. Refutation and rejection of false prophets (12:21–13:23)

21Again a message came to me from the
LORD: 22"Son of man, you've heard that
proverb they quote in Israel: 'Time passes,
and prophecies come to nothing.' 23Tell
the people, 'This is what the Sovereign
LORD says: I will put an end to this prov-
erb, and you will soon stop quoting it.'
Now give them this new proverb to re-
place the old one: 'The time has come for
every prophecy to be fulfilled!'
24"There will be no more false visions
and flattering predictions in Israel. 25For I
am the LORD! If I say it, it will happen.
There will be no more delays, you rebels of
Israel. I will fulfill my threat of destruc-
tion in your own lifetime. I, the Sovereign
LORD, have spoken!"
26Then this message came to me from
the LORD: 27"Son of man, the people of
Israel are saying, 'He's talking about the
distant future. His visions won't come true
for a long, long time.' 28Therefore, tell
them, 'This is what the Sovereign LORD
says: No more delay! I will now do every-
thing I have threatened. I, the Sovereign
LORD, have spoken!'"

CHAPTER 13

Then this message came to me from the
LORD: 2"Son of man, prophesy against the
false prophets of Israel who are inventing
their own prophecies. Say to them, 'Listen
to the word of the LORD. 3This is what the
Sovereign LORD says: What sorrow awaits
the false prophets who are following their
own imaginations and have seen nothing
at all!'
4"O people of Israel, these prophets of
yours are like jackals digging in the ruins.
5They have done nothing to repair the
breaks in the walls around the nation.
They have not helped it to stand firm in
battle on the day of the LORD. 6Instead,
they have told lies and made false predic-
tions. They say, 'This message is from the
LORD,' even though the LORD never sent
them. And yet they expect him to fulfill
their prophecies! 7Can your visions be
anything but false if you claim, 'This mes-
sage is from the LORD,' when I have not
even spoken to you?
8"Therefore, this is what the Sovereign
LORD says: Because what you say is false
and your visions are a lie, I will stand
against you, says the Sovereign LORD. 9I
will raise my fist against all the prophets
who see false visions and make lying pre-
dictions, and they will be banished from
the community of Israel. I will blot their
names from Israel's record books, and they
will never again set foot in their own land.
Then you will know that I am the Sover-
eign LORD.
10"This will happen because these evil
prophets deceive my people by saying, 'All
is peaceful' when there is no peace at all!
It's as if the people have built a flimsy
wall, and these prophets are trying to re-
inforce it by covering it with whitewash!
11Tell these whitewashers that their wall
will soon fall down. A heavy rainstorm will
undermine it; great hailstones and mighty
winds will knock it down. 12And when the
wall falls, the people will cry out, 'What
happened to your whitewash?'
13"Therefore, this is what the Sovereign
LORD says: I will sweep away your white-
washed wall with a storm of indignation,

with a great flood of anger, and with hailstones of fury. 14 I will break down your wall right to its foundation, and when it falls, it will crush you. Then you will know that I am the LORD. 15 At last my anger against the wall and those who covered it with whitewash will be satisfied. Then I will say to you: 'The wall and those who whitewashed it are both gone. 16 They were lying prophets who claimed peace would come to Jerusalem when there was no peace. I, the Sovereign LORD, have spoken!'

17 "Now, son of man, speak out against the women who prophesy from their own imaginations. 18 This is what the Sovereign LORD says: What sorrow awaits you women who are ensnaring the souls of my people, young and old alike. You tie magic charms on their wrists and furnish them with magic veils. Do you think you can trap others without bringing destruction on yourselves? 19 You bring shame on me among my people for a few handfuls of barley or a piece of bread. By lying to my people who love to listen to lies, you kill those who should not die, and you promise life to those who should not live.

20 "This is what the Sovereign LORD says: I am against all your magic charms, which you use to ensnare my people like birds. I will tear them from your arms, setting my people free like birds set free from a cage. 21 I will tear off the magic veils and save my people from your grasp. They will no longer be your victims. Then you will know that I am the LORD. 22 You have discouraged the righteous with your lies, but I didn't want them to be sad. And you have encouraged the wicked by promising them life, even though they continue in their sins. 23 Because of all this, you will no longer talk of seeing visions that you never saw, nor will you make predictions. For I will rescue my people from your grasp. Then you will know that I am the LORD."

NOTES

13:9 *record books.* The reference is probably to works similar to those that Persian kings later kept to record noteworthy events and persons—the so-called *seper hazzikeronoth* [TH2146, ZH2355], "historical records" or "book of memorable deeds" (see Esth 6:1-2, RSV; Mal 3:16).

13:10 *This will happen because.* This translates the emphatic causal connective, *ya'an ubeya'an* [TH3282, ZH3610], underscoring the following indictment as the cause of the preceding judgments.

13:18-19 *magic charms on their wrists . . . magic veils . . . trap others . . . barley.* No explanation of the obscure expressions in this paragraph is "wholly satisfactory," even though the general ideas seem clear (Brownlee 1986:195). For "magic charms," perhaps we are to think of "bands on wrists" (Block 1997:410; Brownlee 1986:193), or "cushions on the joints of every arm" (Greenberg 1983:233). For "magic veils," perhaps we should think of "amulets for heads" (Block 1997:410), "rags for heads" (Greenberg), or "veils" to place on heads (Brownlee). Although there is some sympathy for seeing the "souls" (NLT, "others") as some reality exterior to the persons involved (Saggs, cited in Block 1997:415), more interpreters take "souls" as a periphrastic reference to persons involved (Eichrodt 1970:160; Greenberg) or "human lives" (Block 1997:410-411). Most likely, the "barley" represents a paltry price of magical "services" rendered (Block 1997:411; Brownlee), but perhaps it signifies the means of performing the magic (Greenberg). NLT follows the Peshitta and Targum (the sense if not the actual reading) and context in translating "their wrists." The MT's "my wrists" is a probable scribal error (dittography).

13:20 *like birds.* The hunting aspect of the similes used here is clear, the context being loaded with the root *ts-w-d* [TH6679, ZH7421], "to hunt, capture." Identification of the prey as birds depends on the meaning of MT's *leporekhoth*. The preposition *le-* apparently carries comparative force (cf. Waltke and O'Connor 1990:§11.2.10d, note 23). The plural noun or substantive participle, *porekhot* [TH6524B, ZH7256], quite likely does mean "birds" (HALOT 3.966; Zimmerli 1979:298, comparing Ps 124:7). But see REB, which reads "the lives you hunt for excitement," and NAB (2nd ed.), which omits the second occurrence of the word as redundant (so also LXX and Targum). The NLT makes sense of the MT as is and is probably the preferable understanding of the term.

COMMENTARY

The oracles rejecting the public response to prophetic warnings stand as a "hinge" paragraph (12:21-25), tied meaningfully to both the preceding and following materials. On the one hand, the "rebel" vocabulary (12:25) ties it to 12:2. Logically, it easily follows as a response to the issues presented in the two sign-acts (12:1-20). The proverb about ongoing failure of prophetic warnings to materialize (12:22) and the popular dismissal of warnings by assigning them to a distant future (12:27) are both aimed at evading the indictments and warnings of prophets like Ezekiel (no doubt Jeremiah and Zephaniah as well). In two short oracles, God rejects both evasions. Fulfilled prophecy will become so widely conceded that the old proverb will be replaced by a new one: "The time has come for every prophecy to be fulfilled" (12:23). Furthermore, there will be "no more delay" (12:28).

On the other hand, the oracles in 12:21-25 formally bring up the topic of prophecy and introduce the matter of "false visions and flattering predictions" (12:24). Both of these figure prominently in 13:1-23, where we see Ezekiel's major treatment of contemporary prophecy in Israel. Repetition of the Hebrew root *kh-z-h* [TH2372, ZH2600] in its verb forms ("to see or have a vision," 12:27) and noun forms ("a vision," 12:22, 23, 24, 27) ties the oracles to chapter 13 where visions—especially *false* visions—become a new leitmotif (13:6, 7, 8, 9, 16, 23; cf. Talmon and Fishbane 1976:136-137). I take 12:21-28 as an introduction to Ezekiel's analysis and rejection of a popular, probably dominant strain of prophecy in Israel reflected in chapter 13.

Ezekiel recounts core accusations that Yahweh leveled against the false prophets and prophetesses, basic indictments that entail other accusations as well, devoting two oracles to each audience. The target was "the prophets of Israel," professional prophets sponsored by Temple and palace. First, says the Lord, both the prophets and prophetesses speak "from their own hearts" (lit., 13:2, 17) or out of their "own spirit" (13:3). As the NLT puts it, they were "inventing their own prophecies" (13:2), "following their own imaginations" (13:3; cf. 13:17). The *source* of their utterances was flawed. They spoke from self-projection, self-invention, or outright deception. In any case, they failed to transcend culturally determined viewpoints. They stood in direct contrast to authentic prophets like Ezekiel, who spoke when prompted and illumined by a spirit beyond their own (cf. chs 2–3, flowing out of 1:26-28). Unlike Ezekiel, they had no extra-mundane, counter-cultural word to offer. Unlike Ezekiel (2:3-4, 9; 3:5-6), God had not commissioned ("sent") them. They used prophetic jargon—"This message is from the LORD"—without authorization or effect (13:6). In fact, they "have seen nothing at all!" (13:3).

The false prophets' lack of access to an authentic word from God led them to employ divination, which, being proscribed in Torah (e.g., Lev 19:31; 20:6, 27; Deut 18:10-11), was more at home in the hands of the king of Babylon than in Israel (21:21-23), isolated texts like 1 Samuel 28 and Hosea 3:4; 4:12 notwithstanding. In Canaanite and ancient Near Eastern culture, divination was associated historically with information gathering, decision making, and (as in 13:18-19) for alluring people (cf. 21:21 again). Diviners employed "any number of manipulative techniques whereby the will of the gods was determined and the course of future events plotted. They drew information from examining the liver or entrails of an animal (hepatoscopy), consulting the dead (necromancy), observing the pattern of oil on water (hydromancy), observing the patterns of fallen sticks or arrows (rhabdomancy), and determining the course of human events by observing the heavens (astrology)" (Block 1997:390).

Divination and associated means of discerning God's will and the course of future events were forbidden in Israel as "detestable customs" (Deut 18:9-14). They stood in contrast to the prophet God would raise up (Deut 18:15). The Urim and Thummim (cf. Exod 28:30; Lev 8:8; 1 Sam 28:6) presented something of a "sanctified" divination instrument in ancient Israel, but disappeared with little account of its use. These "manipulative, mechanical techniques" were fundamentally at odds with the nonmanipulative, personal, relational means of communication used by the living God of Israel (inspired oracles, visions, dreams). They addressed gods of a fundamentally different sort from the covenant-making Lord. Israel's sovereign Lord could not be manipulated into a response. The result of all this was lies, false predictions, specious visions (13:6-7).

God's second core indictment thus followed clearly from his first indictment. These prophets and prophetesses were liars (13:10-12). The *character* of the prophets and the *content* of their "word from Yahweh" were outright falsehoods. Although they were indeed profoundly "false" (13:2-3), Yahweh, through Ezekiel, actually called them "foolish" or "worthless" prophets (13:3; NLT, "false prophets"). They dealt in falsehood and deception to be sure (13:6, 17), but the adjective chosen (Heb., *nabal* [TH5036, ZH5572]) covers much more ground. *Nabal* persons are morally stupid, worthless as spiritual guides, no matter how clever or expert in esoteric manipulations they may appear.

Their message betrays and feeds the larger delusion they foster. "All is peaceful," they claim, while God says through prophets like Ezekiel that "there is no peace at all!" (13:10). They mislead God's people on several critical counts: They reinforce the proverb that Yahweh has rejected (12:22), undermining the warnings of imminent danger facing Jerusalem and Judah. They tell "clients" what they want to hear and perpetuate false hopes that the whole Babylonian problem will somehow go away (cf. 11:2-12; Isa 5:19). It is as though, says Yahweh, they daub whitewash on the "flimsy wall" of false hopes the people have patched together (13:10). In the coming storm of God's fury, this patchwork wall will come crashing down, leaving God's people dismayed (13:11-12). Ezekiel's call as a watchman for God's people (3:16-21; 33:1-9) indicates his people should be able to depend on a prophet of Yahweh to speak in ways that help them "stand firm in battle" (13:5). The prophet's word in the end should be salvific, edifying for them, whether they agree with the message or appreciate it at the moment or not. Prophets should be building a dependable "wall" in their utterances. The "foolish prophets" promote a view of Yahweh that totally misrepresents his person; indeed they "bring shame on" him (13:19). They obscure his sovereign freedom, his actions, and covenant purposes. Against the whole Mosaic tradition, they foster a view of a covenant free of moral accountability and of a God of uncertain will.

For the false prophetesses, the indictment for self-generated, fraudulent prophecies (13:17, 19) focuses on trafficking in magic, soothsaying, and witchcraft. The reference to their prophesying seems to poke fun at their prophetic pretense (13:17). The precise nature and use of the "magic charms" and "magic veils," and the meaning of what may be technical expressions remain unclear (see note on 13:18-19), in spite of abundant magical literature and paraphernalia from the biblical world, including Babylon (13:18, 20-21). The general contours, however, are clear enough. The sorceresses claim life-and-death power over others, pronouncing bogus "sentences" or "protections" and "cures" ("you . . . trap others," 13:18; "you kill," "you promise life" 13:19), duping those who want to exercise such control over others. Sadly, their fake "ministry" directly counters the purposes of God, encouraging the wicked and discouraging the righteous (13:22), treating persons like prey to be hunted down (13:18, 20). Herein lies Yahweh's final indictment: These persons are predators, parasites on God's precious people.

These women and their male colleagues, indicted earlier in the chapter, are not necessarily all simple charlatans, deliberately ransacking God's people. Some may have been sincere but tragically confused and theologically compromised members of Judean establishment religion. However, Ezekiel's comment that the women operate "for a few handfuls of barley or a piece of bread" sounds very much like Micah's accusation that the prophets in his day tailored their messages, good news or bad news, depending on the fee paid (Mic 3:5). It also sounds like Amaziah's wrongheaded notion that Amos was a prophet for hire like the northern, Israelite, sanctuary prophets he knew (Amos 7:12; cf. 2 Kgs 4:42). Whatever the motivation, the results for God's people were disastrous.

The Lord's explicit response to all these false prophets is a foreboding threat of doom. Yahweh's most ominous statements—"I will stand against you" (13:8) and "I am against all your magic charms" (13:20)—set the context for the specific consequences announced. God will "raise [his] fist" in the catastrophe that will envelop Jerusalem (13:9). He will banish them from Israel, blot out their names from Israel's record books, and permanently expel them from the land (13:9). The Lord's fury will sweep away the flimsy wall of false hopes they have daubed (13:11). As for the prophetesses, God will tear off their magical trappings and bring their parasitic visions and predictions to a halt (13:18, 23). The entirely unexpected catastrophes (that is, unexpected by the foolish prophets and prophetesses) will produce awareness and acknowledgment that Yahweh—*as understood by Ezekiel and his compatriots in authentic covenant faith*—manifests his will, his character, and his sovereign person in these events (13:9, 14, 21, 23). None of their assurances of good times or their manipulative incantations would be able to stop him.

Against the emphasis on the coming fury, Ezekiel briefly introduced the insight that the Lord's judgment includes saving intentions. God wanted not only to judge the prophetesses but also to rescue his people from their grasp (13:21, 23). The "save" and "rescue" vocabulary underscores the plight of persons trapped in the worldview and lifestyle promoted by these women (and, one presumes, by the false prophets as well). It offers a paltry option compared to vibrant covenant faith. It also unveils something of the complexity of Ezekiel's theology of judgment—much more than fury on the loose.

As for demolishing false hopes, Ezekiel leveled a broadside attack on the troop of professional prophets, male and female, in Jerusalem and in the exile, who contributed to the delusion that all would be well with Jerusalem. That hope was a mirage, said Ezekiel. By the time readers had Ezekiel's book in hand, they would already have seen the destruction of the city and Temple by the Babylonians just as Ezekiel had said. Ezekiel had stood his ground against public rejection and professional prophetic repudiation *and had been proven right by the course of events*. This vindication of his warnings argued that his promises of restoration also should be taken seriously. Thus, inclusion of these warnings in the book built prophetic capital for the moral instruction and the vision of restoration yet to come in the book.

◆ 3. No righteous hero could save Israel (14:1-23)

**Then some of the leaders of Israel visited
me, and while they were sitting with me,
2this message came to me from the LORD:
3"Son of man, these leaders have set up
idols* in their hearts. They have embraced
things that will make them fall into sin.
Why should I listen to their requests? 4Tell
them, 'This is what the Sovereign LORD
says: The people of Israel have set up idols
in their hearts and fallen into sin, and then
they go to a prophet asking for a message.
So I, the LORD, will give them the kind of
answer their great idolatry deserves. 5I will
do this to capture the minds and hearts of
all my people who have turned from me to
worship their detestable idols.'**

**6"Therefore, tell the people of Israel,
'This is what the Sovereign LORD says: Re-
pent and turn away from your idols, and
stop all your detestable sins. 7I, the LORD,
will answer all those, both Israelites and
foreigners, who reject me and set up idols
in their hearts and so fall into sin, and
who then come to a prophet asking for my
advice. 8I will turn against such people
and make a terrible example of them,
eliminating them from among my people.
Then you will know that I am the LORD.**

**9'And if a prophet is deceived into giving
a message, it is because I, the LORD, have
deceived that prophet. I will lift my fist
against such prophets and cut them off
from the community of Israel. 10False proph-
ets and those who seek their guidance will
all be punished for their sins. 11In this way,
the people of Israel will learn not to stray
from me, polluting themselves with sin.
They will be my people, and I will be their
God. I, the Sovereign LORD, have spoken!'"**

**12Then this message came to me from
the LORD: 13"Son of man, suppose the peo-
ple of a country were to sin against me,
and I lifted my fist to crush them, cutting
off their food supply and sending a fam-
ine to destroy both people and animals.
14Even if Noah, Daniel, and Job were there,
their righteousness would save no one but
themselves, says the Sovereign LORD.**

**15"Or suppose I were to send wild ani-
mals to invade the country, kill the people,
and make the land too desolate and dan-
gerous to pass through. 16As surely as I
live, says the Sovereign LORD, even if those
three men were there, they wouldn't be
able to save their own sons or daughters.
They alone would be saved, but the land
would be made desolate.**

**17 "Or suppose I were to bring war against
the land, and I sent enemy armies to de-
stroy both people and animals. 18 As surely
as I live, says the Sovereign LORD, even if
those three men were there, they wouldn't
be able to save their own sons or daugh-
ters. They alone would be saved.**

**19 "Or suppose I were to pour out my
fury by sending an epidemic into the land,
and the disease killed people and animals
alike. 20 As surely as I live, says the Sover-
eign LORD, even if Noah, Daniel, and Job
were there, they wouldn't be able to save
their own sons or daughters. They alone
would be saved by their righteousness.**

**21 "Now this is what the Sovereign LORD
says: How terrible it will be when all four
of these dreadful punishments fall upon
Jerusalem—war, famine, wild animals, and
disease—destroying all her people and
animals. 22 Yet there will be survivors,
and they will come here to join you as
exiles in Babylon. You will see with your
own eyes how wicked they are, and then
you will feel better about what I have
done to Jerusalem. 23 When you meet them
and see their behavior, you will under-
stand that these things are not being
done to Israel without cause. I, the Sover-
eign LORD, have spoken!"**

14:3 The Hebrew term (literally *round things*) probably alludes to dung; also in 14:4, 5, 6, 7.

NOTES

14:3 ***idols.*** Heb., *gillulim* [TH1544, ZH1658] (lit., "round things") probably alludes to dung; also in 14:4-7. See the note on 5:9 for Ezekiel's vocabulary for idolatry.

Why should I listen to their requests? The specific requests are for divine direction through the prophet, "inquiring" of the prophet. God literally responds, "Should I allow myself to be inquired of by them?" This assumes an emphatically negative answer to the rhetorical question.

14:14 ***Noah, Daniel, and Job.*** Interpreters have long observed that the list of these three men presents for some readers a certain discontinuity in an otherwise painstakingly parallel paragraph. Noah and Job are ancient, non- or pre-Israelite men, whereas Daniel, the exceptionally wise and righteous youth deported by Nebuchadnezzar in 604 BC, was neither of ancient lore nor Gentile extraction. It was also noted that the MT spelling here and in 28:3 also might signal a disconnect from the Daniel for whom the biblical book is named. The MT has the consonants *dn'l* [cf. TH1840A, ZH1971], instead of the *dny'l* [TH1840, ZH1975] used in all other spellings of the name outside of Ezekiel.

Discovery of a Canaanite legendary character, *dn'l* (Danel), seems to explain the apparent disjuncture. Already in second millennium BC, literature from the city of Ugarit celebrated this storied *dn'l* in the *Legend of Aqht,* as a just judge who cared for widows and orphans (ANET 149-155, especially pp. 150-151). This figure seems to match the antiquity, character, and non-Israelite origins of Noah and Job, balancing the list perfectly. Many have drawn this conclusion or regarded it as quite probable, as some modern translations reflect. Although the NASB, RSV, and ESV translate "Daniel" and carry no textual note, the NIV, NRSV, and NAB translate "Daniel," adding a note that the reference is probably to the legendary Danel. The NEB uses "Danel" in its text, with a note that the name may alternatively be read as Daniel, and the JB translates "Danel" with no reference to the biblical Daniel. Among interpreters of the past 50 years, Allen (1994:218), Blenkinsopp (1990:72-73), Darr (2001:1213), Eichrodt (1970:188-189, 391), Greenberg (1983:57), Taylor (1969:129), Zimmerli (1979:314-315), all conclude the reference is to the Canaanite Danel. Block (1997:447-450) argues well for reference to the biblical Daniel, emphasizing the sole criterion Ezekiel actually mentions is these persons' righteousness (14:14, 20), not their antiquity or reputation as intercessors. Block notes also the fact that scholars wishing to date the book of Daniel very late may prematurely dismiss Ezekiel's contemporary. Alexander

(1986:807-808) also defends a traditional interpretation. While the reference might indeed be to the Daniel for whom a biblical book is named, the evidence pointing to the more ancient, Canaanite legendary figure, Danel, inclines me toward that conclusion.

COMMENTARY

Two "word events" (introduced by "this message came to me from the LORD," 14:2, 12) and three oracles related to them (14:4-5, 6-11, 21-23) present the dramatic climax of the larger unit (chs 12–14). Elaboration of Ezekiel's understanding of divine retribution holds these "word events" together. The character, requests, and apparent assumptions of leaders of the exilic community who have gathered around Ezekiel (14:1) prompted these words from the Lord.

The circumstance of men from the exilic leadership gathered around Ezekiel provides the setting for the chapter (14:1). Judging from Yahweh's response (14:2-11), they have come to "a prophet [Ezekiel] asking for a message [from the LORD]" (14:4). Yahweh indicts these leaders and rejects communication with them, saying they have "set up idols in their hearts" and "embraced things that will make them fall into sin" (14:3-4, 7). They situated these idols in their lives in such ways that they had come to occupy center stage in their hearts. The various self-interests deified in their idolatry had captured them and especially their faculties for making faithful commitments, judgments, decisions, and assessments.

The question that drives the paragraph is whether Yahweh will respond to such idolaters when they come to his prophet seeking divine direction. The leaders' spiritual commitments stand directly opposed to Ezekiel and the will of God revealed through him. From 13:1-23 the reader knows the sort of "divine" directions and assurances these men had come to expect from Israel's prophets (e.g., "All is peaceful," 13:10). And the reader knows the methods—divination techniques—these leaders had come to expect from professionals. (See commentary on ch 13 and the foolish prophets' use of divination.) One wonders if their attempts to "inquire" of the Lord through Ezekiel may actually have been insults, toying with this unusual prophet.

Yahweh himself actually deceived prophets who played this game with the leaders of Israel (14:9), says Ezekiel. Modern sensibilities and even other passages in Ezekiel (e.g., 14:6) make us wish for a statement acknowledging the role of human response in such situations. On the one hand, we do not want God to seem brutally arbitrary or cavalier. (He deceives the prophet and then punishes that prophet for being deceived!) On the other hand, repeatedly Ezekiel informs us that it is because of Israel's sin, for which she is fully responsible, that God is bringing judgment. The prophet, however, granted no territory to alien gods to account for the events he encountered. So Ezekiel put all of the transactions in God's hands: the false prophets' misplaced confidence (recall ch 13), the compromised search of idolaters for "divine direction," and the punishment for both (14:9-10). Other passages in Ezekiel will emphasize the human side of transactions like these.

The incongruity between the inquirers' idolatrous commitments and lifestyle and their seeking advice (14:7) from the God of Israel constitutes the heart of the indictment. It shows either pitiful ignorance of or full disregard for the covenant God offered to Israel. Ezekiel could not guarantee a response from God, for only God determines whether or not he will respond to inquiries. He will not respond directly through the prophet, but he will indeed respond with dreadful irony—to everyone, "Israelites and foreigners" (14:7). He will respond in the historical events threatened through Ezekiel (chs 4–7, 9–10), bringing the judgments that Israel's idolatry deserves (14:4).

The Lord's just and specific retribution also drives this paragraph. Yahweh's rhetorical question, "Why should I listen to their requests?" implies that God owes them no attention at all, let alone a response (14:3). But, surprisingly and ironically, God says he will indeed answer them, though not with the sort of response hoped for (14:4). In sum, God responds that the guilt and punishment of the inquirer is like the guilt and punishment of the false prophet (14:10b). Emphasis is on the fact that every single idolater who dares make inquiry of Yahweh and every prophet who plays that theological game will suffer God's judgment (note "all" in 14:5, 6, 10, along with "both Israelites and foreigners," 14:7, and additional specification in the MT of 14:4, 7-8).

God's "answer" has purpose, however. Positively (14:5), God wishes to "capture the minds and hearts of all [his] people." Negatively, he will make a "terrible example" of those who reject him (14:8). These purposes logically support the surprising invitation to "repent and turn away from your idols" (14:6). As we shall see, the land and the city are beyond rescue. Even so, God's brief entreaty assumes the desire on his part even yet to save those who will turn to him. The invitation specifically targets the idols and detestable sins that the leaders have made the center of their attention. The turn to God entails a turn away from these competing allegiances. But the invitation stands, nevertheless, and may be the point toward which the unit has been heading rhetorically. Beyond these purposes, God's judgment of false prophets and those who seek them out aims at instruction, at teaching Israel not to stray. He even envisions a day of authentic covenant relationship after this judgment (14:11).

Ezekiel carefully crafts his record of the second word event (14:12-23). He casts it as a hypothetical moral case put forward by God ("suppose the people of a country were to sin against me," 14:13). This "a country" case implies God's sovereignty over all nations, but select vocabulary also ties the case to his people by context (cf. 14:9, 12). And clearly the case assumes the backdrop of the covenant curses we know from Leviticus 26 and Deuteronomy 28. Near-verbatim repetitions and a summary tie the unit together. Ezekiel recounts: (1) possible responses by God (14:13, 15, 17, 19); (2) the goal of destroying both people and animals (14:13, 17, 19, 21); (3) the possibility of rescue because of the presence of the "paragons of virtue," Noah, Daniel, and Job (14:14, 20; Greenberg 1983:257); (4) the designation of them as "these three men" and their hypothetical presence (14:14, 16, 18); (5) finally, underscoring the point of the entire message, their righteous presence would save only themselves, not even their own children (14:16, 18, 20).

Marching through this repetitive structure, the threats from God move the message along, one blow of Yahweh's "fist" after another (14:13). He deliberately sends a series of destructions. The end result remains unaltered in the hypothetical case, whether he sends famine (14:13; cf. Deut 28:48), wild animals (14:15; Lev 26:6), war (14:17; Lev 26:16-18, 25, 33, 36; Deut 28:52, 65), or epidemics (14:19; Lev 26:25) upon the land. The end result underscores the twin points of the whole message introduced at 14:13. First, this hypothetical country was beyond hope. Righteous persons, even moral heroes, present in the city would not save it. They would save no one beyond themselves, not even their offspring—the point emphasized with God's oath (14:20). Second, the doctrine of direct, specific divine retribution remained in place and would prove just. God categorically denied hopes for a "soft option," as Allen puts it (1994:218)—hopes apparently harbored by the exiles (and no doubt Jerusalemites as well). Perhaps citing stories like Abraham's barter with God (Gen 18:22-23) or the Torah implying a saving "solidarity" with the righteous (Exod 20:5; 34:7; Deut 5:6), Ezekiel's audience hoped against hope that the children they had been forced to leave behind in 597 BC would somehow be saved.

One might be tempted to compare God's word to Jeremiah denying that intercessory prayer for the city was appropriate (Jer 15:1-3). Jerusalem was beyond the reach of intercession. God's rejection of prayer seeking direction in 14:1-11 might support such a move. Ezekiel may well have agreed with Jeremiah's view and may, as a prophetic intercessor and an obviously righteous man in the community, be implicitly included in this case study. But the explicit issue is rather the possibility of the many being saved by the presence of a righteous few.

The "application" offered in 14:21-23 gains energy from what it surprisingly omits. After the tightly parallel claims of 14:13-20, one anticipates a clear reference to these righteous persons and heroic intercessors to clinch the pronouncement of judgment on Judah. Lines such as "Even if Noah, Daniel, and Job were in the land of Judah, they would save no one but themselves—indeed perhaps not even themselves!" are notably absent. Instead, Ezekiel's closing oracle gathers all four covenant punishments just rehearsed into a single exclamation lamenting the prospects of all of them falling on Jerusalem (14:21). Judah is the land full of idolatry, and Jerusalem is beyond the reach of salvation. Ezekiel set popular illusions regarding prophetic fulfillment aside (12:21-25). He dashed hopes of rescue because of the presence of famous persons whom even Ezekiel might consider righteous (e.g., Jeremiah, Huldah, or others). It would not happen!

A final word (14:21-23) seeks to temper the prophet's anguish at the message he must give, anguish that has surfaced already at 9:8 and 11:13. When exiles from the collapse of Jerusalem began to arrive in Babylon, Ezekiel and the people (MT has plural "you" in 14:22-23) would see for themselves the behavior and character of the deportees. Yahweh implies confidence that Ezekiel shared his understandings of covenant life with respect to commitments and behaviors that are and are not appropriate to covenant faithfulness. The prophet knew and accepted the will of God; he knew that the judgment of Jerusalem was fully deserved.

◆ D. Pictures of Jerusalem's Doom (15:1–19:14)

1. Allegory of the useless vine (15:1-8)

Then this message came to me from the
LORD: 2"Son of man, how does a grapevine
compare to a tree? Is a vine's wood as
useful as the wood of a tree? 3Can its
wood be used for making things, like pegs
to hang up pots and pans? 4No, it can only
be used for fuel, and even as fuel, it burns
too quickly. 5Vines are useless both before
and after being put into the fire!

6"And this is what the Sovereign LORD
says: The people of Jerusalem are like
grapevines growing among the trees of the
forest. Since they are useless, I have thrown
them on the fire to be burned. 7And I will

see to it that if they escape from one fire, they will fall into another. When I turn against them, you will know that I am the LORD. 8And I will make the land desolate because my people have been unfaithful to me. I, the Sovereign LORD, have spoken!"

NOTES

15:1 The section title for the outline, "Pictures of Jerusalem's Doom," flags the metaphorical nature of the majority of this unit. The collection of metaphorical oracles implies Ezekiel's awareness of the genre. Except for 17:2, Ezekiel does not flag each entry according to its genre. The more general term for metaphorical expressions would be *mashal*, but with the exceptions of 17:2 and 24:3, *mashal* [TH4912, ZH5442] designates a proverb, as in 12:22-23; 16:44; 18:2-3; and perhaps 20:49 [21:5]. *Khidah* [TH2420, ZH2648], as in 17:2, seems to designate the more specific sort of extended metaphor that we might call "allegory," or, perhaps better, "a fable" (Greenberg 1983:22). Even though I have used the term "allegory" in the outline titles as a way of tying the oracles of chs 15–19 together, some of the pieces should perhaps more accurately be called "extended metaphors" or "narrative metaphors," especially chs 16 and 23, as Galambush argues (1992:10-11).

15:2-4 See Greenberg 1983:264-265 for excellent resources on syntactic anomalies in these brief verses.

15:7 ***if they escape from one fire, they will fall into another.*** Because of the heavy historical reference present in the other allegories gathered at this point of the book, it may be legitimate to ask whether the two fires—the one past and the second one coming—may not refer, respectively, to the events surrounding the surrender of Jehoiachin (597 BC) and the capture of Zedekiah (586 BC). Zimmerli (1979:320) accepts the possible reference to Jehoiachin, while shying away from the second. Greenberg (1983:266) thinks the reference is to vines and burning alone, and declines specific historical reference for the general claim about coming disaster.

COMMENTARY

Ezekiel's allegory of the useless vine (15:1-5) packs prophetic "punch" far out of proportion to its size. Part of its impact grows from the surprising directions in which Ezekiel takes the metaphor. First, in biblical tradition, the vine had usually been connected to the land and God's people in a positive light (Gen 49:11; Num 13:23; Judg 9:12; Ps 80:8 [9]; Isa 5:1ff; Hos 10:1). But here Ezekiel used the metaphor in an indictment (cf. Jer 2:21). Second, reference was made usually to the luxuriant *fruit* of the vine (cf. 17:5-10; 19:10-14). Here, Ezekiel focuses on the *wood* of the vine itself—and that in a highly uncomplimentary manner!

Everyone knew that wood from vines, say a grapevine or perhaps just a wild vine, was virtually useless even in "mint" condition. It has crooked, twisted, fibrous, weak-grained wood—one could not even make a good peg from which to hang wares (15:3). It was not even worth much as fuel. It burned both ends, leaving little pieces of charred wood left. How much less could one dream of using it for anything but more burning, when it had been consigned to the fire (15:5)!

Yahweh gives his own "reading" of the allegory with an explicit conclusion, not just regarding Jerusalem as a city but specifically regarding her inhabitants (15:6-8). Ominously, God either had or was going to "turn against them" (15:7). For the purposes of the God of Israel in the world, his people were at this point useless (recall Gen 12:2-3). They had abandoned his way and shamed his name, as we know from the chapters leading to this allegory. Here Yahweh names the lack of covenant faithfulness as the accusation warranting judgment (15:8). They had been consigned to the fire that would sweep the land at the hands of the Babylonians, who had already ravaged the land once in the action leading up to Jehoiachin (and Ezekiel's) deportation. This coming, complete conflagration stands as a declared reality (15:8). As frequently stated elsewhere in Ezekiel, God's purpose in his actions is that the people acknowledge that these events are the work of the sovereign Lord of the historic covenant with Israel (15:7).

The allegory and its interpretation present another "hinge" unit. Its potent declaration of Israel's fiery end could function as a substantiating word of Yahweh, supporting the dismantling of false hopes in chapters 12 through 14. The change in literary genre to allegory would underscore that substantiation. At the same time, its literary genre tends to tie it to the succeeding chapters, where allegory abounds.

◆ 2. Allegory of Jerusalem, the orphan harlot (16:1-63)

Then another message came to me from the LORD: 2"Son of man, confront Jerusalem with her detestable sins. 3Give her this message from the Sovereign LORD: You are nothing but a Canaanite! Your father was an Amorite and your mother a Hittite. 4On the day you were born, no one cared about you. Your umbilical cord was not cut, and you were never washed, rubbed with salt, and wrapped in cloth. 5No one had the slightest interest in you; no one pitied you or cared for you. On the day you were born, you were unwanted, dumped in a field and left to die.

6"But I came by and saw you there, helplessly kicking about in your own blood. As you lay there, I said, 'Live!' 7And I helped you to thrive like a plant in the field. You grew up and became a beautiful jewel. Your breasts became full, and your body hair grew, but you were still naked. 8And when I passed by again, I saw that you were old enough for love. So I wrapped my cloak around you to cover your nakedness and declared my marriage vows. I made a covenant with you, says the Sovereign LORD, and you became mine.

9"Then I bathed you and washed off your blood, and I rubbed fragrant oils into your skin. 10I gave you expensive clothing of fine linen and silk, beautifully embroidered, and sandals made of fine goatskin leather. 11I gave you lovely jewelry, bracelets, beautiful necklaces, 12a ring for your nose, earrings for your ears, and a lovely crown for your head. 13And so you were adorned with gold and silver. Your clothes were made of fine linen and were beautifully embroidered. You ate the finest foods—choice flour, honey, and olive oil—and became more beautiful than ever. You looked like a queen, and so you were! 14Your fame soon spread throughout the world because of your beauty. I dressed you in my splendor and perfected your beauty, says the Sovereign LORD.

15"But you thought your fame and beauty were your own. So you gave yourself as a prostitute to every man who came along. Your beauty was theirs for the asking. 16You used the lovely things I gave you to make shrines for idols, where you played the prostitute. Unbelievable! How could such a thing ever happen? 17You took the very jewels and gold and silver ornaments I had given you and made statues of men and worshiped them. This is adultery against me! 18You used the beautifully embroidered clothes I gave you to dress your idols. Then you used my special oil and my incense to worship them. 19Imagine it! You set before them as a sacrifice the choice flour, olive oil, and honey I had given you, says the Sovereign LORD.

20"Then you took your sons and daughters—the children you had borne to me—and sacrificed them to your gods. Was your prostitution not enough? 21 Must you also slaughter my children by sacrificing them to idols? 22 In all your years of adultery and detestable sin, you have not once remembered the days long ago when you lay naked in a field, kicking about in your own blood.

23"What sorrow awaits you, says the Sovereign LORD. In addition to all your other wickedness, 24 you built a pagan shrine and put altars to idols in every town square. 25 On every street corner you defiled your beauty, offering your body to every passerby in an endless stream of prostitution. 26 Then you added lustful Egypt to your lovers, provoking my anger with your increasing promiscuity. 27 That is why I struck you with my fist and reduced your boundaries. I handed you over to your enemies, the Philistines, and even they were shocked by your lewd conduct. 28 You have prostituted yourself with the Assyrians, too. It seems you can never find enough new lovers! And after your prostitution there, you still were not satisfied. 29 You added to your lovers by embracing Babylonia,* the land of merchants, but you still weren't satisfied.

30"What a sick heart you have, says the Sovereign LORD, to do such things as these, acting like a shameless prostitute. 31 You build your pagan shrines on every street corner and your altars to idols in every square. In fact, you have been worse than a prostitute, so eager for sin that you have not even demanded payment. 32 Yes, you are an adulterous wife who takes in strangers instead of her own husband. 33 Prostitutes charge for their services—but not you! You give gifts to your lovers, bribing them to come and have sex with you. 34 So you are the opposite of other prostitutes. You pay your lovers instead of their paying you!

35"Therefore, you prostitute, listen to this message from the LORD! 36 This is what the Sovereign LORD says: Because you have poured out your lust and exposed yourself in prostitution to all your lovers, and because you have worshiped detestable idols,* and because you have slaughtered your children as sacrifices to your gods, 37 this is what I am going to do. I will gather together all your allies—the lovers with whom you have sinned, both those you loved and those you hated—and I will strip you naked in front of them so they can stare at you. 38 I will punish you for your murder and adultery. I will cover you with blood in my jealous fury. 39 Then I will give you to these many nations who are your lovers, and they will destroy you. They will knock down your pagan shrines and the altars to your idols. They will strip you and take your beautiful jewels, leaving you stark naked. 40 They will band together in a mob to stone you and cut you up with swords. 41 They will burn your homes and punish you in front of many women. I will stop your prostitution and end your payments to your many lovers.

42"Then at last my fury against you will be spent, and my jealous anger will subside. I will be calm and will not be angry with you anymore. 43 But first, because you have not remembered your youth but have angered me by doing all these evil things, I will fully repay you for all of your sins, says the Sovereign LORD. For you have added lewd acts to all your detestable sins. 44 Everyone who makes up proverbs will say of you, 'Like mother, like daughter.' 45 For your mother loathed her husband and her children, and so do you. And you are exactly like your sisters, for they despised their husbands and their children. Truly your mother was a Hittite and your father an Amorite.

46"Your older sister was Samaria, who lived with her daughters in the north. Your younger sister was Sodom, who lived with her daughters in the south. 47 But you have not merely sinned as they did. You quickly surpassed them in corruption. 48 As surely as I live, says the Sovereign LORD, Sodom and her daughters were never as wicked as you and your daughters. 49 Sodom's sins were pride, gluttony,

and laziness, while the poor and needy
suffered outside her door. 50She was proud
and committed detestable sins, so I wiped
her out, as you have seen.*
51"Even Samaria did not commit half
your sins. You have done far more detest-
able things than your sisters ever did.
They seem righteous compared to you.
52Shame on you! Your sins are so terrible
that you make your sisters seem righ-
teous, even virtuous.
53"But someday I will restore the for-
tunes of Sodom and Samaria, and I will
restore you, too. 54Then you will be truly
ashamed of everything you have done, for
your sins make them feel good in com-
parison. 55Yes, your sisters, Sodom and
Samaria, and all their people will be re-
stored, and at that time you also will be
restored. 56In your proud days you held
Sodom in contempt. 57But now your
greater wickedness has been exposed to
all the world, and you are the one who is
scorned—by Edom* and all her neighbors
and by Philistia. 58This is your punishment
for all your lewdness and detestable sins,
says the LORD.
59"Now this is what the Sovereign LORD
says: I will give you what you deserve, for
you have taken your solemn vows lightly
by breaking your covenant. 60Yet I will re-
member the covenant I made with you
when you were young, and I will establish
an everlasting covenant with you. 61Then
you will remember with shame all the evil
you have done. I will make your sisters,
Samaria and Sodom, to be your daughters,
even though they are not part of our cov-
enant. 62And I will reaffirm my covenant
with you, and you will know that I am the
LORD. 63You will remember your sins and
cover your mouth in silent shame when I
forgive you of all that you have done. I,
the Sovereign LORD, have spoken!"

16:29 Or *Chaldea.* **16:36** The Hebrew term (literally *round things*) probably alludes to dung. **16:50** As in a few Hebrew manuscripts and Greek version; Masoretic Text reads *as I have seen.* **16:57** As in many Hebrew manuscripts and Syriac version; Masoretic Text reads *Aram.*

NOTES

16:2 ***detestable sins.*** Heb., *to'eboth* [TH8441, ZH9359] (detestable things), one of Ezekiel's favorite words for idols and all the apparatus of idolatrous worship, it occurs 43 times over 17 chapters in Ezekiel (e.g., 5:9; 6:9; 7:8).

16:3 ***Your father was an Amorite and your mother a Hittite.*** This could be just a simple insult, or slander by reference to Israel's complex history. More likely it carries an unflattering reference to Jerusalem's origins, though one cannot be certain. The allegory's focus on Jerusalem herself is the best support for this reading. In addition, biblical memory and archaeological evidence give some support as well. As early as the Amarna texts (fourteenth century BC) names easily taken as Amorite appear in connection with the city. The book of Joshua also includes Jerusalem in a list of entities with Amorite kings (Josh 10:1-5). And we know of Hittites resident in Canaan and in Jerusalem ever since patriarchal times (Gen 23:10; 25:9; 27:46; 1 Sam 26:6; 2 Sam 11:3, 6).

16:5 ***No one had the slightest interest in you.*** For my approach to this kind of statement with respect to feminist concerns, see the Introduction, "Ezekiel's View of Women"; see also Raymond Ortlund, Jr., on feminist interpretive issues here (1996:171-185).

16:6 ***As you lay there, I said, "Live!"*** The MT repeats this line, followed by the Targum and Vulgate among the ancient versions, and the KJV, NKJV, NASB, and ESV among English translations. The NLT follows the LXX and the Syriac versions (as do RSV, NRSV, NIV, NAB, REB) in regarding the repetition in the MT as a scribal error (dittography), and hence not to be repeated.

16:29 ***Babylonia.*** Or Chaldea (NLT mg). See notes on 1:3; 23:14.

16:36 *idols.* Heb., *gillulim* [TH1544, ZH1658] (lit., "round things") probably alludes to dung (also in 18:12, 15). See note on 5:9 for Ezekiel's vocabulary of idolatry.

16:37 *I will strip you naked.* We have no historical precedent for the stripping of an adulteress as part of her punishment or as a prelude to execution. Mention of this punishment appears only in passages such as this one where the adulteress represents Israel (cf. 16:39; 23:26, 29; Jer 13:22-26; Hos 2:3, 9 [5, 12]; see also Nah 3:5 of Nineveh). Whether it represented actual judicial practice or is included here mainly to shock the reader we do not know. If the Mishnah's provision for treatment of a woman suspected of adultery reflects historically distant preexilic practice, it could support the former (*b. Sotah* 1.5, cited by Greenberg 1983:286).

16:38 *I will cover you with blood.* Again, we do not know whether this threat reflects historical practice for punishing adulteresses. The NLT translates the same expression referring to the judgment of Edom in 35:6 as "I will give you a bloodbath." This might indicate that our line in 16:38 presents one of those places where the allegory bleeds over into the language of warfare and the military catastrophe facing Jerusalem. It also evokes the bloody situation of her childhood (16:6).

16:46 *older sister . . . Samaria . . . younger sister . . . Sodom.* "Sister" personifies these well-known cities as related to Jerusalem in a family of wickedness. The Hebrew ("big sister . . . little sister") behind the descriptions "older" and "younger" is perhaps better translated as "big" and "little" sister, since Samaria was larger than Jerusalem, and Sodom reduced to rubble for centuries by Ezekiel's time, whereas Samaria was much younger and Sodom older than Jerusalem, at least in the biblical narratives. Of the two, Samaria was the capital of a state; Sodom a smaller city-state (so Allen 1994:225, 244; Greenberg 1983:272, 288-289).

daughters. This refers to settlements surrounding the larger cities, Samaria and Sodom.

16:50 *as you have seen.* This is the reading in a few Hebrew and LXX mss; MT reads "as I have seen."

16:57 *Edom.* Many ancient manuscripts read "Aram."

16:60 *I will remember the covenant.* See de Vaux (1961:1.34-37) on marital repudiation, divorce, adultery, and fornication in Israel.

COMMENTARY

Ezekiel's central task in the oracles of chapter 16 was to "confront Jerusalem," and by implication all Israel, "with her detestable sins" (16:2). He aimed to educate and hopefully to persuade his audience to acknowledge Jerusalem's sins, centrally her idolatry (lit., "detestable things," see note on 16:2). This collection of oracles was apparently received between September 592 (8:1) and August 591 (20:1), even though it was read years later. It aims to vindicate God's destruction of Jerusalem by documenting the covenant betrayal of Israel. In the process, Ezekiel hoped also to validate his own prophetic ministry and to accredit the vision for the future that he was also going to expound.

Chapter 16 is an allegory, but in contrast to the parabolic "story" beginning in 17:2, it is not explicitly tagged as a *mashal* [TH4912, ZH5442] (proverb, parable). The unit unfolds as follows: Ezekiel 16:3-14 pictures Jerusalem as a castaway orphan whom Yahweh rescues, marries, and adorns. Verses 15-34 narrate, in concessionary logic, Jerusalem's trust in her own beauty and consequent, unbridled harlotry. In spite of Israel's utter dependence upon Yahweh for her life and beauty, she trusted herself instead of him.

Yahweh's angry response to this betrayal through Jerusalem's "lovers" follows in 16:35-43. The story is resumed and expanded in 16:44-52, unfavorably comparing Jerusalem to her "sisters," Samaria and Sodom. Then follows Yahweh's promise of restoration (16:53-58). A separate, but related, oracle promising an everlasting covenant closes the literary unit (16:59-63).

The story's opening lines about Jerusalem's ancestry and infancy are shocking and sad (16:3-5). The NLT captures the uncomplimentary tone in Ezekiel's words about her parents and ancestry: "You are nothing but a Canaanite" from Amorite and Hittite stock (16:3)! Whether Ezekiel referred to Jerusalem's own Canaanite pedigree (16:45) or to strands of the Israelite people's complex origins, or just intended an insult without these historical realities in mind one cannot be certain. More likely the former, I think (see note on 16:3). Worse still, Jerusalem was a throwaway child, abandoned by her parents immediately upon birth. They gave her none of the rudimentary, "neonatal" care normally provided newborns, but instead threw her out. Ezekiel stresses the tragedy of the situation by repetition: "No one cared about [her]"—not even her parents. They wanted her dead (16:4-5). From every perspective her situation looked hopeless: her "unfortunate" past, her present dreadful plight, and her horrible future. In this attempted infanticide, Ezekiel may have been recalling the genocide facing Israel at the time of her birth and her desperate plight in Egypt (Exod 1–2).

Ezekiel places the sovereign love and compassion of Yahweh in stark contrast to Jerusalem's pitiful situation (16:6-14). Passing by, Yahweh saw the castaway and spoke life into her deathly situation (16:6). Reminiscent of the creative power of God's word in Genesis 1, his word here also came unbidden, bringing abundant life into being for reasons of his own. He not only enabled life where certain death loomed ahead, but enabled her to "thrive" (16:7). And he did so while she was yet "unwanted . . . dumped . . . left . . . helplessly kicking about in [her] own blood" (16:5-6). This has been the story of Yahweh's gracious, sovereign election of Israel, presumably through Abraham, Isaac, and Jacob, and climaxing in the Exodus and covenant at Sinai.

Ezekiel moved directly from Jerusalem's/Israel's origins and the Lord's earliest interactions with her in her "infancy" to the time of her attractiveness for marriage. He narrated the marriage itself, Yahweh's lavish gifts for his bride, and her striking, regal beauty thus graced by Yahweh (16:6-14). This involved a marriage covenant, made with the pubescent girl, even though she was yet unwashed, unclothed, and unwanted (16:8). Ezekiel emphasized here the marvel of Israel's election, and especially the fact and implications of Yahweh's historic covenant entered with his people at Sinai (16:59; Exod 19:1-8).

Patterned after a vassal treaty between a great king and a lesser ruler, the Mosaic covenant held significant reciprocity in the context of Yahweh's loving initiative. Further, in Exodus and Deuteronomy, the Great King who was offering the covenant, unlike ancient sovereigns, did not offer the covenant to formalize relationships after a real or impending *conquest*. Instead, Israel's God had actually *rescued* her from the hand of the world's most powerful sovereign, Egypt's Pharaoh, *and had done so expressly for a liberating relationship with himself* (Exod 15:1-18;19:4-5). These were Yahweh's lavish gifts. These features open the historic Mosaic covenant beautifully to Ezekiel's presentation of it as a marriage covenant, a move similar to the prophet Hosea's interpretation (Hos 2).

The rest of the allegory Ezekiel devotes to Israel's unfaithfulness to this marriage covenant (16:15-34, 43, 45-52) and to Yahweh's response to her harlotry in jealous anger (16:35-44). Over 60 percent of the verses of the chapter are devoted to these sober topics. In this allegory, marital unfaithfulness—adultery and prostitution—pictures Israel's unfaithfulness to the Mosaic covenant, especially in the embracing of other gods and the practices entailed in worshiping them.

Jerusalem's root sin, however, was not the worship of other gods but the worship of herself and amnesia regarding her past, forgetting the source of her beauty (16:15, 22, 43). Yahweh's charge of adultery referenced betrayal of the marriage (i.e., Mosaic) covenant (16:17, 22, 38). The charge of prostitution focused on Israel's eagerness and wanton indiscretion in forsaking Yahweh (16:20, 25, 28, 35, 41). Finally, Ezekiel charged that Israel, sick at heart, offered herself to others without charge (16:31) and actually hired lovers to satisfy her lust (16:30, 33-34; cf. 16:28, 31, 41). These twists in the story imply Jerusalem's (and Israel's) thoroughgoing departure from the Lord and/or confusion regarding the Lord as well as the compromised faith and life that followed. Even Israel's "good" kings failed to reverse these evils (e.g., Jehoshaphat in 1 Kgs 22:41-44). Ezekiel could even have in mind Ahaz's "selling" himself for Assyrian aid against the urging of Isaiah to trust the Lord (2 Kgs 16:5-18; Isa 7:1-17).

Ezekiel's allegory is profoundly tragic, all the more because it shares or appears to share features of the truly "sad stories" Phyllis Tribble places among the Old Testament's "texts of terror." She treats historical narratives in which women suffer as victims, "used, abused, rejected" (1984:1-2). Katheryn Darr concludes Ezekiel has created "some of the Bible's most misogynistic texts" in his elaboration here and in chapter 23 (1998:92). The fact that God himself is the angered husband only deepens the problem. For my discussion of this issue, see the Introduction, "Ezekiel's View of Women."

Ezekiel's "historical" allegory complicates the reading of the story. The boundary between allegory and actual historical reference seems permeable, with Ezekiel moving unpredictably back and forth between the two fields of reference. The allegory is of a man (representing Yahweh) who found a castaway, and transformed her pitiful situation by marrying her and luxuriantly providing for her (16:6-14). When she rejected his astounding love in a trail of unbridled profligacy (16:15-34, 43-58) and violence (16:20-21, 36), he promised in his heated anger to punish her (16:35-43). But when his anger subsided, he promised to reaffirm again his covenant with her (16:42, 59-63). The historical reference is to the nation of Israel and especially Judah and Jerusalem, to her covenant-breaking behavior, and to the travesties of war suffered at the hands of invading Assyrians, Philistines, Egyptians, and Babylonians.

Both Israel's idolatrous behaviors and the violence she suffers become increasingly repugnant to readers as Ezekiel portrays the historical realities through allegory. Israel made human statues and worshiped them (16:17, 36), dressed the idols with embroidered cloth (16:18), worshipping them with oil, incense, fine flour, and honey (16:18-19), engaged in child sacrifice (16:20-21, 36), and built pagan shrines and altars in town squares (16:24). Yahweh promised that the invading "lovers/nations" would destroy her, knocking down her pagan shrines and idolatrous altars (16:39). The enemies would stone her and run her through "with swords" (16:40), "burn [her] homes" [note the plural, national reference] (16:41), and leave her scorned by her neighbors (16:57).

In the allegory, the man punishes his violent and unfaithful wife, not only for adultery, but also for the murder of her own children (16:38), both capital offenses. In that process, the husband strips her publicly (16:37, see note), and covers her with blood (16:38). The violence in the allegory depicts not only an enraged husband, but also an aggrieved member of the community exercising his responsibility. The violence at the hands of the nations is a historical reference to the atrocities of war, not the raging of a misogynist husband. We may note, however, that even if Ezekiel should be found to picture Yahweh as a misogynist husband, the shocking metaphor does not condone misogyny any more than Jesus' parabolic presentation of God as a "godless man who had great contempt for everyone" (Luke 18:2, TLB) should be taken as a straightforward description of the character of God. Nevertheless, the emphasis does fall on Yahweh's angry response—he will fully repay Jerusalem for her sins (16:42-43, 59).

Once more Ezekiel underscored the legitimacy of Yahweh's response, this time by comparing Jerusalem unfavorably to two other cities allegorized as Jerusalem's sisters and known to all Jerusalemites as disgraceful places (16:46-52). The "older sister," Samaria, was the infamous capital of the kingdom of Israel, built by Omri and made the mecca of Baal worshipers in Israel by Jezebel (1 Kgs 16:23-28; 18:18-19; 2 Kgs 11:18-19). The "younger sister," said Ezekiel, was Sodom, touted in Israel's patriarchal stories as so wicked as to deserve God's fiery destruction (Gen 19). Ezekiel shockingly claimed that Jerusalem was viler than these wicked cities—an inconceivable thought for lovers of Jerusalem (16:56). She was so wicked she made Samaria and Sodom look innocent (16:52)! Part of her punishment was the contempt her neighbors now had for her (16:56-58). According to ancient Near Eastern theology, the collapse of Judah and her defeat before Nebuchadnezzar meant either that her God, Yahweh, was unable to protect her (cf. Joel 2:17), or that Jerusalem and Judah were so reprobate that their God Yahweh gave them up to judgment. In either case, they suffered the disdain of their neighbors. Thus the allegorical oracle ends.

Even so, the undeserved restoration that Yahweh promises receives substantial coverage (16:53-63). Between that closing note of disdain (16:56-58) and the unfavorable comparison of Jerusalem to her sister cities (16:52), Ezekiel sounds a note of hope unusual in its extraordinary breadth (16:53-55). God promises the restoration not only of Jerusalem but also of Sodom and Samaria, as well as their "daughters"! The emphasis here seems to be on the restoration of these infamous sinners, with Jerusalem restored along with them. At the conclusion of this chapter, filled with horrendous threats of deserved judgment, the prophet underscores by contrast the lavish grace of God. In his sovereignty he will find a way to restore even these parade examples of sinful cities. If he can do that, surely he can restore Jerusalem. Such announcements of salvation for the nations are rare in Ezekiel (cf. 29:13-15 for Egypt).

An oracle with its own introductory formula closes the unit (16:59-63). It extends the note of hope that just surfaced in the allegory, and it serves as counterpoint to the dreadful threats in it. These notes of restoration stand at odds with the threats of death seen earlier (vv. 37-38). This disjuncture arises in part from the fact that the historic realities being presented allegorically will actually involve both death and survival, both destruction of the city and restoration after exile. It flows from the allegory with talk of a covenant in Israel's youth and her flippant disregard for the vows of her youth (16:59-60). Incorporation of Jerusalem's "sisters" into Jerusalem's sphere as "daughters" (16:61) also draws on the allegory. At the same time, the promise of an "everlasting covenant" (16:60) anticipates a later, fuller presentation of covenantal hope (cf. 34:23-31; 37:24-27). The oracle makes a brief but theologically clear comment on the allegory, clearly tying it to Mosaic covenant thought. Israel will have a bright future because of Yahweh's unconditional faithfulness to that covenant, a covenant already broken by Israel, and thus technically no longer binding upon Yahweh. The allegorical interpretation of the Sinai covenant as a marriage covenant accentuates the startling grace in Yahweh's restoration of the covenant. For adultery, death for the unfaithful party would normally have been the expected outcome (Lev 20:10; Deut 22:22). But unfaithful Israel will only be chastened, not put to death. Nor will Yahweh divorce Israel (in contrast to Hos 2:1-4). Instead, in his own sovereign love, he chose not only to reestablish the broken covenant but also to inaugurate an everlasting bond with Israel (16:60). Israel would feel shame and would stand appropriately silent, her true condition unmasked by the grace of Yahweh (16:63). She would also acknowledge that the God accomplishing all of these things is Yahweh, the historic God of the covenant (16:62). Her restoration and the renewal of the covenant were both the result of Yahweh's gracious forgiveness (16:63).

◆ 3. Allegories of eagles and a vine (17:1-24)

Then this message came to me from the LORD: 2"Son of man, give this riddle, and tell this story to the people of Israel. 3Give them this message from the Sovereign LORD:

"A great eagle with broad wings and
long feathers,
covered with many-colored plumage,
came to Lebanon.
He seized the top of a cedar tree
4 and plucked off its highest branch.
He carried it away to a city filled
with merchants.
He planted it in a city of traders.
5He also took a seedling from the land
and planted it in fertile soil.
He placed it beside a broad river,
where it could grow like a willow
tree.
6It took root there and
grew into a low, spreading vine.
Its branches turned up toward the
eagle,
and its roots grew down into the
ground.
It produced strong branches
and put out shoots.
7But then another great eagle came
with broad wings and full plumage.
So the vine now sent its roots and
branches
toward him for water,
8even though it was already planted
in good soil

and had plenty of water
so it could grow into a splendid vine
and produce rich leaves and
luscious fruit.

9 "So now the Sovereign LORD asks:
Will this vine grow and prosper?
No! I will pull it up, roots and all!
I will cut off its fruit
and let its leaves wither and die.
I will pull it up easily
without a strong arm or a large
army.
10 But when the vine is transplanted,
will it thrive?
No, it will wither away
when the east wind blows against it.
It will die in the same good soil
where it had grown so well."

11 Then this message came to me from the
LORD: 12 "Say to these rebels of Israel:
Don't you understand the meaning of this
riddle of the eagles? The king of Babylon
came to Jerusalem, took away her king
and princes, and brought them to Bab-
ylon. 13 He made a treaty with a member
of the royal family and forced him to take
an oath of loyalty. He also exiled Israel's
most influential leaders, 14 so Israel would
not become strong again and revolt. Only
by keeping her treaty with Babylon could
Israel survive.

15 "Nevertheless, this man of Israel's
royal family rebelled against Babylon,
sending ambassadors to Egypt to request
a great army and many horses. Can Israel
break her sworn treaties like that and get
away with it? 16 No! For as surely as I live,
says the Sovereign LORD, the king of Israel
will die in Babylon, the land of the king
who put him in power and whose treaty he
disregarded and broke. 17 Pharaoh and all
his mighty army will fail to help Israel
when the king of Babylon lays siege to Je-
rusalem again and destroys many lives.
18 For the king of Israel disregarded his
treaty and broke it after swearing to obey;
therefore, he will not escape.

19 "So this is what the Sovereign LORD
says: As surely as I live, I will punish him
for breaking my covenant and disregard-
ing the solemn oath he made in my name.
20 I will throw my net over him and capture
him in my snare. I will bring him to Bab-
ylon and put him on trial for this treason
against me. 21 And all his best warriors*
will be killed in battle, and those who sur-
vive will be scattered to the four winds.
Then you will know that I, the LORD, have
spoken.

22 "This is what the Sovereign LORD says:
I will take a branch from the top of a tall
cedar, and I will plant it on the top of Is-
rael's highest mountain. 23 It will become
a majestic cedar, sending forth its branch-
es and producing seed. Birds of every sort
will nest in it, finding shelter in the shade
of its branches. 24 And all the trees will
know that it is I, the LORD, who cuts the
tall tree down and makes the short tree
grow tall. It is I who makes the green tree
wither and gives the dead tree new life. I,
the LORD, have spoken, and I will do what
I said!"

17:21 Or *his fleeing warriors.* The meaning of the Hebrew is uncertain.

NOTES

17:2 *give this riddle.* A "riddle" (*khidah* [TH2420, ZH2648]) is "an obscure saying from which something else is to be understood" (Greenberg 1983:309); it seems to designate a sort of extended metaphor that we might call "a fable" (Greenberg 1983:22).

17:9 *I will cut off its fruit. . . . I will pull it up.* This refers to the transplanted seedling. Most translations, ancient and modern, have third-person action here (e.g., RSV, "Will he not pull up its roots and cut off its branches?"). The "he" refers either to one of the eagles, probably the first one in retaliation (so LXX, ESV, NAB, NJPS; Block 1997:532; Darr 2001:1246-1247; Greenberg 1983:318; Zimmerli 1979:363) or to Yahweh (so NLT). The NIV and REB translate the verbs as passives, also retaining the ambiguity of the MT. The

NLT, which seems idiosyncratic, takes the actor as Yahweh and removes the ambiguity from the Hebrew text.

17:12 *The king of Babylon came to Jerusalem.* For an excellent summary of the history of Judah's final days, a discussion of problems involved in reconstructing that history, and note of pertinent sources outside of Scripture that bear upon this history, see Provan, Long, and Longman 2003:276-284 along with their notes on pp. 380-381. See also the Introduction, "Date and Occasion of Writing," especially "Josiah, the Collapse of Judah, and the Call of Ezekiel" for a more "Ezekiel focused" coverage of the historical background for ch 17.

17:13 *He made a treaty with a member of the royal family.* See ANET 308 for a tablet documenting Nebuchadnezzar's provision for Jehoiachin's family in Babylon.

17:17 Psammeticus II's (595–589 BC) military successes at home in uniting upper and lower Egypt in 592 and the appearance of his troops in Palestine in 591 no doubt stirred Judean (and some exilic) hopes for success against Nebuchadnezzar.

17:19-21 Greenberg argues for taking these verses as referring to the breaking of the Sinai covenant, the treaty with Yahweh par excellence (1983:320-322). The NLT allows such an interpretation, though it tends toward the interpretation that 17:19-21 refers to the broken treaty with Nebuchadnezzar (the view of Allen 1994:259; Blenkinsopp 1990:80-81; Block 1997:347-348; Darr 2001:1250; Zimmerli 1979:365-366). I agree with Allen that the word "so" of 17:19, which represents the explicit causal marker *laken* [TH3651A, ZH4027], flows most naturally as a direct conclusion from the immediately preceding verses.

17:22 *branch.* Heb., *tsammereth* [TH6788, ZH7550]; this was a common prophetic messianic figure already by Ezekiel's time (Isa 11:1; Jer 23:5; 33:15; Zech 3:8; 6:12). Ezekiel shared the semantic reference but not the vocabulary; the word "branch" is elsewhere generally *tsemakh* [TH6780, ZH7542].

COMMENTARY

This literary unit is comprised of a riddle (17:1-10), two explanations of the riddle (17:11-18 and 19-21), and a concluding, messianic extension of the riddle (17:22-24). Both the riddle and the interpretation open with the revelation formula, "this message came to me from the LORD" (17:1, 11), and they conclude with a variation of the acknowledgment formula, "all the trees will know" (17:24). In 17:2, Ezekiel is told to give a *mashal* [TH4912, ZH5442] (a "metaphor," here extended), more specifically a parabolic riddle (*khidah* [TH2420, ZH2648]). Perhaps a *mashal* passes over into a *khidah* when it is not self-evident and requires explanation (Eichrodt 1970:292). Here the *mashal* is a fable (Block 1997:525), where plants and animals act like human beings, not every detail necessarily corresponding to historical reality. The eagle, known for its strength and speed, provides a fitting image for the Babylonian and Egyptian kings (cf. Deut 28:49; Jer 48:40; Lam 4:19; Hab 1:8). Ezekiel had already seen the eagle related to one of the creatures associated with the divine throne (ch 1). The cedar of Lebanon, known from time immemorial in the ancient Near East for its towering strength and beauty, imaged Davidic royalty well. Read in its present context, the general meaning of the parable seems self-evident. But Block is no doubt right to point out the ambiguity of the fable heard strictly on its own and thus rightly called a "riddle" (17:2). The present literary context would remove most of the ambiguity for Ezekiel's first readers.

The first eagle, colorful and strong (17:3), as a Babylonian king (17:12), can only have been Nebuchadnezzar in this context. The "highest branch" plucked away to the economic center of the empire, that is, to the city of Babylon, would have been Jehoiachin, son of Josiah (2 Kgs 24:6-8). Ezekiel himself was among the intelligentsia and leadership of the nation deported when this "highest branch" was carried away to Babylon (17:13). Ezekiel reflects public regard for Jehoiachin by dating his oracles to the deportation of Jehoiachin—rather than, for example, to the regnal years of his successor, Zedekiah.

Ezekiel's early listeners and readers would have recognized King Zedekiah in the (contrasting) seedling transplanted by the eagle (17:5-6). Nebuchadnezzar installed him as king at the deportation of Jehoiachin and swore him to loyalty in a treaty reestablishing Judah as a satellite state of the Babylonian Empire (17:14). His identity as a seedling, not a lofty cedar branch (17:5-6), registers the fact that Zedekiah was not in the ruling branch of Josiah's line. He was not Jehoiachin's father or son but his uncle. Jehoiachin's father, Jehoiakim, had been made king by Nebuchadnezzar in 604 BC. By 601 he rebelled against Nebuchadnezzar (2 Kgs 23:34–24:2), presumably seeking an alliance with Egypt against the Babylonians, an alliance that did not deliver promised aid when Jehoiakim had to face Nebuchadnezzar (2 Kgs 24:7). Prophetic warnings against reliance upon Egypt were already known to the royal house (Isa 30:1-5; 31:1-3; Jer 2:17-19, 36-37; Hos 7:11).

According to the fable and the related accounts in Jeremiah (Jer 27:1-7), Zedekiah became involved in talks with neighboring states about the possibility of revolt. This almost certainly would have involved aid from Egypt for the counteralliance against Babylon. He finally rebelled in 591 when the Egyptian Psammeticus II invaded Palestine. In fact, a letter from the fortified city of Lachish contemporary with these events reports a trip to Egypt by a certain "Coniah ben Elnathan," most likely, one may reasonably speculate, as part of anti-Babylonian collaborations (ANET 322). As noted before, the royal family surely knew of the repeated prophetic warnings. Given the unreliable loyalties of the Judean crown with Babylon, a devastating response by Nebuchadnezzar was inevitable.

Two moral failures brought Yahweh's judgment upon Zedekiah. First, Zedekiah broke the treaty he had made with Nebuchadnezzar (17:15, 18-19). Zedekiah had taken an oath in Yahweh's name to remain loyal to Babylon. Breaking that treaty trivialized the oath and shamed the name of Yahweh, whose character allegedly guaranteed Zedekiah's loyalty. For this crime he would be deported and die one day in Babylon (17:16, 19-20). Second, his conspiracy with Egypt, intended to secure "a great army and many horses," exposed Zedekiah's true faith. He trusted in military armaments, not in the protection of Yahweh, Lord of Hosts (17:15). Faithful covenant life with Yahweh meant confessing the inadequacy of warhorses and massive troops to save God's people (cf. Hos 14:1-3 on the northern kingdom and her reliance upon Assyrian arms). Perhaps 17:19-20 should refer not to the treaty with Nebuchadnezzar but to the Sinai covenant. If so, Ezekiel pointed to the breaking of Yahweh's own treaty with Judah—the Mosaic covenant—as a prominent breach of faith, which would cause the dreadful demise of Zedekiah.

The allegory concludes with a brief, striking oracle full of hope (17:22-24). Yahweh continues the riddle propounded earlier but with himself as the central character. On Israel's highest mount he plants a branch taken from a tall cedar (17:22). The branch grows into a majestic tree, so large and lush it provides home and shelter to all sorts of birds (17:23). Seeing this astounding event, all the trees acknowledge this must be the work of Israel's God, Yahweh (17:24).

The theology of history that implicitly structures the earlier part of the riddle becomes explicit in this oracle. The great eagles and the planted trees act earlier in the chapter. But we are to know that in their actions the God of Israel was himself at work, achieving his purposes. Here that action is explicitly claimed. Furthermore, for the first time in the book we have a messianic hope in the sense that God's future deliverance is associated with a singular person of his choosing—the single branch that grows into a majestic cedar on Israel's highest mount. The mount is Jerusalem, not literally Israel's highest point, but loftiest in the extravagant language of royal hope. When this happens, all the nations will acknowledge Yahweh as the central figure in the rise and fall of empires. Ezekiel makes another anticipatory entry on a theme he will pursue at some length later (chs 36–37).

◆ 4. The one who sins dies (18:1-32)

Then another message came to me from the LORD: 2"Why do you quote this proverb concerning the land of Israel: 'The parents have eaten sour grapes, but their children's mouths pucker at the taste'? 3As surely as I live, says the Sovereign LORD, you will not quote this proverb anymore in Israel. 4For all people are mine to judge—both parents and children alike. And this is my rule: The person who sins is the one who will die.

5"Suppose a certain man is righteous and does what is just and right. 6He does not feast in the mountains before Israel's idols* or worship them. He does not commit adultery or have intercourse with a woman during her menstrual period. 7He is a merciful creditor, not keeping the items given as security by poor debtors. He does not rob the poor but instead gives food to the hungry and provides clothes for the needy. 8He grants loans without interest, stays away from injustice, is honest and fair when judging others, 9and faithfully obeys my decrees and regulations. Anyone who does these things is just and will surely live, says the Sovereign LORD.

10"But suppose that man has a son who grows up to be a robber or murderer and refuses to do what is right. 11And that son does all the evil things his father would never do—he worships idols on the mountains, commits adultery, 12oppresses the poor and helpless, steals from debtors by refusing to let them redeem their security, worships idols, commits detestable sins, 13and lends money at excessive interest. Should such a sinful person live? No! He must die and must take full blame.

14"But suppose that sinful son, in turn, has a son who sees his father's wickedness and decides against that kind of life. 15This son refuses to worship idols on the mountains and does not commit adultery. 16He does not exploit the poor, but instead is fair to debtors and does not rob them. He gives food to the hungry and provides clothes for the needy. 17He helps the poor,* does not lend money at interest, and obeys all my regulations and decrees. Such a person will not die because of his father's sins; he will surely live. 18But the father will die for his many sins—for being cruel, robbing people, and doing what was clearly wrong among his people.

19"'What?' you ask. 'Doesn't the child pay for the parent's sins?' No! For if the child does what is just and right and keeps

my decrees, that child will surely live. 20The person who sins is the one who will die. The child will not be punished for the parent's sins, and the parent will not be punished for the child's sins. Righteous people will be rewarded for their own righteous behavior, and wicked people will be punished for their own wickedness. 21But if wicked people turn away from all their sins and begin to obey my decrees and do what is just and right, they will surely live and not die. 22All their past sins will be forgotten, and they will live because of the righteous things they have done.

23"Do you think that I like to see wicked people die? says the Sovereign LORD. Of course not! I want them to turn from their wicked ways and live. 24However, if righteous people turn from their righteous behavior and start doing sinful things and act like other sinners, should they be allowed to live? No, of course not! All their righteous acts will be forgotten, and they will die for their sins.

25"Yet you say, 'The Lord isn't doing what's right!' Listen to me, O people of Israel. Am I the one not doing what's right, or is it you? 26When righteous people turn from their righteous behavior and start doing sinful things, they will die for it. Yes, they will die because of their sinful deeds. 27And if wicked people turn from their wickedness, obey the law, and do what is just and right, they will save their lives. 28They will live because they thought it over and decided to turn from their sins. Such people will not die. 29And yet the people of Israel keep saying, 'The Lord isn't doing what's right!' O people of Israel, it is you who are not doing what's right, not I.

30"Therefore, I will judge each of you, O people of Israel, according to your actions, says the Sovereign LORD. Repent, and turn from your sins. Don't let them destroy you! 31Put all your rebellion behind you, and find yourselves a new heart and a new spirit. For why should you die, O people of Israel? 32I don't want you to die, says the Sovereign LORD. Turn back and live!

18:6 The Hebrew term (literally *round things*) probably alludes to dung; also in 18:12, 15. **18:17** Greek version reads *He refuses to do evil.*

NOTES

18:2 *The parents have eaten sour grapes.* Block (1997:560) rightly notes the MT has an imperfect tense verb, which one would normally translate "eat" in a proverb like this: "the fathers eat sour grapes—the children's mouths pucker." The NLT could have retained the present tense, more proverbial language, in spite of the aorist used in the LXX and the perfect form adopted in Jer 31:29. Block, however, presses proverbial language too far, I think, in concluding that here we have now "an inevitable and uncontrollable determinism" (1997:560). It seems to me that Block drives too large a wedge between the theological and general interpretation of the proverb because the proverb, as interpreted by Yahweh, clearly addresses intergenerational judgment for sin. But Block is correct that the actual issue is the *use* to which Ezekiel's audience was putting the proverb. See ANET 207-208 and 395 for ancient Near East versions of the proverb's judicial theory (cited by Greenberg 1983:339).

mouths pucker. Translators ancient and modern have struggled to capture the precise sense of the second half of the proverb. The MT has "the children's teeth *tiqhenah*" (a form of *qahah* [TH6949, ZH7733]), with the proverb hanging on *qahah*, the precise meaning of which remains uncertain. The LXX translates "the children's teeth ached" (from *gomphiazō*) here in Ezekiel, but uses *haimōdiō* ("the children's teeth were set on edge") in the citation of the same proverb in Jer 31:29 [38:29 LXX], the only other occurrence of *qahah* in the stem used here. The Vulgate translates *obstupescunt,* "became senseless, numb." In late Hebrew and Aramaic, the root *q-h-h* conveys "become blunt, dull." Anyone who has felt the unpleasant sense registered by one's teeth after eating acidic food knows what the proverb is getting at. Describing it accurately is the problem. The biblical proverb that puts "vinegar that sets the teeth on edge" parallel to "smoke in the eyes" evokes the same experience (Prov 10:26). The NLT changes the physiological referent but captures the unpleasant experience delightfully by rendering "the children's mouths pucker at the taste."

18:4 ***all people are mine. . . . The person who sins is the one who will die.*** Readers of the KJV recall here, "all souls are mine . . . the soul that sinneth, it shall die." The RSV, NIV, ESV, and NASB translate similarly. The NRSV and NAB translate along the lines of the NLT. At issue is translation of the Hebrew word *nepesh* [TH5315, ZH5883]. Generally in the Hebrew Bible the *nepesh* is not something a person has, independent of a body, but rather something a person is. *Nepesh* names the person viewed from the perspective of its creaturely, flesh-and-blood, living, breathing existence (HALOT 2.712-713). Thus, God breathed into Adam the breath of life, and he became a living *nepesh*, "a living creature," a living, breathing human being (Gen 2:7; cf. plural in Gen 1:20, 24 for similar designation of living creatures God creates). The NLT interprets these texts well, as expounded by the following oracle. Whole persons and all that pertains to them belong to God, not just their lives or destinies or some aspect of them. And whole persons choose to act righteously and live, or to act sinfully and die.

18:5 ***Suppose a certain man is righteous and does what is just and right.*** See Block (1997:567, note 57), for an extensive bibliography on proposed sources of the catalogs of righteous and wicked behavior cited by Ezekiel. Block (1997:568) follows Weinfeld in seeing Temple and priestly background behind the lists and also suggests ties with a royal "code of honor," here democratized in application to all Israel.

18:6 ***idols.*** Heb., *gillulim* [TH1544, ZH1658] (lit., "round things") probably alludes to dung (also in 18:12, 15). See note on 5:9 for Ezekiel's vocabulary of idolatry.

COMMENTARY

Chapter 18 contains the theological centerpiece for this section of Ezekiel. Chapters 15–19 present a collection of oracles with unusual attention to their literary form and genre, a collection of *meshalim* [TH4912, ZH5442] and *khidoth* [TH2420, ZH2648] (i.e., of allegories and riddles, and here a standard proverb). Chapter 19 contains another allegory, with attention given there not to the proverbial or allegorical character of the oracle but to its form as a "lament" (*qinah* [TH7015, ZH7806]). Chapter 18 provides the theological foundation for the allegorical, parabolic work around it.

Yahweh opens the first section of his message to Ezekiel (18:1-20) by reference to a proverb, a standard *mashal* (18:2). It is a typical poetic 3 + 3 bicolon of the sort encountered in the book of Proverbs, in this case, with three Hebrew words on each side of the poetic line: *'aboth yo'kelu boser // weshinne habbanim tiqhenah*, meaning "the parents have eaten sour grapes // and the children's mouths pucker." The proverb describes the intergenerational consequences of sin. One generation eats the grapes; the next generation has the puckered mouth.

Yahweh cites the use of the proverb in order to repudiate in strongest terms (with an oath) its continued currency in Israel (18:3). He then provides two reasons for his rejection of the proverb. The first reason: Yahweh's sovereign "ownership" of all persons and generations, a relationship grounded in his role as creator (not pursued in Ezekiel) and as covenant partner of Israel. As creator he can construe the relationship between generations as he pleases. Second, Yahweh rejects the proverb because his "rule" of life is actually contrary to the proverb: The person who sins—not his children or others—is the one who suffers the consequences for the sin (18:4; already in Deut 24:16).

What is the consequence of sin? The sinner "dies." Then, if we reverse the proverb, the one who does not sin but rather does Yahweh's will would "live." It is highly unlikely that Ezekiel had in mind afterlife experiences of "death" as eternal separation from God and "live" as meaning "eternal life." Following covenant thought, "die" and "live" most likely refer to actual physical death (perhaps premature or violent death), and to deliverance from such a fate (Lev 26; Deut 28–29). (Notice "allowed to live," and "save their lives," 18:24, 27.) It is also true that this covenantal understanding had in it the sense that part of living with Yahweh was life now under his blessing (Hab 2:4; 3:17-19).

Yahweh particularizes and supports the general claim in 18:4 with three case studies (18:5-9, 10-13, and 14-18). He then deals with an anticipated question and repeats and expands his claim from 18:4 (18:19-20). In the second section of his message (18:21-32) he examines intragenerational applications of the rule (18:21-24) and refutes an accusation of injustice (18:25-29). The unit closes with a passionate appeal, based on the theological foundation of the chapter: Israel should turn to him and live (18:30-32).

There was, however, covenant tradition that Ezekiel's listeners and readers could cite in support of the proverb, most notably the famous words from Yahweh's historic self-revelation: "Yahweh! The LORD! The God of compassion and mercy! I am slow to anger and filled with unfailing love and faithfulness. I lavish unfailing love to a thousand generations. I forgive iniquity, rebellion, and sin. But I do not excuse the guilty. I lay the sins of the parents upon their children and grandchildren; the entire family is affected—even children in the third and fourth generations" (Exod 34:6-7; cf. Num 14:18). Even though the emphasis in this disclosure falls clearly on Yahweh's unfathomable love and faithfulness, the claim regarding the intergenerational consequences of sin is also strong. In addition, there was the threat that Jerusalem's fate was already sealed because of the sins of Manasseh (2 Kgs 21:10-15; 23:26-27; 24:3), a threat that seemed inexorably to be unfolding in the decimation of Judah by Nebuchadnezzar.

Texts in Exodus, Numbers, and 2 Kings report Yahweh's self-revelation and prophetic threats against Jerusalem in words consonant with the proverb in Ezekiel. The proverb itself, however, comes from an entirely different literary tradition and source of wisdom. In the prophetic and Torah traditions, revelation is from above, so to speak, with God taking the initiative to break into human experience and perception. The wisdom traditions, in contrast, present revelation from below, insight derived from observing God's creation, including human experience—such insight was often presented as a proverb. The idea here embodied such common human experience that it had come to proverbial expression. Each generation does indeed live with the consequences of those it follows. The proverb reports human experience that is wider than sin-judgment issues, addressing all sorts of negative, intergenerational consequences.

This oracle presumes, however, that the proverb and quite possibly the traditions we now have in Exodus and 2 Kings were being used to evade the preaching of Ezekiel and other prophets (cf. Jer 31:29-30). They apparently claimed that accusing

Judah and Jerusalem (both exiles and "left behinds") of being a rebellious house was preaching to the choir. Ezekiel had the wrong audience—it was the last generation, not their own, that was responsible for the present judgment. Against such misuse of folk wisdom and sacred tradition, Yahweh presented hypothetical case histories and their implications. Against this same proverb, but to a different point, Jeremiah declared the hope of a new covenant (Jer 31:27-34). Jeremiah insisted the judgment reflected in the proverb did not exhaust God's plan for Judah. True, he would judge her, but he would surely restore her as well.

Yahweh addressed the intergenerational moral consequences issue with contrasting hypothetical scenarios. First he presented a righteous person who did righteous deeds (18:5), defining him first by specific sinful behaviors he does not engage in (18:6-7a) and by righteous behaviors he does (18:7b-9). The behaviors confirm the man's righteousness and lead to the promise of life (18:9).

The second case study, in parallel contrast to the first, supposes the righteous man begets a murderous thief as a son (18:10-11). As with the man, the son's wickedness is particularized both by what he does and does not do. This son does none of his father's righteous deeds (18:10b), but he does do the wickedness his father eschewed and much more (18:11-13a). The sinful character of such a one stands confirmed with the judgment that this sinner "must die" with "full blame" (18:13).

In the third case study (18:14-18), yet another intergenerational reversal is hypothesized. The wicked son of the righteous man begets in turn a righteous son! The proverb is now explicitly denied, for, although the "father will die for his many sins" (18:18), this righteous son will "surely live" (18:17).

Ezekiel anticipated the surprise, if not outrage, of his listeners and readers at such a scenario (18:19). As noted above, ancient Israelite tradition, while emphasizing Yahweh's lavish mercy, claimed a generation's sin held consequences for three and four following generations (Exod 34:6-7). And clan solidarity spread consequences of a person's sin over the entire clan or family, as in the case of Achan, whose children perished with him in judgment (Josh 7:16-26). Thus, several different streams of cultural influence would have led Ezekiel's hearers to side with the proverb at issue. Against this, Ezekiel denied that this righteous son of the wicked one should die (18:19). He repeats the rule of life cited at the outset (18:4 and 18:20). The bracketing rhetorical device (inclusio) emphasizes the rule: "The person who sins is the one who will die." Finally, he expounds the rule, claiming that parents and children are not punished for each other's sins (18:20) and that righteous persons and sinners will be rewarded or punished for their own behavior.

Yahweh pushed the case studies another step, moving from *inter*generational connections for reward or punishment to *intra*generational situations (18:21-29). He propounds what one might call dynamic individual moral accountability—dynamic in the sense that persons are not locked into certain destinies either by their parents' behaviors or their own personal record. So if righteous persons turn away from their righteous ways and adopt wicked behavior, such persons will die for their sins (18:24, 26). However, wicked persons will live if they turn away from their wickedness and live exhibiting righteous deeds (18:28).

But Ezekiel's listeners and readers have imbibed the theology of the proverb and its tradition so rigidly that they accuse Yahweh of injustice in his rule that the person who sins is the one who will die and not another—specifically in the case studies of dynamic individual moral responsibility (18:25, 29). Yahweh's response is that the rebellious house's notion of intergenerational moral consequences is the unjust option (18:29). On one level the rule and the case studies represent a revision of earlier covenantal revelation and history writing by denying the third and fourth generation consequences of sin, at least as the congregation was construing it. Yahweh here plainly denies that intergenerational connection (18:17-20), at least if it is separated from the awareness that persons die for their own sin, not another's (18:4, 20, 24, 26), no matter what intergenerational connections there may be. It is also possible that Ezekiel's emphasis could be used to question the sort of clan discipline seen in the case of Achan (Josh 7:22-26), though Ezekiel does not pursue such possibilities. The conclusion Yahweh draws in 18:30 shows that the congregation's *use* of earlier revelation and wisdom to deny their own accountability is Yahweh's major concern in the oracle. No matter what the repercussions of intergenerational connections, and there are many, each generation stands before God judged on its own merits. None can use an earlier generation's behaviors as an excuse for their own sin, and none need conclude that their destiny is fixed and all hope of change and redemption is lost.

The conclusion Yahweh draws uses few words but carries huge theological freight along several lines. First, he directly and plainly applies the rule of dynamic personal responsibility to the people of Israel, making explicit the point implicit all along: Yahweh will judge each Israelite for his or her own actions (18:30). No confusion on Yahweh's part or hiding in tradition on their part will save sinners among them. The rule Yahweh follows applies both corporately and individually. Then follows an open invitation for Israel to turn away from their wicked deeds, and, by inference from the case studies considered, to turn to live by the law of the Lord (18:30-31). No impediment can be raised, either in their own lives or in some alleged determination by prior generations that need prevent this redirection of their lives. Although the focus throughout the oracle to this point has been on human behavior, Yahweh here addresses their rebellious hearts, from which flow their sinful deeds. Without specifying how it would happen, Yahweh directs Israel to put away her rebellion—all of it—and find a new heart and new spirit (18:31). Earlier Yahweh claimed that he himself would provide Israel with a new heart and spirit in his restoration of them after judgment (11:19-20). Perhaps they were invited at that moment to live in that anticipated reality. A rhetorical question underscores and supports acceptance of the opportunity before them: "For why should you die, O people of Israel?" (18:31).

Finally, Yahweh urges their repentance by revealing his own passionate desire in this matter. Yahweh's desire was implicit in the warnings and invitations already recorded in the book, but had yet to be put into words. Earlier, Yahweh forcefully laid out his desire for persons to live, not die (18:23). First a probing question: "Do you think that I like to see wicked people die?" Then a direct denial: "Of course not!" Finally, there is a clear statement of his divine preference: "I want them to turn from their wicked ways and live" (18:23). After this the oracle ends, where we see Yahweh directly addressing his desire to the people: "I don't want *you* to die" [emphasis added]. The two passages are tied together by the word formula, "says the

Sovereign LORD" (18:30 and 32). The chapter ends with a two-word (in Hebrew), climactic plea: "Turn back and live!" Yahweh put the crucial repentance and the consequent life both in hortatory form. Here is what Yahweh really wants!

Throughout the chapter human behavior plays a critical role. In the three case studies, the righteous and the wicked are defined by specific sets of behavior. On the one hand, the person "*is* righteous and *does* what is just and right" (18:5, emphasis added; cf. 18:14ff). The behaviors done and refrained from all come from select historic Torah (variously called "decrees," "regulations," and "what is just and right" in this setting, 18:9, 17, 21, 27) and from other writings (cf. Pss 5:2-7 [3-8]; 24:3-6; Isa 33:14-16). They did not come from a single set of laws or wisdom or other ethical instruction. Their selection, one suspects, is determined by the setting being addressed here in the case studies. The hypothetical persons are not known as righteous or wicked because of a particular doctrinal confession or claim to believe Yahweh. On the one hand, Yahweh clearly cares about the faith and inner disposition of persons—their repentant stance, their rebellious heart, and their new heart and spirit (18:30-31). But in this chapter, on the other hand, destiny hinges and character is defined by one's life habits and behaviors. The one who does right *is* righteous; the one who does wicked deeds *is* wicked.

Scripture nowhere sets aside this theological insight. Sensitivities about "works righteousness" should not blind us to Ezekiel's assumption that behavioral patterns do in the end reveal character. We know about hypocrites and moral frauds who are not what they appear to be; but they are the exceptions that prove Ezekiel's rule. And we know also that *earning* life (or death!) is not the calculus of Ezekiel's treatise or of Scripture elsewhere. One cannot keep God's Torah with sufficient rigor or perfection to "deserve" or "earn" life. "Earning" or "deserving" salvation is not on the table. Instead, persons who do righteous deeds are righteous in Ezekiel's understanding, and these persons live. Persons who do wicked deeds are wicked, and they, not their parents or their children, die. The New Testament retains the claim that God judges human beings by what they do, not what they profess (e.g., Matt 25:31-46; Rom 2:6-10), with the presumption that by grace people can actually be righteous, and others, by rejecting divine grace, can be rebels.

◆ 5. Lamentation riddles: the lioness and the vine (19:1-14)

"Sing this funeral song for the princes of Israel:

2 "What is your mother?
A lioness among lions!
She lay down among the young lions
and reared her cubs.
3 She raised one of her cubs
to become a strong young lion.
He learned to hunt and devour prey,
and he became a man-eater.
4 Then the nations heard about him,
and he was trapped in their pit.
They led him away with hooks
to the land of Egypt.

5 "When the lioness saw
that her hopes for him were gone,
she took another of her cubs
and taught him to be a strong young lion.
6 He prowled among the other lions
and stood out among them in his strength.

He learned to hunt and devour prey,
and he, too, became a man-eater.
7 He demolished fortresses*
and destroyed their towns and cities.
Their farms were desolated,
and their crops were destroyed.
The land and its people trembled
in fear
when they heard him roar.
8 Then the armies of the nations
attacked him,
surrounding him from every
direction.
They threw a net over him
and captured him in their pit.
9 With hooks, they dragged him into
a cage
and brought him before the king
of Babylon.
They held him in captivity,
so his voice could never again
be heard
on the mountains of Israel.

10 "Your mother was like a vine
planted by the water's edge.
It had lush, green foliage
because of the abundant water.
11 Its branches became strong—
strong enough to be a ruler's
scepter.
It grew very tall,
towering above all others.
It stood out because of its height
and its many lush branches.
12 But the vine was uprooted in fury
and thrown down to the ground.
The desert wind dried up its fruit
and tore off its strong branches,
so that it withered
and was destroyed by fire.
13 Now the vine is transplanted to
the wilderness,
where the ground is hard and dry.
14 A fire has burst out from its branches
and devoured its fruit.
Its remaining limbs are not
strong enough to be a ruler's
scepter.

"This is a funeral song, and it will be used in a funeral."

19:7 As in Greek version; Hebrew reads *He knew widows.*

NOTES

19:7 *He demolished fortresses.* This follows the Greek version in part. MT reads "he knew widows." The Hebrew makes fine sense separated from its immediate context, but makes little sense in this context. Block tries to salvage the Hebrew by translating "he consorted with his widows" (1997:596 and notes 29 and 30 for full discussion and bibliography). Though this is technically possible, it seems little better than the interpretation it replaces. It appears the text may have become garbled by two consonantal confusions. The LXX suggests a text with *yr'* (possibly parsed as one of three roots: [TH7462/7489/7489A, ZH8286/8317/8318]) instead of *yada'* [TH3045, ZH3359] (to know), that is, "he demolished" rather than "he knew." This is likely, based on the common confusion of the consonants *r* and *d* in Hebrew and in the Targum. Context (cities being destroyed) suggests one should read *'rmnwt* [TH759, ZH810] (fortresses) for *'lmnwt* [TH490, ZH530] (widows), taking *'lmnwt* as a by-form of *'rmnwt,* by an attested substitution of *r* for *l* (HALOT 1.58, 89; again with the Targum).

19:10 *like a vine planted.* MT reads "like the vine in your blood," which seems unlikely, though Vulgate, KJV, and NKJV ("in your blood/bloodline") follow it. The LXX translated this as "like a vine, like a blossom on a pomegranate," but conflates the text while trying to deal with "in your blood." Some Hebrew mss have "like a vine in your vineyard" (so NASB, NIV, RSV, NRSV, ESV). The most probable solution yet proposed (because of its simplicity and ties to the paragraph's vocabulary) involves redivision of the consonantal text, reading "like a grapevine full of tendrils" (Brewer, cited and adopted by Allen 1994:284). Because the sense of the line seems clear without this word, the NLT, along with the NAB and REB, has elected not to choose a solution until better evidence for translation is available.

19:14 ***and it will be used in a funeral.*** The future tense in the MT is difficult, though this is followed by LXX, NIV, and NLT. I think it is better (with RSV, NJPS, NEB) to translate this line using the past perfect tense: "and has become a lamentation" (NASB). This means that the events Ezekiel prophesied in his lament have occurred and are memorialized in the very *qinah* [TH7015, ZH7806] that predicted them. Some translate with the present tense, thereby making a similar point: "it is used as a lamentation" (NRSV, NAB).

COMMENTARY

Chapter 19 contains two stanzas of a single composition (19:2-9 and 10-14) about the final kings of Judah (i.e., the "princes of Israel," 19:1). Although not so designated, the poem is an allegory (*mashal* [TH4912, ZH5442]) and a riddle (*khidah* [TH2420, ZH2648]), as was chapter 17. Ezekiel, however, calls attention to the poem's genre—it is a funeral song, a dirge (*qinah* [TH7015, ZH7806]; 19:1, 14), whose form itself says, "Judah and its kings are dead!" Not only so, but Ezekiel turns the lament on its head, condemning, not eulogizing, the (about to be) departed. Furthermore, the poem (especially the first half) uses vocabulary from the traditional blessing of Judah (Gen 49:8-12), and then it reverses that blessing in this elegy.

In both stanzas, each starting with mention of "your (masc. sg.) mother," Ezekiel addresses a single person, most likely Zedekiah, the last Davidic king of Judah (597–587 BC). Some have taken the mother in both stanzas to be Hamutal, queen mother of Jehoahaz and Zedekiah (2 Kgs 23:30-31; 24:17-18; Jer 52:1). Note of her (otherwise undocumented) influence at the royal court and in "king making" would then be one of the poem's accents. Others have objected, citing lack of evidence and trivialization of the point of the dramatic lament. They suggest the mother who produces these tragic royal figures must be either Judah itself, or Jerusalem (Allen 1994:287; Blenkinsopp 1990:84; Greenberg 1983:357).

There is general agreement that the first cub (19:3-4) must be Jehoahaz, son of Josiah by Hamutal. The people of the land had made him king when Pharaoh Neco II killed Josiah at Megiddo. Neco had been en route to join the Assyrians against Babylon at Carchemish in north Syria (2 Kgs 23:29-30). Returning from defeat in the north, Neco deposed Jehoahaz after a three-month reign and installed his half-brother Jehoiakim in his place. Neco took Jehoahaz to Egypt where he died (2 Kgs 23:34).

The identification with Jehoahaz, secure because of the reference in 19:4 to being "led . . . away with hooks to the land of Egypt," also shows something of the stereotypical nature of the referents in this lament and its transcendence of strict historical description for the sake of dramatic portrayal. Jehoahaz could have hardly built a reputation as a "man-eating lion" in just three months on the throne. His successors Jehoiakim and Zedekiah would be more likely candidates for rapacious reputations, but neither died in Egypt. The point, instead, made also by repetition (19:6-7), appears to be the violent, power-hungry character of the last kings of Judah, who brought judgment upon themselves.

The second lion could be Jehoiakim, Jehoiachin, or Zedekiah. All three may have been taken to Babylon (19:9), though the time and place of Jehoiakim's death is debated (2 Kgs 24:6; 2 Chr 36:6). Jehoiachin, like Jehoahaz, reigned only three months. All the sources agree in indicting Zedekiah and placing blame for the collapse of Judah and the Davidic throne squarely on his shoulders. His capture and deportation by Nebuchadnezzar, together with his death in Babylon, are dramatically recalled (2 Kgs 24:20–25:7). Zedekiah is the most likely candidate here.

The appearance of the vine metaphor in 19:10-14 seems a bit abrupt, until one recalls that genre (*qinah* [TH7015, ZH7806], "lament," cf. 19:1, 14) and theme (indictment of Judah's last kings), and not metaphorical medium (beast or vine), give the segment coherence. The vine stanza emphasizes also the strength and influence of the king—reflecting not so much geopolitical realities as the royal pretensions of Judah's final kings. Jehoiakim's attempts at political influence proved short-lived and disastrous! Neither Jehoiachin nor Zedekiah wielded strong influence. Lamentably their destructive impact on kingship in Judah and on the nation itself (19:12-14) overshadowed any appearance of greatness they may have suggested early on. The destruction of kingship in Judah must be laid squarely at the feet of the last kings themselves. Not only the vine but also the fruit was burned by the fire (19:14); thus, no one remained with sufficient strength of will or character to be king. Consequently, the kingdom ended in disgrace (19:12). The "desert wind" as God's instrument conveys the intervening judgment of God (Allen 1994:290; cf. 17:10).

Most striking, we get a concluding note by the writer that the lament Ezekiel composed prior to the fall of Jerusalem and the removal of Zedekiah actually came to be used as a lament (19:14b). As the NJPS reads: "it has become a [familiar] dirge." The events actually transpired and were remembered with Ezekiel's words! The future events announced in the *qinah* [TH7015, ZH7806] with it being as certain as if it happened in the past (the so-called prophetic perfect) now actually were past. God had spoken and God had acted! Not even the king or the Davidic dynasty could stand above the will of God.

◆ E. The Lord Draws His Sword (20:1–24:27)

1. The Lord rejects an inquiry from the elders of Israel (20:1-44)

**On August 14,* during the seventh year of
King Jehoiachin's captivity, some of the
leaders of Israel came to request a mes-
sage from the LORD. They sat down in
front of me to wait for his reply. [2]Then
this message came to me from the LORD:
[3]"Son of man, tell the leaders of Israel,
'This is what the Sovereign LORD says: How
dare you come to ask me for a message?
As surely as I live, says the Sovereign LORD,
I will tell you nothing!'**

**[4]"Son of man, bring charges against
them and condemn them. Make them re-
alize how detestable the sins of their
ancestors really were. [5]Give them this
message from the Sovereign LORD: When
I chose Israel—when I revealed myself to
the descendants of Jacob in Egypt—I took
a solemn oath that I, the LORD, would be
their God. [6]I took a solemn oath that day
that I would bring them out of Egypt to a
land I had discovered and explored for
them—a good land, a land flowing with
milk and honey, the best of all lands any-
where. [7]Then I said to them, 'Each of you,
get rid of the vile images you are so
obsessed with. Do not defile yourselves
with the idols* of Egypt, for I am the LORD
your God.'**

**[8]"But they rebelled against me and
would not listen. They did not get rid of
the vile images they were obsessed with,
or forsake the idols of Egypt. Then I
threatened to pour out my fury on them
to satisfy my anger while they were still
in Egypt. [9]But I didn't do it, for I acted to**

protect the honor of my name. I would not allow shame to be brought on my name among the surrounding nations who saw me reveal myself by bringing the Israelites out of Egypt. 10So I brought them out of Egypt and led them into the wilderness. 11There I gave them my decrees and regulations so they could find life by keeping them. 12And I gave them my Sabbath days of rest as a sign between them and me. It was to remind them that I am the LORD, who had set them apart to be holy.

13"But the people of Israel rebelled against me, and they refused to obey my decrees there in the wilderness. They wouldn't obey my regulations even though obedience would have given them life. They also violated my Sabbath days. So I threatened to pour out my fury on them, and I made plans to utterly consume them in the wilderness. 14But again I held back in order to protect the honor of my name before the nations who had seen my power in bringing Israel out of Egypt. 15But I took a solemn oath against them in the wilderness. I swore I would not bring them into the land I had given them, a land flowing with milk and honey, the most beautiful place on earth. 16For they had rejected my regulations, refused to follow my decrees, and violated my Sabbath days. Their hearts were given to their idols. 17Nevertheless, I took pity on them and held back from destroying them in the wilderness.

18"Then I warned their children not to follow in their parents' footsteps, defiling themselves with their idols. 19'I am the LORD your God,' I told them. 'Follow my decrees, pay attention to my regulations, 20and keep my Sabbath days holy, for they are a sign to remind you that I am the LORD your God.'

21"But their children, too, rebelled against me. They refused to keep my decrees and follow my regulations, even though obedience would have given them life. And they also violated my Sabbath days. So again I threatened to pour out my fury on them in the wilderness. 22Nevertheless, I withdrew my judgment against them to protect the honor of my name before the nations that had seen my power in bringing them out of Egypt. 23But I took a solemn oath against them in the wilderness. I swore I would scatter them among all the nations 24because they did not obey my regulations. They scorned my decrees by violating my Sabbath days and longing for the idols of their ancestors. 25I gave them over to worthless decrees and regulations that would not lead to life. 26I let them pollute themselves* with the very gifts I had given them, and I allowed them to give their firstborn children as offerings to their gods—so I might devastate them and remind them that I alone am the LORD.

27"Therefore, son of man, give the people of Israel this message from the Sovereign LORD: Your ancestors continued to blaspheme and betray me, 28for when I brought them into the land I had promised them, they offered sacrifices on every high hill and under every green tree they saw! They roused my fury as they offered up sacrifices to their gods. They brought their perfumes and incense and poured out their liquid offerings to them. 29I said to them, 'What is this high place where you are going?' (This kind of pagan shrine has been called Bamah—'high place'—ever since.)

30"Therefore, give the people of Israel this message from the Sovereign LORD: Do you plan to pollute yourselves just as your ancestors did? Do you intend to keep prostituting yourselves by worshiping vile images? 31For when you offer gifts to them and give your little children to be burned as sacrifices,* you continue to pollute yourselves with idols to this day. Should I allow you to ask for a message from me, O people of Israel? As surely as I live, says the Sovereign LORD, I will tell you nothing.

32"You say, 'We want to be like the nations all around us, who serve idols of wood and stone.' But what you have in mind will never happen. 33As surely as I live, says the

Sovereign LORD, I will rule over you with an
iron fist in great anger and with awesome
power. 34And in anger I will reach out with
my strong hand and powerful arm, and I
will bring you back* from the lands where
you are scattered. 35I will bring you into the
wilderness of the nations, and there I will
judge you face to face. 36I will judge you
there just as I did your ancestors in the
wilderness after bringing them out of
Egypt, says the Sovereign LORD. 37I will ex-
amine you carefully and hold you to the
terms of the covenant. 38I will purge you of
all those who rebel and revolt against me.
I will bring them out of the countries where
they are in exile, but they will never enter
the land of Israel. Then you will know that
I am the LORD.

39"As for you, O people of Israel, this is
what the Sovereign LORD says: Go right
ahead and worship your idols, but sooner
or later you will obey me and will stop
bringing shame on my holy name by wor-
shiping idols. 40For on my holy mountain,
the great mountain of Israel, says the Sov-
ereign LORD, the people of Israel will
someday worship me, and I will accept
them. There I will require that you bring
me all your offerings and choice gifts and
sacrifices. 41When I bring you home from
exile, you will be like a pleasing sacrifice
to me. And I will display my holiness
through you as all the nations watch.
42Then when I have brought you home to
the land I promised with a solemn oath to
give to your ancestors, you will know that
I am the LORD. 43You will look back on all
the ways you defiled yourselves and will
hate yourselves because of the evil you
have done. 44You will know that I am the
LORD, O people of Israel, when I have hon-
ored my name by treating you mercifully
in spite of your wickedness. I, the Sover-
eign LORD, have spoken!"

20:1 Hebrew *In the fifth month, on the tenth day,* of the ancient Hebrew lunar calendar. This day was August 14, 591 B.C.; also see note on 1:1. **20:7** The Hebrew term (literally *round things*) probably alludes to dung; also in 20:8, 16, 18, 24, 31, 39. **20:25-26** Or *I gave them worthless decrees and regulations. . . . I polluted them.* **20:31** Or *and make your little children pass through the fire.* **20:34** Greek version reads *I will welcome you.* Compare 2 Cor 6:17.

NOTES

20:1–24:27 This section of Ezekiel, like the others, is structured coherently. Four of the five major segments focus mainly on the end—judgment (20:1-44; 22:1-31; 23:1-49; 24:1-27). One segment identifies the means—the sword of the Lord, i.e., Babylon (20:45–21:32 [21:1-37]). Rhetorically and logically, 24:1-27 provides the climax for both the section (20:1–24:27) and the division (3:16–24:27). The ominous dated announcement of the launch of Nebuchadnezzar's siege of Jerusalem (24:1-6), set beside the tragic silence in the "unmourned" death of Ezekiel's wife (24:15-27), presents climactic drama, especially in a section so full of lamentation over various aspects of the demise of Jerusalem. Ezekiel's repeated warnings to Jerusalem, accentuated in this unit, find powerful, if not complete, substantiation in the word of Babylon's decisive move against the city.

Under this logical coherence, select vocabulary and expressions recur, knitting the section together: *shapat* [TH8199, ZH9149], "judge, condemn" (12 of 29 occurrences in the book occur in 20:1–24:27: 20:4, 35-36; 21:30 [35]; 22:2; 23:24 [cf. "punishment"], 36 [cf. "accuse"], 45; 24:14); *mishpat* [TH4941, ZH5477], "regulation, justice, punishment" (these four chapters contain 14 of 43 occurrences in the book: 20:11, 13, 16, 18-19, 21, 24-25; 21:27 [32]; 22:29; 23:24, 45); *'ir* [TH5892, ZH6551], "city" (21:19 [24]; 22:2-3; 24:6, 9); *'ir haddamim* [TH1818, ZH1947], "violent/murderous city" (only 22:2 and 24:6, 9 in MT); *shapak* [TH8210, ZH9161], "pour out" (cf. NLT, "sheds, spill"; 20:8, 13, 21, 28, 33-34, 36; 21:22 [27]; 22:3-4, 6, 9, 12 [cf. MT], 22, 27; 23:8, 45 [cf. KJV]; 24:7); *shapak za'am,* "pour out fury" (21:31 [36]; 22:31; elsewhere in MT only at Ps 69:24 [25]; Zeph 3:8); *zimmah* [TH2154, ZH2365] (cf. NLT, "obscene, defile, lewdness"; 11 of 14 occurrences in the book: 22:9, 11; 23:21, 27, 29,

35, 44, 48, 49; 24:13); *lehakkoth kap* [TH5221/3709, ZH5782/4090], "to clap the hands" (21:14 [19], 17 [22]; 22:13; elsewhere in Ezekiel only at 6:11); *'esh* [TH784, ZH836], "fire" (20:31, 47 [21:3]; 21:31-32 [36-37]; 22:20-21, 31; 24:10, 12); *Babel* [TH894, ZH951], "Babylon" (21:19 [24], 21 [26]; 23:15, 17, 23; 24:2); *shem* [TH8034, ZH9005], "name" (20:9, 14, 22, 29, 39, 44; 22:5; 23:4, 10; 24:2); *shabbath* [TH7676, ZH8701], "Sabbath" (20:12-13, 16, 20-21, 24; 22:8, 26; 23:38), *shabath* [TH7673, ZH8697], "stop, rest, end" (23:27, 48); and *'ishah* [TH802, ZH851], "woman, wife" (22:11; 23:2, 10, 44 [cf. KJV], 48; 24:18).

20:4 ***Son of man, bring charges against them and condemn them.*** These are interrogatives in Hebrew, perhaps to be understood rhetorically: "Will you judge them, mortal, will you judge them?" (NRSV; similarly RSV, NASB, NIV). The NLT has taken the interrogative particle to indicate "an indignant affirmation," as Block puts it (1997:618; also HALOT 1.236).

20:7 ***idols.*** Heb., *gillulim* [TH1544, ZH1658] (lit., "round things") probably alludes to dung (also in 20:8, 16, 18, 24, 31, 39). See note on 5:9 for Ezekiel's vocabulary of idolatry.

20:25-26 ***I gave them over to worthless decrees and regulations. . . . I let them pollute themselves.*** Or, "I gave them worthless decrees and regulations. . . . I polluted them" (NLT mg). Here, Ezekiel writes perhaps the most difficult lines in the book. The MT, LXX, Vulgate, the KJV and revisions of it, NJPS, and NAB all have God claiming that *he* gave these rebels "bad laws" that would not sustain life, that *he* polluted them through child sacrifice (cf. also NASB). The Targum has the people following "their own stupid inclinations," with God giving them over to their enemies, because of their refusal to obey his word or listen to his prophets (cited by Block 1997:638). The NIV and NLT have God acting not directly in the giving of bad laws, but indirectly. Thus NLT reads, "I *gave them over* to worthless decrees. . . . I *let them* pollute themselves. . . . I *allowed them* to give their firstborn children as offerings to their gods." Block lists seven major proposals for rendering this passage (1997:638-639, notes 130-137). His own proposal is that the "bad laws" represent something of an "anti-gift" in contrast to 20:10-11. As such, they press a favorite theme in Ezekiel: "Yahweh's indisputable authority 'to determine and interpret the course of human history'" (1997:639-640, following Ellen Davis 1989:114-116). With Davis, Block considers translations like that in the NLT among unsuccessful attempts to "domesticate" Ezekiel. Block then seeks to separate the "bad laws" God gave from the Mosaic covenant and stresses Ezekiel's rhetorical strategy, which does not necessarily entail an objective history. Instead, Ezekiel aimed to convince the exiles that they, like their ancestors, were rebels facing the warranted wrath of God (1997:640). Part of Yahweh's strategy is precisely the logical nonconformity of the claims. "Although Israel must carry the responsibility for its own fate, Yahweh retains full authority to determine its destiny, and to achieve that goal by whatever means he chooses" (1997:640-641).

Block's interpretation relies heavily on a particular understanding of God's sovereignty. Admittedly, if sovereignty were going to weigh significantly in interpreting any biblical writer, it would surely be Ezekiel. Even so, there may be self-imposed moral limits to God's sovereignty, limits that God himself cannot breach without calling his character (as he himself has revealed it) into question.

Another part of Block's exposition points in a better direction, I believe: Acts God claims to be doing directly are commonly lived out historically by some *intermediate* action in biblical revelation. Block points this out, but does not really put much weight here. In these situations, a theologically uninformed observer would not attribute the actions to God, because God acts through the actions of others whom he "allows" to carry out his will. In the immediate context, Babylon would actually wield the sword that Yahweh claimed to have drawn (21:1-5, 18-23). The NLT and NIV go this direction and catch the rhetorical intent of Ezekiel. This is not "domestication"; it's good interpretation.

The idea "I gave them over," however, cannot rest on the Heb., *beha'abir* [TH5674, ZH6296] (20:26; "by passing over"), as "giving over," because this verb, as a technical term, is part of a formula that refers to the enactment of child sacrifice (cf. 20:31 along with Lev 18:21; Deut 18:10; 2 Kgs 16:3; Jer 32:35). Instead, the interpretation in this translation relies on the rhetoric of Ezekiel's theology. Paul states explicitly in Rom 1:24-28 the theology that Ezekiel 20:25-26 implicitly conveys.

Or, quite possibly perhaps we are dealing here with Ezekiel's own awareness of texts or traditions in Torah that appear, divorced from context, to ask for or at least allow sacrifice of the firstborn (Exod 13:2, 15 and 22:29, qualified and revised in Exod 13:13, 15e, and other texts referring to the redemption of the firstborn male, e.g., Num 3:11-13; 8:17-18; 18:15). In that case, Ezekiel writes assuming his audience's proof texting in support of their abominable behavior. God here accuses Israel of trying to legitimize its own perversion by appeal to early laws long since qualified under his inspiration (Darr 2001:1284; Eichrodt 1970:271-272).

20:31 ***give your little children to be burned as sacrifices.*** Or "and make your little children pass through the fire." See Ackerman (1992:117-142) for treatment of the slaughter of children in the ancient Near East, as well as in certain streams of Yahweh worship.

COMMENTARY

Dates bracket chapters 20–24, placing the text between August 591 and January 588. These years follow on the heels of a renewed Egyptian presence in Palestine in the person of Psammeticus II (595–591) and, during Nebuchadnezzar's siege of Jerusalem, Hophra (aka Apries; 591–570). These stirrings of false hope may have prompted the desire on the part of the exiles to get Yahweh's word on the prospects for independence or on the probable length of the exile. Hence, they came to Ezekiel "inquiring" of Yahweh's word (20:1). As seen in 17:7-10, Yahweh's message rejected hopes for deliverance from the Babylonian army because he himself had sent it.

The prophet's vocation could include discerning God's will for persons who came seeking it. This was true in Israel and also among her neighbors, as attested in cultures from Egypt in the west to Mari and Sippur in the east, from the early second millennium BC on up through Neo-Assyrian times and beyond (Begg 1992; Huffmon 1976; cf. ANET 441-451). Prophets in Israel were known for their participation in the divine council (Jer 23:16-22) and their intercessory prayer. In Amos's day, his northern protagonist, Amaziah, considered prophecy a way of making a living (Amos 7:12). False prophets were known to have their "price" for rendering a positive message (Mic 3:5-6). We are not well-informed on general expectations regarding remuneration for prophetic "services" in Israel or elsewhere.

Ezekiel had already castigated such prophets for making up their own messages instead of speaking God's words (13:1-7). The technical language for this process of "getting a message" appears in the opening lines of this chapter. The one seeking the word from Yahweh was said literally to be "inquiring of Yahweh," whereas Yahweh was said to be "allowing himself to be inquired of" (20:1, 3). The NLT uncovers the dynamics of this process in translating "to request a message from the LORD" (20:1) and then having the Lord "tell you [something]" (20:3).

But Yahweh altered the whole equation for this inquiry process. Covenant fidelity, not money, community standing, or simple demand, was the prerequisite for discerning Yahweh's will. The leaders of Israel could not pay Ezekiel or Yahweh enough to allow them access to Yahweh's word simply upon request, especially given their blatant disregard for what they already knew of the will of God. "How dare you come to ask me for a message?" Yahweh challenges them (20:3). These leaders, their children back in Judah, and their ancestors had all been rebels, as God claimed at the outset of Ezekiel's mission (2:3-8) and underscores again in 20:8, 13, 21. They will get no answer from him (20:3). Clearly, God's "I will tell you nothing" does not mean he will refuse to speak to them. The entire segment is packed with Yahweh's speaking to his people. Instead, he apparently means that he will not speak at their whim. He will not respond to persons who are already agnostic about the validity of Ezekiel's message (20:49). Instead, God will speak through Ezekiel whatever *he*, Yahweh, judges appropriate for them to hear.

Yahweh instructed Ezekiel to arraign these inquirers and convince them "how detestable the sins of their ancestors really were" (20:4). By implication, this conviction would also validate judgment being linked to previous generations; it would also indict the present generation engaged in the same abominations. In a repetitive cadence, as though in stanzas, Yahweh traces Israel's rebellion (20:8, 13) from the pre-Exodus Israelites (20:5-12), to those in the wilderness (20:13-17), to the second generation who entered the Promised Land (20:18-26), to those in the land (20:27-29), and then in a leap to the present generation and its entanglement in the very same sins (20:30-31).

The arraignment summarizes the various indictments as "detestable sins" (lit., "abominations," *to'aboth* [TH8441, ZH9359], 20:4), terminology associated with the nations whose behaviors Yahweh consistently rejected (e.g., Lev 18:27; Deut 12:31; 18:12; 20:18; 1 Kgs 14:24; 2 Kgs 16:3). The stanzas then particularize these detestable sins as defilement with idols (20:7, 8, 18, 24, 26, 31), such as sacrifice and worship at high places (20:26-28), rejection of the regulations and decrees Yahweh had given (20:11, 13, 19, 21, 24; cf. 20:25), and dishonoring Yahweh's Sabbaths, which were given as a sign of their unique covenant relationship with him, the mark of their holiness (20:12-13, 20-24).

Stanza by stanza these detestable behaviors prompt Yahweh to contemplate judgment, and even the destruction of his people (20:8, 13, 15, 21), but in his mercy, he relents and withholds judgment (20:9-10, 14, 17, 22). The repetitions provide a litany of grace. But the accent falls on Yahweh's mercy as an expression of his sovereign concern for his own reputation among the nations (20:9, 14, 22). He acts for the sake of his "name," protecting the legacy of power and gracious liberation he established when he rescued his people from bondage in Egypt.

Three oracles (20:27-44) follow the arraignment (20:1-26). All three are introduced by the "message formula" *koh 'amar* [TH3541/559, ZH3907/606] *'adonay yhwh*: "This is what the Sovereign LORD says" (20:27, 30, 39), perhaps tying them to the arraignment that also opens with this rubric (20:3, 5). All three are addressed to "the people of Israel." Two oracles (20:27-29 and 30-38) proceed causally from the indictments rehearsed in 20:1-26. First, on the basis of the preceding arraignment of Israel from its earliest days, Yahweh issues a reminder that the pagan shrines (lit., "high places") still scattered around the country have a trail of blasphemy and betrayal running back to pagan roots. In effect, Yahweh asks, "What place have these detestable practices in my people's life?" (20:27-29).

Then, in the second oracle (20:30-38), Yahweh asks, perhaps rhetorically, about Israel's plans. He implies that their plans include no repentance or change from the polluting worship of their past (20:30-31). Yahweh shuts the door on their request for a message from him, repeating in 20:31 his words in 20:3: "I will tell you nothing!" This pronouncement brings the reader back to the opening verses of the segment and may mean that the oracle ends here, with the inclusio (20:3 and 31) bracketing it. The following verses (20:32-38), however, appear to involve a response by Israel dismissing the indictments of 20:4-31, linking it closely to those words.

In language reminiscent of Israel's yen for a king centuries earlier, Yahweh reports the exiles now want to "be like the nations all around us" with regard to the worship of idols (20:32; cf. 1 Sam 8:5, 19). But he will not let that happen! The historic covenant placed him in the position of the Great King over Israel. He would now exercise that rule by judging those with such desires, no matter how scattered they may be. He would gather them "into the wilderness of the nations" and judge them there as he had their "ancestors in the wilderness" after the Exodus. The puzzling phrase, "wilderness of the nations" (20:35), probably describes not an actual place but a state of being under the judgment of God, judgment such as can only happen in the desert—conjuring memories of the historic years in the wilderness. Thus in Ezekiel's day, the "wilderness" was wherever God placed his people (Eichrodt 1970:279).

The third oracle (20:39-44) foresees a day when God's people will worship him obediently on his holy mount. In the process, Ezekiel touches once more on several themes of the larger unit. Addressed are the topics of idol worship and its impact on Yahweh's reputation (20:39), undivided devotion to Yahweh (20:40), Yahweh's initiative in bringing Israel to the land he promised their ancestors (20:42), and the exiles' awareness of their sin and of their sovereign Lord through the experience of mercifully being brought back to the land (20:43-44). In a strange redirection, however, the oracle, though hopeful, is sober and implicitly accusatory.

◆ 2. The Lord's sword drawn and polished (20:45–21:32 [21:1-37])

**45*Then this message came to me from the
LORD: 46"Son of man, turn and face the
south* and speak out against it; prophesy
against the brushlands of the Negev. 47Tell
the southern wilderness, 'This is what the
Sovereign LORD says: Hear the word of the
LORD! I will set you on fire, and every tree,
both green and dry, will be burned. The
terrible flames will not be quenched and
will scorch everything from south to
north. 48And everyone in the world will
see that I, the LORD, have set this fire. It
will not be put out.'"**

**49Then I said, "O Sovereign LORD, they are
saying of me, 'He only talks in riddles!'"**

CHAPTER 21

**1*Then this message came to me from the
LORD: 2"Son of man, turn and face Jerusalem and prophesy against Israel and her
sanctuaries. 3Tell her, 'This is what the
LORD says: I am your enemy, O Israel, and**

I am about to unsheath my sword to de-
stroy your people—the righteous and the
wicked alike. 4 Yes, I will cut off both the
righteous and the wicked! I will draw my
sword against everyone in the land from
south to north. 5 Everyone in the world will
know that I am the LORD. My sword is in
my hand, and it will not return to its
sheath until its work is finished.'

6 "Son of man, groan before the people!
Groan before them with bitter anguish and
a broken heart. 7 When they ask why you
are groaning, tell them, 'I groan because of
the terrifying news I have heard. When it
comes true, the boldest heart will melt
with fear; all strength will disappear. Every
spirit will faint; strong knees will become
as weak as water. And the Sovereign LORD
says: It is coming! It's on its way!'"

8 Then the LORD said to me, 9 "Son of
man, give the people this message from
the Lord:

"A sword, a sword
is being sharpened and polished.
10 It is sharpened for terrible slaughter
and polished to flash like
lightning!
Now will you laugh?
Those far stronger than you have
fallen beneath its power!*
11 Yes, the sword is now being sharpened
and polished;
it is being prepared for the
executioner.

12 "Son of man, cry out and wail;
pound your thighs in anguish,
for that sword will slaughter my
people and their leaders—
everyone will die!
13 It will put them all to the test.
What chance do they have?*
says the Sovereign LORD.

14 "Son of man, prophesy to them
and clap your hands.
Then take the sword and brandish it
twice,
even three times,
to symbolize the great massacre,
the great massacre facing them on
every side.
15 Let their hearts melt with terror,
for the sword glitters at every gate.
It flashes like lightning
and is polished for slaughter!
16 O sword, slash to the right,
then slash to the left,
wherever you will,
wherever you want.
17 I, too, will clap my hands,
and I will satisfy my fury.
I, the LORD, have spoken!"

18 Then this message came to me from the
LORD: 19 "Son of man, make a map and
trace two routes on it for the sword of
Babylon's king to follow. Put a signpost on
the road that comes out of Babylon where
the road forks into two—20 one road going
to Ammon and its capital, Rabbah, and
the other to Judah and fortified Jerusa-
lem. 21 The king of Babylon now stands at
the fork, uncertain whether to attack Je-
rusalem or Rabbah. He calls his magicians
to look for omens. They cast lots by shak-
ing arrows from the quiver. They inspect
the livers of animal sacrifices. 22 The omen
in his right hand says, 'Jerusalem!' With
battering rams his soldiers will go against
the gates, shouting for the kill. They will
put up siege towers and build ramps
against the walls. 23 The people of Jerusa-
lem will think it is a false omen, because
of their treaty with the Babylonians. But
the king of Babylon will remind the people
of their rebellion. Then he will attack and
capture them.

24 "Therefore, this is what the Sovereign
LORD says: Again and again you remind
me of your sin and your guilt. You don't
even try to hide it! In everything you do,
your sins are obvious for all to see. So now
the time of your punishment has come!

25 "O you corrupt and wicked prince of
Israel, your final day of reckoning is here!
26 This is what the Sovereign LORD says:

"Take off your jeweled crown,
for the old order changes.
Now the lowly will be exalted,

and the mighty will be brought
down.
27 Destruction! Destruction!
I will surely destroy the kingdom.
And it will not be restored until the
one appears
who has the right to judge it.
Then I will hand it over to him.

28"And now, son of man, prophesy concerning the Ammonites and their mockery. Give them this message from the Sovereign LORD:

"A sword, a sword
is drawn for your slaughter.
It is polished to destroy,
flashing like lightning!
29 Your prophets have given false visions,
and your fortune-tellers have
told lies.
The sword will fall on the necks
of the wicked
for whom the day of final
reckoning has come.

30 "Now return the sword to its sheath,
for in your own country,
the land of your birth,
I will pass judgment upon you.
31 I will pour out my fury on you
and blow on you with the fire
of my anger.
I will hand you over to cruel men
who are skilled in destruction.
32 You will be fuel for the fire,
and your blood will be spilled
in your own land.
You will be utterly wiped out,
your memory lost to history,
for I, the LORD, have spoken!"

20:45 Verses 20:45-49 are numbered 21:1-5 in Hebrew text. **20:46** Hebrew *toward Teman.* **21:1** Verses 21:1-32 are numbered 21:6-37 in Hebrew text. **21:10** The meaning of the Hebrew is uncertain. **21:13** The meaning of the Hebrew is uncertain.

NOTES

20:45–21:32 Verses 20:45-49 are numbered 21:1-5 in the MT and LXX; verses 21:1-32 are numbered 21:6-37 in MT and LXX. In the following notes and commentary the verse numerals for the Hebrew and Greek texts are given inside brackets.

21:13 [18] The meaning of the Hebrew is uncertain. Block translates, "For the testing [is over]. Now what? Even if the staff . . . ! It despises . . . it will not be!" and says the verse is "totally obscure" (1997:674 and notes 92-94).

21:14 [19] ***clap your hands.*** Block (1997:679) understands this sign-act as an expression of anger, as in 6:11. Citing Friebel (1999:712-716), Block notes a wide range of interpretation: "an expression of enthusiasm accompanying the sword song; a gesture involved in a sword dance; a gesture of victory; a magical act designed to enhance the effectiveness of the sword; an expression of scornful glee; a summons for a servant or the onslaught of battle; an echo of the sword's blows" (1997:679, note 131).

21:21-22 [26-27] ***to look for omens.*** These verses picture the Babylonian "magicians" (professional diviners, assumed but not actually mentioned in the Hebrew text) employing three of their numerous divination techniques. They used arrows strewn from a quiver to cast lots (i.e., belomancy), they read livers and entrails (i.e., hepetoscopy), and used some other method that put lots in Nebuchadnezzar's hands. (See ANEP, pictures 594 and 595 for model livers used to learn the art of "reading livers.") These methods of discerning the will of God, or similar techniques, were known also in Israel, and were increasingly forbidden for the people of God (cf. Deut 18:9-14; Judg 17:5; 18:14-20; 1 Sam 15:23; Zech 10:2; see also Meyers and Meyers 1993:185-190 for a helpful discussion of this complex issue.) Livers and other entrails from sacrifices were to be burned, not saved for divination (Lev 3:4; 4:8; 7:4; 8:16). Although divination played a part in Israel's religion from earliest times, its inferiority to divine revelation became increasingly clear to spiritual people.

21:23 [28] ***because of their treaty with the Babylonians.*** The Hebrew is cryptic: "oaths of oaths to them." The NLT's interpretation of 21:23-24 is reasonable. See (e.g.) the RSV and NASB for translations showing the difficulty of the Hebrew text. The LXX omits the phrase "oaths of oaths," probably through haplography.

COMMENTARY

The concluding paragraph of chapter 20 ends with the exiles' dismissal of Ezekiel with the condescending, "he only talks in riddles" (20:49). The lines are not really a riddle (like ch 17), but they pack in imagery about fire and plants (20:45-49 [21:1-5]) sufficient to draw the slander. God sets a fierce fire in the Negev, the brush land in the south of Palestine. The fire God kindles from south to north burns hot enough to devour bushes like tinder and trees both dry and green (i.e., everything). It will rage widespread with unstoppable destruction. The judgment, repeatedly delayed, is on its way! The whole world will know this is Yahweh's doing, just as they knew he had brought Israel out of Egypt (as emphasized earlier in 20:5, 9, 14).

The reader may puzzle over the connections of this Negev oracle to the surrounding text. Does it conclude the preceding or launch the following messages from Yahweh? Logically, it could underscore the announcements of judgment in 20:4-44. This emphasis on pervasive, unstoppable judgment could also introduce the judgment claims of chapter 21. Several formal indicators also tie the Negev oracle to the following material. First, the Masoretic Text numbers 20:45 as 21:1, signaling the Masoretes' inclusion of it with the following materials. Second, like 20:2, the verse carries the major revelation event formula: "Then this message came to me from the LORD" (20:45 [21:1]). Third, as in 21:2 [7], 20:46 [21:2] has Yahweh commanding the prophet to "turn and face" a direction or place. Perhaps the connection with the following materials is the certainty and irreversibility of God's judgment. The term "fire" (*'esh* [TH784, ZH836]) is used in 20:31 in connection with child sacrifice, but appears now in this oracle against the Negev (20:47 [21:3]) and again in 21:31-32 [36-37] in judgment against Judah and Jerusalem. This gives an ironic twist to the word, marking out the unit 20:45–21:32 [21:1-37]. The "global" scope of the vision of the judgment also ties the Negev oracle to the sword oracles and related materials. "Everyone in the world" will acknowledge the events here proclaimed as Yahweh's doing (20:48 [21:5]; 21:5 [21:10]), and "everyone in the land" will be targets for Yahweh's drawn sword (21:4 [21:9]).

I understand the paragraph's main connection with the following materials to be the last line: "He only talks in riddles!" (20:49 [21:5]). Although this is an acceptable translation, the Hebrew *memashshel meshalim* [TH4911/4912, ZH5439/5442] deals technically not just with riddles but more commonly with general, figurative material (cf. commentary on 17:1-2). As such, the line appropriately introduces the striking use of the sword in chapter 21 as a figure par excellence of coming judgment. It also expresses the skepticism this whole unit finally addresses. Yahweh will have the last laugh (21:10 [15]).

Four dramatic oracles comprise the unit. The first three open with the standard revelation notice, literally, "the word of the LORD came unto me saying" (21:1, 8, 18 [6, 13, 23]). The omission of that rubric before the clearly related oracle to Ammon (21:28 [33]) suggests that the final oracle on Yahweh's sword may at one time have continued from 21:17 without interruption. It opens with the command to prophesy (21:28 [33]), relating it closely to 21:2 [7] and 14 [19]. If so, the intervening oracle about maps and omens (21:18-27 [23-32]) would bear particular weight as an interpretive insert by Ezekiel or an editor.

In 21:1-7 [6-12], we see that the divine enemy draws his sword. Ezekiel hears the frightful announcement that Yahweh is the *enemy* of Israel and her sanctuaries (21:3 [8]); this introduces the theme of Yahweh's sword, which will dominate the chapter. Yahweh is about to draw (21:3 [8])—no! He *has* drawn his sword to slaughter everyone—righteous, wicked, from south to north (21:3-4 [8-9]). Each of these claims brings horrible news. Yahweh, the God celebrated for centuries as Israel's faithful redeemer and deliverer (see Exod 15; Ps 18) now confronts her as enemy. The God who talked at length about the righteous living and the wicked dying (ch 18) has drawn the sword to slay everyone in sight with indiscriminate judgment!

In this oracle Yahweh commands the first of four sign-acts found in the chapter, the command for Ezekiel to "groan before the people" (21:6 [11]). In the other three acts Ezekiel will brandish a sword (21:14 [19]), clap his hands (21:14 [19]; cf. 21:17 [22]), and later trace a map with routes for Nebuchadnezzar to follow (21:19 [24]). His groan will be sufficiently dramatic as to prompt request for an explanation (21:7 [12]). In response he will emphasize the terrifying news he bears. The strongest, like Ezekiel, will have "bitter anguish and a broken heart" (21:6 [11]), paralyzed with trauma. The oracle about the king of Babylon's making military decisions based on manipulation and reading of divination and omen materials (21:21-22 [26-27]) is a reminder of the perceived power of acts by authorized persons in the ancient world. Prophetic sign-acts were potent.

The second major oracle (21:8-17 [13-22]) extends several themes generally treated in 21:1-7 [6-12]—the extent of the slaughter, the terrifying nature of the news, the groaning, the wailing response, and the sword itself. The genre shifts from prose to poetry beginning at 21:9 [14], underscoring the prophetic, oracular nature of Ezekiel's speech. The oracle opens with the repetition of its key words for emphasis: "a sword, a sword" (21:9 [14]; cf. "Destruction! Destruction!" in 21:27 [32]).

This second oracle features Yahweh's sword itself—sharpened for lethal efficiency (21:9-11 [14-16]), burnished for fearful flashing in battle (21:15 [20]), brandished in simulated attack (21:14, 16 [19, 21]). The sword symbol needs minimal interpretation, for it can only speak of death and destruction in the hands of an enemy. The informed reader will be drawn back to the Mosaic covenant, recalling "sword" as one member of the classic triads of covenant curses (along with famine and disease; Lev 26:25, 33, 36-37; Deut 28:21-22, 48). The symbol is then embellished with poetic improvisation on the theme of execution by sword and with dramatic sign-acts. Ezekiel addresses the sword itself (21:16 [21]), and the sword of Babylon's king acts (21:19 [24]). Before brandishing a sword, Ezekiel is to "clap [his] hands" (21:14 [19]). Then in 21:17 [22], Yahweh himself claps his hands in satisfaction of his angry judgment. Clapping the hands in Ezekiel occurs only in negative contexts and expresses a range of emotional outbursts. In 6:11 it is a response to the horror of destruction coming. In 25:3 and 6 clapping the hand with the expression *he'akh* [TH1889, ZH2027] signals "malicious glee" at anger finally satisfied (Greenberg

1983:135). Here, as Greenberg puts it, the act expresses "vexation," being "fed up and about to act" (1997:423-424).

Sandwiched between the second sword oracle and its continuation in the Ammon oracle (21:28-32 [33-37]) stands a message finally focused on Zedekiah, king of Jerusalem (21:18-27 [23-32]). Yahweh instructs Ezekiel to draw a map with a road coming out of Babylon and diverging at a fork, with roads leading on the one hand to Jerusalem (ominously called "fortified Jerusalem"), and on the other to Rabbah, capital of Ammon, a neighbor on the plateau in the Transjordan. Such a fork could be located at several points on historic roads, but we are not told which fork Ezekiel is to draw or if it reflects real-life topography. (See ANEP, illustration 260, for an example of an ancient map.)

The truly scary news follows. Even as Ezekiel draws his map, Nebuchadnezzar, king of Babylon, and his invasion forces actually do stand at just such a fork. When the king asked his professional magicians to decide by various divination techniques whether he should invade Ammon or lay siege to Jerusalem, their answer pointed him to Jerusalem (21:19-22 [24-27])! Then follows a rather technical picture of what the ruthless Babylonian army will do when they lay siege to Jerusalem, complete with battering rams, siege towers, and assault ramps (21:22 [27]; cf. 4:1-3; see ANEP, illustrations 368 and 377 for pictures of ancient war machines). The king of Babylon would not be talked out of his assault by appeal to a treaty that Israel herself had not kept. Israel had been led into full-blown rebellion and was about to reap the consequences (21:23 [28]).

In a separate part of the oracle introduced with the message formula, Ezekiel brings the weight of the sword oracles and the map message in this chapter directly to bear on Zedekiah, the "corrupt and wicked prince"—the last king—of Judah (21:25 [30]). One could think of the term "prince" (*nasi'* [TH5387, ZH5954]) perhaps as an insult. But Ezekiel also used the epithet *nasi'* positively in reference to the David who will come (34:24; 37:25), so one hesitates to press too much here. What must be pressed is the announcement to Zedekiah: "your final day of reckoning is here!" (21:25 [30]). Speaking as Yahweh himself via the messenger formula (21:26 [31]), Ezekiel "removed" Zedekiah from the throne by ordering him to take off his "jeweled crown" (21:26 [31]). No more second chances. Because of Zedekiah's wretched leadership, the kingdom was lost. The crown jewels may as well be removed now.

Ezekiel's theology of history also bears here on the wicked prince. What we were told allegorically in 17:24, the prophet here says plainly: Yahweh exalts and brings down. When new orders rise, it is the work of Yahweh. In his judgment of Zedekiah and the destruction of the kingdom, he was bringing to a crashing halt the old order of corrupt and violent power. That kingdom will remain in disarray until Yahweh himself hands it over to another (21:26-27 [31-32]).

The emphasis here and throughout the whole collection of oracles in 20:45–21:32 [21:1-37] pertains to judgment, not hope. Nevertheless, a glimmer of hope shines in the implication that one day Yahweh will restore the kingdom and "the one" whom Yahweh deems worthy of exercising restorative judgment will appear. Yahweh, who works his will in the rise and fall of nations, will hand the rule of his people over to this one (21:27 [32]). Here we see "messianic hope" in the making. Ezekiel did not speak explicitly of the birth of a savior in Bethlehem or other Christian messianic ideas. The key "messianic" move here is the joining of the promised restoration with the appearance of a person who will be the agent of that hope. Yahweh himself will accomplish it.

Finally, this segment comes to a conclusion with the resumption of the sword oracles, now against Ammon (21:28-32 [33-37]). The repetitive exclamation, "A sword, a sword" (21:28 [33] parallel to 21:9 [14]), ties the oracle against the Ammonites directly to that against the people of Israel, as do numerous other expressions common to both. The parallel exclamations ("a sword, a sword!") likely imply that we should understand Ammon as the target of the drawn sword (21:28 [33]). Ammon earned this fate by participating with Judah in a western coalition rebellion against Nebuchadnezzar not long after Zedekiah had been put on the throne by the Babylonian. Then, when the political fallout began to materialize, Ammon tried to reverse policy and become "loyal subjects" of Nebuchadnezzar, aiding and abetting in the capture and harassment of Judahites and Jerusalemites. Ezekiel was particularly angry at Ammon's glee at the destruction of the Temple and her mockery of defeated Judah (25:1-7). The fact that her prophets had misled her would not lesson her judgment (21:29 [34]).

God's agent wielding the sword as depicted in these oracles has been Babylon's Nebuchadnezzar (21:1-17 [6-22]). He would be the one most likely to be told to return the sword to its sheath. Thus, the focus returns to Babylon in the closing oracle lines (21:30-32 [35-37]). Even though he executed God's purposes, Nebuchadnezzar and the Babylonians would experience judgment in their own land. Yahweh's word guaranteed it (21:32 [37]; cf. Hab 2:4-20).

◆ 3. Jerusalem's abominations cataloged and requited (22:1-31)

**Now this message came to me from the
LORD: 2"Son of man, are you ready to judge
Jerusalem? Are you ready to judge this
city of murderers? Publicly denounce her
detestable sins, 3and give her this mes-
sage from the Sovereign LORD: O city of
murderers, doomed and damned—city of
idols,* filthy and foul—4you are guilty be-
cause of the blood you have shed. You are
defiled because of the idols you have
made. Your day of destruction has come!
You have reached the end of your years. I
will make you an object of mockery
throughout the world. 5O infamous city,
filled with confusion, you will be mocked
by people far and near.**

**6"Every leader in Israel who lives within
your walls is bent on murder. 7Fathers and
mothers are treated with contempt. For-
eigners are forced to pay for protection.
Orphans and widows are wronged and op-
pressed among you. 8You despise my holy
things and violate my Sabbath days of
rest. 9People accuse others falsely and
send them to their death. You are filled
with idol worshipers and people who do
obscene things. 10Men sleep with their
fathers' wives and have intercourse with
women who are menstruating. 11Within
your walls live men who commit adultery
with their neighbors' wives, who defile
their daughters-in-law, or who rape their
own sisters. 12There are hired murderers,
loan racketeers, and extortioners every-
where. They never even think of me and
my commands, says the Sovereign LORD.**

**13"But now I clap my hands in indigna-
tion over your dishonest gain and blood-
shed. 14How strong and courageous will
you be in my day of reckoning? I, the**

LORD, have spoken, and I will do what I said. [15]I will scatter you among the nations and purge you of your wickedness. [16]And when I have been dishonored among the nations because of you,* you will know that I am the LORD."

[17]Then this message came to me from the LORD: [18]"Son of man, the people of Israel are the worthless slag that remains after silver is smelted. They are the dross that is left over—a useless mixture of copper, tin, iron, and lead. [19]So tell them, 'This is what the Sovereign LORD says: Because you are all worthless slag, I will bring you to my crucible in Jerusalem. [20]Just as copper, iron, lead, and tin are melted down in a furnace, I will melt you down in the heat of my fury. [21]I will gather you together and blow the fire of my anger upon you, [22]and you will melt like silver in fierce heat. Then you will know that I, the LORD, have poured out my fury on you.'"

[23]Again a message came to me from the LORD: [24]"Son of man, give the people of Israel this message: In the day of my indignation, you will be like a polluted land, a land without rain. [25]Your princes* plot conspiracies just as lions stalk their prey. They devour innocent people, seizing treasures and extorting wealth. They make many widows in the land. [26]Your priests have violated my instructions and defiled my holy things. They make no distinction between what is holy and what is not. And they do not teach my people the difference between what is ceremonially clean and unclean. They disregard my Sabbath days so that I am dishonored among them. [27]Your leaders are like wolves who tear apart their victims. They actually destroy people's lives for money! [28]And your prophets cover up for them by announcing false visions and making lying predictions. They say, 'My message is from the Sovereign LORD,' when the LORD hasn't spoken a single word to them. [29]Even common people oppress the poor, rob the needy, and deprive foreigners of justice.

[30]"I looked for someone who might rebuild the wall of righteousness that guards the land. I searched for someone to stand in the gap in the wall so I wouldn't have to destroy the land, but I found no one. [31]So now I will pour out my fury on them, consuming them with the fire of my anger. I will heap on their heads the full penalty for all their sins. I, the Sovereign LORD, have spoken!"

22:3 The Hebrew term (literally *round things*) probably alludes to dung; also in 22:4. **22:16** Or *when you have been dishonored among the nations.* **22:25** As in Greek version; Hebrew reads *prophets.*

NOTES

22:3 ***idols.*** Heb., *gillulim* [TH1544, ZH1658] (lit., "round things"), probably alludes to dung; also in 22:4. See note on 5:9.

22:4 ***the blood you have shed.*** The word *shapak* [TH8210, ZH9161] (to pour) abounds here, with 18 of its 33 occurrences in the book appearing in this section, and 8 of those in this chapter. Chapter 20 emphasizes the "pouring out" of Yahweh's anger (20:8, 13, 21, 33-34 [MT]) mentioned also in 22:22. *Shapak* also expresses the *reason* for the Lord's anger, as ch 22 hammers at the theme of Jerusalem as the bloody, violent city, where persons "*shapak* [shed] blood" (22:3-4, 6, 9, 12, 27; cf. 23:45; 24:7).

22:17-22 ***slag that remains after silver is smelted.*** "Slag" or "dross" refers to the material containing the impurities removed from silver in the refining process. To be used in making jewelry or other decoration, native silver (and gold) had to be refined. A process of washing and crushing was followed by one of heating the metal in a crucible with another metal, usually lead. In the crucible the impurities from the silver bonded with the lead. This impurity could either be oxidized and blown off (as in Jer 6:29), or removed with the use of sodium hydroxide, which turned the impurity into slag or dross that floated on the pure silver. Being called "slag" or "dross" is clearly no compliment! See van der Steen's helpful article on metallurgy (2000), and Forbes's more technical presentation (1964:172-177).

22:25 ***princes.*** This follows the LXX; Hebrew reads "prophets." The words could have been easily confused in a Hebrew consonantal text: *nsy'ym* [TH5387, ZH5954] (princes) versus *nby'ym* [TH5030, ZH5566] (prophets). The redundancy with "prophet" in 22:28, in view of the diversity apparently intended in the oracle, makes "princes" the better reading.

COMMENTARY

Chapter 22 offers a collection of three oracles with key connections to their sectional context and a literary structure focused yet again on Yahweh's verdict regarding Jerusalem. As for connections with their sectional context, particularly striking is the use again of Yahweh's question to Ezekiel, "Are you ready to judge Jerusalem? Are you ready to judge this city of murderers?" (22:2; cf. 20:4, where NLT, however, does not show the verbatim parallel of the Hebrew). These are chapters emphasizing that Yahweh's verdict is about to be carried out.

Regarding the literary structure of this chapter, the collection's central contention appears at the start in the verdict expressed through Ezekiel: "O city of murderers, doomed and damned—city of idols, filthy and foul—you are guilty because of the blood you have shed. You are defiled because of the idols you have made. Your day of destruction has come!" (22:2-4). The rest of the chapter elaborates on the sentence and the verdict with its implied accusations; the second oracle does so by means of comparing Israel with "the smelting furnace," another of Ezekiel's symbols (22:17-22). Ezekiel continues to work away at the argument that, whatever the connection between the fate of Jerusalem and the sins of previous generations, the present population and their exiled relatives carry sufficient guilt themselves to sink the city.

Yahweh's summary accusation, that Jerusalem is murderous and idolatrous (22:3-4), leads the assault, and is then generalized in 22:13 as "dishonest gain and bloodshed." Calling Jerusalem a murderous city (lit., "city of blood" in 22:2) may have been shocking, because of its use also by the prophets as a name for Nineveh, Assyria's major city (Nah 3:1), which had by this time fallen to the Babylonians and Medes.

Ezekiel's first move in substantiating the verdict and sentence is to list the specific, detestable sins leading to it:

- Murder by every leader (22:6; cf. Exod 20:13; Deut 5:17; 27:25)
- Parents treated with contempt (22:7; cf. Exod 20:12; Deut 5:16)
- Foreigners forced to pay "protection fees" (22:7; cf. Deut 24:17)
- Orphans and widows wronged, oppressed (22:7; cf. Exod 22:22; Deut 24:17)
- Yahweh's holy things despised (22:8; cf. Lev 20:1-3; 22:10-11)
- Yahweh's Sabbaths violated (22:8; cf. Exod 20:8-11; Deut 5:12-15)
- False accusation, even in capital cases (22:9; cf. Exod 20:16; Deut 5:20)
- Idol worship (22:9; cf. Exod 20:3-5; Deut 5:7-9)
- Obscene behavior (related to idolatry? 22:9; cf. Lev 20:13-14)
- Incest with stepmother (22:10; cf. Lev 20:11)
- Intercourse with menstruating women (22:10; cf. Lev 20:18)
- Adultery (22:11; cf. Exod 20:14; Lev 20:10; Deut 5:18)

- Incest with daughter-in-law (22:11; cf. Lev 20:12)
- Incestuous rape of sister (22:11; cf. Lev 20:17)
- Loan racketeering (22:12; cf. Exod 22:25; Lev 25:36)
- Extortion (22:12; cf. Lev 19:13; Deut 24:14)

All of the Ten Commandments were breached, either explicitly, as in murder and dishonoring of parents, or implicitly, as in the frivolous use of Yahweh's name (in false witness) and coveting (in all the predatory actions). His list of infractions of the case laws in Exodus, the Levitical Holiness Code (Lev 17–26), and the Deuteronomic materials show Ezekiel's wide acquaintance and concern with Torah and covenant law, even though we may not be certain regarding the precise literary form in which he found these materials. Ezekiel made no ethical and moral distinction between priestly concerns for clean and unclean and other more forensic covenant law. Idolatry, injustice, and covenant unfaithfulness defile and pollute people and land, as surely as do infractions of sacral boundaries. All of this was a result of "forgetting" Yahweh, failing even to think of God (22:12), let alone follow in his way.

Accompanied by the clapping of his hands as a sign of strong anger (cf. 21:14, 17), Yahweh summarized Israel's sin as "dishonest gain and bloodshed." He promised he would execute the threats of judgment he was making through Ezekiel and other prophets (22:13-14). The public indication of Yahweh's anger, pictured as the clapping of his hands, would be the exile of Judah, scattering her among the nations (22:15). All of her neighbors would see this exhibition of Yahweh's anger. When Yahweh's name was "dishonored among the nations because of" Judah's wickedness (22:16), it would be an indication that what had happened to them was significant and traumatic enough to have an impact on international opinion (as did the Exodus). It would be large enough to get Israel's attention and lead them to acknowledge that the one acting in their circumstances was none other than the ancient God of Israel (22:16).

The segment's concluding oracle (22:23-31) carries in its core (22:25-29) essentially the same indictments as those pronounced in 22:6-12, with the additional charge that prophets are accomplices in the moral pollution of the land (22:28). Here, however, Ezekiel singles out key sectors of the culture for particular accusation. He addresses princes (22:25), priests (22:26), leaders (22:27), prophets (22:28; cf. ch 13), and "even common people" (22:29), essentially charging that each group had abandoned its main covenantal and social responsibility. The oracle targets pervasive violence, oppression, and abuse of power. The entire culture had proven unfaithful.

On either side of this core of accusations, Ezekiel pronounced consequent judgment, a day of Yahweh's indignation (22:24) and fury (22:31). On one hand, the land would be polluted because it would receive no cleansing rains (22:24)—drought itself a covenant curse (Lev 26:19; Deut 28:22-23). On the other hand (22:31), Yahweh would consume the people in his fiery anger.

Between these two judgment oracles packed with specific indictments, Ezekiel placed the oracle of "the LORD's Refining Furnace" or "the LORD, the Relentless Smelter" (22:17-22). The oracle trades on ancient metallurgical technology presumably known to Ezekiel's readers, in this case technology for extracting silver from ore. In a first phase, ore thought to contain silver was heated in a process that produced a metallic, lead-silver alloy. A second phase of the smelting removed lead, other metals, and impurities from the lead-silver alloy, leaving the refined silver. The impurities were either oxidized or skimmed off the surface as dross (which contains mostly lead and other materials). The dross is waste from the refinement process.

Ezekiel's oracle starts with the second part of the smelting process, where we would expect the emergence of refined silver (22:17-18). Instead—nothing but dross! Against the notion that Judah and Jerusalem were the Lord's special possession, prized above other nations (Exod 19:5), Ezekiel claimed they were just dross—not precious at all. Against the claim by many that those remaining in the land were better than the exiles (obviously sinners deported for their sins), the oracle spoke a resounding "No! Just dross!" If Ezekiel's readers knew Isaiah 1:25 or Proverbs 25:4, they would recognize this as a very negative use of a metaphor that usually carried good news (cf. Jer 6:29).

Ezekiel 22:19-22 seems to rely on the first part of the smelting process, whereby metals and other materials were melted down. We notice there is no silver in the process at all. Only other metals are thrown in the furnace according to the metaphor (22:20-21). Clearly we are to see this not as refinement but as judgment, since the causal reasoning from 22:18 to 22:19 is explicitly from indictment to consequence. Judah and Jerusalem in this part of the metaphor are not silver, but they will melt down *like* silver under the heat of the Lord's fury. In these verses the emphasis has shifted from the disappointing *quality* or *character* of Judah and Jerusalem (dross) to the *severity of the fiery judgment*. In this case, the metaphor of the oracle would come literally true in the fire of Nebuchadnezzar's attack on the land and city. "When the instrument of Yahweh's destruction comes upon the city, Jerusalem will be turned into a raging blast furnace" (J. Bunn 1971:299). Against the backdrop of oracles like these, those who experience or hear of the coming conflagration will recognize it as an expression of the fury of the Lord (22:22).

The concluding two verses of the third oracle and of the segment (22:30-31) close the unit with pronouncement of judgment by consuming fire; they interpret these events explicitly as the "full penalty" for the sins of Israel. We are told that prior to the announcement of judgment, Yahweh had tried to find a person who would "rebuild the wall of righteousness that guards the land" and "stand in the gap in the wall" (22:30). The expression "stand in the gap" sets an ominous tone, since the term "gap" (*perets* [TH6556, ZH7288]) used in this context would refer to gaping holes in walls breached by enemy forces.

◆ 4. The harlots Samaria and Jerusalem punished (23:1-49)

This message came to me from the LORD:
2"Son of man, once there were two sisters
who were daughters of the same mother.
3They became prostitutes in Egypt. Even
as young girls, they allowed men to fon-
dle their breasts. 4The older girl was
named Oholah, and her sister was Oholi-
bah. I married them, and they bore me
sons and daughters. I am speaking of Sa-
maria and Jerusalem, for Oholah is Sa-
maria and Oholibah is Jerusalem.

5"Then Oholah lusted after other lovers
instead of me, and she gave her love to the
Assyrian officers. 6They were all attractive

young men, captains and commanders dressed in handsome blue, charioteers driving their horses. 7And so she prostituted herself with the most desirable men of Assyria, worshiping their idols* and defiling herself. 8For when she left Egypt, she did not leave her spirit of prostitution behind. She was still as lewd as in her youth, when the Egyptians slept with her, fondled her breasts, and used her as a prostitute.

9"And so I handed her over to her Assyrian lovers, whom she desired so much. 10They stripped her, took away her children as their slaves, and then killed her. After she received her punishment, her reputation was known to every woman in the land.

11"Yet even though Oholibah saw what had happened to Oholah, her sister, she followed right in her footsteps. And she was even more depraved, abandoning herself to her lust and prostitution. 12She fawned over all the Assyrian officers—those captains and commanders in handsome uniforms, those charioteers driving their horses—all of them attractive young men. 13I saw the way she was going, defiling herself just like her older sister.

14"Then she carried her prostitution even further. She fell in love with pictures that were painted on a wall—pictures of Babylonian* military officers, outfitted in striking red uniforms. 15Handsome belts encircled their waists, and flowing turbans crowned their heads. They were dressed like chariot officers from the land of Babylonia.* 16When she saw these paintings, she longed to give herself to them, so she sent messengers to Babylonia to invite them to come to her. 17So they came and committed adultery with her, defiling her in the bed of love. After being defiled, however, she rejected them in disgust.

18"In the same way, I became disgusted with Oholibah and rejected her, just as I had rejected her sister, because she flaunted herself before them and gave herself to satisfy their lusts. 19Yet she turned to even greater prostitution, remembering her youth when she was a prostitute in Egypt. 20She lusted after lovers with genitals as large as a donkey's and emissions like those of a horse. 21And so, Oholibah, you relived your former days as a young girl in Egypt, when you first allowed your breasts to be fondled.

22"Therefore, Oholibah, this is what the Sovereign LORD says: I will send your lovers against you from every direction—those very nations from which you turned away in disgust. 23For the Babylonians will come with all the Chaldeans from Pekod and Shoa and Koa. And all the Assyrians will come with them—handsome young captains, commanders, chariot officers, and other high-ranking officers, all riding their horses. 24They will all come against you from the north* with chariots, wagons, and a great army prepared for attack. They will take up positions on every side, surrounding you with men armed with shields and helmets. And I will hand you over to them for punishment so they can do with you as they please. 25I will turn my jealous anger against you, and they will deal harshly with you. They will cut off your nose and ears, and any survivors will then be slaughtered by the sword. Your children will be taken away as captives, and everything that is left will be burned. 26They will strip you of your beautiful clothes and jewels. 27In this way, I will put a stop to the lewdness and prostitution you brought from Egypt. You will never again cast longing eyes on those things or fondly remember your time in Egypt.

28"For this is what the Sovereign LORD says: I will surely hand you over to your enemies, to those you loathe, those you rejected. 29They will treat you with hatred and rob you of all you own, leaving you stark naked. The shame of your prostitution will be exposed to all the world. 30You brought all this on yourself by prostituting yourself to other nations, defiling yourself with all their idols. 31Because you have followed in your sister's footsteps, I will force you to drink the same cup of terror she drank.

32 "Yes, this is what the Sovereign LORD says:

"You will drink from your sister's
cup of terror,
a cup that is large and deep.
It is filled to the brim
with scorn and derision.
33 Drunkenness and anguish will fill you,
for your cup is filled to the brim
with distress and desolation,
the same cup your sister Samaria
drank.
34 You will drain that cup of terror
to the very bottom.
Then you will smash it to pieces
and beat your breast in anguish.
I, the Sovereign LORD, have spoken!

35 "And because you have forgotten me and turned your back on me, this is what the Sovereign LORD says: You must bear the consequences of all your lewdness and prostitution."

36 The LORD said to me, "Son of man, you must accuse Oholah and Oholibah of all their detestable sins. 37 They have committed both adultery and murder—adultery by worshiping idols and murder by burning as sacrifices the children they bore to me. 38 Furthermore, they have defiled my Temple and violated my Sabbath day! 39 On the very day that they sacrificed their children to their idols, they boldly came into my Temple to worship! They came in and defiled my house.

40 "You sisters sent messengers to distant lands to get men. Then when they arrived, you bathed yourselves, painted your eyelids, and put on your finest jewels for them. 41 You sat with them on a beautifully embroidered couch and put my incense and my special oil on a table that was spread before you. 42 From your room came the sound of many men carousing. They were lustful men and drunkards* from the wilderness, who put bracelets on your wrists and beautiful crowns on your heads. 43 Then I said, 'If they really want to have sex with old worn-out prostitutes like these, let them!' 44 And that is what they did. They had sex with Oholah and Oholibah, these shameless prostitutes. 45 But righteous people will judge these sister cities for what they really are—adulterers and murderers.

46 "Now this is what the Sovereign LORD says: Bring an army against them and hand them over to be terrorized and plundered. 47 For their enemies will stone them and kill them with swords. They will butcher their sons and daughters and burn their homes. 48 In this way, I will put an end to lewdness and idolatry in the land, and my judgment will be a warning to others not to follow their wicked example. 49 You will be fully repaid for all your prostitution—your worship of idols. Yes, you will suffer the full penalty. Then you will know that I am the Sovereign LORD."

23:7 The Hebrew term (literally *round things*) probably alludes to dung; also in 23:30, 37, 39, 49. **23:14** Or *Chaldean.* **23:15** Or *Chaldea;* also in 23:16. **23:24** As in Greek version; the meaning of the Hebrew is uncertain. **23:42** Or *Sabeans.*

NOTES

23:1-4 ***They became prostitutes. . . . they allowed men to fondle their breasts.*** Ezekiel's development of the harlot metaphor in this unit has drawn criticism as misogynous and pornographic. See the Introduction, "Ezekiel's View of Women," and especially the notes and commentary on ch 16 for treatment of these matters.

23:4 ***I married them.*** Ezekiel reflected his ethical environment in the acceptance of polygamy as legitimate behavior for Yahweh in the story. Before any readers could take these lines as warrant for polygamy, the claim would need to find support in the Christian canon as a whole regarding the Creator's will for marriage. Scripture as a whole seems to mandate monogamy. Numerous biblical passages allow or at least assume polygamy. The narratives of Jacob (Gen 29:21-30) and David (2 Sam 5:13-16), and the legal assumptions in Exod 21:10 and Deut 21:15 may be cited. The NT explicitly mandates monogamy only for select church leaders (1 Tim 3:2, 12; Titus 1:6). On the other hand, one can find legal material (e.g., Exod 20:17; 21:5), prophetic instruction (e.g., Mal 2:14), wisdom teaching (e. g., Prov 12:4; 18:22), and more supporting monogamous marriage. Of hermeneutic importance is the creation account of Gen 2:15-25, which clearly assumes a monogamous pair as the Creator's original design. Jesus' teaching, and generally that of the apostles' as well, everywhere assumes the marriage of one man and one woman for life (e.g., Luke 14:26; 1 Cor 7:2). These passages tip the balance clearly toward monogamy as God's highest will for his people in marriage.

23:5-6 *Assyrian officers . . . captains and commanders.* Assyrian (and later Babylonian) military and administrative terminology for these personnel came into the Hebrew language as Akkadian loan words whose precise meaning, once borrowed, remains unclear. Thus they are variously translated. Greenberg renders them "guardsmen . . . governors and prefects" (1997:471); Zimmerli as "warriors . . . Ambassadors and governors" (1979:472); Block as "staff officers . . . governors, prefects" (1997:737). See Yadin (1963:2.293-301, 380-463) and Parrot (1961:106-107; plates 115-117, cited in Greenberg 1997:475) for lavish and often colorful illustration of Assyrian (and to a lesser extent, Babylonian) military hardware, personnel, and exploits.

23:7 *idols.* Heb., *gillulim* [TH1544, ZH1658] (lit., "round things"), probably alludes to dung; also in 23:30, 37, 39, 49. Cf. note on 5:9.

23:14 *pictures that were painted on a wall.* Lit., "men engraved on the wall" and "engraved in red/vermillion." Some Judeans had direct contact with Babylonians as early as the emissaries from Merodach-baladan under Hezekiah (2 Kgs 20:12). Ezekiel himself may well have seen the public art that he here calls "engraved." But just what the Jerusalemites as an audience had seen is puzzling. Perhaps Ezekiel exaggerated to underscore Oholibah's (Jerusalem's) unspeakable betrayal of Yahweh.

Babylonian. Lit., "Chaldean." The Chaldeans were a West Semitic people whose tribes gained control of southern Mesopotamia, territory to that point ruled by native Babylonians (Kassites). Ezekiel's use of this term shows awareness of social structures in the Neo-Babylonian Empire, where rulers and the ruling classes were predominantly Chaldean. See Arnold 2004:87-105 on the Chaldeans, Babylonians, and the rise of the Neo-Babylonian Empire.

23:15 *Handsome belts . . . flowing turbans.* For Ezekiel's accuracy in attention to distinctively Babylonian garb, see Greenberg 1997:478.

23:24 *They will all come against you from the north.* As in the LXX; the meaning of the Hebrew is uncertain. The MT as pointed reads "and they will come against you *hotsen* [TH2021, ZH2210] chariot and wheel, even with a host of people." The meaning of *hotsen* remains unknown.

chariots, wagons, and a great army prepared for attack. See Yadin (1963:2.380-463) for illustrations from Mesopotamian art of these war machines and troops.

23:37 *burning as sacrifices the children they bore to me.* For treatments of child sacrifice in ancient Israel, see Matthews and Benjamin 1993:21, 223; Miller 2000:59, 240, note 63.

COMMENTARY

Ezekiel's allegory of the two sisters (23:1-49) contains the second of three major units related to the earlier announcement that Yahweh had drawn his sword (20:45–21:32 [21:1-37]). The drawn sword metaphor trumpeted the means of Yahweh's judgment—

invasion by the king of Babylon (21:19, 21 [21:24, 26]). The immediately following units, climaxing in chapter 24, underscore the purpose or the goal of that invasion—judgment. Repeatedly throughout these units Ezekiel reiterates the causal link between Israel's sin and Yahweh's judgment. His hearers and readers needed to make this same theological connection in order to understand their situation in light of the fact that Jerusalem was in ruins and the Temple was destroyed.

Ezekiel did not call his allegory of the two sisters (23:1-49) a riddle (*khidah* [TH2420, ZH2648]) or a story (*mashal* [TH4912, ZH5442]), as he did with similar "stories" earlier (17:2). Nevertheless, in the very first lines we clearly enter "story" and "metaphor" territory, with attendant demands on the reader and interpreter. Ezekiel again raised the contention that Israel and Judah's sin was tantamount to harlotry; he underscored that claim by means of the story of the sister harlots, Oholah and Oholibah.

Ezekiel named the older sister Oholah, meaning "her tent." This is Samaria (i.e., Israel), the northern kingdom, seen quintessentially in its capital city. The younger he called "Oholibah," "my tent is in her" (cf. HALOT 1.19 on the names). "Tent" in these names should probably be taken as a reference to a cultic tent, a sacred tent, or place of worship. Perhaps Ezekiel was playing on ties with the ancient Tabernacle. Oholah's name might indicate that the shrines in Samaria were hers, not Yahweh's. Oholibah's name, on the other hand, would underscore the particular ownership Yahweh claimed of the Jerusalem Temple. In the allegory, both girls have, from their earliest days, names associated with their later days when they were known by their chief cities, Samaria and Jerusalem. Ezekiel carried their dual identity back into the centuries of Israel's history prior to the division of the monarchy. The story form allows these liberties to underscore his point.

As in chapter 16, Ezekiel again used the prostitute metaphor to picture poignantly his people's breach of covenant with him. Hosea had already shown the aptness of adultery and harlotry as images with which to expound unfaithfulness to the Mosaic covenant (Hos 1–3, especially Hos 2:1-13 [2:3-15]). He had also offered hope for a renewed covenant in the image of God's new and lasting marriage to his people (Hos 2:14-20 [2:16-22]). Here Ezekiel extends Hosea's metaphor. He traces the unfaithfulness of Israel and Judah all the way back to their days in Egypt (23:3, 8, 27). In doing so, he was perhaps implying a lack of clear faithfulness to what Israel knew of the God of the patriarchs, even before their covenant relationship with him at Sinai.

Moving quickly beyond Israel's early history, Ezekiel focused on Samaria's response to her encounters with the Assyrians. On the one hand, "Oholah" (23:4) feared these brutal imperialists. Already in the time of Ahab (mid-ninth century BC), Israel had confronted Assyrians at a distance. Ahab contributed significantly to a coalition that held off Shalmaneser III's move to take territory along the eastern Mediterranean, stopping the Assyrians at Qarqar on the upper Orontes River. By the time of the prophet Hosea and the last kings of Israel, the Assyrians had seized 80 percent of Israelite territory, dividing the conquered land into Assyrian provinces. The pitifully reduced kingdom surrounding Samaria fell to the Assyrians under Sargon II in 721 BC. In those last decades, Assyrian forces under Adad-nirari III, Tiglath-pileser III (biblical "Pul"), Shalmaneser V, and finally Sargon had marched the length and breadth of Israel with frightful destruction and violence for all who resisted Assyrian expansion (cf. 2 Kgs 15:19-20, 29).

On the other hand, "Oholah" could not resist the charm of the Assyrians. Their royal art, celebrating the Assyrian military machine and her heroic kings, echoes Ezekiel's picture of the Assyrians (23:6-7). Powerful, technologically advanced, culturally and spiritually "cosmopolitan," colorful and dashing—Israel lusted after them. Out of political expediency and theological compromise, willingly embracing and pursuing idolatry (perhaps in part imposed upon her by treaty), she rejected her faithful lover Yahweh (23:7-8).

As stipulated in the Sinai covenant in both its priestly and Deuteronomic renderings, Israel suffered the consequence of her covenant unfaithfulness (Lev 26:23-35; Deut 28:25-26, 49-52). Yahweh "handed her over" to the advancing Assyrians (23:9). They totally destroyed what was left of the kingdom of Israel and deported massive sectors of the population, repopulating the land with persons conquered elsewhere (2 Kgs 17:1-24).

The first 10 verses of chapter 23 constitute a rhetorical setup for the "real" punch. Ezekiel had opened the "two sisters" story with a brief telling of Israelite history that many of the prophet's audience might well have applauded. Samaria was clearly and famously unfaithful, and Yahweh did bring well-deserved judgment upon her. His audience would have agreed. But Ezekiel devoted the major space in his allegory to the younger sister, Oholibah (i.e., Jerusalem and Judah), the audience he was addressing in exile and back home. First he describes her covenant unfaithfulness (23:11-21), then the consequent judgment (23:22-35). Concluding oracles address judgment again to both sisters (23:36-45, 46-49).

In spite of her historical advantage as witness to Israel's fate, Jerusalem's infatuation with things foreign and her lust to pursue forbidden relationships outstripped that of her older sister (23:11-12). The reader knows already from chapter 8 that Jerusalem's embrace of Babylonian culture reached all the way to Temple practice and theological compromise. She pursued her promiscuous cravings with a pornographic twist, falling in love with pictures of Babylonian officers: "pictures . . . painted on a wall" (23:14). What historical referent might lie behind this accusation of Jerusalem's lust after *pictured* Babylonian officers now escapes us. Ezekiel may have been punctuating Oholibah's culpability by allegorical exaggeration. The following lines regarding the equine size of the Babylonians' genitals (23:20) seem to show that sort of sensual distortion, underscoring the lust and depravity of all parties. Ezekiel the priest wrote here no doubt out of "anguished revulsion at the pollution of Yahweh's Temple and its quickly approaching destruction" (Galambush 1992:124). Further, the outrageous imagery may also underscore this unit's place toward the climax of Ezekiel's portrayal of the sin and coming judgment of Jerusalem (chs 4–24).

Judah's infatuation with the Babylonians proved short-lived. What she craved so ardently, she then spurned (23:17, 22, 28). She turned away from Babylon, drawn away by promises of aid from Egypt. In league with other rebels, she withheld tribute and sued for independence from Babylonian sovereignty. The result was predictable, marked in 23:22 with an explicit causal ("therefore") marker and two formally introduced oracles ("this is what the Sovereign LORD says," 23:22-27 and 23:28-31).

Politically it was inevitable: Babylon would retaliate. Allegorically and theologically it seems predictable: Spurned lovers will rage; the God of the covenant will act. In the geopolitical realities of Babylonian retaliation, Yahweh would be at work. He would "send" the Babylonians against Jerusalem (23:22). *He* will hand Jerusalem over to her enemies (i.e., erstwhile lovers) (23:28). Once again the allegory bursts historical boundaries for emphasis, as Yahweh sends not only Babylon to come against Judah but also the Assyrians (23:23), a people by now long passed from the stage of international interventions. Marauding troops from as far as Pekod, Shoa, and Koa come prepared to attack (23:23). These names can reasonably be identified with tribes from far eastern Babylon (see references to Neo-Assyrian and Babylonian royal texts in Block 1997:748-750; ANET 307-308).

The role of the international lovers in punishing Oholah and Oholibah is prominent. Their role as lovers pursuing their own lusts is less prominent, but still important. The Egyptians "slept with her [Oholah], fondled her breasts, and used her as a prostitute" (23:8). The Babylonians "came and committed adultery with her [Oholibah]" (23:17). Alas! They had "used her" for their own imperial purposes, with no thought of her welfare.

In 23:22-31, as in the allegory of chapter 16, Ezekiel moves without warning between the "real world" of Iron Age warfare, the allegorical world of a jealous husband punishing a wayward wife, and the theological world of the Lord of Israel's ancient covenant. Tracing Ezekiel's path carefully between these worlds lets the text stand in its own historical world with all of its ruggedness.

Ezekiel then underscores the consequences of Jerusalem's unfaithfulness by inserting another metaphor within the two sisters story—Yahweh's "cup" (23:32-34). Used by Isaiah (Isa 51:17, 22) and Jeremiah (Jer 16:7; 25:15, 17, 28; 49:12; 51:7), the cup symbolizes its owner's pervasive influence on the party who drinks it. Here Yahweh will make Oholibah drink from a cup of wrath, unleashing Yahweh's wrath in her. The same horrific fate that befell Samaria will come to Jerusalem (23:33). The size of the cup ("large and deep") and its fullness ("to the brim") emphasize the magnitude of this event. "Terror," "scorn," "derision," "distress," "desolation," and "anguish" pack these few lines with the realities of military defeat at the hands of the Babylonians. It will be unspeakably terrible. They describe the stupor into which Jerusalem will fall as though drunk. Though it's the same cup that Samaria drank, it presents an unprecedented horrible event, so the cup will be smashed (23:34). Following the cup oracle, a one-line pronouncement of judgment in the allegorical mode ends the section devoted to Jerusalem (23:11-35). It parallels 23:22 as an explicit conclusion: "You must bear the consequences" (23:35).

The concluding oracles (23:36-45 and 23:46-49) draw out the implications of this story of the two sisters in several important ways. Ezekiel begins by tying this segment (ch 23) into the preceding entries in the larger unit (chs 20–24) by a formal accusation (23:36-39), using the language of arraignment, seen also at 20:4 and 22:2 (cf. also 23:45). The NLT's "accuse" gets at the nub of the judicial term. At this point, explicit, Torah-based accusation clarifies allegory. The sisters have committed murder through child sacrifice, adultery through idolatry, desecration of Yahweh's Temple, and violation of his Sabbaths (23:36-39, 49). "My incense" and "my special oil" (23:41) clearly speak of liturgical oils and incense that should have been given to Yahweh. The sisters have compromised faith in Yahweh by merging it with the local and international religions competing for their loyalties right in Jerusalem, as earlier in Samaria. Furthermore, this opinion is no private whim of the prophet. Righteous persons will concur in this arraignment (23:45).

The accusations make clear that the sisters' sins have polluted Yahweh's Temple (23:38-39). Their entry into "alternative" religions rendered Yahweh's own dwelling unfit for meeting him. The Jerusalem Temple was no longer a sacred place. Yahweh declared that he would bring judgment by handing them over to the "natural" consequences of their behaviors. Their own lovers, now equally vicious enemies, would accomplish Yahweh's judgment by getting their own vengeance (23:46-49). This full payment for their prostitution would thus carry a supreme irony. In this catastrophe, here interpreted and anticipated, Ezekiel's audience and readers would know that Yahweh had once again revealed himself for all who desire to see him. Yahweh will reveal himself in history—their history—by action accompanied by his prophetic word.

This knowledge of Yahweh stands as the positive outcome of the punishment of Oholibah. Hosea and Jeremiah had used the imagery of Samaria and Jerusalem as Yahweh's wife for both negative and positive ends, portraying not only their unfaithfulness but also a restored relationship, a new covenant, within the metaphor (Jer 31; Hos 2). At this point Ezekiel made a striking revision of the prophetic tradition, offering relatively muted promises of restoration. But the hope that is offered should not be negated (contra Galambush). The fact that in 16:60-63 Yahweh's new, eternal covenant evokes the memory of Jerusalem's shameful past is not a marriage metaphor run amok. Rather, it anticipates the promises that Yahweh will give in 36:22-27. Furthermore, the recognition of Yahweh should not be despised as "the only positive result" of the punishment detailed in chapter 23 (Galambush 1992:86). It may be the one positive result noted here, but that result constitutes the single, most important outcome of Yahweh's present intervention in Israel's history, judging by its repetition in almost every one of the first 39 chapters of the book.

◆ 5. The delightful one's death not mourned (24:1-27)

On January 15,* during the ninth year of
King Jehoiachin's captivity, this message
came to me from the LORD: 2"Son of man,
write down today's date, because on this
very day the king of Babylon is beginning
his attack against Jerusalem. 3Then give
these rebels an illustration with this message from the Sovereign LORD:

"Put a pot on the fire,
and pour in some water.
4Fill it with choice pieces of meat—
the rump and the shoulder
and all the most tender cuts.
5Use only the best sheep from
the flock,
and heap fuel on the fire
beneath the pot.
Bring the pot to a boil,
and cook the bones along with
the meat.

6"Now this is what the Sovereign
LORD says:
What sorrow awaits Jerusalem,
the city of murderers!
She is a cooking pot
whose corruption can't be
cleaned out.
Take the meat out in random order,
for no piece is better than another.
7For the blood of her murders

is splashed on the rocks.
It isn't even spilled on the ground,
where the dust could cover it!
8 So I will splash her blood on a rock
for all to see,
an expression of my anger
and vengeance against her.

9 "This is what the Sovereign LORD says:
What sorrow awaits Jerusalem,
the city of murderers!
I myself will pile up the fuel
beneath her.
10 Yes, heap on the wood!
Let the fire roar to make the
pot boil.
Cook the meat with many spices,
and afterward burn the bones.
11 Now set the empty pot on the coals.
Heat it red hot!
Burn away the filth and corruption.
12 But it's hopeless;
the corruption can't be cleaned out.
So throw it into the fire.
13 Your impurity is your lewdness
and the corruption of your idolatry.
I tried to cleanse you,
but you refused.
So now you will remain in your filth
until my fury against you has
been satisfied.

14 "I, the LORD, have spoken! The time
has come, and I won't hold back. I will not
change my mind, and I will have no pity
on you. You will be judged on the basis of
all your wicked actions, says the Sovereign
LORD."

15 Then this message came to me from
the LORD: 16 "Son of man, with one blow I
will take away your dearest treasure. Yet
you must not show any sorrow at her
death. Do not weep; let there be no tears.
17 Groan silently, but let there be no wail-
ing at her grave. Do not uncover your
head or take off your sandals. Do not per-
form the usual rituals of mourning or ac-
cept any food brought to you by consoling
friends."

18 So I proclaimed this to the people the
next morning, and in the evening my wife
died. The next morning I did everything I
had been told to do. 19 Then the people
asked, "What does all this mean? What
are you trying to tell us?"

20 So I said to them, "A message came to
me from the LORD, 21 and I was told to give
this message to the people of Israel. This
is what the Sovereign LORD says: I will
defile my Temple, the source of your se-
curity and pride, the place your heart de-
lights in. Your sons and daughters whom
you left behind in Judah will be slaugh-
tered by the sword. 22 Then you will do as
Ezekiel has done. You will not mourn in
public or console yourselves by eating the
food brought by friends. 23 Your heads will
remain covered, and your sandals will not
be taken off. You will not mourn or weep,
but you will waste away because of your
sins. You will mourn privately for all the
evil you have done. 24 Ezekiel is an example
for you; you will do just as he has done.
And when that time comes, you will know
that I am the Sovereign LORD."

25 Then the LORD said to me, "Son of
man, on the day I take away their strong-
hold—their joy and glory, their heart's de-
sire, their dearest treasure—I will also take
away their sons and daughters. 26 And on
that day a survivor from Jerusalem will
come to you in Babylon and tell you what
has happened. 27 And when he arrives,
your voice will suddenly return so you can
talk to him, and you will be a symbol for
these people. Then they will know that I
am the LORD."

24:1 Hebrew *On the tenth day of the tenth month,* of the ancient Hebrew lunar calendar. This event occurred on January 15, 588 B.C.; also see note on 1:1.

NOTES

24:1 ***January 15.*** The date is probably among the celebration days proclaimed by Zechariah (Zech 8:19), but taken up again as fast days after the fall of Jerusalem in AD 70 (Moore 1927:1.65-66, cited by Zimmerli 1979:498).

the ninth year of King Jehoiachin's captivity. Lit., "the ninth year." The NLT supplies the reference to Jehoiachin's captivity, which is how Ezekiel customarily dates his oracles. This would be January 15, 588 BC (see NLT mg), but this date poses a problem. We know that the siege of Jerusalem lasted approximately 18 months. If one reads 24:1 plainly (i.e., as dated nine years after Jehoiachin's deportation in April 597), then Nebuchadnezzar launched the siege in January 588. The fall of the city, 18 months later, would have been in mid-July 587. We know, however, from 2 Kgs 25 and from the Babylonian Chronicles that Nebuchadnezzar took the city in July 586 and razed the city and organized deportations a month later. Dating the fall of the city to July 587 gives a full 18 months for the journey of the survivor mentioned in 33:21, which seems much too long. (Ezra 7:9 shows that the journey from Babylon to Jerusalem could be made by a group in five months, following the standard route that passed along the upper Euphrates and back south. Moreover, in 605, Nebuchadnezzar and a relatively small number of troops pressed hard from Palestine to Babylon in less than a month [Thiele 1965:166].) Some texts harmonize the dates by changing the reading in 33:21 to the "eleventh year" (Lucianic LXX, Syriac, and a few Hebrew mss), an emendation that most current scholars resist (see note on 33:21). More likely the difficulty should be resolved by leaving both this text and 33:21 as they stand, while understanding 24:1 to be uniquely dated, for emphasis, to the "official" calendar following the reign of Zedekiah and not to the deportation of Jehoiachin (Block 1998:772-774; Thiele 1965:165-172). This moves the 24:1 date up one year from January 588 to January 587. The fall would then be in the summer of 586, the deportation in August of 586, and the survivor's journey would take about five months.

24:3-13 The NLT presents 24:3b-13 as poetry. BHS presents only 24:3b-5 as poetic. Contemporary versions differ, because here as in many other places in Ezekiel the boundary between poetry and lofty prose proves difficult to delineate with confidence.

24:3 *give . . . an illustration.* This renders *meshol . . . mashal*. The recitation of the *mashal* [TH4912, ZH5442] should probably not be regarded as a sign-act in itself. That is, Ezekiel himself is not told to cook meat in a caldron. The words for "sign" used by Ezekiel to this point do not occur (*'oth* [TH226, ZH253], 4:3; 14:8; 20:12, 20 and *mopeth* [TH4159, ZH4603], 12:6, 11; 24:24, 27). Ezekiel's withholding of all public tokens of mourning at the shocking death of his wife and the sudden return of voice (i.e., full liberty to speak beyond times of special revelation) would be signs with their own nonverbal message underscoring or dramatizing Ezekiel's spoken word (see *mopeth* in 24:24 and 27).

24:4, 5, 10 *cuts . . . heap fuel . . . bones . . . bones.* The MT uses two forms of the word *'etsem* [TH6106, ZH6795] (bone) in these verses. The NLT rightly takes the masc. pl. form (*'etsamim*, which can mean "limb"; Judg 19:29; Eccl 11:5) in 24:4 to designate "cuts" of meat. In 24:10, its fem. pl. form apparently refers to bones themselves, there added to fuel the fire. In 24:5, the first occurrence of *'etsamim* is probably a corruption from *'etsim* [TH6086, ZH6770] (pieces of wood). Thus, the NLT translates "and heap fuel on the fire." The second appearance in 24:5, "cook the bones (*'etsamim*)," would perhaps better be taken as "tender cuts," as in v. 4.

24:17 *Do not uncover your head.* Lit., "do not cover/wrap (your) mustache."

COMMENTARY

With chapter 24 we reach the climax of the book's announcement of judgment upon the rebellious house of Israel stretching from 3:16 through 24:27. Dramatic action in the chapter itself and important intertextual references to other key passages in the book mark this climax. Next, Ezekiel will turn his attention to Yahweh's judgment of the nations (chs 25–32), which we are to see as good news for Israel (28:25-26; 29:21). Concluding oracles and visions of restoration and hope bring this book to a climactic end (chs 33–48).

The prophet devotes the first half of this segment to a cooking pot allegory (24:2-5) and two oracles elaborating upon it (24:6-8 and 24:9-13), carrying the allegory forward and transforming it (24:6, 9-11). This focus concludes with a brief pronouncement underscoring the warnings of judgment (24:14). The cooking pot metaphor takes the reader back to 11:2-12 and an earlier use of this picture. The address to "rebels" (lit., "the rebellious house") refers us all the way back to Ezekiel's commission to this crowd (2:5-9) and to the first sign-act in the book (3:26-27). The last half of the segment centers around a dramatic sign-act Ezekiel is to perform (24:15-19)—no mourning at the sudden loss of his wife—followed by two oracles interpreting that act (24:20-24 and 24:25-27).

Ezekiel records the date of the day he received instructions to deliver the cooking pot allegory because it was a truly significant day—the day Nebuchadnezzar laid siege to Jerusalem (24:1-2). It was January 15, 588 BC, the ninth year of Jehoiachin's exile. The community eventually marked this frightful day with a fast. Zimmerli puzzles over how a prophet in exile would know the timing of the onset of the siege hundreds of miles away in Judah. He concludes, relying on the unusual pattern of the date formula here and certain assumptions limiting prophetic awareness, that the date as given is a later redaction (1979:498-499). Allen attributes Ezekiel's prescience to the interaction between divine revelation and human history (1990:56). In either case, the issue is the vindication of Yahweh and his prophet. What they threatened years earlier in oracles with uncontested date formulae had come to pass!

Some see the cooking pot instructions as delivery of a prophetic sign-act. More likely, we should see the cooking pot passage as an allegory or parable. The Lord tells Ezekiel, *meshol . . . mashal* [TH4912, ZH5442], terminology used earlier with reference to a proverb (12:23; 16:44) and an allegory (17:2). If it is a recitation or a song rather than a dramatic act (Zimmerli 1979:498-499), the addressee is in question. Perhaps Nebuchadnezzar is to light and stoke the fire; perhaps Ezekiel. The referent could be indefinite, thereby drawing readers and listeners into the action. In any case the addressee is to put a pot on a fire, pour in some water, fill it with choice pieces of meat, heap fuel on the fire, bring the pot to a boil, and cook everything in it (24:2-5).

Though the theological punch is not clear in the allegory itself, it is crystal clear in the interpretation (24:6-8 and 9-14). Both elaborating oracles highlight Jerusalem's violent, murderous culture. Pronouncing "woe" (NLT, "What sorrow") on the city, Yahweh addresses Jerusalem as "the city of murderers" (24:6, 9; cf. 24:7-8). The designation, applied by Nahum to Nineveh (Nah 3:1), has a sad irony when applied to Yahweh's city. The oracle extends the metaphor to picture exile (the meat taken out of the pot at random, 24:6). The all-too-public loss of life in the defeat of the city will mirror the brazen nature of Jerusalem's homicidal ways, with blood splashed on bare rock for all to see (24:7-8). Theological interpretation sees this catastrophe as an expression of Yahweh's anger and vengeance (24:8). The prophet's construal is critical, because the events are open to various interpretations.

Carrying the metaphor further, Ezekiel introduces (24:6) and then pursues (24:11-13) the notion that the cooking pot is "corrupt." The city itself, not just its contents, is morally and spiritually corroded, not only murderous but also idolatrous (24:13). And the outlook is bleak, for in spite of extreme measures proposed to purify the pot, nothing dislodges or clears out the corrosion. Again Ezekiel scores a key interpretive insight: The city remains corrupt because of refusal to be cleansed by Yahweh (24:13).

Before changing subjects, Ezekiel warns again that time has run out. No divine change of mind should be anticipated—the siege that had started would not end happily for Jerusalem. Comprehensive judgment on "all your wicked actions" certainly comes. Yahweh promises this (24:14)!

Throughout the first half of the book (chs 1–24), Ezekiel labors to subvert false hopes for Jerusalem's survival and to counter attempts to absolve both the exile community and those yet in the city from responsibility for her threatened destruction. The concluding three passages focus on the death of Ezekiel's wife and the eerie implications of her death for all who love Jerusalem.

Ezekiel reports a divine word (24:15-17) in which Yahweh warned him that he was going to "take away" Ezekiel's wife "with one blow" (i.e., suddenly? dramatically?). This trauma Yahweh couples with a second: Though Ezekiel may "groan silently," he must forgo all normal and expected signs of mourning! Yahweh describes Ezekiel's wife as his "dearest treasure," (lit., "the delight of your eyes") and, in so doing, links her fate to that of Jerusalem, the exiles' heartfelt "delight" (*makhmad* [TH4261, ZH4718], the common word in 24:16 and 21). Then follow four staccato lines covering two days (24:18a, b, c, and 19). Ezekiel reports Yahweh's word in the morning. The prophet's wife dies in the evening. Ezekiel obeys Yahweh's instructions for austerity the next morning. The people ask for an explanation.

Ezekiel then reports a five-part message from Yahweh responding to the exiles' questions and aimed at the symbol par excellence of their false hopes (24:20-24). First, Yahweh himself will defile their beloved Temple (recall the lexical link with *makhmad* above). The exiles and those left back in Judah defiled it with their breach of Yahweh's covenant; Yahweh would now "corrupt" it with the corpses of the Jerusalemites (cf. 9:7; 11:6) and with trampling by foreign invaders. Second, the exiles' children back home would perish in the siege of Jerusalem that was under way. Third, the exiles themselves would be so overcome with grief that they, like Ezekiel, would be unable to carry on the rudimentary rituals of grief. Fourth, their unbearable grief would remind them of Ezekiel's enactment of Yahweh's word and would be a confirmation of the prophet and his claim to speak for Yahweh. Finally, picking up perhaps the most prominent theme of the whole book, Yahweh promises that through these events the community would acknowledge that the force at work in these events, as interpreted by Ezekiel, is none other than Yahweh, the historic God of the covenant.

The chapter's final lines (24:25-27) emphasize (by chiastic repetition) two major claims made already in the immediate context. Yahweh promises to destroy the whole fortress of Jerusalem, including their beloved Temple. Still worse, perhaps, Yahweh will "take away" their children left behind in Jerusalem (24:25). The labored, extended language employed here signals the profound loss entailed in these promised events. In addition, the closing lines make a twofold loop back—they tie in to the present chapter and also hark back to the opening of this whole division of the book. First, they bracket this immediate segment by giving attention to significant days (24:1

and 24:26). Yahweh promises that on the day Jerusalem falls to the Babylonian siege (i.e., on the day Yahweh makes good on these threats) a survivor from the besieged city will arrive in exile with a report of "frontline" events. Second, Ezekiel refers the reader back to the opening paragraphs of this book division and the speech limitation imposed on the newly commissioned prophet (3:26-27). When the survivor arrives, on that day Yahweh will lift Ezekiel's dumbness so he may speak freely.

Our passage also bridges ahead to 33:21-22, where arrival of the survivor with news of the fall of the city contributes to materials preparing for the oracles and visions of hope in chapters 33–48. In this predicted restoration of speech and in the just-promised similarity between the people's inability to grieve and Ezekiel's austerity at the death of his beloved—in both of these matters Ezekiel will be a *mopeth* [TH4159, ZH4603], translated "an example" in 24:24 and "a symbol" in 24:27. His behavior, *presaged in these messages from Yahweh,* will carry a nonverbal message that will reveal Yahweh as the God at work in these events.

Theological Reflections on Ezekiel 1:4–24:27. Oracles scattered over the first five years of Ezekiel's ministry and other materials organized around these dated pieces in the first 24 chapters of the book do not, and perhaps need not, present an entirely coherent theological stance. But major emphases are clear, if not easily integrated.

To this point the book of Ezekiel has argued primarily for (1) the credibility of Ezekiel as a prophet of Yahweh and (2) the legitimacy of viewing the destruction of the Temple and Jerusalem as the consequence of Israel's broken covenant. The author grounded the credibility of Ezekiel as a prophet first in the credibility of Yahweh, then in the integrity of Ezekiel's commission, and finally in the predictions of Jerusalem's demise. Though resident in Jerusalem, Yahweh had manifested himself in Babylon as the one who speaks in continuity with historic revelation and gives his Spirit to enable reception and proclamation of his word.

The assertion that the broken covenant was a legitimate explanation for the destruction of the Temple and its host city elicited a variety of interlocking claims. Israel and Judah's history of idolatry and forsaking of Yahweh's Torah had come to fruition in the catastrophe at the hands of the Babylonians. Both the ancestors and the present generation stood accountable for this invitation of the covenant's curses. Theological and popular tradition could not be stretched to erase this culpability. Idolatry, violence, murder, and forsaking the Sabbath repeatedly surface in specific indictments (e.g., 18:10-13). Failure of priestly and prophetic leadership to speak for Yahweh also figures among the causes of destruction (e.g., 13:4 and 22:26).

On the one hand, Ezekiel was sent as a sentinel to promote repentance by his warnings, even though the destruction of the city itself was sure. Yahweh had no thirst for the death of the wicked and sought their repentance as well as the rescue of the righteous. On the other hand, the situation seemed so dire that neither the repentant nor the righteous had hope. Yahweh would punish the city until his anger found rest. And Yahweh's concern for his own reputation would lead to sovereign, destructive, and restorative initiatives quite apart from anyone's repentance.

In counterpoint to the dominant themes of indictment and warning, brief but repeated glimpses of hope anticipate the final chapters of the book (e.g., 11:14-20; 16:59-63). These anticipations of life after the fall of Jerusalem, indeed after a return of exiles to Jerusalem, invite the reader to persevere in reading the book and in being faithful to Yahweh. Even though Yahweh had vacated the Temple and even his city, he had not deserted his people. He hallowed even their exile with his presence and was himself a sanctuary for them in a foreign land. Yahweh, who left his city to the Babylonians, would again rule from Jerusalem.

Scripture nowhere surrenders Ezekiel's basic stance regarding the credibility of God's servants and God's people. Their credibility is based first in the credibility of God himself and his sovereign choice to engage his people to reveal his will, to call them to faithful life with him. Secondarily, but significantly, their credibility rests on the integrity and authenticity of their covenant relationship with God, enabled and sustained by his Spirit. Further, although Old Testament covenantal theology receives canonical critique regarding the nature of the consequences of obedience and disobedience (e.g., Job, Ecclesiastes, Rom 8, and elsewhere), biblical writers do not in the end surrender the idea that God actually works in history, saving and judging his creation. Nonetheless, the final vindication of both God and his people awaits the eschaton.

Furthermore, almost without exception, the behaviors and attitudes that stir the wrath of Yahweh according to Ezekiel remain offenses to the God and Father of Jesus. For example, idolatry, extortion, murder, abuse of the poor and marginalized, adultery, incest, self-serving and self-generated "prophecy," and culturally compromised worship all stand as repugnant to Christian conscience (e.g., Rom 1:28-32; 1 Cor 6:9-11). False confidence drawn from distorted views of election, misuse of theological tradition to subvert moral accountability, and religious and civil leadership that fosters all these abominations—these concerns of Ezekiel remain concerns in the apostolic community (e.g., Luke 3:7-8; Rom 6:1,15; 1 Cor 8:4-13). They stand in direct opposition to Kingdom values as taught and lived by Jesus of Nazareth.

Ezekiel's glimpses of hope also find resonance in the rest of the canonical dialogue. We will return to this at the conclusion of Ezekiel's fuller treatment of hope, yet to come in the book. For now we can observe God's continuing quest to bring not only Israel but all persons to repentance. Hope abounds not only for the forgiveness of sin but the conquest of sin's power in creation. Further, this hope stands not because of a failure to take sin seriously but because of confidence in the power of God unleashed in the life, death, and resurrection of the Lord Jesus and his Spirit poured out in the world.

◆ IV. Oracles against Israel's Neighbors (25:1–32:32)

Ezekiel now turns his readers' attention to Yahweh's judgments against neighboring countries that took part in the destruction of Jerusalem and its Temple. Seven addressees receive attention in 24 oracles. Several features of these oracles make them a deliberately "transitional read" between an extended collection of oracles almost entirely given to judgment themes (3:16–24:27) and lengthy materials given almost entirely to coming salvation (33:1–48:35). The selection of seven addressees marks the collection as important. The theological awareness that the "bad news" announced here for Israel's enemies actually registers as "good news" to the home crowd evokes a transitional ambience, simultaneously pointing backward and forward. Departure at three points from the generally chronological arrangement of the dated oracles shows the intent to keep these pieces together and to put them at this point in the book (26:1; 29:17; and 32:1), squarely between the major judgment (3:16–24:27) and restoration (33:1–48:35) units. Ezekiel plainly states in 28:25-26 what editorial selection and arrangement imply by anchoring these oracles at this transitional point in the book and providing a key construal of the judgment against the nations as restoration at the midpoint of the collection.

In the mind of the prophet, Yahweh's relationship with his own people raised questions of what kind of relationship he had with other nations. Yahweh's ability (or lack thereof) to provide for his people and protect them from outsiders shaped his international reputation (20:9, 14, 22; Joel 2:17). If Yahweh proved unconvincing in his claim to rule the nations, his claim on Israel's covenant loyalty weakened accordingly. For Amos, Yahweh's sovereignty among the nations formed the context from which he pressed Yahweh's peculiar covenant demands upon Israel (Amos 1:3–3:3; 9:7-8). In the book of Jeremiah, Yahweh's promised judgment of the nations seems to provide theological credibility and moral justification for the prophet's announcements of doom and restoration for Judah. As he did with Judah, the Lord will punish the nations for their hubris, their wickedness (Jer 50:14, 29), and their idolatry (Jer 46:25-26; 48:13, 46; 49:1; 50:2; 51:44), to say nothing of their destruction of Judah and God's Temple (Jer 50:18, 28-29; 51:11, 24, 36). Jeremiah strengthens this word by including Babylon, Yahweh's instrument in the judgment of Judah (Jer 50:1–51:58). Ezekiel appears to use these oracles to integrate his overall message theologically, providing a bridge between oracles of doom for his people and the visions of restoration yet to appear in the book.

Conspicuously absent from these international oracles is any word against Babylon. Perhaps Ezekiel edited his work at this point with an eye to avoid unnecessarily provoking the exiles' "hosts" in Babylon. It is also conceivable that Ezekiel later addresses "the Babylon question" cryptically through a form of gematria involving substitution of letters to form a "secret" alphabet. Here, letters are magnified one level in the alphabet and then reversed. Thus *bbl* (Babylon) became *ggm* and then *mgg* (Magog). See note on 38:2. (For an accessible treatment of recent scholarship on all of the nations addressed in chs 25–32, see Hoerth, Mattingly, and Yamauchi 1994.)

◆ A. Oracles against Immediate Neighbors (25:1-17)

1. Oracle against Ammon, who celebrated the Temple's defilement (25:1-7)

Then this message came to me from the LORD: 2"Son of man, turn and face the land of Ammon and prophesy against its people. 3Give the Ammonites this message from the Sovereign LORD: Hear the word of the Sovereign LORD! Because you cheered when my Temple was defiled, mocked Israel in her desolation, and laughed at Judah as she went away into exile, 4I will allow nomads from the eastern deserts to overrun your country. They will set up their camps among you and pitch their tents on your land. They will harvest all your fruit and drink the milk from your livestock. 5And I will turn the city of Rabbah into a pasture for camels,

and all the land of the Ammonites into a resting place for sheep and goats. Then you will know that I am the LORD.

6"This is what the Sovereign LORD says: Because you clapped and danced and cheered with glee at the destruction of my people, 7I will raise my fist of judgment against you. I will give you as plunder to many nations. I will cut you off from being a nation and destroy you completely. Then you will know that I am the LORD.

NOTES

25:2, 3, 5 ***land of Ammon. . . . Ammonites.*** Both words translate the literal "sons of Ammon," depending on whether the land or the ethnic group appears to be the referent.

25:3 ***Hear the word of the Sovereign LORD!*** The message to the Ammonites actually divides into two brief oracles carrying this introduction in the MT (25:3-5 and 25:6-7).

25:4 ***nomads from the eastern deserts.*** This identifies the MT's *bene qedem* [TH6924, ZH7710] (people of the east) as nomads inhabiting the vast desert to the east of the Transjordan highlands. Ammon's origins were from a similar cultural location.

25:6 ***my people.*** This renders *'admath yisra'el* [TH127, ZH141] ("the land of Israel"; so RSV, NIV) with an emphasis on population over against territory.

COMMENTARY

A close reading of the text indicates that the shorter oracles against Judah's immediate neighbors—Ammon, Moab, Edom, and Philistia—form something of an introductory collection to the international oracles as a whole. The same rubrics and logic appear in each collection: "Hear the word of the Sovereign LORD!" or "This is what the Sovereign LORD says," which is followed by a causal conjunction ("because" or "therefore": *laken* [TH3651A, ZH4027], not translated in 25:4, 7, 9 in NLT), followed by "behold me" (*hineni* [TH2009, ZH2180]; cf. NLT, "I will"), followed by "you [or they] will know that I am the LORD."

In the first oracle, Yahweh indicts the Ammonites for their unseemly delight at the defilement of the Jerusalem Temple and the exile of Judah—the destruction of God's people (25:3, 6). The Ammonites actually cheered with extravagant celebration at these catastrophes and mocked Yahweh's people. The indictment may even reach back to Ammon's response to the fall of the northern kingdom, depending on how we understand "Israel in her desolation" (25:3). We have no record of these deplorable behaviors outside of Ezekiel. We do know from Obadiah the sort of response Judah's neighbors might have had to the fall of Jerusalem, if they shared Edom's sentiments. Focus here is clearly on Ammon's participation in the horrible events that left Jerusalem and the Temple in rubble. For the moment, this scene takes precedence even over the oft-maligned worship of the Ammonite "abomination," Milcom, and the child sacrifice associated with it (1 Kgs 11:5-8; 2 Kgs 23:13; Zeph 1:5).

The indictment shows that the Scripture traces the Ammonites to an ancestor, Ben-ammi, son of Lot by union with his younger daughter (Gen 19:38). Evidence exists for an Ammonite presence in the Transjordan highlands north of Moab and south of Gilead from the mid-second millennium BC through the Persian period and beyond. Ammon developed from a territory of pastoralists on the fringes of the eastern desert (cf. 25:4-5) to a people sufficiently urbanized to support kingship and chief cities (Rabbah, 25:5). Bounded on the north by the Jabbok River and straddling the King's Highway east of the Jordan, Ammon's affairs were tied up with those of Israel and Judah from the period of the judges on through the administration of Nehemiah. At the time of Israel's possession of the land, Ammon received special consideration because of her ancestral link with Lot (Deut 2:19, 37). But by the period of the judges, Ammonites were among the neighbors jeopardizing stability in the Israelite tribal league (Judg 3, 10–12). David brought them under Israelite rule, as did other kings in periods of Israelite or Judahite resurgence (2 Sam 11–13). The Ammonites receive very negative press in the Old Testament because Solomon introduced (within sight of the Jerusalem Temple) the worship of their god, Milcom or Molech (1 Kgs 11:5-8; 2 Kgs 23:10), for whom devotees sacrificed children.

◆ 2. Oracle against Moab, who ridiculed Judah's distinction (25:8-11)

8"This is what the Sovereign LORD says: Because the people of Moab have said that Judah is just like all the other nations, 9I will open up their eastern flank and wipe out their glorious frontier towns—Beth-jeshimoth, Baal-meon, and Kiriathaim. 10And I will hand Moab over to nomads from the eastern deserts, just as I handed over Ammon. Yes, the Ammonites will no longer be counted among the nations. 11In the same way, I will bring my judgment down on the Moabites. Then they will know that I am the LORD.

NOTES

25:8 *the people of Moab have said.* The MT reads "Moab and Seir," attributing the slander also to peoples of the territory south of Moab, east of the Gulf of Aqabah (i.e., Edom). Following the LXX and BHS editors, the NLT omits "and Seir," as extraneous to the Moab oracle, though most English versions retain "and Seir."

25:9 *Beth-jeshimoth, Baal-meon, and Kiriathaim.* These were towns in the northern reaches of Moabite territory. Moab's king Mesha mentions the latter two in his ninth-century BC inscription (Arnold and Beyer 2002:160-162). See the Mesha Inscription for a Moabite rendering of Israel's and Yahweh's dealings with Moab (ANET 320-321).

25:10-11 *Ammon. . . . Ammonites.* These both appear in MT twice in these brief verses about Moab (so also LXX, KJV, NASB, JPS). Some have thought these two mentions of Ammon awkward, with one or the other perhaps best taken as glosses intruding into the text (cf. RSV, NAB). The NLT shows how these terms could be understood as authentic parts of the Moab oracle.

COMMENTARY

Ezekiel's focus moves south along the Transjordanian highlands to Moab. This kingdom sat below Ammon roughly between the brook Zered and the wadi Arnon, with the upper boundary moving north beyond the Arnon in periods of Israelite weakness. Yahweh's central concern with Moab was her taunt that Israel was "just like all the other nations" (25:8). We know from Obadiah (Obad 1:11-14) the sorts of taunts Israel's neighbors hurled at her at the fall of Jerusalem. Apparently Moab mocked Israel's claims to be under Yahweh's special protection or in special relationship with her God. However, the Moabite insult spoke truth insofar as Judah misinterpreted Yahweh's commitment to Jerusalem as a false warrant for rejecting Ezekiel's warnings (cf. Jer 7:4). But Yahweh did maintain a particular covenant with his people, which others parodied or mocked at their own peril.

◆ 3. Oracle against Edom, who acted vengefully against Judah (25:12-14)

[12]"This is what the Sovereign LORD says: The people of Edom have sinned greatly by avenging themselves against the people of Judah. [13]Therefore, says the Sovereign LORD, I will raise my fist of judgment against Edom. I will wipe out its people and animals with the sword. I will make a wasteland of everything from Teman to Dedan. [14]I will accomplish this by the hand of my people of Israel. They will carry out my vengeance with anger, and Edom will know that this vengeance is from me. I, the Sovereign LORD, have spoken!

NOTES

25:12 ***The people of Edom.*** The Edomites were descendants of Esau (Gen 25:30; 36:1, 8, 16-21, 35-43; Num 20:14ff).

COMMENTARY

Scripture tells us that the Edomites came from Esau, Jacob's brother (see note on 25:12). As such, Moses assumed the Edomite "brothers" would grant them safe passage through their territory as Israel marched from Kadesh-barnea, hoping to pass beneath the Dead Sea and up the Transjordanian highlands to Canaan. Edom refused and conflict ensued (Num 20:14-21). From that time there was considerable acrimony in Edomite–Judean/Israelite relationships, culminating especially in Edom's unseemly glee at and eagerness to profit from Jerusalem's destruction under Nebuchadnezzar (Obad 1:11-14). The animosity between the two "brother" kingdoms appears dramatically in Psalm 137:7 and Malachi 1:2-4. This unwarranted "vengeance" evoked Yahweh's wrath (25:13). Destruction of everything from Edom's heartland to the frontier regions of her influence (Teman to Dedan) signals Yahweh's full judgment. Like Obadiah (Obad 1:18-21), Ezekiel anticipated this judgment at the hands of Israel when they were restored as a military presence in the region (25:14). They would be a vehicle of Yahweh's anger and judgment. The full reversal of Edom's situation would prompt acknowledgment of Yahweh's work in history, both theirs and Judah's.

◆ 4. Oracle against Philistia, who perpetuated animosity (25:15-17)

[15]"This is what the Sovereign LORD says: The people of Philistia have acted against Judah out of bitter revenge and long-standing contempt. [16]Therefore, this is what the Sovereign LORD says: I will raise my fist of judgment against the land of the Philistines. I will wipe out the Kerethites and utterly destroy the people who live by the sea. [17]I will execute terrible vengeance against them to punish them for what they have done. And when I have inflicted my revenge, they will know that I am the LORD."

NOTES

25:15 ***The people of Philistia.*** With this oracle against Philistia, Ezekiel completes a semicircle of accusation and announced judgment on every side. Beginning with the Ammonites to the east/northeast (25:1-7), the prophet moves to the Moabites just below them (25:8-11), the Edomites just south of Moab (to Judah's southeast, 25:12-14), and the Philistines along the coast to the southwest (25:15-17). Ezekiel's approach here is in some ways analogous to that in the book of Amos (Amos 1:3–2:8).

acted . . . out of bitter revenge. Biblical Hebrew has three words for "avenging," "vengeance," "revenge," and the like: *naqam* [TH5358, ZH5933], a verb, and two nouns from the same root, *naqam* [TH5359, ZH5934], and *neqamah* [TH5360, ZH5935]. These words occur 12 times in the book of Ezekiel. After two appearances in 24:8, the other 10 uses of these words by Ezekiel are packed into this oracle against the Philistines and the immediately preceding one against the Edomites, three times in 25:15 alone. In both 25:12 and 15, the syntax expresses particularly bitter vengeance, "to take revenge with vengeance." A wooden translation of verse 15 sounds clumsy but retains the *naqam* theme clearly: "Because the Philistines acted in *vengeance*, and took *revenge* in *vengeance* with heartfelt disdain, to destroy with eternal animosity." The NLT's treatment of the verse retains the potent note of revenge while avoiding the plodding redundancy of the MT. The concentration of this vengeance vocabulary in Ezekiel's treatment of Moab and Philistia is probably not accidental. More likely it reflects the particularly acrimonious relationships sustained over many centuries between these two nations and the people of Israel and Judah. Yahweh's response to both enemies would be to take vengeance. In fact, these people's anticipated acknowledgment of Yahweh as Lord hinges on their awareness of his capacity to bring his own vengeance (25:17).

COMMENTARY

The final brief oracle against Israel's neighbors targets the Philistines, who alone of the four neighbors lack a genealogical link with Israel. Their association with the Kerethites (25:16, probably from Crete), reflects their Aegean, non-Semitic origins. Unhappy relationships with Philistia appear already in the period of the Judges, and perhaps even with the patriarchs (Gen 21, 26). Ezekiel singles out their long-standing animosity with Israel as the cause of Yahweh's judgment to come (25:15). Apparently they used the years of Judah's suffering under Nebuchadnezzar as yet another opportunity for vengeance, though we lack information about these matters.

◆ B. Oracles against Tyre and Her King (26:1–28:24)

1. Unthinkable responses to Tyre's taunt (26:1–21)

On February 3, during the twelfth year of King Jehoiachin's captivity,* this message came to me from the LORD: 2"Son of man, Tyre has rejoiced over the fall of Jerusalem, saying, 'Ha! She who was the gateway to the rich trade routes to the east has been broken, and I am the heir! Because she has been made desolate, I will become wealthy!'

3"Therefore, this is what the Sovereign LORD says: I am your enemy, O Tyre, and I will bring many nations against you, like the waves of the sea crashing against your shoreline. 4They will destroy the walls of Tyre and tear down its towers. I will scrape away its soil and make it a bare rock! 5It will be just a rock in the sea, a place for fishermen to spread their nets,

for I have spoken, says the Sovereign LORD. Tyre will become the prey of many nations, [6]and its mainland villages will be destroyed by the sword. Then they will know that I am the LORD.

[7]"This is what the Sovereign LORD says: From the north I will bring King Nebuchadnezzar* of Babylon against Tyre. He is king of kings and brings his horses, chariots, charioteers, and great army. [8]First he will destroy your mainland villages. Then he will attack you by building a siege wall, constructing a ramp, and raising a roof of shields against you. [9]He will pound your walls with battering rams and demolish your towers with sledgehammers. [10]The hooves of his horses will choke the city with dust, and the noise of the charioteers and chariot wheels will shake your walls as they storm through your broken gates. [11]His horsemen will trample through every street in the city. They will butcher your people, and your strong pillars will topple.

[12]"They will plunder all your riches and merchandise and break down your walls. They will destroy your lovely homes and dump your stones and timbers and even your dust into the sea. [13]I will stop the music of your songs. No more will the sound of harps be heard among your people. [14]I will make your island a bare rock, a place for fishermen to spread their nets. You will never be rebuilt, for I, the LORD, have spoken. Yes, the Sovereign LORD has spoken!

[15]"This is what the Sovereign LORD says to Tyre: The whole coastline will tremble at the sound of your fall, as the screams of the wounded echo in the continuing slaughter. [16]All the seaport rulers will step down from their thrones and take off their royal robes and beautiful clothing. They will sit on the ground trembling with horror at your destruction. [17]Then they will wail for you, singing this funeral song:

"O famous island city,
once ruler of the sea,
how you have been destroyed!
Your people, with their naval power,
once spread fear around the world.
[18] Now the coastlands tremble at
your fall.
The islands are dismayed as
you disappear.

[19]"This is what the Sovereign LORD says: I will make Tyre an uninhabited ruin, like many others. I will bury you beneath the terrible waves of enemy attack. Great seas will swallow you. [20]I will send you to the pit to join those who descended there long ago. Your city will lie in ruins, buried beneath the earth, like those in the pit who have entered the world of the dead. You will have no place of respect here in the land of the living. [21]I will bring you to a terrible end, and you will exist no more. You will be looked for, but you will never again be found. I, the Sovereign LORD, have spoken!"

26:1 Hebrew *In the eleventh year, on the first day of the month,* of the ancient Hebrew lunar calendar year. Since an element is missing in the date formula here, scholars have reconstructed this probable reading: *In the eleventh [month of the twelfth] year, on the first day of the month.* This reading would put this message on February 3, 585 B.C.; also see note on 1:1. **26:7** Hebrew *Nebuchadrezzar,* a variant spelling of Nebuchadnezzar.

NOTES

26:1 *On February 3, during the twelfth year.* See NLT mg. The month is missing in the date formula here. The NLT follows the reading reconstructed by some scholars (Allen 1990:71; Block 1998:34; Eichrodt 1970:368-369) following the LXX, which puts the date at February 3, 585 BC. See also Greenberg (1997:115), Taylor (1969:190), and Zimmerli (1983:33-34), who decline this solution, as do most modern versions.

26:12 *They will plunder.* The MT switches to third-person pl. verb forms (i.e., "they will"), without naming the subjects. The simplest and most direct understanding is that the antecedents of these verbs are the masc. designations in the immediately preceding verses—the charioteers and horsemen of Nebuchadnezzar (vv. 10-11). The LXX, however, continues third-person sg. verbs from the preceding paragraph and the references to Nebuchadnezzar. The LXX translator either had a text with the sg. verbs or translated with the sg. form in order to make his understanding of the text clear. In the first case, it would function as a textual witness, in the second, perhaps more important, it would function as our earliest commentary on the text and witness to an interpretive tradition that saw Nebuchadnezzar as the referent from 26:7 on through 26:14 (see Thompson 1981). In this case one text is as likely as the other.

26:20 *You will have no place of respect here in the land of the living.* The MT (lit., "So that you may not be inhabited and I will give beauty/glory in the land of the living") seems unlikely, but improving upon it proves difficult. Consequently, some versions more or less let MT stand (ASV, ESV, NKJV). Some repoint MT's verb "dwell/be inhabited" to read "return" (hence "you will not return"), and redivide and emend the consonants of MT's "I will give beauty/glory" to read "take one's place" or "have a place" (NIV, NAB), or some combination of these alternatives (RSV, NRSV, REB). The LXX reads "in order that you may not be inhabited [with the MT] and not take your stand in the land of the living" (redividing and emending the second clause). The NLT follows the LXX in the second clause and rightly construes "take your stand" richly as "taking a place of dignity and recognition." The NLT omits the first clause, considering it assumed by or easily assimilated to the second.

COMMENTARY

Having given the oracles against the nations with four staccato words to Judah's immediate neighbors (Ammon, Moab, Edom, and Philistia), Ezekiel turns now to two major players in the unfolding drama of Judah's destiny—Tyre (26:1–28:26) and Egypt (29:1–32:32).

The date formula and the amount of space devoted to Tyre indicate the importance Ezekiel placed on this rival and adversary of Judah. By Ezekiel's time Tyre was the preeminent Phoenician city, the center of a seafaring commercial empire covering the whole Mediterranean. Tyre itself was an island fortress, situated less than a half mile offshore, with dependent villages opposite her on the mainland (the "daughters" referred to in most versions).

The date adopted by the NLT (26:1) places this oracle against Tyre within a year of the fall of Jerusalem. Whenever one finally dates the oracle (see note on 26:1), the prophecy assumes either the actual fall of the city or its imminent, unavoidable destruction. Tyre's gleeful exclamation contains two points of contention for Ezekiel. Tyre celebrates the tragic destruction of Jerusalem. Further, she gloats at the prospect of taking over Judah and Jerusalem's commercial holdings (26:2). The catalog of Tyre's trading contacts in chapter 27 reminds us that trade in agricultural and horticultural products passed through Jerusalem, "the Gateway of the Peoples" (26:2, according to MT and most modern versions; cf. 27:17). Because of goods she produced and trade routes she controlled, Judah presented a prize coveted by Tyre. For that gleeful lust, God pronounces the frightful news: "I am your enemy" (26:3)!

Consequently, Yahweh would bring nations to destroy Tyre under Nebuchadnezzar, his chief instrument of that judgment (26:3, 7; note the logic by which the claims regarding Nebuchadnezzar in 26:7-14 explain the more general opening paragraph in 26:3-6). Describing the devastation the Babylonian's forces will inflict upon both the mainland villages and the island fortress, Ezekiel employs language typical of warfare on dry land (26:7-11). The language is not poetic or simply symbolic. Ezekiel used standard terminology relating to land battles and military strategy for the assault on island Tyre—including mention of cavalry, chariots, a siege wall, a siege ramp, battering rams, and invading troops. Nebuchadnezzar would completely demolish Tyre.

Threat of Tyre's demolition continues in 26:12-14 with a change to third-person plural verbs, triggered by the plural reference to horsemen who would trample the city's streets (26:11). Reference to Nebuchadnezzar continues, with focus now on his plundering troops. Ezekiel foresaw the total destruction of the city in the picture of the rocky island scraped bare, "a place for fishermen to spread their nets" (26:14). As Ezekiel himself notes, Nebuchadnezzar did not himself capture or destroy insular Tyre (cf. 29:17-20), but, after a 13-year siege, managed only to exact tribute from the king and savage the outlying areas on the mainland. The task of demolishing Tyre was left for Alexander the Great, whose troops did level the city, just as Ezekiel had anticipated. (The failure of Ezekiel's threat—indeed, God's threat!—to materialize as prophesied raises obvious theological questions. See the commentary on 29:17-21 for treatment of this matter.)

Over several centuries Tyre had resisted assault by invading armies from the south, east, and north. She had managed to carry on her maritime commerce and stay relatively disentangled from imperial designs of Egyptian, Canaanite, and Mesopotamian powers. She had submitted to tribute but had not actually been conquered or permanently disrupted. So Ezekiel anticipated widespread horror at the news of Tyre's complete obliteration (26:15-18). Erstwhile trading partners and rival rulers would wail for Tyre with a funeral song, lamenting its totally unforeseen change from an awe- and fear-inspiring naval power to a bare rock for drying fishing nets.

Ezekiel closed this message from the Lord with an oracle raising a new theme in these judgments against the nations—their fate in the grave (26:19-21; cf. 31:14; 32:17-32). Waves of destruction would overwhelm Tyre, says the Lord, with a word picture especially fitting for this sea power. Reduced to the fate of all the dead, without special treatment in the grave, Tyre would also be left without a trace of her greatness in the world of the living. The message about Tyre is backed by the singular warrant of Yahweh's own word. He has spoken (26:14, 21)!

◆ 2. Lamentation over the shipwreck of Tyre (27:1-36)

Then this message came to me from the
LORD: 2"Son of man, sing a funeral song
for Tyre, 3that mighty gateway to the sea,
the trading center of the world. Give Tyre
this message from the Sovereign LORD:

"You boasted, O Tyre,
'My beauty is perfect!'
4You extended your boundaries into
the sea.
Your builders made your beauty
perfect.
5You were like a great ship
built of the finest cypress
from Senir.*
They took a cedar from Lebanon
to make a mast for you.
6They carved your oars
from the oaks of Bashan.
Your deck of pine from the coasts
of Cyprus*
was inlaid with ivory.
7Your sails were made of Egypt's
finest linen,
and they flew as a banner above you.

You stood beneath blue and purple
awnings
made bright with dyes from the
coasts of Elishah.
8 Your oarsmen came from Sidon
and Arvad;
your helmsmen were skilled men
from Tyre itself.
9 Wise old craftsmen from Gebal
did the caulking.
Ships from every land came with
goods to barter for your trade.

10 "Men from distant Persia, Lydia, and
Libya* served in your great army. They
hung their shields and helmets on your
walls, giving you great honor. 11 Men from
Arvad and Helech stood on your walls.
Your towers were manned by men from
Gammad. Their shields hung on your
walls, completing your beauty.

12 "Tarshish sent merchants to buy your
wares in exchange for silver, iron, tin, and
lead. 13 Merchants from Greece,* Tubal,
and Meshech brought slaves and articles
of bronze to trade with you.

14 "From Beth-togarmah came riding
horses, chariot horses, and mules, all in
exchange for your goods. 15 Merchants
came to you from Dedan.* Numerous
coastlands were your captive markets;
they brought payment in ivory tusks and
ebony wood.

16 "Syria* sent merchants to buy your
rich variety of goods. They traded tur-
quoise, purple dyes, embroidery, fine
linen, and jewelry of coral and rubies.
17 Judah and Israel traded for your wares,
offering wheat from Minnith, figs,* honey,
olive oil, and balm.

18 "Damascus sent merchants to buy
your rich variety of goods, bringing wine
from Helbon and white wool from Zahar.
19 Greeks from Uzal* came to trade for your
merchandise. Wrought iron, cassia, and
fragrant calamus were bartered for your
wares.

20 "Dedan sent merchants to trade their
expensive saddle blankets with you. 21 The
Arabians and the princes of Kedar sent
merchants to trade lambs and rams and
male goats in exchange for your goods.
22 The merchants of Sheba and Raamah
came with all kinds of spices, jewels, and
gold in exchange for your wares.

23 "Haran, Canneh, Eden, Sheba, Asshur,
and Kilmad came with their merchandise,
too. 24 They brought choice fabrics to
trade—blue cloth, embroidery, and multi-
colored carpets rolled up and bound with
cords. 25 The ships of Tarshish were your
ocean caravans. Your island warehouse
was filled to the brim!

26 "But look! Your oarsmen
have taken you into stormy seas!
A mighty eastern gale
has wrecked you in the heart
of the sea!
27 Everything is lost—
your riches and wares,
your sailors and pilots,
your ship builders, merchants,
and warriors.
On the day of your ruin,
everyone on board sinks into the
depths of the sea.
28 Your cities by the sea tremble
as your pilots cry out in terror.
29 All the oarsmen abandon their ships;
the sailors and pilots on shore come
to stand on the beach.
30 They cry aloud over you
and weep bitterly.
They throw dust on their heads
and roll in ashes.
31 They shave their heads in grief for you
and dress themselves in burlap.
They weep for you with bitter anguish
and deep mourning.
32 As they wail and mourn over you,
they sing this sad funeral song:
'Was there ever such a city as Tyre,
now silent at the bottom of the sea?
33 The merchandise you traded
satisfied the desires of many
nations.
Kings at the ends of the earth
were enriched by your trade.
34 Now you are a wrecked ship,
broken at the bottom of the sea.

All your merchandise and crew
have gone down with you.
35 All who live along the coastlands
are appalled at your terrible fate.
Their kings are filled with horror
and look on with twisted faces.
36 The merchants among the nations
shake their heads at the sight of you,*
for you have come to a horrible end
and will exist no more.'"

27:5 Or *Hermon.* **27:6** Hebrew *Kittim.* **27:10** Hebrew *Paras, Lud, and Put.* **27:13** Hebrew *Javan.* **27:15** Greek version reads *Rhodes.* **27:16** Hebrew *Aram;* some manuscripts read *Edom.* **27:17** The meaning of the Hebrew is uncertain. **27:19** Hebrew *Vedan and Javan from Uzal.* The meaning of the Hebrew is uncertain. **27:36** Hebrew *hiss at you.*

NOTES

27:5 ***Senir.*** According to Deut 3:9, Senir was an Amorite name for Mount Hermon. In Song 4:8 it appears to designate one of the peaks of the Anti-Lebanon range, other than Hermon and Amana. Here, in parallel with Lebanon, Senir probably refers to the Anti-Lebanon range as a whole.

Lebanon. This was the mountain range running parallel to the Mediterranean coast, between it and the interior rift valley, famous for prize cedars (cf. 17:3; 31:3; Isa 2:13; 14:8; 37:24; Jer 22:23).

27:6 ***Bashan.*** This was a Transjordan plateau extending from Gilead to Mount Hermon, famous for grain and cattle production (39:18; Deut 32:14).

Your deck . . . was inlaid with ivory. The MT has "your deck they made of ivory (of/from?) the daughter of the Assyrians (*bath-'ashurim* [TH1323/804A, ZH1426/855], consonantal *bt-'shrym*) from the islands/coasts of Cyprus," which seems confused. In spite of its difficulty, the ancient versions retain the reference to ivory. None, however, retain a reference to "Assyria." The Ugaritic *t'shr* (HALOT 4:1677), meaning "Cyprus, cedar," suggests redividing the MT's problematic *bt-'shrym* to *b-t'shrym,* paving the way for a rendering like the NLT (so also with various identifications of the wood, NJPS, NIV, NASB, RSV, NRSV, NAB, ESV).

Cyprus. Heb., *kittim* [TH3794, ZH4183], a chief port on Cyprus, here naming the whole island by means of a chief city.

27:7 ***Elishah.*** This is the island of Cyprus, ancient Alashiya.

27:8 ***Sidon.*** This was the chief rival of Tyre among Phoenician port cities; it was located 25 miles north of Tyre.

Arvad. This was the northernmost of the main Phoenician cities and, like Tyre, was situated on an island just off the coast. It was known in Assyrian royal annals as the city "in the sea" (ANET 276), and also as a contributor of 200 troops to a coalition organized against Shalmaneser III (ANET 279).

27:9 ***Gebal.*** This was an ancient Phoenician city located 25 miles north of modern Beirut. It was known as an exporter of prize cedars even before Sidon and later Tyre came to prominence.

27:10 ***Persia.*** Heb., *paras* [TH6539, ZH7273]. Even before the rise of its empire, Persia was known as an international power on Tyre's far eastern horizon.

Lydia. Heb., *lud* [TH3865, ZH4276]. In Gen 10:13 this name belongs to a son of Egypt, thus located in North Africa, and in Gen 10:22 it designates a son of Shem, located in Asia Minor. Here, Lydia in west-central Asia Minor is probably intended, which was by Ezekiel's time proverbially wealthy.

Libya. Heb., *put* [TH6316A, ZH7033]. This was in North Africa west of Egypt. Ezekiel touched three horizons in his reference to Persia, Lydia, and Libya.

27:11 ***Helech.*** The NLT transliterates the Hebrew name for Cilicia. Cilicia/Helech was a region in southeast Asia Minor, bounded on the north by the Taurus Mountains, on the east by the Amanus, and on the west by Pamphylia.

27:12 ***Tarshish.*** This was a city or region in the far western Mediterranean, probably in Spain, judging from the association with tin and other metals. The name itself appears to be formed on a root having to do with smelting (Block 1998:71).

27:13 ***Greece.*** Heb., *yawan* [TH3120, ZH3430] (cf. the alternate spelling Javan in NLT mg). Land of the Ionians on both sides of the Aegean, this was the designation of the Greek world in the OT. *Yawan* is known elsewhere also in the OT for trafficking slaves (Joel 3:6; cf. Amos 1:6, 9).

Tubal. This is associated in the OT and Neo-Assyrian royal inscriptions with place names that would locate it in south-central and eastern Anatolia. The name itself may have to do with metal casting, appropriate to the bronze merchandise Tubal offered.

Meshech. This is to be identified with *Mushku* of Neo-Assyrian sources and located immediately to the west of Tubal. Booty taken from Meshech and Tubal by Assyrian kings included metal vessels (Block 1998:73).

27:14 ***Beth-togarmah.*** Ezekiel locates Beth-togarmah in "the distant north" (38:6) along with Meshech and Tubal. It should probably be taken as the name of a city known from Hittite texts as *Tegarama,* from Akkadian sources as *Til-garimmu,* and from classical sources as *Gauraena,* part of a region famous in Neo-Assyrian documents as a source of well-bred horses (cf. 1 Kgs 10:28; Block 1998:73-74).

27:15 ***Dedan.*** The LXX reads *Rhodiōn* [TG4499, ZG4852] (Rhodes). The site's association in 27:14 with Anatolia and here with seacoasts points away from Dedan, the well-known trading post in the northwest Arabian desert. The LXX reflects this awareness in its translation, which seems to have read *rdn* for *ddn.* Probably better, some have suggested understanding *ddn* as Danuna, the land of the Danunites, north of Tyre, attested in the Amarna letters (Block 1998:74 and note 125).

27:16 ***Syria.*** Heb., *'aram* [TH758A, ZH806] (Aram); some mss read *'edom* [TH123A, ZH121] (Edom), an interchange of the similar-looking letters Resh and Daleth in the Hebrew consonantal text.

27:17 ***Minnith.*** The NLT reads the MT as a place name, a site in Ammon mentioned also in Judg 11:33. The term should perhaps be read as an Indian loan word (HALOT 2:602), the name of a sort of grain, "minnith-wheat." The LXX also rejected reading this as a place name.

27:18 ***Helbon.*** This was a city north of Damascus known in Neo-Assyrian sources for its wine trade.

Zahar. This is probably a place name. If so, it is a site or area of uncertain identification, perhaps *Zuhur* attested in the Amarna Letters, or modern Es-Sakhra north of Damascus.

27:19 ***Greeks from Uzal.*** Lit., "Vedan and Javan from Uzal." The meaning of the Hebrew is uncertain (so NLT mg). Millard's emendation that produces "casks of wine from Izalla," is very attractive (1962:201-203). Izalla designates a place joined with Helbon in cuneiform records of wine trade (Greenberg 1997:557).

27:20 ***Dedan.*** As a territory, it was the home of Arabian tribes settled along the Red Sea in the northwest sector of the Arabian Peninsula. Here, it likely refers to the inland oasis on the trading route through the same area.

27:21 ***Arabians.*** This is the biblical name for a number of nomadic tribes that moved on the eastern and southern fringes of Israelite and Judean settled land. They provided sheep, goats, camels, and asses to the sedentary populations and also traded in spices, incense, dates, embroidered cloth, various metals, and precious stones, moving along the trade routes of the Arabian peninsula (cf. 1 Kgs 10:14; Isa 11:14; 21:11-17; Jer 25:23-24; 49:28-33).

Kedar. This refers either to the most powerful of a set of Arabian tribes that flourished from the eighth to the fourth century BC or to their land. Jeremiah knew them as "warriors from the East," self-sufficient nomadic tribes (Jer 49:28, 31). They were famous as sheep breeders and traders (Isa 60:7).

27:22 *Sheba.* This is probably known best as the homeland of the "Queen of Sheba," who visited King Solomon accompanied by a caravan bearing gifts of gold, precious jewels, and spices (1 Kgs 10:1-2). As noted elsewhere in Scripture, Sheba was famous in the ancient Near East for its far-flung trade in gold, gems, incense, and myrrh (38:13; Ps 72:15; Isa 60:6). Sheba was located in the southwest corner of the Arabian peninsula (modern Yemen) and was home to a well-developed culture in the early years of the Israelite monarchy.

Raamah. This was an Arabian trading center, perhaps to be identified as Ragmat, the capital of the oasis of Najran, north of Sheba (northern Yemen) on the incense route connecting Sheba and Ragmat in the south with Dedan, Tema, and other trading centers to the northwest in the Arabian peninsula (cf. Job 6:19; Jer 25:23).

27:23 *Haran.* This was a major city situated on the Balikh River 60 miles north of the Euphrates in upper Mesopotamia, the gateway for goods flowing west out of Mesopotamia to the Mediterranean along the trade route that traversed the northern steppes of upper Mesopotamia.

Canneh. This should probably be identified with *Kannu'*, a site of uncertain location known in Neo-Assyrian sources as a home of merchants.

Eden. This is a short form of Beth-eden (Assyrian *Bit-Adini*), an Aramean state southwest of the Balikh.

Asshur. Asshur can designate the nation of Assyria, but in this list it is likely the name of a capital city of Assyria that was a regional hub funneling numerous northern trade routes into the single road down the Tigris Valley, over to Babylon and south.

Kilmad. This is an unknown site. The Syriac OT omits this word. Targum divides it (*kl mdy* [TH3605/4074A, ZH3972/4512]) and reads "all the Medes." Some manuscripts read *klmr* (assuming the easy confusion of Daleth for Resh) and identify the site with *Kulmer*, northeast of Diyarbakir and known from Neo-Assyrian sources (Block 1998:79).

27:25 *Tarshish.* See note on 27:12.

COMMENTARY

This second, extended message that Ezekiel received concerning the destruction of Tyre has a remarkably simple but powerful structure. God levels two core accusations from which the rest of the message follows (27:3-4a). First, God claims that Tyre boasted in her own beauty—the beauty of her situation, development, economic and cultural achievements, her nearly imperial beauty—as though she were self-made, with no debt at all to the Lord (27:3). Second, she "extended [her] boundaries into the sea." That is, she had built a financial empire extending her control throughout the length and breadth of the Mediterranean (27:4a). The pervasive extension of Tyre's influence was itself not really the wrong. Their shipping skill even proved beneficial to Israel at times (1 Kgs 5; 9:26-28). The oracle makes clear that it was

Tyre's arrogance and sense of indestructibility that triggered her fall. Ezekiel then elaborates upon Tyre's beauty using the metaphor of a great and beautiful ship, the great ship *Tyre* (27:4b-9). This paves the way for a powerful depiction of the destruction of Tyre as the wreck of this great ship and of "global" reaction to that catastrophe (27:26-36). In between these two poems on the great ship *Tyre*, Ezekiel celebrates the greatness of Tyre by means of a catalog of her far-flung merchant enterprises (27:10-25), as gateway to the Mediterranean and the trading center of the world (27:3a).

Ezekiel wrote his prophecy in the lament genre (27:2), announcing Tyre's demise not only by the content of the message but also in its literary form, which drones the death of the city. Ezekiel maintained a rough funeral song meter (a 3:2 meter) in 27:3-10, which is resumed again in 27:25-36. The funerary meter brackets the oracle and makes the whole prophecy a lament. Two sections of the message read like encyclopedia articles and may actually reflect sources the prophet used. The first section presents the construction of an excellent ship (27:4-9), the second, a catalog of the trading centers around the entire Mediterranean, Arabian, and Mesopotamian worlds with whom Tyre conducted her lucrative commerce (from Tarshish in Spain to Persia beyond the Tigris, from Greece in the north to southern Arabia).

The arrogance in Tyre's claim to great beauty (27:3) can perhaps be captured by paraphrasing it. She boasted, "I am fully and completely beautiful," or "I am quintessential beauty itself." Ezekiel skillfully used his ship metaphor to particularize Tyre's beauty. "Your builders made your beauty perfect. You were like a great ship built of the finest cypress from Senir" (27:4b-5). He described how the critical parts of the gorgeous ship *Tyre* were made from the finest materials, acquired from places known from ancient sources to be outlets of premier quality materials for each part. Thus, the builders used cypress from Senir for the main hull, cedar from Lebanon for her mast, carved oak from Bashan for her oars, and so on (27:6-7). The opening dirge closes with a note that the ship was staffed by oarsmen and helmsmen from Phoenicia itself, skilled from long naval experience in rope handling and navigation. Finally, experienced sea craftsmen from Gebal, another ancient Phoenician trade center, caulked or repaired her (Greenberg 1997:551), shoring up her seaworthiness (27:8-9a; cf. 2 Kgs 12:6, 8). Of course, we readers are being set up. The more perfect the beauty and more excellent the quality of the ship *Tyre*, the more terrible and unexpected her loss will be.

While the second catalog continues the theme of Tyre's beauty (27:10-11), Ezekiel also shifts focus to the second indictment, Tyre's spreading of terror through her naval and mercantile empire (cf. 26:17). Tyre has hired mercenaries from far and near to help staff her army and guard critical assets. Their shields and helmets, hung on Tyre's battlements, accentuate her beauty. Listing the source of troops for particular military tasks provides an easy transition into naming centers from which traders and merchants come to bring their particular goods and wares to enrich Tyre. As with the construction and outfitting of the great ship *Tyre*, here also trading and manufacturing centers or regions are linked with products and goods for which the respective centers are famous. Thus, Tyre procured metals including tin from Tarshish, probably a Phoenician colony on the Guadalquivir River in western Spain, known in classical sources for deposits of silver, iron, tin, and lead (Greenberg 1997:553). Neo-Assyrian documentation of booty taken or of tribute and gifts received enhances our ability to identify and sometimes also to locate these sites and understand the goods or products linked with them. Thus, Ezekiel claims merchants from Meshech "brought slaves and articles of bronze to trade" with Tyre (27:13). Like Ezekiel, Assyrian sources pair *Tabala* and *Mushku* (i.e., Tubal and Meshech) and associate them, among other things, with metal products (Block 1998:73). Through Tyre's developed commerce, she became the most profusely stocked warehouse of the ancient world—"filled to the brim" with common and luxury holdings of all sorts (27:25).

Ezekiel's announcement of the coming destruction of Tyre returns to the motif introduced in his poem on the building of the great ship *Tyre* (27:4a-9); it is a worldwide response to her destruction, a lament of her tragic loss at sea (27:26-36). Her navigators made a fatal mistake, taking the ship *Tyre* into open seas in gale-force winds (27:26). The "eastern gale" that wrecked *Tyre* would surely be the Babylonians under Nebuchadnezzar. The miscalculation brought a total loss—crew, cargo, and passengers disappeared into the depths (27:27). Tyre's clientele and personnel trembled in traumatic response, standing on shore, watching wreckage wash up on the beach (27:28-29). Signs of grief and utter dismay appear throughout her network of cities and dependents—weeping, dust on heads, rolling in ashes, donning burlap, shaving heads, wailing (27:29-31). Finally, we hear the dirge these mourners themselves intone (27:32-36). Emphasis on her greatness underscores the trauma of her destruction. The lament fits well the ambivalent situation in which persons were both enriched and exploited by Tyre's powerful commercial kingdom (27:33-36). Leaders and merchants worldwide would shake their heads in confused disbelief and speak one last time of her horrible, final end (27:36). This "terrible end" will receive a second airing in 28:19.

◆ 3. The destiny of Tyre and her proud prince (28:1-19)

Then this message came to me from the LORD: 2"Son of man, give the prince of Tyre this message from the Sovereign LORD:

**"In your great pride you claim,
'I am a god!
I sit on a divine throne in the heart of the sea.'
But you are only a man and not a god,
though you boast that you are a god.
3You regard yourself as wiser than Daniel
and think no secret is hidden from you.
4With your wisdom and understanding
you have amassed great wealth—
gold and silver for your treasuries.
5Yes, your wisdom has made you very rich,
and your riches have made you very proud.**

**6"Therefore, this is what the Sovereign LORD says:
Because you think you are as wise as a god,
7 I will now bring against you a foreign army,
the terror of the nations.
They will draw their swords against your marvelous wisdom
and defile your splendor!**

[8] They will bring you down to the pit,
and you will die in the heart
of the sea,
pierced with many wounds.
[9] Will you then boast, 'I am a god!'
to those who kill you?
To them you will be no god
but merely a man!
[10] You will die like an outcast*
at the hands of foreigners.
I, the Sovereign LORD, have spoken!"

[11] Then this further message came to me
from the LORD: [12] "Son of man, sing this
funeral song for the king of Tyre. Give him
this message from the Sovereign LORD:

"You were the model of perfection,
full of wisdom and exquisite in
beauty.
[13] You were in Eden,
the garden of God.
Your clothing was adorned with every
precious stone*—
red carnelian, pale-green peridot,
white moonstone,
blue-green beryl, onyx, green jasper,
blue lapis lazuli, turquoise, and
emerald—
all beautifully crafted for you
and set in the finest gold.
They were given to you
on the day you were created.
[14] I ordained and anointed you
as the mighty angelic guardian.*
You had access to the holy mountain
of God
and walked among the stones of fire.

[15] "You were blameless in all you did
from the day you were created
until the day evil was found in you.
[16] Your rich commerce led you to
violence,
and you sinned.
So I banished you in disgrace
from the mountain of God.
I expelled you, O mighty guardian,
from your place among the stones
of fire.
[17] Your heart was filled with pride
because of all your beauty.
Your wisdom was corrupted
by your love of splendor.
So I threw you to the ground
and exposed you to the curious
gaze of kings.
[18] You defiled your sanctuaries
with your many sins and your
dishonest trade.
So I brought fire out from within you,
and it consumed you.
I reduced you to ashes on the ground
in the sight of all who were
watching.
[19] All who knew you are appalled at
your fate.
You have come to a terrible end,
and you will exist no more."

28:10 Hebrew *will die the death of the uncircumcised.* **28:13** The identification of some of these gemstones is uncertain. **28:14** Hebrew *guardian cherub;* similarly in 28:16.

NOTES

28:3 ***Daniel.*** See note on 14:14.

28:12 ***model of perfection.*** The NLT, like most modern versions, follows the LXX and early versions in repointing the MT's participle *khothem* [TH2856, ZH3159] (to seal) as the related noun *khotham* [TH2368, ZH2597] (seal, model).

28:13 ***every precious stone.*** The identification of some of these gemstones is uncertain. See Block (1998:105-112) for an extended review of present interpretive options for these gemstones and two helpful charts summarizing his findings.

28:19 ***You have come to a terrible end.*** Heb., *ballahoth* [TH1091, ZH1166] *hayitha* (A calamity you have become) accentuates by word order the calamitous future Tyre faces. In this terrifying refrain, Ezekiel dramatically presents Tyre's future demise both as complete (lit., "have become") and independent; see Waltke and O'Connor 1990:§30.5.1e (along with §29) for a recent, extended treatment of this so-called "prophetic perfect."

COMMENTARY

Ezekiel brings two oracles together here (28:1-10 and 11-19) to conclude his presentation of the Lord's word against Tyre. The first is a standard judgment oracle, the second a dirge (Heb., *qinah* [TH7015, ZH7806]) that rehearses the fate of the king and his city. In both oracles, the prophet's extravagant language and diverse cultural references have generated interesting interpretive approaches. In his balanced treatment of these passages, Block identifies three such ways of reading the prophet (1998:117-121): First, some have emphasized the obvious parallels between Ezekiel's king of Tyre and the first human in the Genesis accounts of creation. Created by God, commissioned as ruler of creation, the first *'adam* [TH120, ZH132] was humiliated and consigned to die for grasping at divine status. Second, interpreters have seen Ezekiel's oracle as based on a primordial "fall" of some sort. Jewish interpreters have understood an angelic "fall" associated with that of humans (*2 Enoch* 29:4-5, cited by Block 1998:118, note 137). Similarly, Christians, under the influence of Isaiah 14:12, have identified the king of Tyre with Lucifer and have seen here the "fall" of Satan. Third, interpreters have found Ezekiel relying on traditional language and motifs from Canaanite (especially as attested at Ugarit) and Mesopotamian mythology.

In spite of its appeal to many conservative Christians, the construal of chapter 28 as an account of a satanic "fall" fails because of its inability to account for the plain historical references in the immediate context that tie the two oracles squarely to the king of Tyre. Calvin's rejection of this approach to Isaiah 14 and its failure to stay with Isaiah's clear references to the Babylonian king, Nebuchadnezzar, applies with equal force here (as quoted by Block 1998:119, note 139).

The reading given here combines Block's first and third approaches. It concludes that Ezekiel presses both biblical (especially Genesis creation materials) and extra-biblical (especially Canaanite) traditions into service to castigate the "larger than life" king of Tyre. This tiny island's far-flung influence, all out of proportion to its size, and its ability to stay relatively independent against the press of empires to the east and south fed hubris that drew a literary and theological broadside from Ezekiel. He couched that broadside in indigenous language, evoking indigenous themes. Although here Ezekiel presses the limits of incarnational communication, we have already seen his boldness in this matter in his use of Canaanite and Mesopotamian iconography in chapter 1 in the depiction of the throne chariot.

The Lord addresses the "prince (*nagid* [TH5057, ZH5592]) of Tyre" in 28:2, a phrase that is to be taken as a reference to the king, as supported by the parallel address in 28:12. The logic of the judgment oracle is straightforward. Yahweh indicts Tyre's leader for his unbridled arrogance (28:2-5). He then draws an explicit conclusion (28:6), repeats the indictment (28:7a), and pronounces the consequent destruction (28:7b-10).

The prince arrogantly claims he is a god (28:2). Even though the Masoretic Text has *'el* [TH410A, ZH446] here, it is unlikely he claims to be El, the Canaanite high-god, since at Tyre, Melqart, not El, was the high-god. Nevertheless, the *nagid* makes an extravagant *genre claim*—to be a divine person. God's rebuttal, "You are only a man and not a god," implies this. Though Egyptians divinized kingship, Canaanites and Mesopotamians did not generally do so, but rather saw their kings as divinely appointed. So the leader's pride takes him beyond convention even in Tyre. He also sees himself *ruling* as a god or with the gods (28:2), claiming the divine throne sits in island Tyre, not on the northern mountain of the gods as Canaanite lore held. He even regards himself as *wiser* than the fabled Daniel (or *Danel,* cf. note on 14:14). So he apparently also claimed divine wisdom (i.e., intelligence and skill).

As we noted, the Lord directly contradicts his claim to be god—"you are only a man!" (see also 28:9). But he acknowledges the leader's brilliance and the role of that brilliance in his financial success. The kings of Tyre clearly presided with unmatched skill over the commercial development of the island giant. The Lord will point to this very genius as the cause of Tyre's peculiar evil (cf. 28:15-17).

Because of Tyre's pride, God would bring destruction on her at the hands of a foreign army (28:7). The judgment would specifically target the trophies of Tyre's skill for plunder and destruction. The prince's boasts would seem terribly hollow then (28:9). The Lord's warranting of this oracle with the pronouncement of his own sovereign voice carries particular force in light of the claims of this self-appointed "deity" (28:9).

The second oracle (28:11-19) reads as though Ezekiel has appropriated lines from mythic and traditional materials to construct a dirge for the king of Tyre. Perhaps it came from a story of a primeval human or royal figure. The mention of Eden, the garden of God, the holy mountain of God, and an angelic guardian seem to suggest a mythic background as well as reliance on materials from or related to the Genesis 2–3 account. This oracle and the preceding one address the character and fate of the city while speaking of its leader. This dirge conforms little if any to metrical or formal expectations for this genre. Even so, we take Ezekiel's guidance (28:12) in hearing it as a funerary oration that transforms into a pronouncement of judgment.

The king's incredible handsomeness, adornment, noble status, and access to the gods is extolled in 28:12-14, projecting present realities into the primordial past. The king of Tyre was the "model of perfection" (28:12). If we understand *khotham* [TH2368, ZH2597] here (see note on 28:12) not as "model" but as "seal" (a signet carrying an individual's distinctive signature or emblems), then we would see royal prerogatives in the image. The king of Tyre "impresses" his own beauty on succeeding generations or perhaps stands appointed as God's imprint on Tyre or even the world. He resided in God's storied place of luxuriance, adorned with exquisite gems. His garment was adorned with precious stones, perhaps echoing the Israelite high priest's pectoral garb (though the priest's garb had 12 rather than 9 stones), or perhaps calling royal regalia to mind (28:13). In either case, these gems signal privilege and status for the king of Tyre. They were part of his created endowment. Further, the king was given guardian tasks elsewhere assigned to the cherubim at the Garden of Eden (28:14; cf. Gen 3:24). Access to "the holy mountain of God" placed him among the council of God, the sacred assembly where the will of God is declared (cf. Pss 2:6; 43:3; 82:1; 87:1). This access is expressed in his walking among "stones of fire"—that is, sparkling, glistening stones.

Ezekiel claimed that God himself had granted the preeminence of the king of Tyre. His pretensions to deity notwithstanding (28:2, 9), the king was a mere creature created by God (28:13, 15). The king functioned under the anointing and appointment of God (28:14). Even his access to divine things was the doing of God. We learn that the celebration of his preeminence was the crux of his demise. His abuse of the very gifts of God caused his destruction. The king of Tyre had been created handsome, intelligent, and skillful, but he chose to preside over commercial practices laced with violence (28:16). The trade he sponsored trafficked in dishonesty (28:18), and infatuation with splendor itself corrupted his competence (28:17). These and other sins defiled Tyre's "sanctuaries"—referring either to the actual defilement of her religious practices or to the king's doings being thought of as sacred because they had been appointed by God. Tyre had prostituted the gifts of God and turned them into an occasion for hubris, a fatal mistake.

In each case Ezekiel links the indictments with acts of God, withdrawing the king's privileged status and bringing the city to complete ruin. The destruction would be so complete and unimaginable that former clients would be appalled. Describing Tyre's horrible future in "as good as done" language, he repeats the refrain that unites his oracles against Tyre: "You have come to a terrible end, and you will exist no more" (28:19; see 26:21; 27:36).

Ezekiel's oracles against Tyre aimed to subvert false hope among the exiles that heard them and later readers who read them. Apparently uttered sometime during Nebuchadnezzar's protracted siege of Tyre, they warned listeners not to look to Tyre for an answer to their exile or the demise of Jerusalem.

◆ 4. The judgment of scornful Sidon (28:20-24)

20Then another message came to me from
the LORD: 21"Son of man, turn and face the
city of Sidon and prophesy against it.
22Give the people of Sidon this message
from the Sovereign LORD:

"I am your enemy, O Sidon,
and I will reveal my glory by what
I do to you.
When I bring judgment against you
and reveal my holiness among you,
everyone watching will know
that I am the LORD.
23 I will send a plague against you,
and blood will be spilled in
your streets.
The attack will come from every
direction,
and your people will lie slaughtered
within your walls.
Then everyone will know
that I am the LORD.
24 No longer will Israel's scornful
neighbors
prick and tear at her like briers
and thorns.
For then they will know
that I am the Sovereign LORD.

NOTES

28:21 ***the city of Sidon.*** In Ezekiel's time, Sidon, like Tyre, was one of the premier Phoenician cities, famous for maritime prowess and mercantile wealth. The city was located at modern Saida, 25 miles above Tyre. In the mid-second millennium BC, Sidon already surfaces in the Amarna Letters (fourteenth century BC) and Ugaritic documents (thirteenth century BC) as a significant city-state. "Sidonians" actually became a common designation for Phoenicians in general. Sidon's early dominance of Tyre appears in the Bible's analysis of the nations (Gen 10:15), a situation reversed from about the time of David and his alliance with Hiram, King of Tyre (2 Sam 5:11). Ezekiel indirectly paid tribute to Sidon's naval preeminence by noting that Tyre's oarsmen came from Sidon (27:8). Though Sidon was destroyed by both the Assyrians and Babylonians, she revived and was a prominent city on into the Greco-Roman period.

28:22 ***I am your enemy.*** Heb., *hineni 'alayik* [TH5921, ZH6584]. The announcement is made powerful by understatement, "I [am] here against you!" It makes the frightful claim that the God of Israel stands before Sidon as an adversary. The phrase appears throughout much of the book, being used against Israel and Jerusalem (e.g., 5:8; 13:8, 20; 21:3) as well as the nations (e.g., 26:3; 29:3; 30:22).

COMMENTARY

During Israel's kingdom period, Tyre exercised preeminence among the Phoenician cities and their commercial hegemony. But before and after these centuries Sidon was the leading Phoenician trade center, a bit farther up the coast but still within easy access of Israel and Judah. We learn as much about Sidon's dealings with Israel by Ezekiel's brief note as we do from other sources. She apparently "scorned" Israel, and, along with other neighbors, "pricked and tore" at her—metaphors that could cover most any of the behaviors singled out as points of contention with any of the other neighbors of God's people (28:24).

God stands as Sidon's enemy (28:22). The military destruction that Sidon was about to suffer would reveal the glory and holiness of Israel's God. Sidon's fate would confirm the identity of Israel's God, Yahweh, as the God who governs the nations for the sake of his people and his glory. We may presume that Israel's neighbors knew of Yahweh her God and some of the main aspects of her ancient faith. As seen in the book of Joel (cf. Joel 2:17), international events with observable, national weal or woe prompted theological claims. God will reveal himself to those who have eyes to see.

◆ C. Israel Gathered to Dwell Safely (28:25-26)

25"This is what the Sovereign LORD says: The people of Israel will again live in their own land, the land I gave my servant Jacob. For I will gather them from the distant lands where I have scattered them. I will reveal to the nations of the world my holiness among my people. 26They will live safely in Israel and build homes and plant vineyards. And when I punish the neighboring nations that treated them with contempt, they will know that I am the LORD their God."

NOTES

28:25 ***the distant lands where I have scattered them.*** The fall of Samaria to the Assyrian Sargon II and the fall of Jerusalem to the Babylonian Nebuchadnezzar II marked the respective destructions of the kingdoms of Israel and Judah. God had given all the land of David and Solomon into the hands of foreigners. Sargon displaced tens of thousands of Israelites, scattering them in communities the length and breadth of the Fertile Crescent, from Hamath in the west to Media in the far east (2 Kgs 17:6, 24). Nebuchadnezzar deported thousands more from Judah, settling them in enclaves between the Tigris and Euphrates south of the city of Babylon (1:1; 3:15; 2 Kgs 24:11-16; 25:11; Ezra 2:59). The vision of these widely displaced peoples being gathered in the Promised Land presented a hope of vast proportions. (For maps of these scatterings, see Rainey and Notley 2001:237; cf. Aharoni and Avi-Yonah 1968, maps 150 and 163.)

COMMENTARY

Precisely at the midpoint in the "oracles against the nations," Ezekiel places a paragraph to reestablish the reader's perspective. Two agendas remain central to an adequate reading of these oracles. First, these indictments and pronouncements of judgment against Israel's neighbors served to announce blessing to Israel. The demise of troublesome neighbors and predatory empires was good news to Israel. These oracles preface the specific proclamations of hope for the Jewish exiles.

Second, we are to keep in mind specific aspects of the hope that has been briefly sketched and will, in due course, be taken up at length. Israel will again thrive in her own land. This assumes God will gather the people he has scattered. He will keep his land promise to Jacob. Just as he judged his own people, he will punish the nations for their disregard of his purposes for them. Furthermore, through these historical developments the Lord will reveal himself as the vindicated God of Israel.

◆ D. Oracles against Egypt and Her King (29:1–32:32)

1. The arrogant king of Egypt to be brought low (29:1-21)

On January 7,* during the tenth year of
King Jehoiachin's captivity, this message
came to me from the LORD: 2"Son of man,
turn and face Egypt and prophesy against
Pharaoh the king and all the people of
Egypt. 3Give them this message from the
Sovereign LORD:

"I am your enemy, O Pharaoh, king
 of Egypt—
you great monster, lurking in the
 streams of the Nile.
For you have said, 'The Nile River
 is mine;
I made it for myself.'
4I will put hooks in your jaws
and drag you out on the land
with fish sticking to your scales.
5I will leave you and all your fish
stranded in the wilderness to die.
You will lie unburied on the open
 ground,
for I have given you as food to the
 wild animals and birds.
6All the people of Egypt will know that
 I am the LORD,
for to Israel you were just a staff
 made of reeds.
7When Israel leaned on you,
you splintered and broke
and stabbed her in the armpit.
When she put her weight on you,
 you gave way,
and her back was thrown out
 of joint.

8"Therefore, this is what the Sovereign
LORD says: I will bring an army against
you, O Egypt, and destroy both people and
animals. 9The land of Egypt will become a
desolate wasteland, and the Egyptians
will know that I am the LORD.

"Because you said, 'The Nile River is
mine; I made it,' 10I am now the enemy of
both you and your river. I will make the
land of Egypt a totally desolate waste-
land, from Migdol to Aswan, as far south
as the border of Ethiopia.* 11For forty
years not a soul will pass that way, neither
people nor animals. It will be completely
uninhabited. 12I will make Egypt desolate,
and it will be surrounded by other deso-
late nations. Its cities will be empty and
desolate for forty years, surrounded by
other ruined cities. I will scatter the Egyp-
tians to distant lands.

13"But this is what the Sovereign LORD
also says: At the end of the forty years I
will bring the Egyptians home again from
the nations to which they have been scat-

tered. [14]I will restore the prosperity of Egypt and bring its people back to the land of Pathros in southern Egypt from which they came. But Egypt will remain an unimportant, minor kingdom. [15]It will be the lowliest of all the nations, never again great enough to rise above its neighbors.

[16]"Then Israel will no longer be tempted to trust in Egypt for help. Egypt's shattered condition will remind Israel of how sinful she was to trust Egypt in earlier days. Then Israel will know that I am the Sovereign LORD."

[17]On April 26, the first day of the new year,* during the twenty-seventh year of King Jehoiachin's captivity, this message came to me from the LORD: [18]"Son of man, the army of King Nebuchadnezzar* of Babylon fought so hard against Tyre that the warriors' heads were rubbed bare and their shoulders were raw and blistered. Yet Nebuchadnezzar and his army won no plunder to compensate them for all their work. [19]Therefore, this is what the Sovereign LORD says: I will give the land of Egypt to Nebuchadnezzar, king of Babylon. He will carry off its wealth, plundering everything it has so he can pay his army. [20]Yes, I have given him the land of Egypt as a reward for his work, says the Sovereign LORD, because he was working for me when he destroyed Tyre.

[21]"And the day will come when I will cause the ancient glory of Israel to revive,* and then, Ezekiel, your words will be respected. Then they will know that I am the LORD."

29:1 Hebrew *On the twelfth day of the tenth month,* of the ancient Hebrew lunar calendar. This event occurred on January 7, 587 B.C.; also see note on 1:1. **29:10** Hebrew *from Migdol to Syene as far as the border of Cush.* **29:17** Hebrew *On the first day of the first month,* of the ancient Hebrew lunar calendar. This event occurred on April 26, 571 B.C.; also see note on 1:1. **29:18** Hebrew *Nebuchadrezzar,* a variant spelling of Nebuchadnezzar; also in 29:19. **29:21** Hebrew *I will cause a horn to sprout for the house of Israel.*

NOTES

29:4 *out on the land.* The NLT captures the point of the MT, which literally reads "from the midst of your waterways." Pharaoh, like a river monster (crocodile?), will be pulled out of his habitat and hiding place, exposed and vulnerable on dry land.

29:7 *her back was thrown out of joint.* The MT has "You made all their hips to stand." The NLT follows probable emendation that corrects a suggested metathesis and reads "cause to shake" rather than "cause to stand." So also NJPS, NRSV, REB, NAB, NIV, ESV, NKJV, NASB, with various understandings of the exact plight envisioned by the text.

29:10 *from Migdol to Aswan, as far south as the border of Ethiopia.* Lit., "from Migdol to Syene as far as the border of Cush." Although its exact location is not known, Migdol (meaning "Fortress" or "Tower") was almost certainly located in the Eastern delta (cf. Exod 14:2; Num 33:7). Aswan is the modern name of the ancient settlement of Syene, located on the bank of the Nile at the first cataract (which is the northernmost of the six). The land below this point was sometimes regarded as Ethiopia. "From Migdol to Syene" marked the north and south extremities of the land, something like "from Dan to Beersheba" in Palestine.

29:21 *I will cause the ancient glory of Israel to revive.* Lit., "I will cause a horn to sprout for the house of Israel." This "horn" is not a *shopar* [TH7782, ZH8795], the ram's horn used for sounding messages; rather, the "horn" is *qeren* [TH7161, ZH7967], the horn of a wild gazelle or ram, which was a symbol of strength. The *qeren* as a symbol of strength often denotes a person or the strength of that person (cf. Pss 89:17, 24; 132:17; 148:14). The NLT highlights the kingdomwide renaissance spawned by the ascendance of a strong king anointed and blessed by Yahweh.

COMMENTARY

Ezekiel dates this oracle against the king of Egypt to January 587 BC, a year and a half before the fall of Jerusalem to the armies of Nebuchadnezzar, king of Babylon (29:1, see NLT mg). Two accusations form the core of the message and account for Yahweh's adversarial stance toward the pharaoh. First, the king of Egypt claimed to have produced the greatness of Egypt on his own. The king's hubris in thinking himself creator and owner of Egypt's central natural resource, the Nile River, put him at loggerheads with the Creator of all that is. (The reference to the Nile River also includes the commerce supported by it and the agricultural prosperity sustained by its irrigation.) Second, Egypt proved to be an undependable ally of Israel, promising aid but failing to deliver at the critical hour. A long history of meddling and empty promises made Egypt a target of prophetic castigation (Isa 30:16; 31:1-3; Jer 2:17-19, 36-37; Hos 7:11; see commentary on ch 17). In the decade preceding this oracle, Egypt had made shows of interest in supporting the southern Levant as a buffer between Egypt and the Babylonians. Even after Nebuchadnezzar placed Jerusalem under blockade (c. January 588 BC), Hophra of Egypt had made a show of strength in Palestine, causing the Babylonians briefly to withdraw their forces from the city (Jer 37:5). But the Egyptians pulled back, and Nebuchadnezzar resumed his siege (2 Kgs 25:1; Jer 52:4), eventually capturing and destroying the city. Though addressed to the pharaoh, Yahweh held both the king and his people liable for the behavior of the Egyptian state (29:3, 6).

Two oracles comprise the message from the Lord (29:2-7 and 29:8-16). The first scans as Hebrew poetry; it pictures God's arrest and judgment of Pharaoh symbolically. The Lord pictures Pharaoh as a water monster, either the primordial dragon or perhaps a huge Nile crocodile. God pictures his judgment upon the king as a divine fishing expedition. Yahweh will do what no human could do. He will hook this foreboding beast, pull him up onto the parched ground, and leave him there as carrion (29:2-5; cf. Job 41:1-2). He pictures the futility of relying on Egypt as analogous to Israel's putting her weight on a staff, only to have it give way, splinter, and stab her (29:6-7).

The second oracle covers the same ground but in straightforward prose (29:8-16). The basic bad news remains: Yahweh is now the enemy of Pharaoh and the people of Egypt (29:10). The charges remain the same—the arrogance of the king's claim that he owns the Nile River (29:9). Ezekiel plainly describes Yahweh's judgment as complete destruction in a military conquest at the hands of an army Yahweh will bring to Egypt (29:8, 10-12; cf. 29:17-20). Full-scale desolation and deportation awaited Egypt. The whole land, from the delta region in the north to the territories at the southern reaches of the nation, would suffer, becoming an uninhabited, untraveled wasteland.

Unique among the oracles against the nations (chs 25–32) is the promise here that Yahweh will eventually restore Egypt (29:13-15). God will bring back to their land the Egyptians he has scattered and will restore their prosperity. But this restoration proves spartan at best, little better than no restoration at all. Nevertheless, any restoration will be the work of Yahweh. The restoration is a full generation in the future. The repatriated exiles will find themselves in Pathros (an Egyptian name meaning "Land of the South"), the territory between Cairo and Aswan. Egypt's territory will be significantly reduced. She will move from being an ancient superpower to the status of being a very marginal nation. One might think of the "liberation" of Egypt by the Persians (343 BC) as fulfilling this expectation.

All of this will prompt insight in Israel (29:16). Trusting *this* Egypt—reduced, impotent—will be no temptation! But in addition, the sight of Egypt stripped of power will expose the folly, indeed the sin, of ever trusting Pharaoh instead of Yahweh. Her power, which seemed so enticing but always proved unreliable, should all along have been seen as vulnerable and essentially weak. On the other hand, Yahweh's restoration of Egypt, even Egypt, *a fortiori* should buttress hope for the sure restoration of his own people.

Ezekiel received the last dated oracle included in this book on April 26, 571 BC (29:17-20). Nebuchadnezzar's 13-year siege of Tyre was now over. In that siege the Babylonian succeeded in extracting tribute from the king of Tyre and brutalized the mainland dependencies of Tyre. But Nebuchadnezzar did not actually succeed in taking, looting, and destroying the island stronghold, the chief city of Tyre. This protracted labor without adequate compensation is described in 29:18. These events posed two problems. First, they raised something of a fairness issue. Nebuchadnezzar, in addition to his own imperialistic motivations, found himself laying siege to Tyre at the behest of God (29:20; so also 26:7). According to this oracle, Yahweh shared Nebuchadnezzar's obligation to pay his troops, though some have found this embarrassing (Eichrodt 1970:409). This "problem" sets the context for the heart of this oracle, the promise that the Lord would give Nebuchadnezzar the land of Egypt and its wealth for his pay (29:19). From this we may learn, says Block, that Yahweh's employment of his servants "is neither arbitrary nor callous" (1998:153).

The second problem underlies the first and proves more potent theologically. As Zimmerli puts it, in the background here is "the question of divine faithfulness and of the validity of the divine word" (1983:119). Clearly the word from Yahweh in 29:17-21 concedes the point that the total, devastating victory of Nebuchadnezzar over Tyre envisioned in God's word to Ezekiel in 585 BC (cf. 26:1-14) did not occur as anticipated. The Lord did not retract his earlier word, nor did he make further reference to it or evaluation of it here. He simply gave another message, taking the situation as it had actually developed into account. Furthermore, in spite of the fact that such a state of affairs could prove embarrassing for the prophet, who was struggling to establish his own credibility and authenticity—in spite of this, faithful scribes and bearers of tradition left these oracles as they were. They passed them on without apology and without further comment for the people of God to ponder.

This state of affairs has prompted a variety of interpretive responses. Some, eager to preserve strong biblical witness to God's divine government of the universe and/or the truthfulness of Scripture, attempt to read both 26:1-14 and 29:17-21 in such a way as to avoid this second theological problem altogether (e.g., Feinberg 1969:148-150, 171). Emphasis falls here on distancing Nebuchadnezzar from the events envisioned in 26:1-14 and on Alexander the Great's remarkable fulfillment of Ezekiel's prophecy. This fails, I think, to read the text as it is. Others, at an opposite pole, seeking to undercut "inerrancy" as an adequate descriptor of scriptural truthfulness, emphasize

Ezekiel's "mistaken" expectations regarding the fate of Tyre (e.g., Beegle 1978). A number of recent interpreters mention the conditional nature of prophetic utterance, obvious in the book of Jonah (Jonah 3:1-10), as a consideration here (e.g., C. Wright 2001:249). While this is certainly true of much prophetic utterance, conditionality does not appear germane to the issue of Tyre's survival of the Babylonian siege. No offer or expectation of repentance figures in this situation.

Many contemporary interpreters across a broad theological spectrum find themselves grappling with the mysteries of divine freedom and providence on the one hand and the truth of God's word and God's faithfulness to it on the other, resisting oversimplification in the process (e.g., Allen, Block, Eichrodt, Greenberg, Tuell, C. Wright, and Zimmerli). For these interpreters, although the book of Ezekiel itself assumes and declares the integrity and dependability of the divine word, including that word given through the prophet Ezekiel, Yahweh remains free and Lord over his word. He can adapt it and adjust it as he will, even if that means lack of fulfillment for some particular word. And the failure of some particular word to find satisfying fulfillment does not count convincingly against the dependability and truthfulness of God's word in general. Thus listeners and readers, ancient and modern, who insist God fulfill his prophetic word literally and minutely to retain credibility will be disappointed or confused. Recent interpreters have also emphasized the understanding of prophetic ministry implied by these texts. Clearly the Deuteronomic test of the true prophet (Yahweh has sent the prophet whose word comes to pass, Deut 18:21-22), though helpful in some circumstances, is not comprehensive. The prophets' loyalty and obedience as servants of God, proclaiming what he gives them, actually proves critical (as the earlier verses in Deut 18 may well imply). Yahweh's prophets cannot be reduced to "accurate fortune-tellers proclaiming a fixed and unchangeable future" (Tuell 2001:207).

Regarding the editing and compositional priorities shaping the book, the persons who have given us the book have clearly subordinated chronological ordering to topical ordering. Even though in general the dated oracles provide an orderly flow of time within which oracles are placed, here topical continuity overruled chronology, allowing the placement of this last oracle in the company of messages dated much earlier.

The last five clauses of this message do give something of a footnote appropriate to the prophetic circumstance. The first promise is for the revitalization of Israel's ancient glory through the provision of a strong king. The second promise, that Ezekiel's words will then be respected, implies that at the time, there was a lack of respect for Ezekiel's prophetic words. This subject is also broached elsewhere (33:32). Here it appears to acknowledge that the need for a revised word on Nebuchadnezzar's dealing with Tyre could have repercussions for the credibility of Ezekiel among the exiles. The promise therefore provided a needed assurance to the prophet, and in its current setting encourages the reader to trust. Complicating these matters even further, so far as we know, Nebuchadnezzar never did achieve large-scale military conquests in Egypt, certainly not anything approximating the compensation promised here. This connection between Nebuchadnezzar, Egypt, and Tyre is not addressed again.

2. The Day of the Lord for Egypt and allies (30:1-19)

This is another message that came to me
from the LORD: 2"Son of man, prophesy and
give this message from the Sovereign LORD:

"Weep and wail
for that day,
3 for the terrible day is almost here—
the day of the LORD!
It is a day of clouds and gloom,
a day of despair for the nations.
4 A sword will come against Egypt,
and those who are slaughtered will
cover the ground.
Its wealth will be carried away
and its foundations destroyed.
The land of Ethiopia* will be ravished.
5 Ethiopia, Libya, Lydia, all Arabia,*
and all their other allies
will be destroyed in that war.

6 "For this is what the LORD says:
All of Egypt's allies will fall,
and the pride of her power will end.
From Migdol to Aswan*
they will be slaughtered by the sword,
says the Sovereign LORD.
7 Egypt will be desolate,
surrounded by desolate nations,
and its cities will be in ruins,
surrounded by other ruined cities.
8 And the people of Egypt will know
that I am the LORD
when I have set Egypt on fire
and destroyed all their allies.
9 At that time I will send swift
messengers in ships
to terrify the complacent Ethiopians.
Great panic will come upon them
on that day of Egypt's certain
destruction.
Watch for it!
It is sure to come!

10 "For this is what the Sovereign LORD says:
By the power of King Nebuchadnezzar*
of Babylon,
I will destroy the hordes of Egypt.
11 He and his armies—the most ruthless
of all—
will be sent to demolish the land.
They will make war against Egypt
until slaughtered Egyptians cover
the ground.
12 I will dry up the Nile River
and sell the land to wicked men.
I will destroy the land of Egypt and
everything in it
by the hands of foreigners.
I, the LORD, have spoken!

13 "This is what the Sovereign LORD says:
I will smash the idols* of Egypt
and the images at Memphis.*
There will be no rulers left in Egypt;
terror will sweep the land.
14 I will destroy southern Egypt,*
set fire to Zoan,
and bring judgment against Thebes.*
15 I will pour out my fury on Pelusium,*
the strongest fortress of Egypt,
and I will stamp out
the hordes of Thebes.
16 Yes, I will set fire to all Egypt!
Pelusium will be racked with pain;
Thebes will be torn apart;
Memphis will live in constant terror.
17 The young men of Heliopolis and
Bubastis* will die in battle,
and the women* will be taken
away as slaves.
18 When I come to break the proud
strength of Egypt,
it will be a dark day for
Tahpanhes, too.
A dark cloud will cover Tahpanhes,
and its daughters will be led away
as captives.
19 And so I will greatly punish Egypt,
and they will know that I am
the LORD."

30:4 Hebrew *Cush;* similarly in 30:9. **30:5** Hebrew *Cush, Put, Lud, all Arabia, Cub. Cub* is otherwise unknown and may be another spelling for *Lub* (Libya). **30:6** Hebrew *to Syene.* **30:10** Hebrew *Nebuchadrezzar,* a variant spelling of Nebuchadnezzar. **30:13a** The Hebrew term (literally *round things*) probably alludes to dung. **30:13b** Hebrew *Noph;* also in 30:16. **30:14a** Hebrew *Pathros.* **30:14b** Hebrew *No;* also in 30:15, 16. **30:15** Hebrew *Sin;* also in 30:16. **30:17a** Hebrew *of Awen and Pi-beseth.* **30:17b** Or *and her cities.*

NOTES

30:4 ***Ethiopia.*** See NLT mg on 30:4, 5. *Kush* [TH3568, ZH3932] names lands of the southern Nile, Nubia, and Sudan, often designating the southern extremities of Egyptian influence, though by Ezekiel's time Cush was a state in its own right.

30:5 ***Libya, Lydia.*** See NLT mg. *Put* [TH6316, ZH7033] designates Libya, a land and people immediately to the west of Egypt, entangled in Egyptian affairs since the third millennium BC. *Lud* [TH3865, ZH4276] most likely refers to Lydia, a kingdom in central Asia Minor. Although it seems out of place geographically in this line of place names, the reference is probably to Lydia as a source of mercenaries for the Egyptian Psammetichus I against the Assyrians (Block 1998:159). *Lud* could refer to an unidentified North African location in view of its place in the table of nations (Gen 10:13; 1 Chr 1:11, so Hamilton 1990:340; HALOT 2:522), but even there the Asia Minor location may be in view (Rainey and Notley 2001:27-28).

all Arabia. The MT can be translated several ways, two of which make sense here: "all Arabia" (so NLT, with NASB, ESV, NIV) and "all the mixed populations" (e.g., LXX, NJPS), referring as in Jer 50:37 to diverse mercenaries (NLT, "allies from other lands"). The NLT's understanding seems more likely in this list of countries or ethnic groups.

30:12 ***I will dry up the Nile River.*** See Currid 1997:229-246 on this prophetic theme.

30:15 ***Pelusium.*** The NLT, along with NIV, ESV, NRSV, and NAB, translates MT's *sin* [TH5512, ZH6096/6097] using the later classical name for this Egyptian entry point on the east delta. The Hebrew *sin* preserves older designations using the Egyptian toponym *swn*, and is transliterated by LXX, NKJV, NASB, JB, REB, and NJPS.

COMMENTARY

Four short oracles comprise this message against Egypt (30:2b-5; 30:6-9; 30:10-12; 30:13-19). Although each of the oracles presents the judgment of Egypt with different foci, considerable repetition emphasizes certain themes across the collection. Perhaps the most pervasive theme is that the land of Egypt will be utterly destroyed and left desolate (30:4, 7, 9, 14-16). All Egypt will suffer—territorially, from north to south (30:6, 14-16), and demographically as rulers (30:13), armed hordes (30:10, 15), and women (30:17-18) will all perish, the slain littering the ground (30:4, 11). Not only Egypt but her allies will fall in this day (30:5-6, 8, 12). The oracles also thoroughly convey that all of this will be the work of Yahweh, his doing in Egypt's history. Note in this regard the repeated first-person singular references by Yahweh—"I have set Egypt on fire," "I will send swift messengers," and so on (30:8, 9, 10, 12 [2 times], 13, 14, 15 [2 times], 16, 18, 19). Repeatedly, Yahweh interprets these events not only as his doing but as expressions of his fury (30:15), punishment, and judgment on Egypt (30:14, 19). Ezekiel points to Egypt's pride as the cause of Yahweh's judgment—pride in her power (30:6) and in her national strength (30:18).

One aspect of Ezekiel's oracles against Egypt perplexes some interpreters: his repeated designation of Nebuchadnezzar, king of Babylon, as the agent of Yahweh's complete destruction and punishment of Egypt (30:10-12, 25; 32:11). So far as we can discover at the present, no solid evidence exists that this complete and humiliating defeat of the Egyptians at the hands of Nebuchadnezzar (or any other Babylonian, for that matter) ever occurred. A fragmentary inscription apparently refers to military activity of some sort in Egypt in Nebuchadnezzar's 37th year (c. 570–568 BC), though its broken condition limits its usefulness in reconstructing Babylonian-Egyptian relationships (ANET 308). Bright sees Nebuchadnezzar's purpose as a punitive campaign, aimed at putting a stop to Egyptian meddling in Asia (2000:352). Later tradition had Nebuchadnezzar campaigning in Libya and even into Iberia (Josephus *Against Apion* 1.20), apparently confusing the Babylonian with the Persian Cambyses (Wiseman 1983:39-41). But no credible evidence links Babylon or any of its later conquerors with the sort of destruction anticipated by Ezekiel. This remains a score to be settled, if ever, most likely in the eschaton.

See the commentary on 29:17-21 for further consideration of these matters and on chapters 47–48 for related reflection. The basic approaches to the apparent lack of fulfillment of Ezekiel's oracle against Tyre (26:1-21) apply here as well. Two matters encourage our reaction. First, Ezekiel and his later editors saw fit to leave these obviously "unfulfilled" prophecies standing just as they were, without editorial adjustment or excuse or apology. Either they did not consider this to be a significant problem for the credibility and usefulness of the book, or they in effect commended the problem to God, awaiting whatever fulfillment his sovereign providence brought to pass. This encourages a waiting posture, freed from the need to "protect" Ezekiel from himself or to get drawn into eisegesis in an effort to avoid these difficulties. Second, judging from John the Revelator's approach to Ezekiel 47–48 (see Rev 21–22), one could see these matters, along with other aspects of Ezekiel's vision, as fulfilled in Christ and his church (without denying a unique destiny for God's historic people).

Beyond the introductory function of the announcement of Yahweh's Day in 30:2-3 (cf. NLT, "the day of the LORD") and the conclusion drawn in 30:19, a clear logical progression does not appear across the oracles. Nevertheless, one can discern some shifts in emphasis. The first oracle (30:2b-5) sets this overall message—that Egypt will surely suffer total destruction as judgment from Yahweh at the hands of Nebuchadnezzar II—in the context of the coming Day of the Lord and Egypt's participation in that monumental upheaval. Ezekiel announced the Day of the Lord in terms reminiscent of Joel's classic prophecy: a call to weep and wail because the terrifying day is almost here, a day of clouds and gloom (cf. Joel 1:5, 13; 2:1-2, 10, 31 [3:4]; 3:15 [4:15]). Messages about the Day of the Lord frequently involve the nations but are not generally directly addressed to a Gentile nation as is this one to Egypt. In addition to setting the context for the Day of Yahweh, the first oracle clarifies the coming destruction as a catastrophic military invasion (30:4) in which not only Egypt but her allies will be ravished.

The second oracle (30:6-9) attributes the judgment to Egypt's pride and then stresses the completeness of the destruction by naming doomed sites at her northern and southern extremities, Migdol and Aswan (see note on 29:10). Migdol was apparently located somewhere in the east delta region; Aswan housed a garrison guarding the first cataract of the Nile in the far south. The fact that desolate Egypt would be surrounded by devastated cities and nations connects these oracles against Egypt to the earlier oracles against the nations, anticipating ruin for all those lands as well. Egypt's complacence would be shattered with panic (30:9).

That complacency rose from her geographic and topographic isolation and the consequent relative lack of threat from military invasion. The times the Egyptian heartland had been invaded by foreign troops were rare and long-remembered events—the Hyksos in the middle Bronze Age, the Sea Peoples in the late Bronze Age, the Assyrians in the seventh century BC. One may contrast this to the repeated hammerings by foreign invaders suffered by the Syro-Palestinian states. But, warned Ezekiel, Egypt's false security would be shattered by naval forces sailing clear up the Nile. Ezekiel underscores the shocking nature of this warning with the admonition to "Watch for it!" and the assurance that "It is sure to come!"

The third oracle (30:10-12) names Nebuchadnezzar and his forces as Yahweh's instrument to punish Egypt (30:10). They are ruthless foreigners—famous already to Habakkuk (Hab 1:5-17), wicked men (30:11-12). The thought of drying up the Nile was surely unimaginable, utterly "impossible" (30:12; cf. Isa 19:5-6). No single geophysical entity embodied the life and power of Egypt more than the Nile. It provided the main path for commerce and for the north–south movement of military forces, and cultic processions. Fishing provided a chief source of meat. The annual inundation of the Nile, a natural wonder known all over the ancient world, sustained Egyptian agriculture by providing fresh alluvial soil and bolstering irrigation. Thus, according to Egyptian thought, Egypt was the gift of the Nile—more precisely, the gift of the god Hapi, and through him, the gift of Pharaoh. Through identification with the river and with deification in Hapi, Pharaoh himself was thought to control the Nile. So, to dry up the Nile was to cut off Egypt's very life and simultaneously to reject Pharaoh's arrogant claims to be the giver of life. And God's word guaranteed this unthinkable thing would happen (30:12).

The fourth and final short oracle in this message event turns attention to Egypt's sprawling religious establishment (30:13-19). Yahweh follows the threat to "smash the idols of Egypt" with specific reference to Memphis and Thebes, two of the most important cities for Egyptian religion. Ancient Thebes straddled the Nile River over 400 miles south of the delta. Along with royal mortuary temples, it included the immense temples of Karnak and Luxor on the east bank, and the Valley of the Kings on the west bank. It was a veritable monument to Egyptian imperial achievement and the gods and rulers that presided over it. By the time of Ezekiel, Memphis in the north was the political and religious hub of Egypt. It housed temples and shrines to numerous deities, but was especially well known as the home of the priests of Ptah, a deity associated later with Apis, the sacred bull.

Ezekiel named cities to be sacked, ravished, and ruined in Yahweh's fury. They are for the most part outposts of the east delta region or sites famous in Israel for other reasons, and thus likely to be known to Ezekiel's exilic audience. In addition to Thebes and Memphis, Zoan, Pelusium, Heliopolis, Bubastis, and Tahpanhes would be judged. Zoan (30:14), though in some decline in Ezekiel's day, was famous as the capital city of first-millennium BC pharaohs, located in the east delta. Pelusium (30:15-16) was an important point of entry to Egypt in the far east delta region, the departure point of roads heading west across the delta from Sinai and Palestine. Heliopolis, "city of the sun-god," was a suburb of Cairo that wielded influence more through its religion than politics. Its wide influence in Egypt came especially from its elaboration of the theology of kingship associated with the god Re, whose divine image the king was thought to be. Bubastis designates another important and prosperous town in the northeast delta region, standing at the juncture of the land route southeast into the Sinai and the water link with the Mediterranean. Numerous pharaohs from the mid-third millennium BC beautified and refurbished Bubastis. Tahpanhes had been substantially occupied only since the early seventh century as one of several forts raised against Assyrian incursions. In the Old Testament, Tahpanhes is best known as the site to which Jeremiah's protagonists dragged him after the assassination of Gedaliah, the governor appointed by the Babylonians after the fall of Jerusalem. Whether Ezekiel knew of these affairs we do not know. When these things transpired, the Egyptians would know that the God of Israel is God of all nations.

◆ 3. The Lord breaks Pharaoh's arms (30:20-26)

[20]On April 29,* during the eleventh year of King Jehoiachin's captivity, this message came to me from the LORD: [21]"Son of man, I have broken the arm of Pharaoh, the king of Egypt. His arm has not been put in a cast so that it may heal. Neither has it been bound up with a splint to make it strong enough to hold a sword. [22]Therefore, this is what the Sovereign LORD says: I am the enemy of Pharaoh, the king of Egypt! I will break both of his arms—the good arm along with the broken one—and I will make his sword clatter to the ground. [23]I will scatter the Egyptians to many lands throughout the world. [24]I will strengthen the arms of Babylon's king and put my sword in his hand. But I will break the arms of Pharaoh, king of Egypt, and he will lie there mortally wounded, groaning in pain. [25]I will strengthen the arms of the king of Babylon, while the arms of Pharaoh fall useless to his sides. And when I put my sword in the hand of Babylon's king and he brings it against the land of Egypt, Egypt will know that I am the LORD. [26]I will scatter the Egyptians among the nations, dispersing them throughout the earth. Then they will know that I am the LORD."

30:20 Hebrew *On the seventh day of the first month*, of the ancient Hebrew lunar calendar. This event occurred on April 29, 587 B.C.; also see note on 1:1.

NOTES

30:24 *Pharaoh, king of Egypt.* Originally, "pharaoh" designated a section of the Egyptian royal residence, "the Great House." Eventually it came to designate the palace and by metonymy came to name the king of Egypt, similar to the way "the White House" may be used to refer to the President of the United States. By the time of Ezekiel, "pharaoh" was used as a title, roughly synonymous with the ruling "king." Throughout the OT this later use of the term consistently appears.

COMMENTARY

Dated April 29, 587 BC (see NLT mg on 30:20), this oracle comes four months after Pharaoh Hophra's aborted effort to relieve Jerusalem during the siege by Nebuchadnezzar. The prophet used the "arm" as a symbol of strength and power, often of military might. The threats are particularly ironic because of the prominent role in Egyptian art of the victorious Pharaoh, with "outstretched arm," slaying his enemies. Ezekiel pressed the image as far as possible. God broke Pharaoh's arm, indeed broke both arms, the good one and the bad! The broken arm was not put in a splint or in a cast. So Pharaoh could not hold his sword. In fact, Pharaoh is here pictured lying on the ground, groaning in pain—Pharaoh lies mortally wounded (30:24; cf. Pss 10:15; 37:17). The broken arm is a metaphor for a fatal defeat in combat.

By contrast, Yahweh will strengthen the arms of the king of Babylon (30:24) and will put his sword in the Babylonian's hand. He will conquer Egypt as Yahweh's agent of judgment. Nebuchadnezzar will scatter the Egyptians, just as he had the Judeans (30:23, 26). These events are to reveal Yahweh to the nations (30:26).

From the vicious tone of the Lord's pronouncement against the pharaoh, king of Egypt, one can gather the disdain in which the Almighty held this meddling neighbor of Judah. Always eager to dabble in Palestinian affairs in order to protect itself from invasion by the greater powers, Egypt rarely delivered on promised aid. Yet another of these betrayals figured in the punitive campaign that brought Nebuchadnezzar to Judah and ended in the deportation of Jehoiachin and company.

◆ 4. Egypt's "towering cedar" plummets to the pit (31:1-18)

On June 21,* during the eleventh year of King Jehoiachin's captivity, this message came to me from the LORD: [2]"Son of man, give this message to Pharaoh, king of Egypt, and all his hordes:

**"To whom would you compare your
greatness?
[3]You are like mighty Assyria,
which was once like a cedar of
Lebanon,
with beautiful branches that cast
deep forest shade
and with its top high among the
clouds.
[4]Deep springs watered it
and helped it to grow tall and
luxuriant.
The water flowed around it like a river,
streaming to all the trees nearby.
[5]This great tree towered high,
higher than all the other trees
around it.
It prospered and grew long thick
branches
because of all the water at its roots.
[6]The birds nested in its branches,
and in its shade all the wild animals
gave birth.
All the great nations of the world
lived in its shadow.
[7]It was strong and beautiful,
with wide-spreading branches,
for its roots went deep
into abundant water.
[8]No other cedar in the garden of God
could rival it.
No cypress had branches to equal it;
no plane tree had boughs to
compare.
No tree in the garden of God
came close to it in beauty.
[9]Because I made this tree so beautiful,
and gave it such magnificent
foliage,
it was the envy of all the other
trees of Eden,
the garden of God.**

[10]"Therefore, this is what the Sovereign LORD says: Because Egypt* became proud and arrogant, and because it set itself so high above the others, with its top reaching to the clouds, [11]I will hand it over to a mighty nation that will destroy it as its wickedness deserves. I have already discarded it. [12]A foreign army—the terror of the nations—has cut it down and left it fallen on the ground. Its branches are scattered across the mountains and

valleys and ravines of the land. All those
who lived in its shadow have gone away
and left it lying there.

13 "The birds roost on its fallen trunk,
and the wild animals lie among
its branches.
14 Let the tree of no other nation
proudly exult in its own prosperity,
though it be higher than the clouds
and it be watered from the depths.
For all are doomed to die,
to go down to the depths of
the earth.
They will land in the pit
along with everyone else on earth.

15"This is what the Sovereign LORD says:
When Assyria went down to the grave,* I
made the deep springs mourn. I stopped
its rivers and dried up its abundant water.
I clothed Lebanon in black and caused the
trees of the field to wilt. 16I made the na-
tions shake with fear at the sound of its
fall, for I sent it down to the grave with
all the others who descend to the pit. And
all the other proud trees of Eden, the most
beautiful and the best of Lebanon, the
ones whose roots went deep into the wa-
ter, took comfort to find it there with
them in the depths of the earth. 17Its al-
lies, too, were all destroyed and had
passed away. They had gone down to the
grave—all those nations that had lived in
its shade.

18"O Egypt, to which of the trees of
Eden will you compare your strength and
glory? You, too, will be brought down to
the depths with all these other nations.
You will lie there among the outcasts*
who have died by the sword. This will be
the fate of Pharaoh and all his hordes. I,
the Sovereign LORD, have spoken!"

31:1 Hebrew *On the first day of the third month,* of the ancient Hebrew lunar calendar. This event occurred on June 21, 587 B.C.; also see note on 1:1. 31:10 Hebrew *you.* 31:15 Hebrew *to Sheol;* also in 31:16, 17. 31:18 Hebrew *among the uncircumcised.*

NOTES

31:3 *You are like mighty Assyria.* Ezekiel's suggested comparison of Egypt to Assyria depended on his readers' knowledge of the story of the collapse of the Assyrian empire. Less than a century before the date of this oracle, the Assyrian empire stood at its zenith. All of the Levant was firmly in its grip. In 664 BC, the great Ashurbanipal (669–627) had marched Assyrian forces all the way up the Nile to Thebes, 300 miles below the delta as the crow flies. He brought even storied Egypt firmly, if briefly, under Assyrian control (Rainey and Notley 2001:248-249). From the mountains east and north of the Tigris, to eastern Asia Minor and on down the Mediterranean and up the Nile as far as Thebes, from horizon to horizon, Assyria ruled. By 656, however, the Egyptians had expelled Assyrian garrisons from Egypt. Before long, discontent in scattered parts of the empire threatened its unity. Ashurbanipal's brother, Shamash-shum-ukin, king of Babylon, rebelled and split the lower Euphrates territories from Assyrian control. By the time Ashurbanipal died, the end was not far away. In 614 the Medes took the major city, Ashur. In 612, Nineveh fell to a Medeo-Babylonian force. Remnants of the Assyrian army fled west and attempted a stand at Hauran and then Carchemish (Aharoni and Avi-Yonah 1968, maps 156 and 157). It was en route to an attempt to prop up the disintegrating Assyrians that Pharaoh Neco defeated Judean king Josiah (Aharoni and Avi-Yonah 1968, map 159). When this tactical move failed, Neco retreated to Egypt. The Assyrian empire was no more—gone from the conquest of Thebes in 664 to disintegration at Carchemish in less than 50 years! This is the story everyone knew. Was this going to be Egypt's story, too, asked Ezekiel?

31:8-9 *the garden of God.* The oracles in this chapter develop the allegory of the cosmic tree, a motif widely attested in ancient cultures. The allegory has the inhabited world as an enormous tree, watered by roots in the cosmic deep and rising with its top in the clouds.

Every living being finds shelter in its boughs and shade. References to the tree of life, to Eden and the garden of God, blend the ancient theme with biblical creation traditions (cf. 31:18; see Allen 1994:125-126).

31:11 *I have already discarded it.* This sudden switch to a past tense reference (via the suffixed form of the Hebrew verb) startles the reader because Ezekiel was obviously talking about events yet future. This disjuncture has been taken as an indication of confusion of some sort. Perhaps the prophet momentarily stepped into the tense of the historical comparison with Assyria's well-known fate taken up in 31:15ff (Block 1998:189-192). Perhaps the incongruities present untidy remainders of a complex compositional history (Zimmerli 1983:143-144, 151-152). Or perhaps, instead, at this critical juncture in the analogy, where Ezekiel has set aside poetic form for a prose rendering of the judgment verdict in 31:10-12, we could expect the prophet's "dramatic" use of both suffixed and prefixed forms to convey the "as good as done" certitude with which he announced the threatened destruction of Egypt (cf. Waltke and O'Connor 1990:§30.5.1e, along with §29; see also Chisholm 1998:88, 98-99).

COMMENTARY

Three oracles comprise this message from the Lord (31:2-9, 10-14, and 15-18). A two-point comparison of Egypt with Assyria holds the oracles together. After asking Pharaoh to name a comparator, the Lord names Assyria as the comparator and follows it up immediately with a specific simile he will pursue: Pharaoh as a cedar of Lebanon. Ezekiel returns to imagery already used in chapters 17 and 27 and to a picture thoroughly indigenous to the Levant. The strength and beauty of the cedars covering the mountains along the eastern Mediterranean all the way from the Amanus in the north to the Lebanons in the south was legendary. Already in the third millennium BC, Sargon the Great boasted of taking cedars from these forests. Their wood was prized for the construction of palaces and other monumental buildings.

The first point of comparison of Pharaoh (and the Egyptians) to the Assyrians, then, is the point of Egypt's grandeur, beauty, and elegant might. Ezekiel used several points of the simile to picture Egypt's influence—it shared water with other trees (31:4), gave roost to birds and shade to animals (31:6), possessed enduring resources—primeval and abundant water (31:4, 7), and had unrivaled magnificence (31:8-9). Ezekiel enhanced the imagery by appeal to primordial themes related to the creation account of Genesis 2 (Eden, the garden of God). All of this, says Ezekiel, was God's doing. The *Lord* made Egypt the beautiful thing that it was (31:9). And lest the reader miss the point, twice in these oracles Ezekiel exits the comparison to speak explicitly of nations (31:6, 11; cf. also 31:14, 16, 18). God through Ezekiel was speaking of the rise and fall of great nations under his sovereignty.

The second oracle (31:10-14) explicitly states the logic of judgment with the indictment that Egypt became "proud and arrogant," setting itself "high above the others" (31:10). Instead of accepting her magnificent place among the nations of the ancient world as a gift from God (31:9), Egypt and her pharaoh arrogantly claimed credit for Egypt's undeserved wealth and influence (cf. 29:3, 9). For this wickedness God would destroy her. Ezekiel underscored this destruction by repeating it as good as done—"I have already discarded it" (31:11)! He then reverses the "cedar of Lebanon" simile to picture this devastation. Egypt will be "cut down"; branches will litter the terrain; birds and animals will scatter (31:12-13).

An intriguing, parenthetic admonition warns unidentified nations against the hubris that will bring Egypt down (31:14). It is possible Ezekiel was addressing aspirations of the exile community already dreaming of greatness upon their return to Judah. Or perhaps Ezekiel obliquely critiqued Babylon here, a dangerous move if made explicitly, because he was living in Babylon.

The final oracle of this set of messages (31:15-18) addresses the second point of comparison with Assyria, the fact that Egypt, like Assyria, would meet a horrible end, her present grandeur notwithstanding (31:15). With a focus broadened to include the world of the dead, God underscored the international trauma and disbelief caused by Assyria's demise. God sent her to the grave with all the others. Other proud trees (i.e., rulers, nations) found comfort that great Assyria was consigned to the grave just as they were (31:16-17).

The final lines of the message (31:18) reiterate the two points of comparison just uttered: (1) Egypt's incomparable, enviable strength and glory and (2) her very unenviable fate—to die by the sword. The logic of this message stands opposite that of Nahum's message to Nineveh. Nahum pronounced Nineveh's (i.e., Assyria's) doom by an implicit comparison to Egypt. Thebes, the architectural wonder of Upper Egypt, had rarely in her history fallen to foreign troops. Situated hundreds of miles up the Nile from the delta region and Egypt's northern and eastern borders, she was virtually out of reach. But the unthinkable did happen, as it had occasionally before, when Assyria's great Ashurbanipal sacked Thebes in 664 BC. Recalling that moment of glory for Assyria, Nahum asked the Assyrians if they really thought they were better than Thebes (Nah 3:8-10). Ezekiel now asks Pharaoh, "Are you better than the Assyrians?" and then emphatically answers "No!"

◆ 5. An international lament over Pharaoh (32:1-16)

On March 3,* during the twelfth year of King Jehoiachin's captivity, this message came to me from the LORD: 2"Son of man, mourn for Pharaoh, king of Egypt, and give him this message:

"You think of yourself as a strong young lion among the nations,
but you are really just a sea monster,
heaving around in your own rivers,
stirring up mud with your feet.
3Therefore, this is what the Sovereign LORD says:
I will send many people
to catch you in my net
and haul you out of the water.
4I will leave you stranded on the land to die.
All the birds of the heavens will land on you,
and the wild animals of the whole earth
will gorge themselves on you.
5I will scatter your flesh on the hills
and fill the valleys with your bones.
6I will drench the earth with your gushing blood
all the way to the mountains,
filling the ravines to the brim.
7When I blot you out,
I will veil the heavens and darken the stars.
I will cover the sun with a cloud,
and the moon will not give you its light.
8I will darken the bright stars overhead
and cover your land in darkness.
I, the Sovereign LORD, have spoken!

9"I will disturb many hearts when I bring news of your downfall to distant

nations you have never seen. [10]Yes, I will
shock many lands, and their kings will be
terrified at your fate. They will shudder in
fear for their lives as I brandish my sword
before them on the day of your fall. [11]For
this is what the Sovereign LORD says:

"The sword of the king of Babylon
will come against you.
12 I will destroy your hordes with the
swords of mighty warriors—
the terror of the nations.
They will shatter the pride of Egypt,
and all its hordes will be destroyed.
13 I will destroy all your flocks and herds
that graze beside the streams.
Never again will people or animals
muddy those waters with their feet.
14 Then I will let the waters of Egypt
become calm again,
and they will flow as smoothly
as olive oil,
says the Sovereign LORD.
15 And when I destroy Egypt
and strip you of everything
you own
and strike down all your people,
then you will know that I am
the LORD.
16 Yes, this is the funeral song
they will sing for Egypt.
Let all the nations mourn.
Let them mourn for Egypt and
its hordes.
I, the Sovereign LORD, have spoken!"

32:1 Hebrew *On the first day of the twelfth month,* of the ancient Hebrew lunar calendar. This event occurred on March 3, 585 B.C.; also see note on 1:1.

NOTES

32:2 *mourn for Pharaoh.* Lit., "raise a funeral dirge for Pharaoh." The Hebrew text refers to a poetic genre, the *qinah* [TH7015, ZH7806]. The genre is generally thought to be marked by a 3 x 2 meter in its bicola. Although such a "meter" is not consistently used in the poetic lines of this oracle, scattered 3 x 2 lines can be found that may give it a *qinah* tone. Note these lines from 32:2 (lit.): "(1) But you—(2) like a sea monster—(3) in the sea // (1) You heave around—(2) in your rivers. (1) You muddy—(2) water—(3) with your feet // (1) You foul—(2) their streams."

just a sea monster. The MT reads *tannim* [TH8565, ZH9478], "you are really just *a jackal.*" Guided by context, the NLT and most modern versions follow two witnesses to MT, as well as the LXX *drakōn* [TG1404, ZG1532] and the Targum, in reading *tannin* [TH8577, ZH9490], "a sea monster."

32:9 *your downfall.* The NLT maintains MT's *shibreka,* from *sheber* [TH7667, ZH8691], "a break(ing)," "collapse," or "destruction," translating in such a way as to particularize very nicely the sort of destruction most likely in mind here; so also NKJV, ESV. Or, less likely, the abstract "destruction" could be taken concretely to refer to "your broken army" (NEB), "your shattered remnants" (NJPS), "broken parts" (Allen 1994:130), or the like. The LXX assumes *shebyeka* [TH7628, ZH8660] (cf. Judg 5:12), "your captivity" or "your captives" (cf. RSV).

32:10-11 *I brandish my sword. . . . The sword of the king of Babylon will come against you.* These parallel lines underscore the Lord's engagement in human historical affairs. In some sense the king of Babylon's sword is Yahweh's sword. Although the king of Babylon retains full responsibility for his own behavior, the Lord accomplishes his purposes through him.

COMMENTARY

Ezekiel dated this message from the Lord to March 3, 585 BC, two months after news of the fall of Jerusalem reached Ezekiel's exile community (33:21). The date underscores again Egypt's failure to make good on promised aid that might have averted catastrophe for Jerusalem. Once again the Lord instructed Ezekiel both to deliver his message in the form of a funeral dirge (lit., "lift a dirge for Pharaoh," 32:2) and to call for the nations to chant a dirge over Egypt (32:16), the funerary language bracketing the message.

The logic of this word of Yahweh is straightforward, launched with another rebuke of Pharaoh for his arrogance and presumption. Pharaoh had a vastly overexalted view of himself (32:2). Consequently (32:3a), Yahweh would destroy him, his people, and his land (32:3b-8), to the horror of other kings (32:9-10).

The charge occupies a single verse in our texts (32:2). We have already seen Ezekiel use the metaphor of a lion to depict kings of Judah and Babylon (cf. ch 19). The metaphor seems entirely fitting in view of the widespread use of leonine iconography to depict royalty in the ancient Near East. Pharaoh thought of himself as a fierce and majestic lion. God says he was actually just an unruly sea monster, muddying his own waters. The monster referenced here (*tannin* [TH8577, ZH9490]) could in some contexts conjure up awesome images of the primordial dragon (cf. Isa 27:1; 51:9). But in this very uncomplimentary context, the word more likely intends a large sea creature or perhaps the Nile crocodile, albeit extravagantly portrayed.

The metaphor established in the charge is extended to portray God's judgment of Pharaoh (32:3-8). Yahweh will capture the monster and leave him stranded on dry land—as food for birds and wild animals (32:3-4), a point that indicates his plan to use many agents to carry out this business. In gruesome detail, the Lord promised to scatter his remains and "drench the earth with [his] gushing blood" (32:5-6). He concludes this part of the dirge with language often associated with the Day of the Lord (cf. commentary on 30:2-5). This will be a momentous event, wherein the heavens will be darkened either by the smoke of battle or the cosmic repercussions of Yahweh's actions against Pharaoh.

Yahweh's demolition of Egypt will destabilize many lands and rock rulers far and wide to the core. The implications are clear. If Pharaoh, king of Egypt, can fall, no ruler can feel safe. If Yahweh, God of Israel, could deal this way with the longest running kingship in the ancient world, no king could think himself secure from Yahweh's sword (32:9-11).

The Lord dropped his controlling metaphor to speak in plainly historic terms. Nebuchadnezzar, king of Babylon, would be Yahweh's agent of destruction. He would wield Yahweh's sword (32:11). Through Nebuchadnezzar and his mighty warriors, Yahweh would destroy Pharaoh's vast forces. The Babylonians had already struck terror in the nations who watched them burst out of Mesopotamia, taking virtually everything in their path. They would shatter Egypt's pride. Emphasis falls on the complete destruction Yahweh would bring: note "all" (32:12, 13, 15), and "everything" (32:15). Later, in Yahweh's sovereignty, he would bring the land to rest again, just as he had brought devastation to it (32:14).

Advancing the most pervasive theme in Ezekiel once more, the prophet claimed that through these mighty acts of Yahweh the nations would acknowledge Yahweh as the actor dominating even mighty Egypt's affairs (32:15). They would know him. Finally, the message ends with emphasis on the dirge genre of Yahweh's word and with exhortation for the nations to mourn "Egypt and its hordes" (32:16). They are called upon to lament both the demise of glorious Egypt and the fragility of their own situations implied in that collapse.

◆ 6. Egypt consigned to the pit (32:17-32)

17 On March 17,* during the twelfth year, another message came to me from the LORD: 18 "Son of man, weep for the hordes of Egypt and for the other mighty nations.* For I will send them down to the world below in company with those who descend to the pit. 19 Say to them,

'O Egypt, are you lovelier than the
other nations?
No! So go down to the pit and lie
there among the outcasts.*'

20 The Egyptians will fall with the many who have died by the sword, for the sword is drawn against them. Egypt and its hordes will be dragged away to their judgment. 21 Down in the grave* mighty leaders will mockingly welcome Egypt and its allies, saying, 'They have come down; they lie among the outcasts, hordes slaughtered by the sword.'

22 "Assyria lies there surrounded by the graves of its army, those who were slaughtered by the sword. 23 Their graves are in the depths of the pit, and they are surrounded by their allies. They struck terror in the hearts of people everywhere, but now they have been slaughtered by the sword.

24 "Elam lies there surrounded by the graves of all its hordes, those who were slaughtered by the sword. They struck terror in the hearts of people everywhere, but now they have descended as outcasts to the world below. Now they lie in the pit and share the shame of those who have gone before them. 25 They have a resting place among the slaughtered, surrounded by the graves of all their hordes. Yes, they terrorized the nations while they lived, but now they lie in shame with others in the pit, all of them outcasts, slaughtered by the sword.

26 "Meshech and Tubal are there, surrounded by the graves of all their hordes. They once struck terror in the hearts of people everywhere. But now they are outcasts, all slaughtered by the sword. 27 They are not buried in honor like their fallen heroes, who went down to the grave* with their weapons—their shields covering their bodies* and their swords beneath their heads. Their guilt rests upon them because they brought terror to everyone while they were still alive.

28 "You too, Egypt, will lie crushed and broken among the outcasts, all slaughtered by the sword.

29 "Edom is there with its kings and princes. Mighty as they were, they also lie among those slaughtered by the sword, with the outcasts who have gone down to the pit.

30 "All the princes of the north and the Sidonians are there with others who have died. Once a terror, they have been put to shame. They lie there as outcasts with others who were slaughtered by the sword. They share the shame of all who have descended to the pit.

31 "When Pharaoh and his entire army arrive, he will take comfort that he is not alone in having his hordes killed, says the Sovereign LORD. 32 Although I have caused his terror to fall upon all the living, Pharaoh and his hordes will lie there among the outcasts who were slaughtered by the sword. I, the Sovereign LORD, have spoken!"

32:17 Hebrew *On the fifteenth day of the month,* presumably in the twelfth month of the ancient Hebrew lunar calendar (see 32:1). This would put this message at the end of King Jehoiachin's twelfth year of captivity, on March 17, 585 B.C.; also see note on 1:1. Greek version reads *On the fifteenth day of the first month,* which would put this message on April 27, 586 B.C., at the beginning of Jehoiachin's twelfth year. **32:18** The meaning of the Hebrew is uncertain. **32:19** Hebrew *the uncircumcised;* also in 32:21, 24, 25, 26, 28, 29, 30, 32. **32:21** Hebrew *in Sheol.* **32:27a** Hebrew *to Sheol.* **32:27b** The meaning of the Hebrew is uncertain.

NOTES

32:22 ***Assyria.*** Since the Old Assyrian period of the early second millennium BC, Assyria was a well-known force in the ancient Near East. After centuries in eclipse, Assyrian culture and kingship revived from the fourteenth to the twelfth centuries BC and again in the ninth century. From then on through her fall at the end of the seventh century, Assyria dominated life in the Fertile Crescent and often throughout the eastern Mediterranean lands, including Israel and Judah. Assyria was infamous for its brute strength and ruthless military conquests. These are the people who perfected hanging people (usually impaling them!) on trees/stakes as a punishment of choice (the precursor of later crucifixion).

32:24 ***Elam.*** This state was situated on the slope of the Iranian Plateau toward the lower Tigris Valley, the territory of the Zagros Mountains. The earliest documents show Elam to be a source of raw materials sought by Mesopotamian cultures (metals, wood, stone, lapis lazuli, tin, etc.). Though Elam is known already in the third millennium BC from numerous contacts with Sumerian rulers and Old Assyrian kings, Elam was on Ezekiel's horizon mainly as an ally of the Babylonians and a partner in the overthrow of the Neo-Assyrian empire. Soon after these events, Elam came under the control of the Medes and finally, under Cyrus II, became part of the Persian Empire.

32:26 ***Meshech and Tubal.*** These lands are known from Neo-Assyrian sources and other ancient Near Eastern attestation. Meshech is to be identified with *Musku* of the cuneiform sources; it was located immediately west of Tubal. These countries were respectively located in south-central and eastern Anatolia and were known for metal working.

32:27 ***fallen heroes.*** With this reference to "fallen heroes" (*nopelim* [TH5307, ZH5877]), Ezekiel may have evoked the memory of the *nepilim* [TH5303, ZH5872], perverse "heroes" of the antediluvian age (Gen 6:1-4). If so, he reinterprets this tradition, or follows some other tradition about these persons because he casts them now in a positive light (Block 1998:227-229). Zimmerli (1983:176) compares them to the Greek heroes in Hesiod, buried in full military armor, which was used as pillow and blanket in the underworld, in contrast to which the bodies of the fallen Egyptians lie strewn on the battlefield (32:26, "slaughtered by the sword").

32:29 ***Edom.*** This names an area and a kingdom southeast of the Dead Sea, the Wadi Arabah being its border on the west. Wadi Hasa was on the north. Both in the OT and in early Egyptian references Edom is associated with Seir, territory south of the Dead Sea. At least from the time of David's conquest of Edom, relationships between Israel (especially Judah) and Edom were continually rancorous (2 Sam 8:13-14; 1 Kgs 11:13-14; Isa 34:5-6; Jer 49:17-22; Amos 1:11-12; Mal 1:2-5). Resentment swirled about Edom's complicity with the Babylonians in the destruction of Jerusalem (Obad 1:9-14).

32:30 ***Sidonians.*** Strictly speaking, "Sidonians" would be residents of Sidon, the ancient and influential Phoenician city located between Tyre and Arvad on the Mediterranean coast. More likely, however, the term here simply means "Phoenicians," as it had for centuries by the time of Ezekiel.

COMMENTARY

The final oracle against the nations and concluding message concerning Egypt came to Ezekiel on March 17, 585 BC. The core message to Ezekiel was to "weep for the hordes of Egypt and for the other mighty nations" (32:18). Whether he wept in genuine sadness over the tragedy soon to overtake these peoples or simply played the part of a mourner appropriate to the circumstance we do not know with certainty. In any case, Ezekiel leads the reader in a proper response—weeping. Although this message focuses on Egypt, the expression "and [weep] for the other mighty nations" calls to mind the similar fate announced for the other nations addressed in chapters 25–31.

The reason Ezekiel is to weep is that Yahweh is sending Egypt's hordes (and the other nations as well) to the underworld. The rest of the message elaborates on this. First, Ezekiel is to consign Egypt to the pit (32:19). God underscores this fate by raising and then rejecting the idea that some quality might be found in Egypt—perhaps "loveliness"—that would keep her from this fate. But Egypt and her hordes must go to the pit, and she will be there with despised outcasts (32:19).

God's message undercuts Egypt's hubris, her arrogant presumptions, and her claims to exceptionality. At Yahweh's hand, Egypt, her Pharaoh, her teeming population, and massive military forces (i.e., her "hordes") would die like every other human being. She would die like her cultured despisers and those she despised. Assyria, Elam, Meshech and Tubal, Edom, and Sidon are mentioned. Egypt's heralded participation in the destiny of all human beings, rich and poor, famous and unknown, completely unmasks her, clearing away impressions of invincibility. Like every other human being, the Egyptians will die and find themselves in the grave in the company of outcasts.

This message from Yahweh rejects theological and cultural claims central to Egypt's identity. From early on Egyptian writers and rulers invested extensively in developing coherent and defining views of the afterlife. The king of Egypt entered the afterlife with massive provisions for continued royal treatment; he anticipated sharing the company of the gods. Privileged persons in the military, government, and religious establishments also anticipated circumstances befitting their station in life. (See ANET 32-36 for Egyptian mortuary texts of interest here.) Ezekiel put all of this aside with the claim that the Egyptians would die like everyone else and find themselves in the grave with outcasts! There would be no place of privilege for them.

Although Assyria, Elam, Meshech, Tubal, Edom, and Sidon are specifically mentioned, the nearly identical claims about them tie them together as participants in a common experience. Each "lies there surrounded by the graves" of its armies or hordes (32:22, 24, 26; cf. 32:30). They lie with "those who were slaughtered by the sword" (32:22, 24, 29; cf. 32:26), often with reference to troops slaughtered in the open field, not a designation of heroes buried with honor (32:27). They all "struck terror in the hearts of people everywhere" (32:23-24, 26; cf. 32:30) but now "lie in shame with others in the pit" (32:25; cf. 32:24, 30). They share a common embarrassment at their pitiful and unprivileged fate. They are outcasts among outcasts (32:25-26, 28, 30).

Ezekiel's picture of Egypt in the underworld here has been compared to Isaiah 14:1-21, where similar themes and vocabulary appear in Isaiah's taunt of the king of Babylon. (For a summary of views, see Block 1998:214, note 8.) Although neither passage presents a fully developed view of the afterlife, the moral failure of the parties named—Pharaoh's pride (32:19), the terrifying conduct of all these nations—seems related in some way to their lack of status in the grave. Thus, Egypt and its hordes will be "dragged away to their *judgment*" (32:20, emphasis added), implying perhaps some afterlife accountability for conduct before death. However, the repeated emphasis falls not on direct punishment in the grave for deeds done before death, but on the grave as the common fate of all these parties, indeed of all who die. The "judgment" seems to be the shocking realization that for all their might and grandeur, these rulers and their armies all suffer the same fate. (A clear concept of reward and punishment in the afterlife awaited further revelation and the development of the idea of the resurrection of the body; cf. Dan 12:1-4; 1 Cor 15; Wis 3:1–5:23.)

Pharaoh could take a certain comfort in learning that he would not be alone in having his forces slain (32:31). But his fate remained sealed—Pharaoh and his hordes would lie in the grave, in the company of outcasts, slaughtered by the sword (32:32). This ends the message, which is certified as Yahweh's word.

◆ V. Oracles and Visions of Israel's Restoration (33:1–48:35)

This final section of Ezekiel's written prophecy closes the circle on the book's major program. Ezekiel aimed to explain adequately the destruction of Judah and Jerusalem and to articulate a credible vision of a hopeful future. This vision of the future dramatically mirrors Ezekiel's prophetic analysis of Israel's recent past (3:22–24:27). There the nation was destroyed, and God's glory departed from the Temple and the land (chs 8–11). In this final prophecy of Israel's future, the glory of God returns to the Temple (43:2–44:4), to the renewed and redistributed land (47:13–48:29), and the rebuilt city (45:1-8; 48:15-35). These are the essential ingredients in Israel's restoration.

Ezekiel's vision in chapters 40–48 picks up six major agendas raised in 37:20-28. When Ezekiel illustrated the coming unification of the southern and northern kingdoms of Israel by joining two sticks together as though they were one, he followed that sign-act with an oracle detailing that promised kingdom. (1) The Lord would gather his people Israel and plant them again in the land (37:21). (2) He would save them from their backsliding and idolatry (37:23-24). (3) David would be their prince (37:25). (4) The Lord would make an everlasting "covenant of peace" with them (37:26). (5) Perhaps most remarkably, he would "put [his] Temple among them forever," thus making his home among them, he their God and they his people (37:26-28). (6) In this way the nations would know that the Lord was the one who "makes Israel holy" (37:25-28). This is a return to previous themes (cf. 20:32-44), an example of the "resumptive exposition" (Block 1998:497) that is a characteristic compositional strategy of Ezekiel's.

Ezekiel expounded upon the last agenda, the hallowing of Israel and Israel's God, in the Gog oracles (chs 38–39; see especially 39:25, 27 on Yahweh's holiness). This accounts in part for the placement of chapters 38–39. Then the prophet turns dramatically to God's promise to put his Temple, his "home," among his restored and united people, picking up the flow directly from 37:27 (40:5–46:18). He takes up the matter of the people's holiness: they will never again defile him or themselves (43:7-12; 44:5-30; 45:9-25). He expands upon the promised Davidic prince (45:9–46:18). Finally and climactically he treats the location of the unified nation in the land (chs 47–48).

Beyond these links with 37:20-28, genre, content, vocabulary, and book-level structure tie this concluding vision to the opening chapters of the book. Like chapters

1–3 and 8–11, chapters 40–48 report "divine visions" (1:1-2; 8:3; 10:1; 40:2). The visions involve divine apprehension of Ezekiel (being "taken hold of" by the hand of the Lord; 1:3; 8:1; 40:1), spiritual transport (3:12-14; 8:3; 40:2), and, especially in chapters 8–11 and 40–48, a guided tour of a temple (8:3; 40:5). All three vision sets are dated (July 31, 593, September 17, 592, and April 28, 573, respectively). Clearly, the reader is expected to connect these three vision reports as important nodes in the flow of the book. Further, the content of these visions presents a grand reversal that anchors the book's overall chiastic structure. Whereas in chapters 9–11 the glory of the Lord dramatically leaves its unique abode in the Jerusalem Temple, with equal drama that glory returns to fill the Temple in Ezekiel's restoration vision (chs 43–44). Thus, the earlier chapters of warning and judgment are here reversed in what amounts to "an extended oracle of salvation" (Allen 1990:213).

In spite of the obvious import placed on these critical chapters by those who gave us Ezekiel's book, they present enormous challenges to interpreters. Not only has Ezekiel's puzzling Hebrew suffered considerably in scribal transmission (note the plethora of textual notes on the translation itself), but also wide disagreement persists over the basic question of what the vision is actually about. Some have taken it to be a virtual blueprint for development of the restoration community, for the building of the Temple, reestablishment of worship, and reconstitution of the community in the land by the returnees, what Taylor calls a "literal prophetic" construal (1969:251). This reading finds support in the fact that chapters 40–48 abound in architectural, geographical, and topological detail and that they reverse earlier pronouncements of judgment that were clearly intended to be taken literally (e.g., 7:2-6, 14-27; 14:1-23)—with this literal context controlling the use of metaphor, symbol, parable, hyperbole, and the like in chapters 4–24 and beyond. Some dispensational interpreters, also inclined to expect a literal fulfillment of this sort of prophecy, read chapters 40–48 as a vision of Christ's millennial reign from Jerusalem. They expect a rebuilt Temple and reestablishment of animal sacrifice. Popularized and widely disseminated by the *Scofield Reference Bible*, Lewis Sperry Chafer gave this reading a theological platform in his *Systematic Theology* (1948:343).

Several aspects of Ezekiel's vision, however, present an apparently impracticable and surreal picture if we imagine it through the eyes of Ezekiel and his contemporaries. They knew only Solomon's Temple and his federal compound, which included the royal palace, the House of the Forest of Lebanon, the Hall of Pillars, the Hall of the Throne (i.e., of Judgment, cf. 1 Kgs 6–7). The Temple, which Ezekiel tours in chapter 8, stood on or just north of Mount Moriah, the hill above the City of David. When Solomon built it, he enlarged the City of David, incorporating an area roughly 300 meters by 420 meters, plus the Ophel (a ridge to the south of the Temple). Ezekiel's Sanctuary (the *miqdash* [TH4720, ZH5219]), containing only the Temple and its courts, measuring 291 meters square, straddles almost the entire east–west width and two-thirds of the north–south length of the Temple Mount, if Jerusalem is in mind (chs 40–42). As these viewers would have seen it, Ezekiel's Temple extends from the hilltop down into the Kidron Valley on the east, the Tyrophean Valley on the west (before it was significantly filled in), and on down the spur toward the City of David. A person in Nehemiah's time would have had a similar view. Not until Herod did architects call for the construction of a gigantic platform (its perimeter measuring 485 x 315 x 470 x 280 meters) that would have allowed Ezekiel's Temple to sit on level ground.

The life-giving stream also bursts the bounds of historical realities (47:1-12). One could envision directing water from the Gihon Spring down to the Dead Sea, as has been considered in modern times. But imagining that flow as a river too deep to walk through within a mile and a third of the Temple far surpasses the capacity of any stream near the Temple Mount (47:3-5). Further, the Gihon flows not from the Temple Mount but from a site down into the Kidron Valley below the City of David.

The distribution of the land among the tribes also seems to stretch reality, though the limited information given demands caution here (47:13–48:35). The distribution of the tribes takes none of their particular needs such as those related to population (e.g., for space and quality of land) into account. Populous Simeon and Judah have the same amount of land as any other tribe (assuming a later population with roughly the same ratios as those seen in Israel's early history; cf. Num 1). It disregards topographical and geographical realities. Zebulon and Gad, for example, have largely less fertile, wilderness land (48:27-29). Although the outer boundaries of the land are given (47:15-20), the east–west boundaries between the various tribes are not given. Seven tribes are located above the national square and the royal land, with five tribes below it. If the national square with the Temple and the national city is to be anchored by tying the city to the site of historic Jerusalem, it does not seem possible to give tribes equal allotments within the exterior boundaries laid out. These features among others make the "literal prophetic" view difficult to carry out consistently.

In addition to these problems, dispensationalists have difficulty accounting for the New Testament's own treatment of these matters and answering the charge that their hermeneutic is skewed by a priori doctrinal commitments (Allen 1990:214-215; Waltke 1988:269-276). Consequently, many readers have taken Ezekiel's vision in chapters 40–48 as fully symbolic, proclaiming the gospel and realities of the Kingdom and Temple fulfilled in the church.

Older interpreters like Fairbairn in the mid-nineteenth century specifically took the "incongruities" and "literal extravagances" noted above to point solely to spiritual realities, specifically to the good in store for Christ's church and people (1979:439, 443). For example, commenting on the rooms for the priests in 40:48–41:11, Fairbairn declines to expound on the details of the passage or pursue matters that Ezekiel has left undefined—details of the Temple itself, its sacred furniture, indeed even the critically important Ark of the Covenant, about which Ezekiel says nothing. Instead, Ezekiel wrote with the object of "securing a far purer and more elevated condition for the covenant-people" (Fairbairn 1979:463). In this way the prophet would "teach that there was to be in the future a conformity to the Divine idea, where there had been little before; that while Jehovah would remain the same in all his essential attributes and manifestations as formerly, he should be otherwise known and glorified by his people; their dwellings should all become true sanctuaries, and their services fragrant with the odour of living piety" (ibid.).

More recent interpreters, while accepting the symbolic nature of aspects of the vision, have also called attention to ways these chapters respond to royal and priestly abuses flagged in Ezekiel's earlier judgment oracles. Literarily and theologically, chapters 40–48 address agendas facing the exilic and early postexilic community. Whatever one makes of the New Testament's appropriation of Ezekiel, one should not ignore the historical context to which these chapters, like the rest of Ezekiel, were addressed. Two factors situate these chapters well in a "between Temples" era: (1) the dating of these visions halfway through a cycle toward the Year of Jubilee and (2) their suitability as a "liturgical manifesto" for a truly reconstituted kingdom of priests and holy nation. Still, we know of no inclinations in the restoration community to turn to Ezekiel for an actual model for rebuilding the community, either architecturally or institutionally. These and other features of chapters 40–48 could incline one to read them as an eschatological picture of the reconstituted nation. Noting the lack of typically eschatological language in these chapters, Block suggests it is an "ideational" vision in which "historical events are described from a theological plane" and spiritual realities are pictured "in concrete terms, employing the familiar cultural idioms of temple, altar, sacrifices, *nasi'* [TH5387, ZH5954], and land" (1998:505-506). Ezekiel presents "a lofty spiritual ideal: Where God is, there is Zion. . . . there is order and the fulfillment of all his promises" (1998:506). These aspects of the text are well accounted for by recognizing the apocalyptic (perhaps "proto-apocalyptic") use of visionary experience, numerical patterns, and symbolism in the proclamation of a "real" future (Taylor 1969:253).

Much like Block, but with a much more complex conception of the compositional history of the unit and less awareness of the unity of the text, Zimmerli sees these chapters simultaneously as new Torah for the restoration community and as a vision of the complete fulfillment of the future Yahweh had promised for Israel, not to be enacted by Israel but miraculously created by God (1983:328-329; similarly Eichrodt, but with even less confidence than Zimmerli in finding meaningful coherence in the disjointed text, 1983:530-531). For Zimmerli, the multifaceted numerical symmetries underscore the proclamational nature of the picture envisioned (1983:343-344). Ezekiel is shown the real future of Israel prepared by God, awaiting them in the Year of Jubilee and following the new exodus and day of liberation promised in 20:34ff (1983:361). But Zimmerli stresses the difficulty of translating the objective language of architecture and measurements into more general language of theological symbolism, addressing persons "lost in imprisonment of exile . . . called to responsibility" (1983:361).

Levenson (1976:18) presents one of the most penetrating recent analyses of chapters 40–48. Working carefully with the abundant intertextuality in these chapters of Ezekiel, he explores the prophet's synthesis of Sinai and Zion theologies, of the living legacies of Moses and David in the exiles' future. Under these heads, both the programmatic and symbolic aspects of the vision receive emphasis. He sees a proleptic revelation of Israel's restoration, "a foretaste of ultimate redemption granted one who must otherwise dwell in history." So Ezekiel provides a "practical program," not simply a vision of grace (ch 45), and in the process addresses the problem of the relationship of divine and human government, which meet in the promised restoration (ch 48).

A particularly fascinating extension of Levenson's approach by Tuell (1992:171) finds numerous points of contact between chapters 40–48 and the realities of provincial life in the Persian Empire. These points of contact include Persian measurement standards, establishment of the Temple as a state-sponsored institution in the empire, the *nasi'* [TH5387, ZH5954] (prince) as a Persian provincial governor, and the boundaries of the new land as those of the Persian province (or subprovince), Abar-Nahara. Whether or not Tuell succeeds fully in making his argument for a setting in the reign of Darius, he demonstrates the possibility of a clearly programmatic presentation in a literary format that is essentially a "theological enterprise," a doctrinal tract reflecting distinct ideas about God, history, and the identity of Israel to be lived out in real time.

This commentary proceeds with the understanding that for the preexilic and exilic prophets, the anticipated return from exile and diaspora was their eschatological hope. Return from exile included for them the complete resolution of all of the problems facing God's people—moral, spiritual, physical, political, and national—often in connection with the rise of a Davidic ruler. Through this scion, Yahweh would shepherd his people, subjecting the nations to his rule, planting his people in their land, and blessing them with unending shalom, justice, and plenty. This was simultaneously their spiritual and physical destiny. Because the specific, historically anticipated hope opened almost seamlessly into a utopian future, their language reflected the permeable boundary between history and eschaton with easy movement in and out of metaphor, hyperbole, and symbol. But the utopian and the ineffable were no less "real" than the prosaic. All of it was expected. All of it had warrant for present decision making or policy formulation.

The fact that not all of these hopes materialized for God's people does not argue against the nature of that hope. The gap between what the prophets had proclaimed and what the returnees actually experienced threw some members of the restoration community into a theological crisis. How that crisis was then (and is now) handled charts the courses of different Jewish and Christian communities to this day (Levenson 1976:99-100, 148).

◆ A. Israel's New Heart; Yahweh's New Name (33:1–37:28)

1. Ezekiel: watchman or singer of love songs? (33:1–33)

Once again a message came to me from the LORD: 2"Son of man, give your people this message: 'When I bring an army against a country, the people of that land choose one of their own to be a watchman. 3When the watchman sees the enemy coming, he sounds the alarm to warn the people. 4Then if those who hear the alarm refuse to take action, it is their own fault if they die. 5They heard the alarm but ignored it, so the responsibility is theirs. If they had listened to the warning, they could have saved their lives. 6But if the watchman sees the enemy coming and doesn't sound the alarm to warn the people, he is responsible for their captivity. They will die in their sins, but I will hold the watchman responsible for their deaths.'

7"Now, son of man, I am making you a watchman for the people of Israel. Therefore, listen to what I say and warn them for me. 8If I announce that some wicked people are sure to die and you fail to tell them to change their ways, then they will die in their sins, and I will hold you responsible for their deaths. 9But if you warn them to repent and they don't repent, they will die in their sins, but you will have saved yourself.

10"Son of man, give the people of Israel this message: You are saying, 'Our sins are heavy upon us; we are wasting away! How

can we survive?' 11As surely as I live, says the Sovereign LORD, I take no pleasure in the death of wicked people. I only want them to turn from their wicked ways so they can live. Turn! Turn from your wickedness, O people of Israel! Why should you die?

12"Son of man, give your people this message: The righteous behavior of righteous people will not save them if they turn to sin, nor will the wicked behavior of wicked people destroy them if they repent and turn from their sins. 13When I tell righteous people that they will live, but then they sin, expecting their past righteousness to save them, then none of their righteous acts will be remembered. I will destroy them for their sins. 14And suppose I tell some wicked people that they will surely die, but then they turn from their sins and do what is just and right. 15For instance, they might give back a debtor's security, return what they have stolen, and obey my life-giving laws, no longer doing what is evil. If they do this, then they will surely live and not die. 16None of their past sins will be brought up again, for they have done what is just and right, and they will surely live.

17"Your people are saying, 'The Lord isn't doing what's right,' but it is they who are not doing what's right. 18For again I say, when righteous people turn away from their righteous behavior and turn to evil, they will die. 19But if wicked people turn from their wickedness and do what is just and right, they will live. 20O people of Israel, you are saying, 'The Lord isn't doing what's right.' But I judge each of you according to your deeds."

21On January 8,* during the twelfth year of our captivity, a survivor from Jerusalem came to me and said, "The city has fallen!" 22The previous evening the LORD had taken hold of me and given me back my voice. So I was able to speak when this man arrived the next morning.

23Then this message came to me from the LORD: 24"Son of man, the scattered remnants of Judah living among the ruined cities keep saying, 'Abraham was only one man, yet he gained possession of the entire land. We are many; surely the land has been given to us as a possession.' 25So tell these people, 'This is what the Sovereign LORD says: You eat meat with blood in it, you worship idols,* and you murder the innocent. Do you really think the land should be yours? 26Murderers! Idolaters! Adulterers! Should the land belong to you?'

27"Say to them, 'This is what the Sovereign LORD says: As surely as I live, those living in the ruins will die by the sword. And I will send wild animals to eat those living in the open fields. Those hiding in the forts and caves will die of disease. 28I will completely destroy the land and demolish her pride. Her arrogant power will come to an end. The mountains of Israel will be so desolate that no one will even travel through them. 29When I have completely destroyed the land because of their detestable sins, then they will know that I am the LORD.'

30"Son of man, your people talk about you in their houses and whisper about you at the doors. They say to each other, 'Come on, let's go hear the prophet tell us what the LORD is saying!' 31So my people come pretending to be sincere and sit before you. They listen to your words, but they have no intention of doing what you say. Their mouths are full of lustful words, and their hearts seek only after money. 32You are very entertaining to them, like someone who sings love songs with a beautiful voice or plays fine music on an instrument. They hear what you say, but they don't act on it! 33But when all these terrible things happen to them—as they certainly will—then they will know a prophet has been among them."

33:21 Hebrew *On the fifth day of the tenth month,* of the ancient Hebrew lunar calendar. This event occurred on January 8, 585 B.C.; also see note on 1:1. **33:25** The Hebrew term (literally *round things*) probably alludes to dung.

NOTES

33:2 *watchman.* For a portrayal of the sort of city tower from which a sentry would keep watch for the enemy, see ANEP, illustration 373. The monumental carvings from Nineveh portray Sennacherib's assault on the Judean fortress city of Lachish. In that portrayal, soldiers trying to defend the city fight from the tower where the sentry would have stood earlier. From such towers persons also kept watch for fire signals from neighboring settlements, as we know from Lachish Ostraca IV. This letter sent from a settlement between Lachish and Azekah poignantly reads: "May my lord be apprised that we are watching out for the fire signals of Lachish according to all the signals which my lord has given, because we cannot see [the signals of] Azekah" (ANET 322).

33:11 *Why should you die?* Ezekiel brings together materials he used earlier, reshaped for this point in the book. Ezekiel's commission as a watchman (33:1-9, from 3:16-20) and the treatment of dynamic moral accountability (33:11-20, from 18:1-32) are brought together here to underscore Ezekiel's role as a prophet of hope and to emphasize the accountabilities of both the prophet and the exiles. In ch 18, the doctrine of individual dynamic moral accountability was used to refute a proverb that evaded the exiles' responsibility for their plight. Here Ezekiel uses that same understanding of dynamic accountability to inspire and support hope among exiles who felt trapped by the consequences of their sins (33:10). For a penetrating analysis of the sentinel image, see Lapsley (2000:68-71).

33:21 *the twelfth year of our captivity.* This was 585 BC (cf. NLT mg). Some texts read the "eleventh year" here (Lucianic LXX, Syriac, and a few Hebrew mss), most likely an emendation to resolve a discrepancy between the dates here, in 24:1, and in 2 Kgs 25 (see note on 24:1). Most current scholars resist this emendation. The difficulty should probably be resolved by leaving both this text and 24:1 as they stand, while understanding 24:1 to be uniquely dated, for emphasis, to the "official" calendar following the reign of Zedekiah and not to the deportation of Jehoiachin as customarily in Ezekiel (Block 1998:772-774; Thiele 1965:165-172). This moves the 24:1 date from January 588 to January 587. The fall of Jerusalem would then be in the summer of 586, the deportation in August of 586, leaving about five months for the journey of the survivor of the catastrophe.

33:25 *You eat meat with blood in it.* This is contrary to Lev 17:10-16.

you worship idols. Lit., "you fix your gaze/attention on idols" (*gillulim* [TH1544, ZH1658]; see note on 5:9 for Ezekiel's vocabulary of idolatry), an act contrary to Exod 20:3.

you murder the innocent. Lit., "you spill [innocent] blood," a deed contrary to Exod 20:13.

33:26 *Murderers!* This translates "You stand by/on your sword," an idiom occurring only here; it points to the inclination to resort quickly to violence to address problems.

Idolaters! This renders "you do abominable things," naming a wide range of lawless behavior, most obviously idolatry.

Adulterers! Ezekiel phrases this in priestly terms of defiling a neighbor's wife, prohibited in Lev 18:11, 15.

COMMENTARY

Here we see a second presentation of the prophet Ezekiel as Yahweh's sentinel for Israel (3:16-21; 33:1-9). This parallel signals the beginning of a major section of the book (33:1–48:35) to be read over against the first 24 chapters. Ezekiel's explanation of the judgment of Judah and Jerusalem began with the presentation of his commission as a prophet (1:3ff). Ezekiel was called upon to proclaim Yahweh's message of indictment and warning to this rebellious nation. Ezekiel and his listeners (and later, readers) were to perceive his prophetic role by analogy to the duties of a town sentinel (3:16-21). Emphasis fell on the responsibilities involved—the sentinel to see and warn, the townspeople to hearken to the alarm and take warning—and on the hope for escape or rescue because of the warning.

These same contentions inform Ezekiel's role as a prophet of hope, just as they did his role as a prophet of judgment. As the book has progressed, with its dated oracles underscoring the correctness of Ezekiel's warnings, Ezekiel's status as a spokesperson for the God of Israel has risen. As God said at the outset, the people should have become aware that a prophet was among them (2:5). The sentinel image applies now to his role as a prophet of hope. God called him to proclaim the message of hope as diligently and clearly as he did the messages of indictment and judgment. Ezekiel will address issues as critical and as important for the life and death of the people of God in his role as a prophet of hope as he did as a prophet of doom. The repetition here of Ezekiel's appointment as a sentinel (33:7-9) should orient the reader to a new beginning in the book—with the original reading assumptions still firmly in place.

Ezekiel put a second oracle here (33:10-20) to draw out the implications of the sentinel metaphor. The sentinel metaphor divides responsibilities so that the sentinel has responsibility to warn promptly and clearly, while the hearers must hearken and take action to save themselves. One could misunderstand this metaphor to signal the disinterest of the sentinel beyond his or her warning task. God clarifies that this would be a misunderstanding both of the sentinel metaphor as an aspect of prophetic call and of the Lord's intentions in illuminating that call. Neither the prophet nor God was disinterested in the listeners' response or their eventual fate. They gave the warning so that God's people would be saved (33:11). God emphasizes his bias for the life (not the death) of his people by first stating it negatively, then positively. God has no delight in the death of the wicked; he has great pleasure when the wicked change their ways and find life (33:11).

This affirmation of God's strong bias for the life of his people came in response to two claims by God's people—both in exile with the prophet and back in Jerusalem (33:10, 17). First, the people were giving up hope. They saw no way out of the consequences of their sins in terms of the destruction of the land and people (33:10). Second, they saw Yahweh's decision to save (only) those wicked who repent and not to save erstwhile righteous persons who turn their back on God as being unjust (33:17-20).

Regarding the hopelessness of their situation (33:10), God made explicit what is implicit in most prophetic messages of indictment and doom. Although the indictments stood and the announced doom would indeed come, God had proclaimed these sober messages with the hope that the wicked would turn from their evil ways and thus live. Indeed, God pleaded for his people to turn from their wicked ways and thus live. He reinforced this with a rhetorical question that implies there is no convincing reason for persisting in sin and therefore dying (33:11).

God extended this discussion by summarizing the word given in chapter 18 repudiating the proverb on sour grapes and puckered mouths (intergenerational consequences of sin). In chapter 18, he argued for dynamic, individual accountability, claiming that neither the character of a person's parents nor even a pattern of behavior earlier in one's life determines one's destiny. At any given point, one lives or dies with God based on a current relationship with God that can be judged by the nature of one's behaviors—righteous or wicked (18:3-32). The person that sins dies, not his or her children or his or her parents. The person that repents and obeys lives—not his parents or children. As Lapsley succinctly puts it, "every decision at any given moment is determinative of the moral status of the self" (2000:71).

Here, in chapter 33 (33:10-16), God argues not so much for accountability but rather for hope based on the liberating power of repentance. The emphasis here is that God wants his people to live. He exposed their sin so they might repent and live according to his revealed will. In order to motivate repentance, he has clarified the consequences sure to come to those who reject his ways. The oracle focuses on "turning" to God, on what this involves, on God's desire to foster such a turn, and on the results of thus turning to God.

Regarding the alleged unfairness of Yahweh's acceptance of persons based on currently demonstrated character, Yahweh simply rejects the accusation out of hand, just as earlier in 18:25-29. He accuses them of wrongdoing in their desire to hide behind their own past conduct or another's deeds. He reaffirms his commitment to judge each person on their own merits (33:17-20).

Contrary to his usual pattern of dating the reception of an oracle, here Ezekiel dates an event, thereby underscoring the import of the day (33:21). On January 8, 585 BC, which was 12 years into the captivity (with Jehoiachin) and six months following the event, a survivor of the siege of Jerusalem came with word that the city had fallen. This constitutes a marker event in the prophet's career and in the organization of the book—the event toward which the first half of the book has been moving. Just as the Lord had foretold (24:27), the city had indeed fallen, a refugee had arrived with eyewitness news, and Ezekiel's speech restriction had been lifted.

The refugee's arrival raises a related question regarding possession of the land. The Babylonians had destroyed major cities and settlements all across the land and were in the process of deporting thousands of Judeans. Thousands had already been killed and driven from the land. This total disruption of property holding and property rights prompted questions regarding possession of the land God had given his people by covenant with Abraham. By a strange turn of logic, persons left in the land capitalized on their desperate plight. They reasoned that if God gave the land to Abraham and he was but one person, surely God was going to give them the land now as a possession, few in number as they were (33:24).

In response, God shifts the point of focus from numbers to character—in keeping with the historic promise. Population count had nothing to do with the patriarchal promise at this point. The fulfillment of the promise to Abraham was tied not to numbers but to his trust in Yahweh expressed in obedience (Gen 12:1-3; 17:4-8; 18:19; 22:15-19). So Yahweh turned their attention away from the survivors' skimpy numbers to their deplorable conduct. They broke the Torah as expressed in Exodus and Leviticus. They rejected the revealed will of God and thereby disqualified themselves as possible recipients of the promise to Abraham. God emphatically rejected their presumptuous claim with a repeated rhetorical question—"Should the land belong to you?" (33:25-26). The assumed answer is clearly, "No!"

The consequence of their breach of covenant law would not be a blessing but a curse (33:27-29). Even though they had survived the fall of Jerusalem, they would suffer the consequences of breaking the covenant. He addressed the ravaged post-siege population, persons living among ruins, in open fields, in deserted forts and caves. Even so, God said he would send them the sword, wild animals, and disease—all historic covenant curses (cf. Lev 26:22, 25, 33). The land itself would suffer, devoid not only of inhabitants but also of travelers (cf. the threats against Egypt in 29:11). As in the oracles against the nations, the demolition of Judah's pride surfaces as an agenda with the Lord (33:28). Also, as everywhere in Ezekiel, Yahweh makes it clear that he will reveal himself in these events (33:29).

As in Ezekiel's original commission, so here again at the outset of his ministry of declaring Yahweh's program for restoration, God addressed the character of Ezekiel's audience (33:30-32). Even after the fall of Jerusalem confirmed Ezekiel's prophetic credentials, he would still deal with a "congregation" of mockers and gainsayers. They pretended to be sincere, but they actually thought he was good entertainment. They even mocked the possibility that the Lord was speaking through him.

Incidentally, in this paragraph we perhaps learn something about prophetic technique. Was Ezekiel actually a musician? Did he sing some oracles (33:32)? It is possible. We know he, like nearly all of the other Old Testament prophets from whom we have written oracles, was a poet—not the Shakespeare of the Hebrew Bible, but nevertheless a poet. (The NLT's printing convention identifies such poetic passages by indentation and the use of poetic cola; e.g., 32:2b-8.) And we know of Ezekiel's knowledge and use of various poetic genres, such as the maxim (*mashal* [TH4912, ZH5442]), the riddle (*khidah* [TH2420, ZH2648]), and the dirge (*qinah* [TH7015, ZH7806]). We might expect the *qinah* to be sung, but we cannot be certain. Like other Hebrew poets, he presses a repertoire of poetic artistry into service in his poems, such as rhyme, alliteration, assonance, use of so-called A and B words, and especially complex varieties of parallelism. So he was an artist of sorts, to be sure. Whether he was really a musician is hard to say. Whatever the case, his audience had no more intention of taking him seriously at this point than they did at the outset of his ministry (cf. 2:3-5).

God identified not only their cynical behavior but also the conditions of their hearts as a key factor in their response to the prophet. "Their hearts seek only after money" (33:31), specifically *betsa'* [TH1215, ZH1299]—gain almost always associated with violence or unlawful means (Exod 18:21; 1 Sam 8:3; Jer 6:13; Hab 2:9). It is possible that Ezekiel here touched upon a theme that integrates chapters 33 through 37. Chapter 36 addresses the fact that God's people need a totally new heart if they are to keep covenant with Yahweh consistently (cf. 36:26-27).

◆ 2. The Lord himself to shepherd Israel (34:1-31)

Then this message came to me from the LORD: [2]"Son of man, prophesy against the shepherds, the leaders of Israel. Give them this message from the Sovereign LORD: What sorrow awaits you shepherds who feed yourselves instead of your flocks. Shouldn't shepherds feed their sheep? [3]You drink the milk, wear the wool, and butcher the best animals, but you let your flocks starve. [4]You have not taken care of

the weak. You have not tended the sick or
bound up the injured. You have not gone
looking for those who have wandered
away and are lost. Instead, you have ruled
them with harshness and cruelty. 5So my
sheep have been scattered without a
shepherd, and they are easy prey for any
wild animal. 6They have wandered through
all the mountains and all the hills, across
the face of the earth, yet no one has gone
to search for them.

7"Therefore, you shepherds, hear the
word of the LORD: 8As surely as I live, says
the Sovereign LORD, you abandoned my
flock and left them to be attacked by ev-
ery wild animal. And though you were my
shepherds, you didn't search for my sheep
when they were lost. You took care of
yourselves and left the sheep to starve.
9Therefore, you shepherds, hear the word
of the LORD. 10This is what the Sovereign
LORD says: I now consider these shepherds
my enemies, and I will hold them respon-
sible for what has happened to my flock.
I will take away their right to feed the
flock, and I will stop them from feeding
themselves. I will rescue my flock from
their mouths; the sheep will no longer be
their prey.

11"For this is what the Sovereign LORD
says: I myself will search and find my
sheep. 12I will be like a shepherd looking
for his scattered flock. I will find my sheep
and rescue them from all the places where
they were scattered on that dark and
cloudy day. 13I will bring them back home
to their own land of Israel from among
the peoples and nations. I will feed them
on the mountains of Israel and by the riv-
ers and in all the places where people live.
14Yes, I will give them good pastureland
on the high hills of Israel. There they will
lie down in pleasant places and feed in
the lush pastures of the hills. 15I myself
will tend my sheep and give them a place
to lie down in peace, says the Sovereign
LORD. 16I will search for my lost ones who
strayed away, and I will bring them safely
home again. I will bandage the injured
and strengthen the weak. But I will de-
stroy those who are fat and powerful. I
will feed them, yes—feed them justice!

17"And as for you, my flock, this is what
the Sovereign LORD says to his people: I
will judge between one animal of the
flock and another, separating the sheep
from the goats. 18Isn't it enough for you
to keep the best of the pastures for your-
selves? Must you also trample down the
rest? Isn't it enough for you to drink clear
water for yourselves? Must you also mud-
dy the rest with your feet? 19Why must my
flock eat what you have trampled down
and drink water you have fouled?

20"Therefore, this is what the Sovereign
LORD says: I will surely judge between the
fat sheep and the scrawny sheep. 21For
you fat sheep pushed and butted and
crowded my sick and hungry flock until
you scattered them to distant lands. 22So
I will rescue my flock, and they will no
longer be abused. I will judge between
one animal of the flock and another. 23And
I will set over them one shepherd, my ser-
vant David. He will feed them and be a
shepherd to them. 24And I, the LORD, will
be their God, and my servant David will be
a prince among my people. I, the LORD,
have spoken!

25"I will make a covenant of peace with
my people and drive away the dangerous
animals from the land. Then they will be
able to camp safely in the wildest places
and sleep in the woods without fear. 26I
will bless my people and their homes
around my holy hill. And in the proper
season I will send the showers they need.
There will be showers of blessing. 27The
orchards and fields of my people will yield
bumper crops, and everyone will live in
safety. When I have broken their chains of
slavery and rescued them from those who
enslaved them, then they will know that I
am the LORD. 28They will no longer be prey
for other nations, and wild animals will no
longer devour them. They will live in safe-
ty, and no one will frighten them.

29"And I will make their land famous
for its crops, so my people will never
again suffer from famines or the insults

of foreign nations. 30In this way, they will know that I, the LORD their God, am with them. And they will know that they, the people of Israel, are my people, says the Sovereign LORD. 31You are my flock, the sheep of my pasture. You are my people, and I am your God. I, the Sovereign LORD, have spoken!"

NOTES

34:2 ***against the shepherds, the leaders of Israel.*** Ezekiel did not engage in an allegory in this chapter. Instead, he made extensive use of a common ancient Near Eastern metaphor, likening kings and leaders to shepherds. Though he pursued the metaphor from several angles, it remains simple and unextended. In the process, he shares language used by Jeremiah (Jer 23:1-6; cf. Jer 22:17ff). Repeated use of the verbs *darash* [TH1875, ZH2011], *biqqesh* [TH1245, ZH1335], and *biqqer* [TH1239, ZH1329] stitches the first half of this segment together. The three terms are used both negatively, in the sense of "requiring, holding accountable" (34:10, 11, 12), and positively, in the sense of "searching for, seeking for [in order to tend]" (34:4, 6, 8, 11, 16).

34:3 ***You drink the milk.*** The NLT (cf. REB, JB, NAB, and NIV [curds?]) follows the readings of the LXX and Vulgate, which suggest *khalab* [TH2461, ZH2692] (milk). This differs only in vowel pointing from the MT's *kheleb* [TH2459, ZH2693] (fat/finest portion), which is followed by NKJV, NASB, RSV, NRSV, ESV, and NJPS.

34:8 ***As surely as I live.*** The Lord emphasizes his accusation of the shepherds by repetition (34:3 and 8) and by buttressing it here with an oath. He then underscores these restoration marvels emphatically as his own acts. The MT uses an independent first-person sg. pronoun in this oath formula (*khay-'ani* [TH589, ZH638]). Ezekiel then punctuates the oracles in this segment with this independent first-person pronoun (34:8, 15, 20, 24, 27, 30, 31) and the "particle of interest," *hinneh* [TH2009, ZH2180], which calls particular attention to the first-person suffix attached to it (*hineni;* 34:10, 11, 17, 20; cf. Arnold and Choi 2003:157-161). The restoration will be Yahweh's accomplishment; only he can keep these promises.

34:10 ***I will rescue my flock from their mouths.*** The shepherds had themselves become predators, ravenous animals from which Yahweh's flock needed to be rescued. Like Jeremiah, Ezekiel held the final kings of Judah, and especially Zedekiah, responsible for the destruction of the nation. Sin was found in every quarter of the population, but kings charged with caring for their subjects bore particular responsibility (cf. Jer 22:13-23 and its denunciation of king Jehoiakim).

34:12 ***I will be like a shepherd. . . . my sheep.*** The Lord's portrayal of himself as a model "shepherd" for his people and his promise of setting "one shepherd" over them in a coming Davidic kingdom provide rich background to Jesus' claim to be "the good shepherd" (John 10:11, 14). Although Jesus pursued the metaphor in some directions not found in Ezekiel, this passage still forms the background for his words, and it makes clear that Jesus was not simply describing his relationship to his own followers but also making a clear claim to be the messianic Good Shepherd. See Raymond Brown's helpful discussion (1966:396-398).

on that dark and cloudy day. Language of this sort, associated with the fall of Jerusalem and the scattering of God's people, evokes thought of the Day of the Lord and its eschatological judgment (cf. Joel 2:2; Zeph 1:15). In this context, it also anticipates the salvation associated with that day.

34:17 ***separating the sheep from the goats.*** Lit., "separating rams from billy goats," using these terms also as metaphors for leaders among the people.

34:23-24 ***I will set over them one shepherd, my servant David. He . . . will be a prince among my people.*** Ezekiel often uses *nasi'* [TH5387, ZH5954] (prince) of the messiah; "it corresponds with his conception of the true David" (NBD 973). References to this David being the prince can be found in 37:25; 44:3; 45:7, 16-17, 22; 46:2-18; 48:21-22.

34:25 ***covenant of peace.*** Elaborating on the Lord's relationship with Israel as "my flock," Ezekiel presents a covenant structure to govern that relationship. The promise here repeatedly echoes language of the Sinai covenant's blessings and curses from Lev 26:3-22. As Allen puts it, "the old Exodus achievement" is "reapplied to future liberation" (1994:163).

34:31 ***You are my flock, the sheep of my pasture. You are my people, and I am your God.*** Ezekiel gives prophetic utterance to realities celebrated liturgically in Pss 95:7 and 100:3.

COMMENTARY

Five related oracles comprise Ezekiel's address to the leadership of Judah and Jerusalem. Most survivors among these leaders lived in the exile community; a few still lived in the land. God employed the shepherd metaphor to speak to Israel's leaders (34:2-16), as the NLT makes explicit in 34:2. The shepherd image is then extended to address the flock, God's people, as well as their leaders (34:17-24). The shepherd metaphor pictures the major responsibilities of leadership so admirably that kings in the ancient Near East used it to describe themselves for centuries. The famous Hammurabi, king of Babylon over a thousand years before Ezekiel, portrayed himself as a "beneficent shepherd" appointed by the gods Enlil and Marduk in the prologue and epilogue to his law code. He purported that under his watchful care, his people prospered, guided by the just and righteous laws he promulgated, living in peace and blessed by the gods (ANET 164-165, 177-178).

Beginning with a standard "woe oracle," Ezekiel delivered the central accusation in the form of an extended direct address: "you shepherds who feed yourselves instead of your flocks" (34:2). Israel's leaders failed at the central point of their identity. Shepherds have no other reason to exist than to care for the sheep in their charge. In other words, claimed Ezekiel, leaders have no more basic responsibility than to care for those they lead. These leaders, however, pressed the flock into the service of their own well-being—taking milk, wool and meat from the flock, while allowing the flock to starve (34:3). Not only had they actively exploited the flock, they had also conspicuously omitted the expected acts of care for those in their charge (34:4). As a result, the sheep were scattered, wandering at the mercy of predators (34:5-6).

Two brief prophetic words introduced by "therefore" (34:7, 9) explicitly draw conclusions that flow from the indictments. The first repeats the central indictment from 34:2-6—self-indulgence by the shepherds instead of care for the sheep (34:7-8). The second announces Yahweh's acts in response to this situation. He responds by taking an enemy stance toward these leaders (34:9-10). He will hold these leaders responsible for their behaviors, just as a shepherd is held responsible for the welfare of the flock. He will terminate their place of privilege with the flock as well as their exploitation of it. Finally, he will rescue his flock from these shepherds, actually "from their mouths" (34:10). Ironically, these shepherds had actually become the predators, the lions and bears from whose mouths the sheep have to be snatched!

The promises of rescue (34:10) no doubt account for the location of these oracles at this point in the book. Although Ezekiel launched these materials with indictments as in a judgment oracle, the direction turns at this point to a proclamation of hope. Yahweh's promises of restoration have four foci. (1) The Sovereign Lord himself will become Israel's shepherd, tending his flock with divine perfection (34:11-16). (2) He will also save the flock from predators actually within the flock (34:17-21). (3) He will give them a Davidic leader (34:24). (4) And he will establish a "covenant of peace" for them (34:25-31).

Yahweh himself will assume the leadership that had previously been delegated to the shepherds now under indictment. As the God of Israel, he will be the quintessential shepherd, doing all that a shepherd should do for the sheep (34:11-16). The main emphasis is on gathering the scattered sheep. Ezekiel shifted in and out of the metaphor here, making it clear that the gathering of the sheep signaled the return of the exiles to their homeland. God would feed them again on the hills of Israel. These rescued sheep would experience the blessed side of Yahweh's justice, while those who had abused their power by making themselves fat on the flock would experience the stern edge of that justice. The series of first person verbs—"I will . . . I will . . ."—emphasizes this turn of events as the doing of Yahweh himself.

A subtheme to be pursued briefly is introduced in 34:16: the reality of abuse within the flock itself. Beyond the atrocities perpetrated by the shepherds, Yahweh exposed the maltreatment carried out by various members of the flock (34:17-19), addressing them as "my flock . . . [my] people" (34:17). Using a metaphor of separating sheep and goats (34:17) or judging between fat and scrawny sheep (34:20), Yahweh promised to isolate those who hoarded resources, abused their privilege, and disregarded their fellows. He would rescue the flock from itself. These comments underscore the fact that the exiles as a body could not blame their whole plight on their leaders, the royal family, and the top figures in the Temple and palace establishment. The population as a whole was responsible for significant aspects of their situation, for Yahweh deals with breach of covenant wherever it is found.

Ezekiel mixed metaphor and historical reference by claiming that God would "set over them one shepherd, my servant David" (34:23). Here, as at other places in the book, Ezekiel moved without warning from speaking metaphorically (the shepherd image presented in the chapter) to speaking historically (an actual Davidic ruler would emerge). Ezekiel spoke of governmental realities with reference to a Davidic ruler, the historical means by which Yahweh himself would be their shepherd, as just promised. Ezekiel here refrains from calling the Davidic ruler "king." Instead, he would be "prince" (Heb., *nasi'* [TH5387, ZH5954]) among God's people (34:24). Perhaps Ezekiel wanted to avoid any connotation of the abuses of power so blatant in the last kings of Judah. But talk of a Davidic ruler can only mean a king, as the language eventually used indicates (see 37:22, 24).

This Davidic ruler would be Yahweh's *servant,* with clear lines of accountability. The ruler's Davidic lineage indicates that Ezekiel expected Yahweh to keep his promise regarding an unending Davidic dynasty (2 Sam 7:11-16; Ps 89:19-52). For a similar vision of Israel's future, following shepherd indictments with Davidic hope, see Jeremiah 23:1-8 (cf. also Jer 33:14-16). There will be *one* shepherd. That is, there will be no divided monarchy with a Davidic house in Judah and random dynasties in the house of Israel. As in the days of David, there would be one kingdom of God's flock and a single, Davidic ruler (cf. Hos 3:3-5).

Christian readers can readily see that these promises informed New Testament expectations. Luke tells us that devout Jews (like Zechariah and Mary) believed that God's definitive rescue of his people would come from a son of David who would restore the kingdom with unprecedented blessings (Luke 1:32-33, 67-79). Ezekiel's word here and other similar passages in Hebrew Scripture (noted above) support such expectations. These expectations were fulfilled in Jesus, the son of David, who claimed to be the Good Shepherd caring for God's flock and uniting them under his royal leadership (John 10:7-18).

Designating this Davidic ruler as "shepherd" and associating him with covenant carries considerable import. "Shepherd" (*ro'eh* [TH7462A, ZH8286]) is not an exact synonym for "king" (*melek* [TH4428, ZH4889]) but calls several considerations to the fore. "Shepherd" sets aside dynastic rise to power and highlights God's appointment of David to the throne. In the case of David and the Davidide rulers, the title recalls the humble beginnings of the king and suggests the conjoining of humility and power characteristic of great leaders. *Ro'eh* underscores the pastoral calling of the king, to tend, heal, lead, and nurture the flock. Association with covenant reminds the reader of the analogy between how Zedekiah became king under Nebuchadnezzar and how this messianic ruler will become king. The great king Nebuchadnezzar elevated Zedekiah to kingship, putting him under oath to loyalty by means of a covenant. Zedekiah ruled *on behalf of* Nebuchadnezzar, by the Babylonian's leave and according to his will. In the same way, the messianic shepherd would be prince by covenant with Yahweh. He would not rule on his own, but on behalf of Yahweh. Yahweh will, in fact, rule through him.

Although the Davidic promise (34:23-24) is not tied explicitly to the following covenant of "peace" (*shalom* [TH7965, ZH8934], 34:25), the Davidic hope takes the promise of restoration to heights that can easily be linked with ultimate salvation. The promise of a "covenant of *shalom*" provides a rubric under which to unveil full and complete blessing for the people of God. "Shalom" designates a state in which all parties and realities of God's world are as they should be. Beyond its designation as a "covenant of peace," information that we often associate with the making of covenants does not appear here—historical prologue, terms of the covenant, witnesses, documentation. Presumably, Ezekiel had in mind a covenant that establishes and guarantees profound peace. Covenants are instruments for formally bringing certain realities into play and providing for the perpetuation of those realities. Often pledges and expectations are included. But in chapter 34 the emphasis is on promise—the guarantee being the person of God himself. Ezekiel did not speak here or elsewhere of a "new covenant," as did Jeremiah (Jer 31:31-34) and Hosea (from a slightly different perspective, Hos 2:18-23). But the concept Ezekiel employed has continuity with his precursors. In coming chapters he will address, as did Jeremiah, his people's ability to act as his people.

All of Israel's ills are here addressed and all her needs met: security, plenty, liberation, protection, tranquility, respect, identity as the flock of God, submission to (acknowledgment of) Yahweh as their God (vv. 25b-31). Those who read chapter 34 with Leviticus 26 and Deuteronomy 28–29 in mind know that covenant blessings abound here. Yahweh's holy hill, the place of his unique presence, would be the center of life and bliss, previewing the return of God's glory portrayed in chapters 42–43. Not only are Israel's present needs to be met lavishly, but Yahweh pronounces an end to all such deprivations. Never again will they suffer as they have. These unprecedented blessings are to bring about an awareness declared here for the first time in the book (34:30-31). God's people will be aware that he is with them, in his saving, restoring presence, revealing himself to them. God's people will be aware of and acknowledge that they are indeed Yahweh's people. They are actually his *flock*, with the privileges and blessings that image implies, because Yahweh himself is their shepherd.

◆ 3. Mount Seir, mountains of Israel: a question of possession (35:1–36:15)

Again a message came to me from the
LORD: 2"Son of man, turn and face Mount
Seir, and prophesy against its people.
3Give them this message from the Sover-
eign LORD:

"I am your enemy, O Mount Seir,
and I will raise my fist against you
to destroy you completely.
4I will demolish your cities
and make you desolate.
Then you will know that I am
the LORD.

5"Your eternal hatred for the people of
Israel led you to butcher them when they
were helpless, when I had already pun-
ished them for all their sins. 6As surely as
I live, says the Sovereign LORD, since you
show no distaste for blood, I will give you
a bloodbath of your own. Your turn has
come! 7I will make Mount Seir utterly
desolate, killing off all who try to escape
and any who return. 8I will fill your moun-
tains with the dead. Your hills, your val-
leys, and your ravines will be filled with
people slaughtered by the sword. 9I will
make you desolate forever. Your cities will
never be rebuilt. Then you will know that
I am the LORD.

10"For you said, 'The lands of Israel and
Judah will be ours. We will take possession
of them. What do we care that the LORD is
there!' 11Therefore, as surely as I live, says
the Sovereign LORD, I will pay back your
angry deeds with my own. I will punish you
for all your acts of anger, envy, and hatred.
And I will make myself known to Israel* by
what I do to you. 12Then you will know that
I, the LORD, have heard every contemptu-
ous word you spoke against the mountains
of Israel. For you said, 'They are desolate;
they have been given to us as food to
eat!' 13In saying that, you boasted proudly
against me, and I have heard it all!

14"This is what the Sovereign LORD says:
The whole world will rejoice when I make
you desolate. 15You rejoiced at the desola-
tion of Israel's territory. Now I will rejoice
at yours! You will be wiped out, you people
of Mount Seir and all who live in Edom!
Then you will know that I am the LORD.

CHAPTER 36

"Son of man, prophesy to Israel's moun-
tains. Give them this message: O moun-
tains of Israel, hear the word of the LORD!
2This is what the Sovereign LORD says:
Your enemies have taunted you, saying,
'Aha! Now the ancient heights belong to
us!' 3Therefore, son of man, give the
mountains of Israel this message from the
Sovereign LORD: Your enemies have at-
tacked you from all directions, making
you the property of many nations and the
object of much mocking and slander.
4Therefore, O mountains of Israel, hear
the word of the Sovereign LORD. He speaks
to the hills and mountains, ravines and

valleys, and to ruined wastes and long-
deserted cities that have been destroyed
and mocked by the surrounding nations.
5 This is what the Sovereign LORD says: My
jealous anger burns against these nations,
especially Edom, because they have shown
utter contempt for me by gleefully taking
my land for themselves as plunder.
6 "Therefore, prophesy to the hills and
mountains, the ravines and valleys of Is-
rael. This is what the Sovereign LORD says:
I am furious that you have suffered shame
before the surrounding nations. 7 Therefore,
this is what the Sovereign LORD says: I have
taken a solemn oath that those nations will
soon have their own shame to endure.
8 "But the mountains of Israel will pro-
duce heavy crops of fruit for my people—
for they will be coming home again soon!
9 See, I care about you, and I will pay atten-
tion to you. Your ground will be plowed
and your crops planted. 10 I will greatly in-
crease the population of Israel, and the
ruined cities will be rebuilt and filled with
people. 11 I will increase not only the people,
but also your animals. O mountains of Is-
rael, I will bring people to live on you once
again. I will make you even more prosper-
ous than you were before. Then you will
know that I am the LORD. 12 I will cause my
people to walk on you once again, and you
will be their territory. You will never again
rob them of their children.
13 "This is what the Sovereign LORD says:
The other nations taunt you, saying, 'Is-
rael is a land that devours its own people
and robs them of their children!' 14 But
you will never again devour your people
or rob them of their children, says the
Sovereign LORD. 15 I will not let you hear
those other nations insult you, and you
will no longer be mocked by them. You
will not be a land that causes its nation to
fall, says the Sovereign LORD."

35:11 Hebrew *to them;* Greek version reads *to you.*

NOTES

35:1–36:15 Focused as it is on the question of land, it is no surprise to see the words "mountain(s)" and "hill(s)" (both representing Heb. *har* [TH2022, ZH2215]) stitch this unit together, occurring in 35:2, 3, 7, 8, 12, 15; 36:1, 4, 6, 8. This vocabulary also ties this unit to the immediately preceding and following materials: 33:28; 34:6, 13, 14 and 37:22; 38:8, 20, 21; 39:2, 4, 17.

35:2 *Mount Seir.* Modern readers can visualize Mount Seir as the red sandstone mountains made famous by pictures of the later Nabatean city of Petra (located in the modern Wadi Musa, Jordan), carved out of that foreboding terrain several centuries after Ezekiel's time. Biblical Mount Seir was south-southeast of the Dead Sea, though there is evidence as early as the Late Bronze Age indicating that Seir also extended west of the Arabah below the Dead Sea (Rainey and Notley 2001:101, 109, 122).

35:6 *a bloodbath of your own.* This is a creative but unlikely rendering of an apparently jumbled Hebrew text whose precise meaning is difficult to catch, as the divergent renderings of ancient and modern versions indicate. For a reasonable attempt at reconstructing the path by which the text came to its present disarray, see Allen 1994:167. The number of likely glosses involved attests to scribal interest in the text.

35:13 *you boasted proudly.* The NLT follows the LXX in omitting a difficult second clause in the MT, which apparently stands in synonymous parallelism with this first colon. The meaning of its main verb, *weha'tartem* [TH6984, ZH6280], is unknown, and proposed emendations fail to persuade.

35:15 *all who live in Edom!* The exclamation mark registers a Hebrew idiom that involves a redundant concluding "all of it!" The repetition of this idiom in 36:10 is another lexical link between the two panels of this unit (35:1–36:15).

36:8-12 Ezekiel echoes language from Gen 2:5-16 and 3:17-19, marking God's restoration of the hills themselves as re-creation. This theme ties the materials of 35:1–36:15 to 36:16-38 where the Lord promises to re-create his people, giving them a new heart and spirit. God will rectify Israel's fundamental moral problem.

36:14 ***rob them of their children.*** The MT here has a verb built on the root *k-sh-l* [TH3782, ZH4173], meaning "stumble, cause to stumble." The NLT reflects the understanding that there was confusion here by metathesis and reads a form built on the root *sh-k-l* [TH7921, ZH8897], "to bereave." This concurs with ancient and modern versions (cf. LXX, Vulgate, KJV, RSV, et al.), and the second root occurs also in 36:13.

COMMENTARY

Two messages comprise this unit, one addressed to "Mount Seir" (35:1-15) and the other addressed to the "mountains of Israel" (36:1-15). Ezekiel pursued the question of possession of the land raised in 33:23-26 and 34:13-16, along with related issues. These issues may well have led the prophet to place the message to "Mount Seir" (which refers to Edom, see 35:15) here in the book rather than locating it earlier with other oracles against surrounding nations. This is not a general oracle against a neighbor but a message that is particularly appropriate in the context of restoration and thoughts of return to the land. Dramatically, the prophet addresses the land itself, the mountains, as a meaningful partner in historical processes governed by Yahweh. This involves a personification in which the land is given personal attributes of speaking, acting, and thinking. Rhetorically, the prophet may be answering slander spoken directly at the land of Israel and its cities (36:3).

The word against Mount Seir opens with an information-packed announcement (35:1-4): (1) Yahweh has assumed an enemy stance toward Mount Seir! (2) Yahweh plans to destroy this land and its cities completely. (3) Through these events Yahweh will be known to Mount Seir. Then follows the indictments for which Yahweh will bring this judgment upon Mount Seir.

Yahweh refers to grievances ancient and recent. He cites Mount Seir's "eternal hatred" of Israel (35:5). He calls to mind a history of animosity between these parties reaching back to the early centuries of their mutual existence as organized lands. "Mount Seir" refers to the territory inhabited by Edom, descendants of Esau, brother of Jacob, the founding patriarch of Israel (Gen 36:8). This identification surfaces in 35:15. Situated south of the Dead Sea at the time of Israel's migration from Egypt to Canaan, the Edomites refused Israel peaceful passage through their territory (Num 20:14-18; Deut 2:4-5). This rebuff launched a history of continuing hostility. Yahweh links this ancient animosity to the more recent atrocities during the years surrounding the fall of Jerusalem to the Babylonians (35:5). Edom took terrible advantage of Israel's already devastated situation, tracking down refugees and killing them or selling them as slaves (cf. Obad 1:10-14). Yahweh said he would repay them in kind; he had punished his people enough and had not designated Edom as an instrument of his judgment against Israel (35:5).

Two indictments carry particular theological freight in this context. First, the Edomites took advantage of Judah's weakened state to grab land depopulated by the slaughter and deportation of its inhabitants. She coveted the land given to Israel by Yahweh. "We will take possession [of the lands of Israel and Judah]" (35:10).

Second and more shocking, the Edomites directly discounted the God of Israel, saying "What do we care that the LORD is there!" (35:10; cf. Amos 9:10). They may have concluded from the fall of Jerusalem that Yahweh lacked the ability—the power and authority—to save his people from Babylon. Or they may have believed he had the ability but not the will or compassion to protect his people (36:9 may imply this). In that case, if Edom cannot accuse Israel of actions worthy of judgment by its God, then God could be viewed as having broken his historic covenant or gone back on his word. Or he may have actively rejected his people, destroying them by the Babylonians, in which case his judgment in selecting such people as his own is called into question. In any case, they rejected Yahweh as a force to be reckoned with in the matter of possessing the land. These were contemptuous and boastful words, says Yahweh, and Mount Seir would pay for them (35:12-13). Both God's people and the Edomites would acknowledge Yahweh for who he is when he "wipes out" the Edomites, leaving Mount Seir desolate (35:11, 15). Ezekiel's treatment of this Edomite theology provides commentary on the claims made in 36:13-15, 20-21, 22-23, 30. Although Edom escaped the destruction that decimated Judah under Nebuchadnezzar, within a few decades, Nabonidus (a successor to Nebuchadnezzar) invaded Edom and destroyed its cities, sending its people back into a pastoral, nomadic existence. Even though Edomite settlements in former Judean territory prospered, the desolation in Edom proper was still evident in the days of Malachi (Mal 1:2-5). (See Hoerth, Mattingly, and Yamauchi 1994:341-343.)

Turning to the mountains of Israel, Ezekiel pursued the same issue, that Israel's enemies had taken advantage of Israel's desolation and depopulation and made good on their taunt to seize the land (36:2). Yahweh acknowledged that the invasion and defeat they had suffered had left them vulnerable to attack and to mockery and slander from every direction (36:2-3, 13, 15). This shame of the land itself is a major concern here. Yahweh regarded these as acts of contempt not just for his land and people but for himself, because the land is his (36:5; cf. Deut 32:8-9). This situation infuriated Yahweh and prompted him to act (36:6). He would shame these predators by their own destruction and by the lavish restoration of his own land (36:8ff). Yahweh anticipated the return of his people and the role of the land in sustaining his people (36:8). But he planned to grace the land itself, attending to the welfare of the land. Under his blessing the land would be lavishly productive (36:8-9). The land would be tilled and cared for (36:9). It would be repopulated and resettled, with cities rebuilt. The land would again support and house God's people (36:10-12). This blessing of Yahweh would flow through the whole land—"the hills and mountains, ravines and valleys, and to ruined wastes and long-deserted cities" (36:4).

◆ 4. The house of Israel's new heart (36:16-38)

**[16]Then this further message came to me
from the LORD: [17]"Son of man, when the
people of Israel were living in their own
land, they defiled it by the evil way they
lived. To me their conduct was as unclean
as a woman's menstrual cloth. [18]They pol-
luted the land with murder and the wor-
ship of idols,* so I poured out my fury on
them. [19]I scattered them to many lands to
punish them for the evil way they had**

lived. 20But when they were scattered among the nations, they brought shame on my holy name. For the nations said, 'These are the people of the LORD, but he couldn't keep them safe in his own land!' 21Then I was concerned for my holy name, on which my people brought shame among the nations.

22"Therefore, give the people of Israel this message from the Sovereign LORD: I am bringing you back, but not because you deserve it. I am doing it to protect my holy name, on which you brought shame while you were scattered among the nations. 23I will show how holy my great name is—the name on which you brought shame among the nations. And when I reveal my holiness through you before their very eyes, says the Sovereign LORD, then the nations will know that I am the LORD. 24For I will gather you up from all the nations and bring you home again to your land.

25"Then I will sprinkle clean water on you, and you will be clean. Your filth will be washed away, and you will no longer worship idols. 26And I will give you a new heart, and I will put a new spirit in you. I will take out your stony, stubborn heart and give you a tender, responsive heart.* 27And I will put my Spirit in you so that you will follow my decrees and be careful to obey my regulations.

28"And you will live in Israel, the land I gave your ancestors long ago. You will be my people, and I will be your God. 29I will cleanse you of your filthy behavior. I will give you good crops of grain, and I will send no more famines on the land. 30I will give you great harvests from your fruit trees and fields, and never again will the surrounding nations be able to scoff at your land for its famines. 31Then you will remember your past sins and despise yourselves for all the detestable things you did. 32But remember, says the Sovereign LORD, I am not doing this because you deserve it. O my people of Israel, you should be utterly ashamed of all you have done!

33"This is what the Sovereign LORD says: When I cleanse you from your sins, I will repopulate your cities, and the ruins will be rebuilt. 34The fields that used to lie empty and desolate in plain view of everyone will again be farmed. 35And when I bring you back, people will say, 'This former wasteland is now like the Garden of Eden! The abandoned and ruined cities now have strong walls and are filled with people!' 36Then the surrounding nations that survive will know that I, the LORD, have rebuilt the ruins and replanted the wasteland. For I, the LORD, have spoken, and I will do what I say.

37"This is what the Sovereign LORD says: I am ready to hear Israel's prayers and to increase their numbers like a flock. 38They will be as numerous as the sacred flocks that fill Jerusalem's streets at the time of her festivals. The ruined cities will be crowded with people once more, and everyone will know that I am the LORD."

36:18 The Hebrew term (literally *round things*) probably alludes to dung; also in 36:25. **36:26** Hebrew *a heart of flesh.*

NOTES

36:17 *a woman's menstrual cloth.* Heb., *niddah* [TH5079, ZH5614]. This noun refers literally either to the woman herself or her menstrual flow (cf. HALOT 2.673). Its use here underscores the revulsion of Yahweh at Israel's evil behavior.

36:18 *idols.* The term *gillulim* [TH1544, ZH1658] (lit., "round things") probably alludes to dung; also in 36:25. See note on 5:9 on Ezekiel's vocabulary of idolatry.

36:26-27 *a new heart. . . . so that you will follow my decrees and be careful to obey my regulations.* The vocabulary brought together here illustrates the blending and appropriating of priestly and Deuteronomistic materials from the Torah available to Ezekiel that we see through much of the book. See Levitt Kohn (2002:25-26, 75-86, 94-95, 103-104,

105-118) for the most recent exhaustive study of the relationship between Ezekiel and the Pentateuchal Priestly Source, on the one hand, and Deuteronomic History on the other. Levitt Kohn concludes that all of these materials substantially precede Ezekiel and that he creatively and independently appropriated them as authoritative texts. Positioning himself as a second Moses, he contributed significantly to the literary shape that these Torah materials eventually achieved in our Pentateuch.

COMMENTARY

The previous message dealt with the shame of the military defeat and exile of God's people from their land (35:1–36:15). For their sake, the Lord would vindicate his name. Ezekiel turns now to the repercussions of exile for Yahweh's own reputation among the nations. In the process, he articulates the radical hope of Yahweh's re-creation of his people, which ties these paragraphs to the preceding unit with its description of a re-creation of the land.

The opening lines explain the crisis. Israel's corrupt behavior led Yahweh to scatter them among the nations as punishment (36:17-19). But in their dispersion they brought shame to Yahweh, prompting concern for his own reputation among the nations (36:20-21). Ezekiel's sensitivities as a priest surface here, as he phrases these concerns in terms of pollution and cleanness. He explains that Israel's evil behavior had polluted the land (36:17-18) and made it unfit for service to Yahweh or for his dwelling.

Ezekiel cites more of the slander prompted by the Exile: "These are the people of the LORD, but he couldn't keep them safe in his own land!" (36:20; cf. 35:10, 12). Yahweh's own entanglement in the problem is clear. His ability to protect and provide for his people was called into question. Recent events had apparently, in the minds of some bystanders, shown that the Lord was inadequate to the task of being God! It would appear that the gods of Babylon had prevailed on the stage of history, as the Assyrian Rabshakeh had claimed of his own gods in the days of Hezekiah (cf. 2 Kgs 18:28-35). The theological calculus of the covenant, whereby Yahweh's actions against his people are legitimized, had either not come to the nations or not been persuasive to them. Hence, the actions he will take in this context will be viewed entirely from the perspective of the impact on his own "name"—his reputation (36:22). He will "protect [his] holy name" (36:22), will "show how holy [his] great name is," and will "reveal [his] holiness" through the return of his people (36:23). "Holy" as applied to Yahweh's reputation indicates his uniqueness, his separation and independence from Israel and all other gods. But "holy" and "holiness" applied to Yahweh himself describe not only his separateness from Israel and other gods but also his separation to Israel, as well as his moral character. As separate from his people, he is wholly other, God and not human. Yahweh is the Sovereign, who in creating his people through the Exodus brought the mighty Pharaoh, his gods, his army, and his people to their knees. At the same time, in establishing his covenant with them at Sinai, he separated himself from the nations and his governance of all the earth to be his people's God and to be uniquely with them (Exod 15:1-18; 19:4-6; 29:46). His holy character rejects Israel's murder and idolatry (36:18) as totally other than himself, totally revolting and inappropriate for this God's people (Thompson 1975:42-43).

Yahweh will demonstrate his holiness in three ways: (1) Geopolitically, he will gather his people from the lands of their dispersion and bring them back to the Land of Promise (36:24, 28). (2) Using liturgical imagery of the priesthood, Ezekiel says he will "sprinkle clean water" upon them and thus make them clean (cf. Lev 15:5-13; 16:24-28; 22:6; Num 19:13, 20)—fit for his presence *and* enabled for his service. Note here that Yahweh will purify his returned people. They will purify the land (cf. 37:23; 39:11-16). (3) Existentially, Yahweh will give his people new hearts and new spirits (36:26). For Ezekiel, "heart" denotes the human capacity to think, feel, judge, decide, and commit. Israel's moral failure—her repeated choices not to keep covenant with Yahweh but to live idolatrously and violently—had revealed that her heart was set on violence (33:31). Israel's behavior and loyalties exposed a misaligned heart, as unresponsive to God's voice as a stony human heart. That is the fundamental problem to which Yahweh now promises an answer. He envisions an unprecedented heart transplant in which that unresponsive, stony heart is removed, and a new, fleshy heart (tender and responsive) is given to Israel (36:26). "Spirit" connotes the dynamic by which the loyalties of the heart will be translated into action. In this case, Yahweh promises to give Israel *his own Spirit,* dramatically enabling them to "follow [his] decrees and . . . obey [his] regulations" (36:27). Ezekiel here resumes the promise of a new, responsive heart and a new, obedient spirit offered already at 11:19-20. He also picks up a critical question prompted by the earlier exhortation to "find yourselves a new heart and a new spirit" (18:31). But where will Israel find a new heart and new spirit? What is it that will move Yahweh's people from aspiration to transformation of character and obedient behavior? The Lord's own provision of a new heart and his impartation of his own Spirit provided the answer to that question.

In these dramatic promises, Ezekiel echoes hopes voiced elsewhere for the moral and spiritual transformation of Israel associated with restoration from exile (11:19). The national catastrophe and the character of the exile community had made it more than clear that if Yahweh were ever to have a people consistently living his covenant, he himself would have to enable them to do so. Deuteronomy 30:1-6 and Jeremiah 31:31-34 are classic expressions of this hope. Joel 2:28-29 voices a related confidence regarding God's effusion of his Spirit into his people and their consequent capacity to discern and declare his will. Unlike Jeremiah, Ezekiel does not associate this with a "new covenant," but clearly he envisions a new order of relationship between the Lord and his people, as is clear from the standard covenant affirmations he anticipates: "You will be my people, and I will be your God" (36:28).

This moral and spiritual transformation will take place in conjunction with their return to the Land of Promise (36:28-30, 33-38). Unprecedented bounty and security in the land once destitute will lead observers to compare Israel to the Garden of Eden itself (36:35). Instead of peddling slander, the nations seeing this unforeseen turn of events will realize that the same God who scattered his people has now brought them back and renewed the land (36:36). Not only the nations, but Israel herself will be astounded at these events, with the result that they will be ashamed of their detestable ways—indeed, they will despise themselves for their sins (36:31). They will recognize that God has again acted, not according to what they deserve, but according to his own purposes (36:32). Once again (cf. 34:25-28), Ezekiel brings together in a marvelous vision the well-being of the land coupled with the obedience of God's people, drawn together in an order permeated by harmony.

Although the emphasis in this message is on the sovereign purposes of Yahweh to protect his holy name, a stream of grace and mercy for his people also flows through this word. Again, Yahweh plans to do for his people what they could not do for themselves. He is ready to answer the exiles' prayers for restoration. The flock imagery that closes this message links it with the oracles in chapter 34, stitching these paragraphs into the larger unit (chs 33–37).

It may surprise some readers to discover that Yahweh's restoration of his people is *in order to shame them* (emphasized in 36:22, 31-32); this constitutes a problem in Ezekiel studies. According to some scholars Yahweh's intent to shame his people through their "restoration" actually means there is no restoration message in Ezekiel. The so-called "restoration" is for Ezekiel actually an outgrowth of and an integral part of God's judgment of his people. Ezekiel never really altered his message—it is judgment from start to finish (Schwartz 2000:52-55). By this view, Yahweh's unilateral decision to gather his people to the land and "reprogram" them so that they will at last obey him is not an expression of God's compassion. On the contrary, it represents an exile plan run amok, since the anticipated repentance did not materialize in exile. This "backfire" left Yahweh with his reputation in shambles—people were unable to obey him, and he was without a people to rule.

In this reading, Yahweh actually decided to restore his people out of his own neediness, following a "more pointed legalism" and a perverse desire to "exact retribution." The decision unilaterally "to maintain his covenant eternally is one of spite. . . . Aimed at causing Israel to feel the eternal remorse that the exile failed to bring about" (Schwartz 2000:48-49). Unlike the God of Jeremiah and Isaiah who promises to restore his people based on his love for them and compassion upon them, in Ezekiel, Yahweh acts "for his own thoroughly egocentric reasons" (Schwartz 2000:59).

Scholars who hold the above view rightly underscore the fact that Ezekiel is not Jeremiah or Isaiah. Although Ezekiel shows influence from both of these prophets, his theological contribution to the canonical dialogue is a distinct voice. Unlike Jeremiah and Isaiah, Ezekiel never explicitly grounds Yahweh's promise of restoration, of an eternal covenant and of a new heart and spirit to obey him, in Yahweh's *love* for Israel. His love is implied in some passages, but it is not explicit. But these are few and are more like whispers of love than ringing declarations. Instead, Ezekiel emphasizes Yahweh's concern for his own "name" (20:9, 14, 22, 44).

It is a mistake, however, to conclude from this that the mercy and grace of Yahweh are not at play in Ezekiel's view. Rather than construing this as Yahweh's "obsession" with his own reputation (Schwartz 2000:57-58), one could just as well see in it a legitimate defense of the sovereignty of Yahweh, exercised in gracious interaction with his people. Passages like 11:18-21 and 18:30-32, which reveal Yahweh's mercy toward Israel in restoration, and which Schwartz finds bewildering and out of place among the judgment oracles, are better read as examples of Ezekiel's "resumptive exposition," a stylistic move the prophet used in his development of several themes, including restoration (Block 1998:24-25, following Greenberg). They are not out of place and need not be collapsed into the surrounding judgments. They sit well as promises of actual restoration. One is hard-pressed to see in the God envisioned by

Schwartz's reading any justification for the community's reception of this work in the Canon, for reading it as a positive and edifying contribution to the prophetic corpus. The canonizers happily did not share Schwartz's hermeneutic of suspicion.

Paul Joyce's reading of these matters accounts for the text much more adequately in my opinion. Joyce emphasizes the "distinctively theocentric" approach Ezekiel takes, an approach so forceful as to defy easy resolution with Israel's responsibility. Still, for Joyce the Lord's gift of a new heart and a new spirit is not a "reprogramming" that guarantees automatic obedience, coercing conformity to God's will. Instead, God granted the "gift of obedience," making obedience possible. Ezekiel underscores the insight that "humankind is ultimately impotent without God" (Joyce 1989:127-129). This need not imply that until this "gift," obedience was impossible. The Sinai covenant seemed to assume the possibility of obedience, and the Psalter regularly celebrates the godly who, unlike the wicked, do appear to live pleasing to God (e.g., Ps 1). But the nation as a whole failed to obey consistently. The day was coming when the nation as a whole would indeed obey the Lord.

In addition, several passages that do not use the words "mercy" or "compassion" nevertheless appear to speak out of divine mercy and grace, for example, the poignant plea, "Why should you die? . . . I don't want you to die. . . . Turn back and live!" (18:31-32; cf. 11:18-21; 16:1-14). In our immediate context, the Lord claims he is furious because the land has "suffered shame before the surrounding nations" (36:6). Moreover, Ezekiel does explicitly tie his unilateral restoration and deliverance of Israel to his mercy (39:25). Finally, the watchman metaphor governs Ezekiel's commission and proclamation of both judgment (3:16-21) and restoration (33:1-9). It eloquently grounds the prophet's mission in the merciful concern of Yahweh.

Moreover, Lapsley (2000:130-145) may well be correct in actually identifying the shame (emphasized in 36:22, 31-32) as an essential feature of Yahweh's restoration plan. Israel's shame, induced by awareness of the grace of God, evidences a level of self-awareness critical to Israel's moral identity. Israel is able now to see herself as Yahweh has seen her all along. This implies not only a knowledge of herself but of Yahweh as well. Out of this knowledge of herself and, more critically, of Yahweh, she has the real possibility of choosing to do the will of God, a possibility that has to this point regularly eluded her.

◆ 5. Can dry bones live again? (37:1-14)

The LORD took hold of me, and I was carried away by the Spirit of the LORD to a valley filled with bones. [2]He led me all around among the bones that covered the valley floor. They were scattered everywhere across the ground and were completely dried out. [3]Then he asked me, "Son of man, can these bones become living people again?"

"O Sovereign LORD," I replied, "you alone know the answer to that."

[4]Then he said to me, "Speak a prophetic message to these bones and say, 'Dry bones, listen to the word of the LORD! [5]This is what the Sovereign LORD says: Look! I am going to put breath into you and make you live again! [6]I will put flesh and muscles on you and cover you with skin. I will put breath into you, and you will come to life. Then you will know that I am the LORD.'"

[7]So I spoke this message, just as he told me. Suddenly as I spoke, there was a rattling noise all across the valley. The bones

of each body came together and attached
themselves as complete skeletons. [8]Then
as I watched, muscles and flesh formed
over the bones. Then skin formed to cover
their bodies, but they still had no breath
in them.
[9]Then he said to me, "Speak a prophetic
message to the winds, son of man. Speak
a prophetic message and say, 'This is what
the Sovereign LORD says: Come, O breath,
from the four winds! Breathe into these
dead bodies so they may live again.'"
[10]So I spoke the message as he com-
manded me, and breath came into their
bodies. They all came to life and stood up
on their feet—a great army.
[11]Then he said to me, "Son of man,
these bones represent the people of Israel.
They are saying, 'We have become old, dry
bones—all hope is gone. Our nation is fin-
ished.' [12]Therefore, prophesy to them and
say, 'This is what the Sovereign LORD says:
O my people, I will open your graves of
exile and cause you to rise again. Then I
will bring you back to the land of Israel.
[13]When this happens, O my people, you
will know that I am the LORD. [14]I will put
my Spirit in you, and you will live again
and return home to your own land. Then
you will know that I, the LORD, have spo-
ken, and I have done what I said. Yes, the
LORD has spoken!'"

NOTES

37:1-14 Does Ezekiel's presentation here imply a belief in individual resurrection? Investigating the possible background of Ezekiel's ideas of resurrection, Block argues convincingly that appeals to Egyptian, Mesopotamian, or Iranian influence to account for Ezekiel's view here, though not impossible out of hand, are not as convincing as the interpretation that sees here "a graphic portrayal of the effects of the covenant curse on his people," i.e., a battlefield (1998:385). That is, Ezekiel deals not simply with "the dead" in general, but with the disarticulated dead scattered over an ancient battlefield.

COMMENTARY

Ezekiel describes experiences here that place these paragraphs in tandem with materials at the opening of the book (1:3; 37:1). The Lord "taking hold" of him (lit., "the hand of Yahweh was upon me"), the Spirit of the Lord carrying him, and his location in a valley (probably the same valley encountered in 3:22) all take the reader back to 3:12, 22, and 8:2-3. The reader expects a significant and defining encounter here as before. Although Ezekiel does not explicitly label this a vision (cf. 1:1; 8:3), that is no doubt how we should understand this experience of spiritual transport.

The valley is littered with disjointed bones—filled with them (37:2). It looks like an old battleground, the scene of such carnage that the fallen were never given burial. This is Ezekiel's "Death Valley." God's opening words raise the question—could these bones become living people again (37:3)? This question was *the* question that must be answered if there was to be any hope for the exiles and any reason to proceed with the book. The exiles, settled in Babylon, had no obvious reason to seriously consider return and national "resurrection." These were virtually impossible. Where in the ancient world was there precedent for the idea that a deported people, exiled for an entire generation and more, would or could return to its land of origin and reconstitute its national institutions? The promise of restoration from the proph- et sounded ridiculous (cf. 33:32) and must surely have raised the question of its possibility. The death of these ancient warriors had nothing directly to do with the exiles' hope. They simply addressed in an unforgettable fashion this key question. Could the impossible occur?

Ezekiel obeyed the Lord's directive to prophesy to the bones (37:4, 7), with the result that they became skeletons, then corpses—no small marvel (37:7-8). Ezekiel details the wonders involved: bones form skeletons, skeletons get muscles, flesh, and skin. But still they had no breath, no life.

A second exhortation has Ezekiel prophesying to the four winds (37:9). The impossible occurs: The corpses come to life and stand as a great army (37:10). Ezekiel's report makes sense because of a wordplay on the Hebrew *ruakh* [TH7307, ZH8120]. Depending on context, *ruakh* denotes either "breath" (Job 12:10; Ps 135:17) or "breeze" (Eccl 1:14) or "wind" (Exod 10:13) or "spirit" (11:5; 13:3), among other related meanings. Thus, the same Hebrew word appears in the following four expressions: "Speak a prophetic message to the *winds*," "Come, O *breath*," "*breath* came," "I will put my *Spirit* in you" (37:9, 10, 14). Ezekiel's report artistically integrates the various meanings of *ruakh*.

Yahweh explained to Ezekiel the meaning of the dry bones brought to life by prophetic utterance (37:11), and directed the prophetic promises for his people (37:12-14). The situation Yahweh has addressed in the visionary experience of Ezekiel is the exiles' hopelessness. The exiles' view of themselves as old, dry bones, without hope, dictated the content of the Lord's revelation. God acknowledged implicitly that the nation was dead and buried—that described the Exile well. But these exiles were still Yahweh's people (37:12-13). Yahweh was not stymied by the impossibilities of exile. Against all odds, he would bring them back to the land of Israel. He will put his *ruakh* in this dead community and bring it to life again in their land. When this happens, they will acknowledge Yahweh and realize he accomplished what he promised (37:13-14). The vision should engender hope and restored confidence in Yahweh's ability and intent to deliver. Much as in 36:25-28, emphasis falls here on the potent, life-giving Spirit of Yahweh as Israel's only hope of life. It also aims to buttress confidence in the word of true prophets. As Ezekiel obeys the Spirit's directive to prophesy to the bones and the wind, the miracle of resurrection occurs. Ezekiel has spoken Yahweh's word.

What this passage implies about Ezekiel's view of the afterlife remains unclear. On the one hand, Ezekiel's prophecies regarding the grave and the underworld present Yahweh as God of the living and of the dead. In this visionary experience, which borders on allegory, God clearly raises the dead by creating new life in them. It would not be at all surprising to discover that Ezekiel saw here not only a useful allegory but an actual expression of faith in resurrection. On the other hand, nowhere do we have a clear expression of that resurrection faith standing on its own, without a larger allegorical "prompt" that carries its own meaning apart from the idea of an afterlife. Nor do we have hints of other ideas easily associated with resurrection, such as final judgment. Such ideas would have contributed significantly to Ezekiel's presentation at various points. One thinks, for example, of the contribution that a final judgment in an afterlife could have made to the question of God's justice in chapters 18 and 33.

◆ 6. Reunion of Israel and Judah (37:15-28)

[15]Again a message came to me from the LORD: [16]"Son of man, take a piece of wood and carve on it these words: 'This represents Judah and its allied tribes.' Then take another piece and carve these words on it: 'This represents Ephraim and the northern tribes of Israel.'* [17]Now hold them together in your hand as if they were one piece of wood. [18]When your people ask you what your actions mean, [19]say to them, 'This is what the Sovereign LORD says: I will take Ephraim and the northern tribes and join them to Judah. I will make them one piece of wood in my hand.'

[20]"Then hold out the pieces of wood you have inscribed, so the people can see them. [21]And give them this message from the Sovereign LORD: I will gather the people of Israel from among the nations. I will bring them home to their own land from the places where they have been scattered. [22]I will unify them into one nation on the mountains of Israel. One king will rule them all; no longer will they be divided into two nations or into two kingdoms. [23]They will never again pollute themselves with their idols* and vile images and rebellion, for I will save them from their sinful backsliding. I will cleanse them. Then they will truly be my people, and I will be their God.

[24]"My servant David will be their king, and they will have only one shepherd. They will obey my regulations and be careful to keep my decrees. [25]They will live in the land I gave my servant Jacob, the land where their ancestors lived. They and their children and their grandchildren after them will live there forever, generation after generation. And my servant David will be their prince forever. [26]And I will make a covenant of peace with them, an everlasting covenant. I will give them their land and increase their numbers,* and I will put my Temple among them forever. [27]I will make my home among them. I will be their God, and they will be my people. [28]And when my Temple is among them forever, the nations will know that I am the LORD, who makes Israel holy."

37:16 Hebrew *This is Ephraim's wood, representing Joseph and all the house of Israel.* **37:23** The Hebrew term (literally *round things*) probably alludes to dung. **37:26** Hebrew reads *I will give them and increase their numbers;* Greek version lacks the entire phrase.

NOTES

37:16 ***This represents Ephraim and the northern tribes of Israel.*** The MT, LXX, and Targums read, "This represents Joseph the stick of Ephraim and all the house of Israel, his associates," a puzzling line. That Ezekiel intended the second stick to represent the northern kingdom seems clear. The syntactical relation of "stick of Ephraim" to the line is unclear. The Targum and a number of modern versions (RSV, NRSV, NAB, JB, ESV) understand "stick of Ephraim" as a gloss or explanation of "Joseph," unusual as a designation for the northern tribes. The NLT omits "Joseph" (but see NLT mg), apparently attempting to simplify the text while expressing the probable meaning of the line as a whole. The northern kingdom or northern tribes were rarely if ever called "Joseph," perhaps eliciting the gloss with the more common designation. See KJV, NKJV, and NASB for a construal less probable in view of the parallel Judah line.

37:23 ***from their sinful backsliding.*** The MT reads "from all their dwellings" (*moshebothehem* [TH4186, ZH4632]), which the Targum and a few contemporary versions retain in one way or another (NASB, NJPS). The LXX rendering assumes Heb. *meshubothehem* [TH4878, ZH5412], "from all their turnings away" or "apostasies" or "backslidings." The NLT, along with most contemporary versions, follows the LXX, translating "backslidings" or "apostasies" or "betrayals."

37:25 ***my servant David will be their prince forever.*** The promised prince will inaugurate a Davidic kingdom (see commentary on 34:23-24).

COMMENTARY

Talk of the restoration of the exiles immediately raises the question of the extent of the "Israel" to be reborn in the Land of Promise. Concern for the whole people of God, including northern Israel, joins the two messages of this chapter together, as the reference to "all the house of Israel" indicates (37:11, 16).

Ezekiel performed another prophetic sign-act (i.e., behavior portraying the deeds of God). Such acts were designed to elicit questions and to pave the way for prophetic instruction. Ezekiel took two sticks and carved the words "This represents Judah and its allied tribes" on one stick and "This represents Ephraim and the northern tribes of Israel" on the other. The two sticks reflected the realities of the nation since its division under Rehoboam. The southern kingdom took its name from the dominant tribe, but the territory of the kingdom of Judah included the tribes of Simeon and Benjamin, as well as the Levites assigned to these three tribes. Though the northern kingdom was not called the kingdom of Ephraim, it was often simply referred to as "Ephraim," again using the name of the dominant tribe. Using "Joseph" as a name for the northern kingdom, as the Hebrew text does, is highly unusual and has prompted the NLT to omit that reference in lieu of the more common Ephraim (see note on 37:16).

Precisely what Ezekiel was to do remains unclear. Disagreement lingers regarding the meaning of the Hebrew word *'ets* [TH6086, ZH6770] (wood, stick). Some have suggested it means here a scepter or rod or leader's staff, an idea perhaps supported by the Septuagint (*rhabdos* [TG4464, ZG4811]; "stick, staff"). Some have proposed wooden writing tablets known especially from Mesopotamia and widely attested in the ancient Near East. But it is more likely that Ezekiel simply had in mind ordinary "sticks" or "pieces of wood" (so NLT). Although lack of certainty precludes confident reconstruction of the act, the general nature and meaning of what was done seems clear.

When the people questioned the meaning of his actions, Ezekiel was to give two messages from Yahweh (37:19 and 20-28). The first message stays within the sign-act: "I will take Ephraim and the northern tribes and join them to Judah. I will make them one piece of wood in my hand" (37:19). Key points are the unity of the two pieces, and the fact that it is in the hand of Yahweh that the two become one. This will be his doing. Note also that Yahweh joins the northern tribes to Judah, not the reverse. This is not a reestablishment of the northern kingdom, but a renewal of the united monarchy under a Davidic king (see below and cf. Hos 3:4-5; Amos 9:11-12). Then, holding the sticks joined as one, Ezekiel is to give Yahweh's second message, explaining in plain terms what the single stick involves (37:20-28).

First, Yahweh will gather the people of Israel from among the nations and put them in their land. In light of the sign-act, "people of Israel" (37:21) must refer to the exiles of all 12 tribes. This would include descendants of the deportees from the northern kingdom at the fall of Samaria (over 130 years before the fall of Jerusalem), as well as recent exiles from Judah (37:21). Note the repetition of this promise in 37:25-26.

Second, God will make them one nation. National, governmental unity will replace the national division that marred God's people for centuries. They will be one nation with one king (37:22; cf. Jer 23:7-8; 33:14-16; Hos 1:11; 3:4-5).

Third, these people will "truly be [God's] people" and he their God (37:23). This means that the returnees will actually conduct themselves as the people of God. They will never again pollute themselves with idolatry and rebellion. They will be the special people, the holy nation they were called to be (cf. Exod 19:3-6). This will transpire because God will, as he says, "save them from their sinful backsliding" (37:23). "Save" and "cleanse" describe interventions in this community that transform it morally and spiritually, describing in different terms the reality promised in 36:25-32. In this context, salvation deals both with the consequences of sin (the deportation) and the power of sin (the propensity to idolatry and murder).

Fourth, David will be their one king—that is, a Davidic son will rule the nation as in the days in Israel's glory (37:24). This also will be Yahweh's doing (34:23). This is the second time Ezekiel's eschatological restoration has involved a Davidic king (34:23-24).

Fifth, once again we hear of the "covenant of peace," underscored as an "everlasting" covenant. God will establish an enduring order where profound harmony and right relations are the norm (37:26).

Finally, raising a brand-new agenda, God promises to put his Temple among them (37:26b-27). This will be the focal point of God's presence, his home among his people. The import of the Temple itself is seen in the order of the promise (Temple first, presence second) and in the critical role of the Temple in bringing insight to the nations. It will signal uniquely to them that it is Yahweh who sets Israel apart from the nations and to himself; he is the one who "makes Israel holy" (37:28). The repeated appearance of the word *'olam* [TH5769, ZH6409] (NLT, "forever," "everlasting") emphasizes the permanence of Yahweh's complete response to the plight of his people.

Jesus and his early followers saw themselves in both continuity and discontinuity with these expectations. Basic to all their conclusions about these matters was the conviction that Jesus of Nazareth was the promised Davidic son, king of Israel—by that time a role associated with the term "Messiah" (Mark 8:27-30; 11:10; Luke 1:32-33, 67-79; 24:44-49; Acts 2:25-36; Rom 1:1-6). Through his life, death, and resurrection, the promised deliverance from the penalty and the power of sin has been realized (Mark 10:45; Rom 8:1-4; 2 Cor 5:14-21; Heb 9:11-14), though final defeat of evil would await the eschaton (Rev 20–22). The apostolic community saw themselves as the inheritors of the promises to Israel, as is clear in their easy appropriation of technical terms for historic Israel to describe the Christian community (the "diaspora," 1 Pet 1:1; the "twelve tribes," Jas 1:1). At the same time, they may well have envisioned that a unique place for historic Israel in the purposes of God would yet emerge, confirming God's faithfulness to his word (Rom 11). The themes of the gathering of all the tribes to the Land of Promise and the building of a Temple for the living God are conspicuously absent from the New Testament's processing of the promises to Israel. Either these themes are to be seen as fulfilled in the messianic community as it is, or they are to be transported to the eschaton as promises yet awaiting fulfillment. The universalizing, "global" impulses of the gospel of Jesus and the identification of the church in some ways with the Israel of promise appear to have made the gathering of the historic tribes actually fulfilled in Christ and therefore unnecessary. Clear fulfillment of the promises regarding the giving of God's Spirit to the church as God's real presence among them, together with the end of the need for sacrifice for sin with Jesus' death, seems to have undercut expectations for a physical temple in an earthly city and paved the way for "temple" as a potent metaphor. Now the church itself and individuals in that church are the temple of God by the Spirit (1 Cor 3:16-17; 6:19-20). Jesus was the temple (John 1:14; 2:19-21) that God established among his people (Comfort 1994:52). The Temple as an expectation for the eschaton is explicitly denied (Rev 21:22) in lieu of life in the immediate presence of God and the Lamb. In that day, the promise of presence substantially realized in the pouring out of God's Spirit on the church reaches its climactic fulfillment.

Thus, the themes of this chapter connect powerfully with New Testament proclamation. But precisely how the Temple (or a temple) is to figure in the hope that Ezekiel envisioned remains to be seen. In several ways, the messages of Ezekiel 37 (i.e., God's promise to resurrect lifeless Israel, to unify again his scattered, fractured people, and to put his presence among them) seem like a climax to the restoration materials to this point, with the reference to the Temple paving the way for the visions of chapters 40–48. Now, however, chapters 38 and 39 call for attention before the tour of the city, the Temple, and the land. Among other things, we surely must attend to possible explanations for this striking intercalation.

◆ B. Destruction of Gog from Magog (38:1–39:29)

1. The Lord marshals and destroys Gog's forces (38:1-23)

This is another message that came to me from the LORD: 2"Son of man, turn and face Gog of the land of Magog, the prince who rules over the nations of Meshech and Tubal, and prophesy against him. 3Give him this message from the Sovereign LORD: Gog, I am your enemy! 4I will turn you around and put hooks in your jaws to lead you out with your whole army—your horses and charioteers in full armor and a great horde armed with shields and swords. 5Persia, Ethiopia, and Libya* will join you, too, with all their weapons. 6Gomer and all its armies will also join you, along with the armies of Beth-togarmah from the distant north, and many others.

7"Get ready; be prepared! Keep all the armies around you mobilized, and take command of them. 8A long time from now you will be called into action. In the distant future you will swoop down on the land of Israel, which will be enjoying peace after recovering from war and after its people have returned from many lands to the mountains of Israel. 9You and all your allies—a vast and awesome army—will roll down on them like a storm and cover the land like a cloud.

10"This is what the Sovereign LORD says: At that time evil thoughts will come to your mind, and you will devise a wicked scheme. 11You will say, 'Israel is an unprotected land filled with unwalled villages! I will march against her and destroy these people who live in such confidence! 12I will go to those formerly desolate cities that are now filled with people who have returned from exile in many nations. I will capture vast amounts of plunder, for the people are rich with livestock and other possessions now. They think the whole world revolves around them!' 13But Sheba and Dedan and the merchants of Tarshish will ask, 'Do you really think the armies you have gathered can rob them of silver and gold? Do you think you can drive away their livestock and seize their goods and carry off plunder?'

14"Therefore, son of man, prophesy

**against Gog. Give him this message from
the Sovereign LORD: When my people are
living in peace in their land, then you will
rouse yourself.* 15You will come from your
homeland in the distant north with your
vast cavalry and your mighty army, 16and
you will attack my people Israel, covering
their land like a cloud. At that time in the
distant future, I will bring you against my
land as everyone watches, and my holi-
ness will be displayed by what happens to
you, Gog. Then all the nations will know
that I am the LORD.**

**17"This is what the Sovereign LORD asks:
Are you the one I was talking about long
ago, when I announced through Israel's
prophets that in the future I would bring
you against my people? 18But this is what
the Sovereign LORD says: When Gog in-
vades the land of Israel, my fury will boil
over! 19In my jealousy and blazing anger,
I promise a mighty shaking in the land of
Israel on that day. 20All living things—the
fish in the sea, the birds of the sky, the
animals of the field, the small animals
that scurry along the ground, and all the
people on earth—will quake in terror at
my presence. Mountains will be thrown
down; cliffs will crumble; walls will fall
to the earth. 21I will summon the sword
against you on all the hills of Israel, says
the Sovereign LORD. Your men will turn
their swords against each other. 22I will
punish you and your armies with disease
and bloodshed; I will send torrential rain,
hailstones, fire, and burning sulfur! 23In
this way, I will show my greatness and
holiness, and I will make myself known to
all the nations of the world. Then they will
know that I am the LORD.**

38:5 Hebrew *Paras, Cush, and Put.* **38:14** As in Greek version; Hebrew reads *then you will know.*

NOTES

38:2 ***Gog.*** Gog designates the leader of a massive coalition set on plundering God's people and land. The identification of Gog remains uncertain. The most attractive option, because of chronological and geographic proximity, is Gyges, king of Lydia—the *Gugu* of cuneiform sources from Ashurbanipal. In this understanding, Ezekiel referred not to a historic figure present during his ministry, but joined the tradition of a devastating foe from the north (see below) with the name of a famous and powerful king from over the northern horizon to construct an apocalyptic figure. Others have suggested *Gaga,* known from the Amarna letters (fourteenth century BC) as nations of the north. The location works for that option, but its chronology is problematic. Other proposals are less probable. Whatever the identity of Gog, Ezekiel appears to use him as the archetypal evil one, the "enemy from the north" famous in prophetic tradition, especially Jeremiah (Jer 1:13-15; 4:6), as *the* enemy of God and his people. Some minor LXX witnesses unnecessarily omit reference to the land of Magog.

Magog. This name appears first in the Bible as son of Japheth (Gen 10:2; 1 Chr 1:5). The NLT (with LXX, Targum, RSV, NRSV, NIV, NASB, and others) rightly takes it as a geographic name, the home of Gog. Association with Meshech and Tubal, known from Neo-Assyrian and other ancient references, would seem to place Magog in Anatolia. Difficulties in the identification and location of Magog may give credence to the idea that Magog may be a coded reference to Babylon by way of an atbash, a type of gematria (cf. Block 1998:434, note 36). In this cipher, each consonant of the word is replaced by the next letter in the alphabet and then reversed, yielding *mgg* (*magog*) from *bbl* (*babel* or Babylon). In this case chs 38 and 39 would at one and the same time be Ezekiel's oracle against Babylon, missing from the oracles of chs 25–32, and it would be his presentation of the Lord's victory over global evil.

the prince who rules over. The expression "who rules over" translates *ro'sh* [TH7218, ZH8031], which generally means "head" or "chief" or the like, much like English "head." The KJV translates it "chief prince of Meshech" (so Allen 1990:199), but this involves very awkward syntax. Others render the Hebrew term as the first of three place names and translate "prince of Rosh" (LXX, NASB, NKJV, REB). Understood thus, Rosh would be identified with a place attested at Ugarit and as Reshu/Rashu in Neo-Assyrian texts. But these references locate Rashu on the Elamite frontier along the Tigris River (Luckenbill 1927:25-26, 41), which does not seem to fit here. Popular identifications of Ezekiel's *ro'sh* with Russia depend on flawed etymology and read modern realities into the text. Perhaps the best solution is that adopted by the NLT, which reads *ro'sh* as standing in apposition to "prince" (so also Block 1998:434-435; Taylor 1969:244).

Meshech and Tubal. These lands are known from Neo-Assyrian sources and other ancient Near Eastern attestation. Meshech is to be identified with *Musku* of the cuneiform sources. It was located immediately west of Tubal. These countries were located in south-central and eastern Anatolia and were known for their metal working.

38:5 ***Persia, Ethiopia, and Libya.*** Lit., "Paras, Cush, and Put." These points from the extremities of the compass—from Persia in the distant east to Ethiopia in the south to Libya in the west—underscore the extent of Gog's influence. From these distant quarters he draws support. The portrayal of Israel's well-being as a matter of global concern and impact is another apocalyptic feature of these chapters.

38:6 ***Gomer.*** This people came from the oldest son of Japheth (Gen 10:2-3) and are probably to be identified with a group known in Neo-Assyrian sources as the *Gimirraa.* They were known to the Greeks as the *Kimmerioi* (i.e., the Cimmerians). These Indo-European nomads invaded the Caucasus and Asia Minor beginning in the late eighth century BC, attacking Tubal and Meshech among other peoples. The Cimmerians still threatened Asia Minor in the late seventh century.

Beth-togarmah. See note on 27:14.

38:11 ***who live in such confidence.*** "Confidence" translates the MT's *betakh* [TH983, ZH1055], whose dominant semantic load is "security." The NLT attempts to register this "security" through the eyes of Gog, who reads their security as overconfidence, naivete and arrogance (v. 12). See Waltke and O'Connor 1990:§9.6b, note 34 on the interesting construct with prepositional phrase behind this line.

38:13 ***Sheba.*** See note on 27:22.

Dedan. See note on 27:15.

Tarshish. See note on 27:12.

COMMENTARY

A major problem confronts the interpreter of chapters 38–39 in the determination of its genre—this forms the expectations with which one reads the text. The radical confrontation of good and evil, the unleashing of cosmic forces, the extensive exaggeration, and the use of symbolism have led many since Hitzig (1847) to read these oracles as apocalyptic literature. At the same time, several of these features are present in varying degrees in clearly nonapocalyptic oracles of Ezekiel. "The Day of the Lord" language indicates that this lens (i.e., "Day of Yahweh" lens) may be important to Ezekiel. Also important for overall construal of these prophecies is the book's own editorial location of these oracles as salvation oracles.

Students have been struck by the helter-skelter nature of the compilation, with its resulting logical inconsistencies (e.g., the villages have no walls, but walls fall in the destruction (38:11 and 20); the corpses of all Gog's hordes are buried (39:9-16); then a sacrificial feast is called for the devouring of the unburied dead (39:17-20).

These are so obvious as to force the conclusion that they are deliberately left in the text and that we are offered a collage of scenes about this cataclysmic event rather than a coherent discourse. Even so, the overall impact is clear and clearly stated (39:25-29). It is this aspect of the literature that Block tries creatively to capture in describing it as "a satirical literary cartoon strip" consisting of a number of frames (1998:431). Allen uses the word "kaleidoscope" to describe the presentation (1990:203). Historical referents do appear in the text—Gog, Meshech, Tubal, and so on—but they seem to be used symbolically or, better, archetypally. Consequently, a clear description of historical events does not emerge. Instead, claims about historical realities are made but used in such a way that they could find actualization in a number of different historical events.

Regarding genre, then, the complexity and idiosyncrasy of these materials caution against certainty or rigidity. Ezekiel has produced apocalyptic-like material, delivered in a literary collage that speaks as though of history, but in terms that transcend or burst historical expectation.

Was placement of these materials merely a compositional matter, an aspect of the book's redactional history? Some, like Josephus, have referred to two books of Ezekiel, presumably books covering chapters 1–37 and chapters 40–48 (*Antiquities* 10.79). The Gog materials would presumably have found their place in the book, then, as these two books were joined into a single scroll. The question of place remains, however. At least one other obvious point for an easy join would have been at the conclusion of the book, following the present chapters 47–48. The final paragraph of the Gog-Magog materials (39:25-29) even offers something of a possible conclusion for the book. But this arrangement would have compromised the overall chiastic structure of the present work and would have weakened the impact of the climactic "The LORD (i.e., Yahweh) Is There" in 48:35. This supports a purposeful placement of these materials at their present location, even if prompted by compositional necessities.

Hermeneutically, we must distinguish the interpreter's task from the historian's (without driving a wedge between the two). If one is attempting to reconstruct the envisioned "history of the return and restoration" of God's people, the Gog materials appear very much out of order, since they assume successful return to the land (cf. 38:8, 11-12). They assume events that will follow the emergence of the realities envisioned in chapters 40–48. In his placement of the second oracle regarding Nebuchadnezzar's siege of Tyre, Ezekiel already set theological and topical considerations ahead of chronological issues in the ordering of materials (cf. 29:17-21). If then, instead of asking about the history of the return and restoration, we ask about the intent of the author or editors in placing the materials here between chapters 33–37 and chapters 40–48, focusing on major theological contentions made in chapters 38–39, other interpretive options arise.

The repeated messenger formula, "this is what the Sovereign LORD says" (Heb., *koh 'amar* [TH3541/559, ZH3907/606] *'adonay yhwh*), would appear to provide the most obvious indicators of structure for the Gog materials (Taylor 1969:242-243). Objection that some topical or lexical affinities across these boundaries render them secondary do not seem persuasive (Allen 1990:202-203; Block 1998:424-432).

While the repeated messenger formulae do mark the unit as divine speech, they also provide reasonable introductions to the seven frames comprising the unit.

In the first oracle (38:1-9), Ezekiel is to prophesy against Gog, the ruler of Meshech and Tubal, announcing that Israel's Sovereign Lord stands as his enemy, a frightful reality! And this enemy has determined to take control of Gog and his whole army, including raiding cavalry with chariots and armed hordes (38:1-4). He would forcefully lead them, like victors "lead" captives with hooks in their jaws (cf. Amos 4:2). It is in light of this heavily theocentric general introduction that the specifics of the action narrated later must be read. The references to the plans and commitments of the parties involved is to be read as exposition of the action of God. Nations from all points of the compass (38:5) and peoples normally at odds with each other (Gomer and Beth-togarmah, 38:6) would join Gog. Here we see a distinctive aspect of these Gog oracles. The events described are wholly God's doing! God would turn Gog around. God would capture him, muster his forces, and later order him to action (38:7). But others would also join as willing participants (e.g., "Persia . . . will join you," 38:5), as presumably would Gog himself (38:10). The first oracle also presents the circumstance in which Yahweh arrests Gog. It is temporally remote, "a long time from now" (38:8)—God's people would then be returned to the land and enjoying peace (as promised in the "covenant of peace" oracles, 34:25ff, and 37:26ff).

The second oracle exposes Gog's evil plan (38:10-13). Gog sees the prosperity of the people and the plenty of the land. He knows of the desolation suffered by the land and the remarkable turnaround evident in the people's newfound tranquility. They also appear vulnerable, without fortification or defenses. But they are confident nevertheless, apparently confident of the Lord's protection (38:11). Gog resents their well-being and their apparent belief that exceptional events have transpired for them. His plan is to plunder this wealth, expecting great gain. Interestingly, nations who have been party to the events assumed by this state of affairs caution Gog regarding his confidence against these settled people. Sheba, Dedan, and Tarshish have been trading partners with Israel, some with Tyre's help. It appears the Gog oracles assume the threats against Tyre have taken place, so that these peoples regard the returnees as dangerous targets, unlike their situation at the fall of Jerusalem (cf. 27:10-24).

The third oracle (38:14-16) essentially repeats material already spoken, with emphasis on "the land" (his people's land in 38:14 and 38:16a, Yahweh's land in 38:16b) and the addition of two new theological agendas. First, Yahweh claims the events involving Gog will be a display of his holiness (i.e., of his unique character and relationship with Israel and all humans). Second, through the events, "all the nations" will have clear insight regarding the force driving the events (i.e., they will know that it was Yahweh's doing; 38:16). The opening "therefore" (38:14) suggests that these insights are causally drawn from the preceding materials. We also learn what the place names implied: that Gog's home is in the "distant north," most likely Anatolia (38:15). Yahweh states the actions that Gog will take, but then notes again his divine agency in those actions. *Yahweh* will "bring" Gog against his land (38:16).

The fourth oracle (38:17-23), like the others, is addressed to Gog in the second person, but also contains third-person references to him. It begins with a hermeneutical question regarding the relationship of these oracles to previous prophetic utterances

(38:17). This could easily touch the question of the reuse or reinterpretation of previous "biblical" materials, such as the adaptation of the "foe from the north" materials known to Jeremiah (Jer 1:13-15; 4:6) and Isaiah (Isa 14:31), though not necessarily so. Yahweh raises the question as to whether or not this foe from the distant north has already been the topic of prophetic proclamation. More than any other prophet, Ezekiel's contemporary Jeremiah makes much of a horrific foe from the north. This dreaded foe from the north figures in his prophecies about the fall of Jerusalem (Jer 1:14-15; 4:16; 6:22; 15:12; 25:9). Jeremiah also saw a foe from the north involved in the Day of Yahweh, sometime after the fall of Jerusalem, when even Babylon would be judged (Jer 25:26; 50:3, 9, 41; 51:48). Jeremiah's scenario is similar to the present setting, but it is not clear precisely whom Ezekiel had in mind.

The message here takes a turn wholly unforeseen to those who failed to take seriously the warning of Sheba, Dedan, and Tarshish (38:13). Yahweh reveals the tone of his own response to Gog's actions—boiling fury (38:18). Yahweh will respond to Gog in his "jealousy and blazing anger" (38:19). And Yahweh reveals the consequences of Gog's actions. Catastrophes await Gog and his hordes in the land of Israel (38:21-22). God will bring an eschatological earthquake with the result that animate creation will tremble at this display (38:20). The cosmos itself will convulse in response to the presence of God. Such consternation will so fill the land that the invading forces will turn on one another in confusion, wielding the sword against their fellows (38:21). God will use the cosmic upheaval to punish Gog. This will be not just a day of misfortune for Gog, but rather a "day of judgment" (as 39:8 has it). The events will be of a scale as to make clear the greatness and holiness of the Lord (38:23). All nations will acknowledge Yahweh as the God at work in these happenings.

◆ 2. Gog's destruction reveals the Lord's ways (39:1-29)

**"Son of man, prophesy against Gog. Give
him this message from the Sovereign
LORD: I am your enemy, O Gog, ruler of the
nations of Meshech and Tubal. 2 I will turn
you around and drive you toward the
mountains of Israel, bringing you from
the distant north. 3 I will knock the bow
from your left hand and the arrows from
your right hand, and I will leave you help-
less. 4 You and your army and your allies
will all die on the mountains. I will feed
you to the vultures and wild animals. 5 You
will fall in the open fields, for I have spo-
ken, says the Sovereign LORD. 6 And I will
rain down fire on Magog and on all your
allies who live safely on the coasts. Then
they will know that I am the LORD.**

**7 "In this way, I will make known my holy
name among my people of Israel. I will not
let anyone bring shame on it. And the na-
tions, too, will know that I am the LORD,
the Holy One of Israel. 8 That day of judg-
ment will come, says the Sovereign LORD.
Everything will happen just as I have de-
clared it.**

**9 "Then the people in the towns of Israel
will go out and pick up your small and
large shields, bows and arrows, javelins and
spears, and they will use them for fuel.
There will be enough to last them seven
years! 10 They won't need to cut wood from
the fields or forests, for these weapons will
give them all the fuel they need. They will
plunder those who planned to plunder
them, and they will rob those who planned
to rob them, says the Sovereign LORD.**

**11 "And I will make a vast graveyard for
Gog and his hordes in the Valley of the
Travelers, east of the Dead Sea.* It will
block the way of those who travel there,**

and they will change the name of the
place to the Valley of Gog's Hordes. 12It
will take seven months for the people of
Israel to bury the bodies and cleanse the
land. 13Everyone in Israel will help, for it
will be a glorious victory for Israel when I
demonstrate my glory on that day, says
the Sovereign LORD.

14"After seven months, teams of men
will be appointed to search the land for
skeletons to bury, so the land will be made
clean again. 15Whenever bones are found,
a marker will be set up so the burial crews
will take them to be buried in the Valley of
Gog's Hordes. 16(There will be a town there
named Hamonah, which means 'horde.')
And so the land will finally be cleansed.

17"And now, son of man, this is what the
Sovereign LORD says: Call all the birds and
wild animals. Say to them: Gather together
for my great sacrificial feast. Come from
far and near to the mountains of Israel,
and there eat flesh and drink blood! 18Eat
the flesh of mighty men and drink the
blood of princes as though they were rams,
lambs, goats, and bulls—all fattened ani-
mals from Bashan! 19Gorge yourselves with
flesh until you are glutted; drink blood un-
til you are drunk. This is the sacrificial feast
I have prepared for you. 20Feast at my ban-
quet table—feast on horses and charioteers,
on mighty men and all kinds of valiant
warriors, says the Sovereign LORD.

21"In this way, I will demonstrate my
glory to the nations. Everyone will see
the punishment I have inflicted on them
and the power of my fist when I strike.
22And from that time on the people of
Israel will know that I am the LORD their
God. 23The nations will then know why
Israel was sent away to exile—it was pun-
ishment for sin, for they were unfaithful
to their God. Therefore, I turned away
from them and let their enemies destroy
them. 24I turned my face away and pun-
ished them because of their defilement
and their sins.

25"So now, this is what the Sovereign
LORD says: I will end the captivity of my
people*; I will have mercy on all Israel, for
I jealously guard my holy reputation!
26They will accept responsibility for* their
past shame and unfaithfulness after they
come home to live in peace in their own
land, with no one to bother them. 27When
I bring them home from the lands of their
enemies, I will display my holiness among
them for all the nations to see. 28Then my
people will know that I am the LORD their
God, because I sent them away to exile
and brought them home again. I will
leave none of my people behind. 29And I
will never again turn my face from them,
for I will pour out my Spirit upon the
people of Israel. I, the Sovereign LORD,
have spoken!"

39:11 Hebrew *the sea.* **39:25** Hebrew *of Jacob.* **39:26** A few Hebrew manuscripts read *They will forget.*

NOTES

39:7 *the Holy One of Israel.* The NLT follows a few MT mss, the Old Greek (cf. LXX Alexandrinus), and some ancient versions; the MT (and LXX Vaticanus) reads (the) Holy One *in* Israel. Found only here in Ezekiel, the appellation "the Holy One of Israel" borrows Isaiah's signature name for the God of Israel. Either reading emphasizes the aspect of God's character of greatest concern to Ezekiel in chs 38 and 39—namely, his holiness.

39:9 *small and large shields, bows and arrows, javelins and spears.* See Yadin 1963:2.293-313 for illustrations and discussions of most of these weapons.

COMMENTARY

The fifth oracle in this message (38:1–39:29) is the longest of the collection; it comprises 39:1-16. Significant repetition from earlier oracles may signal something of a new beginning in the presentation, perhaps a second panel. The first of the two panels (38:2-23, oracles 1–4) focuses on the conscription of Gog and his forces.

This second panel focuses on the complete destruction of Gog and the theological implications of it all (39:1-29, oracles 5–7). Yahweh's declaration of enemy status against Gog and the "turn around" of Gog (39:1-2) reach back to 38:3-4. The surprise that destruction awaits Gog and his hordes (39:3-5) picks up 38:21-22, while adding fresh detail. Gog and forces will die in the open field and be left as carrion for birds of prey (39:4; cf. 37:2-3). This will be Yahweh's doing, not just a happenstance of war. They will later become a sacrificial feast (39:17ff). Not only so, but the people in the towns of Israel will go out and gather the weapons left on the field, and these weapons will provide seven years worth of fuel (39:9-10)! Shields large and small, bows and arrows, javelins and spears litter the landscape, so that God's people will reverse the tables on Gog, plundering the hordes that aimed to plunder.

The unanticipated slaughter of Gog's forces will call for a vast graveyard, which Yahweh will provide. It is located in a "Valley of the Travelers," a site not identified with certainty. The graveyard will be so large that it blocks traffic, prompting travelers to rename the route "The Valley of Gog's Hordes" (39:11). The people of Israel will also bury the bodies of Gog and his hordes, stripped of their weapons and other plunder (39:12). This will be a seven-month process, after which teams will be sent out to locate skeletons missed in the burial effort so that all remains of Gog and his forces will be buried. The point of this seven-month effort will be to cleanse the land (twice emphasized, 39:12, 16). We have seen already in Ezekiel the defiling force of corpses and bones (6:5; 9:7). God's people must meticulously cleanse this massive defilement. All together, the destruction of Gog and his hordes and the purification of the land represent a "glorious victory" for the people of Israel—and for their God. These events constitute a demonstration of God's glory on a huge scale (39:13).

The sixth oracle adds yet another scene of apocalyptic proportions (39:17-24). Ezekiel is to summon "all the birds and wild animals" far and near for a "great sacrificial feast" sponsored by Yahweh (39:17-19). Emphasis falls on the menu: the flesh and blood of mighty men, rulers, warriors and charioteers, even horses (39:18-20); it is a lavish gorging offered by Yahweh (39:19). All of this puts an apocalyptic twist on Yahweh's sacrificial feast as a Day of Yahweh theme (Zeph 1:7-8). Such a striking and public victory will demonstrate God's glory to the onlooking nations and respond to two aspects of the shame heaped on Yahweh's name by the fall of Jerusalem and the exile of God's people (cf. 39:21-24 against 36:19-24); the idea that either Yahweh was unable to protect his people (weak), or he was unwilling to do so (malicious) would be shown false. It will be clear that the glorious Yahweh has the capacity to move and govern nations. His people went into exile not because he was unable to care for them or lacked the will to do so, but rather because of their own breach of covenant. The logic of the Exile will now be convincing to international onlookers. Its repetition suggests that the concern of Yahweh for his glory is *the* paramount theological agenda driving the entire Gog project; it is a concern registered seven times in the message as a whole (38:16, 23; 39:6, 7, 13, 22, 28).

Ezekiel devotes the seventh oracle (39:25-29) to a loose summary of key aspects of chapters 38–39 that includes aspects of chapters 33–37 as well. Demonstration of the logic of the Exile depends on demonstration of the logic of the return to the land. Thus, when God's people saw that he had brought all of them home as an act of powerful mercy, they would understand also that he took them out of the land because of their shameful unfaithfulness to him (as in 36:31). This would constitute a revelation of Yahweh's holiness—of his moral character and of his complete "otherness" (39:27). It would display Yahweh's mercy as well as his zealous concern for his own reputation (39:25; cf. 36:32). The Lord promises never again to turn away from his people; he bases that promise on his plan to pour out his Spirit upon the people of Israel (39:29; cf. 36:25-27)—he will not turn away because his people will not give him reason to do so.

In spite of the fact that 37:15-28 could provide a fitting climax to chapters 33–37 and a fitting introduction to the materials in chapters 40–48, the oracles against Gog (chs 38–39) now stand as the bridge between the two. The fact that scribes have suffered the disjuncture, allowing it to stand, testifies to the importance of these two chapters in the flow of Ezekiel. First, God plans to return his people (all of them) from the lands to which he has scattered them over the centuries. By his own initiative, his own grace and power, and apart from repentance in his people, he will do this. Second, these chapters emphasize in unparalleled fashion the peaceful, imperturbable life to which Yahweh leads his people through exile. They will live in unparalleled *shalom* [TH7965, ZH8934], which not even the infamous foe from the north will be able to shatter. Should *any* foe come against them, their God will not only protect them but extravagantly demonstrate his grace and power in the process. Third, in these remarkable and impossible events, Yahweh will vindicate his nature and establish his holy name once more as the God of the nations, the God of Israel, and the God of Ezekiel. Chapters 38–39 are for Ezekiel a major prophetic theodicy, a vision of conclusive vindication of God and his people as well. These claims and the defense of God here tie the Gog materials all the way back to the question of the fairness and implied adequacy of Yahweh raised in 33:17-20. This summary also recalls the overview of the logic of restoration offered at 28:25-26, in the midst of the oracles against the nations.

But what finally are we to make of Gog? What sort of "fulfillment" or lack thereof should we expect for the astounding realities pictured in chapters 38–39? If we read consistently, the major contours of our response to these questions will already have been anticipated. The way forward is indicated by the hermeneutic explored in the introduction to the Oracles and Visions of Israel's Restoration (33:1–48:35), which should be reviewed here (pp. 195-199).

In chapters 38 and 39, Ezekiel composes an apocalyptic-like collage, drawing heavily on "Day of Yahweh" language, writing with archetypal symbolism of anticipated realities, realities that could find concrete expression in a number of different historical scenarios. Here and in chapters 40–48 as well, Ezekiel provides numerous clues that we should not anticipate a detailed, literal fulfillment of what he has seen—the appearance of a real Mr. Gog who rules an actual land of Magog, an actual military invasion of Israel by virtually the entire known world. But the theological claims he makes seem clear. The God of Israel will bountifully restore his people. He will protect them and grant them unparalleled blessing. In the process he will ultimately defeat evil, vindicating himself and the trust of his people.

Ezekiel's apocalyptic approach signals that he is not content to write of a singular historical event. Instead, he looks behind historical realities anticipated and perceives the ultimate forces of evil and God at work in them. And although we do not look for a literal and precise fulfillment of the Gog-Magog affair, these icons of restoration and blessing and protection and vindication should not be thought of as unreal or unhistorical. Indeed, they will have to be lived out in historical or beyond-historical realities. If John the Revelator's handling of these chapters (Rev 19:17-21; 20:7-10) and of the river of life and new city of God (48:15-35; Rev 21:1–22:5) are any clue, the ultimate expression of the archetypal conflict Ezekiel treats here will have to do with the ultimate victory of God in the Messiah. What one thinks that might mean for present-day Israel will depend largely on hermeneutical conclusions reached from the study of Scripture as a whole regarding the nature of biblical prophecy and how it works in the providence of God.

◆ C. Vision of the Lord's New Temple (40:1–42:20)

1. Temple tour (40:1–41:26)

On April 28,* during the twenty-fifth year of our captivity—fourteen years after the fall of Jerusalem—the LORD took hold of me. 2In a vision from God he took me to the land of Israel and set me down on a very high mountain. From there I could see toward the south what appeared to be a city. 3As he brought me nearer, I saw a man whose face shone like bronze standing beside a gateway entrance. He was holding in his hand a linen measuring cord and a measuring rod.

4He said to me, "Son of man, watch and listen. Pay close attention to everything I show you. You have been brought here so I can show you many things. Then you will return to the people of Israel and tell them everything you have seen."

5I could see a wall completely surrounding the Temple area. The man took a measuring rod that was 10½ feet* long and measured the wall, and the wall was 10½ feet* thick and 10½ feet high.

6Then he went over to the eastern gateway. He climbed the steps and measured the threshold of the gateway; it was 10½ feet front to back.* 7There were guard alcoves on each side built into the gateway passage. Each of these alcoves was 10½ feet square, with a distance between them of 8¾ feet* along the passage wall. The gateway's inner threshold, which led to the entry room at the inner end of the gateway passage, was 10½ feet front to back. 8He also measured the entry room of the gateway.* 9It was 14 feet* across, with supporting columns 3½ feet* thick. This entry room was at the inner end of the gateway structure, facing toward the Temple.

10There were three guard alcoves on each side of the gateway passage. Each had the same measurements, and the dividing walls separating them were also identical. 11The man measured the gateway entrance, which was 17½ feet* wide at the opening and 22¾ feet* wide in the gateway passage. 12In front of each of the guard alcoves was a 21-inch* curb. The alcoves themselves were 10½ feet* on each side.

13Then he measured the entire width of the gateway, measuring the distance between the back walls of facing guard alcoves; this distance was 43¾ feet.* 14He measured the dividing walls all along the inside of the gateway up to the entry room of the gateway; this distance was 105 feet.* 15The full length of the gateway passage was 87½ feet* from one end to the other. 16There were recessed windows that narrowed inward through the walls of the

guard alcoves and their dividing walls. There were also windows in the entry room. The surfaces of the dividing walls were decorated with carved palm trees.

17Then the man brought me through the gateway into the outer courtyard of the Temple. A stone pavement ran along the walls of the courtyard, and thirty rooms were built against the walls, opening onto the pavement. 18This pavement flanked the gates and extended out from the walls into the courtyard the same distance as the gateway entrance. This was the lower pavement. 19Then the man measured across the Temple's outer courtyard between the outer and inner gateways; the distance was 175 feet.*

20The man measured the gateway on the north just like the one on the east. 21Here, too, there were three guard alcoves on each side, with dividing walls and an entry room. All the measurements matched those of the east gateway. The gateway passage was 87½ feet long and 43¾ feet wide between the back walls of facing guard alcoves. 22The windows, the entry room, and the palm tree decorations were identical to those in the east gateway. There were seven steps leading up to the gateway entrance, and the entry room was at the inner end of the gateway passage. 23Here on the north side, just as on the east, there was another gateway leading to the Temple's inner courtyard directly opposite this outer gateway. The distance between the two gateways was 175 feet.

24Then the man took me around to the south gateway and measured its various parts, and they were exactly the same as in the others. 25It had windows along the walls as the others did, and there was an entry room where the gateway passage opened into the outer courtyard. And like the others, the gateway passage was 87½ feet long and 43¾ feet wide between the back walls of facing guard alcoves. 26This gateway also had a stairway of seven steps leading up to it, and an entry room at the inner end, and palm tree decorations along the dividing walls. 27And here again, directly opposite the outer gateway, was another gateway that led into the inner courtyard. The distance between the two gateways was 175 feet.

28Then the man took me to the south gateway leading into the inner courtyard. He measured it, and it had the same measurements as the other gateways. 29Its guard alcoves, dividing walls, and entry room were the same size as those in the others. It also had windows along its walls and in the entry room. And like the others, the gateway passage was 87½ feet long and 43¾ feet wide. 30(The entry rooms of the gateways leading into the inner courtyard were 14 feet* across and 43¾ feet wide.) 31The entry room to the south gateway faced into the outer courtyard. It had palm tree decorations on its columns, and there were eight steps leading to its entrance.

32Then he took me to the east gateway leading to the inner courtyard. He measured it, and it had the same measurements as the other gateways. 33Its guard alcoves, dividing walls, and entry room were the same size as those of the others, and there were windows along the walls and in the entry room. The gateway passage measured 87½ feet long and 43¾ feet wide. 34Its entry room faced into the outer courtyard. It had palm tree decorations on its columns, and there were eight steps leading to its entrance.

35Then he took me around to the north gateway leading to the inner courtyard. He measured it, and it had the same measurements as the other gateways. 36The guard alcoves, dividing walls, and entry room of this gateway had the same measurements as in the others and the same window arrangements. The gateway passage measured 87½ feet long and 43¾ feet wide. 37Its entry room faced into the outer courtyard, and it had palm tree decorations on the columns. There were eight steps leading to its entrance.

38A door led from the entry room of one of the inner gateways into a side room, where the meat for sacrifices was washed.

39On each side of this entry room were two tables, where the sacrificial animals were slaughtered for the burnt offerings, sin offerings, and guilt offerings. 40Outside the entry room, on each side of the stairs going up to the north entrance, were two more tables. 41So there were eight tables in all—four inside and four outside—where the sacrifices were cut up and prepared. 42There were also four tables of finished stone for preparation of the burnt offerings, each 31½ inches square and 21 inches high.* On these tables were placed the butchering knives and other implements for slaughtering the sacrificial animals. 43There were hooks, each 3 inches* long, fastened to the foyer walls. The sacrificial meat was laid on the tables.

44Inside the inner courtyard were two rooms,* one beside the north gateway, facing south, and the other beside the south* gateway, facing north. 45And the man said to me, "The room beside the north inner gate is for the priests who supervise the Temple maintenance. 46The room beside the south inner gate is for the priests in charge of the altar—the descendants of Zadok—for they alone of all the Levites may approach the LORD to minister to him."

47Then the man measured the inner courtyard, and it was a square, 175 feet wide and 175 feet across. The altar stood in the courtyard in front of the Temple. 48Then he brought me to the entry room of the Temple. He measured the walls on either side of the opening to the entry room, and they were 8¾ feet thick. The entrance itself was 24½ feet wide, and the walls on each side of the entrance were an additional 5¼ feet long.* 49The entry room was 35 feet* wide and 21 feet* deep. There were ten steps leading up to it, with a column on each side.

CHAPTER 41

After that, the man brought me into the sanctuary of the Temple. He measured the walls on either side of its doorway, and they were 10½ feet* thick. 2The doorway was 17½ feet* wide, and the walls on each side of it were 8¾ feet* long. The sanctuary itself was 70 feet long and 35 feet wide.*

3Then he went beyond the sanctuary into the inner room. He measured the walls on either side of its entrance, and they were 3½ feet* thick. The entrance was 10½ feet wide, and the walls on each side of the entrance were 12¼ feet* long. 4The inner room of the sanctuary was 35 feet* long and 35 feet wide. "This," he told me, "is the Most Holy Place."

5Then he measured the wall of the Temple, and it was 10½ feet thick. There was a row of rooms along the outside wall; each room was 7 feet* wide. 6These side rooms were built in three levels, one above the other, with thirty rooms on each level. The supports for these side rooms rested on exterior ledges on the Temple wall; they did not extend into the wall. 7Each level was wider than the one below it, corresponding to the narrowing of the Temple wall as it rose higher. A stairway led up from the bottom level through the middle level to the top level.

8I saw that the Temple was built on a terrace, which provided a foundation for the side rooms. This terrace was 10½ feet* high. 9The outer wall of the Temple's side rooms was 8¾ feet thick. This left an open area between these side rooms 10and the row of rooms along the outer wall of the inner courtyard. This open area was 35 feet wide, and it went all the way around the Temple. 11Two doors opened from the side rooms into the terrace yard, which was 8¾ feet wide. One door faced north and the other south.

12A large building stood on the west, facing the Temple courtyard. It was 122½ feet wide and 157½ feet long, and its walls were 8¾ feet* thick. 13Then the man measured the Temple, and it was 175 feet* long. The courtyard around the building, including its walls, was an additional 175 feet in length. 14The inner courtyard to the east of the Temple was also 175 feet wide. 15The building to the west, including its two walls, was also 175 feet wide.

The sanctuary, the inner room, and the entry room of the Temple [16]were all paneled with wood, as were the frames of the recessed windows. The inner walls of the Temple were paneled with wood above and below the windows. [17]The space above the door leading into the inner room, and its walls inside and out, were also paneled. [18]All the walls were decorated with carvings of cherubim, each with two faces, and there was a carving of a palm tree between each of the cherubim. [19]One face—that of a man—looked toward the palm tree on one side. The other face—that of a young lion—looked toward the palm tree on the other side. The figures were carved all along the inside of the Temple, [20]from the floor to the top of the walls, including the outer wall of the sanctuary.

[21]There were square columns at the entrance to the sanctuary, and the ones at the entrance of the Most Holy Place were similar. [22]There was an altar made of wood, 5¼ feet high and 3½ feet across.* Its corners, base, and sides were all made of wood. "This," the man told me, "is the table that stands in the LORD's presence."

[23]Both the sanctuary and the Most Holy Place had double doorways, [24]each with two swinging doors. [25]The doors leading into the sanctuary were decorated with carved cherubim and palm trees, just as on the walls. And there was a wooden roof at the front of the entry room to the Temple. [26]On both sides of the entry room were recessed windows decorated with carved palm trees. The side rooms along the outside wall also had roofs.

40:1 Hebrew *At the beginning of the year, on the tenth day of the month,* of the ancient Hebrew lunar calendar. This event occurred on April 28, 573 B.C.; also see note on 1:1. **40:5a** Hebrew *6 long cubits* [3.2 meters], *each being a cubit* [18 inches or 45 centimeters] *and a handbreadth* [3 inches or 8 centimeters] *in length.* **40:5b** Hebrew *1 rod* [3.2 meters]; also in 40:5c, 7. **40:6** As in Greek version, which reads *1 rod* [3.2 meters] *deep;* Hebrew reads *1 rod deep, and 1 threshold, 1 rod deep.* **40:7** Hebrew *5 cubits* [2.7 meters]; also in 40:48. **40:8** Many Hebrew manuscripts add *which faced inward toward the Temple; it was 1 rod* [10.5 feet or 3.2 meters] *deep.* [9]*Then he measured the entry room of the gateway.* **40:9a** Hebrew *8 cubits* [4.2 meters]. **40:9b** Hebrew *2 cubits* [1.1 meters]. **40:11a** Hebrew *10 cubits* [5.3 meters]. **40:11b** Hebrew *13 cubits* [6.9 meters]. **40:12a** Hebrew *1 cubit* [53 centimeters]. **40:12b** Hebrew *6 cubits* [3.2 meters]. **40:13** Hebrew *25 cubits* [13.3 meters]; also in 40:21, 25, 29, 30, 33, 36. **40:14** Hebrew *60 cubits* [31.8 meters]. Greek version reads *20 cubits* [35 feet or 10.6 meters]. The meaning of the Hebrew in this verse is uncertain. **40:15** Hebrew *50 cubits* [26.5 meters]; also in 40:21, 25, 29, 33, 36. **40:19** Hebrew *100 cubits* [53 meters]; also in 40:23, 27, 47. **40:30** As in 40:9, which reads *8 cubits* [14 feet or 4.2 meters]; here the Hebrew reads *5 cubits* [8¾ feet or 2.7 meters]. Some Hebrew manuscripts and the Greek version lack this entire verse. **40:42** Hebrew *1½ cubits* [80 centimeters] *long and 1½ cubits wide and 1 cubit* [53 centimeters] *high.* **40:43** Hebrew *a handbreadth* [8 centimeters]. **40:44a** As in Greek version; Hebrew reads *rooms for singers.* **40:44b** As in Greek version; Hebrew reads *east.* **40:48** As in Greek version, which reads *The entrance was 14 cubits* [7.4 meters] *wide, and the walls of the entrance were 3 cubits* [1.6 meters] *on each side;* Hebrew lacks *14 cubits wide, and the walls of the entrance were.* **40:49a** Hebrew *20 cubits* [10.6 meters]. **40:49b** As in Greek version, which reads *12 cubits* [21 feet or 6.4 meters]; Hebrew reads *11 cubits* [19¼ feet or 5.8 meters]. **41:1** Hebrew *6 cubits* [3.2 meters]; also in 41:3, 5. **41:2a** Hebrew *10 cubits* [5.3 meters]. **41:2b** Hebrew *5 cubits* [2.7 meters]; also in 41:9, 11. **41:2c** Hebrew *40 cubits* [21.2 meters] *long and 20 cubits* [10.6 meters] *wide.* **41:3a** Hebrew *2 cubits* [1.1 meters]. **41:3b** Hebrew *7 cubits* [3.7 meters]. **41:4** Hebrew *20 cubits* [10.6 meters]; also in 41:4b, 10. **41:5** Hebrew *4 cubits* [2.1 meters]. **41:8** Hebrew *1 rod, 6 cubits* [3.2 meters]. **41:12** Hebrew *70 cubits* [37.1 meters] *wide and 90 cubits* [47.7 meters] *long, and its walls were 5 cubits* [2.7 meters] *thick.* **41:13** Hebrew *100 cubits* [53 meters]; also in 41:13b, 14, 15. **41:22** Hebrew *3 cubits* [1.6 meters] *high and 2 cubits* [1.1 meters] *across.*

NOTES

40:1 ***twenty-fifth year . . . fourteen years.*** Ezekiel exhibits a fascination with numerical patterns and combinations associated with scribal and priestly expertise. The use of five and multiples of five (25, 50, 150, 500, 550, 5,000, 10,000, and 25,000) is most prominent. Seven (along with its multiples) and three and four are also featured. This patterned use of numbers by Ezekiel indicates to Zimmerli (1983:327, 343) the symmetry and harmony of the scene and underscores the proclamational aims of the revelation.

40:2 ***In a vision from God.*** The Hebrew expression *mar'oth 'elohim* [TH4759, ZH5261] is translated variously by the NLT depending on context. In 1:1 it is rendered "visions *of* God," in 8:3 and 40:2, "a vision *from* God" (emphasis added), based on the differing emphases of the visions. Although the precise sense of the phrase may vary, it is important to note that the identical expression ties the chapters together.

40:5 ***measuring rod . . . 10½ feet long.*** See NLT mg. The "long cubits, each being a cubit and a handbreadth" mentioned in the MT presumably contrast with a shorter cubit, an old (?) measure (2 Chr 3:3). Whether this indicates Mesopotamian or Egyptian influence is uncertain (ABD 6.899-900). Tuell's proposal (1992:29) that Persian standard measurements are evident here remains unproven.

40:10 ***three guard alcoves on each side of the gateway passage.*** Ezekiel's six-chamber gate design closely resembles the six-chamber fortified city gates known from the Solomonic cities of Gezer, Megiddo, and Hazor, as well as Ashdod and Lachish (Mazar 1990:380-387, see p. 384 for diagrams).

40:13 ***back walls.*** The NLT follows LXX in reading Heb. *gaw* [TH1458, ZH1567], "back or inside (walls)," instead of MT's *gag* [TH1406, ZH1511], "roof," which does not seem to make sense as a boundary for measurement here. Although Block's translation of *gag* as "ceiling" could work (1998:521), both "roof" and "ceiling" seem to move suddenly to a very different plane of measurement.

40:14 The NLT has Ezekiel's guide measuring a distance of 105 feet (60 long cubits) along "the dividing walls all along the inside of the gateway up to the entry room of the gateway." The LXX, NASB, NKJV, and NJPS also have 60 cubits, but measure height. The NIV has 60 cubits "all around the inside of the gateway." The very different renderings offered here reflect the difficulty of the MT at this point and the challenge of picturing exactly what Ezekiel sees. The RSV, NRSV, REB, JB, and ESV have 20 cubits (this can be reconstructed from the LXX's "20 alcoves"; cf. Allen 1990:220), and the NAB has 25, under the influence of v. 13. They take the MT to be corrupt, which is entirely possible in light of the fact that this measurement occurs with none of the other gates. It is difficult to match the 105 feet with the gate dimensions given, unless the measurement includes not only the gate proper but also the steps, whose dimensions we are not given. The different numbers adopted do not so much affect the overall picture of the east gate as the specific aspect being measured.

40:16 ***palm trees.*** Palm trees were ubiquitous in the art and iconography of the ancient biblical world, often associated with fertility figures of one sort or another, and by no means odd in temple decor. By the Solomonic period, however, the palm tree began to appear alone without gender indicators. In these situations it no longer represented a *Dea nutrix* (a maternal, nursing goddess) but its "own unique form of numinous power" (Keel and Uehlinger 1998:153). In Yahweh's Temple it would be a symbol of his life-giving and sustaining power.

40:48 The NLT, along with almost all modern English versions, includes a phrase from the LXX that seems to translate a Hebrew line dropped from the MT by homoioteleuton (i.e., scribal confusion between lines with similar endings). Without it, the concluding measurements seem to dangle, as in the NASB translation of this verse.

41:15 ***The sanctuary . . . of the Temple.*** Instead of "temple," MT has "the courtyard"; the LXX reads "outer vestibule/entryway." The NLT's "Temple" seems demanded by context.

41:18-20 ***cherubim.*** The cherubim that figure prominently in the decoration of the new Temple recall the same decor in Solomon's Temple (1 Kgs 6:23-29, 32-35; 8:6-7) and also the use of cherubim in the ancient Ark of the Covenant (cf. Exod 25 and 26, 36 and 37;

Num 7:89 and 1 Sam 4:4). Ezekiel's two-faced cherubim (one face a man, the other that of a lion) adapted the historic cherubim that had only a man's face. These cherubim carried and guarded the throne of Yahweh. Ezekiel's more frequent deployment of the cherub-figures features four-faced creatures (as in chs 1, 10, and 11). These also were associated with the throne of the Shekinah (i.e., of the Lord's glorious presence), as chariot attendants holding and guarding that throne. Their four-faced appearance probably reflected Mesopotamian and Canaanite art more than Israelite tradition.

41:22 *base.* The NLT follows LXX, reading Heb. *'eden* [TH134, ZH149], "base," rather than *'orek* [TH753, ZH802], "length." The two Hebrew words look similar and would be easily confused in some consonantal scripts, so the MT may well be a corruption of *'eden*, which occurs frequently in the instructions for the Tabernacle in Exod 25–40, and is usually translated by the LXX as *basis* [TG939, ZG1000], the same word used here.

an altar . . . the table. This beautifully decorated table (also called an "altar" in this verse) stood in the Great Hall at the separation between the Holy Place and the Most Holy Place. It acknowledged the continuing presence of Yahweh in his Temple. In the Tabernacle and Solomon's Temple this furnishing was known as the Table of Show Bread or of the Bread of the Presence (Exod 25:23-30; Num 4:7; 1 Kgs 7:48). It should not be confused with the altar standing in the inner court; rather, it stood outside of the Temple and squarely in front of it, where sacrifices of all sorts having to do with the people's relationship with Yahweh were offered.

COMMENTARY

The opening paragraph (40:1-4) ties these chapters to the preceding materials, especially to the extended vision reports in chapters 1–3 and 8–11. (See the Introduction, "The Debate over the Fate of Solomon's Temple" and "The Future Temple," for details.) Each section shares the same genre: divine vision report. They each involve Ezekiel being seized by the Lord. They entail spiritual transport, carry a date, and include significant attention to the glory of the Lord. The reader is to recall the earlier revelation of the exalted one commissioning Ezekiel to be a prophet to rebellious Israel (chs 1–3). We are to remember the scathing critique of the Jerusalem Temple in chapters 8–11, the startling departure of the Glory of the Lord from the Temple and from Jerusalem itself, and the warnings of total destruction, which by now have come to pass (cf. 24:2; 33:21). With these sights in mind we proceed. What Ezekiel saw earlier in the Temple was a present reality. What he sees now is the future as though already in place—we may say it is "symbolic of the future," so long as we do not think "unreal" when we say "symbolic."

The date of this latest "apprehension" of Ezekiel by Yahweh was April 28, 573 BC. The prophet comments that 25 years had passed since he and the other exiles had been deported with King Jehoiachin and the royal family. And it had been 14 years since the fall of Jerusalem. The fascination with numerical symmetries shown throughout the vision leads one to note here that 25 is 5 x 5 and half of 50, that is, halfway from the deportation in 597 to the Jubilee of that event, the 50-year mark—at which time one might expect release from captivity (cf. Lev 25:8-23). Note also that Jubilee (50) is the square of 7 plus 1 (7 x 7 + 1) and that the 14th year is also 2 x 7. On this auspicious date, the Lord again dramatically apprehended the prophet for a revelation so important that Ezekiel made it the climax of his entire literary work. Although one could take such striking numerical convergences as pure symbolism, the apparent historical realism of the other dates used to place oracles in the book leads one to expect this date also to designate the actual date Yahweh granted the vision. In this case, we confront complex providence, not just numerology or symbolism.

Yahweh situated Ezekiel on a "very high mountain" (40:2). Except for Mount Hermon in the far north, there are no "very high mountains" in the land of Israel. This topography speaks the language of tradition associated with two major streams of theology in Israel, the Sinai (Mosaic) traditions and the Zion (Davidic) traditions. The Zion traditions, especially, appropriated ancient Canaanite concepts of the sacred mount in the far north to express the claims of Yahweh. That mount was the home of the Canaanite high god, El, and of the divine assembly over which he presided. From there the gods ruled, and sacred streams fructified the earth (Levenson 1985:111-142). Out of this tradition, psalmists and prophets celebrated Mount Zion as the Temple Mount (Pss 24, 36, 46, 48, 132), the place from which Yahweh—not the gods of the nations!—ruled and blessed the world. Ezekiel is brought to that sacred place.

To the south, Ezekiel saw what looked like a city (40:2). Remarkably, the city remains nameless until the last line of the book (48:35). Interpreters generally assume the city to be Jerusalem (i.e., Zion). If so, it represents a totally reconstituted Jerusalem, quite unlike past historic realities. This would be a Zion *without* Yahweh's Temple, which we will learn stands in a compound of its own, separate from the city (42:16-20; 45:2; 48:16-20). Ezekiel saw what appeared to be "a man," identified as a heavenly messenger by his shining countenance (40:3; cf. 1:26; 8:5ff, where the Lord himself guides Ezekiel through the vision). This figure is the only person Ezekiel will see in the entire vision. The "man" guides Ezekiel, bringing him to each successive point of view and addressing him with language elsewhere reserved for Yahweh's speech.

Finally (40:4), Ezekiel receives instructions that explain the reason for the visionary transport and the purpose of the revelation he is receiving. The man speaks for Yahweh as the one doing the revealing; he urges the prophet's careful attention to what he sees and hears because he is given the task of conveying to the exiles everything he will see in the vision (cf. 44:5-6, where the instruction is repeated). He will even write it down for careful study (43:11). This pattern of being brought to the mount, receiving revelation from Yahweh, and returning to the people of Israel as a mediator of divine revelation, oral and written, seems to present Ezekiel in the role of Moses—a second, latter-day Moses. In the whole of Hebrew Scripture, other than Moses, only Ezekiel actually revealed Torah (statutes and ordinances) on behalf of Yahweh (42:13-14; 43:7-12, 18-27, etc.; cf. 43:10). This underscores the importance of what Ezekiel was about to see and hear, and marks it as part of the new exodus and national inauguration promised earlier (cf. 20:39-44).

The vision's itinerary moves as follows. Brought to the land of Israel, to a very high mountain, Ezekiel sees a city (40:2), then a man (40:3), then a walled Temple area (40:5). Ezekiel's tour of the Temple compound begun at 40:5 occupies the writer's concern through 42:20. After this detailed tour of the Temple, brief notations of place locate the prophet at the east gate of the inner court (43:1), the east gate of the outer court (44:1), the front of the Temple via the north gate (44:4), the priests' rooms in the outer court (46:19), the corner kitchens of the outer court (46:21), then finally the Temple entrance and spots scattered at intervals of one-third of a mile along the flow of the stream from the entrance heading out toward the valley of the Dead Sea and back to the Temple (47:1-6).

Scattered through this itinerary two types of speech appear. First, periodic commentary and explanation by the tour guide laces the account (40:45-46; 41:4; 42:13-14; 46:20; 47:6, 8-12). This commentary is relatively brief compared to the extensive description of what Ezekiel was seeing. Second, at various points extended oracles appear, often introduced by the standard rubrics of prophetic oracular revelation: "The LORD said to me" (43:7-17; 44:2-3; 44:5-8), or "This is what the Sovereign LORD says" (43:18-27; 44:9–45:17; 45:18-25; 46:1-15; 46:16-18; 47:13–48:35).

Thus, although chapters 40–42 cover the major tour of the Temple area, the entire nine chapters (chs 40–48) focus on the Temple. The Temple pervades the vision and is the centerpiece of the restored community. The destruction of Solomon's Temple was a deathblow to old ways. The new Temple will be the heart of the promised restoration. The vision closes with the prophet en route back to the Temple (47:7). Just like the Mosaic Torah, Ezekiel's "Torah" is set in a narrative frame, part of the story of the tour. The Temple itself becomes a site of revelation.

As the Temple tour begins in 40:5, Ezekiel observes a striking feature: a 10½-foot exterior wall (as wide as it was tall) surrounding the entire Temple compound, including the inner and outer courts. The Solomonic Temple also had inner and outer courts (1 Kgs 7:8-9, 12; 8:64), but we have no precise information about the dimensions and configurations of the walls delimiting them. If this indicates narrative interest in the theological issues at stake in separating sacred from profane space, Ezekiel was clearly more concerned with such separation than the historian responsible for 1 Kings.

The man in Ezekiel's vision then moves to the exterior east gateway (40:6-16). One approached the gateway by a series of seven steps leading to the elevated Temple compound's exterior court (40:22, 26). After passing through the gate's threshold, one proceeded between a set of guard alcoves, three matching chambers on the right and left, then past a second threshold and through an entry room, also with matching chambers on the right and left of the center walkway. All told, the east gateway complex measured 43¾ feet between the back walls of the matching chambers and 87½ feet from end to end of the walkway, 105 feet if measured from the first step outside to the interior face of the gateway (40:14-15). The Solomonic Temple presumably included gateways of some sort, but the accounts in 1 Kings and 2 Chronicles omit description of them. Ezekiel's gate design, with its six matching guard alcoves, does remind us, however, of the six-chamber, fortified gates famous from the Solomonic cities of Gezer, Megiddo, and Hazor (1 Kgs 9:15; cf. NIDB 5:318-319; Pritchard 1997:54-55). The design suggests the Temple compound was itself something of a sacred fortress, with serious attention paid to guarding its sacred space. Here, as at several other points, the vision given to Ezekiel aims to rectify the failure of first-Temple patrons to guard the Temple's sacred space and to preserve the distinction between things sacred and things profane (cf. 42:13-14; 43:7-9, 12; 44:5-14, 23).

Ezekiel's guide brought him through the exterior east gateway into the Temple's outer courtyard (40:17). He could see 175 feet across the outer courtyard to a matching inner east gate that led into the Temple's inner court (40:18-19). Bypassing that inner east gate for the moment, the tour went from the outer east gate to an outer north gate (40:20-23), and around to an outer south gate (40:24-27). The outer north and south gates matched exactly the design of the east gate (40:21, 23-24). At both of these gates, as at the east gate, a matching inner gate stood 175 feet across the outer court and emptied into the inner court. In other words, the outer court wrapped around three sides of the inner court, a 175-foot band around its north, east, and south sides.

The tour then proceeded to each of the gates that opened from the Temple's outer court into the inner court, first the south gate, then the east gate, and finally the inner north gate. With the exception of the fact that the inner gates had eight steps leading up to their outer threshold (not seven as at the outer gates), and that the gates' entry rooms faced into the outer courtyard (as opposed to emptying into the inner court as one might have expected), the design and dimensions of these inner gates matched those of their corresponding outer gates (40:28-37). The eight-step rise to the inner gates indicates that the Temple compound as a whole rose as one proceeded toward its center, perhaps imitating a mountain, the sacred mount. This ascent continued with another rise (10 steps) into the entry room of the Temple building itself (40:49; 41:8), placing it at the pinnacle of the Temple Mount. The inner court itself was a 175-foot square space where the altar was to stand in front of the Temple (40:47; 43:13-17).

As one entered the north and south inner gates, stone tables were arranged for the slaughter and preparation of sacrificial animals (40:39, 41). Their respective entry rooms gave access to side rooms where meat for sacrifices could be washed (40:38). Precisely how these rooms stood with reference to the wall separating the outer from the inner courts is not clear. Also beside the interior entrances to these north and south gates, two rooms were provided for priests on duty in the Temple, the one by the inner north gate for Levites supervising Temple maintenance and the other by the inner south gate for Levites in charge of the altar (40:44-46). Ezekiel does not specify how the Levites will use these rooms. The position of these rooms could support the idea that in them the priests changed clothing, so as not to wear holy clothes used to perform their priestly functions in the inner court when they move to the outer court and places open to the public (42:13-14). The rooms may have held gear needed for their duties or places to rest and refresh; we simply do not know. From these rooms Ezekiel's guide brought him to the Temple edifice (40:48-49), noting that the altar stood in front of it (40:47; cf. 43:13-17). For reasons not apparent, Ezekiel delays description of that altar until Temple Torah begins, and the institution of altar service is described (43:13-17, 18-27).

The new Temple (40:48–41:26), like Solomon's, was a long, rectangular, three-part structure composed of a front entry room with a wooden canopy (the *'ulam* [TH361, ZH395]), the sanctuary (*hekal* [TH1964, ZH2121]), and the Most Holy Place, literally "the Inner Place" (*penimah* [TH6441, ZH7163], cf. 41:3). Situated on a terrace 10½ feet above the inner court and oriented on an east-west axis, the Temple's exterior dimensions measured 87½ feet wide by 175 feet deep, including auxiliary rooms attached on three sides of the Temple (41:5-7). Behind the Temple to the west was another large building, 122½ feet by 157½ feet, whose purpose remains unclear (41:12). In spite of its imposing size, not a word is said regarding its function. Block suggests one should think of it as an architectural response to "the excesses of the Judean monarchy, whose claims for space tended to encroach upon sacred temple territory" (1998:553). The area within the Temple compound's inner wall measured 175 feet by 525 feet, composed of three areas each measuring 175 feet square: (1) the inner courtyard directly in front of the Temple, (2) the Temple itself, and (3) the space directly behind the Temple holding the large, undesignated building just noted (41:13-15).

Ezekiel notes the whole interior of the Temple was paneled with wood and the panels themselves decorated with carvings of cherubim. Each cherubim had two faces (that of a human and a lion), each face looking toward a palm tree standing on either side of the cherubim (41:15b-20). Cherubim and palm trees were also carved on the double swinging doors at the entrances to the sanctuary and the Most Holy Place (41:23-26).

◆ 2. Rooms for the priests (42:1-20)

**Then the man led me out of the Temple
courtyard by way of the north gateway. We
entered the outer courtyard and came to a
group of rooms against the north wall of
the inner courtyard. 2This structure, whose
entrance opened toward the north, was
175 feet* long and 87½ feet* wide. 3One
block of rooms overlooked the 35-foot*
width of the inner courtyard. Another block
of rooms looked out onto the pavement of
the outer courtyard. The two blocks were
built three levels high and stood across
from each other. 4Between the two blocks
of rooms ran a walkway 17½ feet* wide. It
extended the entire 175 feet of the com-
plex,* and all the doors faced north. 5Each
of the two upper levels of rooms was nar-
rower than the one beneath it because the
upper levels had to allow space for walk-
ways in front of them. 6Since there were
three levels and they did not have support-
ing columns as in the courtyards, each of
the upper levels was set back from the
level beneath it. 7There was an outer wall
that separated the rooms from the outer
courtyard; it was 87½ feet long. 8This wall
added length to the outer block of rooms,
which extended for only 87½ feet, while
the inner block—the rooms toward the
Temple—extended for 175 feet. 9There was
an eastern entrance from the outer court-
yard to these rooms.**

**10On the south* side of the Temple there
were two blocks of rooms just south of the
inner courtyard between the Temple and
the outer courtyard. These rooms were
arranged just like the rooms on the north.
11There was a walkway between the two
blocks of rooms just like the complex on
the north side of the Temple. This complex
of rooms was the same length and width
as the other one, and it had the same en-
trances and doors. The dimensions of each
were identical. 12So there was an entrance
in the wall facing the doors of the inner
block of rooms, and another on the east at
the end of the interior walkway.**

**13Then the man told me, "These rooms
that overlook the Temple from the north
and south are holy. Here the priests who**

offer sacrifices to the LORD will eat the
most holy offerings. And because these
rooms are holy, they will be used to store
the sacred offerings—the grain offerings,
sin offerings, and guilt offerings. [14]When
the priests leave the sanctuary, they must
not go directly to the outer courtyard.
They must first take off the clothes they
wore while ministering, because these
clothes are holy. They must put on other
clothes before entering the parts of the
building complex open to the public."

[15]When the man had finished measur-
ing the inside of the Temple area, he led
me out through the east gateway to mea-
sure the entire perimeter. [16]He measured
the east side with his measuring rod, and
it was 875 feet long.* [17]Then he measured
the north side, and it was also 875 feet.
[18]The south side was also 875 feet, [19]and
the west side was also 875 feet. [20]So the
area was 875 feet on each side with a wall
all around it to separate what was holy
from what was common.

42:2a Hebrew *100 cubits* [53 meters]; also in 42:8. **42:2b** Hebrew *50 cubits* [26.5 meters]; also in 42:7, 8. **42:3** Hebrew *20-cubit* [10.6-meter]. **42:4a** Hebrew *10 cubits* [5.3 meters]. **42:4b** As in Greek and Syriac versions, which read *Its length was 100 cubits* [53 meters]; Hebrew reads *and a passage 1 cubit* [18 inches or 53 centimeters] *wide.* **42:10** As in Greek version; Hebrew reads *east.* **42:16** As in 45:2 and in Greek version at 42:17, which reads *500 cubits* [265 meters]; Hebrew reads *500 rods* [5,250 feet or 1,590 meters]; similarly in 42:17, 18, 19, 20.

NOTES

42:16 *875 feet long.* As noted in NLT mg, the Hebrew of the MT has the Temple compound as 500 rods (5,250 feet or 1,590 meters) square—i.e., just under a square mile! The NLT's "cubits" follows the lead of the LXX's reading at 42:17. Further, in MT at 45:2, the measure of what is apparently the land for the Temple is 500 cubits (not rods). Fairbairn regards the LXX at 42:15-17 as having been subject to tampering because of the extravagant measure of the MT, but regards that measure itself as a "palpable" indication of the vision's symbolic nature (1979:468-470).

Both LXX and NLT also agree with the Qere of MT in this verse, which reads "five hundred" rather than the Kethiv "five cubits" (which makes no sense); this supposes that the written consonants in MT *'mwt* [TH520, ZH564] (cubits) are a metathesis for *m'wt* [TH3967, ZH4395] (hundred).

COMMENTARY

The Temple tour draws to a close with a survey of rooms along the north and the south walls of the inner and outer courtyards and looking onto both courtyards (42:1-12). In them, the priests who offer sacrifice will eat the most holy offerings, and sacred offerings will be stored there; so the rooms will be considered holy (42:13). The account of the guide's measuring of each side of the exterior perimeter forms the literary conclusion to the main Temple tour (42:15-20).

Because of Ezekiel's earlier, extended attention to the Temple of Solomon and the abominations in that Temple (ch 8), the reader inevitably experiences this "tour" against the backdrop of that earlier Temple. Ezekiel's Temple building closely resembles the general design and dimensions of Solomon's Temple, but the two are not identical (cf. 1 Kgs 6–7; 2 Chr 3). The significance of the differences between the two remains unclear at most points, especially the differences in specific dimensions. Both Temples feature carved palm trees and carved cherubim in their decor. Palm trees were a widely used icon of nurture and fertility, often associated with a mother goddess in Canaanite iconography. But in Solomon's Temple, and Ezekiel's as well, the palm trees occur without the constellation of related figures that would give the palm tree gendered significance. They apparently stood as symbols of Yahweh's life-giving energy. The cherubim, as used in the book of Ezekiel and in the Solomonic Temple, should probably be understood as guards associated with thrones royal and divine (see notes on 1:5-9; 41:18-20). The carved gourds and open flowers prominent on the doors and wood panels of Solomon's Temple do not appear in Ezekiel's Temple (cf. 1 Kgs 6:18, 29), nor do the pomegranates featured on the two columns (known as Jachin and Boaz) that stood at the entry to the sanctuary (1 Kgs 7:18; 2 Chr 3:16; 4:13). We do not know the precise identity of the gourds and flowers and therefore do not venture comment on their significance. The pomegranates, it is thought, would evoke ideas of prosperity and blessing, without tying that theme to deities besides Yahweh (Keel and Uehlinger 1998:360).

The superior quality of building materials used for Solomon's Temple is striking. Both Temples employed stone, with significant use of wood paneling. But the historian in 1 Kings makes a good bit of Solomon's use of prefinished, quarried stone (1 Kgs 6:7) and his employment of cedar planks, paneling, and boards for walls and ceilings (1 Kgs 6:15-20), cypress floors (1 Kgs 6:15), cherubim of olive wood (1 Kgs 6:23), olive wood doors at the Most Holy Place (1 Kgs 6:31-32), and cypress doors at the sanctuary entrance (1 Kgs 6:33-35). None of the kinds of wood in Ezekiel's Temple are designated. Solomon's lavish use of pure gold for overlay and for actual building most obviously differentiates the first Temple from the one in Ezekiel's vision. Solomon's Temple featured pure gold overlay on its walls, ceilings, and floor, as well as on the cherubim and doors, with actual gold construction material (not just overlay) for lampstands, basins, and chains (1 Kgs 6:20-35; 2 Chr 3:3–4:8, including overlay with jewels!; 2 Chr 3:6). In addition, an altar, "the Sea" (2 Chr 4:15), oxen, water basin, and tables were cast out of bronze (2 Chr 4:11-22). In contrast, no mention of gold or jewels or bronze appears in the entire description of Ezekiel's Temple compound. Whatever glory or dazzling beauty the Ezekiel Temple possesses, it will not be in gold, jewels, and exquisite woods, but rather in the glory of God filling it.

◆ D. Vision of the Lord's New Worship (43:1–46:24)

1. Glory returns to the Temple, Torah, and the altar (43:1-27)

After this, the man brought me back around to the east gateway. [2]Suddenly, the glory of the God of Israel appeared from the east. The sound of his coming was like the roar of rushing waters, and the whole landscape shone with his glory. [3]This vision was just like the others I had seen, first by the Kebar River and then when he came to destroy Jerusalem. I fell face down on the ground. [4]And the glory of the LORD came into the Temple through the east gateway.

[5]Then the Spirit took me up and brought me into the inner courtyard, and the glory of the LORD filled the Temple. [6]And I heard someone speaking to me from within the Temple, while the man who had been measuring stood beside me. [7]The LORD said to me, "Son of man, this is the place of my throne and the place where I will rest my feet. I will live here forever among the people of Israel. They and their kings will not defile my holy name any longer by their adulterous wor-

ship of other gods or by honoring the relics of their kings who have died. 8They put their idol altars right next to mine with only a wall between them and me. They defiled my holy name by such detestable sin, so I consumed them in my anger. 9Now let them stop worshiping other gods and honoring the relics of their kings, and I will live among them forever.

10"Son of man, describe to the people of Israel the Temple I have shown you, so they will be ashamed of all their sins. Let them study its plan, 11and they will be ashamed* of what they have done. Describe to them all the specifications of the Temple—including its entrances and exits—and everything else about it. Tell them about its decrees and laws. Write down all these specifications and decrees as they watch so they will be sure to remember and follow them. 12And this is the basic law of the Temple: absolute holiness! The entire top of the mountain where the Temple is built is holy. Yes, this is the basic law of the Temple.

13"These are the measurements of the altar*: There is a gutter all around the altar 21 inches deep and 21 inches wide,* with a curb 9 inches* wide around its edge. And this is the height* of the altar: 14From the gutter the altar rises 3½ feet* to a lower ledge that surrounds the altar and is 21 inches* wide. From the lower ledge the altar rises 7 feet* to the upper ledge that is also 21 inches wide. 15The top of the altar, the hearth, rises another 7 feet higher, with a horn rising up from each of the four corners. 16The top of the altar is square, measuring 21 feet by 21 feet.* 17The upper ledge also forms a square, measuring 24½ feet by 24½ feet,* with a 21-inch gutter and a 10½-inch curb* all around the edge. There are steps going up the east side of the altar."

18Then he said to me, "Son of man, this is what the Sovereign LORD says: These will be the regulations for the burning of offerings and the sprinkling of blood when the altar is built. 19At that time, the Levitical priests of the family of Zadok, who minister before me, are to be given a young bull for a sin offering, says the Sovereign LORD. 20You will take some of its blood and smear it on the four horns of the altar, the four corners of the upper ledge, and the curb that runs around that ledge. This will cleanse and make atonement for the altar. 21Then take the young bull for the sin offering and burn it at the appointed place outside the Temple area.

22"On the second day, sacrifice as a sin offering a young male goat that has no physical defects. Then cleanse and make atonement for the altar again, just as you did with the young bull. 23When you have finished the cleansing ceremony, offer another young bull that has no defects and a perfect ram from the flock. 24You are to present them to the LORD, and the priests are to sprinkle salt on them and offer them as a burnt offering to the LORD.

25"Every day for seven days a male goat, a young bull, and a ram from the flock will be sacrificed as a sin offering. None of these animals may have physical defects of any kind. 26Do this each day for seven days to cleanse and make atonement for the altar, thus setting it apart for holy use. 27On the eighth day, and on each day afterward, the priests will sacrifice on the altar the burnt offerings and peace offerings of the people. Then I will accept you. I, the Sovereign LORD, have spoken!"

43:11 As in Greek version; Hebrew reads *if they are ashamed.* **43:13a** Hebrew *measurements of the altar in long cubits, each being a cubit* [18 inches or 45 centimeters] *and a handbreadth* [3 inches or 8 centimeters] *in length.* **43:13b** Hebrew *a cubit* [53 centimeters] *deep and a cubit wide.* **43:13c** Hebrew *1 span* [23 centimeters]. **43:13d** As in Greek version; Hebrew reads *base.* **43:14a** Hebrew *2 cubits* [1.1 meters]. **43:14b** Hebrew *1 cubit* [53 centimeters]; also in 43:14d. **43:14c** Hebrew *4 cubits* [2.1 meters]; also in 43:15. **43:16** Hebrew *12 cubits* [6.4 meters] *long and 12 cubits wide.* **43:17a** Hebrew *14 cubits* [7.4 meters] *long and 14 cubits wide.* **43:17b** Hebrew *a gutter of 1 cubit* [53 centimeters] *and a curb of ½ a cubit* [27 centimeters].

NOTES

43:3 ***when he came to destroy Jerusalem.*** The MT and LXX have "when *I* came to destroy," a difficult reading, since no other reference in the book has Ezekiel coming to destroy Jerusalem. The NLT's third-person reading ("he") takes the MT as the result of a confusion of the similar-looking letters Waw and Yodh, a mistake easily made at some stages of the book's transmission in Hebrew. The reference is probably to the vision event in 9:3-4.

43:9 ***the relics of their kings.*** "Relics" (*pegarim* [TH6297, ZH7007]) may refer to royal stelae, judging from an Ugaritic cognate (Allen 1990:257; see bibliography cited there). Such objects would introduce alien, competing claims to glory in the Temple compound. The term *pegarim* normally refers to corpses (as e.g., in 6:5); several translations render along this line (e.g., KJV, NRSV, ESV, NASB).

43:11 ***and they will be ashamed.*** On the problem of Yahweh shaming his people, see the commentary on 36:16-32. Perhaps the conditional clause of the MT should be retained (with NKJV, NIV, NASB, NRSV, ESV, REB), instead of following a common emendation with LXX and Vulgate: "and if they are ashamed of all they have done" (NIV). Lapsley (2000:179) suggests that in Ezekiel's understanding of Israel's moral transformation, Israel's shame is a "necessary precondition of a full, detailed knowledge of the Temple."

Describe to them all the specifications of the Temple. . . . Tell them about its decrees and laws. This makes it clear that Ezekiel was to write about what he had seen in the preceding Temple tour and also to write about the more instructive, "Torah-like" material that follows. Hence these verses serve simultaneously as a conclusion to the preceding narrative and as an introduction to the oracles to follow (Allen 1990:250; Keil and Delitzsch 1989:282-283).

43:12 ***this is the basic law of the Temple.*** Heb., *zo'th torath* [TH8451, ZH9368] *habbayith.* Does this line describe the preceding tour report (chs 40–42) or the instruction to follow regarding Temple personnel and protocol (43:13ff)? Some think *torah* and the earlier title "decrees" (*khuqqoth* [TH2708, ZH2978]) make poor descriptors for the foregoing report of the Temple tour (chs 40–42), a narrative with major attention to architectural features of the Temple compound (Block 1998:590-591; Eichrodt 1970:556). As such, 43:10-12 should be taken as introductory for the following oracles. Similar priestly formulae known from Leviticus as *introductory* superscriptions support such a view (e.g., Lev 6:9, 14, 25; 7:1, 11). At the same time, the use of such formulae as *concluding* subscripts in Leviticus makes the appeal to priestly usage there inconclusive and at least opens 43:10-12 to construal as a conclusion of the Temple tour report (cf. Lev 11:46; 13:59; 14:32, 54; Zimmerli 1983:419).

43:13 ***There is a gutter all around the altar.*** "Gutter" here translates MT's *kheq* [TH2436, ZH2668], a technical architectural term (HALOT 1:313) having to do with the bottom of the altar (thus RSV, "base"); so also v. 14. In 43:14, however, where the NLT also translates "gutter," the MT has an expanded form, *kheq ha'arets* [TH776, ZH824]. This has prompted some, following W. F. Albright (1968:146-147), to translate "Bosom of the Earth," comparing Akkadian ziggurat (i.e., step pyramid) terminology.

43:15 ***The top of the altar, the hearth.*** This is called *hahar'el* [TH2022, ZH2215] in MT, but the versions read it as *ha'ari'el* [cf. TH738, ZH787], a term that occurs later in this verse, evidently as a reference to the same object. The meaning of both phrases is a puzzle; we would expect their respective meanings to be "the mountain of God/El" and "the lion of God/El," but one wonders at such a name for an altar hearth. A completely different etymology associates the word with burning and thus the simple meaning of "(altar) hearth" (HALOT 1:87). Albright's suggestion that this terminology reflects Akkadian ziggurat terminology, "mountain of God," should not yet be dismissed, especially if *har'el* is a gloss on *'ari'el* (Tuell 1992:48-51). Block's review of recent possible explanations shows how tentative any conclusion must be (1998:600-601).

43:18 ***These will be the regulations.*** This is another scribal superscription known from Levitical style (Lev 6:9, 14, 25; 7:1, 11).

43:24 ***sprinkle salt.*** Being the preservative par excellence in the world of the OT, salt also functioned as a symbol of things that last, that have or require durability or faithfulness. The connection here is quite likely that given in Lev 2:13, "salt to remind you of God's eternal covenant" (lit., "the salt of the covenant of your God"). Thus, turning the words around, "a covenant of salt" (i.e., "a covenant administered with salt" or "solemnized with a liturgy including salt") indicated a covenant regarded as enduring, dependable. The salt underscores both the covenant itself and the particular offering as a significant facet of honoring it (Milgrom 1991:191-192).

COMMENTARY

The dazzling appearance of the glory of the God of Israel dramatically interrupted Ezekiel's guided tour at the exterior east gateway (43:1-2). As had happened first at the Kebar River in chapters 1–3, the appearance of the glory of the Lord was a preface to the programmatic giving of the word of the Lord (1:28ff). Upon the return of the glory of the Lord to the Temple (43:4-5), the Glorious One spoke from within the Temple (43:6). Thus, the narrative interruption provides an introduction to a series of oracles giving "Temple Torah" (43:12). The oracles stretch from 43:6 through 46:18, with only brief narrative notes at 44:1 and at 46:19-24. The tour becomes primarily the setting for hearing the word of Yahweh.

As Ezekiel's guide brought him back to the exterior east gateway where the tour had begun (43:1; cf. 40:5), the glory of the Lord appeared without warning, approaching from the east, in which direction it had departed in the previous Temple vision (9:3; 10:3-4, 18-19; 11:22-23). Ezekiel explicitly compared this visionary experience of the Shekinah to those described in chapters 1–3 and 8–11, thus encouraging readers to make the obvious connection to the vision of the earlier experiences (43:3). The arrival of the Glory of the Lord in Solomon's grand Temple climaxed its dedication four centuries earlier (1 Kgs 8:10-11). The departure of the Glory of the Lord carried away by the cherubim proclaimed the demise of the Temple (10:18-19; 11:22-23). The removal of Yahweh's throne and his presence from that Temple signaled his dramatic abandonment of the corrupt Temple. The sanctuary of the Temple, the *hekhal* [TH1964, ZH2121], actually constituted Yahweh's "palace"; according to Temple theology, the Most Holy Place was the throne room of the divine King. In 43:2-5 Yahweh "re-hallows" the Temple, making it his home, entering via the gate by which he had left earlier.

Ezekiel is transported to the inner courtyard, and the Lord speaks to him from within the Temple (43:6). The guide stands beside Ezekiel, listening as the Lord himself speaks. To this point in the tour, only the man has spoken, presumably on behalf of Yahweh (40:4, 45; 41:22; 42:13). Now, significantly, the Lord himself speaks to Ezekiel from the Temple. Ezekiel introduces it with language echoing the speaking glory in 1:28: "I fell face down on the ground, and I heard someone's voice speaking to me" (cf. 43:4, 6).

In the first of these oracles the Lord reclaims the Temple as his throne and footstool (43:7-9). Of course, throne and footstool are royal furniture, the throne bespeaking sovereign rule, and the footstool imaging enemies now under the sovereign's feet. Thus, Yahweh interprets his reappearance in the Temple as the resumption of his rightful rule among his people and the world. Not that he forfeited his kingship in his departure from the Temple—he continued accomplishing his purposes among the nations. But the return of the Glory to his throne signals a turn in salvation history as epochal as the establishment of his people at Sinai, as significant as his commitment to rule through a Davidic son, and to own Solomon's Temple as the seat of his governance of the earth (1 Kgs 8:10-21).

Yahweh then excludes from the new Temple any of the national or royal behaviors that defiled his holy name and brought about the destruction of the first Temple (43:7b-9). He specifically excludes the introduction of idolatrous practices or architectural modifications compromising or breaching the sanctity of his Temple. While we do not know what particular incidents Ezekiel had in mind here, the Temple modifications under King Ahaz and desecrations sponsored by Manasseh come immediately to mind (2 Kgs 16:10-18; 21:1-6).

There may even be a causal relationship between the two aspects of this paragraph: Because Yahweh will live among them forever, his people will stop defiling his holy name. Here is a point where Ezekiel's vision, whatever its symbolic nature or eschatological tack, seems aimed directly at some abuse in the exilic or early postexilic community. Although Ezekiel names no particular abuse, he could well have had in mind something like the offering of defective animals and the compromise of worship by tolerance toward domestic violence that, according to Malachi, showed contempt for Yahweh's name (Mal 1:6-9; 2:13-16).

The Lord reextends the charge given by the guide in 40:4 (43:10-12). Ezekiel is to describe accurately for the people all that he has been shown and to write it *all* down before the exiles' eyes, with an emphasis on comprehensive reporting. Yahweh specifies the content to be conveyed: the Temple's plan, especially entrances, exits, and traffic flow, as well as regulations (43:11-12, "decrees," *khuqqoth* [TH2708, ZH2978], "laws," *toroth* [TH8451, ZH9368], "specifications" *tsuroth* [TH6699, ZH7451]) governing the use of the Temple.

Although modern readers have lost some of the information needed to make clear sense of the text, Ezekiel assumed his readers would be instructed and influenced toward holy living by study of the Temple's design, dimensions, and accompanying explanations. Such a response is possible, says Zimmerli, because of "the proclamation of salvation encoded in the architectural plan" itself (1983:419). Ezekiel underscores the import of the aspects of the Temple to be described by placing the list of them before the verb (43:11; i.e., NLT's "all the specifications of the Temple—including its entrances and exits—and everything else about it . . . its decrees and laws" precedes the verb "tell/describe" in the MT). Additionally, the Lord's instructions to write a document to support the study of this revelation assumes or perhaps confers upon the text a certain canonicity. This text of Ezekiel's would be worthy of preservation and study by the community. The sorts of goals one might associate with oral prophetic ministries, the Lord here transfers to prophetic writing. One thinks of the same phenomenon involving the writing of Jeremiah's first scroll (Jer 36), where the reading of the scroll written at Jeremiah's dictation was tantamount to hearing the prophetic word directly.

A twofold intent prompted Ezekiel's writing of these instructions. Yahweh indicates (1) that his people will be ashamed of their past sins, especially their desecration of the first Temple, and (2) that consequently they will in the future observe the new Temple's decrees and laws (43:10-11). The theme that Yahweh would bring his people back to the land in order to shame them into obedience surfaces for the last time in these verses (cf. 16:53-54, 61-63; 20:26; 36:32). On the problem of Yahweh's restoration of his people in order to shame them, see the commentary on 36:16-32.

Important as 43:10-12 is, its precise role is contested (see note on 43:12). In the end, it appears the paragraph functions both as a conclusion for the preceding Temple tour narrative (chs 40–42) and as an introduction for the following oracles (Allen 1990:238, 250; Keil and Delitzsch 1989:282-283). Emphasis falls (43:12) on the "basic law of the Temple," a *torah* [TH8451, ZH9368] expressed architecturally in the Temple and safeguarded by statutes and decrees regarding Temple personnel and protocol soon to follow in the text. That "basic law" mandates a reality that shall pertain to the entire mountaintop containing the Temple—"absolute holiness" (43:12). Translated literally, "absolute holiness" would be "holiest of holy things." The sanctity reserved for the Most Holy Place in Solomon's Temple will cover the entire Temple compound and environs of the new Temple! This basic law is sandwiched between the twice-pronounced rubric, "This is the basic law of the Temple" (43:12).

The Temple's main and only exterior altar is the first item treated following this "basic law" of the Temple (43:10-12). (Recall an interior, much smaller altar/table for the Bread of the Presence in 41:22.) Strangely, the altar is never actually shown to Ezekiel, though it arises within Ezekiel's vision experience. Instead, the one speaking from the Temple describes the altar and prescribes its dimensions to Ezekiel, commencing with the formal introductory formula, "these are the measurements of the altar" (43:13). This is the sort of formulaic superscript appealed to in our attempt to understand "this is the basic law of the Temple" in 43:12 (e.g., Lev 7:1). The dimensions themselves constitute part of Temple Torah.

Shaped like a step pyramid, 17½ feet high, the altar dominated the inner court space in front of the Temple. Its foundation measured 35 feet square, with the succeeding levels and then the hearth measuring 31½ feet, 28 feet, and 21 feet square, respectively (43:13-17). Steps led up the east side of the altar, orienting worship to the Temple itself, and not to the east as the elders had bowed in Ezekiel's earlier Temple vision (8:16). Atop the altar, the sacrifice stood between the priest and the presence of Yahweh.

All sacrifices were burned on the hearth of this solitary altar. Years ago it was claimed that both the altar in Solomon's Temple and this one in Ezekiel's Temple evoked the mountainesque shape of a Babylonian ziggurat (i.e., a step pyramid); this idea was buttressed with an appeal to cognate Akkadian terminology related to the cosmic mountain (Albright 1968:147). Albright's linguistic evidence has been undercut by Block (1998:600) and Zimmerli (1983:426-429), but Ezekiel's naming of the altar's foundation as "Bosom of the Earth" and its hearth as "Mountain of God" still should perhaps be taken to indicate a Temple theology that locates the cosmic mountain, the mountain of God, at the Temple (Levenson 1985:139). Here heaven and earth meet in the worship of Yahweh and transactions of cosmic significance occur. (See notes on 43:13-15 for details of the NLT's rendering.)

The placement of the altar's description could indicate the import or necessity of preserving the sanctity of the altar and with it the Temple. It is the only major cult object (other than the small altar for the Bread of the Presence at 41:22) treated in the tour and the first instance of explicit three-dimensional measuring, where not only width and breadth but also height receives note. Other cult objects such as lampstands or lavers known from earlier Tabernacle or first Temple construction do not figure here. Block notes the altar's central import in purifying the Temple grounds (1998:596). Clearly the altar, and the purified worship it represented, had special import for Ezekiel.

The precise measurements for the altar likely imply use of hewn blocks for the altar's construction, and steps flank the east side of the altar. Against this, Mosaic Torah called for *un*hewn stone construction and forbade steps for the altar (Exod 20:24-26). Moses may well assume construction of a much smaller altar, in deliberate contrast to large altars known already from Egypt and some Canaanite installations. But an altar the size of Ezekiel's needed steps or some such means for reaching the hearth on top, Yahweh's provision of "an effective means of service," as Block says (1998:601). We have no information on the presence or absence of steps for the altar in either the Solomonic or the Second Temple (1 Kgs 8:22; 2 Chr 4:1; Ezra 3:2-3), so comparison there fails. What are we to make of this difference between the altar here and that prescribed through Moses? Even if we do not look for a literal fulfillment of Ezekiel's altar, we cannot evaporate the problem through some sort of symbolism. One would still have to ask about the meaning of the symbol. Perhaps the cleansing of the altar was thought to atone for these breaches of Torah (Bunn 1971:358). More likely, we have here another feature of the new word spoken by Yahweh through Ezekiel.

Another Temple Torah superscription marks out 43:18-27: "These will be the regulations for the burning of offerings and the sprinkling of blood when the altar is built" (43:18). Interestingly, in this oracle the altar is yet to be built, unlike the surrounding realities shown to the prophet as already in place. This lapse in the logic of the vision may signal redactional activity. Or perhaps we have a place here where Ezekiel moves momentarily out of a visionary stance into a historical view, something like the several movements between allegory and history in chapters 16 and 23. Except for 43:27, these regulations pertain not to the general offerings (for which see 45:13–46:15) but to the purification and inauguration of the altar, the liturgical hallowing of it. This is in keeping with the Temple Torah underscoring the particularly sacred nature of the Temple and its whole area. The central focus of the compound above all must be marked as holy (43:12).

Anticipating the personnel restrictions yet to follow (44:5-16), only the Zadokite Levites will officiate at the dedication (43:19). No explanation of the various offerings appears. The designations come from traditional priestly practice in Israel, and the instructions assume knowledge of the sin offering, the whole burnt offering, and the peace offering (cf. Lev 1–7).

The purification of the altar would be a seven-day ceremony. In this regard it would follow the purification of the ancient altar of burnt offering for the Tabernacle (Exod 29:36-37, 44) and the seven-day ordination ceremony of Aaron and his sons as well (Exod 29:10-18). The dedication of Solomon's Temple also covered seven days, but accounts available make no note of a special dedication of the altar (1 Kgs 8:62-65; 2 Chr 7:1-10). Ezekiel calls for more extensive attention to the consecration of the altar itself than did Solomon at the dedication of his Temple. In other matters as well, the regulations for the dedication of the new Temple's altar reach behind Solomon's practice to the more ancient Torah for the Tabernacle.

The ceremony commences with a sin offering to "cleanse and make atonement for the altar" (43:19-20). As with the ordination of Aaron, the blood of the sin offering will be applied to the altar, but the animal itself will be burned *outside* of the sacred area involved (there the camp, here the Temple precinct; see 43:21; cf. Exod 29:14). The ultimate purpose of the cleansing of and atoning for the altar is to "[set] it apart for holy use" (43:26). The Hebrew expression is identical for the "ordination" of Aaron (Exod 29:9)—"to fill its hands" for a specific task. Why this requires cleansing and atoning Ezekiel does not say. The ancient explanation of atoning for the altar to be used on the Day of Atonement was to "cleanse it from Israel's defilement and make it holy" (Lev 16:19). Some such phrasing would likely explain Ezekiel's instruction. In restored Israel and in the strictly hallowed new Temple compound, movement from profane to sacred space or use would require deliberate cleansing from the contamination of human contact.

Just how the progression of offerings in 43:18-24 should be reconciled with the apparent summary statement of 43:25 remains unclear. The summary seems plain enough: For each of the ceremony's seven days, "a male goat, a young bull, and a ram from the flock," all without defect, will be offered as a sin offering and for the hallowing of the altar. In contrast to this, 43:18-24 has a young bull as a sin offering on day one (v. 19), a young male goat and then another young bull and a ram on day two (v. 22-23), and no other specific directions for days three through seven. Perhaps verse 25 is not a summary for all the days, but rather direction for the remaining days (i.e., three through seven). The purpose for all of this is to set the altar apart for holy use by cleansing and making atonement for the altar (43:26). On the eighth day, the daily sacrifices to be offered in perpetuity for the community in general begin: the burnt offerings and the peace offerings of the people. The result will be Yahweh's acceptance of the people (43:27), implying their continuing need for such acceptance. As in the Levitical sacrifices, acceptance by Yahweh remains an important effect even of those offerings that do not deal with sin or guilt or explicit breaches of covenant.

◆ 2. The priesthood (44:1-31)

Then the man brought me back to the east
gateway in the outer wall of the Temple
area, but it was closed. 2And the LORD said
to me, "This gate must remain closed; it
will never again be opened. No one will
ever open it and pass through, for the
LORD, the God of Israel, has entered here.
Therefore, it must always remain shut.
3Only the prince himself may sit inside
this gateway to feast in the LORD's pres-
ence. But he may come and go only
through the entry room of the gateway."

4Then the man brought me through the
north gateway to the front of the Temple.
I looked and saw that the glory of the
LORD filled the Temple of the LORD, and I
fell face down on the ground.

5And the LORD said to me, "Son of man,

take careful notice. Use your eyes and ears, and listen to everything I tell you about the regulations concerning the LORD's Temple. Take careful note of the procedures for using the Temple's entrances and exits. 6And give these rebels, the people of Israel, this message from the Sovereign LORD: O people of Israel, enough of your detestable sins! 7You have brought uncircumcised foreigners into my sanctuary—people who have no heart for God. In this way, you defiled my Temple even as you offered me my food, the fat and blood of sacrifices. In addition to all your other detestable sins, you have broken my covenant. 8Instead of safeguarding my sacred rituals, you have hired foreigners to take charge of my sanctuary.

9"So this is what the Sovereign LORD says: No foreigners, including those who live among the people of Israel, will enter my sanctuary if they have not been circumcised and have not surrendered themselves to the LORD. 10And the men of the tribe of Levi who abandoned me when Israel strayed away from me to worship idols* must bear the consequences of their unfaithfulness. 11They may still be Temple guards and gatekeepers, and they may slaughter the animals brought for burnt offerings and be present to help the people. 12But they encouraged my people to worship idols, causing Israel to fall into deep sin. So I have taken a solemn oath that they must bear the consequences for their sins, says the Sovereign LORD. 13They may not approach me to minister as priests. They may not touch any of my holy things or the holy offerings, for they must bear the shame of all the detestable sins they have committed. 14They are to serve as the Temple caretakers, taking charge of the maintenance work and performing general duties.

15"However, the Levitical priests of the family of Zadok continued to minister faithfully in the Temple when Israel abandoned me for idols. These men will serve as my ministers. They will stand in my presence and offer the fat and blood of the sacrifices, says the Sovereign LORD. 16They alone will enter my sanctuary and approach my table to serve me. They will fulfill all my requirements.

17"When they enter the gateway to the inner courtyard, they must wear only linen clothing. They must wear no wool while on duty in the inner courtyard or in the Temple itself. 18They must wear linen turbans and linen undergarments. They must not wear anything that would cause them to perspire. 19When they return to the outer courtyard where the people are, they must take off the clothes they wear while ministering to me. They must leave them in the sacred rooms and put on other clothes so they do not endanger anyone by transmitting holiness to them through this clothing.

20"They must neither shave their heads nor let their hair grow too long. Instead, they must trim it regularly. 21The priests must not drink wine before entering the inner courtyard. 22They may choose their wives only from among the virgins of Israel or the widows of the priests. They may not marry other widows or divorced women. 23They will teach my people the difference between what is holy and what is common, what is ceremonially clean and unclean.

24"They will serve as judges to resolve any disagreements among my people. Their decisions must be based on my regulations. And the priests themselves must obey my instructions and decrees at all the sacred festivals, and see to it that the Sabbaths are set apart as holy days.

25"A priest must not defile himself by being in the presence of a dead person unless it is his father, mother, child, brother, or unmarried sister. In such cases it is permitted. 26Even then, he can return to his Temple duties only after being ceremonially cleansed and then waiting for seven days. 27The first day he returns to work and enters the inner courtyard and the sanctuary, he must offer a sin offering for himself, says the Sovereign LORD.

28"The priests will not have any prop-

erty or possession of land, for I alone am their special possession. 29Their food will come from the gifts and sacrifices brought to the Temple by the people—the grain offerings, the sin offerings, and the guilt offerings. Whatever anyone sets apart* for the LORD will belong to the priests.
30The first of the ripe fruits and all the gifts brought to the LORD will go to the priests. The first samples of each grain harvest and the first of your flour must also be given to the priests so the LORD will bless your homes. 31The priests may not eat meat from any bird or animal that dies a natural death or that dies after being attacked by another animal.

44:10 The Hebrew term (literally *round things*) probably alludes to dung; also in 44:12. **44:29** The Hebrew term used here refers to the complete consecration of things or people to the LORD, either by destroying them or by giving them as an offering.

NOTES

44:3 ***the prince.*** This is the Davidic ruler, the shepherd-king (see commentary on 34:23-24).

44:9 ***foreigners.*** The identity of the "foreigners" named here remains unclear. One might think of the Temple servants listed among the returnees from exile in Ezra 2:43-58 and Neh 7:46-60, but one would expect these to have been incorporated into the Yahweh-fearing community. Perhaps the Carites, who served David and later were loyal to Davidic rulers, are a more likely identification (2 Kgs 11:4-7; Allen 1990:260-261, but see Hobbs 1985:139).

have not surrendered themselves to the LORD. Lit., "not circumcised in heart," as in most versions ancient and modern (cf. not circumcised "in mind" [REB], or "in spirit" [NJPS]). According to Deut 10:16 (cf. NLT mg), to be "circumcised in heart" is to be finished with the stubbornness associated with disobedience and idolatry. "Uncircumcised in flesh" meant the foreigners had not become proselytes, joined the covenant community, or taken its sign on themselves.

44:19 ***transmitting holiness.*** "Transmitting" holiness by contact turns out to be much less pervasive in the OT than often thought. Generally, when unholy or unconsecrated persons touched holy things, they did not become holy; they became dead (Thompson 1975:38-47). Nevertheless, preventing the transmission of holiness by contact does seem to be the point here.

COMMENTARY

Ezekiel's tour of the Temple, suspended at 43:1-5, now resumes at 44:1. The tour narrative had stopped for the hearing of the Lord's word regarding Temple Torah (43:6-12), the measurement of the altar (43:13-17), and the inaugural consecration of the altar (43:18-27). Now the guide conducts Ezekiel from the inner court (43:5) to the east gate of the Temple's outer wall (44:1). As in 43:1-5, the narrative provides a new literary context, shifting the vantage point from which to hear Yahweh speak. As a perpetual reminder of the return of the glorious one to his Temple, the east gateway through which the glory of the Lord returned to the Temple (44:2) would remain closed to all traffic. Not even the prince, who is the Davidic ruler (see 34:24; 37:25), would traverse that gateway, though he would be allowed "to feast in the LORD's presence" there (44:3). This would refer to the eating of the various peace offerings that involve feasting on meat from those sacrifices (cf. Lev 7:11-16).

After being brought through the inner north gate to the front of the Temple,

Ezekiel again fell on his face at the sight of the glory of the Lord filling the Temple. It is the posture of worship, submission, and petition (44:4; cf. 43:3). In this posture Ezekiel heard the ensuing words from the Lord (44:5–46:18), perhaps inviting the reader to an equally submissive posture in the hearing of the message. The Lord spoke to a wide range of issues, including the issue of admittance to the Temple and its spheres of service for foreigners, Levites, and Zadokite priests (44:6-16); the protocol for priestly clothing, hair, duties, defilement, and holding of property (44:17-31); land for a national sacred area (45:1-5); a sector for a city and all Israel (45:6); and the land for the prince (45:7-8; see 34:24; 37:25). The continued description of Ezekiel's audience as "rebels" (44:6) brings the reader back to the purpose of the book as a whole. Although the period of restoration is under discussion, the publication of the book, like the prophetic word itself, was aimed at penetrating the rebellious mind-set of the exilic and early postexilic audience.

Admittance to the Temple receives attention first (44:7-8). Unassimilated and unincorporated foreigners are barred from the Temple. The ethnic or professional identity of these persons remains a mystery, but the criteria leading to their exclusion do not. They are foreigners, and although they live among God's people, they have not joined that covenant community by physical circumcision and have resisted the way of the Lord, remaining unsubmissive to him (lit., "uncircumcised in heart"). Their entry to the Temple would be a serious breach of the new Temple Torah. A similar prohibition blocked foreigners from the Herodian Temple. Clear notices at intervals in the wall that separated the Court of the Women from the Court of (Israelite) Men and of the Priests declared: "No foreigner may enter within the barricade which surrounds the temple and enclosure. Anyone who is caught doing so will have himself to blame for what follows—death!" (Clermont-Ganneau 1871; Josephus *Antiquities* 15.418-419 [15.11.5]; *War* 5.194 [5.5.2]).

The Levites were permitted to serve as Temple guards and gatekeepers, but were not to function as priests, approaching the Lord or touching holy things, including all offerings (44:10-14). They could help the people by slaughtering the sacrifice and giving other assistance, but could not actually "present" the offering to the Lord at the altar. This constituted a restriction of their access and work authorization as a consequence of their history of unfaithful leadership. (Early on, a similar restriction allowed Aaron and his sons [a subset of the Levites] to bring offerings to the altar, but restricted non-Aaronide Levites to other worship service; Lev 8:6-7; Num 3:1-3; 18:2-6.) The Levites had led the people into idolatry and sin (cf. 14:1-11). What specific historical episodes we should call to mind are not clear. Early recollections of Levite zeal for the Lord were positive (Exod 32:26-28). But if, as seems likely, the priests whom King Josiah brought to Jerusalem from the shrines around Judah were Levites, then the Levites had become compromised in their loyalty to the Lord and stumbling blocks to faithful worship (2 Kgs 23:4-8). Also, the historic proscription of non-Aaronide priests from offering sacrifice had been breached (Num 18:6). Their apostasy could be traced back into the earlier kingdom period. The fact that these priests from shrines outside Jerusalem were not allowed to participate in altar service in the Jerusalem Temple indicates their probable censure (2 Kgs 23:9). The Deuteronomic historian calls these individuals "priests," but in Ezekiel they are simply Levites, the designation "priest" reserved for Zadokites.

Historically, the Elide branch of the Aaronides rose to ascendency and then, because of corruption within the Elides (1 Sam 3:11-15), they were replaced by the Zadokites. Zadokite priests were Aaronide Levites descended from Zadok, a priest in Davidic service who superseded Abiathar as high priest when the latter was banished to Anathoth for supporting Adonijah instead of Solomon as David's successor (1 Kgs 2:21-27). In Deuteronomic teaching, Levites and Zadokites shared priestly duties (Deut 12:2-18; 14:27; 16:11; 18:6-8). Although Ezekiel's earlier accounts of proceedings in the Jerusalem Temple have implicitly not been complimentary of Zadokite service (chs 8, 9, 11, etc.), they apparently should not be taken as a rejection of the Zadokites in general. Here they are remembered as faithful and rewarded for it. According to Ezekiel, unlike the Levites, the Zadokites would function as bona fide priests, with full access to most holy things and spaces (44:15-16).

In 44:17-31 various regulations follow to minimize priestly defilement by the Zadokites, to reinforce their calling, and to provide for their support in food and dwelling. They are to wear only linen in the inner court (44:17; cf. Exod 39:27-29; Lev 6:10; 16:4) in order to avoid perspiring and presumably to avoid uncleanness through bodily secretions. This clothing would be taken off and left in the sacred changing rooms so as to protect others from having holiness transmitted to them through it (cf. 42:13-14). As stipulated in Leviticus 10:6 and 21:5, 10, the Zadokites were not to shave their heads or let their hair grow long (44:20). The prohibition against drinking wine before entering the sanctuary replicates Leviticus 10:9. The permission to marry only Israelite virgins or widows of priests comes from Leviticus 21:7, 13-14. Their charge to teach the Lord's people the difference between what is holy and common, ceremonially clean and unclean, carries on the central task of the Levitical priesthood established by Moses (44:23; Lev 10:10-11). They will also adjudicate in disagreements among God's people (44:24), transferring an earlier practice of the Levitical priests to the Zadokites (Deut 17:8-13). The priests are to be models for the community by their own obedience and observance of Torah (44:24). Earlier Levitical custom will govern their contact with the dead (44:25-27; Lev 21:1-2). The more stringent restriction prohibiting the chief priest from contact even with his parents in their death is not adopted, quite likely because no chief priest appears among the Temple personnel of Ezekiel's vision (Lev 21:11). This may not be significant, however, since no chief priest appears here or elsewhere in Ezekiel.

Finally, the Lord speaks regarding provision of food and shelter for Temple personnel (44:28–45:6). These stipulations are grounded theologically in the *Lord's* role as the priests' sole inheritance (44:28). They will have no other property or possession of land. Two consequences follow from their peculiar situation. First, they will have their food from the gifts and sacrifices brought to the Temple—grain offerings, sin offerings, and guilt offerings, as well as firstfruits where appropriate (44:29, adapting Num 18:8-20). Second, they are not to eat any animals that die on their own or by attack from other animals (44:31; cf. Lev 22:8). This prohibition applied to the whole community in early tradition (Lev 7:24).

◆ 3. Land allotment (45:1-25)

"When you divide the land among the tribes of Israel, you must set aside a section for the LORD as his holy portion. This piece of land will be 8 1/3 miles long and 6 2/3 miles wide.* The entire area will be holy. 2A section of this land, measuring 875 feet by 875 feet,* will be set aside for the Temple. An additional strip of land 87 1/2 feet* wide is to be left empty all around it. 3Within the larger sacred area, measure out a portion of land 8 1/3 miles long and 3 1/3 miles wide.* Within it the sanctuary of the Most Holy Place will be located. 4This area will be holy, set aside for the priests who minister to the LORD in the sanctuary. They will use it for their homes, and my Temple will be located within it. 5The strip of sacred land next to it, also 8 1/3 miles long and 3 1/3 miles wide, will be a living area for the Levites who work at the Temple. It will be their possession and a place for their towns.*

6"Adjacent to the larger sacred area will be a section of land 8 1/3 miles long and 1 2/3 miles wide.* This will be set aside for a city where anyone in Israel can live.

7"Two special sections of land will be set apart for the prince. One section will share a border with the east side of the sacred lands and city, and the second section will share a border on the west side. Then the far eastern and western borders of the prince's lands will line up with the eastern and western boundaries of the tribal areas. 8These sections of land will be the prince's allotment. Then my princes will no longer oppress and rob my people; they will assign the rest of the land to the people, giving an allotment to each tribe.

9"For this is what the Sovereign LORD says: Enough, you princes of Israel! Stop your violence and oppression and do what is just and right. Quit robbing and cheating my people out of their land. Stop expelling them from their homes, says the Sovereign LORD. 10Use only honest weights and scales and honest measures, both dry and liquid.* 11The homer* will be your standard unit for measuring volume. The ephah and the bath* will each measure one-tenth of a homer. 12The standard unit for weight will be the silver shekel.* One shekel will consist of twenty gerahs, and sixty shekels will be equal to one mina.*

13"You must give this tax to the prince: one bushel of wheat or barley for every 60* you harvest, 14one percent of your olive oil,* 15and one sheep or goat for every 200 in your flocks in Israel. These will be the grain offerings, burnt offerings, and peace offerings that will make atonement for the people who bring them, says the Sovereign LORD. 16All the people of Israel must join in bringing these offerings to the prince. 17The prince will be required to provide offerings that are given at the religious festivals, the new moon celebrations, the Sabbath days, and all other similar occasions. He will provide the sin offerings, burnt offerings, grain offerings, liquid offerings, and peace offerings to purify the people of Israel, making them right with the LORD.*

18"This is what the Sovereign LORD says: In early spring, on the first day of each new year,* sacrifice a young bull with no defects to purify the Temple. 19The priest will take blood from this sin offering and put it on the doorposts of the Temple, the four corners of the upper ledge of the altar, and the gateposts at the entrance to the inner courtyard. 20Do this also on the seventh day of the new year for anyone who has sinned through error or ignorance. In this way, you will purify* the Temple.

21"On the fourteenth day of the first month,* you must celebrate the Passover. This festival will last for seven days. The bread you eat during that time must be made without yeast. 22On the day of Passover the prince will provide a young bull as a sin offering for himself and the people of Israel. 23On each of the seven days of the feast he will prepare a burnt offering to the LORD, consisting of seven

young bulls and seven rams without defects. A male goat will also be given each day for a sin offering. [24]The prince will provide a basket of flour as a grain offering and a gallon of olive oil* with each young bull and ram.

[25]"During the seven days of the Festival of Shelters, which occurs every year in early autumn,* the prince will provide these same sacrifices for the sin offering, the burnt offering, and the grain offering, along with the required olive oil.

45:1 As in Greek version, which reads *25,000 cubits* [13.3 kilometers] *long and 20,000 cubits* [10.6 kilometers] *wide;* Hebrew reads *25,000 cubits long and 10,000 cubits* [3 1/3 miles or 5.3 kilometers] *wide.* Compare 45:3, 5; 48:9. **45:2a** Hebrew *500 cubits* [265 meters] *by 500 cubits, a square.* **45:2b** Hebrew *50 cubits* [26.5 meters]. **45:3** Hebrew *25,000 cubits* [13.3 kilometers] *long and 10,000 cubits* [5.3 kilometers] *wide;* also in 45:5. **45:5** As in Greek version; Hebrew reads *They will have as their possession 20 rooms.* **45:6** Hebrew *25,000 cubits* [13.3 kilometers] *long and 5,000 cubits* [2.65 kilometers] *wide.* **45:10** Hebrew *use honest scales, an honest ephah, and an honest bath.* **45:11a** The *homer* measures about 40 gallons or 182 liters. **45:11b** The *ephah* is a dry measure; the *bath* is a liquid measure. **45:12a** The *shekel* weighs about 0.4 ounces or 11 grams. **45:12b** Elsewhere the *mina* is equated to 50 shekels. **45:13** Hebrew *1/6 of an ephah from each homer of wheat and 1/6 of an ephah from each homer of barley.* **45:14** Hebrew *the portion of oil, measured by the bath, is 1/10 of a bath from each cor, which consists of 10 baths or 1 homer, for 10 baths are equivalent to a homer.* **45:17** Or *to make atonement for the people of Israel.* **45:18** Hebrew *On the first day of the first month,* of the Hebrew calendar. This day in the ancient Hebrew lunar calendar occurred in March or April. **45:20** Or *will make atonement for.* **45:21** This day in the ancient Hebrew lunar calendar occurred in late March, April, or early May. **45:24** Hebrew *an ephah* [20 quarts or 22 liters] *of flour . . . and a hin* [3.8 liters] *of olive oil.* **45:25** Hebrew *the festival which begins on the fifteenth day of the seventh month* (see Lev 23:34). This day in the ancient Hebrew lunar calendar occurred in late September, October, or early November.

NOTES

45:12 ***sixty shekels will be equal to one mina.*** For some reason, the MT follows the Babylonian sexagesimal system of 60 shekels to the mina, rather than the traditional Phoenician/Israelite measure of 50 to one (as in LXX).

45:13 ***tax to the prince.*** "Tax" renders *terumah* [TH8641, ZH9556], a term that provides thematic unity to this part of Ezekiel's vision. The word refers to offerings or gifts brought to the Lord (44:30), and in Ezekiel it usually designates the portion of land set apart as sacred to the Lord (45:1, 7; 48:8, 9, 10, 12, 18, 20, 21). Here it names the regular provisions the people are to supply to the prince to underwrite his support of national worship, hence the rendering "tax." Since this is not one of the common words for "tax" (*mas* [TH4522, ZH4989], *mas'eth* [TH4864A, ZH5368], *minkhah* [TH4503, ZH4966], *middah* [TH4503, ZH4501], or *mekes* [TH4371, ZH4830]), we should probably keep in mind the "contribution" nuance carried by the term.

45:25 ***Festival of Shelters.*** The NLT makes explicit the identity of the feast that is implicit in the MT. Traditionally known as the Feast of Booths or Feast of Tabernacles, this festival is known especially from Lev 23:39; Num 29:12-39; and Deut 16:13-15. Living for a week in makeshift shelters (booths, tents), Israel celebrated the Lord's yearly agricultural provision for them by recalling God's miraculous provision for Israel in the wilderness. For a full treatment of the sorts of exegesis involved in the reappropriation of Mosaic Torah offered by Ezekiel in ch 45 and its surrounding context, see Fishbane 1985, chs 9 and 14.

COMMENTARY

The Zadokites will be given space for housing on land devoted to the Lord *for* them but not belonging to them. Pursuit of this topic takes Ezekiel into a summary of the division of the land that he will address further in chapter 48 (Tuell 1992:62). The portion designated for the Zadokites will include a square of land for the

Temple (45:3). The Lord's concern for protecting the sacral purity of the Temple appears graphically here. Thus, even though the Temple is situated on land already specially devoted to the Lord, it is nevertheless to have an 87½ foot wide strip of land bordering it on all sides and separating its place within the already sacred land (45:2). Parallel to this land on the north, a strip of the same shape and dimensions will be for the Levites and their cities (45:5). This will constitute their possession, even though it belongs peculiarly to the Lord (45:5). An adjacent strip of the same length but half the width will be reserved for a city open to anyone in Israel (45:6). These three strips of land together comprise a square 8⅓ miles on each side (48:20). On either side of this special square of property, territory stretching to the eastern and western borders of the land will be set aside for the prince (45:7-8). The theme of the Temple's holiness receives emphasis in this layout with the city and the prince separated from the Temple. The Lord registers concern to prevent repetition of the abuses perpetrated upon God's people by the kings of Israel and Judah (e.g., 1 Kgs 21:1-19; Mic 3:1-10). A final note in this oracle anticipates the allocation of land to the tribes yet to be detailed (45:8; cf. 47:13–48:29), with Judah's allotment immediately to the north of the Temple area and Benjamin's to the south.

The oracle of 45:9-25 is devoted to the behavior of the princes of Israel (45:9-12) and the funding for the special responsibilities of the prince in providing offerings for Israel's worship and celebrations (45:13-25). The Lord again references the sorry history of royal violence and oppression and calls for an end to this injustice (45:9). He charges the crown with guarding standard weights and measures for the community (45:10). The number of royal stamp and seal impressions on pottery from kingdom period archaeological sites shows the widespread opportunity leaders had either to aid or to prevent the business fraud Ezekiel challenged here. The variety of weights and measures unearthed and evidence for the use of varying systems simultaneously underscores the need for this standardization (Stern 2001:189-200; Dever 2001:221-230). The new community is to have none of the corrupt weights and measures that the prophets condemned centuries earlier (e.g., Amos 8:4-6; Mic 6:10-11; cf. also Lev 19:35-36; Deut 25:13-16). Additionally, sufficient provision is made for the prince that there should be no pretext for royal confiscation of the citizens' lands. This era of economic justice would mean the "realization at long last of a royal ideal" (Allen 1990:265, citing 22:25; 1 Kgs 21:1-16; and Jer 22:1-5, 13-17).

The Lord calls for a proportional "tax" (or, "contribution"; see note on 45:13) by which the people provide grain and animals appropriate for offerings to be used to make atonement for them (45:13-17). This general atonement for the people seems to function in the restored community as the Day of Atonement traditionally would have (Lev 16). Grain offerings, burnt offerings, peace offerings, and sin offerings would be needed to make atonement for the people (45:17). Thus, although the prince has responsibility to make sure these offerings are made (45:17), the people provide the goods for the community's atonement. The grain offerings and libation offerings, traditionally of wine but here of oil, would have been auxiliary gifts accompanying the burnt, peace, and sin offerings (the latter omitted in 45:15; cf. Num 15:1-10).

Ordinances for select festivals appear next (45:18-25). Ezekiel calls first for a purification of the Temple on the first day of each new year. The requirement echoes similar cleansings of the Holy Place, the tent, and the altar in connection with the Day of Atonement in Leviticus 16:15-19 and reminds us of the consecration of the altar (43:18-21). This atonement underscores the need for the furniture and instruments of worship to be purified in preparation for being in the presence of the Lord and also the contaminating impact of human use on these items. Unique to Ezekiel's Temple Torah is the requirement of an additional cleansing of the Temple on the seventh day of the new year for persons who may have sinned inadvertently (45:20).

Finally, provision is made for celebration of the Passover (45:21-24; cf. Exod 12; Lev 23:5-8; Num 28) and the Festival of Shelters (or "booths," "tabernacles"; 45:25; cf. Num 29). Ezekiel's sacrificial provisions for Passover are more extensive than those in the Mosaic Torah (Exod 12:1-20; Num 28:16-22). Ezekiel's provisions for sacrifices in the Festival of Shelters is less extensive and less elaborate than those in the Mosaic tradition (Num 29:12-38). The types of sacrifices required are nearly the same (burnt offering, sin offering, grain offerings in both traditions). The number of animals to be offered and the schedule for offering differs. Unlike the Mosaic legislation that stipulated quite different sacrificial provisions for these two festivals, Ezekiel provides the same sacrifices for both (45:25).

We can make these observations of similarities and differences between Moses's and Ezekiel's treatment of these festivals, but what we should conclude from this data remains unclear. One thing seems probable: Though regarded as authoritative and as the Lord's word, the Mosaic Torah was amenable to revision and adaptation by succeeding communities, at least up to the time of Ezekiel's compilation. This adaptation and revision was not a freewheeling, arbitrary process. But persons sufficiently accredited as reliable students of Moses and authentic spokespersons of the Lord, persons like Ezekiel and later individuals speaking in Ezekiel's name, could offer such revision for the good of the people of God. Both Jesus and the apostles handled the Hebrew Scriptures in this stream of tradition (e.g., Matt 5:17-48; Mark 7:19). This freedom for scriptural revision *theoretically* remains open. Since the formation of the Christian canon, however, works exercising this function have failed to achieve the universal acceptance necessary to be regarded as an inspired, new word from the Lord.

◆ 4. Duties of the prince (46:1-24)

"This is what the Sovereign LORD says: The east gateway of the inner courtyard will be closed during the six workdays each week, but it will be open on Sabbath days and the days of new moon celebrations. [2]The prince will enter the entry room of the gateway from the outside. Then he will stand by the gatepost while the priest offers his burnt offering and peace offering. He will bow down in worship inside the gateway passage and then go back out the way he came. The gateway will not be closed until evening. [3]The common people will bow down and worship the LORD in front of this gateway on Sabbath days and the days of new moon celebrations.

[4]"Each Sabbath day the prince will present to the LORD a burnt offering of six lambs and one ram, all with no defects. [5]He will present a grain offering of a basket of

choice flour to go with the ram and whatever amount of flour he chooses to go with each lamb, and he is to offer one gallon of olive oil* for each basket of flour. 6At the new moon celebrations, he will bring one young bull, six lambs, and one ram, all with no defects. 7With the young bull he must bring a basket of choice flour for a grain offering. With the ram he must bring another basket of flour. And with each lamb he is to bring whatever amount of flour he chooses to give. With each basket of flour he must offer one gallon of olive oil.

8"The prince must enter the gateway through the entry room, and he must leave the same way. 9But when the people come in through the north gateway to worship the LORD during the religious festivals, they must leave by the south gateway. And those who entered through the south gateway must leave by the north gateway. They must never leave by the same gateway they came in, but must always use the opposite gateway. 10The prince will enter and leave with the people on these occasions.

11"So at the special feasts and sacred festivals, the grain offering will be a basket of choice flour with each young bull, another basket of flour with each ram, and as much flour as the prince chooses to give with each lamb. Give one gallon of olive oil with each basket of flour. 12When the prince offers a voluntary burnt offering or peace offering to the LORD, the east gateway to the inner courtyard will be opened for him, and he will offer his sacrifices as he does on Sabbath days. Then he will leave, and the gateway will be shut behind him.

13"Each morning you must sacrifice a one-year-old lamb with no defects as a burnt offering to the LORD. 14With the lamb, a grain offering must also be given to the LORD—about three quarts of flour with a third of a gallon of olive oil* to moisten the choice flour. This will be a permanent law for you. 15The lamb, the grain offering, and the olive oil must be given as a daily sacrifice every morning without fail.

16"This is what the Sovereign LORD says: If the prince gives a gift of land to one of his sons as his inheritance, it will belong to him and his descendants forever. 17But if the prince gives a gift of land from his inheritance to one of his servants, the servant may keep it only until the Year of Jubilee, which comes every fiftieth year.* At that time the land will return to the prince. But when the prince gives gifts to his sons, those gifts will be permanent. 18And the prince may never take anyone's property by force. If he gives property to his sons, it must be from his own land, for I do not want any of my people unjustly evicted from their property."

19In my vision, the man brought me through the entrance beside the gateway and led me to the sacred rooms assigned to the priests, which faced toward the north. He showed me a place at the extreme west end of these rooms. 20He explained, "This is where the priests will cook the meat from the guilt offerings and sin offerings and bake the flour from the grain offerings into bread. They will do it here to avoid carrying the sacrifices through the outer courtyard and endangering the people by transmitting holiness to them."

21Then he brought me back to the outer courtyard and led me to each of its four corners. In each corner I saw an enclosure. 22Each of these enclosures was 70 feet long and 52½ feet wide,* surrounded by walls. 23Along the inside of these walls was a ledge of stone with fireplaces under the ledge all the way around. 24The man said to me, "These are the kitchens to be used by the Temple assistants to boil the sacrifices offered by the people."

46:5 Hebrew *an ephah* [20 quarts or 22 liters] *of choice flour . . . a hin* [3.8 liters] *of olive oil;* similarly in 46:7, 11. **46:14** Hebrew 1/6 *of an ephah* [3.7 liters] *of flour with* 1/3 *of a hin* [1.3 liters] *of olive oil.* **46:17** Hebrew *until the Year of Release;* see Lev 25:8-17. **46:22** Hebrew *40 cubits* [21.2 meters] *long and 30 cubits* [15.9 meters] *wide.*

NOTES

46:1-2 The architectural terminology here does not match that in 40:32-34. Zimmerli is correct in thinking the "entry room" (*'ulam* [TH361, ZH395]) and "door post" (*mezuzah* [TH4201, ZH4647]) must refer to areas at the inner threshold of the gate, since from this vantage point the prince is to observe the offering of his sacrifices (1983:490).

46:3 *The common people.* These "people of the land" (*'am-ha'arets* [TH5971A, ZH6639]) are not simply inhabitants of the land but are citizens, comprising the cultic community other than the prince and the Temple officials themselves (Block 1998:671).

COMMENTARY

The series of oracles launched at 44:2 (with the Lord speaking in the context of the return of the Shekinah to the Temple) draws to a close at 45:25 (see 44:2-3; 44:5-8; 44:9–45:8; 45:9-25). Two final oracles conclude Ezekiel's Temple Torah; they are focused on the duties of the restored community's civic and cultic leader, the prince. The first oracle outlines the prince's participation in the worship going on in the Temple (46:1-15). The second aims to foster justice in the community by regulating the prince's acquisition and disposition of land (46:16-18).

The east gate of the outer wall was to remain closed perpetually because it was through that gate the Glory of God reentered the Temple (44:2-3). This closed gate would remind worshipers of that significant event and its monumental import. The Lord also regulates use of the east gateway into the inner courtyard (46:1-3). Closed during the workweek, the gate would be open on Sabbath days and the days of the new moon. Only the prince could enter this gate, but he was only to go so far as the inner gatepost, observing the priests' offering of his sacrifices from there. He would also fall prostrate in worship there, a posture befitting a mortal in the presence of the Lord (cf. 44:4). Having worshiped inside the east gateway, the prince was to turn around and exit by his path of entry. On these Sabbath and new moon days, when the east inner gate is open, the people could also worship at this gate, but they must stay in the outer courtyard, outside of the gate. Though at a distance, they would share some of the prince's visual access to the inner court. The specific offerings the prince was to present on these Sabbath and festival day occasions are also given (46:4-7). No mention is made of the people's offerings, perhaps because the prince presents offerings both for himself and for the people (45:22). On these occasions the prince appears to be worshiping as a leader of the people—as Block has it, "guardian and patron of the cult" (1998:671), with some tokens of deference. The same directions pertain when the prince offers voluntary sacrifices for himself (46:12).

The prince and the people alike were to access the *outer* court of the Temple by either the north or the south exterior gateways. Contrary to the preferential protocol for the prince's entry *and* exit in the east interior gateway, both the prince and the people should never leave the outer court by the gate through which they entered. Having entered through the north exterior gateway, they were to leave by way of the south gateway, and vice versa (46:8-10). Here the prince has no preeminent position but enters and exits with other worshipers. Beyond simple crowd control, we do not know the reason for these strict regulations for the entry and exit of worshipers in the new Temple. Nonetheless, the significant affirmation of solidarity in the restoration community is evident.

The concluding oracle of this section (46:16-18) regulates the land allotment given to the prince in order to preserve it as a family inheritance and to limit the prince's land claims. It brings forward 45:7-8 and anticipates 48:21-22. Samuel's ancient warning about the land-grabbing abuses the people could expect if they were to have a king (1 Sam 8:10-18) and the memory of actual confiscation of property suffered at the hands of leaders (cf. 1 Kgs 21; Mic 2:2) provide background to these lines. So to prevent piecemeal compromise of the prince's land, any gift of his allotment to persons other than family members must be returned to the prince in the Year of Jubilee (46:16-17; cf. Lev 25). Furthermore, any land gifts he does give can only come from his allotted land. A strict prohibition against the unjust eviction of God's people from their land makes the concern crystal clear and underscores the point (46:18).

Turning from proclamation of the Temple Torah, Ezekiel resumes narrating the Temple tour (46:19-24). This takes the reader back to 44:4, situated with Ezekiel in the inner court, in the front of the Temple (cf. previous major junctures in the tour at 43:3 and 40:2). As was the case in Mosaic legislation, two features of Ezekiel's renewed cult practice will involve cooking and baking. First, priests will receive meat from the guilt offerings and sin offerings over which they preside, and grain from the cereal offerings (46:20; cf. 42:13; 44:11, 15, 28-31; Lev 6:16-30; 7:6-10, 28-36). Second, worshipers themselves are to feast on portions of their peace offerings (46:24; cf. Lev 7:15-18). So "the man" leads Ezekiel first to a place on the far west end of the Temple compound where the Zadokite priests will prepare their portions from the offerings for consumption (46:19-20). Access to this installation apparently runs along the north face of the inner wall, on a walkway that is on the level of the inner courtyard and thus is sacred space. Then, he showed Ezekiel the kitchens reserved for the preparation of portions for consumption by the people (46:21-24). Here the Levites, now confined to the role of "Temple assistants," will assist worshipers.

◆ E. Vision of the Lord's New Land (47:1–48:35)

1. Life-giving stream from the Temple (47:1-12)

In my vision, the man brought me back to the entrance of the Temple. There I saw a stream flowing east from beneath the door of the Temple and passing to the right of the altar on its south side.
[2]The man brought me outside the wall through the north gateway and led me around to the eastern entrance. There I could see the water flowing out through the south side of the east gateway.

[3]Measuring as he went, he took me along the stream for 1,750 feet* and then led me across. The water was up to my ankles.
[4]He measured off another 1,750 feet and led me across again. This time the water was up to my knees. After another 1,750 feet, it was up to my waist.
[5]Then he measured another 1,750 feet, and the river was too deep to walk across. It was deep enough to swim in, but too deep to walk through.

[6]He asked me, "Have you been watching, son of man?" Then he led me back along the riverbank.
[7]When I returned, I was surprised by the sight of many trees growing on both sides of the river.
[8]Then he said to me, "This river flows east through the desert into the valley of the

Dead Sea.* The waters of this stream will
make the salty waters of the Dead Sea
fresh and pure. 9 There will be swarms of
living things wherever the water of this
river flows. Fish will abound in the Dead
Sea, for its waters will become fresh. Life
will flourish wherever this water flows.
10 Fishermen will stand along the shores of
the Dead Sea. All the way from En-gedi to
En-eglaim, the shores will be covered with
nets drying in the sun. Fish of every kind
will fill the Dead Sea, just as they fill the
Mediterranean.* 11 But the marshes and
swamps will not be purified; they will still
be salty. 12 Fruit trees of all kinds will grow
along both sides of the river. The leaves of
these trees will never turn brown and fall,
and there will always be fruit on their
branches. There will be a new crop every
month, for they are watered by the river
flowing from the Temple. The fruit will be
for food and the leaves for healing."

47:3 Hebrew *1,000 cubits* [530 meters]; also in 47:4, 5. **47:8** Hebrew *the sea.* **47:10** Hebrew *the great sea;* also in 47:15, 17, 19, 20.

NOTES

47:1 ***In my vision.*** This is not in the MT or ancient versions; the NLT supplies this gloss to make explicit the evident but implicit connection of this line to the Temple vision.

47:9 ***wherever this water flows.*** Even though the MT regularly refers to the stream in ch 47 with the singular term, *nakhal* [TH5158, ZH5707], at this point it has a dual form (preceded by a sg. verb), which we would normally translate "(two) rivers." The LXX reads a sg., "the river," as do the other ancient versions and most modern English versions. REB apparently points as a pl. and understands it as an intensive (cf. Waltke and O'Connor 1990:§7.4.3), translated "torrent."

47:10 ***En-gedi.*** This is a famous, picturesque oasis (modern 'Ain Jidi) halfway up the west shore of the Dead Sea, fed by a perpetual and bountiful spring, celebrated in Song 1:14.

En-eglaim. This is a place name known from Isa 15:8 as a site perhaps to be located near the south border of Moab. If, with Aharoni, we identify it with Al Mazra', roughly across from En-gedi, it would form something of a geographic merism, highlighting the totality of the reach of the life-giving stream (Aharoni 1967:32; Block 1998:695).

COMMENTARY

Ezekiel's visionary Temple tour continues as the guide brings him back to the entrance of the Temple (47:1). The opening note ties the following narrative back to similar rubrics that describe the tour; it locates Ezekiel at specific points in the envisioned Temple compound (e.g., 40:3; 43:1, 4; 44:1, 4; 46:19).

Facing the main Temple door, Ezekiel saw an unexpected sight—"a stream flowing east from beneath" that door (47:1). No spring or stream on the Temple Mount itself has ever been found; there has been no water source there on the surface to our knowledge. Still, issuing from the presence of Yahweh comes a trickling stream. Flowing east, it passes to the south side of the altar and then out the eastern gates. (Only the outer east gateway is mentioned, but passage through the inner east gate is assumed; see 47:2.)

From the outer east gate, the man leads Ezekiel to follow the stream as it flows east. Every third of a mile (1,750 feet) he takes Ezekiel across the stream. What strikes Ezekiel in this process is the rapid increase in the stream's depth. First just ankle deep (47:3), then up to his knees (47:4), then to his waist (47:4) and finally, within no more than a mile and a third, the trickle from the Temple door becomes a river too deep to be crossed on foot (47:5). Without note of additional springs or tributaries, this multiplication of the water manifests the stream's supernatural origins. The guide called attention to this rapid increase in the stream by asking whether or not Ezekiel had been watching (47:6). Clearly he had!

Led back along the riverbank, Ezekiel was stunned to see many trees growing along both sides of the stream (47:7). While Ezekiel was pondering the trees, the man told him what became of the water as it flowed east toward the Dead Sea and out of sight (47:8). As the waters enter the Dead Sea, they purify it and produce astounding, abundant life—fish and swarms of living creatures (47:8-9). Along the seashore, known since time immemorial for its lifeless, brackish water and crystalline deposits, fishermen will dry their nets, with fish of every kind filling the sea. (At the same time, in an interesting sidebar, it is noted that the useful salt marshes will be preserved [47:11] since they produce salt useful for food preservation and worship.) Wherever the water of this stream goes, it brings life (47:9).

Having brought Ezekiel's attention back to the riverbanks and the trees teeming along them, the guide called attention to the amazing variety of the trees, to their perpetual verdancy, and to their abundant, accelerated fruitfulness (47:12). Beyond that, the leaves have healing power. All of this stems from being watered by the river that flows from the Temple, the throne of God. The source is critical.

This vision plays off of traditions that surface elsewhere in the Old Testament. One thinks immediately of the account of Eden's primal river, lush enough to water the primordial garden and powerful enough to split into four mighty rivers (Gen 2:10-14). One also thinks of the celebration of a stream gladdening God's holy mount (Ps 46:4-5). In Ezekiel the river speaks of the life-giving presence of the Lord. Obviously that vital presence centers in the Temple, the focus of this massive vision (chs 40–48). At the same time, that Temple cannot contain the presence of God. Instead, from this sanctuary the Lord's presence will fructify the land, bringing life and blessing wherever it flows. Finally, stress falls on the life-giving nature of the Lord's presence. Tied heretofore primarily with judgment, now the Lord's presence is linked with abundant life. Few pictures of this vital power could be more dramatic than its transformation of the Dead Sea into a teeming "Sea of Life."

Whereas Ezekiel was shown the Temple as God's throne and unique dwelling place (43:7), in his revelation, John sees the throne of God and of the Lamb open to view, not hidden in a temple (Rev 22:1). Thus, the stream Ezekiel sees issuing from the Temple's threshold (47:1), John sees flowing from the very throne of God (Rev 22:1). Whereas Ezekiel sees "many trees growing on both sides of the river" (47:7), John sees a single tree of life associated with the river, picking up the imagery of Eden (Gen 2:9), construed on both sides of the stream under Ezekiel's influence (Rev 22:2, NIV). The stream itself has life-giving properties (47:9; Rev 22:1). And the tree(s) watered by the stream bring healing (47:12; Rev 22:2). Fruit appears on the trees monthly—in Ezekiel fresh fruit each month (47:12), in Revelation a different fruit each month (Rev 22:2).

◆ 2. Borders and division of the land (47:13–48:35)

13 This is what the Sovereign LORD says: "Divide the land in this way for the twelve tribes of Israel: The descendants of Joseph will be given two shares of land.* 14 Otherwise each tribe will receive an equal share. I took a solemn oath and swore that I would give this land to your ancestors, and it will now come to you as your possession.

15 "These are the boundaries of the
land: The northern border will run
from the Mediterranean toward
Hethlon, then on through Lebo-
hamath to Zedad; 16 then it will run
to Berothah and Sibraim, which are
on the border between Damascus and
Hamath, and finally to Hazer-hatticon,
on the border of Hauran. 17 So the
northern border will run from the
Mediterranean to Hazar-enan, on
the border between Hamath to the
north and Damascus to the south.

18 "The eastern border starts at a
point between Hauran and Damascus
and runs south along the Jordan River
between Israel and Gilead, past the
Dead Sea* and as far south as Tamar.*
This will be the eastern border.

19 "The southern border will go west
from Tamar to the waters of Meribah
at Kadesh* and then follow the
course of the Brook of Egypt to the
Mediterranean. This will be the
southern border.

20 "On the west side, the
Mediterranean itself will be your
border from the southern border to
the point where the northern border
begins, opposite Lebo-hamath.

21 "Divide the land within these boundaries among the tribes of Israel. 22 Distribute the land as an allotment for yourselves and for the foreigners who have joined you and are raising their families among you. They will be like native-born Israelites to you and will receive an allotment among the tribes. 23 These foreigners are to be given land within the territory of the tribe with whom they now live. I, the Sovereign LORD, have spoken!

CHAPTER 48

"Here is the list of the tribes of Israel and the territory each is to receive. The territory of Dan is in the extreme north. Its boundary line follows the Hethlon road to Lebo-hamath and then runs on to Hazar-enan on the border of Damascus, with Hamath to the north. Dan's territory extends all the way across the land of Israel from east to west.

2 "Asher's territory lies south of Dan's and also extends from east to west. 3 Naphtali's land lies south of Asher's, also extending from east to west. 4 Then comes Manasseh south of Naphtali, and its territory also extends from east to west. 5 South of Manasseh is Ephraim, 6 and then Reuben, 7 and then Judah, all of whose boundaries extend from east to west.

8 "South of Judah is the land set aside for a special purpose. It will be $8\frac{1}{3}$ miles* wide and will extend as far east and west as the tribal territories, with the Temple at the center.

9 "The area set aside for the LORD's Temple will be $8\frac{1}{3}$ miles long and $6\frac{2}{3}$ miles wide.* 10 For the priests there will be a strip of land measuring $8\frac{1}{3}$ miles long by $3\frac{1}{3}$ miles wide,* with the LORD's Temple at the center. 11 This area is set aside for the ordained priests, the descendants of Zadok who served me faithfully and did not go astray with the people of Israel and the rest of the Levites. 12 It will be their special portion when the land is distributed, the most sacred land of all. Next to the priests' territory will lie the land where the other Levites will live.

13 "The land allotted to the Levites will be the same size and shape as that belonging to the priests—$8\frac{1}{3}$ miles long and $3\frac{1}{3}$ miles wide. Together these portions of land will measure $8\frac{1}{3}$ miles long by $6\frac{2}{3}$ miles wide.* 14 None of this special land may ever be sold or traded or used by others, for it belongs to the LORD; it is set apart as holy.

15"An additional strip of land 8⅓ miles long by 1⅔ miles wide,* south of the sacred Temple area, will be allotted for public use—homes, pasturelands, and common lands, with a city at the center. 16The city will measure 1½ miles* on each side—north, south, east, and west. 17Open lands will surround the city for 150 yards* in every direction. 18Outside the city there will be a farming area that stretches 3⅓ miles to the east and 3⅓ miles to the west* along the border of the sacred area. This farmland will produce food for the people working in the city. 19Those who come from the various tribes to work in the city may farm it. 20This entire area—including the sacred lands and the city—is a square that measures 8⅓ miles* on each side.

21"The areas that remain, to the east and to the west of the sacred lands and the city, will belong to the prince. Each of these areas will be 8⅓ miles wide, extending in opposite directions to the eastern and western borders of Israel, with the sacred lands and the sanctuary of the Temple in the center. 22So the prince's land will include everything between the territories allotted to Judah and Benjamin, except for the areas set aside for the sacred lands and the city.

23"These are the territories allotted to the rest of the tribes. Benjamin's territory lies just south of the prince's lands, and it extends across the entire land of Israel from east to west. 24South of Benjamin's territory lies that of Simeon, also extending across the land from east to west. 25Next is the territory of Issachar with the same eastern and western boundaries.

26"Then comes the territory of Zebulun, which also extends across the land from east to west. 27The territory of Gad is just south of Zebulun with the same borders to the east and west. 28The southern border of Gad runs from Tamar to the waters of Meribah at Kadesh* and then follows the Brook of Egypt to the Mediterranean.*

29"These are the allotments that will be set aside for each tribe's exclusive possession. I, the Sovereign LORD, have spoken!

30"These will be the exits to the city: On the north wall, which is 1½ miles long, 31there will be three gates, each one named after a tribe of Israel. The first will be named for Reuben, the second for Judah, and the third for Levi. 32On the east wall, also 1½ miles long, the gates will be named for Joseph, Benjamin, and Dan. 33The south wall, also 1½ miles long, will have gates named for Simeon, Issachar, and Zebulun. 34And on the west wall, also 1½ miles long, the gates will be named for Gad, Asher, and Naphtali.

35"The distance around the entire city will be 6 miles.* And from that day the name of the city will be 'The LORD Is There.'*"

47:13 It was important to retain twelve portions of land. Since Levi had no portion, the descendants of Joseph's sons, Ephraim and Manasseh, received land as two tribes. **47:18a** Hebrew *the eastern sea.* **47:18b** As in Greek version; Hebrew reads *you will measure.* **47:19** Hebrew *waters of Meribath-kadesh.* **48:8** Hebrew *25,000 cubits* [13.3 kilometers]. **48:9** As in one Greek manuscript and the Greek reading in 45:1: *25,000 cubits* [13.3 kilometers] *long and 20,000 cubits* [10.6 kilometers] *wide;* Hebrew reads *25,000 cubits long and 10,000 cubits* [3⅓ miles or 5.3 kilometers] *wide.* Similarly in 48:13b. Compare 45:1-5; 48:10-13. **48:10** Hebrew *25,000 cubits* [13.3 kilometers] *long by 10,000 cubits* [5.3 kilometers] *wide;* also in 48:13a. **48:13** See note on 48:9. **48:15** Hebrew *25,000 cubits* [13.3 kilometers] *long by 5,000 cubits* [2.65 kilometers] *wide.* **48:16** Hebrew *4,500 cubits* [2.4 kilometers]; also in 48:30, 32, 33, 34. **48:17** Hebrew *250 cubits* [133 meters]. **48:18** Hebrew *10,000 cubits* [5.3 kilometers] *to the east and 10,000 cubits to the west.* **48:20** Hebrew *25,000 cubits* [13.3 kilometers]; also in 48:21. **48:28a** Hebrew *waters of Meribath-kadesh.* **48:28b** Hebrew *the great sea.* **48:35a** Hebrew *18,000 cubits* [9.6 kilometers]. **48:35b** Hebrew *Yahweh Shammah.*

NOTES

47:13 ***in this way.*** Heb., *geh gebul* [TH1366, ZH1473], lit., " ?? border." If *geh* is a real Hebrew word, its meaning was lost before the LXX was made. Ancient and modern versions treat it as a scribal error, probably for *zeh haggebul,* "this is the boundary" by which the land will be divided, as Block explains (1998:705, note 5). The NLT catches the sense of the line well.

47:15 *Hethlon.* This is a place of uncertain location on the north border of the restored land as Ezekiel saw it. It is situated either on the Mediterranean coast or between it and Lebo-hamath in the upper Beqa'a Valley.

Lebo-hamath to Zedad. The word order in MT is puzzling: *lebo' tsedadah khamat* seems to insert "to Zedad" between "Lebo" and "hamath." Further, the MT also features a verse break before "hamath," prompting some translations to list it separately (cf. KJV, NASB in contrast to NLT, NIV, RSV, ESV). Perhaps the text has been compromised by the misplacement of "hamath" as a gloss on "Lebweh toward Sedad" (see note on Zedad below) under the influence of v. 20.

The anchor point of the traditional north border of the land of Israel, Lebo-hamath is generally identified with Lebweh, in the upper end of the Beqa'a Valley. Paired with the Brook of Egypt (Wadi el-'Arish) on the southern border, these boundaries marked out the extremities of Egypt's "province of Canaan" as early as the Amarna Period (fourteenth century BC). Israel's traditional narrative used these same two points in marking out the boundaries of the land viewed by the spies (Num 34:1-12), allotted by Joshua (Josh 15:1-4), ruled by Solomon (1 Kgs 8:65), and reclaimed, at least the northern portion, by Jeroboam II (2 Kgs 14:25).

Zedad. This was a place 35 miles east-northeast of Lebweh (Lebo-hamath), 62 miles north of Damascus, just east of the road from Damascus to Aleppo near Riblah. The modern village of Sedad probably preserves its name. In spite of the LXX's spelling (*Seddada*), a proposed identification with Khirbet Serada near sources of the Jordan River seems unlikely given the location of Lebo-hamath (Aharoni 1967:66-67; Block 1998:713; ABD 6.1068).

47:16 *Berothah.* This is a place on the restored land's northern boundary, a city of Hadadezer, king of Aram-Zobah, usually identified with modern Bereitan, south of Baalbek in the Beqa'a (HALOT 1.155; Block 1998:713). It is perhaps to be identified with Berothai in 2 Sam 8:8.

Sibraim. This place name is completely unknown and was apparently unfamiliar to early readers as well, judging from the inserted (or perhaps original) explanation (". . . which is/are on the border between . . .") that locates it between Damascus and Hamath. The NLT connects this explanation to both Berothah and Sibraim. The LXX retains the explanation, but ties it to Eliam, a town not included in the MT here, perhaps known from 2 Sam 10:16.

Damascus. The best known of the cities Ezekiel lists in his vision, Damascus appears first in Scripture among David's conquests from the Aramean Hadadezer, ruler of the kingdom of Zobah (2 Sam 8:3-8). During the ninth century the Aramean kingdom centered in Damascus became a major rival of Israel under Ben-hadad and his successors, but it eventually succumbed to Assyrian imperialism in the mid-eighth century, never to regain its earlier influence.

Hamath. This city, 130 miles north of Damascus on the Orontes River in central Syria, gave its name to a significant Amorite (and later Aramean) state. Hamath enters OT history when its king, Toi, sends congratulations to David upon his defeat of the Aramean Hadadezer (2 Sam 8:9-10; 1 Chr 18:9-10). Solomon is said to have built installations in Hamath, and Jeroboam II is also said to have defeated Hamath (2 Kgs 14:28; 2 Chr 8:4). Like Israel, Hamath eventually lost its identity in the Assyrian conquest.

Hazer-hatticon. This city should mark the northeast corner of Ezekiel's ideal boundary. According to Aharoni and Avi-Yonah (1968:73), this site is to be identified with Qaryatein, a desert oasis east of Zedad. The ancient versions, however, cannot agree on the meaning, let alone the location of the name. Block says the site "defies identification" (1998:713).

Hauran. This area east of Galilee and the Jordan River and north of the Yarmuk River is known from Egyptian texts of the 19th Dynasty and Neo-Assyrian texts as well. The fertile region served as Palestine's granary in late antiquity.

47:17 ***Hazar-enan.*** Generally equated in recent scholarship with Qaryatein, and perhaps another name for Hazer-hatticon, the site remains unknown. Identifications of Hazar-enan with modern Hadr at the foot of Mount Hermon assume a totally different and unlikely construal of the boundary line in Ezekiel (Block 1998:714).

48:8 ***the land set aside for a special purpose.*** Ezekiel used technical sacrificial language, *terumah* [TH8641, ZH9556], to designate this land, a term built on the verb *rum* [TH7311, ZH8123], meaning "to be high, elevated," and in some forms "to present" (as a gift or offering). Following the MT and LXX, the NIV better conveys the interesting transaction involved here: "Bordering the territory of Judah . . . will be the portion *you are to present* as a special gift" (emphasis added). However, the entire land belongs to the Lord. In this context he is graciously distributing his own inheritance to the tribes as their allotments. Simultaneously he instructs them to present this land to him as a special gift. The Lord provides the land, which Israel will present to him as an offering.

48:9 ***set aside for the* L*ORD's Temple.*** The MT and versions ancient and modern here lack "Temple," indicating that the entire area set aside in the national square uniquely belongs to the Lord. Of course, the Lord's Temple is to be situated in this land (48:10), but that is probably not the thrust of this verse.

48:30 ***the city.*** See Richter's treatment of Ezekiel's influence on John the Revelator's vision of the New Jerusalem; both John and Ezekiel see the eschaton as a return to Eden (2008:122-129).

48:35 ***"The* L*ORD Is There."*** The Hebrew name of the city is *yhwh shammah* [TH3068/8033, ZH3378/9004]. The second word, *shammah,* is actually the adverb *sham* (there) plus a deictic *-ah* [TH1886.5, ZH2025], which would ordinarily give the word a locative force, "to there" or "thither." One could thus wonder if the name does not indicate the city as the place *toward which* the Lord's presence is directed or headed, a dynamic hope even beyond the coming of the city (whatever that might mean). The LXX understood the consonants *shammah* (there) to read "her name" (i.e., the city's name), and took the consonants *yhwh* not as the Lord's name but as a verb of being, yielding "the name of the city . . . will be her name." The Targum follows MT, "His Shekinah Is There," as do modern English versions. This is acceptable, as Keil and Delitzsch concluded (1989:381-382), showing that, although Ezekiel ordinarily uses simple *sham* when this word is in play, he does twice use *shammah* meaning simply "there," not "thither" (in 23:3 and 32:29, 30; so HALOT 4:1547). They comment tellingly that this makes "no material difference," since "the city can only bear the name from the time when Jehovah is *shammah,* and can only bear it so long as Jehovah is *shammah*" (1989:382). Still, the two forms are not identical and one wonders why the extended form is used here. Perhaps the Vulgate gives a clue in its rendering *Dominus ibidem,* "The LORD is in *this very* place," taking the form as emphatic rather than deictic—"there, really there."

COMMENTARY

The preceding narrative of the stream of life is anchored in the Temple tour (47:1-2) and yet has horizons in the land beyond the Temple (47:8-12). As such, it serves as a literary bridge between the preceding vision of the Temple and the following division of the land (47:13–48:35). The introduction to the present section includes the note that Joseph's descendants will be given two shares of the land (47:13). In the allotment list we discover this refers to Joseph's two sons, Ephraim and Manasseh (48:4-5; cf. Gen 48).

The allotment of the land commences by establishing its boundaries on all four points of the compass, beginning with the northern border. "Border" here may conjure up too precise a line in the minds of modern readers—a presentation of territories that implies boundaries between them may be more appropriate. Thus, the sites are said to lie "on the border between [the territories of] Damascus and Hamath" (47:16). Unfortunately, even though these boundaries are obviously important to Ezekiel, "none of the places named in this [northern boundary] list can be identified with certainty" (Block 1998:712), so precision eludes us.

Points on the line that do seem more securely identified—Lebo-hamath, Zedad, and Hauran—lead us to put the northern boundary in the upper reaches of the traditional "land of Canaan," still north of the Huleh Basin and Damascus (Aharoni 1967:61-63). Ezekiel seems to reflect the boundary set for reconnaissance of the 12 spies under Joshua (Num 13:21), as well as the land to be possessed (Num 33:7-9). This also harkens back to the northern extent of David's influence (2 Sam 8:3-12) and Solomon's "empire" (1 Kgs 8:65), as well as the extent of Jeroboam II's conquests (2 Kgs 14:25). King Josiah's aspirations, cut short by his untimely death, may well have had this territory in view as well (2 Kgs 23:19).

Ezekiel's vision calls to mind the far-flung boundaries for the land given in the time of Moses (Num 34:1-12) and the heralded reach of Solomon's kingdom (1 Kgs 4:20-21), thus emphasizing the full extent of the restoration. The former recalls the founding vision of Moses, the latter the marvel of the empire never seen again. But Ezekiel's land is not just a duplicate of earlier tradition. David, Solomon, and Jeroboam II wielded influence as far as "the gates of Hamath," but this land to our knowledge was never settled by Israelites. In Ezekiel's vision, this land will be allotted to tribes for settlement. And, if the tentative identifications of Zedad and Hazer-hatticon are correct, the restored land includes a significant "bulge" of land north and east of Damascus, more than compensating for Transjordan land from Reuben, Gad, and Manasseh not included in the new allotment. In addition, although we cannot identify the exact spot where Ezekiel's northern boundary meets the Mediterranean Sea, it does appear to be well north of Tyre and Sidon, incorporating coastlands never held by Israel.

The eastern border (47:18; cf. Num 34:10-12) presents fewer difficulties, once a decision is made about the northeast anchor point. Presumably the site referenced "between Damascus and Hamath" would be Hazer-hatticon, the last oasis on the northern boundary (cf. 47:16). The Jordan River and the east side of the Dead Sea make a line leading down to Tamar in the Arabah south of the Dead Sea. Interestingly, Ezekiel called the sea along this boundary "the eastern sea" (47:18, NLT mg; Joel 2:20; Zech 14:8), translated "the Dead Sea" by the NLT to make a clearer geographic reference. Ezekiel's choice of words underscores the boundary function of the sea in this particular passage. Ezekiel set aside "Dead Sea" or "Salt Sea" language because these references were inappropriate in view of the envisioned transformation by waters from the Temple (cf. 47:8-10).

The southern border proceeds from Tamar in the Arabah west to Meribah at Kadesh and on to the Mediterranean Sea by way of the Brook of Egypt (47:19; cf. Num 34:3-5). Meribah-kadesh is apparently another name for Kadesh-barnea and is to be identified with modern 'Ain el-Qudeirat, the richest and most central of the springs on the southern edge of the Negev (Aharoni 1967:65). This "Brook/Wadi of Egypt" is the Wadi el-'Arish, *nakhal mitsrayim* in Hebrew (as in Isa 27:12), the southern boundary of the historic "Land of Canaan." It flows into the Mediterranean about 50 miles south of Gaza and is to be distinguished from the *River* of Egypt (*nehar mitsrayim;* cf. Gen 15:18, NLT mg), which designates the Pelusiac branch of the Nile still farther to the west.

Finally on the west, the Great Sea constitutes the border, reaching all the way from the Wadi el-'Arish in the south to a point above Byblos on the level of Lebo-hamath in the north (47:20).

The "boundaries of the land" (47:15-20), the "list of the tribes of Israel and the territory [for] each" (48:1-29), and the list of city exits (48:30-35) appear to be either written *from* traditional lists or written *as* set lists, each having a scribal superscription (47:15; 48:1, 30), and the second having a scribal subscription (48:29). They are enclosed by hortatory material as follows:

A. Instruction: "Divide the land . . . for the twelve tribes of Israel" (47:13-14)
  B. The boundaries of the land (47:15-20)
A'. Instruction: "Divide the land within these boundaries" (47:21-23)
  B'. The list of tribes and their allotments (48:1-29)
    C. The list of city exits (48:30-35)

The hortatory material in 47:13-14 prescribes "the way" in which the allotment will proceed. Joseph's descendants (from his two sons) will each be given a share (47:13), with each of the other tribes except Levi (cf. 44:28; 45:4-5; 48:12) receiving a share, and all of them equal shares. Then the Lord ties this restoration promise to the ancient oath to the ancestors, a promise reaching all the way back to Abraham and his entry to the "land of Canaan" (Gen 12:5b-7). The promise was elaborated, nurtured, repeated, and passed on for centuries but without definitive fulfillment (Gen 15:18-21; 17:8; 26:4; 28:13-15; 35:12; 50:24; Exod 3:7-8; 6:2-9; 23:23-33; Lev 26:41-42; Num 14:20-24; 33:50-56; Deut 1:6-8; 4:1; 11:23-25). According to Ezekiel the new land—new allotments, new fertility, new security, spiritually new inhabitants—would at last bring the complete fulfillment of that promise (47:14).

The hortatory lines in 47:21-23 give particular attention to just treatment of foreigners in the land who have joined the covenant people. This assumes the males had been circumcised and that the families would live by God's covenant. These would be persons totally unlike the "uncircumcised foreigners . . . who have no heart for God," whom God excludes from Temple service in 44:7. On the contrary, these would be circumcised persons who *do* "have a heart for God," not persons temporarily in the land as sojourners, but families who had settled and become like native-born Israelites. They are to receive equal treatment in the distribution of the land, says the Lord, in another move to guarantee justice and mercy in the new land.

The list of the tribes and their allotments runs from 48:1 through 48:29, intercalating the description of the prince's land and the national square between the treatment of Judah and Benjamin in the list (48:8-22). Within the external boundaries just established (47:15-20), the tribal allotments are simply listed from north to south: Dan, Asher, Naphtali, Ephraim, Reuben, Judah, Benjamin, Simeon, Issachar, Zebulun, and Gad, with the prince's land and the national square (i.e., "the land set aside for a special purpose," 48:8) placed between Judah and Benjamin. Ezekiel calls these allotments *khalaqim* [TH2506, ZH2750] (48:8), language associated with Joshua's division of spoil from holy war (cf. *khalaq* [TH2505, ZH2745] in Josh 22:8). Note that Dan's northern boundary follows the northern boundary of the whole land (following the Hethlon road to Lebo-hamath and on to Hazar-enan, cf. 47:15-17) and that Dan's allotment "extends all the way across the land of Israel from east to west" (48:1), taken with the information that all the allotments likewise run all the way from the west to the east boundaries (48:2, 3, etc.); this tells us that the allotments are strips of land, oriented horizontally from east to west. There are 13 such strips, one for each tribe and one for the land of "special purpose" (48:8).

Unlike the external boundaries, the borders between the tribes are not geographically or topographically specified. Nor is the north–south width of each tribe's allotment given. We are told that the land set aside for special purpose is 8⅓ miles wide, its length stretching from the west boundary to the east boundary, just like the other allotments. If we assume that each of the tribal allotments is also 8⅓ miles wide, the land would stretch about 108 miles from north to south, less than half the actual distance from Lebo-hamath in the north to Kadesh-barnea in the south. Whether and how the allotments actually fit historical realities does not appear to have concerned the writer.

We know from the explicit instruction in 47:14 that each tribe is to have an equal share of the land. The list of allotments expresses this emphasis on equality by its symmetry and verbatim repetition, not by actual measurements given. In the original allotment at the time of the conquest, fairness was addressed by making the inheritances in proportion to the relative size of the various tribes (Num 26:52-56). We are not told precisely how the issue of proportion to the size of each tribe will be addressed here, but other manifestations of a just distribution appear. The east–west orientation of the allotments guarantees that each tribe has access to topographically and geologically similar land: coastline, coastal lowlands, high land, wilderness, and the great rift. No tribe monopolizes the most desirable land. Also, north–south travel between the tribes is also facilitated by this array.

Between the northern allotments for Dan, Asher, Naphtali, Ephraim, Reuben, and Judah, and the southern ones for Benjamin, Simeon, Issachar, Zebulun, and Gad, Ezekiel literarily and actually situates the "land set aside for a special purpose" (48:8-22). This *terumah* [TH8641, ZH9556], property given to the Lord (see note on 48:8), encompasses a strip of land 8⅓ miles wide, north to south, stretching like the allotment of each tribe across the entire land from west to east, with the Temple in the center (48:8). This term, which elsewhere designates offerings, or the area given to the priests (48:10), here designates the whole allotment from the Sea to the Arabah.

The national square, 8⅓ miles on a side, situated in the middle of this special-purpose land, includes, from north to south, a strip 8⅓ miles long by 3⅓ miles wide for the Levites and their cities, another strip of the same dimensions for the Zadokite priests and the Temple precinct, and a third strip, 8⅓ miles by 1⅔ miles, for public land, including land for a city in the center. The land given to the Levites and the priests belongs uniquely to the Lord and can never be sold, traded, or used by persons other than those named in the promised allotment (48:14). Remarkably, the national city and the Temple stand outside the tribal allotments. No tribe can claim the Temple or the principal city. They belong to the Lord, not to any privileged tribe.

The remainder of the land set aside for special purposes, all of the strip on either side of the national square, belongs to the prince (48:21-22). Though it is not repeated here, earlier we are told that the prince's land is also inalienable. This land is not to leave the royal family (46:16-18) and is to satisfy the crown's need for land, so that abuse of the people's land by the prince will cease (45:8).

Placement of the tribes has but few reminiscences of the historic locations—these appear not to govern the restoration allotments much at all. Judah and Benjamin remain closest to the central city and to the Temple, though their historic positions are reversed. And Dan remains at the far north, its location after migrating from the south. Instead of focusing on their historic locations, Ezekiel arrayed the tribes around the national square and the Temple according to their genealogical and familial proximity to the patriarch Jacob (cf. Block 1998:723; Eichrodt 1970:593). Thus, Judah, son of Jacob by his first wife, Leah, the son who gained royal preeminence (Gen 49:8-12), borders the special-purpose land on the north. Benjamin, beloved son by his favored wife, Rachel, stands immediately to the south of that land. Other sons of Leah and Rachel appear next, and finally, farthest from the Temple, the sons of the handmaidens, Zilpah and Bilhah. The order is as follows (Block 1998:723-724):

Dan	(Bilhah)
Asher	(Zilpah)
Naphtali	(Bilhah)
Manasseh	(Rachel)
Ephraim	(Rachel)
Reuben	(Leah)
Judah	(Leah)
The Sacred Terumah	
Benjamin	(Rachel)
Simeon	(Leah)
Issachar	(Leah)
Zebulun	(Leah)
Gad	(Zilpah)

Although the emphasis in the vision is on the equal blessing of the allotments, and no explicit remarks evaluate their relative status, some preferential treatment can be detected in this order. The Levites, not named, are actually placed in sacred space, with those from Zadok situated closest to the Temple! Also, the tribes descended from Jacob's wives, not their handmaids, cluster around the sacred Terumah. Traditional boundaries and tribal lists have in some cases been respected, but the former north-south divisions of the tribes occasioned by the division of the monarchy have been ignored, the historic locations jumbled. Emphatic restoration of the tribal lands rectifies the monarchy's persistent attempts to undermine tribal claims in favor of royal control of lands (famously under Solomon and Ahab; 1 Kgs 4:7-19;

21:1-19). As Block notes (1998:724), Ezekiel hearkened to the old theocratic ideal in which Yahweh as Israel's king parcels out to each tribe its inheritance (*nakhalah* [TH5159, ZH5709]; NLT, "allotments," 48:29). The prince not only does not establish these boundaries and allotments, but also is himself subject to the will of Yahweh who gives him, just like the others, an inheritance.

The Temple vision and the book close with a description of the national city under a superscription regarding its exits: "These will be the exits to the city" (48:30-35; cf. 45:6; 48:15-20). The city will be a square, 1½ miles on each side—these dimensions emphasized by repeated mention—with twelve gates, each side having three. Each gate will carry the name of a son of Jacob. The list repeats the names just used in assigning allotments of the land, except that, with the inclusion of Levi, Joseph is substituted for his two sons, Ephraim and Manasseh. The gates thus carry the names of Jacob's biological sons.

As with the ordering of the tribal allotments, so also in the naming of the exit gates, genealogical and familial matters appear most determinative for the order of the names assigned. On the north and on the south sides, the gates carry the names of the six sons of Leah, Jacob's first wife: Reuben, Judah, and Levi on the north; Simeon, Issachar, and Zebulun on the south. The gates on the east side of the city are named for the two sons of Jacob's favorite wife Rachel, Joseph and Benjamin, and for Dan, the firstborn of Rachel's handmaid Bilhah. Pride of place may perhaps belong to the east side of the city, though nothing is made of this. On the west side, exits are named for Gad and Asher (sons of Zilpah, Leah's handmaid) and for Naphtali (the second son of Bilhah, Rachel's handmaid). (See Gen 29:32–30:24; 35:16-19 and 35:22-26 for the traditional account of the birth of these sons.) Actual birth order does not appear to be the issue here: the first, fourth, and third appear on the north; eleventh, twelfth, and fifth on the east; second, ninth, and tenth on the south; seventh, eighth, and sixth on the west. Instead, birth mother seems to determine groupings.

What motivates this ordering cannot be said with certainty. No point from which one might assign preeminence seems obvious. Perhaps the array is a picture of egalitarian utopia. The inclusion of Levi and Joseph and exclusion of Ephraim and Manasseh take the reader back to the ancient accounts in Genesis 29, 30 and 35, grounding this part of Ezekiel's vision in the earliest stages of God's fulfillment of the promises, emphasizing again God's faithfulness to his promise and the present vision as the announcement of that longed-for fulfillment.

Block suggests Ezekiel's scheme—a square city with 12 gates—may carry an implicit comparison to the precinct of Marduk in Babylon, with its square layout and nine gates named after Babylonian deities (1998:738, note 23). This may be overly subtle. But we know from the opening of the book that Ezekiel was sensitive to Babylonian art and iconography. If Marduk's precinct was sacred by virtue of the named gates, this city is definitely "the people's city," with its gates named after its historic patriarchs. This city is not the Temple—the land's sacred center. That was to be situated just north of this city in the priests' land. Over against that national anchor point, the city celebrates its openness to citizens from all over the land, to live and work as they wish.

But precisely what city is in view? What is its name? Over the entire concluding section of the book, the vision of Israel's restoration in chapters 40–48, Ezekiel has assiduously refrained from actually naming the place of the vision. Ezekiel is carried to the land of Israel and to a "very high [but nameless] mountain" (40:2). In 40:2 and then from 45:6 on, we hear of "a city" never named. According to Levenson (1976:7-53), readers who have heard Ezekiel to this point know he has clearly identified Mount Zion as the mount of God's revealing, judging, and redeeming actions. This Mount Zion is larger than the geophysical place; it is filled with overtones of the mythic cosmic mountain, the Garden of Eden, and even Mount Sinai. This is the almost mythic Jerusalem of the Psalter's "Songs of Zion" (e.g., Pss 46, 48, 76). "The city" can only be that city. Still, if so, why not say so? *Yahweh Shammah* sounds a tad like *Yerushalayim* (Jerusalem) though noticeably different. And Ezekiel's survey of the reapportioned tribal lands and national square has not given clues sufficient to equate the city with historic Jerusalem. The Temple, contrary to historical experience, is not even located in a city.

The city is "profane" (*khol* [TH2455, ZH2687]; 48:15) in the sense of not being set apart for worship or as a place of peculiar divine presence analogous to the Temple or the Most Holy Place, which is God's very throne and footstool. The city is not sacred, but it is emphatically civic. This is its glory. In spite of this, the concluding two words of the book announce the name of the city as "Yahweh [is] There!"—emphatically there! Significant realities fall into place with this utterance. Traversing almost the entire length and breadth of the book, the theme of the presence and absence of the Glory of God has structured this work, providing dramatic and thematic unity and movement. The city's name carries that theme to the very last words of the book, asking that all of the book's major themes be held accountable to this dominating concern. Beyond that, the name underscores the good news of Ezekiel's rather hidden gospel. Not the absence but the presence of the Lord has the last word—literally and theologically. This advances the argument beyond the startling return of the Lord's glory to the Temple (43:1-5 and 44:4). Yahweh returns not simply to his Temple but to the life of the people. In the city's name, Ezekiel unexpectedly hallows the common place, neither sanctifying it as a place like the Temple, nor ignoring the civic nature of the place, but proclaiming the Lord uniquely present beyond the Temple in the common life of Israel (cf. Zech 14:20-21).

Ezekiel and John the Revelator. The Christian reader of Ezekiel cannot close this scroll without pondering John the Revelator's appropriation of Ezekiel's Temple vision (especially portions of chs 47–48) in Revelation 21–22. There are too many obvious allusions and cross-references to dismiss the links as accidental or as mere artistic borrowing or archaizing for effect. There are too many meaningful adaptations to say we have simple borrowing without critical reinterpretation.

As John sees "a new heaven and a new earth," a "holy city, the new Jerusalem, coming down from God out of heaven" captures his attention (Rev 21:1-2). Like Ezekiel, John is carried away by the Spirit to "a great, high mountain" where he is shown this remarkable city (Rev 21:10; cf. Ezek 40:2). (We note that, like Ezekiel, John is shown the city by an angelic guide with a measuring rod; Rev 21:15; cf. Ezek 40:3.) The radiance of the city John sees (Rev 21:11) is "the glory of God . . . like a precious stone—like jasper as clear as crystal" (cf. 43:1-4; 44:4, echoing language from Ezekiel's inaugural vision of the glory of God, 1:26-28). Like Ezekiel's city, the new Jerusalem is square (Rev 21:16; cf. Ezek 48:20, 30-34), actually cubed, adding a vertical dimension to Ezekiel's two-dimensional vision. Measuring 12,000 stadia (c. 1,400 miles) on a side, the new Jerusalem dwarfs Ezekiel's 1½-mile square. Like Ezekiel's city, the new Jerusalem has 12 gates, three on a side, each named for one of the tribes of Israel, their specific locations not given (Rev 21:12-13; cf. Ezek 48:31). Each gate of the new Jerusalem is made of a single pearl (Rev 21:21). Unlike Ezekiel's city, the foundation stones of the new Jerusalem are described—twelve stones, each named for one of the apostles and each made of a different jewel stone (Rev 21:14, 19-20; the splendor of the city reflects Isa 54:11-12).

Most startling to the reader of Ezekiel, whose final visions begin with a new temple, the new Jerusalem has no temple (Rev 21:22). Ezekiel's promise emphatically linked God's eternal dwelling among his people with the temple that God would put among them (37:26-28). John is told in the new Jerusalem "God's home is now among his people! He will live with them, and they will be his people." John is also told that the Lord God the Almighty and the Lamb are themselves the new Jerusalem's temple (Rev 21:3, 22).

One comes away from reading these texts with the suspicion that Revelation 22 presents a self-conscious adaptation and exposition of Ezekiel 47 and 48 (among other passages). John made clear allusions to the text and concepts in these passages, perhaps with the Hebrew text in mind more than any Greek version, but following neither the proto-Masoretic Text nor the Septuagint slavishly. (On the larger question of John's use of the OT, see especially Beale 1998.) John the Revelator, it appears, saw Ezekiel's promise of the life-giving presence of Yahweh and his Spirit as ultimately fulfilled in the new Jerusalem, which for John represented the consummation of all God's redeeming work in history. The two visions—Ezekiel's and John's—mark the presence of God and the life-giving Spirit (see commentary on 47:1-12) as the chief features of the eternal city/land and the rule of God. This makes participation in these dimensions of the life of God of utmost import now, linking us with the ancient hopes and the promised destiny of the Lord's own people.

In both Ezekiel and Revelation, focus is on the people of God and God's saving, sovereign residence, glorious among them, expelling sin and sadness. The new Jerusalem is the bride, the church (Rev 21:9). That is, John's whole vision expounds the reality of the triumphant church as the creation of God that bridges the aeons to the new creation. In John, as in Ezekiel, this hope is pastorally motivated, seeking to inspire and undergird faithfulness and courage in the face of suffering and the threats of despotic rule and demonic forces. John's hermeneutic universalizes the prophecy of Ezekiel by interpreting it Christocentrically and ecclesiocentrically, and by incorporating Ezekiel's vision of the decisive restoration of Israel into the climax of all human history and the redemption of all God's people, drawn from all the nations of the earth.

BIBLIOGRAPHY

Ackerman, Susan
1992 *Under Every Green Tree: Popular Religion in Sixth-century Judah.* Atlanta: Scholars.

Aharoni, Yohanan
1967 *The Land of the Bible: A Historical Geography.* Translator, A. F. Rainey. Philadelphia: Westminster.

Aharoni, Yohanan, and Michael Avi-Yonah
1968 *The Macmillan Bible Atlas.* New York: Macmillan.

Albright, William Foxwell
1968 *Archaeology and the Religion of Israel.* 5th ed. New York: Doubleday.

Alexander, Ralph H.
1986 Ezekiel. Pp. 737-996 in *Expositor's Bible Commentary*, vol. 6. Editor, F. E. Gaebelein. Grand Rapids: Zondervan.

Allen, Leslie C.
1990 *Ezekiel 20–48.* Word Biblical Commentary 29. Waco: Word.

1994 *Ezekiel 1–19.* Word Biblical Commentary 28. Waco: Word.

Almada, Samuel E.
2004 Ezekiel 1–39. Pp. 234-245 in *Global Bible Commentary.* Editor, Daniel Patte. Nashville: Abingdon.

Amiet, Pierre, Christiane Desroches Noblecourt, Alain Pasquier, François Baratte, and Catherine Metzger
1981 *Art in the Ancient World: A Handbook of Styles and Forms.* Translator, Valerie Bynner. New York: Rizzoli International.

Andersen, Francis I.
1970 *The Hebrew Verbless Clause in the Pentateuch.* Journal of Biblical Literature Monograph Series No. 14. Nashville: Abingdon.

Archer, Gleason L., Jr.
1964 *A Survey of Old Testament Introduction.* Chicago: Moody.

Arnold, Bill T.
2004 *Who Were the Babylonians?* Archaeology and Biblical Studies 10. Editor, Andrew G. Vaughn. Atlanta: Society of Biblical Literature.

Arnold, Bill T., and Brian E. Beyer
2002 *Readings from the Ancient Near East: Primary Sources for Old Testament Study.* Grand Rapids: Baker Academic.

Arnold, Bill T., and John H. Choi
2003 *A Guide to Biblical Hebrew Syntax.* Cambridge: Cambridge University.

Baudissin, Wolf Wilhelm Graffen
1876 *Studien zur Semitischen Religionsgeschichte*, vol. 1. Leipzig: Fr. Wilh. Grunow.

Beale, G. K.
1998 *John's Use of the Old Testament in Revelation.* Journal for the Study of the New Testament Supplement 166. Sheffield: Sheffield Academic.

Beckwith, R. T.
2000 The Canon of Scripture. Pp. 27-34 in *New Dictionary of Biblical Theology.* Downers Grove, IL: InterVarsity.

Beegle, Dewey M.
1978 *Prophecy and Prediction.* Ann Arbor, MI: Pettengill.

Begg, Christopher T.
1992 Inquiring of God. Pp. 417-418 in *Anchor Bible Dictionary*, vol. 3. Editor, David Noel Freedman. New York: Doubleday.

Berry, George Ricker
1939 The Composition of the Book of Ezekiel. *Journal of Biblical Literature* 58:163-175.

Bertholet, Alfred
1937 *Das Buch Hesekiel.* Freiburg: J.C.B. Mohr.

Blenkinsopp, Joseph

1990 *Ezekiel.* Interpretation: A Biblical Commentary for Teaching and Preaching. Louisville: John Knox.

Block, Daniel I.

1997 *The Book of Ezekiel: Chapters 1–24.* Grand Rapids: Eerdmans.

1998 *The Book of Ezekiel: Chapters 25–48.* Grand Rapids: Eerdmans.

Boadt, Lawrence

1986 Rhetorical Strategies in Ezekiel's Oracles of Judgment. *Ezekiel and His Book. Textual and Literary Criticism and Their Interrelation.* Editor, J. Lust. Bibliotheca Ephemeridum Theologicarum Lovaniensium 74. Leuven: Leuven University Press.

Bright, John

2000 *A History of Israel with an Introduction and Appendix by William P. Brown.* 4th ed. Louisville: Westminster/John Knox.

Broome, E. C.

1946 Ezekiel's Abnormal Personality. *Journal of Biblical Literature* 65:277-292.

Brown, Raymond E.

1966 *The Gospel according to John (i-xii).* Anchor Bible 29. New York: Doubleday.

Brownlee, William H.

1986 *Ezekiel 1–19.* Word Biblical Commentary 28. Waco: Word.

Brueggemann, Walter

2001 *The Prophetic Imagination.* 2nd ed. Minneapolis: Fortress.

Bunn, John T.

1971 *Ezekiel.* Broadman Bible Commentary 6. Nashville: Broadman.

Burnside, Jonathan P.

2003 *The Signs of Sin: Seriousness of Offence in Biblical Law.* Journal for the Study of Old Testament Supplement 364. London: Sheffield Academic.

Calvin, John

1948 *Commentaries on the First Twenty Chapters of the Book of Ezekiel Now First Translated from the Original Latin and Collated with the French Version.* Translator, Thomas Myers. 2 vols. Grand Rapids: Eerdmans.

Chafer, Louis Sperry

1948 *Systematic Theology,* vol. 5. Dallas: Dallas Theological Seminary.

Childs, Brevard S.

1979 *Introduction to the Old Testament as Scripture.* Philadelphia: Fortress.

1986 *Old Testament Theology in a Canonical Context.* Philadelphia: Fortress.

Chisholm, Robert B., Jr.

1998 *From Exegesis to Exposition: A Practical Guide to Using Biblical Hebrew.* Grand Rapids: Baker.

Clermont-Ganneau, C.

1871 Discovery of a Tablet from Herod's Temple. *Palestine Exploration Fund* 3:132-133.

Comfort, Philip

1994 *I Am the Way: A Spiritual Journey through the Gospel of John.* Grand Rapids: Baker.

Cooke, G. A.

1936 *A Critical and Exegetical Commentary on the Book of Ezekiel.* The International Critical Commentary. Edinburgh: T&T Clark.

Cornill, Carl

1907 *Introduction to the Canonical Books of the Old Testament.* Translator, G. H. Box. London: Williams & Norgate.

Cotterell, P., and M. Turner

1989 *Linguistics and Biblical Interpretation.* Downers Grove, IL: InterVarsity.

Cross, Frank Moore, and Shemaryahu Talmon

1975 *Qumran and the History of the Biblical Text.* Cambridge, MA: Harvard University Press.

Currid, John D.

1997 *Ancient Egypt and the Old Testament.* Grand Rapids: Baker.

Darr, Katheryn Pfisterer

1998 Ezekiel. Pp. 192-200 in *Women's Bible Commentary: Expanded Edition.* Editors, Carol A. Newsom and Sharon H. Ringe. Louisville: Westminster/John Knox.

2001 *The Book of Ezekiel: Introduction, Commentary, and Reflections.* The New Interpreter's Bible, vol. 6. Nashville: Abingdon.

Davis, Ellen

1989 *Swallowing the Scroll: Textuality and the Dynamics of Discourse in Ezekiel's Prophecy.* Journal for the Study of the Old Testament Supplement 78. Sheffield: Almond.

De Wette, Wilhelm Martin Liberecht

1858 *A Critical and Historical Introduction to the Canonical Scriptures of the Old Testament,* vol. 2. Translator, Theodore Parker. Boston: Little, Brown & Co.

Dever, William G.

2001 *What Did the Biblical Writers Know and When Did They Know It?* Grand Rapids: Eerdmans.

2005 *Did God Have a Wife? Archaeology and Folk Religion in Ancient Israel.* Grand Rapids: Eerdmans.

Dijkstra, Meindert

1986 The Glosses in Ezekiel Reconsidered. Pp. 55-77 in *Ezekiel and His Book: Textual and Literary Criticism and Their Interrelation.* Editor, J. Lust. Bibliotheca Ephemeridum Theologicarum Lovaniensium 74. Leuven: Leuven University Press.

Driver, S. R.

1909 *An Introduction to the Literature of the Old Testament.* International Theological Library. New York: Charles Scribner's Sons.

Duguid, Iain M.

1994 *Ezekiel and the Leaders of Israel.* Supplement to Vetus Testamentum 56. Leiden: Brill.

Eichrodt, W.

1970 *Ezekiel: A Commentary.* Translator, Cosslet Quin. Old Testament Library. Philadelphia: Westminster.

Eissfeldt, Otto

1965 *The Old Testament: An Introduction, Including the Apocrypha and Pseudepigrapha, and also the Works of Similar Type from Qumran.* New York: Harper & Row.

Fairbairn, Patrick

1979 *An Exposition of Ezekiel.* Minneapolis: Kloch & Kloch. (Orig. pub. 1851.)

Feinberg, Charles Lee

1969 *The Prophecy of Ezekiel: The Glory of the Lord.* Chicago: Moody.

Fishbane, Michael

1985 *Biblical Interpretation in Ancient Israel.* Oxford: Clarendon Press.

1987 Sin and Judgment in the Prophecies of Ezekiel. Pp. 170-187 *Interpreting the Prophets.* Editors, James Luther Mays and Paul J. Achtemeier. Philadelphia: Fortress.

Fohrer, George

1952 *Die Hauptprobleme des Buches Ezechiel.* Beihefte zur Zeitschrift fur die alttestamentliche Wissenschaft 72.

Forbes, R. J.

1964 *Studies in Ancient Technologies,* vol. 9. Leiden: Brill.

Freedy, K. S., and D. B. Redford

1970 The Dates in Ezekiel in Relation to Biblical, Babylonian and Egyptian Sources. *Journal of the American Oriental Society* 90:462-485.

Friebel, Kelvin G.

1999 *Jeremiah's and Ezekiel's Sign-acts.* Journal for the Study of the Old Testament Supplement 283. Editors, David J. A. Clines and Philip R. Davies. Sheffield: Sheffield Academic.

Galambush, Julie

1992 *Jerusalem in the Book of Ezekiel: The City as Yahweh's Wife.* Atlanta: Scholars Press.

García Martínez, Florentino

1992 *The Dead Sea Scrolls Translated: The Qumran Texts in English.* 2nd ed. Translator, Wilfred G. E. Watson. Grand Rapids: Eerdmans.

Greenberg, Moshe

1983 *Ezekiel 1–20.* Anchor Bible 22. New York: Doubleday.

1987 The Design and Themes of Ezekiel's Program of Restoration. Pp. 215-236 in *Interpreting the Prophets.* Editors, James Luther Mays and Paul J. Achtemeier. Philadelphia: Fortress.

1997 *Ezekiel 21–37.* Anchor Bible 22A. New York: Doubleday.

Halperin, David J.

1993 *Seeking Ezekiel: Text and Psychology.* Pennsylvania State University Press.

Hamilton, Victor P.

1990 *The Book of Genesis: Chapters 1–17.* New International Commentary on the Old Testament. Grand Rapids: Eerdmans.

Harford, John Battersby

1935 *Studies in the Book of Ezekiel.* Cambridge: Cambridge University Press.

Harrison, R. K.

1969 *Introduction to the Old Testament with a Comprehensive Review of Old Testament Studies and a Special Supplement on the Apocrypha.* Grand Rapids: Eerdmans.

Hartley, John E.

1992 *Leviticus.* Word Biblical Commentary 4. Waco: Word.

Hitzig, F.

1847 *Der Prophet Ezekiel Erklärt.* Kurzgefasstes exegetisches Hand buch zum Alten Testament. Leipzig: Weidmannsche.

Hobbs, T. R.

1985 *2 Kings.* Word Biblical Commentary 13. Waco: Word.

Hoerth, Alfred J., Gerald L. Mattingly, and Edwin M. Yamauchi

1994 *Peoples of the Old Testament World.* Grand Rapids: Baker.

Hölscher, Gustav

1924 *Hesekiel, der dichter und das buch: eine literarkritische untersuchung.* Beihefte zur Zeitschrift für die alttestamentliche Wissenschaft 39. Giessen: A. Töpelmann.

Howie, C. G.

1950 *The Date and Composition of Ezekiel.* Philadelphia: Society of Biblical Literature.

Huffmon, Herbert

1976 The Origins of Prophecy. Pages 171-186 of *Magnalia Dei, the Mighty Acts of God: Essays on the Bible and Archaeology in Memory of G. Ernest Wright.* Editors, Frank Moore Cross, Werner E. Lemke and Patrick D. Miller, Jr. New York: Doubleday.

Irwin, William A.

1943 *The Problem of Ezekiel: An Inductive Study.* Chicago: The University of Chicago Press.

Jastrow, Marcus

1927 *A Dictionary of the Targumim, the Talmud Babli and Yerushalmi, and the Midrashic Literature.* 2 vols. New York: Pardes.

Josephus

1926 *Josephus: The Life, Against Apion.* Translator, H. St. J. Thackeray. Loeb Classical Library. Cambridge, MA: Harvard University Press.

1937 *Josephus: Jewish Antiquities IX-XI.* Translator, Ralph Marcus. Loeb Classical Library. Cambridge, MA: Harvard University Press.

Joyce, Paul

1989 *Divine Initiative and Human Response in Ezekiel.* Journal for the Study of the Old Testament Supplement 51. Sheffield: Sheffield Academic.

Keel, Othmar, and Christoph Uehlinger

1998 *Gods, Goddesses, and Images of God in Ancient Israel.* Translator, Thomas H. Trapp. Minneapolis: Fortress.

Keil, C. F., and F. Delitzsch.

1989 Ezekiel, Daniel. *Commentary on the Old Testament,* vol. 9. Translator, James Martin. Peabody, MA: Hendrickson.

Klein, Ralph W.

1974 *Textual Criticism of the Old Testament: The Septuagint after Qumran: Old Testament Series.* Editor, Gene M. Tucker. Philadelphia: Fortress.

1988 *Ezekiel: The Prophet and His Message.* Studies on Personalities of the Old Testament. Editor, James L. Crenshaw. Columbia, SC: University of South Carolina Press.

Kraetzschmar, R.

1900 *Das Buch Ezechiel: übersetzt und erklärt.* Handkommentar zum Alten Testament. Abteilung 3, Die prophetischen Bücher; Bd. 3, T. 1. Göttingen: Vandenhoeck & Ruprecht.

Kutsch, Ernst

1985 *Die chronologischen Daten des Ezekielbuches.* Orbis Biblicus et Orientalia 62. Frieburg Schweiz: Universtäts Verlag.

Lang, Bernhard

1986 Street Theater, Raising the Dead, and the Zoroastrian Connection in Ezekiel's Prophecy. Pp. 297-316 in *Ezekiel and His Book: Textual and Literary Criticism and Their Interrelation.* Editor, J. Lust. Bibliotheca Ephemeridum Theologicarum Lovaniensium 74. Leuven: Leuven University Press.

Lange, John Peter

n.d. *Ezekiel.* Commentary on the Holy Scriptures Critical, Doctrinal and Homiletical. Grand Rapids: Zondervan.

Lapsley, Jacqueline E.

2000 *Can These Bones Live? The Problem of the Moral Self in the Book of Ezekiel.* Band 301. Beihefte zur Zeitschrift fur die alttestamentliche Wissenschaft. New York: Walter de Gruyter.

Levenson, Jon Douglas

1976 *Theology of the Program of Restoration of Ezekiel 40–48.* Harvard Semitic Series 10. Editor, Frank Moore Cross, Jr. Missoula, MT: Scholars Press.

1985 *Sinai and Zion: An Entry into the Jewish Bible.* New Voices in Biblical Studies. Editors, Adela Yarbro Collins and John J. Collins. New York: HarperSanFrancisco.

Levitt Kohn, Risa

2002 *A New Heart and a New Soul: Ezekiel, the Exile and the Torah.* Journal for the Study of the Old Testament Supplement 358. New York: Sheffield Academic.

2003 Ezekiel at the Turn of the Century. *Currents in Biblical Research* 2.1:9-13.

Luckenbill, Daniel D.

1927 *Ancient Records of Assyria and Babylon,* vol 2. Historical Records of Assyria. Repr., New York: Greenwood, 1968.

Lust, Johan

1986a Ezekiel Manuscripts in Qumran. Preliminary Edition of 4Q Ez a and b. Pp. 90-101 in *Ezekiel and His Book: Textual and Literary Criticism and Their Interrelation.* Editor, J. Lust. Bibliotheca Ephemeridum Theologicarum Lovaniensium 74. Leuven: Leuven University Press.

1986b The Final Text and Textual Criticism: Ez 39,28. Pp. 48-54 in *Ezekiel and His Book: Textual and Literary Criticism and Their Interrelation.* Editor, J. Lust. Bibliotheca Ephemeridum Theologicarum Lovaniensium 74. Leuven: Leuven University Press.

Lust, Johan, Erik Eynikel, and Katrin Hauspie

2003 *Greek-English Lexicon of the Septuagint.* Rev. ed. Stüttgart: Deutsche Bibelgesellschaft.

Matthews, Victor H., and Don C. Benjamin

1993 *Social World of Ancient Israel 1250–587 BCE.* Peabody, MA: Hendrickson.

May, Herbert G.

1952 The Book of Ezekiel. *Interpreter's Bible,* vol 6. Editor, George Arthur Buttrick. Nashville: Abingdon.

Mazar, Amihai

1990 *Archaeology of the Land of the Bible 10,000–586 B.C.E.* New York: Doubleday.

McCarter, P. Kyle

1986 *Textual Criticism: Recovering the Text of the Hebrew Bible.* Guides to Biblical Scholarship: Old Testament Series. Editor, Gene M. Tucker. Philadelphia: Fortress.

Meyers, Carol L., and M. O'Connor, editors

1983 *The Word of the Lord Shall Go Forth: Essays in Honor of David Noel Freedman in Celebration of His Sixtieth Birthday.* American Schools of Oriental Research Special Volume Series 1. Winona Lake, IN: Eisenbrauns.

Milgrom, Jacob

1991 *Leviticus 1–16.* Anchor Bible 3. New York: Doubleday.

1992 Priestly ("P") Source. Pages 456-461 in *Anchor Bible Dictionary,* vol. 5. Editor, David Noel Freedman. New York: Doubleday.

Millard, A. R.
1962 Ezekiel 29:17: The Wine Trade of Damascus. *Journal of Semitic Studies* 7:201-203.

Miller, J. Maxwell, and John H. Hayes
1986 *A History of Ancient Israel and Judah.* Philadelphia: Westminster.

Miller, Patrick D.
2000 *The Religion of Ancient Israel.* Library of Ancient Israel. Editor, Douglas A. Knight. Louisville: Westminster John Knox.

Moore, George Foot
1927 *Judaism in the First Centuries of the Christian Era. The Age of the Tannaim.* 3 vols. New York: Schocken Books.

Mulder, Martin Jan
1986 Die Neue Pesitta-Ausgabe von Ezechiel. Pp. 101-110 of *Ezekiel and His Book: Textual and Literary Criticism and Their Interrelation.* Editor, J. Lust. Bibliotheca Ephemeridum Theologicarum Lovaniensium 74. Leuven: Leuven University Press.

Meyers, Carol L., and Eric M. Meyers
1993 *Zechariah 9–14.* Anchor Bible 25C. New York: Doubleday.

Neusner, Jacob
1994 *Hagigah.* The Talmud of Babylonia: An Academic Commentary 12. Atlanta: Scholars Press.

1996a *Bavli Tractate Baba Batra A. Chapters I through VI.* The Talmud of Babylonia: An Academic Commentary 22. Atlanta: Scholars Press.

1996b *Bavli Tractate Menahot A. Chapters I through VI.* The Talmud of Babylonia: An Academic Commentary 29. Atlanta: Scholars Press.

Newsom, Carol A.
1987 A Maker of Metaphors: Ezekiel's Oracles against Tyre. Pp. 188-199 in *Interpreting the Prophets.* Editors, James Luther Mays and Paul J. Achtemeier. Philadelphia: Fortress.

Oppenheim, A. Leo
1964 *Ancient Mesopotamia: Portrait of a Dead Civilization.* Chicago: University of Chicago Press.

Ortlund, Raymond C., Jr.
1996 *Whoredom: God's Unfaithful Wife in Biblical Theology.* New Studies in Biblical Theology. Editor, D. A. Carson. Grand Rapids: Eerdmans.

Parrot, Andre
1961 *Nineveh and Babylon.* Translators, Stuart Emmons and James Emmons. London: Thames & Hudson.

Patton, Corrine L.
2000 Should Our Sister Be Treated Like a Whore? A Response to Feminist Critiques of Ezekiel 23. Pp. 221-238 in *The Book of Ezekiel: Theological and Anthropological Perspectives.* Editors, Margaret Odell and John T. Strong. Atlanta: Society of Biblical Literature.

Pfeiffer, R. H.
1941 *Introduction to the Old Testament.* New York: Harper & Brothers.

Poole, Matthew
1962 *A Commentary on the Holy Bible.* 3 vols. London: The Banner of Truth Trust.

Pritchard, James B.
1997 *HarperCollins Concise Atlas of the Bible.* New York: HarperOne.

Provan, Iain, V. Philips Long, and Tremper Longman III
2003 *A Biblical History of Israel.* Louisville: Westminster/John Knox.

Rainey, Anson F., and R. Steven Notley
2001 *The Sacred Bridge: Carta's Atlas of the Biblical World, an Overview of the Ancient Levant.* Jerusalem: Carta.

Rehm, Merlin D.
1992 Levites and Priests. Pp. 297-310 in *Anchor Bible Dictionary,* vol. 4. Editor, David Noel Freedman. New York: Doubleday.

Rendtorff, Rolf
2005 *The Canonical Hebrew Bible: A Theology of the Old Testament.* Translator, David E. Orton. Tools for Biblical Study 7. Leiden: Deo Publishing.

Richter, Sandra L.

2008 *The Epic of Eden: A Christian Entry into the Old Testament.* Downers Grove, IL: IVP Academic.

Schniedewind, W. M.

2004 *How the Bible Became a Book: The Textualization of Ancient Israel.* Cambridge: Cambridge University Press.

Schwartz, Baruch

2000 Ezekiel's Dim View of Israel's Restoration. Pp. 42-68 in *The Book of Ezekiel: Theological and Anthropological Perspectives.* Editors, Margaret S. Odell and John T. Strong. Atlanta: Society of Biblical Literature.

Smith, Mark S.

1990 *The Early History of God: Yahweh and the Other Deities in Ancient Israel.* San Francisco: Harper.

Soggin, J. Alberto

1989 *Introduction to the Old Testament from Its Origins to the Closing of the Alexandrian Canon.* 3rd ed. Old Testament Library. Translator, John Bowden. Louisville: Westminster/John Knox.

Steen, Eveline J. van der

2000 Metallurgy. Pp. 68-70 of *New Interpreter's Dictionary of the Bible,* vol. 4. Nashville: Abingdon.

Stern, Ephraim

2001 *Archaeology of the Land of the Bible: The Assyrian, Babylonian, and Persian Periods 732–332 BCE.* New York: Doubleday.

Swartley, Willard M.

1983 *Slavery, Sabbath, War & Women: Case Issues in Biblical Interpretation.* Scottsdale, PA: Herald.

Talmon, S., and M. Fishbane

1976 The Structuring of Biblical Books: Studies in the Book of Ezekiel. Pp. 129-253 in *Annual of the Swedish Theological Institute 10.* Editor, Bengt Knutsson. Leiden: E. J. Brill.

Taylor, John B.

1969 *Ezekiel: An Introduction and Commentary.* Tyndale Old Testament Commentaries. Leicester, U.K.: Inter-Varsity.

Thiele, Edwin R.

1965 *The Mysterious Numbers of the Hebrew Kings: A Reconstruction of the Chronology of the Kingdoms of Israel and Judah.* Rev. ed. Grand Rapids: Eerdmans.

Thompson, David L.

1975 Old Testament Bases of the Wesleyan Message. *Wesleyan Theological Journal* 10:38-47.

1981 A Problem of Unfulfilled Prophecy in Ezekiel: The Destruction of Tyre. *Wesleyan Theological Journal* 16/1:93-106.

1996 Women, Men, Slaves and the Bible: Hermeneutical Inquiries. *Christian Scholar's Review* 25/3:326-349.

Torrey, Charles Cutler

1930 *Pseudo-Ezekiel and the Original Prophecy.* Yale Oriental Series 18. Researches in the Library of Biblical Studies. Editor, Harry M. Orlinski. Prolegomenon by Moshe Greenberg. New York: KTAV.

Tov, Emmanuel

1986 Recensional Differences between the MT and the LXX of Ezekiel. *Epherimerides theologicae lovaniensis* 62:89-101.

1992 *Textual Criticism of the Hebrew Bible.* Minneapolis: Fortress.

Tribble, Phyllis

1984 *Texts of Terror: Literary-feminist Readings of Biblical Narratives.* Overtures of Biblical Theology. Philadelphia: Fortress.

Tromp, Nicholas J.

1986 The Paradox of Ezekiel's Prophetic Mission: Towards a Semiotic Approach of Ezekiel 3,22-27. Pp. 201-213 in *Ezekiel and His Book: Textual and Literary Criticism and Their Interrelation.* Editor, J. Lust. Bibliotheca Ephemeridum Theologicarum Lovaniensium 74. Leuven: Leuven University Press.

Tuell, Steven Shawn

1992 *The Law of the Temple in Ezekiel 40–48.* Harvard Semitic Monographs 49. Editor, F. M. Cross. Atlanta: Scholars Press.

2001 *Ezekiel.* New International Biblical Commentary. Peabody, MA: Hendrickson.

Vaux, Roland de

1961 *Ancient Israel.* 2 vols. New York: McGraw-Hill.

Waltke, Bruce K.

1988 Kingdom Promises as Spiritual. Pp. 263-288 in *Continuity and Discontinuity: Perspectives on the Relationship between the Old and New Testaments.* Editor, John S. Feinberg. Westchester, IL: Crossway.

Waltke, Bruce K., and M. O'Connor

1990 *An Introduction to Biblical Hebrew Syntax.* Winona Lake, IN: Eisenbrauns.

Weems, Renita J.

1995 *Battered Love: Marriage, Sex, and Violence in the Hebrew Prophets.* Overtures to Biblical Theology. Minneapolis: Fortress.

Weinfeld, Moshe

1991 *Deuteronomy 1–11.* Anchor Bible 5. Editors, William F. Albright and David N. Freedman. New York: Doubleday.

Weiser, Artur

1961 *The Old Testament: Its Formation and Development.* Translator, D. Barton. New York: Association.

Wenham, Gordon H.

1981 *Numbers: An Introduction and Commentary.* Tyndale Old Testament Commentaries. Editor, D. J. Wiseman. Leicester, U.K.: Inter-Varsity.

Wilson, Robert R.

1987 Prophecy in Crisis: The Call of Ezekiel. Pp. 157-169 in *Interpreting the Prophets.* Editors, James Luther Mays and Paul J. Achtemeier. Philadelphia: Fortress.

Wiseman, D. J.

1956 *Chronicles of the Chaldean Kings (626–556 BC) in the British Museum.* London: British Museum.

1983 *Nebuchadnezzar and Babylon.* London: Oxford University Press for the British Academy.

Wright, Christopher J. H.

2001 *The Message of Ezekiel.* The Bible Speaks Today. Downers Grove, IL: InterVarsity.

Wright, John W.

1995 Toward a Holiness Hermeneutic: The Old Testament against Israelite Religion. *Wesleyan Theological Journal* 30.2:68-90.

Würtwein, Ernst

1979 *The Text of the Old Testament: An Introduction to the Biblia Hebraica.* Translator, Erroll F. Rhodes, from the 4th ed. of Des Text des Alten Testaments. Grand Rapids: Eerdmans.

Yadin, Yigael

1963 *The Art of Warfare in Biblical Lands.* 2 vols. Translator, M. Pearlman. New York: McGraw-Hill.

Young, Edward J.

1949 *An Introduction to the Old Testament.* Grand Rapids: Eerdmans.

Zimmerli, Walther

1979 *Ezekiel 1: A Commentary on the Book of the Prophet Ezekiel, Chapters 1–24.* Translator, Ronald E. Clements. Hermeneia—A Critical and Historical Commentary on the Bible. Philadelphia: Fortress. From *Ezechiel Teilband,* Biblischer Kommentar Altes Testament, Band XIII/1. Neukirchen-vluyn: Neukirchener Verlag des Erziehungsvereins GmbH, 1969.

1982 *I Am Yahweh.* Editor, Walter Brueggemann. Translator, Douglas W. Stott. Atlanta: John Knox.

1983 *Ezekiel 2: A Commentary on the Book of the Prophet Ezekiel, Chapters 25–48.* Translator, James D. Martin. Hermeneia—A Critical and Historical Commentary on the Bible. Philadelphia: Fortress. From *Ezechiel 2, II Teilband,* Biblischer Kommentar Altes Testament, Band XIII/2. Neukirchen-vluyn: Neukirchener Verlag des Erziehungsvereins GmbH, 1969.

Daniel

EUGENE CARPENTER

INTRODUCTION TO

Daniel

THE BOOK OF DANIEL fascinates people and rightly so. It is *sui generis* in the Old Testament and even among its noncanonical competitors (Knibb 2001:34). But that assertion must be defined and qualified in various ways, for it is also like other books in the Old Testament: The Joseph narrative in Genesis and portions of Esther are similar to the first six chapters of Daniel; certain prophetic passages (e.g., Isa 24–27; Zech 9–14) have the ambiance and style (basic genre) of chapters 7–12 of Daniel and may be termed protoapocalyptic. In general, it can be said that Daniel combines features found in these other books in a new and powerful presentation and adds much more.

As noted, the book contains stories reminiscent of the stories about Joseph and Esther as well as visions such as were seen by the prophets, but in Daniel, these are narrated in an unprecedented way. The book combines history, court tales (historical, but crafted in a certain way), wisdom illustrations, declarations (of the mantic variety as well as practical),[1] prophecy (he does foretell the future, 2:28; 10:14; and declare words of judgment to the kings in the present, 4:27 [24]; 5:26-27), and apocalyptic visions and dreams into a powerfully crafted presentation of God's intentions and interaction with history and history's response and interaction with the heavenly world. The book speaks theologically and practically to a people that had and would again experience siege, attack, and oppression in order to give them hope.

The wisdom and prudence of Daniel as a witness for Israel's God, even in the court of the great king Nebuchadnezzar, stands out in this dynamic and intriguing document. The heroic stories of Daniel and his contemporaries (chs 1–6) standing firm in the face of death as witnesses for the Lord in a pagan, idolatrous culture are a great example for God's people of all generations. Daniel's visions of the crumbling kingdoms of this world (chs 7–12) as they move inexorably toward destruction and his vision of the everlasting Kingdom of God ruled by the Son of Man and the saints of the Most High God provide a spectacular and awesome background for the New Testament revelation of the Kingdom of God ruled by Jesus Christ. Daniel's visions also prepare the way for an understanding of two resurrections—one that leads to judgment and one that leads to everlasting life—a truth that became central to the message of the book for many who read it in the intertestamental period and for those who would later read it as a part of the Christian canon.

AUTHOR

The author-compiler (hereafter "author" means author-compiler unless specifically qualified) of the final form of this book could have been Daniel (he certainly authored large portions of the book), but it was more likely another person of the Judahite royal family or other noble families (1:3, 6) based on the compositional indicators in the book. It is clear that several Jewish young men were trained in the language and literature of the Babylonians (1:4), and they probably would have learned through oral or written tradition the stories of Daniel and his companions. There were more than four of them (1:6), and at least one of them was inspired by God to compile and craft the book in its final form (cf. Beckwith 1985:416-417). This person could have put the book into its final form, but the book also clearly indicates that Daniel was the author of several portions of the book (see below, "Date and Place of Writing" and "Literary Unity") so that Daniel remains the major and most important contributor to the composition of the book. Under the scenario described in chapter 1, based on the previous training and natural aptitudes of Daniel and the other young Jewish captives (1:4-7), and based upon their completion of the prescribed course of study (1:4), it appears that any one of them could have been the author-compiler of the final form of the book.

The author indicates that Daniel wrote down a substantial summary of his dreams and visions in chapters 7–12 (7:1, 8; 10:1), doing so in the first person (7:2; 8:1; cf. 8:26; 12:4, 9). In chapter 9 he writes his own prayer in the first person (9:4b-19), as well as the introduction (9:1-4a) and the vision that follows (9:20-27). The references that imply Daniel's writing in 12:4, 9 refer at least to the long visions of 10:2–12:4. They may refer to an entire scroll (*seper* [TH5612, ZH6219]; NLT, "book") that Daniel had maintained (12:4) to record the visions of chapters 7–12. Daniel wrote down the final vision and the concluding comments in 12:4-13. Daniel's special ability (1:17) to understand dreams and visions was complemented by the writing skill he had acquired in Imperial Aramaic, Hebrew, and probably Akkadian. His mastery of the language and literature of the Babylonians rivaled the accomplishments of Moses, who was taught all the language and learning of the Egyptians (Exod 2:9-11; Acts 7:22).

The introduction to the book (1:1-21), along with the dreams and stories of 2:1–6:28 [29], focus on Daniel and stem from the sixth-century BC diaspora in Babylon. They are written in the third person, as are the introductions in 7:1 and 10:1. These chapters could still have been written by Daniel, who was still engaged in diligent and energetic physical and spiritual disciplines at 80 to 83 years of age (6:3 [4]; 10:2), but they were more likely put together with the material in chapters 7–12 by a contemporary of Daniel near the end of his life or soon thereafter, during the time of the Persian Empire. The book states that Daniel's visions would become more relevant sometime after Daniel's death (8:26; 12:4, 9). The final author had in hand the material recorded by Daniel in 7:2–12:13. Similarly, the author had in hand the court stories in 2:1–6:28 [29] from written or oral tradition and composed the introduction in 1:1-21, all in the third person. By the same Spirit who had inspired Daniel, he composed the book as we have it, making Daniel the inspired, but also human hero of the book, but God the ultimate author of the book. The original genius and inspiration of the book is evident throughout, and its historicity, literary quality, and theological insights far surpass those portrayed in Daniel's pedestrian successors or imitators (e.g., *1 Enoch, Sibylline Oracles,* Baruch, 2 Esdras, *Assumption of Moses,* and the apocalyptic sections of *The Testaments of the Twelve Patriarchs*).

DATE AND PLACE OF WRITING

Daniel's writing of his accounts and the shaping of the final form of the book may have occurred in Babylon (7:1; 8:1) and/or Persia (1:21; 6:1 [2]; 9:1; 10:1), although this is not certain in either case.[2] More importantly, however, the dreams, visions and events in the book took place at a particular time—during and immediately following the Jews' exile in Babylon (see 1:21 and 10:1). Both events—the Exile and its end—were foretold as a part of God's plan (Deut 4:25-31; 28:64-68; 2 Chr 36:22-23; Ezra 1:1-11; Jer 25:8-14) for a disobedient people (9:4-19). This, ironically, is what makes the book of Daniel a book of hope, a book for people under siege, for at the nadir of their existence God spoke a word of anticipation to his people, a message that assured them that the Lord would yet establish his kingdom with them by exalting them above the superpowers of the day. The ruling superpowers would eventually fall, and God's Kingdom would be established in the end. Even in their exile, they should know that God was supreme among the gods and able to deliver his people against all odds (chs 3, 6).

In contrast with the suggestions of Babylon and Persia as places of composition for the book, many scholars today, including some conservative scholars, believe the book was composed in Judah during the Maccabean Era, being completed around 164 BC. Others have argued the book was composed in various stages, each stage meeting the needs of its contemporary audience. These views will be addressed briefly below.

Chapters 1–6 show their place of origin in many ways: While the Hebrew of Daniel cannot be dated to any particular century with certainty and convincing detail, it does "fit" better with the Hebrew of Ezra, Nehemiah, and Chronicles than with that of Ezekiel (Lucas 2002:307). This, however, does not rule out the suggestion above that the final author framed and formed the materials in the early Persian period or soon thereafter. The Aramaic of Daniel (2:4b–7:28) is most likely Imperial Aramaic, datable to roughly 700–200 BC (Stefanovic 1992:307), but Stefanovic argues that Daniel's Aramaic shows an impressive relationship with some Old Aramaic inscriptions. Also, the general word order of the Aramaic (the verb in last position) strongly suggests Akkadian syntax, which would place Daniel's Aramaic in the period of early Imperial Aramaic (c. seventh to fourth centuries BC) or earlier (Stefanovic 1992:106).[3] While Aramaic was probably used in Palestine at this time, the syntax suggests a Mesopotamian (e.g., Babylonian) origin rather than a western, Maccabean one. An origin for the book in Mesopotamia is very likely (Baldwin 1978a:31-32). Neither the Persian (probably Old Persian) words in the book nor the Greek words prohibit a sixth-century date for the book (Lucas 2002:307-308).

Chapters 1–6 portray a picture of pagan rulers that would not have been acceptable in the time of Antiochus Epiphanes (175–164 BC), for the Babylonian and Persian rulers are presented as much too benevolent toward Daniel and his Jewish friends. Although two of them have character flaws that foreshadow features of the chief players of the book in chapters 7–12, they also demonstrate fear and humility before the Most High as well, a feature that is not descriptive of Antiochus (11:21-35; cf. 11:36-45). Certain features, such as Babylonian ambiance, the religious officials involved and their use of omens, the genre of the court tale, the author's knowledge about Nebuchadnezzar as the builder of the Neo-Babylonian Empire (4:30 [27]) and his correct assertion about Belshazzar as "King" (5:1), all suggest the book's author knew intimately the workings of the eastern Akkadian cultures of the Babylonian and Persian empires (Baldwin 1978a:35-38).[4] Richard Patterson has recently argued that the "court-tale" motif may have taken on new force at the time the Jews returned from Babylonian exile and endured fierce opposition from their adversaries (539–432 BC). These tales of success at the court of pagan kings would have become stories of hope at that time. He concludes that data from various areas—historical background, political scenarios, cultural features, literary genre, setting—all combine to add integrity to the book's own claim to be presenting material and events from the sixth century (Patterson 1993:445-454).

Chapters 7–12 also have been shown to have features that suggest an eastern provenance as opposed to a western, Palestinian one. Chapter 7 presents a succession of two ancient Near Eastern empires (cf. Swain 1940:1-21) and two empires yet to arise from the west (which prove to be Greece and Rome). The Maccabean origin of these chapters is by no means certain. The most detailed chapter concerning Antiochus Epiphanes, chapter 11 (cf. 8:9-14), is at times not precise enough about the Maccabean crisis (11:36-45). If it were written only months or weeks after these events occurred (Ferch 1983:134-136), it should be even more precise. There is no established heuristic tool by which prophecy can be judged to be "too specific" to be considered prophecy before the event rather than prophecy after the event (*vaticinium ex eventu*). Daniel was given a message that outlined in broad strokes the Maccabean crisis as a model and foretaste of the ultimate onslaught against God's people. But his major concern was to illustrate God's divine providence within that period of political, military, and religious strife.

Daniel and his contemporaries needed to know that God was in control of all future history and would deliver his people in the face of all future attempts of annihilation (cf. 2 Thess 2:4; Rev 1:3). This message of future deliverance, however, indicated to some of God's people of the sixth century that they too would make it through their immediate times of trouble, just as earlier Nebuchadnezzar's dream and the decree to kill the wise men of Babylon were shared by Daniel with his three compatriots (2:17-19). Daniel and his friends did not work in a vacuum, and there was no charge to not share the events that they encountered in chapters 1–6.

In spite of the support for an eastern provenance and an early date, many scholars today believe Daniel was composed in the Maccabean era and probably arrived at its present form around 164 BC. It is argued that the final author-editor had chapters 2–6 and probably chapter 7 at hand in some written form, to which he appended his own compositions: chapter 1 and chapters 8–12.[5] (Note that many of these scholars affirm an earlier date for large portions of the book. Hence, there must have been a need for and use of those portions at an earlier time as well.) Some who hold this position do regard the book as holy Scripture—these chapters being considered inspired interpretations of history that had already passed in the plan of God. Some critics who hold to a Maccabean dating of the book, however, do so because they rule out any possibility of predictive prophecy. Other critics have argued that the book was composed in various stages, each stage meeting the needs of its contemporary audience. This view seems hard to sustain, given the literary unity and excellence of the final composition (Gammie 1976:191-204). Santoso is a recent example of this continuing approach (2007:284).

The claim for a Maccabean origin of the book, and even for chapters 7–12, has its problems (Ferch 1983:134-136), as does any claim for the date of this challenging book of the Canon. Gordon Wenham has summarized various arguments for a sixth-century date. These include the book's own claim to be predictive prophecy (2:29-31; 4:24 [21]; chs 7–12; see G. Wenham 1977:49-52), the author's claim that Daniel lived in the sixth century (2:1; 5:1; 10:1), the author's excellent knowledge of Babylonian history—unequaled in any other apocalypse, and the fact that information in 11:40-45 does not fit the known facts about Antiochus IV Epiphanes. The last point would seem to force those who hold to the second-century date to say that either Daniel or the heavenly interpreter erred as he shared from the Book of Truth (10:21).

Additionally, Daniel's apocalyptic character does not demand a second-century date for the book. The book was rather a model and source for later apocalypses. It is qualitatively superior to other apocalyptic literature, although it shares many features with them in whole or in part, for example, genre, eschatology, imagery, concern for history (in some), and use of other Old Testament books for concepts and imagery. There is quasiapocalyptic literature that precedes Daniel and attempts to foretell the future in a way similar in some ways to Daniel 11 (Longman 1999:311; Longman 1991:131-195; ANET 431-432, 605-607; Grayson and Lambert 1964; Arnold and Beyer 2002:207-217).

The problem of alleged historical inaccuracies in Daniel is challenging, but the presence of this problem in itself does not date the book to the second century BC, and the issues can be resolved in most cases based on the genre of the book and on a continuing increase in our knowledge of the world of the ancient Near East. One of the burdens of the book, and one of its major themes, is God's astonishing ability to predict the future (2:27-29). If the book was written as late as some claim, this point would fall flat, although some choose to view certain chapters (e.g., 11) as inspired interpretations of history after the fact. Another issue with a late date is the unproven idea of the acceptance of pseudonymity among the inspired biblical writers.[6] Pseudonymity and false theological claims do not make acceptable bedfellows with the integrity demanded of one of God's inspired prophets. In addition to this, certain theological concepts that link Daniel to the Old and New Testaments in an organic way,[7] the relationship of Mesopotamian texts as old as the seventh century to certain prophetic/apocalyptic aspects of Daniel,[8] and the probable date of the close of the Canon, which could be as early as 132 BC (Beckwith 1985:357-358, 415-417),[9] all support its antiquity. (See further, "Canonicity and Textual History" below.)

Joyce Baldwin, who dates the final form of the book to the sixth century, has noted that the interpretation of the book is not greatly changed just because we are not able to date its composition precisely (NIDOTTE 4.499). This sentiment is shared by Goldingay (1989:xl), who dates the final form of the book in the era of Antiochus Epiphanes (c. 164 BC). Not all commentators would agree with this sentiment, however, as it assumes much concerning the worldview of the individual interpreter. This commentary accepts an early date for the entire book (cf. Miller,

Longman, Young, McComiskey), but does not depreciate the work of those (such as Collins, Bruce, Goldingay, Lucas)[10] who are convinced that the book should be dated to the time of Antiochus. Their insights into the text and background of Daniel are invaluable. Although favoring the late date, Lucas (2002), for example, discusses the alleged historical inaccuracies, linguistic issues, the possibility of predictive prophecy in the book over against a prophetic inspired interpretation of history, the implications of an apocalyptic genre for dating, and Daniel's place in the Hebrew canon (versus its LXX placement).

OCCASION OF WRITING

Several reasons for the creation of the book of Daniel can be identified. The primary cause was theological: In his supreme act of judgment, God had sent his people into exile as he had said he would. The cause was therefore also historical and social, for God judged his people by means of the Babylonians in the sixth century BC. Certain ancient Akkadian apocalypses that preceded Daniel share this social setting of oppression, which has often engendered apocalyptic writings, although, as several studies have cautioned, the social setting was not the only factor at work. A certain theological milieu and worldview was necessary, and anthropological and sociological studies must be used with great caution when describing the origins of apocalypticism (Hanson 1979; Grabbe 1989; Collins 1991; S. L. Cook 1995; Sim 1995). Further, the Akkadian texts mentioned do not, in the materials now available, employ the highly developed imagery of Daniel, his periodization of history, or his apocalyptic eschatology, which reaches to the final consummation (see Longman 1991:189 for dating and details of these texts; cf. Hallo 1966:231-242).

Many of the particular historical acts that are important in Daniel have universal effects because they are brought about by Israel's God, who is shaping all of history to reach his goals. Another cause for the book's composition was to recount God's preservation of his people in the Exile, as depicted in his deliverance of them and certain of their pagan contemporaries (2:12-19). The book was also occasioned by the Lord's revelation of himself more fully to his own people (Daniel, Hananiah, Mishael, Azariah) and to pagan kings in dreams, visions, and mysteries, and through earthly and divine interpreters of these events. It was motivated by the challenge to be faithful in a pagan land and culture (cf. Deut 4:25-31) in the presence of pagan politics and false religion. It was necessary because of the failure of God's people. The book of Daniel was the Lord's promise to his people that there was a future for them if they would repent (7:22; 9:4-19; 12:2-3). It was the need for a model or pattern to follow in times of great crisis that called this book forth. It was finally time for God to give his people a word of hope and a view of the future Kingdom of God with its ruler, the Son of Man. It was the critical mass of all these things that combined to produce the events of Daniel's life and the book that bears his name. Daniel realized that the desolations of Jerusalem came because of his failure and the failure of his people (9:14, 16), but he also knew that these desolations would end (9:2). He implored God, as he had been doing all along (6:11 [12]). His plea for the Lord to hear and to act for the Lord's sake on behalf of his people (9:19) was answered: The Lord gave him further visions and words to impart insight and understanding (9:22-23; 10:1). God imparted mantic wisdom[11] to Daniel to help him and his people understand the puzzling circumstances that he had allowed to befall them.

In short, God revealed that he would not only judge his people, but also encourage them and redeem them according to his word—according to the promises in the covenant he had established with them in Abraham, in Moses at Mount Sinai, in the Davidic covenant, and in the promised new covenant (Jer 31:31-34). The Exile was traumatic; in Daniel's evaluation, it was unparalleled in God's dealings with his people (9:12). Just as the Exodus (Deut 4:32-34) was the Lord's salvific event par excellence on behalf of his people, so the Exile was the Lord's nadir of judgment against the people that he had given birth to (cf. Ezek 37). God not only supplied help for those among Daniel's immediate group, but he gave even more hope to persons in the future. New and progressive revelation was given—death would be overcome (12:2), even the death of exile (9:2; cf. Ezek 37), and both national and individual resurrection were revealed. All kingdoms, the Babylonian and Persian empires, even the future Greek and Roman kingdoms, would bow to the Kingdom of God at the appointed time. This unprecedented crisis for God's people became the occasion for him to reveal afresh his great mercy (9:18-19). Daniel was comforted to learn from Jeremiah's prophecy that the Exile would end soon, and lived to see its end (1:21; 10:1) in Babylon. Similarly, in a vision he saw the ultimate exodus from the grave in a powerful new way (12:2-3, 13) and was comforted and assured that he would experience that event (12:13).

The occasion for the book is not only historical or sociological conditions, it is theological. God acts both among and above his people to fulfill and sustain his goals and promises, not just for them, but for the nations. The occasion for the book is God's movement among the nations (Ezra 1:1-2) to accomplish his goals for his people. History will reflect his will (7:13-14). "Metahistory"—God and other spiritual forces working behind the events taking place in the flow of observable history—is a powerful influence in the shaping of the worldview in Daniel 7–12 and in many apocalyptic visions. But even in the court stories of chapters 1–6, the empires, featuring Babylon and Persia especially (also implied for two additional kingdoms and a fifth kingdom whose origin is God), present a movement toward a denouement of earthly kingdoms and a rise of a kingdom that will not fall (ch 2). And in the introduction, 1:3-5, 17, 18-20 prepare the reader for the interpretation of the dreams and visions of these chapters, as well as Daniel's and his friends' practical behavior in the royal court.

AUDIENCE

Whether the book has a Babylonian provenance and audience (sixth century BC) or, instead, a Maccabean provenance (second century BC), pales before the significance it has for God's people in all cultures and kingdoms. The book is a unity in its final form and, while it features two major sections, they are intrinsically bound together in places by theme, style, and form. In its final form the book is a didactic theological history told in apocalyptic form that binds earthly history and heavenly involvement together.[12] It employs a crafted introduction to prepare the reader for the stories and apocalyptic dreams and visions that have been skillfully woven together. The book teaches God's people how to position themselves in a hostile environment and how they should expect the course of world history to interface with them and their faith and traditions. Those who are truly wise and faithful will learn and will remain faithful to their Lord and traditions in whatever age they live; many will be successfully delivered in this life (chs 3, 6), some may die for their faith, but they will take their allotted place in the end just as Daniel will (12:13). The book is not only for God's people during the Babylonian exile, the Maccabean period, or the New Testament era—it is for the people of God through all of human history, and it will speak until history and heaven reach the omega point, the Kingdom of God.

The book's original audience was Daniel's three friends (1:6) and others of the royal and noble Israelites deported from Judah; but just as importantly, the book indicates that both a Babylonian and a Persian king and some people in their courts were aware of portions of chapters 2, 3, 4, and 6. Nebuchadnezzar was deeply affected by incidents in the lives of both Daniel and his friends (2:46-49; 3:28–4:3 [3:33]; 4:34-37 [31-34]). His actions resulted in others becoming aware of the God of Daniel and his friends (4:1-3 [3:31-33]; 4:34-37 [31-34]). Darius issued a decree extolling the God of Daniel (6:26-28). Others at the royal court, aware of some of the materials eventually included in the book, conspired to destroy Daniel and his three friends (chs 3, 6). Some among Daniel's people knew the stories and collected oral and written materials that were put into the book later by the author, but these materials (oral or written) also served to inform and aid those who encountered them before they were put into the final form of the book.

In the Maccabean era, the book's relevance was recognized and its influence consequently felt on a large scale. People living in the time of the Maccabean kingdom used the book to sustain them against the forces that were threatening to destroy God's people and assimilate them to the Hellenistic pagan culture of that time. Undoubtedly, some readers in between these two eras were helped as well—not just by the book's "how it will end" theme, but primarily by the picture the book gives of how to live successfully in God's sight until the end arrives (11:40; 12:1). Daniel's influence continued at Qumran, where it was a powerful influence (see "Canonicity and Textual History"), and in the era of the New Testament (see "The Prophetic Value of Daniel as Evidenced in the New Testament Writings"). We, as twenty-first-century Christians, need this book, perhaps more than any previous generation of God's people, because of the wisdom (both practical and revelatory) it reveals to those who wait for the coming of God's Kingdom. It will come at its appointed time, a fact that gives hope to the moral, religious, and ethical positions we are called upon to take in this present age (12:1-3; 1 Cor 15:12-19) as we live life with an eye on the future.

CANONICITY AND TEXTUAL HISTORY

The Masoretic Text of Daniel is written in Hebrew and Aramaic, a feature that has puzzled scholars for centuries. This dual-language feature helps give the book an evident "envelope" structure. The book of Job, which features prose in its introductory chapters (Job 1–2), poetry in its central dialogical/monological section (Job 3:1–42:6), and prose again in its epilogue (Job 42:7-16), has a similar threefold structure. Also, the Code of Hammurabi features an introduction in prose, laws written in legal form and terminology, and an epilogue in prose. This strongly suggests that the author of Daniel had this envelope pattern ready at hand in the literary tradition of his day, but it does not solve the puzzle surrounding the language pattern in Daniel.

Several viable suggestions have been put forth about the writer's use of two Semitic languages in the book. A relatively simple solution is probably better than many of the elaborate suggestions that have been offered (Baldwin 1978a:29-30): The introductory material in 1:1-21 concerns the destiny of Daniel, the three Hebrew youths, and the nation of Israel in exile. It is written in Hebrew. While 2:1-4a is also in Hebrew, 2:4b–7:28 is composed in Aramaic for the following reasons: (1) It primarily concerns the rise and fall, the ebb and flow of the kingdoms of this world. (2) Aramaic, the international language of the day (used in all international correspondence), gave an international flavor and supporting linguistic context to these court stories. (3) Chapter 7 begins to introduce Israel prominently again in the Son of Man figure (7:13-14, 18, 21-27) and in the presentation of the holy people of God (7:22, 25-27; cf. NIV, "saints of the Most High"), but the universal nature of the chapter ties it intimately to chapter 2, and appropriately the author presents the material in Aramaic to link the chapters together. Both chapters 2 and 7 are concerned with the future and God's ultimate control over its unfolding: Nebuchadnezzar was thinking about things to come, and God, who reveals mysteries, presented a magnificent panoramic view of the future (2:28-29). A similar view was presented to Daniel in the time of Belshazzar (7:1, 16-17). The "two halves" of the book are tied together at several levels by the official Aramaic of chapter 7 and its basic parallel content and ambiance to chapter 2. Thus, chapters 2 and 7 are the linchpins that link the first half of the book (1–6) and the second half (7–12). Finally, (4) the pagan Babylonian Nebuchadnezzar is introduced in chapter 2, and as the reader enters the royal court to hear the dialogue, it is natural to find him and his astrologers speaking Aramaic.

Chapters 8–12 return to Hebrew since they (1) center around Daniel, a Hebrew, and his visions, in contrast to pagan kings (chs 2, 4), and (2) these chapters develop the material in chapters 2 and 7 concerning Israel in greater detail (e.g., the kingdom symbolized by the rock; 2:34-35, 44-45; 7:13, 22, 25, 27). The plight of Daniel's people is highlighted by the use of repetition and an expanding and developing parallelism of what has gone before. More detail is presented in a theological historical account in an apocalyptic style. Finally, (3) chapter 6 features Darius (Cyrus, most likely) and the Persian Empire, and this becomes a link with chapters 9 and 10, as they all mention Darius (Cyrus), under whom Daniel had visions (9:22-23; 10:1). Persia, the second kingdom in chapter 6, spread a new language and culture across the ancient Near East and west to Greece (though it still used Aramaic as its official language) and south in Egypt. The third kingdom, Greece, spread a new universal language and culture from Greece to India. The international flavor and heartbeat of the book is felt as the narrative moves though languages and cultures.

In the historical flow of the book, Aramaic gradually took a back seat to Greek. But for Daniel and his people, Hebrew was the language in which they found the laws of God, as well as their holy traditions. They found the wisdom they needed primarily in those written and oral traditions, but augmented by the visions and dreams that God shared with them. These chapters conclude with the absolute victory of Daniel's people Israel (12:1-3), not a temporary victory as in the days of Antiochus (8:9-14).[13] When understood correctly, the dual-language feature of the book actually helps demonstrate the unity of the book and reflects the gradual shift of languages and cultures in the ancient Near East and Greece into the time of the Roman Empire.

This commentary employs the Masoretic Text (MT) as its basis. The text, both the Aramaic and the Hebrew, is in good condition, but needs careful critical scrutiny. There are several readings that are more difficult to decipher than the mysterious writing on the wall of chapter 5.

The Septuagint (LXX) translation (also called the Old Greek translation, although they are not always the same [Meadowcroft 1995:29]) is sometimes a puzzle and contains interpretive intrusions into the text. It survives in only two main manuscripts, Codex Chisianus (c. AD 900) and the Chester Beatty Papyrus X (c. AD 200). A more reliable Greek text of Theodotion survives and replaced the Septuagint at an early date in the Christian church (c. AD 200). The Theodotionic text follows the MT somewhat slavishly, but is overall very reliable. The relationship between the Old Greek of Daniel and Theodotionic Daniel is debated (Di Lella 2001:586). The Septuagint tradition and the versions following it contain material not in the Masoretic Text or the text of Theodotion: At 3:23 a passage giving the prayer of the three Hebrew youths is inserted; the story of Susanna is an apocryphal tale found in chapter 13 of the Septuagint (but at the beginning of the version of Theodotion and the Latin Vulgate translation). Bel and the Dragon, another apocryphal story, appears in the Vulgate and other Greek versions (cf. also Grabbe 2001:236).

Peter Flint and Craig Evans (1997:41-45) note that there is an abundance of material about Daniel in the Dead Sea Scrolls. These finds basically support the Masoretic Text tradition (Collins 1993:3; Lucas 2002:19), but some also witness other traditions closer to the Septuagint or Theodotion.[14] Eugene Ulrich (2001:573-575, 580) lists eight manuscripts of Daniel and fragments from seven other manuscripts. All of the chapters of Daniel are represented in the biblical manuscripts from Qumran except chapter 12, which is attested in 4QFlorilegium (12:10). Only a few other books—the Pentateuch, Psalms, Isaiah, *1 Enoch*, and *Jubilees*—have more manuscript copies preserved at Qumran. This situation is impressive—in fact, amazing if the book were written around 164 BC—for given the size of Daniel, one would not expect the extent of its presence among the Dead Sea Scrolls to easily exceed most of the books of the Hebrew Bible. It was accepted as Holy Scripture. It was quoted and alluded to often at Qumran. Ulrich (2001:579) affirms that the Qumran copies also shift from Hebrew to Aramaic (2:4b) and from Aramaic back to Hebrew (8:1) and that no variants reflect sectarian biases—in fact, the variants that are present in these copies of Daniel indicate "virtually nothing of significance" (2001:580). The text of Daniel was Holy Scripture, not to be changed (Ulrich 2001:583). As Flint and Evans (1997) summarize, this abundance of Danielic material shows how the content, form, and individual readings of these manuscripts reflect Daniel closely and assert convincingly the important and authoritative status Daniel enjoyed among the Qumran inhabitants. The book of Daniel was regarded as Scripture, and Daniel was regarded as a prophet. Schiffman observes that the Canon appears to have been closed by the time of the Dead Sea Scrolls and Daniel was part of that Canon. None of the so-called "additions" to Daniel are included in the Danielic materials discovered so far (Schiffman 1995:167-169). These have traditionally included the works known as The Prayer of Azariah, The Song of the Three Young Men, Susanna, and Bel and the Dragon. These apocryphal Danielic stories evidently grew up in Egypt alone.

The book of Daniel was placed among "the Writings" in the Hebrew canon rather than in "the Prophets," where it stands in the Septuagint. Our English Bibles, following the arrangement of the Septuagint, place Daniel among the prophets (cf. Matt 24:15).[15] Although the varied placement and its placement among the writings suggests to some a late date for its canonization, this is not the case. The book was considered canonical (not just quasicanonical) as evidenced by the way even the sectarians at Qumran treated the text (Ulrich 2001:573, 580, 583). Beckwith has noted that Daniel may be among "the Writings" because of its literary character—that is, the fact that it reports the words and actions in writing and contains a great amount of wisdom content, ambience, and form.[16]

LITERARY STYLE

The narrative of Daniel is didactic apocalyptic and didactic theological historiography, although depending upon what definition of apocalyptic is used, one could apply the term apocalyptic to the entire book (as does Baldwin 1978a:46-47; see further discussion below). While chapter 1 is not apocalyptic per se, it is an integral part of the final form of the book since it prepares for and foreshadows what is to come in the book. The chapter includes the assertion that God controls the events of history (1:2) and that Daniel has been given the special ability to interpret all kinds of dreams and visions (1:17) and is trained in the language, wisdom, and literature of Babylon (1:4, 20). The cultural context of Daniel and his compatriots indicates that we can expect interaction with visions and dreams—means of mantic wisdom and knowledge in Babylon. Above all, Daniel presents apocalyptic eschatology and theology that is a result of God's breaking into history and using heavenly messengers to convey this content through visions and dreams.

The book was written to impart theological truths about God and his dealings with his people until the end of history and the establishment of a new order (12:3-4). It is didactic (i.e., it teaches), for it demonstrates to its readers (as well as those involved in the book itself) the connection between the actions of God in history and above history. It also instructs God's people how to respond to the circumstances we find ourselves in, whether religious, political, cultural, or moral. The lessons learned in chapters 1–6 are not to be forgotten in chapters 8–12, but to be remembered and applied. The book is historical. The didactic theological aspects of the book are not mere literary constructs, but are based upon the experiences of sixth-century Jewish exiles whose historical experiences, correctly understood, bear the weight of the didactic theological narratives and poetic truth of the book. Daniel and his friends responded appropriately according to their traditions (oral and written) and according to the new wisdom the Lord was imparting to them. They lived in a culture and affirmed it (1:18-21; 2:48-49), but they were ready at the right time to challenge it and reject it if necessary (1:8-15; 3:1-30). They ultimately responded to the challenges or opportunities that faced them as citizens of the Kingdom of God.

Daniel 7–12 has been termed apocalyptic literature.[17] Apocalyptic is an adjective coming from the Greek verb *apokaluptō* [TG601, ZG636] (to reveal, to unveil). The visions of chapters 7–12 reveal and unveil the history of God's people and the kingdoms of the world as they are intermeshed with each other and, more particularly, as they are intermeshed with the spiritual world of God, his servants, and his enemies. A great amount of symbolism is found in this kind of literature, as can be vividly seen in the New Testament book of Revelation, as well as in Matthew 24; Mark 13; Luke 21:5-36; 1 Thessalonians 4–5; 2 Thessalonians 2:1-12; and Jude. In the Old Testament, certain sections of the prophetic materials are often suggested as examples of apocalyptic literature or at least proto-apocalyptic: Isaiah 24–27; sections of Isaiah 55–66; 65:17-25; 66:22-24; Ezekiel 38–48; Joel; and Zechariah 9–14. Daniel, with its apocalyptic emphasis in large portions of the book and in its larger thematic and literary arrangement, is the example of apocalyptic par excellence in the Old Testament (as Revelation is in the New Testament). Its imagery (horns, animals, statues of metals, cosmic trees, divine beings), its concern with the end of history and a new world's breaking in from beyond history, and its clear assertion of a resurrection of the dead (even into two categories of persons) make the book of Daniel unparalleled in the Old Testament (though not without close connections to it as well as certain connections with the pagan world of the time).

The phenomenon of apocalyptic literature is difficult to pin down and define. A definition of apocalyptic has been slow and laborious in coming, and it is wise to realize that the literary genre apocalyptic cannot ever be described or pinned down exhaustively by a single set of distinguishing criteria that appear in every apocalyptic text (Hess 2007:343). Any attempt to do so would cut off the creative possibilities in the work being described. Beckwith (1985:345) has offered the following attempt:

> *Apocalyptic is literature akin to prophecy, concentrating on one aspect of prophecy, the revealing of secrets, and setting forth great secrets revealed by God to a favoured saint or prophet, whether about his purpose for the future, about the constitution of nature or about the unseen world, the mode of the revelation being sometimes highly symbolical but sometimes literal and unusually detailed.*

A broad and well-researched description of the apocalyptic genre is provided by John Collins (1989:1-32). Some of his characterizations, however, do not apply to Daniel, and some dimensions of the apocalyptic aspects of Daniel are absent from other apocalyptic productions (Longman 1999:386). Still, some remarks about the genre as a whole are in order. An apocalyptic document provides a framework that describes and contains the manner of revelation involved. Angelic interpreters are often present and interpret visions, dreams, or heavenly journeys. In all apocalypses the human recipient is a venerable figure, and often pseudonymity is involved, although this is a moot point with respect to Daniel. There are usually temporal and spatial dimensions to the world of the document, respectively presenting perspectives on history (past and future) and insights into the heavenly realms. There is often a final judgment scene, books are involved, and retribution beyond the grave is set forth. As indicated, apocalyptic eschatology involves retribution that reaches beyond the confines of history, although this is found in a less developed form in some prophetic materials (Isa 26:19; Ezek 37). The Jewish apocalypses have an abundance of biblical allusions and certain adapted and controlled mythological allusions. The wisdom features of apocalypses are of a special direct revelatory type (mantic), not merely the common wisdom of daily life, although this may be present to some extent (as in Daniel). Apocalyptic literature was the response of a group of persons to severe social settings, and that response often had theological motivations from prior traditions and current events that shaped a response to that social, cultural setting. The messianic expectations of a group may surface in an anointed figure in Jewish apocalypses, both from the royal line of David (e.g., the *Psalms of Solomon* 17–18) or from a heavenly origin, as in Daniel 7:13-14 (cf. Hess 2007:343; Collins 1998a:1-31).

As noted, the development of apocalyptic literature has been an object of much debate, but a careful examination of the apocalyptic features of Daniel indicates that the wisdom of the book, mantic and practical, is also connected to the teachings of the Torah (1:8-14; 3:16-18; 4:27 [24]; 5:22-24; 6:5 [6]; 7:25; 8:11-12; 9:10-11; 11:28), for the grounding of Daniel in the Torah certainly informed his prayers (9:1-19). Passages such as Deuteronomy 28 guided him as he responded to surrounding events. Those who were wise were not only wise in responding to the mantic wisdom given them through dreams and visions, but were wise because they followed the times and seasons and the traditions of the Torah and would not deviate from them. The apocalyptic features of Daniel also reflect the prophets (9:1-3, 10) and the psalms and wisdom teachings of God's people (1:4; 2:23; 4:27 [24]; 5:12; 6:23 [24]; 11:35; 12:3). It appears that apocalyptic literature was an innovation, but was also intimately connected with the past traditions of God's people. It sprang (1) from a new message of hope from God in the cultural milieu of the Exile and the following period, which featured the amazing rise of world empires that threatened Israel, and also (2) from the interaction of that message with the Old Testament documents and the contemporary realpolitik.

Between 300 and 50 BC, a great deal of apocalyptic literature was produced, and production continued into the New Testament era. Charlesworth (1983, 1985) lists more than 65 works from the intertestamental period, 27 of them apocalyptic literature or literature with apocalyptic sections and others with smaller portions that have an apocalyptic aspect to them. Second Esdras (cf. *4 Ezra*, about AD 90), an ancient source, records the number of apocalyptic writings as 70 (2 Esdr 14:37-47). Daniel precedes all of these if a sixth-century dating is accepted, and most of them even if a later date is taken (Beckwith 1985:358). Comparison of the eschatology of this literature with eschatological aspects of Daniel reveals the quality and the original genius and inspiration of Daniel (Carpenter 1978:97-109;

cf. Collins 1989:1-21, especially p. 21). Thus, apocalyptic literature has been traced by some scholars back to the sixth century BC, the catastrophic period of the Exile, or early postexilic period. The fall of Jerusalem in 586 BC was a divinely orchestrated event (Deut 28:58-68; Jer 25; 29:10-23) that created a milieu in which apocalyptic thinking became a reality (Baldwin 1978a:51). The devastating, unthinkable fall of Jerusalem is the central catastrophe of the books of 1–2 Kings, Jeremiah, Lamentations, Ezekiel (Ezek 33:21), and Habakkuk. At that time the "unveiling" of history gave a hopeful glimpse of the realities behind history and began to present it "as it looks in divine perspective" (Baldwin 1978a:54). Dreams, visions, mysteries, angels, horns, crowns, animals, composite beasts, trees, statues, metals, thrones, fire, clouds, beings like men, beings like gods—all these, sometimes actual but more often symbolic, became the stock-in-trade of the apocalyptic writer as he struggled to present a view of the realities concerning heaven and earth, God and creation in a panoramic view. Satan, dragons, serpents, demons, angels (both good and bad), natural and supernatural, evil and good, were other concepts, realities, and symbols used to describe the cosmic struggle (Miller 1994:46-47).

The canonical book of Daniel stands out from all these compositions and demonstrates an ambiance and development of revelation that stems from the other Old Testament canonical writers (Beckwith 1985:357-358). Daniel was canonized and put on a par with the core books of the Old Testament at Qumran. The pagan sources of apocalyptic thought in Daniel are, at best, peripheral and nonessential, although they do provide contextual motivation for Daniel's carefully shaped canonical response. The book's ultimate source is the God of Israel, and it records his unfolding plans for establishing his people Israel, even his people from among all nations and tongues, in the universal Kingdom of God. That was his covenantal goal from the beginning (Gen 12:3; 14:18-24; Exod 18; Josh 6:22-23; Dan 2:46-47; 3:28-29; 4:34-37 [31-34]; 5:22-24; 6:24-27 [25-28]; 7:12, 14, 27; 12:1).

The unity of the book calls for a genre identification of Daniel that can accommodate the whole book. The early chapters are not merely court tales, popular romances, or wisdom dramas, but have become part of the broader apocalyptic and theological ambience of Daniel, subordinated to that style and message. Behind the deliverance of Daniel and his friends at the king's court was the sovereign Lord of history and his servants (Gabriel, Michael, Son of Man, one like a son of God), who gave Daniel the skills and understanding to master the language and learning of the Babylonians and to interpret dreams and visions of all manner. Apocalyptic deliverance, foreshadowed in the deliverance of Daniel and his friends from death (chs 3, 6), would mark the final and eternal deliverance of God's people from the grip of death (12:1-3).

The entire book of Daniel can be taken as theological apocalyptic literature (Baldwin 1978a:46-47), because from the first verse to the last, it features the revealing and unveiling of God and his heavenly realm in the flow of history (1:2; 12:13) with an emphasis not found in other Old Testament literature; yet it is also an extension of that literature. (God's deliverance of his people is found both in nonapocalyptic literature and apocalyptic literature.) This emphasis is different in degree, not kind. Daniel's scenarios of supernatural deliverance for his people is a thoroughgoing dynamic feature of apocalyptic, for it overcomes the grave on the individual level (1:15; 2:44; 3:28; 4:34-37 [31-34]; 6:22 [23]; 7:21-22; 8:25; 9:27; 11:32, 35, 45; 12:1, 6, 13).

Literary Unity. The unity, though not necessarily the uniformity, of the book of Daniel is demonstrable. Many competent scholars have asserted this unity and continue to do so, although they may date the book much later. S. R. Driver, R. H. Pfeiffer, and especially H. H. Rowley have all argued convincingly for the unity of the book.[18] James A. Montgomery (1927:88-99) held to a unity of chapters 1–6 and 7–12, respectively, each having its own final author. According to him, the book's final author-editor put the two units together in the Maccabean Era (c. 164 BC) (see "Canonicity and Textual History"). There have also been "fragmentary" or hodgepodge theories of the composition of the book.

In particular, the unity of Daniel is evident in the structure of the book, with later parts developing and assuming earlier sections and key phrases of the book. Earlier portions of the book foreshadow and anticipate the later sections, sometimes in subtle ways. The later parts of the book expand upon and clarify earlier topics much as lines of Hebrew parallelism develop earlier poetic lines.

The introduction to the book in 1:1-21 is, as Montgomery asserts, absolutely necessary in order to introduce the following stories in chapters 2:1–6:28 [29]. The introductory verses were skillfully composed, for their organic unity with what follows is clearly evident, even sharing the same tone with the later material. These early materials share the original genius and inspiration of those chapters. However, 1:1-21 also resonates intimately with chapters 7–12. It develops the potential themes inherent in what the author has set up in 1:1-21, one of which is Daniel's ability to understand and to interpret visions and dreams, a skill he employs throughout the entire book. Daniel and his friends are described in 1:4 as insightful or perceptive (*maskilim* [TH7919, ZH8505]; cf. NLT, "gifted with knowledge"); the same Hebrew term is used again at the close of the book in the stating that the "wise" will shine as the brightness of the sky (12:3). From the beginning, the wise court actions and attitudes of Daniel prepare for his amazing success (1:8-14). The employment of Daniel and his compatriots at the courts of kings corresponds to the excellence they demonstrate during their training (1:17, 20). The use of dreams and visions in 2:1–12:13 is anticipated (1:17), as is the ability of God to deliver and save those who exercise their faith in him and his teachings (cf. 1:5, 8, 15). And finally, the assertion of God's control of history (1:2) anticipates the *coup de grace* for the Babylonian Empire (1:2, cf. ch 5). In short, the book "gives the appearance of being a unity" (Beckwith 1985:416, note 76) as its introduction prepares summarily for the unfolding of God's intervention among his people.

While chapters 7–12 form a separate emphasis in the book, they are tied intimately to both the introduction in chapter 1 and the stories in chapters 2–6. One way of describing the way the author has tied 7–12 to 2–6 is through progressive parallelism, or, perhaps more accurately, repeated and expanded parallelism.[19] Chapters 2, 7, 8, 9, and 11:1–12:4 parallel each other in an expanding repetitive development of key themes, as each succeeding chapter unveils and enlarges upon the content and imagery of the preceding chapter. Chapter 12:7-13 returns to the chief character in 1:17, enclosing the book with the figures of Daniel and of God's ultimate sovereignty over history, thus serving as a literary and theological *inclusio*. Daniel 1:17 gives a key adumbration of what is coming in both 2–6 and 7–12 by asserting the special capabilities God had given to Daniel and the three Hebrew youths with him, but especially to Daniel. A total mastery of the literature, language, and "sciences" (i.e., omen literature; cf. COS 1.90) of the times is asserted so that the reader is prepared for the amazing performances of Daniel and the three youths in the coming chapters. The three Hebrew youths called upon their God, as did Daniel, and trusted their traditions and knowledge of their God in order to survive their ordeal. Daniel 1:17 speaks of Daniel's special ability to understand "visions and dreams." This is, of course, descriptive precisely of the major contents of the sections in chapters 2–6 and 7–12, but in good Hebrew style, these two words chiastically reverse the order of "dreams and visions," as they are presented in 2–6. Finally, it is important to note that not only is the absolute sovereignty of God portrayed in 2–6 (e.g., with the rise of the final everlasting kingdom, 2:44-45) and 7–12 (e.g., 7:13-14, 27), but it is asserted explicitly in the introduction: "The Lord gave him [Nebuchadnezzar] victory over King Jehoiakim of Judah" (1:2). The dates of chapters 7, 8, 9 place these visions within the time scheme of chapters 5–6 (539 BC) or before, thus tying the chapters together chronologically. Chapters 6 and 10–12 (constituting one vision) close their respective sections and also record the latest event in their respective sections. They join the Aramaic of chapter 6 to the Hebrew of chapter 10. It can therefore be observed that the author tied his document together by interlocking the chronology and languages (see "Canonicity and Textual History") and so intends thereby to help the reader interject the visions chronologically into chapters 2–6.

Chapter 7 was written in Aramaic, as was 2:4b–6:28 [29]. By this link, the material in 2–6, which deals with the destiny of the nations of the world, is tied organically to the materials centering more on Israel in chapters 8–12. Chapters 8–12 are an expanded exposition of chapter 7, which develops chapter 2 and also demonstrates themes included in 3:1–6:28 [29]. The New Testament writers clearly understood chapter 7 to be the pivotal chapter in the book. Through the use of literary style and the choice of Aramaic as the language of chapter 7, the author ties the book together in content. The introduction in 1:1–2:4a has adequately prepared for all of this.

HISTORICAL ACCURACY

Scholars, liberal and conservative, have noted several historical assertions in the book that seem inaccurate or at best anachronistic.[20] The major issues center around Darius the Mede (son of Xerxes, a Mede by descent; cf. 5:31 [6:1]; 6:1, 27-28 [2, 28-29]; 9:1; 11:1); the third year of Jehoiakim (1:1); identifying Belshazzar as a king (ch 5); the use of the term "Chaldean" as a class of magicians; and the Ugaritic Daniel (or Dan'el). Other historical and critical issues will be discussed in the commentary notes.

Concerning the hard-to-identify character Darius the Mede (5:31 [6:1]; 6:1, 6, 9, 25, 28 [2, 7, 10, 26, 29]; 9:1; 11:1), it is clear that the writer intended to distinguish this Darius from any other Darius to guard against his readers' thinking he was confusing the two. (It is possible that we have a later scribal update distinguishing this Darius from Darius I Hystaspes, 522–486 BC, but there is not strong evidence for it.) And 6:28 [29] may identify this Darius with Cyrus the Great. Darius the Mede's age is evidently important, for it is given as 62. The writer knows he must make some distinguishing remarks about his Darius. Three solutions have been offered, the second of which seems the simplest and most reasonable: (1) Daniel's Darius is Gubaru (or more commonly, Gobryas, from the Greek), the governor Cyrus placed in charge of Babylon for about a year after its capture (see Dillard and Longman 2006:378-380). Relatively strong and cogent criticism has been leveled at this suggestion (Grabbe 1988:205). (2) D. J. Wiseman suggests both on historical and linguistic evidence that Cyrus was also known as Darius the Mede, carrying two throne names and being around 60 years of age when he took the throne (Baldwin 1978a:26). He translates the biblical text (Dan 6:28 [29]) as in the NLT footnote: "of Darius, that is, the reign of Cyrus the Persian."[21] The use of two names for kings, a throne name (cf. Xerxes in 9:1; Lucas 2009:556; Kuhrt 1995:297) and a nickname, is recorded for several ancient kings (e.g., 2 Kgs 15:19; 1 Chr 5:26). This is, in fact, a sound linguistic and cultural position and may be correct. It fits in the biblical context well, for in chapter 6, Darius rules over Media, Persia, and Babylon and issues decrees with universal significance (6:25-27 [26-28]). (3) W. H. Shea has argued that Darius the Mede was an earlier Gubaru (or Ugbaru, not the same as Gobryas) who conquered Babylon under Cyrus, but who died a few days after Babylon was conquered according to Whitcomb (1959). By taking a different tack in reading the relevant death report, Shea claims that Ugbaru died a year and some days after the capture of Babylon. During this year he was "king of Babylon." Only after the death of Ugbaru did Cyrus take on the additional title of "king of Babylon," as well as "king of Lands." So according to the Nabonidus Chronicle, Cyrus ruled as king of Babylon through Ugbaru for a short period of time. However, Shea later changed his position when it was argued convincingly that Gubaru died shortly after Cyrus took Babylon,[22] and Cambyses was in fact known as "King of Babylon" for about a year under Cyrus (Lucas 2002:135-137).

Darius the Mede is mentioned in Josephus (*Antiquities* 10.11.2, 4 [10.232, 248-249]), but Josephus is dependent upon the book of Daniel here. He does, however, add two points: (1) This Darius was the son of Astyages, king of the Medes, and (2) he was called by another name in Greek. This Darius could have been a son of Astyages, king of the Medes and Persians (594–559 BC) (Provan, Long, and Longman 2003:285). Cyrus (the Great) was, according to Herodotus (*Histories* 1.108-109), the son of Astyages' daughter Mandane and Cambyses the Persian. Hence in Herodotus, Cyrus is of mixed blood of the Medes and Persians, and as in Josephus, he is said to have borne another name (*Histories* 1.113; Lucas 2009:247). Also, there is a less-often-mentioned report by the Roman historian Appian (c. AD 160) of Nicomedia in Bithynia (Grant 1970:344, 459): In one account he describes a tablet displayed in a triumph by Pompey the Great after he returned from successful campaigns in the Middle East. The tablet lists kings conquered by Pompey, and Darius the Mede is among those listed (also an Antiochus of Syria). In this late context (61 BC), the name is odd. Was the name simply being used after the book of Daniel? Or was there an ancient tradition about such a king of the Persians (Lewis 2007:81)? At this time we simply do not know anything about the background of this reference that helps answer these questions.

Another historical issue that is not yet resolved regards the third year of Jehoiakim (1:1) as the year of Daniel's capture; Daniel's chronology seems not to match that of Jeremiah (Jer 25:1). The seeming inconsistency between Jeremiah's "fourth year" (Jer 25:1) and Daniel's "third year" is explained, however, by Jeremiah's use of the nonaccession year system of dating in which the accession year of a king's reign is counted as his first year, and Daniel's use of the Babylonian accession year of dating, in which the remaining time of the accession year of a king was not counted in figuring the years of his reign.[23] Some scholars believe that the event described here took place in 605 BC, while others are persuaded that it took place in 597 BC. It is not easy to decide, and some have argued it best to date the event to 601 BC. It is also argued that the events mentioned in Daniel 1:1 did not happen until 597 BC, the twelfth year of Jehoiakim's reign (2 Chr 36:5-6). But based on information from the Babylonian Chronicles (a clay tablet that records the Battle of Carchemish in 605 BC and the capture of Jerusalem in 597 BC, though it does not mention Jehoiakim's capture), it does remain possible that the third year mentioned here was the time when King Jehoiakim was bound and became Nebuchadnezzar's servant for three years (2 Kgs 24:1; 2 Chr 36:6). The biblical text of Daniel probably records additional information that could fall within the reasonable but somewhat obscure time scheme presented by the Babylonian Chronicles (Baldwin 1978a:20-21), although the event in Daniel is not mentioned in the Chronicle (Wiseman 1961:18; Dillard and Longman 2006:277). This, however, must remain tentative (cf. Jer 36:9). The year 601 BC seems to be the most probable date for Daniel's "third year" (1:1) (Provan, Long, and Longman 2003:381, note 112).

That Belshazzar is called king in chapter 5 can no longer be considered a historical error, and the author of Daniel has been vindicated by historical research. Nabonidus, the actual king of Babylon *de jure*, was voluntarily absent from his throne and resident in Arabia (Teima) for 10 years. Belshazzar was appointed by him to be king *de facto* during this time. And, Belshazzar's designation as the son (5:22; cf. 5:18) of Nebuchadnezzar has also been shown to reflect the historical semantic range of the Aramaic word for son (Millard 1977:71-72; ANET 309-310).

The argument that the use of "Chaldean" (Heb., *kasdim* [TH3778B, ZH4169] and Aramaic *kasday* [TA/ZA10373, S3779]) to refer to astrologers at Nebuchadnezzar's court is anachronistic is not cogent. The word describes the Semitic peoples of southern Babylon who had settled there as early as the eleventh or twelfth centuries. The term Chaldea describes regions in southern Babylonia and is found in Assyrian inscriptions from the ninth century on (Lucas 2002:528). The Chaldeans eventually ruled the nation in the Chaldean dynasty (625–539 BC). Nebuchadnezzar himself was a Chaldean in this sense (5:30; 9:1), but not in the sense of referring to a professional priest, which is a second meaning of the word. Herodotus used the term to describe the professional priests of Bel still in his day (c. 450 BC), who functioned as astrologers, magicians or soothsayers. Its use in Daniel in a technical sense for the Chaldean wise men is valid and does not date this material in the Hellenistic era (Collins 1993:137-138; Lucas 2002:53).

The Daniel of Ezekiel 14:14, 20; 28:3 was traditionally thought to be the Daniel of the book of Daniel. This has been questioned since the discoveries at Ugarit and the appearance in Ugaritic literature of the figure *dan'el*. He was an ancient ruler who practiced pagan magical rituals, but judged wisely for the orphan and the widow. His name is spelled differently from Daniel in the book of Daniel (*dan'el* versus *daniye'l* [TH1840/1841, ZH1975/10181]). But the name in Ezekiel is spelled *dani'el* [TH1840A, ZH1971] (according to the Kethiv; the Qere reading spells the name with a Yodh). Ezekiel may be referring to someone who lived earlier than Daniel, possibly from the patriarchal age (Beckwith 1985:417, note 78; so also the NIV mg). But the three men mentioned in Ezekiel—Job, Noah, and Daniel—were alike in important ways. They were intercessors for their people, and they all experienced a miraculous deliverance by their God (Gen 6–9; Job 1:5; 42:8-9). Goldingay (1989:7) concludes that the links between the Daniel of Ezekiel and the Daniel of the book of Daniel are more convincing than any links between the Daniel of the book of Daniel and the Danel of Ugaritic literature or the angelic Daniel of *1 Enoch* (COS 1.103:343-356; Charlesworth 1983:29-50).[24] H. H. Dressler (1979:159) has argued convincingly that the Daniel of Ezekiel is the wise, just, righteous, and devoted Jew of the book of Daniel rather than an idolater named Danel of Ugaritic fame. It is not cogent to identify a faithful Jewish worshiper (cf. chs 1, 6) who seeks his God through prayer with a pagan righteous man who employed pagan worship rituals to serve his gods.

THE PROPHETIC VALUE OF DANIEL AS EVIDENCED IN THE NEW TESTAMENT WRITINGS

Of the two halves of the book, chapters 7–12 are alluded to or used most often in the New Testament. Chapter 7 is used more than any other chapter of Daniel by far. It is used in many places in Revelation.[25] Chapter 9 simply enlarges on the little horn of chapter 7, and parts of it (especially 9:25-27), are found quoted in Matthew 24:15 and Mark 13:14 and are alluded to in 2 Thessalonians 2:4 and throughout Revelation. Chapters 1–6 are alluded to in the New Testament much less than chapters 7–12. Of chapters 1–6, chapter 2 is alluded to most (e.g., Matt 6:13b; Dan 2:37; Mark 14:58; Dan 2:34, 45), followed by chapters 4 and 6 (Heb 11:33). Chapter 2 is organically connected to chapter 7, which develops its thought, so its frequent use relative to chapters 1–6 is understandable. (As noted under "Literary Unity" above, chapters 2 and 7 are literarily and thematically connected. The presentation of four kingdoms is a leitmotif in each, and both share the final denouement of human history: a fifth, everlasting Kingdom set up by an act of God. Chapter 7 expands upon the fifth Kingdom as it makes its nature even clearer.)

Daniel influenced the writer of Revelation more than any other Old Testament book, especially by providing a framework for much of that book. R. A. Anderson notes that the "Little Apocalypse" of Mark 13 has about 30 uses or echoes of the text of Daniel in it (cf. Matt 24; Luke 21).[26] Hence, the authors of the New Testament consider the entire book of Daniel to be theologically and historically authoritative and to contain significant predictive prophecy and moral, ethical, and religious guidance. No other apocalypse informs and shapes the book of Revelation or any other New Testament book in this way. (Jude quotes from *1 Enoch* and *The Assumption of Moses* but in no way adopts these books themselves as canonical.) Daniel was called a prophet by Christ in Matthew 24:15 (cf. Mark 13:14, KJV); likewise, the author of Revelation evidently regarded Daniel as a prophet. In Revelation 1:7 he conflates some of Daniel's words (7:13) with those of the prophet Zechariah (Zech 12:10) to express a prediction regarding the return of Christ. In addition, the descriptions of the two beasts of Revelation 13, especially the first one, draw on imagery from the four beasts of Daniel 7. The Revelator's beast becomes a composite beast summing up the secular forces of the nations that will oppose God. And the dragon imagery (Rev 12:9; 20:1-2) is at least partially drawn from the imagery of the fourth beast of Daniel 7. The resurrection of individuals into two groups presented in Revelation 20 is foreshadowed in Daniel 12:1-3. David Wenham argues for a greater part for Daniel, perhaps the major part, in the concept of the Kingdom of God in the New Testament.[27] If this can be maintained (cf. Beale 1984), the influence of Daniel becomes even more impressive in its influence on the ideas of the Son of Man, the desolating sacrilege, and the Kingdom of God.

THEOLOGICAL CONCERNS

If there is one theological theme that is dominant in a book that has so many theological lessons, it is the sovereignty of God as it is expressed in his ultimate purpose for humankind and the rest of creation—the inexorable, unrelenting pulse of all creation as it moves toward the final establishment of the Kingdom of God (2:35, 44-45; 7:14, 18, 26-28; 12:1-3, 13).[28] He will rule over his people in his Kingdom, he will live among them (Ezek 48:35), and he will rule over the nations (Dan 7:12, 14). Even though the nations, and even his people in exile, were in rebellion, he would eventually be king over them all in the person of the Son of Man (7:9-14), giving authority to his holy people (7:27; 12:1). Even the realm of divine beings will be brought into his Kingdom (4:35 [32]; 10:20-21; 12:1). God will fulfill his prophetic word. Indeed, history is directed by his dynamic prophetic word, as in the book he continues to describe the future contours of world history in essence and, in some cases, in detail (cf. Merrill 1991:387-395).

God's sovereignty is demonstrated as he deals with his own people. He judged them by sending them into exile (1:2; 9:11-12). But he also preserved and delivered them (1:15; 3:16-18; 6:22, 27 [23, 28]) in Daniel's time. This pattern will be repeated in the future of God's people until final deliverance occurs (7:21-22; 11:35; 12:1). He will ultimately render judgment for his people (7:9-10; 12:1). He rescued his people in Daniel's time by one who looked like a divine being (3:25), a son of the gods, but he would bring ultimate deliverance through the one who looks like a son of man (7:13-14) but rides on the clouds as a divine being. God, as the Ancient of Days, is pictured as the final great Judge of all the earth (7:9; Gen 18:25). The march of world powers will not destroy or ultimately engulf God's people, but he will destroy these powers and establish his people and Kingdom (2:34-35, 44; 7:11-14). He will deliver his people (11:36-45; 12:1), even after they have been shattered for a time, times, and half a time (12:7). Even death will be overcome, as the final deliverance of his people is affected (12:2-3) and the evil forces that oppose his Kingdom are destroyed

(12:1). His Kingdom is eternal and his dominion forever (4:3 [3:33]). Yet by God's command, the exact time of these events is concealed (12:9, 13).

God's sovereignty is revealed on a universal scale even more clearly as he raises up and brings down the pagan kingdoms and kings of this world. He did this in the lifetime of Daniel and his friends, when the Exile ended as Babylon was judged (5:30-31), and the Lord established the Persian Empire under Cyrus (1:21; 6:28 [29]; 10:1). Plutarch, an ancient Roman historian, recorded the awareness of both Alexander the Great and Darius IV, last king of Persia, that the passing of one era and the dawning of a new one was more than they could control or fathom (Plutarch 1986:242, 256, 259, 269). Jeremiah had asserted that the Lord's dynamic prophetic word functioned to build up and tear down nations and kingdoms (Jer 1:10; cf. Ezra 1:1-2). Daniel makes it clear that it is God who gives limited "dominion" to the fallen kings of the nations (4:27-37 [24-34]).

The presentation of all of history under the march of four world empires (chs 2, 7) and in greater detail in "seventy sets of seven" (9:24) is given not to confuse but to assure the people of God that history is not an unending capricious flow of kingdoms rising and falling, but a definite march toward the rule of God who "controls the course of world events; he removes kings and sets up other kings" (2:21a), all by his unmatched wisdom and power, partly revealed and partly shrouded in mystery. All of this is demonstrated not only in the flow of events in chapters 2 and 7, but in the march of history throughout chapters 8–12 and the passing of the torch from Babylon to Persia (5:29-31). Although these four kingdoms can best be identified as Babylon, Medo-Persia, Greece, and Rome, the entire panorama of pagan world empires lurks behind them.

The recorded splendor of these kingdoms—Babylon, Persia, Greece, and Rome—at the height of their power and influence remains embedded and marveled at in the history books of today, as well as in the writings of the ancient historians.[29] The achievements of these kingdoms has been catalogued for centuries, yet they were all finally found lacking. God rejected and judged them as inadequate, unrighteous, and ripe for punishment. In spite of all their great contributions to the humanities, arts, and other fields, these kingdoms ultimately all failed. Human apotheosis, hubris, violence, greed, wealth—technical, artistic, intellectual, military, social, political, and religious genius—all these things rose and fell. The essential character of God's people must be radically different from the character of the peoples of these representative kingdoms of the earth, as different as their king is different from the prideful potentates of these empires. The righteous Kingdom of God, in which *shalom* [TH7965, ZH8934] (peace) will be the way of life, will be realized in and among God's own people.

God's sovereignty does not negate any person's moral and ethical accountability to him—the Lord of the universe—as Daniel's message to Nebuchadnezzar makes clear (4:27 [24]). Nonetheless, even a king's failure to act as he should have did not thwart God's ongoing goal for his creation. There is a certain synergism of God and mankind in the rise and fall of nations (Jer 4:1-4; 7:5-8; 18:8). God did not and does not act arbitrarily as he guides history to his goals and purposes, and his guiding standards include wisdom, justice, righteousness, truth, holiness, faith, and love.

God's sovereignty is illustrated as he defeats the powers of evil, and a major manifestation of wickedness is the hubris of the kings of this world (4:30, 32 [27, 29]), who mistakenly think that they have elevated themselves and created their kingdoms. But also a cosmic personal evil lurks behind the magicians, enchanters, astrologers, diviners, soothsayers, and insipid wisdom of the kings' cronies and supporters. This evil lurks also in the governmental structure per se, in the kings, satraps, prefects, governors, advisers, treasurers, judges, magistrates, and all the other government officials that constitute the royal courts. The entire world system is pictured as passing away, since it is held captive to its own corrupt nature and to spiritual evil beyond itself (10:13). The abomination of desolation (11:31; NLT, "the sacrilegious object that causes desecration") and the little horn (7:8, 20-21) become the symbols of the center of the opposition of the world's systems to God and his people (11:28, 30-32). Although the rulers of the nations may recognize Israel's God in important ways, a fact made possible as God bore witness to himself and his ways through Daniel and his friends, they will more truly know him in the future (4:36-37 [33-34]). The dominions of the world come and go (2:21; 5:28); they are not like the Kingdom of God (4:3, 34 [3:33; 4:31]; 6:26 [27]). They will all ultimately bow to the Son of Man (7:27).

God's sovereignty is also demonstrated as he subordinates even the heavenly powers to serve his goals in history, now and forever. He does what he wants "among the angels of heaven"—that is, he controls the powers of the divine world (4:35 [32]). Angels do his bidding, as do divine beings (3:28; 4:23 [20]; 5:5; 6:22 [23]; 10:11; Gabriel, 8:16; 9:21; Michael, 10:13; 12:1), as well as mankind (4:35 [32]). The gods of the nations, even mighty Marduk of Babylon, were quieted as the Lord acted out his plans. Only Daniel's God could create an eternal Kingdom.

God's sovereignty is evident in his surpassing wisdom and the wisdom he gives to his people—particularly Daniel, Shadrach, Meshach, and Abednego—and to those who are wise to withstand evil and resist it (11:35). God grants wisdom to his people through Daniel, and through the book of Daniel, to inform them about how to live in a hostile world and pagan culture, for the wisdom of God and his people is far beyond the wisdom and wise men of this age. Whether he chooses to deliver his people or whether he decides to deliver them to temporary humiliation and defeat in this age, his wisdom is to be followed (3:18).

The sovereignty of God is visible in his ending the Exile, as is recognized in Daniel's prayer (9:18-19). As in Exodus 33:19-20 and 34:5-7, God chooses to have mercy on whom he will have mercy. The Exile had not been an accident of history but a mighty sovereign act of God's working out of his judgment upon his people to their ultimate benefit (9:11-16). The end of the Exile was implied in God's decree to Jeremiah (Jer 25:11-12), and studied diligently by Daniel (9:1-3). The greatest tragedy of Israel's history occurred in 586 BC, the nation defeated, the people exiled, the city of Jerusalem destroyed, the holy Temple devastated—but it too was part of God's redemptive plan for his people. Greater tragedies may yet happen to them, but they will not keep God from establishing his Kingdom (2:44-45; 4:34-35 [31-32]; 7:13-14, 18, 21-22, 26-27).

God's sovereignty is displayed in his method of dealing with evil in history. The march of the timeline of the empires of history shows that history is marked decisively by the outpouring of God's judgment upon kings and kingdoms. In this sense, even within the biblical linear view of history, as God moves creation toward his Kingdom, there is a cyclical pattern of judgment: epochs of obedience and disobedience, blessing and cursing for Israel. For example, Judges 3–16 presents Israel's religious, moral, and ethical behavior in a six-step cycle: Israel sins, is sent by God into servitude, and cries out for deliverance; God graciously raises up a deliverer (judge), delivers his people, and rest is attained. The cycle is repeated. But there will be an end to such cycles. And, finally, God's sovereignty is demonstrated in the fact that he has left for his people a tract, the book of Daniel, a book that presents the reader with shocking-but-true scenarios in stories, dreams, and visions, and heavenly and human battles that, in the end, assure the reader of the triumph of God on behalf of his people. God's reign will be universal; Daniel's people and their anointed leader will stand supreme. The author of Daniel has shown foreign rulers and kings who declare their recognition of the God of Daniel and the Jews with him. Daniel's people will be triumphant over all obstacles. They will eventually become the head and not the tail, as God had told Moses (Deut 28:1, 13, 44).

The book of Daniel demonstrates the connection between God's sovereign willingness to deliver his people and the outstanding moral, ethical, and religious character the Lord expects of his people. His people should be wise, prudent, faithful, dependable, and unswerving in their devotion to the Lord. Daniel was a man of prayer (chs 6 and 9) whose prayers made a difference. He was humble, and God was touched by this disposition. Daniel fulfilled Micah 6:8: He did justice, loved mercy, and walked (and talked) humbly before his God. Daniel was and is a model of spiritual stability for all ages and all peoples. He was truly a subject of the Kingdom of God. But behind Daniel stands the real hero of the book—Daniel's God, the Lord (9:4).

OUTLINE

- I. The Lord's Sovereignty and Faithfulness (1:1-21)
    - A. The Lord Gives Judah over to Nebuchadnezzar (1:1-2)
    - B. The King Selects, Trains, and Proselytizes Capable Young Men for His Court (1:3-7)
    - C. How Shall We Live in a Foreign Land? (1:8-14)
    - D. The Results: *Summa cum Laude* and Then Some (1:15-21)
- II. Dreams and Stories for the Present and Future: Daniel's Faithfulness and Wisdom Demonstrated before the Kingdoms of This World (2:1–6:28)
    - A. Daniel's Divine Wisdom concerning All World History: The Establishment of God's Kingdom (2:1-49)
        1. A dream that troubles Nebuchadnezzar (2:1-3)
        2. "Only the gods can tell you your dreams" (2:4-11)
        3. Nebuchadnezzar's lethal decree and Daniel's wise response (2:12-16)
        4. Daniel's prayer and praise to a God who reveals secrets (2:17-24)
        5. Daniel informs the king of a God who can answer him (2:25-28)

6. Daniel presents the dream to Nebuchadnezzar (2:29-35)
7. Daniel presents the revealed interpretation of the dream (2:36-45)
8. The king's response to Daniel's unveiling of the dream and its meaning (2:46-49)

B. Three Hebrew Men Divinely Delivered from a Furious King (3:1-30)
1. The challenge of pagan worship in the Babylonian culture (3:1-7)
2. The Jews Shadrach, Meshach, and Abednego defy the king (3:8-18)
3. God's deliverance from fury and fiery furnace (3:19-27)
4. Nebuchadnezzar acknowledges the God of Shadrach, Meshach, and Abednego (3:28-30)

C. The Exile and Restoration of a Proud Pagan (4:1-37)
1. Nebuchadnezzar's praise of the Most High God, and a terrifying dream (4:1-8)
2. Daniel interprets the dream (4:9-27)
3. The king is humbled and restored to his kingdom (4:28-37)

D. The Demise of the Kingdom of Babylon and the Rise of Persia (5:1-31)
1. Belshazzar's hubris and defilement of the Temple vessels (5:1-4)
2. The handwriting on the wall (5:5-9)
3. The queen mother remembers Daniel; Belshazzar's interview and offer (5:10-16)
4. Interpretation, application, and fulfillment of the handwriting (5:17-31)

E. Daniel's Deliverance from Destruction (6:1-28)
1. Daniel's ability and success against religious opposition (6:1-5)
2. The entrapment of Daniel (6:6-13)
3. "May your God rescue you!" (6:14-24)
4. Darius's praise of God for Daniel's rescue (6:25-28)

III. Visions and Interpretations for the Present and Future: Daniel's Faithfulness and Wisdom Demonstrated on Behalf of His People, Israel (7:1-12:7)

A. Daniel's Divine Wisdom concerning Israel and the Nations in World History: The Establishment of God's Kingdom (7:1-28)
1. Daniel's vision of the four beasts (7:1-14)
2. The four beasts are four kingdoms (7:15-18)
3. Interpretation of the fourth beast, little horn, Ancient One, and holy people (7:19-28)

B. The Israelite Nation Divinely Delivered from a Furious King (8:1-27)
1. Daniel's vision of the ram, he-goat, and small horn (8:1-14)
2. Gabriel interprets the vision (8:15-27)

- C. The Exile and Restoration of a Rebellious Nation (9:1-27)
  1. Daniel's prayer for his people in exile (9:1-19)
  2. Daniel's prayer answered (9:20-23)
  3. Seventy weeks decreed and described (9:24-27)
- D. The Fall of the Kingdom of Persia and the Rise of Greece (10:1–11:1)
  1. Daniel's vision by the Tigris River in Cyrus's reign (10:1-9)
  2. Daniel's encounter with a manlike being (10:10-19)
  3. The manlike being explains his visitation (10:20–11:1)
- E. The Deliverance of Israel from Destruction, Resulting in the Triumph of God's People (11:2–12:7)
  1. The truth concerning the kingdoms of Persia and Greece (11:2-4)
  2. The kings of the south triumph (11:5-12)
  3. The rise of the king of the north (11:13-20)
  4. The rise of Antiochus IV Epiphanes (11:21-24)
  5. Antiochus Epiphanes opposes the holy covenant (11:25-35)
  6. The despicable king who does as he pleases (11:36-45)
  7. The deliverance of God's people (12:1-7)

IV. Conclusion: The Lord's Sovereignty and Rewards (12:8-13)

ENDNOTES

1. Daniel displayed the gamut of wisdom in its various forms in the Old Testament; he was the consummate wise man before both God and man. His mantic wisdom (the ability to solve the mysteries presented to him and the kings; see endnote 11) is noted in 1:17 and seen throughout the book as he receives the interpretations to dreams and visions. In addition to this mantic wisdom, Daniel also illustrated in his everyday life the more traditional wisdom of the Israelites as reflected in the book of Proverbs, which stressed wisdom for living successfully before God and man, principles that enlightened rulers and guided a person through life (Prov 8). Daniel wisely honored his God as a servant; he tactfully handled himself at the court of the kings he served. In chapter 2 he was able to gain an audience with the king, and he wisely dealt with him in order to deliver the wise men from death (2:16); he displayed wisdom and common sense and administrative ability. God honored him, and the king promoted and trusted him. God added to Daniel's wisdom, and he increased in wisdom as a true wise man would (Prov 1:1-5). He displayed a deep commitment to the law of his God and the call to holiness (1:8-9; 6:10 [11]) and prayerful intercession (9:1-19). In addition to his excellence in these two spheres of wisdom, Daniel exercised the gift of prophecy by foretelling the future and by challenging King Nebuchadnezzar to stop sinning and to do what is righteous and care for the poor (4:27 [24]). These features of his work will be pointed out in the commentary.
2. The statement in 1:21 does not conflict with 10:1, which says that Daniel was alive in the third year of Cyrus. Daniel 1:21 simply asserts that he continued throughout the period of the Neo-Babylonian Empire—that is, he lived through the period of the Exile.
3. See Lucas 2002:307; Stefanovic 1992:11-27; Meadowcroft 1995:272-280; Kitchen 2003; Kitchen 1965:75-76. Also see further discussions in the Introduction. The syntax of the Aramaic in Daniel can be compared to the different syntax of, e.g., the Genesis Apocryphon in the Dead Sea Scrolls, of western provenance.
4. For the historical value of chs 1–6, see especially A. R. Millard 1977:69-71; Montgomery 1927:73-75; Soggin 1980:408-411; Collins 1975:218-234; Lucas 2000:73; Paul 2001:55-68; Dillard and Longman 2006:373-390.

5. As noted in Young 1949:25; cf. Lacocque 1979:9-10; Delcor 1971:13-16; Miller 1994:24-42.
6. See Joyce Baldwin 1978b; Walton 1986:217-226.
7. David Flusser (1972:148-175) has shown that Daniel need not be dated late because of claims that there is Persian influence in chapters 2 and 7. Persian apocalyptic ideas and genre are notoriously difficult. There appears to be some Persian influence in the book of Daniel, but as Collins notes (1989:22-26), any Persian motifs have been adapted and reconceived by the Jewish traditions in the book. See also Lucas 2009:545 for the difficulty of dating Persian materials.
8. Longman 1991:167-190; Longman 1999:22. See further COS 1.150; 1.149; Walton 1986:220-226 for excellent discussions of similarities and contrasts between Daniel and these Akkadian prophecies.
9. Cf. Longman 1999:22-24; Wallace 1979:19-22. Randall Price (1996:150-151, 157-163) presents the case ably and clearly, reviewing the evidence for an early date of Daniel and against the Maccabean dating. The book purports to present a historical Daniel in a sixth-century setting as the person who experienced the events in the book; that the book was written in the sixth century is not proven, nor is it proven that it was written in the second century BC, but the author of the book purports to be speaking from the sixth century. For a helpful and respectful review of the current issues surrounding the dating and other matters, see Collins 2001:1-15, who holds firmly to a date for the final form of the book in the Hellenistic era.
10. See F. F. Bruce 1988:291, 325. See also Goldingay 1989:xi; note his sagacious assertion about the essential exegesis of the book no matter which position is taken—Babylonian (sixth century BC) or Palestinian (second century BC); see also Longman 1999:23-24 and Lucas 2002:312. I concur with the sentiments expressed by Longman and Lucas.
11. "Mantic wisdom" is a term common in recent commentaries dealing with apocalyptic literature and with Daniel. It is distinct from practical or traditional wisdom, which centered on transmitting wise sayings and teachings regarding a life well lived to each new generation, as exemplified in the book of Proverbs. In general, the term "mantic" refers to a wide variety of forms of divination, including those involving the interpretation of omens, dreams, and visions. In Daniel, however, it is the manner of his mantic wisdom that makes all the difference—he gets it not by pagan divination, but by humble prayer to his God. In this commentary, "mantic wisdom" refers to the wisdom that God gives to Daniel in order to solve the riddles and mysteries presented to him through dreams and visions that contain direct and immediate revelation to Daniel.

    Two recent evangelical commentators refer to this type of wisdom being given to Daniel. Lucas notes that 1:17 refers to "Daniel's skill in an aspect of 'mantic' wisdom—the ability to understand visions and dreams" (2002:56). Longman notes that Daniel had a "kind of mantic wisdom ('Daniel could understand visions and dreams of all kinds,' v. 17)." He notes that "[God] uses Daniel's specialized knowledge as an instrument for the revelation he gives him later in the book" (1999:55). This type of wisdom is regularly featured in apocalyptic literature, but is not wholly lacking in the prophets. Heavenly messengers spoke to Daniel and gave him understanding in answer to his prayers. God spoke to him in immediate ways that made him aware of the interpretation of a dream or vision. Daniel received direct revelation from God in visions, dreams, messages (2:26-30; 4:18-19 [15-16]; 5:17; 7:1-2; 8:1-2; 9:21; 10:1), and by the Spirit of God in him he discovered the meaning of the cryptic writing on the wall (5:11, 17). The other nations thought that they could do the same, but the book of Daniel makes it clear that only Daniel, through his God, really had this special knowledge (cf. Longman 1999:55).

    Daniel's wisdom was such that Nebuchadnezzar made him chief of the Babylonian wise men (magicians, conjurers, Chaldeans, and diviners). Daniel must have studied divination (ch 1), but in the book of Daniel he does not use the techniques of divination to get his "direct mantic knowledge" from the Lord. God spoke to him by dreams, visions, and direct heavenly interpreters, sometimes as a result of prayer and sometimes without any preceding prayer (e.g., ch 7). Dreams and visions had been used by God to reveal himself since the time of Abraham (Gen 15) and Joseph (Gen 41). These had been acceptable ways for the Lord to communicate to patriarchs, prophets, and wise men in Israel, and the Lord supplied interpretations and explanations for these dreams and visions.

12. Some convenient and readable general histories of the ancient Near East include Kuhrt 1995; J. M. Cook 1983; Provan, Long, and Longman 2003; Chavalas 2006.
13. See the remarks of Beckwith (1985:416, note 76).
14. For a brief discussion of textual and canonical issues, see Lucas 2002:19-21; Baldwin 1978a:68-72; Harrison 1969:1132-1134; Montgomery 1927:24-56; Koch 1985:117-130.
15. E. Earle Ellis notes a quotation from Daniel at Qumran, 4QFlor [4Q174] 2:3, which asserts "As it is written in the book of Daniel the prophet" (1988:683). Hence, he suggests an older tradition of the Hebrew canon that placed Daniel among the prophets. Grabbe notes this (2001:237) and observes that several portions of this scroll quote and exegete the passages. Jesus calls Daniel a prophet (Matt 24:15) as does Josephus (*Antiquities* 10.11.4 [10.249]). LaSor, Bush, and Hubbard support this position and reject the distinctions that have been used to disqualify Daniel as a prophet: He was a seer, not a prophet; and, he did not hold the prophetic office, only the gift. These distinctions cannot be maintained based on Scripture (1996:575). Longman holds that Daniel was prophetic because he foretold the future (1999:1-31, 200-206). The NT writer of Revelation pairs Dan 7:13 with Zech 12:10, a recognized OT prophet. Hence, Daniel is paired with a prophet and presents material that looks into the future. K. Koch has argued that Daniel should be called a prophet based on the placement of the book in the prophets in the Septuagint and Christian Bibles. And he argues that the placement of the book among the writings in the Hebrew canon took place because of a desire to stress Daniel as a role model.
16. Beckwith, whose arguments have not been generally accepted, argues for a canonization of Daniel much earlier than the second century BC, and for the antiquity of the book as a whole; see Beckwith 1985:74-75, 138-139, 415-416.
17. For a discussion of scholarly opinions about the origins of apocalypses, see Baldwin (1978a:48-59). She notes that Zoroastrianism, ancient wisdom sources, prophetic books of the OT, and Hellenism have been put forth as the sources of apocalyptic literature; Collins (1989:1-32) updates Baldwin's materials well; see also Lucas 2009:568; 2002:268-270. This whole area remains a matter of intense research. It seems that Daniel would be among the earliest examples of the genre.
18. Nearly everyone sees a unity in the book of Daniel. See Collins 1989:70-72; Dillard and Longman 2006:391-392; Baldwin 1978a:38-46; Pfeiffer 1952:760-764; Rowley 1949:249-280; Young 1949:19-20. However, Soggin (1980:38-46) asserts that "the book is not a unity in either content or language."
19. This literary device is found in Hebrew poetry and was formerly referred to as synthetic parallelism. The phenomenon is a type of parallelism in which following lines develop or repeat in various ways preceding statements. But more than repetition is featured in Daniel's narrative expansions on themes previously introduced; there is development and an unfolding of these themes. There is narrative progression and thematic intensification (Alter 1981:27-63, 137-162). For a visual presentation of the phenomenon in Daniel, see Doukhan 1987:54-55. Doukhan also sees a literary unity to the book in which 1:1 and 12:13 frame the book and function as inclusions. Chapter 1 serves as a general introduction to the entire book. There is an overall interlocking literary structure as well for the remaining chapters: 2/7, 3/6, 4/5, 7/12, 8/11, 9/10. The centrality of chapter 7 both in content and literary form and placement is evident.
20. On these issues, see Dillard and Longman 2006:375-384; R. K. Harrison 1969:1112-1122; A. R. Millard 1977:72-73; Lucas 2009:519-575.
21. Wiseman 1965:9-18; Lucas 2009:574, notes 106, 107.

22. See three articles by W. H. Shea (1971:51-57; 1972:177; 1982:229-247). Whitcomb in fact identified two men named Gubaru, one the conqueror of Babylon and the other a later governor of the province. While Whitcomb equated Darius the Mede with the latter, Shea asserted that the former Gubaru is the correct identification, but he has retracted that statement now (1991:235-237; cf. Lucas 2002:135-136). See Yamauchi 1990:59 for an excellent summary of Shea's position. Note also L. L. Grabbe's (1988:198-213) rejoinders. The intimate, intriguing, but tortuous historical, political, and familial relationships between the Medes and the Persians are relevant to understanding the multivalent potential and qualities of a title like "Darius the Mede."
23. See LaSor, Bush, and Hubbard 1982:662, note 7, for full documentation. They assert that "the 'third year of Jehoiakim' (1:1) would end on 6 Oct., 605 (using a Tishri–Tishri year), which would fit Nebuchadnezzar's invasion of summer 605."
24. See Flint 2001 for a discussion of the Daniel tradition at Qumran and Stuckenbruck 2001:368-386 for a discussion of Daniel and early Enoch materials in the DSS; finally, see Ulrich 2001:573-585 for the Daniel texts present at Qumran.
25. For references in Revelation, see Beale and Carson 2007:1081-1083. Montgomery (1927:5) lists Matt 21:44; 1 Cor 1:24; 2:14 as other NT references to consider. Also note Matt 24:26; Mark 13:14; 14:62; Luke 22:69; Col 1:13-15; 2 Thess 2:4; Heb 11:33ff; Rev 1:7, 12-16; 13; 19:11-21.
26. See R. A. Anderson 1984:153-155 for a brief summary of the influence of the book of Daniel in the NT and history; for recent extended discussions of the extent of the influence of Daniel in the NT and elsewhere see Evans 2001:490-527; Dunn 2001:528-549.
27. See D. Wenham 1987:132-134; see also Merrill 1986:211-225; see preceding note.
28. For a recent discussion of theology and theological ethics see, respectively, Goldingay 2001:660 and Barton 2001:661-670.
29. For selections of such ancient historical writers, see Grant 1992:v-xii, 1-686; Oates 1986:163-198; Starr 1991:3-713; von Soden 1992.

COMMENTARY ON

Daniel

◆ I. The Lord's Sovereignty and Faithfulness (1:1–21)

A. The Lord Gives Judah over to Nebuchadnezzar (1:1–2)

During the third year of King Jehoiakim's reign in Judah,* King Nebuchadnezzar of Babylon came to Jerusalem and besieged it. 2The Lord gave him victory over King Jehoiakim of Judah and permitted him to take some of the sacred objects from the Temple of God. So Nebuchadnezzar took them back to the land of Babylonia* and placed them in the treasure-house of his god.

1:1 This event occurred in 605 B.C., during the third year of Jehoiakim's reign (according to the calendar system in which the new year begins in the spring). 1:2 Hebrew *the land of Shinar.*

NOTES

1:1 *third year of King Jehoiakim's reign.* Most likely 605 BC, but 601 and 597 are also possible dates for this event (see "Historical Accuracy" in the Introduction).

1:2 *The Lord.* Heb., *'adonay* [TH136, ZH151]. Some mss read *yhwh* [TH3068, ZH3378] (Yahweh), but God's covenantal name is not used in Daniel except in 9:2, 4, 8, 10, 13, 14 (twice), 20. *'Adonay* is probably best translated "O Lord of All" in Daniel (Waltke and O'Connor 1990:123-124). The LXX renders this as *kurios* [TG2962, ZG3261] (Lord), but the LXX tended to use "Lord" instead of "God" when translating both the Aramaic and Hebrew sections of Daniel (Meadowcroft 1995:254).

gave him victory over King Jehoiakim. Lit., "gave Jehoiakim into his hand," with "hand" signifying power or authority. Cyrus later asserted that the Babylonian god Marduk had given Babylon into his hand because Nabonidus, the last king of Babylon, had not worshiped Marduk as supreme (Brown 1995:149). Starr (1991:395-410), in his standard history of the ancient world, does not even list Daniel as a source for the Babylonian period, an indication of the unfortunate way the historical aspects of the book are given little weight or discussion by many secular writers. The gods of the ancient world were often cited as giving enemies into the hand (power) of their own people: Enlil gives victory to Urnammu (2110–2095 BC; COS 2.138D; Carpenter 2009:430 and notes 82-86); cities were destroyed and given to the enemy because of disobedience of the people of the city toward their gods.

the Temple of God . . . treasure-house of his god. The Hebrew contrasts the house of God with the house of Nebuchadnezzar's god (lit., "his gods"), where the captured Temple vessels were placed.

the land of Babylonia. This is a good rendering (cf. Gen 11:2). The Hebrew reads "the land of Shinar" (see NLT mg) and intends to remind the reader of the exact same expression in Gen 11:2, regarding the place where the Tower of Babel was built (see Zadok 1984:240-244).

COMMENTARY

These two verses set the historical and theological backdrop for the events of the Exile that are recorded in the book of Daniel. Daniel and Ezekiel are the only books in the Old Testament in which all of the events take place during the exilic era (605?/597?–539 BC) or immediately after it (10:1). We learn that the great king Nebuchadnezzar laid siege to Jerusalem, capital of Judah, and was successful. He may have taken its reigning king Jehoiakim into temporary exile, although this is not clearly asserted (See Introduction, "Historical Accuracy"). However, there is much more to this story than the mere facts that are recorded on the historical level. It is the theological backdrop of the Lord's sovereignty that gives the historical event its eternal significance, an event already predicted by the Lord before it happened (9:1-2). While most modern historians do not see divine providence in history, the inspired author of Daniel saw it everywhere, from the life of the ordinary villager to the feats of Nebuchadnezzar. Nebuchadnezzar the king came and besieged the city—but the Lord of all (see note on 1:2) was the one who gave Nebuchadnezzar his victory, not Nebuchadnezzar himself, nor his gods. He, however, thought that he was the master of his fate and the builder of his empire (4:28-30 [25-27]). He was, rather unwittingly, the Lord's servant (Jer 25:9; 27:6).

The writer emphatically asserts that Jehoiakim, Judah's king, was given into Nebuchadnezzar's hand by the Lord. The Lord of all also gave some of the vessels of the house of Israel's God, the Temple, into Nebuchadnezzar's hand, who took them to the land of Shinar (NLT, "Babylonia") to the house of his god. The treasure-house of the king was indeed impressive. Its name Etemenanki means "the house that is the foundation of heaven and earth," and its accompanying temple of Marduk, Nebuchadnezzar's chief god, was named Esagila (meaning "the temple with its head raised"). The structure was over a hundred feet tall at its peak (Lucas 2009:526-527; 572, note 15). The holy vessels of the Lord were defiled by being deposited in this pagan temple; they will surface again to be further abused and made unclean on the day that Babylon falls (5:1-4, 31 [6:1]).

Abraham, the father of the nation of Israel, had come out of that pagan cultural area (Gen 11:31; 15:7; Neh 9:7). The Exile represented a devastating reversal of the exodus of Abraham out of Babylon and of Israel out of Egypt. Ironically, just as Pharaoh had given a free state education to Moses, who helped devastate the gods of Egypt, so Nebuchadnezzar would educate Daniel whom the Lord would use to display a greater and final exodus (9:24-27; 12:1-3).

Throughout these verses it is the sovereign Lord of Israel who brings about these events, not the Babylonian king or his gods. This is the beginning of Israel's exile into Babylonia because of her refusal to follow her faithful God and to obey his righteous laws. The Exile was a sovereign act of the Lord based upon his laws of governance for his people. It was discussed and threatened in the law (Deut 28:64) and the prophets (Jer 25:8-14; cf. Dan 9:2).

Jehoiakim was exiled because of the wicked policies he unrelentingly pursued (see 2 Kgs 23:36–24:6; 2 Chr 36:5-8; Jer 25:1-38). The rebelliousness of Jehoiakim and Judah are shockingly portrayed in the book of Jeremiah (Jer 1, 22, 24, 25–28, 35–37, 45–46, 52). One must ask, "Could anything good come out of this catastrophe that happened to Judah, Jerusalem, and her anointed king?" The Lord's answer was a resounding yes! He promised his new action would cause even the exodus from Egypt to pale in comparison (Isa 43:18).

◆ B. The King Selects, Trains, and Proselytizes Capable Young Men for His Court (1:3-7)

3Then the king ordered Ashpenaz, his chief of staff, to bring to the palace some of the young men of Judah's royal family and other noble families, who had been brought to Babylon as captives. 4"Select only strong, healthy, and good-looking young men," he said. "Make sure they are well versed in every branch of learning, are gifted with knowledge and good judgment, and are suited to serve in the royal palace. Train these young men in the language and literature of Babylon.*" 5The king assigned them a daily ration of food and wine from his own kitchens. They were to be trained for three years, and then they would enter the royal service.

6Daniel, Hananiah, Mishael, and Azariah were four of the young men chosen, all from the tribe of Judah. 7The chief of staff renamed them with these Babylonian names:

Daniel was called Belteshazzar.
Hananiah was called Shadrach.
Mishael was called Meshach.
Azariah was called Abednego.

1:4 Or *of the Chaldeans.*

NOTES

1:3 *Ashpenaz.* This name may be Old Persian and mean "guest master"; but it has also been found as a personal name in Aramaic (c. 600 BC; Lucas 2009:528, 572, note 17).

chief of staff. This phrase *rab sarisayw* [TH7227B/5631, ZH8042/6247] follows "Ashpenaz," standing in apposition to it, and can mean "chief eunuch"; however, the Akkadian equivalent (lit., "he of the head [of the kind]"; cf. Lucas 2002:47; cf. COS 2.117D) refers to a confidant of the king or leading courtier of the king. The Hebrew phrase likewise can refer to others besides eunuchs—a larger group of persons surrounding the king and loyal to him (cf. Buchanan 1999:21). The NLT and most modern translations render along these lines.

Judah's royal family. The MT doesn't actually mention Judah in this verse, but instead indicates Israelites and then specifies those who were "royal" and "noble." This implies the families of Judah. Although Jerusalem had fallen, the royal line would be preserved.

1:4 *strong, healthy.* The words attempt to render the phrase "who have no blemish" of the Hebrew text (cf. NIV, "without any physical defect"). It may suggest, but I would not press the issue, that we are to see Daniel and these young men as sacrifices for Yahweh (the Lord), fully dedicated to him and ready, if necessary, to suffer death in order to be faithful. The language recalls Lev 21:16-24; 22:17-25.

well versed in . . . learning, are gifted with knowledge and good judgment . . . suited to serve. The underlying wording in the MT comes from Israel's wisdom tradition. The piling up of words in the semantic domain of wisdom emphasizes the great inherent ability of these youths, even before their three-year educational program. Gerald H. Wilson (1985:373-381) gives a helpful survey of some of the wisdom words used in Daniel. But it seems that Daniel was more influenced by divine wisdom than Wilson would allow.

are suited to serve. Heb., *koakh* [TH3581, ZH3946], referring to the strength or capability to endure the rigors of serving in the highest levels of governmental administration (see Yamauchi 1990:259-260 for what it took to have proper court etiquette; also cf. Neh 2).

the language and literature of Babylon. Lit., "the literature and language of the Chaldeans." The LXX renders *seper* [TH5612, ZH6219] as *grammata* [TG1121, ZG1207] (writing, literature). Babylonian literature was extensive at this time, especially wisdom and esoteric literature. For a survey of Mesopotamian culture and literature, see Hallo and Simpson 1971:151-183; Saggs 1962:157-483. The term "Chaldeans" simply refers to the ruling people of Babylon (cf. 2:5 and "Historical Accuracy" in the Introduction).

1:5 ***food and wine.*** This phrase seems to connote "the king's own food" (cf. 11:26, see note).

1:7 ***Belteshazzar . . . Shadrach . . . Meshach . . . Abednego.*** These Babylonian names are difficult to decipher (see the other possible suggestions in the commentary), but more recent suggestions may be helpful: Belteshazzar, "Bel protects the king (or life)," (cf. 4:9 [6]; some prefer "Lady, protect the king," which is less certain); Shadrach, "I am fearful [of God]"; Meshach, "I am of little account"; Abednego, "a servant of the Shining One [Nabu]." However, these are not entirely certain and given the context of the book of Daniel, are suspicious. Perhaps a mocking perversion of original names of Babylonian deities is present. See especially Montgomery 1927:129-130. See also Lucas 2002:53; Baldwin 1978a:81-82; Delcor 1971:64-65; Millard 1977:72; Longman 1999:50-51.

COMMENTARY

God did not leave himself without a witness to the nations even in Babylon, for he employed Daniel and the three Hebrew young men of royal or noble lineage to serve him as his ambassadors in the pagan stronghold of the city of Babylon. Daniel (meaning "God is my Judge" or "God has judged"), Hananiah ("The LORD is grace"), Mishael ("Who is God?"), and Azariah ("The LORD helps") are now introduced to us as the major Israelite players in the book. In 1:6 their names are changed by Ashpenaz to Belteshazzar ("Bel protects his life"; Bel is Marduk, the Babylonian god), Shadrach (possibly "command of Aku"), Meshach ("Who is it that is Aku?"), and Abednego ("servant of Nego"—i.e., Nebo/Nabu). It is not possible to be certain about these meanings (see note on 1:7). The exile of these descendants of the royal line fulfilled Isaiah 39:7 (cf. 2 Kgs 24:12-16). Daniel was a young man, perhaps 14–17 years of age when he was taken into Babylonian captivity. If he was 14 in 605 BC and then lived into the third year of Cyrus the Great (10:1; 536 BC), that would make him about 80 at that time, a rather advanced age for that historical era. The idea that Daniel and these youths were made eunuchs is a mere assumption that finds no evidence in Daniel and is not demanded by Isaiah 39:7. The name Ashpenaz, as translated here, could be a title meaning "guest master" or "innkeeper" (cf. Lucas 2002:45, 47), or it can simply be a personal name (see notes on 1:3).

Some have thought that the name changing reported here implies that Daniel and his friends may have capitulated to the religious milieu in which they found themselves. But 1:8 dispels this notion. Ultimately, it was what was in these Israelites' hearts that counted then as now (Rom 2:28-29), not what external label was attached to them. True religion is an issue of the heart, but the heart ultimately effects behavior that shows the reality and trust of faith in the heart.

As the first referent to God's judgment, Daniel's name itself is intended to cause the reader to understand the judgment of God as depicted in this book—with his taking Israel into exile. God also judges in favor of Daniel and his companions several times before the book has ended. He judges against those who would oppose him or his people, as recorded throughout the book.

These young men were chosen because of their evident natural abilities and aptitudes, but a wisdom and understanding far beyond human capability would be theirs. No amount of teaching from the Babylonian sages and soothsayers could provide it (cf. 1:17). From the human point of view, these gifted young men could master all of the educational challenges presented to them, but they would still find themselves unable to fathom the mysteries that the sovereign Lord would present to them, although Daniel is highlighted as the one who could understand dreams and visions (1:17). They were young men chosen by God, "without blemish" (see note on 1:4), possibly to indicate their potential as living sacrifices for God if necessary (cf. Lev 21:16-24; 22:17-25; Rom 12:1-2). They did in fact become living sacrifices, living examples of how God's people should serve him in oppressive hostile circumstances (chs 3, 6).

The young men chosen were already considered to be the most promising new students around; they were already in the highest percentile of their class, both in their innate abilities and in what they had already accomplished (1:4). They did not enter into their new program of study and indoctrination as blank slates; they were already well versed "in every branch of learning" and "gifted with knowledge and good judgment" (1:4). Their moral character was already sharp; they knew their own traditions well. These assertions about them indicate that there is a connection between their traditional wisdom, in which they were already well versed, and the new program of study in Babylon. To their traditional knowledge, considerable character development, and inherent gifts of wisdom, they will have more added.

Their three years of intensive training in the extensive wisdom and literature of the Babylonians, including languages, would have helped give them a mastery of the topics and problems they would face. But they would decide to work within the new system only as their worldview would permit. The Lord's willingness to work through dreams and visions would make this possible, for he would impart to them mantic knowledge (see Introduction, endnote 11). With their new mastery of the Babylonian language and literature, their new names, their superb diets of the king's food, the best living quarters available in Babylon, their innate capabilities to handle themselves in the royal palace, and the king's blessing, they would be ready to solve all the problems the king could pose to them. Undoubtedly, they all graduated *summa cum laude.* But was this enough to answer the really tough issues of dream and vision interpretation, solving cryptic puzzles, and surmounting challenges to their faith? Would they even be able to understand the mysteries of God revealed to his prophets (9:1-2)? Who would help them interpret the visions and dreams? The God of the captives made the ultimate difference.

Their education rivaled that of Moses under Pharaoh, and Daniel's special God-given abilities parallel those of Joseph to a significant extent (Gen 40–41). As in the Joseph narrative, it is as they allow God to work through them that these three men were given high-standing positions (Gen 41:37-40). Daniel and the other youths would have been exposed to cuneiform writing, Babylonian wisdom literature, creation stories, legal corpora, ancient histories, religious rituals and epics, prophecies and the destinies of the nations, letters, dream journals, vision manuals, and undoubtedly a profound introduction to the chief "science" of the day—divination through the study and interpretation of omens. There were various kinds of omens and numerous ways of interpreting them (Lucas 2009:530, 533; COS 1.120:421-426). This education in Babylon opened the door for Daniel to be involved in mantic wisdom—in Daniel's case, wisdom from God, gained through dreams, visions, and divine interpreters, and closely tied to prophetic insight from the Lord. This training also qualified Daniel and his friends to serve and function in the king's court, a highly regarded position in the ancient Near East. The famous Egyptian instructions *Amenemope* (thirteenth century BC) contain 30 sections and conclude with the assertion that the person who studies these books will be "found worthy to be a courtier" (COS 1.47:122).

Although Daniel studied and understood divination, he did not employ it to solve the dilemmas presented him in dreams and visions. Divination was specifically banned from Israel as a means of inquiring of God or knowing his will (Lev 19:26; Deut 18:10, 14; cf. Carpenter 2009:472 and notes 96-99). This Babylonian indoctrination program was countered by Daniel's Jewish education from the Holy Scriptures and his faithful prayer life (Dan 6; 9:2-19). Armed with prayer and humility, and a firm grasp on his own Jewish tradition, he would speak according to the prophetic message the Lord provided, by and large rejecting this "toxic education" in its use and basic axioms. But there were points of contact such as dreams and visions, where Daniel's God would step in and overpower the system, so to speak, communicating with Daniel directly (cf. Balaam in Num 22–24).

Daniel engaged in prayer with a God who actually answered him and gave him understanding in these matters, and even supplied a heavenly interpreter as needed. By his rejection of most typical divination practices and reliance on prayer, Daniel advanced the message of the God of gods and King of kings and his coming Kingdom immensely. Daniel came from a tradition in which God inspired prophets to speak forth judgment and to report the future. Daniel would do that, but with an apocalyptic twist to it (in some cases being instructed to seal up the message for a time). And like the prophets of Israel, he also declared judgment and justice to those in his day, including kings (4:27 [24]; 5:22-29). In this task, Daniel's education prepared him to be relevant to the world of his day; he infiltrated the system, serving as a wise courtier as well a mantic wise man, knowing both to influentially employ the practical wisdom he had learned (2:16, 24-28, 48) and to reveal mysteries in the name of his God. But he also boldly warned Nebuchadnezzar and future kings (5:22-24) to "Stop sinning and do what is right. Break from your wicked past and be merciful to the poor. Perhaps then you will continue to prosper" (4:27 [24]).

◆ C. How Shall We Live in a Foreign Land? (1:8–14)

8But Daniel was determined not to defile himself by eating the food and wine given to them by the king. He asked the chief of staff for permission not to eat these unacceptable foods. 9Now God had given the chief of staff both respect and affection for Daniel. 10But he responded, "I am afraid of my lord the king, who has

ordered that you eat this food and wine. If you become pale and thin compared to the other youths your age, I am afraid the king will have me beheaded."

[11]Daniel spoke with the attendant who had been appointed by the chief of staff to look after Daniel, Hananiah, Mishael, and Azariah. [12]"Please test us for ten days on a diet of vegetables and water," Daniel said. [13]"At the end of the ten days, see how we look compared to the other young men who are eating the king's food. Then make your decision in light of what you see." [14]The attendant agreed to Daniel's suggestion and tested them for ten days.

NOTES

1:8 ***But Daniel was determined.*** Lit., "Daniel set upon his heart"—an attitude that Pharaoh had refused to take with regard to the 10 plagues (Exod 7:13, 23; 8:15).

not to defile himself. One view of this phrase is that the cultic language concerning Daniel and his friends continues (see note on 1:4), for eating the king's food would make them ritually unclean. However, this is not the only possible way of understanding this (see commentary). By contrast, Nehemiah was the wine taster for King Artaxerxes (Neh 2:1).

1:12 ***test us for ten days.*** This was the normal period of time during which any given thing might be checked.

1:13 ***make your decision in light of what you see.*** The phraseology of Daniel's suggestion shows great politeness and respect toward the attendant.

COMMENTARY

These verses show the character and attitude of Daniel and his three friends toward the pagan environment in which they found themselves. But, whereas the chief official fears the king, Daniel and his friends fear God (cf. ch 3). Their immediate challenge was to stay true to the law of their God whom they served. Even in this period of exile in Babylon, they could serve him and turn to him by showing faith in his protection of them and by acting on that faith through accepting his instructions, while rejecting the king's demands.

Daniel's actions followed upon his strong resolve not to eat the king's food. It is nevertheless difficult to discern his reason for not eating the king's food. Perhaps to have done so would have meant partaking of food not properly prepared according to the instruction in the law; further, it may have meant eating food that had been offered to pagan idols and drinking wine that had been poured out upon pagan altars. Ancient Near Eastern kings could partake of the "food of the gods" (Kuhrt 1995:577). Kuhrt notes that as a sign of recognition and submission the "inhabitants of Babylon and Cutha sent the Assyrian king 'the remnants' of divine meals," which were normally presented to the Babylonian king only. It is not clear that this was the dilemma for Daniel, though it may have been part of it. When the situation had changed under Cyrus of Persia (10:1-2), and the threatening religious milieu surrounding the taking of this food was evidently removed, Daniel ate and drank freely. It seems more likely that Daniel was in this case declaring both a religious and moral independence from the king that was personal, but necessary to him (otherwise he would defile himself); he did not want to become obligated to the king by eating "the food of the gods" (i.e., remnants of pagan sacrifice) at his table and thereby affirm a certain unity with, or religious submission to, his pagan court (cf. 1 Sam 20:30-34; 2 Kgs 25:27-29; Dan 11:26). Daniel knew there were dangers lurking in the situation, and he protected himself from them. Even the king did not know that he was refusing to eat the food prepared for him, and the minor official overseeing him didn't dare to tell anyone (cf. Longman 1999:53).

His refusal to drink wine recalls the Nazirite vow of complete dedication to the Lord (Num 6:1-8), but nowhere is there evidence that he took a Nazirite vow. Here, however, Daniel's vow not to defile himself is clearly evident, something that could end at a set time. In principle, it appears he could have eaten these items if he had not so vowed (10:3), but some items mentioned above create an ambiance that seems threatening to the captives. Perhaps he took this vow because he was in exile in a strange land and could not rejoice at the king's table nor drink his wine under these conditions, much as the psalmist could not sing the songs of Zion by the rivers of Babylon (Ps 137:1-4).[1] Even the land where he was captive was unclean. We are assured by Daniel's vow that no program of cultural accommodation will be effective to win him or the other captives over to the worldview of pagan Babylon. This action was needed at the moment, although later (we are not told when) he ended this vow (cf. 10:3). At the time of Cyrus the Great, when the Persians came to power and the Exile was ended (10:1-2), he was in a different cultural milieu. Then, like Nehemiah, he could enjoy the king's wine and food (Neh 2:1). Evidently no threatening demands were being put upon him by Cyrus at that time—and the exodus from Babylon had taken place three years earlier.

Daniel's integrity and character certainly played a role in the chief official's gracious and kind attitude to him (1:9), but this section also reminds us of the favorable and compassionate attitude God purposefully gave to the Egyptians toward the Israelites and which led, likewise, to the high respect the Egyptians held for Moses (Exod 11:3). God knows his faithful followers and makes their enemies to be at peace with them (Prov 16:7).

Ashpenaz stated his dilemma truthfully and openly—if the young men did not appear well fed, he could lose his head (1:10). He assumed that if Daniel and the other young men did not eat the king's food, but only vegetables, they would become weak and malnourished compared to the other youths. Daniel, then, as part of his tact and wisdom (an aspect of traditional wisdom that is stressed about Daniel's character in the book, cf. 2:14), established the sufficiency of his God to care for himself and his friends and to rescue them from a compromising situation. This anticipates the many times God will deliver the Jewish captives throughout the book. Daniel did not live by bread alone (Deut 8:3); rather, he fed his essential spiritual nature by trusting his God for his needs. He would remain free of the political and religious intrigues of the king's ritualistic programs.

Daniel's wisdom was illustrated in the way he refused to push the chief official and showed genuine concern for the man's dilemma. He worked with his immediate attendant to set up a trial run that would allow everyone involved to be protected, while giving his God time to show his care for his people, for these four youths become representative of what God will do in general for his people who trust him (cf. 1:4; 7:18, 22). Daniel's politeness and sagacity are emphasized in the attitude he had toward the attendant. He did not give up his convictions, although he acted with great respect toward the attendant. Ten days were long enough to carry out the needed effects—perhaps before they would be seen by the chief official or the king again. Daniel shrewdly and tactfully closed his suggestions with a statement that the attendant should make the final decision. The attendant agreed to Daniel's trial run exactly as suggested.

During this time only vegetables and water were served to Daniel and his friends. Not only did they not eat the king's rich meats, but they ate no meat at all, something their own laws did not demand. This abstinence emphasized their total dependence upon their God. The attendant (and even Ashpenaz, one would think) must have been impressed, for Daniel had clearly tied his diet to the faithfulness of his own God. Daniel's actions effectively negated the goal of the "rite of passage" into the Babylonian world that Nebuchadnezzar had planned for him, Hananiah, Mishael, and Azariah. Their well-being lay with their God; he would supply their needs, not the Babylonian system. The royal seed of Judah would remain loyal to their own names, their own Jewish way of life, and the traditions that they had already imbibed as members of their own people, risking death if necessary. God has judged (the meaning of Daniel), and Yahweh is their helper (Azariah), who gives them grace (Hananiah)—Who is like (their) God (Mishael)?

ENDNOTE

1. For a helpful discussion of the theological implications of the Exile, see Klein 1979.

◆ D. The Results: *Summa cum Laude* and Then Some (1:15-21)

15At the end of the ten days, Daniel and his three friends looked healthier and better nourished than the young men who had been eating the food assigned by the king. 16So after that, the attendant fed them only vegetables instead of the food and wine provided for the others.

17God gave these four young men an unusual aptitude for understanding every aspect of literature and wisdom. And God gave Daniel the special ability to interpret the meanings of visions and dreams.

18When the training period ordered by the king was completed, the chief of staff brought all the young men to King Nebuchadnezzar. 19The king talked with them, and no one impressed him as much as Daniel, Hananiah, Mishael, and Azariah. So they entered the royal service. 20Whenever the king consulted them in any matter requiring wisdom and balanced judgment, he found them ten times more capable than any of the magicians and enchanters in his entire kingdom.

21Daniel remained in the royal service until the first year of the reign of King Cyrus.*

1:21 Cyrus began his reign (over Babylon) in 539 B.C.

NOTES

1:15 ***healthier and better nourished.*** Lit., "they looked good and healthy of flesh."

food assigned by the king. See note on 1:5.

1:16 ***fed them only vegetables.*** The MT reads, "The attendant took away their rich food and banqueting wine." The NLT interprets this in light of Daniel's suggestion in 1:12.

1:17 ***And God gave Daniel.*** This translates a disjunctive Waw preceding "Daniel," which draws attention to Daniel's special gifts from God. God gave his wisdom to certain select persons in the OT and to chosen individuals according to some rabbinic writings (Mulder and Sysling 1988:723, note 188).

visions and dreams. Lit., "In every kind of vision (*khazon* [TH2377, ZH2606]) and dreams (*khalomoth* [TH2472, ZH2706])." "Visions" is the usual word for describing a prophetic vision. "Dreams" immediately recalls Joseph. And many parallels exist between Daniel and Joseph in the area of wisdom and dream interpretation (Gen 37; 40:8–41:32).[1] Hallo and Simpson (1971:158-163) observe that the prediction and control of events was a major concern of Babylonian literature, and divination and dreams were the most common means of learned speculation.[2]

1:19 ***The king talked with them.*** The Heb. *wayedabber* [TH1696, ZH1819] *'itam* indicates more than a brief conversation or merely speaking with them; "he discussed with them" catches the thought (see 1:20). He talked to all of the young men, not just Daniel and his three friends.

entered the royal service. This translates the idiom "to the face of the king," which means "in the presence of the king." This was indeed a place of great honor and prestige (cf. Gen 50:4-5; Exod 5:1).

1:20 ***magicians and enchanters.*** The *khartummim* [TH2748, ZH3033] (magicians) were some kind of soothsayer priests who could interpret dreams (Gen 41:8) and perform wonders (Exod 7:11). The word *'ashapim* [TH825, ZH879] (enchanters) is from an Akkadian word, *'ashipu*. It is found only in the book of Daniel; their rituals featured utterances of spells.

COMMENTARY

Daniel and his friends are an excellent model for the integration of faith and higher learning. Although they were forced to be involved in the most challenging and pagan curriculum of the day, they kept their vital piety and were successful in every way. They already knew and continued to involve themselves in the study and language and literature and traditions of their own people and God (3:16-18; 4:27 [24]; 5:22-24; 6:5, 10-11, 16, 19 [6, 11-12, 17, 20]; 9:2-19) and worshiped *only* their Lord and God (chs 3, 6). The king and people of the nation knew it (2:46-47; 3:28-29; 4:34-37 [31-34]; 5:23-24; 6:25-28 [26-29]). All of this was ordained by their God (1:2). Their diet not only helped in their educational and spiritual endeavors, but it may have helped their longevity (even though it was only temporary)—Daniel lived to be a healthy old man (1:21; 10:1; Deut 8:3).

The aptitude for the language and literature and science of the times was a gift from God, much like the gifts of Joseph (Gen 41:38) and of Bezalel and Oholiab, the skilled artisans called and equipped by God to construct the Tabernacle and its furnishings (Exod 31:1-6; 35:30-35). Like them, Daniel was possessed by the "Spirit of the Holy God" (4:8-9 [5-6]; 5:11). But Daniel's special gifts are pointed out to prepare the reader for what is to come in the rest of the book (see note on 1:17). In good Hebrew style, the writer mentions "visions and dreams," while the order of presentation in the larger structure of Daniel is dreams (chs 1–6) and then visions (chs 7–12). The writer was careful to point out that these gifts were not a mere result of completing the prescribed courses of study, but were abilities given by God himself (1:17). They will be featured extensively in the rest of the book of Daniel.

Daniel and the three Hebrew youths passed their oral exams with flying colors; in fact, they did much better than any of the other young men (1:19). As a result, it is they who were privileged to stand in the king's presence. They were placed by the unwitting king into the position their God wanted them to have. They were not afraid of the intellectual and spiritual challenges of the day; they conquered them. They were placed where God wanted them, both by his divine sovereignty and by their willingness to study and conquer the curricula placed before them. Because of their commitment to excellence, their God caused them to stand before the nations because through them he would declare his kingdom to the kingdoms and kings of the world. God could use them in the highest position in the land to reveal himself through them and give a true understanding of himself. Through them, both Israel and the nations would be blessed (Gen 12:1-3).

They did not betray themselves or their faith or their God, but they gained respect because of their expertise in the language, literature, and science of the day. They did not embrace this alien culture, but they mastered it and subordinated it to their God and faith. They were "ten times" better than the others—*summa cum laude*, to say the least. They were far better than the magicians and enchanters of this famed empire of diviners and soothsayers. Like Joseph, they were guided by the true God; even as they worked through their Babylonian curriculum, they did not accept its central concepts or become enamored with polytheism, nor were they impressed with the hubris of kings who thought they controlled the course of history and established cities and empires. Joseph had astounded the Egyptians and his brothers (Gen 41:38; 43:33). God worked through Joseph, who employed a divining cup in that religious and cultural setting (Gen 44:5, 15), but recognized that God gave his abilities and gifts to him. The pagan kings found in Daniel skills and mantic wisdom that went far beyond the abilities he gained by finishing his prescribed course of study and practice. Most important of all, they caught a sufficient glimpse of the God of Daniel and his friends that they declared great things about him, though they did not fully grasp who the source of Daniel's skills and wisdom was. Even on the natural plane of knowledge, Daniel and the three friends excelled the Babylonian wise men; their gifts were from the true God who alone truly predicts and controls the events of the future and gives wisdom and tact for living daily life (1:17, 20).

Daniel would live to exercise his gifts for many years under foreign kings, including some of the best known in world history (Nebuchadnezzar and Cyrus). He lived until at least 537 BC (10:1), rendering unto Caesar the things that were Caesar's and unto God the things that belonged to God (6:2-3, 10 [3-4, 11]; cf. Mark 12:17).

ENDNOTES

1. John Sailhamer (1990) discusses the parallels between Daniel and Joseph in his treatment of Gen 37, 40, 41.
2. For a recent summary of these areas of Babylonian culture, see von Soden 1992:45-231; see also Oppenheim 1977:206-207, 288-310; Bertman 2003.

◆ II. Dreams and Stories for the Present and Future: Daniel's Faithfulness and Wisdom Demonstrated before the Kingdoms of This World (2:1–6:28)

A. Daniel's Divine Wisdom concerning All World History: The Establishment of God's Kingdom (2:1-49)

1. A dream that troubles Nebuchadnezzar (2:1-3)

One night during the second year of his reign,* Nebuchadnezzar had such disturbing dreams that he couldn't sleep.
2He called in his magicians, enchanters, sorcerers, and astrologers,* and he demanded that they tell him what he had dreamed. As they stood before the king,
3he said, "I have had a dream that deeply troubles me, and I must know what it means."

2:1 The second year of Nebuchadnezzar's reign was 603 B.C. 2:2 Or *Chaldeans;* also in 2:4, 5, 10.

NOTES

2:1 ***second year of his reign.*** This would probably be 602 BC, which is arrived at by using the accession year dating system in Babylon. The year of accession was not counted as one of the years of the king's reign. Hence, 605 is not counted, 604/3 and 603/2 are. This indicates that the three-year training period for Daniel and his friends could have been completed by now. It is assumed to have been completed by the writer in 2:48. In 1:20 Daniel completes the course of study, but is not placed into any position by the king. Other solutions are plausible as well (see Montgomery 1927:140-141; Porteous 1965:39). Baldwin (1978a:85-86) prefers to use March/April 603 BC as the date referred to here and employs the nonaccession year dating system, in which the accession year is counted as the first year of a king's reign.

disturbing. Lit., "and his spirit was disturbed."

had . . . dreams. Heb. *khalam . . . khalomoth* [TH2492A/2472, ZH2731/2706] employs the cognate noun of the verb (lit., "dreamed dreams"), helping to recall the same activity and grammatical construction used of Joseph (Gen 37:9). The noun and verbal forms of the root *khalam* are found 17 times in this chapter, effectively making Nebuchadnezzar's dream the focus of the chapter.

he couldn't sleep. This translates a difficult construction that says literally "but his sleep was/became upon him" (cf. Goldingay 1989:32; he cites Gen 41:4-5). HALOT 1.234 supports the traditional translations as in NLT, NIV. But NJPS gives "was overcome by sleep" with a note. This fits the way (*'al* [TH5921, ZH6584]) would usually be translated as an adversative in this context—"but his sleep came [back] upon him."

2:2 ***magicians, enchanters.*** See note on 1:20. NJPS renders the second term "exorcists," which indicates the difficulty of translating some of these obscure technical titles and terms.

sorcerers, and astrologers. NIV also has "astrologers" here. NJPS, NASB, RSV, NRSV, and KJV favor "Chaldeans" for the last term (cf. 1:4, NLT mg). (See "Historical Accuracy" in the Introduction concerning the unsound argument of some that this word usage implies a late date for the book of Daniel.)

The Hebrew terms underlying magicians, enchanters, sorcerers, and astrologers are technical words that are difficult to render accurately today with great precision. The Akkadian behind the second and third Hebrew terms may have been "warlocks" and "incantation priests," respectively, but the Akkadian terms are likewise difficult to render accurately

(Saggs 1962:305, 346; von Soden 1992:200; see Holladay 1988:30, 116, 165-166). For an excellent, easy-to-read article on this topic, see W. Farber 1995:1895-1909.

2:3 *deeply troubles me.* This reflects the Niphal verb *wattippa'em* [TH6470, ZH7192], and the same root is used in the Hithpael in 2:1 (cf. NLT, "disturbing"). These verbal forms make an *inclusio* of these three verses, laying the emphasis upon the troubled spirit of the king. The king wanted to know his disturbing dream because he had reason to fear the overthrow of his throne by various enemies (Oates 1986:129-130).

COMMENTARY

The dream Nebuchadnezzar could not recall and Daniel's revelation and interpretation of it go to the heart of the issue in the book of Daniel—the assured establishment of the Kingdom of God as the ultimate goal of all history, both divine and human (cf. Acts 1:6). The second chapter raises the issue of the end (2:45), which will be developed in chapters 7–12. Meanwhile, chapters 3–6 record the passing of the head of gold and the appearance of the shoulders and chest of silver. Although the kingdom of Israel ended in 586 BC, this chapter asserts, through the imagery of a rock, that it will appear again dramatically and powerfully at the culmination of all earthly nations, but in universal garb. The universality of the kingdom (it "covers the whole earth," 2:35) is important; the original call of Abraham included the assertion that in his descendants all of the nations would be blessed (Gen 12:1-3). But Israel was to be the head of the nations (Deut 28:13), not the tail as during the Exile (Deut 28:44). This situation would change, and the rock in this chapter will prove to be the Kingdom of God, not merely Israel reigning alone over the earth (cf. 7:13-14, 18, 21, 26-27); the image recalls the mountain of the house of the Lord and the filling of the earth with the glory and knowledge of the Lord (Isa 2:2; 6:3; 11:9; Mic 4:1; cf. Lucas 2002:74).

The chapter presents a sweeping, panoramic view of the flow of history that causes the reader to turn his attention to the future and the denouement of all things. As history passes (2:1; 5:1; 5:31 [6:1]; 6:1, 28 [2, 29]), chapters 3–6 portray the demise of Babylon, the head of gold, and the rise of Persia, the chest and shoulders of silver. History moves inexorably to its fulfillment.

These chapters describe the sovereignty and uniform goal and purpose of God; these purposes and goals remain fixed upon the establishment of God's kingdom amidst the change and flux of world rulers, kingdoms, and authority—all of which occur under his authority. He had originally endowed persons with the ability to be his regents on earth, and he gave them the authority to rule in the Garden of Eden (Gen 1–3). Because of who this God of Daniel is and because of the final end of all things, the lives of Daniel and his three Hebrew friends are set within a particular political and religious worldview. That same worldview gave them a perspective to guide them as they are forced to act and react to the false and misguided challenges that confront them in the Exile. Through them God was fulfilling part of his promises to Abraham and David that through their descendants the nations would come to know him, some through blessing, some through judgment (Gen 12:1-3; 15:1-21; 17:1-27; 2 Sam 7:5-16; 1 Kgs 11:12-13; Isa 9:7; 11:1).

The mention of Nebuchadnezzar's second year (603 or 602 BC, see 2:1, NLT mg; Longman 1999:76; Lucas 2002:62) recalls Genesis 41:1, which dates Pharaoh's puzzling dream to "two full years later." Pharaoh's spirit also was agitated (Gen 41:8), and he related the dreams to his magicians and wise men who could not interpret them. But Joseph did interpret them, attributing the dreams to God's revelation. The scope of Nebuchadnezzar's dream and the difficulty of presenting and interpreting the dream go far beyond the dreams of Pharaoh. These kings' presentation of a difficult question to their wise men, along with the the success of a particular and gifted wise man, are also paralleled in the extrabiblical story of Ahikar, who served at the Assyrian court (Niditch and Doran 1977:179-193; Longman 1999:73).

These three verses effectively present the event that raises the problem in the chapter: the need for someone to interpret a dream that Nebuchadnezzar had, and his determination to have it both re-presented and interpreted. By leaving the magicians, enchanters, sorcerers, and astrologers standing in anticipation before the king, the author encourages the reader to anticipate their wise answer to the problem presented by the king—an answer they are unable to deliver.

The basic issue is presented in 2:1 and 2:3, enclosing 2:2 with Nebuchadnezzar's call for the help of his coterie of advisers. He has dreamed a dream, but it is more. It is a dream that troubles him and has disturbed his spirit. Therefore, he must know it. The word "dream" occurs six times in these three verses. The statement that his spirit was disturbed by the dream is emphasized twice, enclosing verse 2. The king's demand to report and declare the dream and his need to know it are also found twice.

According to most translations, the dream was so disturbing that it caused his sleep to leave him (cf. Gen 41:4-5). There is evidence that Nebuchadnezzar's rulership was contested early in his reign and several times thereafter. He had to constantly deal with the Medes and entertained suspicions of their intentions. These concerns fit well with the idea that the king could not sleep after his dream.

The king, however, wanted his group of Babylonian advisers to tell him the dream itself, as we see in the following verses, and not just to interpret the dream. The alternative translation suggested by some—that his sleep returned to him—may therefore have some merit. Perhaps he went back to sleep after awakening, highly agitated by the dream, and forgot the dream itself. That is why he would demand his court experts to tell him the dream as well as to interpret it, so that he might understand it. This interpretation could also imply that he dreamed the dream again, for in 2:2 he literally calls the experts together to declare to him "his dreams" (cf. Pharaoh's two dreams in Gen 41:1-7). However, his motive for not relating the dream may be intentional (2:4-6) rather than due to a lack of recall. There are instances of Assyrian kings testing their dream experts to keep them from deceiving the king (Oppenheim 1977:277). According to some ancient Near Eastern texts, relating the dream itself could in some instances cause it to lose its influence on the person who had the dream (Oppenheim 1956:219; cf. Lucas 2002:70-71). In this instance, it seems that if the king in fact remembered the dream, he was taking the opportunity to test the accuracy of his court professionals.

Verse 2 leaves the impressive coterie of pagan magicians, enchanters, sorcerers, and astrologers standing in the presence of the king anticipating the king's instructions and the reader anticipating their explanation of the whole affair. God had earlier declared Nebuchadnezzar to be his servant to judge not only Judah but also Egypt and all the surrounding nations (Jer 25:9; 27:6; 43:10). In Daniel's time, we see God putting dreams into the mind of the greatest king on earth during the time of the Exile and using his mind to declare a message of instruction and hope—but also of judgment—to Daniel's own people and the nations of the world. Nebuchadnezzar could not resist the desire to grasp the significance of this great dream, though he did not know its source. In the ancient Near East, dreams and magic were weapons given to humans to protect themselves from evil events, and kings were usually chosen to be the dream conduits of the gods. So, Nebuchadnezzar wanted to recover the dream and know its interpretation. His ultimate source for doing that was to be the God who placed the dream in his mind in the first place, the one who had made Nebuchadnezzar his servant to Israel and the nations.

◆ 2. "Only the gods can tell you your dreams" (2:4-11)

4Then the astrologers answered the king in Aramaic,* "Long live the king! Tell us the dream, and we will tell you what it means."

5But the king said to the astrologers, "I am serious about this. If you don't tell me what my dream was and what it means, you will be torn limb from limb, and your houses will be turned into heaps of rubble!
6But if you tell me what I dreamed and what the dream means, I will give you many wonderful gifts and honors. Just tell me the dream and what it means!"

7They said again, "Please, Your Majesty. Tell us the dream, and we will tell you what it means."

8The king replied, "I know what you are doing! You're stalling for time because you know I am serious when I say,
9'If you don't tell me the dream, you are doomed.' So you have conspired to tell me lies, hoping I will change my mind. But tell me the dream, and then I'll know that you can tell me what it means."

10The astrologers replied to the king, "No one on earth can tell the king his dream! And no king, however great and powerful, has ever asked such a thing of any magician, enchanter, or astrologer!
11The king's demand is impossible. No one except the gods can tell you your dream, and they do not live here among people."

2:4 The original text from this point through chapter 7 is in Aramaic.

NOTES

2:4 ***in Aramaic.*** This translates Heb. *'aramith* [TH762, ZH811], which is used to introduce the speech of the astrologers. Their statements were probably in some dialect of Neo-Babylonian, but are reported in the text in Aramaic. Cf. Hartman and Di Lella (1978:138) who assert "it seemed only natural to let the 'Chaldeans' speak in their own languages." Beginning with this verse, Aramaic continues to the end of chapter 7 (see NLT mg). Biblical Aramaic was part of international Aramaic, the *lingua franca* of that day, also termed Royal or Imperial Aramaic (see "The Aramaic of Daniel" in Stefanovic 1992). The shift from Hebrew to Aramaic in this verse is represented in the Dead Sea Scroll 1QDan[a] (1Q71), and Aramaic material from the middle of the book is found in 1QDan[b] (1Q72) and in 4QDan[a, b, d] (4Q112, 113, and 115). 4QDan[a, b] also contain the transition from Aramaic back to Hebrew at 7:28–8:1.

Tell us the dream. If he were to have done that, they could have consulted an omen manual. For an example, see COS 1.120. In that document alone nine different means of divination are described: extispicy (examining entrails), behavior patterns, lecanomancy (oil in water), anomalous births (*summa izbu*), celestial bodies, changes to the human environment, cledonomancy (divine sounds), oneiromancy (dreams), and bodily changes. Of these, the OT recognizes only dreams as a possible way of receiving a message/sign from God.

tell you what it means. Lit., "and its interpretation we will declare." The Aramaic *peshar* [TA/ZA10600, S6591] (interpretation) is similar to the "Pesher" interpretation of texts employed popularly in the Dead Sea Scrolls (e.g., 1QpHab 7:3-5; 1QpMic [1Q14]; 4Qpap pIsa[c] [4Q163]; cf. Charlesworth 2002:9.67, 77, 119-128, 162-165). The word is found 6 times in 2:4-11. Three times it is paired with the word for "dream" or in close conjunction with "dream," which occurs 7 times in this section. Dreams and their interpretations were part of the ancient Sumerian saga of Gilgamesh (von Soden 1992:216-217), but see especially Lucas 2009:531, 575, note A-10 (cf. COS 1.32; 1.33; 2.3, lines 20b-22a; 2.155; Longman 1999:74; Oppenheim 1956; Farber 1995).

2:5 *astrologers.* See note on 1:4. Here the term refers to the king's professional "Chaldeans," or astrologers. About Chaldean astrologers in the time of Alexander the Great (in Babylon), see Plutarch 1986:330-331.

I am serious about this. Lit., "The matter by me is settled/gone forth/promulgated" (*'azda'* [TA/ZA10014, S230]), using an old Persian word used before 200 BC and also found in Imperial Aramaic—i.e., in the sixth and fifth centuries BC (Hartman and Di Lella 1978:138; Holladay 1988:396).

heaps of rubble. This renders *newali* [TA/ZA10470, S5122], a word of uncertain origin.

2:8 *I am serious.* See note on 2:5.

2:9 *you have conspired.* The MT's Kethiv can be read as a Hitpaal, "you have agreed" (*hizzammintun* [TA/ZA10231, S2164]). The Qere reading is a Hitpeel of the same root, *hizdemintun* [TA/ZA10231, S2164], with the same or similar meaning.

2:10 *No one on earth.* Lit., "There is not a person on earth." A human being on earth contrasts with the gods who do not dwell among men of flesh and blood (2:11).

2:11 *impossible.* The word *yaqqir* [TA/ZA10330, S3358] is closely related to *yeqar* [TA/ZA10331, S3367], (honor, wonder). Here it means "difficult" in the sense of "too wonderful" to understand.

the gods. Aramaic, *'elahin* [TA/ZA10033, S426] (divine beings). According to some Sumerian myths, the gods had once dwelt upon earth (Brown 1995:141).

people. The Aramaic has *bisra'* [TA/ZA10125, S1321], lit., "the flesh," meaning humanity.

COMMENTARY

King Nebuchadnezzar made a demand that was impossible for human beings to fulfill. Since dreams originate with the "gods" and not humans, only a god could do what Nebuchadnezzar was asking—or someone in touch with the gods, for the gods do not live among men, but in a heavenly realm (2:11). We are not told why the wise men could not meet the king's challenge, but evidently they could not. Ancient Near Eastern kings did not always trust their religious subjects (Oppenheim 1977:227). Their system and their gods failed. But Daniel had access to his God through prayer, and he would request supernatural wisdom to interpret by direct revelation. He was seeking esoteric wisdom, mantic wisdom.

Of course, this scenario is exactly what the inspired writer wished to convey in order to make it unequivocally clear that the man who could meet the king's demand would show himself to be delivering divine wisdom. Daniel's gifts and abilities to understand and interpret dreams and visions (1:17) did not expressly include the ability to recall the dreams of others in order to interpret them. So the situation demanded more of Daniel than he was capable of doing, even though God had endowed him with the "special ability" to interpret dreams and with the ability to learn and understand Akkadian and Aramaic, the language used from 2:4b to 7:28. The dream had to be recalled before it could be interpreted. Could the dream be merely the production of a troubled king's mind? That is, a production of an especially oppressive set of political, social, military, or economic factors? The false prophets of Jeremiah's day produced lying dreams from their own deceitful minds and hearts (Jer 23:25-26; 27:9). The text will dispose of this possibility: God is the one who creates the dream, and this is what gives the dream its integrity.

The interpretation of the dream is vital, for only a sure interpretation of the dream after the dream itself was recalled would be of any value for knowing the significance of the dream. An inspired dream requires an inspired explanation. Thus, the source of the interpretation must be God himself. A mere human answer would not suffice.

Whether the king knew the dream and was merely testing his wise men or whether he had actually forgotten it is of little importance as the story develops, but it does drive home the inability of the great wise men of Babylon to meet this challenge. God will confirm through Daniel that the dream was from him (2:28), and God will give its meaning.

The astrologers (Chaldeans) had to have the king give them the dream before they could interpret it, for they had no god who could reveal the dream itself to them. The king's offer of "many wonderful gifts and honors" assures the reader that had they been able to recount the dream to Nebuchadnezzar, they would have done so. But they could not; they failed and this cast doubt upon their gods. Perhaps these gods, since they had not generated the dream, really knew nothing about it. Even though they did not give the dream, should they not have been able to discern it since they were the most high gods? Chaldean astrologers were a feature of Babylon's social makeup, even in the time of Alexander the Great, when they warned him to stay away from Babylon, where he eventually died. Alexander, too, had been beset with dreams (Plutarch 1986:295).

Astrologers, magicians, sorcerers, and enchanters in the ancient Near East had many manuals to help them interpret dreams, but all these manuals assumed that the dream was already known. They rightly, in that culture, accused the king of dealing deceitfully with them (2:10, see note) by demanding such an unusual performance from them. According to them, there was literally "not a man upon the earth" who could meet his unreasonable request. Only the "gods" could break into the situation in order for the dilemma to be solved, but they do not dwell among human beings (according to the theology of these wise men).

3. Nebuchadnezzar's lethal decree and Daniel's wise response (2:12-16)

[12]The king was furious when he heard this, and he ordered that all the wise men of Babylon be executed. [13]And because of the king's decree, men were sent to find and kill Daniel and his friends.

[14]When Arioch, the commander of the king's guard, came to kill them, Daniel handled the situation with wisdom and discretion. [15]He asked Arioch, "Why has the king issued such a harsh decree?" So Arioch told him all that had happened. [16]Daniel went at once to see the king and requested more time to tell the king what the dream meant.

NOTES

2:12 ***was furious.*** Two verbs *benas* [TA/ZA10113, S1149] (become angry); *qetsap* [TA/ZA10633, S7108] (become furious), plus a strong adverb *saggi'* [TA/ZA10678, S7690] are used to emphasize the outrageous disposition of the king.

2:13 ***decree.*** This renders the MT's *dath* [TA/ZA10186, S1882], which was used in 2:9 to describe the judgment the wise men would receive if they did not meet the king's demand. This word is found 8 times in Daniel (2:9, 13, 15; 6:5 [6], 8 [9], 12 [13], 15 [16]; 7:25) meaning "decree," "judgment," "law," and "law of God." For a brief discussion of this word and its use in Babylonian and Persian legal terminology, see Olmstead 1948:119-134. Hammurabi, Nebuchadnezzar, Darius the Mede, Cyrus, and especially Darius the Great were creators and developers of the great law codes in the ancient Near East (cf. note on 4:27 [24]).

2:15 ***Arioch.*** He is further described in the MT as the *shallit* [TA/ZA10718, S7990], meaning "chief officer" (of the king).

told. This translates the Haphel stem of *yeda'* [TA/ZA10313, S3046], lit., "he caused to know"—that is, he informed Daniel.

2:16 ***more time.*** "Time" translates a key word in Daniel, *zeman* [TA/ZA10232, S2166] (cf. 2:21; 3:7, 8; 4:36 [33]; 6:10 [11], 13 [14]; 7:12, 22, 25). See note on 2:21.

COMMENTARY

Daniel demonstrates conflict management—the ability to deal with the king's demand and the resultant conflicts—at the highest level of governmental and religious administration. The basic framework of this short passage is instructive:

2:12-13	The king's response—a decree of death issued.
2:14	Arioch delivers the decree to Daniel.
2:15	Daniel responds to the king's decree with Arioch.
2:16	Daniel responds to the king himself, and surprisingly, a temporary reprieve of the decree's enactment is granted.

Nebuchadnezzar responded to the rather aggressive and defensive response of these particular wise men. He became exceedingly angry and outrageously furious, so that he used his ultimate threat of power—death to those who would not succumb to his demands. His actions and attitude foreshadow the hatred and fury of the "king of the north" (Antiochus IV Epiphanes, 175–164 BC) against the Jews (11:21-35), as well as his own fury in chapter 3. But Nebuchadnezzar shows a magnanimous attitude toward Daniel, a Jew, in this chapter—and a highly reverent attitude toward his God (2:47). At this time when things were on the verge of total disaster for the wise men of Babylon, including Daniel and his three friends, Daniel responded with wise, calm counsel and a clear understanding of what needed to be done. A soft word can turn away wrath (Prov 15:1). Daniel dealt successfully with Arioch and gained insight into the situation.

Daniel went to the king and gained what his own wise men could not—a reprieve of the decree for a period of time (2:16; cf. 1:9)! Daniel knew where and how to resolve the dilemma. He employed a methodology that he did not learn in his training in the pagan courts of Babylon—sharing and prayer (2:17-23). He went to his friends and shared with them; then they all sought God, who could solve their dilemma. And so the tragic destruction of all the wise men of Babylon was thwarted by Daniel and his three friends. They accomplished this through wisdom, counsel, patience, and prayer, accompanied by a spirit of humility (cf. Mic 6:8). These behaviors and attitudes resulted in approval from God and even—though it is not guaranteed—success in their service to this earthly king, for they knew that he was ruling by the decree of their own God.

Nebuchadnezzar was true to his threat in 2:9, "If you don't tell me the dream, you are doomed." His decree (see note on 2:13) was about to fulfill it. Although Daniel and his friends were not among those who denied that the king's request could be answered, he and his comrades were also going to die. Presumably, all of the wise men of Babylon were going to die because of the king's decree, whether they were present when the king threatened the wise men or not.

Daniel's question about why the severity of the decree was so harsh was a serious one. Arioch informed Daniel and his friends of the circumstances surrounding the decree. The decree was indeed harsh because the wise men (1) could not answer, thus frustrating the king, (2) they argued with the king and demanded that he tell them the dream, (3) they called his demand irrational and something that only the gods could answer, and (4) they seemed to be stalling for time (2:8). The expense the Babylonian state had put out to train these various types of government counselors and supporters certainly appeared wasted since they could not produce answers when they were asked to do so. Their responses to the king approached disrespect and certainly a lack of wisdom and tact when dealing with him. Daniel had previously established a wise policy and line of communication from the beginning of his stay in Babylon with the representatives of the king and had even spoken with Nebuchadnezzar himself (1:8, 11, 14, 18, 20).

His access to the king enabled Daniel to approach Nebuchadnezzar and obtain an extension of the time period, which the king would not grant to the other wise men (2:8). After this time Daniel would answer his inquiry and tell him his dream. Undoubtedly, the reader is to understand that the wisdom, tact, and patience of Daniel, and his prior behavior before the king, enabled him to have respectful access to him. The recognition of Daniel's excellence and moral, ethical, and academic success also made such a direct line of access to Nebuchadnezzar feasible (1:18-21). Daniel's diligent application of his entire self—body, soul, mind, and spirit—to his opportunities paid off. He had access to the king, and God could use him to reveal more of his mysteries to mankind. Daniel's approach and demeanor, and his promise of success to the king in solving his problem, contrast with the folly, insecurity, and lack of respect demonstrated by the group of wise men the king had just encountered. The wise men were undoubtedly amazed and yet angry at the success Daniel had with Nebuchadnezzar. But they could not protest too much. His wise actions had saved their lives.

Daniel's assertion to Nebuchadnezzar was that if given more time, he would "tell the king what the dream meant" (2:16). His promise to answer him is an unequivocal demonstration of his faith in his God to solve the mystery. While Nebuchadnezzar placed the acquisition of an answer to his dream above the life of his servants, Daniel sought an answer to Nebuchadnezzar's dream in order to rescue and give life back to his friends. These actions by the two men reveal their character. Daniel will do all he can to rescue the Babylonian experts, not just himself and his fellow Jewish friends; this sends a message about his character and his attitude toward the sovereignty of his God.

◆ 4. Daniel's prayer and praise to a God who reveals secrets (2:17-24)

17 Then Daniel went home and told his
friends Hananiah, Mishael, and Azariah
what had happened. 18 He urged them to
ask the God of heaven to show them his
mercy by telling them the secret, so they
would not be executed along with the
other wise men of Babylon. 19 That night
the secret was revealed to Daniel in a vi-
sion. Then Daniel praised the God of heav-
en. 20 He said,

"Praise the name of God forever
and ever,
for he has all wisdom and power.
21 He controls the course of world events;
he removes kings and sets up
other kings.
He gives wisdom to the wise
and knowledge to the scholars.
22 He reveals deep and mysterious things
and knows what lies hidden in
darkness,
though he is surrounded by light.
23 I thank and praise you, God of
my ancestors,
for you have given me wisdom
and strength.
You have told me what we asked
of you
and revealed to us what the
king demanded."

24 Then Daniel went in to see Arioch,
whom the king had ordered to execute the
wise men of Babylon. Daniel said to him,
"Don't kill the wise men. Take me to the
king, and I will tell him the meaning of his
dream."

NOTES

2:17 ***Hananiah, Mishael, and Azariah.*** Regarding the names of Daniel's three companions, see the notes and commentary on 1:6-7.

2:18 ***mercy.*** This translates *rakhamin* [TA/ZA10664, S7359]—cf. Heb. *rakhamim* [TH7356, ZH8171], which has, as does the Aramaic word, the connotation of loving, compassionate attitudes and feelings.

secret. *Razah* [TA/ZA10661, S7328] is a Persian loanword that appears eight times in ch 2 (2:18, 19, 27, 28, 29, 30, 47 [twice]), as well as in 4:6 [3], making a total of nine times. It refers to secrets and mysteries in Daniel that are connected with the dreams of King Nebuchadnezzar. It is used twice in 2:17-24 to refer to the recovery of Nebuchadnezzar's dream and the revelation of its meaning. There are about 19 Persian loanwords in Daniel (cf. Baldwin 1978a:89-90). These loanwords do not necessarily date the book late, but must be taken into account (Lucas 2002:307-308; see Introduction, "Date and Place of Writing"). Lawson (1997) argues well that these words suggest a Mesopotamian milieu and that Daniel here fits the mold of a mantic wise man in that setting. Cf. Longman 1999:74.

2:20 ***wisdom and power.*** These words (*khokmetha' ugeburtha'* [TA/ZA10266/10130, S2452/1370]) occur here and in 2:23, forming an *inclusio* around the lines of poetry in 2:20-23.

2:21 ***the course of world events.*** This is a good translation of two semantically related Aramaic words for "time, season, circumstance, period of time, set time, indefinite time" (*'iddanayya' wezimnayya'* [TA/ZA10530/10232, S5732/2166]). Context determines the exact meaning. The first word is used 13 times in Daniel (2:8-9, 21; 3:5, 15; 4:16 [13], 23 [20], 25 [22], 32 [29]; 7:12, 25); the second is found 10 times (2:16, 21; 3:7, 8; 4:36 [33]; 6:10, 13 [11, 14]; 7:12, 22, 25). These words express God's sovereignty over the times, reasons, and flow of history and nature. See note to 4:16 [13].

COMMENTARY

The author presented the incident in two instances of *inclusio*. One set, in narrative prose (2:17-18, 24), encloses the paean of praise Daniel raises to his God for answering their prayer (2:20-23). The other *inclusio* is part of Daniel's praise (2:20, 23) and encloses the key verses that exalt God as the one who revealed the answer to their prayer (2:21-22). In the text, it is thus emphatically Daniel's God who resolves and solves the dilemma. Daniel and his friends receive the answer; they do not produce it. Their God reveals everything that Daniel and his friends need to know to answer Nebuchadnezzar and to rescue themselves (and the wise men of Babylon).

Mesopotamian divination practices (cf. COS 1.90-93) included the interpretation of dreams, and Daniel operated within this worldview. He was thus "relevant" to his contemporaries, Jewish and non-Jewish. But the source of his revelation was his God alone, in response to the effective "method" of simple humble prayer. God responded and gave him direct revelatory knowledge and (mantic) wisdom through a vision (2:19). Now this wisdom would become a part of Daniel's own worldview, and he would place it into the context of his knowledge and service of his God (cf. Longman 1999:74; Lawson 1997). Daniel's God, who has all wisdom, shares it with his servants. The wise men of Babylon are proven wrong because there is a God who, though he is "surrounded by light" (2:22) and dwells in heaven, shares his wisdom and power with humans, especially with his chosen servants who petition him. He does not answer them because he has to; he answers because he is a God of mercy (2:18) who willingly shares with his people. If any of his servants lack wisdom, they can seek their God, for he willingly shares it (1 Kgs 3:9-12; Jas 1:5-7).

This passage is an adumbration of what is to come in the rest of the book of Daniel, including the near context (2:45b-47). Daniel's God is able to answer all the questions the mighty kings of the world may have, for he is not just the sovereign of the history of his people Israel, but of all nations. He is not just sovereign over specific events in Israel's history, but over the entire flow of history itself and its appointed denouement and fulfillment. He establishes times and seasons, and no one can change them, even though the contemptuous little horn (7:8) and the furious Greek kings (11:2-35) who arise against God's covenant and people will seek to change them.

The titles used for Daniel's God in this passage are significant. In 2:18 Daniel calls his God the "God of heaven," a title taken up again in 2:28. This asserts that God does indeed dwell in the heavens apart from men, but Daniel says here (2:19, 21-22) and in 2:28 that Israel's "God of heaven" does indeed communicate with his faithful servant, and even with the pagan world. The dream was given to the pagan king, but its significance was shared with the servants of God's chosen people. The name of God (2:20) is to be praised forever and ever because he compassionately communicated with his servants and he has delivered them from death at the hands of the king. And this great "God of heaven" (Gen 24:37; cf. Gen 24:3) whose name is to be praised forever and ever, is none other than the God of Daniel's fathers (2:23), namely the God of Abraham, Isaac, and Jacob (Exod 3:14-15). So while "God of heaven" was used for the worship of "God" in Old Testament times, and especially during the Persian period (Chronicles, Ezra, Nehemiah) the author refers by this title to Yahweh (cf. Gen. 14:22), the Lord, without writing the name (2:20). (Yahweh, the covenant name of God, does appear in Dan 9:1-19.) The "God of heaven" is used in ancient Persian documents to refer to Ahura Mazda (the uncreated creator in Zarathustra's teachings), and it is found in Jewish documents from Elephantine in Egypt (Lucas 2002:72). God reveals his mysteries to those upon earth who seek him with humility. Revelation to the nations becomes intertwined with revelation to Israel; in fact, they are one and the same in this case, echoing the goal of God to bless all nations through the descendants of Abraham (Gen 12:1-3).

While Daniel petitioned the God of heaven to disclose the mystery of the king's dream, he got an answer that went far beyond what he or Nebuchadnezzar probably expected. Daniel had a practical purpose in mind: to not perish with the wise men of Babylon. But he got a preview of certain aspects of history that would lead to the eventual establishment of the Kingdom of God. The wise men, magicians, diviners, enchanters, sorcerers, and astrologers would have used divination, dream books, magic, or witchcraft to obtain an answer for the king, but not to discover the content of the dream itself. Daniel, while functioning within the system, used the most powerful tool available to him to interpret the dream—prayer. His God answered his petition. Daniel's use of prayer is a model for any age; he prayed in all circumstances (cf. 1 Thess 5:17).

In chapter 2, Daniel's God is the God of revelation. Six times the Aramaic word meaning "to reveal" is used in this chapter (2:19, 22, 28, 29, 30, 47), though it occurs nowhere else in Daniel. In this passage, God discloses the dream of Nebuchadnezzar and its meaning, which is the secret or mystery that needs a solution (2:19, 23). The vehicle the "God of heaven" used this time was a vision (2:19, 28) communicating Nebuchadnezzar's dream and its interpretation. With this information, he thwarted the king's rash plan to destroy all the wise men of Babylon. As the book develops, Daniel's God will be one who reveals more and more of his plans for history and his ultimate goals for history to his people as needed. Daniel would undoubtedly ponder these things (cf. 7:28) and relate them to his own understanding of the Hebrews' written and oral traditions (cf. 1:4a; 9:2).

Verses 21-22 are amazing for their succinct yet comprehensive and powerful assertion of the omnipotence and omniscience of the God who answers Daniel. These verses assert his presence in heaven and upon earth. Six present active participles (with a seventh one understood as repeated in 2:21b) drive home his total control over the course of world kings and kingdoms, his impartation of wisdom and knowledge to all kinds of "wise men," his total control of the difficult, deep, and mysterious things—even those things in the darkness itself, although God himself is "surrounded by light." Yet perhaps the most comforting truth of this passage is that he compassionately shares all this with his servants at the right time, in the right place, to rescue them from certain execution. This passage, with its little paean of praise, sets the theological tone for the rest of the book. Daniel's God far surpasses all the gods of Babylon and the gods of all other nations. He is sovereign, and that sovereignty will be shown to extend over all the nations, peoples, and tongues by the end of the book.

5. Daniel informs the king of a God who can answer him (2:25-28)

25Arioch quickly took Daniel to the king and said, "I have found one of the captives from Judah who will tell the king the meaning of his dream!"

26The king said to Daniel (also known as Belteshazzar), "Is this true? Can you tell me what my dream was and what it means?"

27Daniel replied, "There are no wise men, enchanters, magicians, or fortune-tellers who can reveal the king's secret. 28But there is a God in heaven who reveals secrets, and he has shown King Nebuchadnezzar what will happen in the future. Now I will tell you your dream and the visions you saw as you lay on your bed.

NOTES

2:25 ***quickly.*** Lit., "in alarm" (using the Hithpeel infinitive *behal* [TA/ZA10097, S927], "to threaten, scare, frighten")—hence, the idea of "haste" in light of the imminent situation is involved.

I have found. This Aramaic Haphel verb is from the root *shekakh* [TA/ZA10708, S7912].

one of the captives. Lit., "one of the men from the sons of the exile." See also 5:13; 6:13; Ezra 6:16.

2:26 ***Belteshazzar.*** See note on 1:7.

Can you tell me. Lit., "Can you make known?" The words used by the king envision the ability to answer as belonging to Daniel, which Daniel denies (2:27).

2:28 ***reveals.*** See comments above on 2:19, 22. See Lawson 1997.

secrets. This is the plural of *raz* [TA/ZA10661, S7328] (cf. 2:18-19, 27); see note on 2:18.

has shown. Daniel uses the same verb the king uses in 2:26 (a Haphel perfect of *yeda'* [TA/ZA10313, S3046]) to emphasize to the king that the God who is in heaven makes things known, not Daniel himself.

in the future. Lit., "in the last days" (cf. 10:14 for the second occurrence of this phrase). Sometimes also rendered "in the coming days," the phrase refers to the days after Nebuchadnezzar with emphasis upon the days of the appearance of the fifth kingdom. Dreams could foretell the future in the ancient Near East: COS 2.155; COS 1.132:460b; Currid (1997:225) cites a passage where dreams were a vehicle of the gods in Egypt to reveal the future: A translation of the original text "Instruction for King Meri-ka-Re" is found in ANET 417 and COS 1.35.

COMMENTARY

These verses, with their typical Hebrew narrative style, are extremely engaging; there is direct speech between the persons involved in each verse. Three short dialogues are reported as follows: Arioch introduces Daniel (2:25); the king replies (2:26); then Daniel replies (2:27-28).

Arioch seems happy when he brings Daniel before the king (see note on 2:25), and he appears to take the credit for finding Daniel. Daniel was part of the captives of Judah (1:3), an important point for the reader to know, for God's covenant came to David who was of the tribe of Judah, the tribe from which the royal line was chosen. David served as the descendant of Abraham through whom God would work his blessings for all nations (Gen 12:1-3; 17:6-8). Through this tribe, God's people would continue to exist and even thrive. Now Nebuchadnezzar would receive the blessing of God's revelation from Daniel, a descendant of Abraham (Gen 12:1-3), through whom all the nations of the earth were to be blessed.

Daniel stated his purpose succinctly and clearly in a way that demonstrated that he was far from acculturated or indoctrinated by his Babylonian education and superiors. The Babylonian divination system had not been his source for solving the dilemma presented to him. He was able to focus on the real source of wisdom and the true God of heaven—the God of his fathers (2:30). He did not take great pride in himself because he was an alumnus of the most prestigious educational system of the day. In no uncertain terms, he evaluated and rejected the Babylonian system; it was incapable of meeting the king's demand—and by implication, any gods they served were incapable of communicating to them and helping them.

Daniel could say "Now I will tell you your dream" because he knew that there is a God who can and does reveal the mysteries he shares with men through dreams and visions. Daniel began with a general statement about the meaning and significance of the dream. God had shown Nebuchadnezzar, a pagan king, what would happen at the end of days, yet in the future. With this assertion, the entire book of Daniel is given a "latter days" slant. Daniel made the implications clear for his audience as well. If this is the way the God of heaven will construct the future and bring about the denouement of all earthly kingdoms, eventually establishing a kingdom that will never pass away (2:44), then the king ought to recognize and honor the true God now (cf. 2:46-49). While the king does obeisance to Daniel, he does so because he recognizes the wisdom and power of Daniel's God (2:47; cf. 4:32, 34, 37 [29, 31, 33]).

Not only did Daniel state that the general interpretive principle for understanding the dream pertains to the future (2:29, 45), but he also asserted that the God of heaven, the God of Daniel's fathers, had shown all of this to this pagan Nebuchadnezzar—to give him a chance to recognize the true God of history who rules over the world's ephemeral kingdoms, which rise and fall with astonishing speed and regularity (2:44-45). The world was already old in Nebuchadnezzar's day. And the king had probably been pondering over the shape of the future. Both he and the last king (Nabonidus) of the Chaldean dynasty were aware of the past. Both were antiquarians who had diligently pursued their interest of studying previous history; their interest in the past implies an interest in the present and the future.

Daniel next proceeds to the specifics. He recounts for the king the dream and his attendant visions. As the Aramaic says, "That was the dream" (2:36). Daniel's faithfulness to his God and his determination to excel even in a strange land now enable him to stand before the King Nebuchadnezzar and declare to him the goal of history—the Kingdom of the God of heaven, the God of Daniel's ancestors.

◆ 6. Daniel presents the dream to Nebuchadnezzar (2:29-35)

29"While Your Majesty was sleeping, you dreamed about coming events. He who reveals secrets has shown you what is going to happen. 30And it is not because I am wiser than anyone else that I know the secret of your dream, but because God wants you to understand what was in your heart.

31"In your vision, Your Majesty, you saw standing before you a huge, shining statue of a man. It was a frightening sight. 32The head of the statue was made of fine gold. Its chest and arms were silver, its belly and thighs were bronze, 33its legs were iron, and its feet were a combination of iron and baked clay. 34As you watched, a rock was cut from a mountain, but not by human hands. It struck the feet of iron and clay, smashing them to bits. 35The whole statue was crushed into small pieces of iron, clay, bronze, silver, and gold. Then the wind blew them away without a trace, like chaff on a threshing floor. But the rock that knocked the statue down became a great mountain that covered the whole earth.

NOTES

2:29 ***you dreamed about coming events.*** Lit., "your thoughts arose about what is to be after this," a reference to the present that places the dream into a future context. Cf. NIV, "O king, your mind turned to things to come."

He who reveals secrets. See comments on 2:19, 22.

has shown you. Lit., "caused you to know." This causative verb indicates that the Revealer (NLT, "He who reveals secrets") is the source of the dream.

2:30 ***that I know.*** Lit., "this secret was revealed to me." This is another repetition of the thematic word "reveal" in this chapter (cf. 2:19, 22, 28, 29, 47).

but because God wants you to understand what was in your heart. Lit., "but that the interpretation may be made known to the king, and that you may understand the thoughts of your heart." The second half of verse 30 (from the *athnach* on) is difficult to render in English. The NLT has caught the essence of the Aramaic grammar and syntax.

2:32 ***thighs.*** This is better rendered "upper thighs" (Holladay 1988:408).

2:33 ***legs.*** This is better rendered "lower legs," given the context (Holladay 1988:365, 424; BDB 1114; see Isa 47:2).

2:34 ***from a mountain.*** This is not in the text at this point, but appears at v. 45. The LXX, Theodotion, and Vulgate also contain such a phrase in this verse. The MT simply asserts that "a stone was cut out" (cf. 2:35).

2:35 ***great mountain.*** See 2:45 (notes and commentary); see also Kaiser (1995:169-171) for a brief review of some possible messianic implications of rock imagery in the OT and NT.

that covered the whole earth. This is better rendered "and filled the whole earth." In either case, the figure of speech recalls the goal of God for humanity in the Garden of Eden (Gen 1:28), his people in Egypt (Exod 1:7), and God's goal for the Kingdom of God in other prophets (Isa 2:1-4; Mic 4:1-3).

COMMENTARY

Daniel wasted no time convincing Nebuchadnezzar that he knew the dream-vision the king had seen, and immediately he set forth the overall context and thrust of the dream. It was a dream that revealed the things to come from that time forth in history. This suggests that past history, probably including the Assyrian Empire, is not in view here. Twice in 2:29 the writer uses verbs that refer to the future. The king's thoughts turned to what would come after him (2:29). The concern of the first six chapters of Daniel is not just about the situation of Daniel and his friends, but is also about the future, and Daniel had been equipped by God to present dreams and visions that dealt with the present and the future (cf. 1:17).

The mystery and secret that was puzzling Nebuchadnezzar and his friends was the dream and its interpretation. It was not a dream brought upon Nebuchadnezzar merely by his own tormented mind. The source of the dream was the Revealer (2:29), who declares what shape the future is going to take. Although the political outlook and realpolitik of the king was such that he probably had pondered what would be after him, it was the God of Daniel, the God of his fathers (2:23), the God of heaven, who shaped the thoughts of the king so that he received truth about the flow of history but could not comprehend it. The king had not been deluded like the false prophets of Jeremiah's day, whose visions and dreams were manufactured by their own minds (Jer 23:25-29; 27:9).

Daniel disavows that he himself had the wisdom to solve the king's dilemma or even that he solved it because he was wiser than any living being, thereby reinforcing for readers that he had received a divine communication about the king's dream and its interpretation. Daniel declares that he has had the solution to the mystery given to him so that the king might know what is to happen in the future (2:29, 45). As things developed, the king would also realize and acknowledge Daniel's God as the God who is over all gods because of his ability to solve this mystery. Isaiah had flaunted the Lord's ability to describe the future before the false gods of Babylon and all the Gentile nations, challenging them to do the same (Isa 41:21-24; 42:9; 43:9; 45:21; 46:9-10; 48:3). Daniel had received the answer so that Nebuchadnezzar could finally know what the thoughts of his mind were. As God had used the exodus from Egypt to inform Pharaoh about who he is, so also he used dreams, visions, and his servant Daniel to declare his name to King Nebuchadnezzar. And there would eventually be a new exodus from Babylon (Jer 29:10-14). God reveals his mysteries, not only to his elect, but through them to the nations.

The central image in Nebuchadnezzar's dream was in the form of a statue of a human being, although a strange-looking representation of a human, composed of various materials. The flow of human history, in which humanity strives to exert itself as ruler and sovereign, is very appropriately here cast in the form of a human image.

Outside of God, humans are the great determiners of history, but only within the parameters God has set for them. Their freedom within those parameters is real. The metals in the statue descend in value from the head to the feet, but at the destruction of the image the weaker, base elements are struck first, toppling the whole image, which is clearly top-heavy. The feet of the image are its weakest point, for they are made of two substances, iron and clay, which do not bond. Clay mingled with iron weakens the basic support of the entire statue. Probably we are not to imagine a new substance in which iron and clay have bonded, but to imagine two feet that are striated with clay and iron interlaced. The human image indicates that human history has a certain cultural unity that binds it together along with a human genericness; but it is in the end a unity that is weak and crumbles when under stress, even containing the seeds of its own demise. The image implies that human history is headed toward a great catastrophe as it degenerates, just as the metals—from head to toe—decreased in value. There is no hope of an upward evolution of human civilization in this picture. Thucydides asserted that "It is the nature of human things to decline" (as quoted in Bury 2006:74). Something outside of the flow of human history breaks in to bring the degenerative process to a sudden end, a fundamental feature of most apocalypses. A new material image of virgin stone, not a man-made idolatrous object, is introduced as established by God himself (2:44).

A great mystery surrounds the rock that destroys the image, reducing it to chaff and crushed particles that are then blown away by the wind (2:35, 44-45). The remains of the image are gone and replaced by the rock that fills the earth. Unlike the image, the rock that becomes a mountain is not a product of human effort and therefore not a kingdom produced by mankind. Nor is it defiled by having human hands or human tools used upon it to shape it, much as only unhewn stones alone could be used to build the altars to the Lord (e.g., Exod 20:24-26). These stones belonged to him alone, for his hand had shaped them. Even Roman pagans, as described by Tacitus, sensed the need to use specially selected stones that were pure from human defilement to construct holy temples (Lewis 2003:216). More to the point, both Micah (Mic 4) and Isaiah (Isa 2) had spoken of the end of days when the mountain of the Lord's house would be exalted above all the other mountains, and the nations would stream to it. Only an inspired interpretation could solve the dilemma of what this imagery meant. No wonder Nebuchadnezzar was puzzled, and no wonder Daniel needed a revelation to solve the mystery. But foreshadowings of the solution had been presented in the traditions of the people of Daniel, in the Torah and in the Prophets.

◆ 7. Daniel presents the revealed interpretation of the dream (2:36-45)

**36"That was the dream. Now we will tell the
king what it means. 37Your Majesty, you are
the greatest of kings. The God of heaven
has given you sovereignty, power, strength,
and honor. 38He has made you the ruler
over all the inhabited world and has put
even the wild animals and birds under your
control. You are the head of gold.**

**39"But after your kingdom comes to an
end, another kingdom, inferior to yours,
will rise to take your place. After that
kingdom has fallen, yet a third kingdom,**

represented by bronze, will rise to rule the world. 40Following that kingdom, there will be a fourth one, as strong as iron. That kingdom will smash and crush all previous empires, just as iron smashes and crushes everything it strikes. 41The feet and toes you saw were a combination of iron and baked clay, showing that this kingdom will be divided. Like iron mixed with clay, it will have some of the strength of iron. 42But while some parts of it will be as strong as iron, other parts will be as weak as clay. 43This mixture of iron and clay also shows that these kingdoms will try to strengthen themselves by forming alliances with each other through intermarriage. But they will not hold together, just as iron and clay do not mix.

44"During the reigns of those kings, the God of heaven will set up a kingdom that will never be destroyed or conquered. It will crush all these kingdoms into nothingness, and it will stand forever. 45That is the meaning of the rock cut from the mountain, though not by human hands, that crushed to pieces the statue of iron, bronze, clay, silver, and gold. The great God was showing the king what will happen in the future. The dream is true, and its meaning is certain."

NOTES

2:36 ***we will tell.*** Daniel alone gives the meaning of the dream; this manner of speech was idiomatic and formal.

2:37 ***the greatest of kings.*** This reflects the MT *melek malkayya'* [TA/ZA10421, S4430] (king of kings), a title that became even more popular in the Persian Empire, which succeeded the Babylonians. The title reflects the status of God's appointed ruler over the earth at this time.

2:38 ***all the inhabited world.*** Lit., "over all the inhabitants of the sons of men."

You are the head of gold. An emphatic position for the "you" is evident from the context. This may have multiplied the megalomania of Nebuchadnezzar (cf. 3:1; 4:30 [27]).

2:39 ***after your kingdom.*** Lit., "after you," indicating there is more to come after Nebuchadnezzar. See the commentary for a discussion of the probable historical sequence of the kingdoms. (For some recent suggestions see Caragounis 1993:387-397; Walton 1986:25-36.)

inferior to yours. The Aramaic indicates downward or "below you," hence, inferior. The silver portion of the statue was below the head of gold both in position and value.

2:41 ***baked clay.*** The Aramaic has "clay of a potter," or workable moist clay (Holladay 1988:417), probably not baked clay as in the NLT and NIV (cf. Lucas 2002:61, 64). Others, however, prefer "baked clay" (Longman 1999:72), and in fact the assertion is not entirely clear; it may refer to iron inlaid with clay (Lucas 2009:533, 572, note 42).

2:42 ***weak as clay.*** That is, breakable or brittle, when dried.

2:43 ***alliances . . . through intermarriage.*** Lit., "mixed together in the seed of mankind." The NLT's translation is possible, but the MT may simply refer to the intermingling or mixing of various peoples and ethnic groups. The inability of the Romans to organize and unify Rome has been noted by ancient and modern historians. Dio Cassius (*Roman History*, LXXII, 35-36) made the "bicultural" nature of Rome evident and spoke of the decline of the empire from a kingdom of gold to iron and then to rust (Grant 1992:570, 573). The great historian Livy often described confusing religious signs and prodigies that rivaled such observations in Babylonia. He speaks of "two snakes gliding in through the door of the temple of Jupiter . . . a two headed pig was born at Caere . . ." (*History* 28:11; cf. Grant 1970:241).

2:44 ***During the reigns of those kings.*** This must primarily refer to the kings that arise within the kingdoms of the composite metaphor of the statue's feet of clay and iron, but possibly also to the kings of the four kingdoms represented by the gold, silver, bronze, and iron mixed with clay. The march of these kingdoms is downward from the gold head of the statue to its toes, yet the whole system of the image is one.

will never be destroyed. This description puts this kingdom into a new category of kingdoms.

or conquered. This kingdom will not pass away or be left to another—unlike the Babylonian Empire, which eventually passed to the Persians without a fight when Cyrus took Babylon (539 BC; cf. Dan 5).

It will crush . . . into nothingness. Lit., "it will crush and it will bring to an end."

2:45 *rock.* See Ford (1978:86, 99) for a possible wordplay between *'eben* [TA/ZA10006, S69], (stone/rock), and *bar* [TA/ZA10120, S1247] (son) = Heb. *ben* [TH1121, ZH1201] (son) in 7:13 (see commentary below). Josephus (c. AD 12–90) believed that the rock and the events surrounding its destruction of the fourth beast, Rome, were yet future to his day (*Antiquities* 10.10.4 [10.209-210]). He did not, however, discuss the rock and its interpretation by Daniel, probably because he did not want to agitate the Roman government.

from the mountain. The Babylonian view of the earth pictured it as a mountain (Archer 1985:49); hence, the rock totally replaced the mountain, since it filled the whole earth (cf. Isa 2:2; Mic 4:1). Cf. Lucas 2009:526-527, 533-534. For this imagery of the stone in the NT, see Evans 2001:514-516.

true . . . certain. "True" translates *yatsib* [TA/ZA10327, S3330], which denotes firmness, certainty, while *meheman* [TA/ZA10041, S540] denotes reliability, trustworthiness. These are both essential aspects of truth. Oates (1986:178-179) notes that a dream needed an authoritative interpretation in order to be considered a legitimate source of information from the gods.

COMMENTARY

What is interpretation? In this case it involved taking a dream image and relating it to the realities of the present and the future—the realities of earthly history and the realities of the metahistorical world, the controlling agencies of the divine realms. And, just as importantly, it involved Daniel's giving a divine interpretation of the dream, since his interpretation was not his own but came from his God.

Daniel began by asserting a clear distinction in his presentation between the replay of the king's dream and his presentation of the true and certain interpretation of the dream (2:45). By presenting the dream, Daniel's interpretation won out over all the other possible interpretations the wise men of Babylon could have presented from their dream manuals or esoteric knowledge. Daniel's interpretation was challenged in 2 Esdras 11:1-13, where a new and different interpretation is presented, in which the imagery of Daniel's fourth kingdom is clearly tied specifically to the Roman Empire and certain emperors. The challenge of the church has been to understand the interpretation Daniel presented and relate it to (1) the New Testament's understanding of Daniel, and to (2) a theology of history, and (3) also to specific kings and kingdoms as they rise and fall (whether secular or divine), while realizing that Daniel is apocalyptic literature in which fluid and suggestive imagery abounds that can be applied as representative symbols of actual historical realities but not exhausted by any particular historical entity. Finally, the church has attempted to distill from this revelation truths to live by under any worldly kingdom.

This grandiose chapter is not limited to four historical kingdoms or entities, but rather displays a model of the kingdoms of this world that attaches to representative historical entities, a model that is universal in its meaning and scope. The book of Revelation employs this imagery to create a picture of the end that takes up all that Daniel says and interprets it in light of the Christ event as past, present, and future (e.g., Rev 13 and 20). The reality is that it is not the four kingdoms of this dream, but the fifth that is the most important in giving meaning to the historical process. Its origin and creation is an act of God (2:44), but in spite of its heavenly origin, this kingdom interacts with history and other historical kingdoms. In this light, the preceding four earthly kingdoms are presented from a partly metahistorical perspective, for it is clear that God has been in charge all the time (2:24, 37-38, 44). These nations embedded in the historical matrix are also connected to the heavenly matrix and operate within that larger matrix.

Daniel wasted little time solving the mystery of the dream. Concerning the head of gold, he boldly and clearly stated to Nebuchadnezzar, "You are the head of gold." Was this emphatic assertion by Daniel partly responsible for the king's construction of a statue of gold only (3:1)? It seems the author reports these words of Daniel's to prepare us for the folly of the king not only in chapter 3 but also in chapter 4. Nebuchadnezzar deduces that he was the builder of Babylon! And he was, on the human level, the one who built the Neo-Babylonian Empire. His reign of 43 years was half of the time the empire existed. But in the same breath, Daniel declared to the king that the God of heaven had established Nebuchadnezzar and his kingdom (2:37-38; cf. 4:26 [23]; 5:20-21). Even this most "earthly" kingdom existed because God had willed it and confirmed it. God had established it, not the king himself (cf. Rom 13:1). That Nebuchadnezzar needed this warning to help him realize that his accomplishments were not his own is confirmed by his own arrogant words in chapters 3–4 (see 4:30 [27]). Both in 4:30 [27] and here there is an echo of the "we" passages in the story of the Tower of Babel (Gen 11:2-4) in Nebuchadnezzar's "I." He embodied the Neo-Babylonian Empire at the height of his hubris. The splendors of the hanging gardens of Babylon are still celebrated by historians today and were depicted as one of the Seven Wonders of the ancient World (Strabo *Geography* 16.1.5). The city's massive walls amazed the Greek historian Herodotus (*Histories* 1.178-186). There are suggestions here of a new Tower of Babel, as well as a new Garden of Eden in the Babylonian Empire.

The head of gold did not blind Daniel to the serious shortcomings of the king, for he was more concerned with asserting the sovereignty of God than the splendor of the king's city. Beauty and splendor without moral and ethical virtue fail God's test of true beauty. Although the arrogance of the king eventually led to his judgment and contributed to the fall of "his" kingdom, it also appears that his reign was extended when he learned the lesson God had for him, as prophetically declared by Daniel (4:27, 34, 36 [24, 31, 33]; 5:21). In the present passage, Daniel simply frames his words with "after your kingdom comes to an end" (2:39) and then moves on to the next kingdom.

According to the biblical authors, Babylon was the beginning and would be the end of the corrupt, rebellious, and false kingdoms of this world (Gen 10:10; 11:1-9; Rev 18). Once the head fell, the feet could not be guided, nor could any other part of the body. And if the portion of the body made of gold fails, then how much more will the parts of lesser quality come to an end. Gold, the "metal of the gods," passes away before Nebuchadnezzar's eyes—and so his own kingdom fades away. The king silently passes off the words of Daniel, for we see his continued hubris expressed in 4:27 [24] and in chapter 3. Judgment falls upon him in his lifetime and would fall upon his kingdom later. He was not as lucky as Hezekiah (cf. 2 Kgs 20:19).

While the sovereignty of God over human history is paramount in this scenario, the message of God through Daniel is that he has placed, to a significant extent, the world of nature at the king's disposal (2:37-38). A second millennium artifact portrays a god by a humanlike statue that stands for a tree that provides food and water for the people (Lucas 2009:540). While this figurative language in Daniel represents the other nations and peoples of the world, the world of nature is also included. Jeremiah had noted that the Lord would give the beasts of the field into Nebuchadnezzar's hand (Jer 27:5-8; see further comments on ch 4). There is no sphere of existence that the sovereign God does not ultimately control through his servants, such as Nebuchadnezzar, and through his kingdoms, such as Babylon. They were and are his regents on earth—answerable to him.

Nebuchadnezzar learned that he was not in control of his rise or his demise, for God brought him up and put him down (Jer 1:10), though he gave him room to "extend" his reign, if he would obey Daniel's instructions (4:27 [24]). God gave mankind the right and ability to rule in the Garden of Eden. Had humanity learned the lesson well? Nebuchadnezzar could have learned that the God of the Jews judged the king of Assyria (Isa 10:12) and that his own crown was in jeopardy, or perhaps his dynasty, as Isaiah had spoken (Isa 44:28; 45:1, 13; cf. Dan 1:21; 6:28 [29]; 10:1). In chapter 3, his continued arrogance and megalomania led him to try to subsume all of history in the head of gold and to maintain the head of gold, thereby regulating the fall of empires—an act of hubris.

The kingdom after Nebuchadnezzar receives short billing—half of a sentence—and it is basically negative. This kingdom receives its share of attention later in the book (6; 7:6; 8; 10; 11). It will be inferior to Nebuchadnezzar's kingdom. This is recognizable in the image itself in that the silver is less valuable than gold and in that it is below the head, indicating both inferiority and the fact that it comes after the Babylonian kingdom. However, the chest and arms imagery suggests the power and strength of this kingdom. This was evident in the way Cyrus the Great of Persia steamrolled the nations of the world in his day, as the Lord gave him victory after victory. Yet all of his victories, unknown to him, were accomplished for the sake of Israel (Isa 45:4-8). Persia never achieved the intellectual and religious dominance that had characterized Babylon. Although Alexander the Great was enamored with Persian splendor, his choice of a capital for his future empire was the city of Babylon.

The third nation to arise would rule the world (2:39), as was asserted about Babylon (2:38). The rulership of this kingdom is the only aspect of its character that is stressed. Greece has often been identified as this kingdom. Given the exploits of Alexander, not merely the military successes but even more so the intellectual and political ones, this is a strong possibility. Alexander disseminated Greek culture, politics, philosophy (especially Aristotle), and religion throughout the ancient Near East, including Egypt. And not only in the ancient Near East, for while the Romans conquered the Greeks, the religion, philosophy, politics, and culture of Greece conquered and seduced the Roman mind.

The fourth kingdom, historically associated with Rome, but signifying still more, is represented by the lower legs of iron of the image and the feet made up of clay and iron and is given more attention than the previous kingdoms (2:40-43), including Nebuchadnezzar's (see ch 7 for more about this kingdom). This is for good reason, for with this fourth kingdom the end of earthly, man-made history and rulership comes to a devastating conclusion, as it encounters a kingdom whose origin is not with men, but with God himself. This fourth kingdom will not be able to unite and maximize its potential for world dominance. As diversity of languages split up the Tower of Babel, so the inability of cultures within this empire to live in peace dismantles this behemoth of destruction. Multiculturalism would become tribalism and the social and political fabric of the empire would not hold. Civil war contributed greatly to the Roman Empire's eventual dissolution (Lewis 2003:363-454; see especially his citations of Augustine and Jerome on pp. 409-414 and 424-427, respectively; cf. Cantor 2003:23-29). (On the decline and fall of the empire, see Ward-Perkins 2006.) The great historian Livy (59/64 BC–AD 12/17) observed and lamented Rome's fall:

> *Contemporary history displays our nation suicidally eating up its own mighty resources. Let it be noted how the moral rot started, how standards were gradually sapped, then crumbled more and more ominously, and finally began to collapse into utter ruin. This is the state we have now reached. Our defects are unendurable to us—and so are their cures. . . . From unlimited self-indulgence has come a longing to pursue vicious extravagance to the point of personal and universal annihilation. (Preface I, quoted in Grant 1970:232)*

The following key assertions are noted about this kingdom: (1) It is as strong as iron (the fourth kingdom of ch 7 has "huge iron teeth"). (2) Because of its ironlike nature, it will destroy the other nations that came before. It will be an exceedingly powerful and devastating military machine. (3) However, weakness is discerned in the composition of this kingdom. It is a composite kingdom whose various components will not, in the end, combine and form a unity. So, it is easily broken and crushed at its most vulnerable points—not its Achilles tendon, but a foundation of weak and unstable feet. Here again are echoes of a divided Tower of Babel. (4) The unstable aspect of the kingdom at its foundation endangers the entire image, so that it falls. All the other nations before it teeter, not only because of the military might of this last kingdom but because the supports of the world system are defective.

This fourth kingdom could not, in the end, sustain the weight of the world systems, even though it contained the strongest metal of the four and should have served as a secure foundation. Yet the clay indicates inherent weaknesses within these solid iron pylons. And even the iron seems to presage a future when iron will be used to pierce the nations (cf. Isa 2:4; Joel 3:10; Mic 4:3). This kingdom and its related world systems contained the seeds of their own demise. A blow to the feet of the image would place the entire structure in danger. The huge image collapsed, not only by the blow to its feet, but because it ultimately had no solid foundation upon which to rest. It produced division within itself; its own foundation succumbed, crumbled, and collapsed. Attempts within the world system to create unity fail; it is destined for certain annihilation. It is no accident that the image was attacked at its feet, not its head (2:34).

This fourth kingdom of iron and clay has most often been interpreted as the Roman Empire by both ancient and modern conservative exegetes and historians (Josephus; Jerome; Miller 1994; Longman 1999; Wood 1973; Young 1949; Yamauchi 1980; Wallace 1979; Baldwin 1978a). However, a sequence of four kingdoms consisting of Babylon, Media, Persia, and Greece has been argued, though less often, both in antiquity and in modern times (Hippolytus; see especially Collins 1993:166-167, excursus; Goldingay 1989:50-51). Some exegetes have argued that the metals represent four Babylonian kings that followed Nebuchadnezzar. Indeed, a staggering number of sequences of kingdoms or kings have been suggested. The first suggested sequence seems the most convincing when an early date is accepted (as in this commentary), and when the prophetic dimension of the book is recognized. But the huge statue of the dream stands not just for four kingdoms, but also for all the kingdoms of this world, all the empires that will arise, for the number 4 may represent completeness, and the related formula 3 + 1 (= 4) refers to something repeated over and over (cf. Amos 1:3, 6, 9, 11, 13, KJV). These kingdoms foreshadow what is to come in the unraveling of human destiny. (They are more fully presented in ch 7.)

During the reign of the kings and kingdoms of this statue, but especially during the last kingdom, God will establish his kingdom, as he has done in the case of all the previous kingdoms. This kingdom is different because it will not end. The fifth kingdom is the most important, and its identity is certain. The goal of history finds its fulfillment in a metahistorical kingdom, yet one that breaks into history itself. It is the Kingdom of God—the Eternal Kingdom, whose origin is from God (2:44). The monotonous rise-and-fall cycle of world kingdoms through the millennia will end; stability will be reached. All the previous kingdoms came to an end as they were conquered by other kingdoms. While this one destroys all the previous kingdoms, it is not destroyed nor does it pass away. The essential difference in the establishment of this kingdom is that it is not created "by human hands" but by God. This Kingdom of God is not something whose origin lies within the creative genius of human beings; its very essence is generated by the God of heaven. A portion of its people were present in Daniel's time (12:13), and others with Daniel will receive their lot within it.

Some Christians see here symbolism pointing toward the virgin birth of Christ, while others discern a reference to the birth of the church or the Kingdom of God in the New Testament. Still others see a reference to the creation of the Kingdom of God at the end of history, or a preliminary millennial kingdom. Rock imagery (2:45) was popular in antiquity. The ancient religion of Mithraism claimed that Mithras had been born of a rock. In ancient Babylon, a husband could pray for the god Shamash to grant his wife the "stone of childbirth," a reference to the ancient practice of using a birthing stone. The function of the stone of this chapter, as we shall see when we look at chapter 7, parallels the "Son of Man" figure in 7:13. Seow (2004:219-246) observes that there is a strong emphasis and agreement presented by the figures of the stone here and the Son of Man in 7:13, specifically in their emphasis on the heavenly origin of the present rule of kingdoms and kings and its current and future submission to the plan of God, who will eventually create and inaugurate a heavenly and eternal kingdom.

Some ancient rabbinic sources held that the Aramaic word for "stone" used here (*'eben* [TA/ZA10006, S69]; 2:34, 35, 45) is employed to recall the Hebrew word for son (*ben* [TH1121, ZH1201]), which created a wordplay that pointed forward to the Aramaic word for "son" (*bar* [TA/ZA10120, S1247]), mentioned in 7:13 (Targum Pseudo-Jonathan to Exod 39:7; cf. *Exodus Rabbah* 29; *Genesis Rabbah* 68:11; for discussion, see Ford 1978:86, 99; see also Evans 2001:507-508). Other rabbinic sources link these passages by other means and go on to establish a messianic reference for the stone and the figure coming with the clouds (Evans 2001:507). Josephus understood the stone to refer to a future act of God (*Antiquities* 10.10.4 [10.209-210]), but refused to describe it, stating that it was a future event and therefore beyond the scope of his historical work (cf. Evans 2001:504-505). Rock imagery is also employed in the New Testament: Jesus Christ became the chief cornerstone, even after being a rejected stone (Mark 12:10; cf. Ps 118:22; Luke 20:18; cf. Isa 8:14; Matt 21:42; 1 Pet 2:6-8); according to the confession of his divinity, he was the rock upon which the church would be built (Matt 16:18). In short, the stone imagery in the Old and New Testaments was used to refer to God, to the Messiah, and here to the Kingdom of God (cf. Gen 49:24; Deut 32:4; Ps 118:22-23; Isa 8:14; 28:16; 1 Pet 2:6-8). In the immediate Jewish setting of the book of Daniel, the stone must represent the Kingdom of the holy people (7:18)—that is, of Israel as it inherits the earth; but both here and in chapter 7, the Kingdom has a universal dimension surrounding it in its context—here it replaces all the kingdoms of the statue.

The rock is not a precious metal or a metal used to shape instruments of war and destruction; rather, it is a natural object of relatively little economic value to men, but here it is cut and shaped without human agency. Therefore, it is able to crush even the iron legs of the image, as well as its unstable feet. In contrast to the head of the huge statue, made of luxurious gold that glitters, this fifth kingdom has a small, but divinely orchestrated beginning. It would endure; it would not be another Tower of Babel made by human hands to magnify themselves (Gen 11:1-9). The rock's stability and endurance and its origin guarantee its endurance and dominion.

This amazing scenario pertains to the future, but clearly impacts the present, as well, because it is not merely a dream whose significance appears and vanishes with the dream itself. The reality of the dream is the shape of the future. Henceforth, even the Babylonian king should know that history is on a mission. Its teleology is reached in the Kingdom of God, a kingdom of eternal and divine qualities.

◆ 8. The king's response to Daniel's unveiling of the dream and its meaning (2:46-49)

[46]Then King Nebuchadnezzar threw himself down before Daniel and worshiped him, and he commanded his people to offer sacrifices and burn sweet incense before him. [47]The king said to Daniel, "Truly, your God is the greatest of gods, the Lord over kings, a revealer of mysteries, for you have been able to reveal this secret."

[48]Then the king appointed Daniel to a high position and gave him many valuable gifts. He made Daniel ruler over the whole province of Babylon, as well as chief over all his wise men. [49]At Daniel's request, the king appointed Shadrach, Meshach, and Abednego to be in charge of all the affairs of the province of Babylon, while Daniel remained in the king's court.

NOTES

2:46 *worshiped him.* The Aramaic *segid* [TA/ZA10504, S5457] is found nine times in Daniel. Eight times it indicates homage, honor, or worship to idols or to God. The translation here probably should be "paid him homage" rather than "worshiped" (see commentary).

sacrifices and . . . sweet incense. This renders the MT *minkhah wenikhokhin* [TA/ZA10432/10478, S4504/5208] (meal offering and pleasing incense), although *minkhah* has a broader semantic range than "meal offering" (see Ezra 7:17; cf. Gen 32:13). These items are indeed presented to Daniel.

2:47 *the Lord over kings.* In like manner, the Qumran sectarians recognized the all-powerful character of God (Schiffman 1995:44).

a revealer of mysteries. This is better rendered "the revealer of mysteries," keeping the parallelism with "the God of gods, the Lord over kings."

2:48 *appointed . . . to a high position.* The Aramaic indicates that the king exalted Daniel.

chief. This translates *signin* [TA/ZA10505, S5460], which usually is taken to mean "prefect" or "governor"; hence, "chief prefect" is a possible rendering of the Aramaic.

2:49 *affairs.* The word refers to administrative responsibilities in this case, since Daniel remained at the king's court; that is, at the king's gate (literally) or palace.

COMMENTARY

While the king paid homage to Daniel, it is certain that Nebuchadnezzar realized that Daniel's God had revealed all of this mystery to Daniel (2:47). He therefore made a distinction between Daniel and Daniel's God. He undoubtedly sensed something unusual about this man of God in whom, he thought, the "spirit of the holy gods" was present (4:8-9 [5-6]). This recognition became a tradition that was passed on into the time of Belshazzar (5:11, 14). The king realized that Daniel had been able to reveal this dream and its interpretation to him because of revelation from his God, not Babylonian gods or divination practices.

Significantly, King Nebuchadnezzar admitted that Daniel's God is Lord over all the kings of the earth. And, of course, he recalled clearly that his own Babylonian wise men, diviners, and all of his retinue of counselors could not do what Daniel had done by the help of his God. One wonders what the king might do with the flattery of being told, "You are the head of gold," albeit he was also told that his kingdom would come to an end (2:39). Chapter 3 answers this question. Daniel very likely found the actions of the king toward him despicable or, perhaps, lamentable; the author did not even need to tell us that he did so. But undoubtedly Daniel took great delight in hearing the king recognize the God of his ancestors as the one who reveals mysteries.

Just as Joseph's successful interpretation of dreams raised him up and caused Pharaoh to pronounce that he was filled with the spirit of the gods and give him great authority (Gen 41:38-40), so Nebuchadnezzar promoted Daniel. The designation as the wisest of the wise was quite an honor in a land known for its wise men (cf. 1 Kgs 4:30). There is a note of hope in the news that Daniel became ruler over the entire province of Babylon, the kingdom that had destroyed Judah and Jerusalem, a much greater honor than Jehoiachin received (2 Kgs 25:27). In a preliminary way, one of God's servants was placed over the kingdoms of this world (cf. 7:14). He was now in a position to make his God known to everyone at Nebuchadnezzar's court.

He was prepared to advise the king on anything. His requests were recognized, for the Lord was with him, much as the Lord's hand was with Ezra and Nehemiah. They requested things from a great pagan king and they were granted, for the hand of the Lord was upon them (Ezra 7:6; Neh 2:4-8). While Daniel influenced the court of Nebuchadnezzar, his three friends faithfully discharged the business of the king in the provinces, placed there at Daniel's request, where he could now help supervise them. Jeremiah would have been delighted and surprised to know that his prophetic words would eventually give hope to this exilic man of God (9:1-2) in a way far beyond what Jeremiah might have imagined.

◆ B. Three Hebrew Men Divinely Delivered from a Furious King (3:1-30)

1. The challenge of pagan worship in the Babylonian culture (3:1-7)

King Nebuchadnezzar made a gold statue ninety feet tall and nine feet wide* and set it up on the plain of Dura in the province of Babylon. 2Then he sent messages to the high officers, officials, governors, advisers, treasurers, judges, magistrates, and all the provincial officials to come to the dedication of the statue he had set up. 3So all these officials* came and stood before the statue King Nebuchadnezzar had set up.

4Then a herald shouted out, "People of all races and nations and languages, listen to the king's command! 5When you hear the sound of the horn, flute, zither, lyre, harp, pipes, and other musical instruments,* bow to the ground to worship King Nebuchadnezzar's gold statue. 6Anyone who refuses to obey will immediately be thrown into a blazing furnace."

7So at the sound of the musical instruments,* all the people, whatever their race or nation or language, bowed to the ground and worshiped the gold statue that King Nebuchadnezzar had set up.

3:1 Aramaic *60 cubits* [27 meters] *tall and 6 cubits* [2.7 meters] *wide.* **3:3** Aramaic *the high officers, officials, governors, advisers, treasurers, judges, magistrates, and all the provincial officials.* **3:5** The identification of some of these musical instruments is uncertain. **3:7** Aramaic *the horn, flute, zither, lyre, harp, and other musical instruments.*

NOTES

3:1 ***King Nebuchadnezzar.*** No date is given in the MT, but the LXX says this court conflict occurred in the eighteenth year of the king. This suggested date remains uncertain. In any case, the best future for Nebuchadnezzar, who was declared to be the "head of gold," was a continuation of the present—the status quo; cf. 4:4 [1]. In this chapter, he appears to be centralizing all of his empire around himself and his god.

ninety feet tall. This translation converts the 60 cubits of the Aramaic into feet (see NLT mg); the cubit referred to here probably was equal to 18 inches.

nine feet wide. The NLT converts the width, "six cubits," into feet.

set it up. The text again stresses in 3:3 that the king set up the image.

plain. This Aramaic word is intended to send the reader's thoughts back to the Tower of Babel (Gen 11:2), where the people settled in a plain.

Dura. This is generally taken to mean a geographical location, but Edward Cook (1989:115-116) has argued with some cogency that *dura'* [TA/ZA10164, S1757] probably refers to the defensive wall called Nimit-Enlil; this was the famous outer wall of Babylon described by Herodotus (*Histories* 1.178-181).

3:2 ***high officers, officials, governors, advisers, treasurers, judges, magistrates.*** The first two categories in this list of groups of governmental officials are preceded by a *le* [TA/ZA10378, S3807.2], here used to mark the direct object. The conjunction Waw stands before "governors," possibly indicating that the first two groups are of higher rank. The first three terms are supposedly well-known, but translations continue to vary for them. Lucas renders them as: satraps, prefects, governors (2009:536; cf. NIV, RSV, NJPS). The last four terms are Persian and uncertain in exact meaning. "Magistrates" probably refers to police or military magistrates (Holladay 1988:425; cf. 6:1-8 [2-9]).

3:3 ***officials.*** The list is repeated for effect in the Aramaic (see NLT mg), serving to impress the reader with the ridiculous importance being attached to this confusing event.

3:4 ***listen to the king's command.*** Lit., "they order you," from a Semitic idiom.

3:5 ***musical instruments.*** The instruments that make up Nebuchadnezzar's orchestra have been discussed much. "Horn" (*qeren* [TA/ZA10641, S7162]; cf. coronet, trumpet) is the same word that refers to an animal's horn (7:7, 11, etc.). "Flute" (*mashroqi* [TA/ZA10446, S4953]) could possibly also be rendered "pipe." "Zither" (*qitharos* [TA/ZA10630, S7030]) is a Greek loanword and may also be rendered as "kithara" (lyre). For "lyre" (*sabbeka'* [TA/ZA10676, S5443]), Holladay (1988:421) suggests a triangular lyre employing four strings and producing a bright, sharp tone. "Harp" (*pesanterin* [TA/ZA10590, S6460]) indicates some kind of triangular stringed instrument. The word is Greek in origin and is known in Greek after the sixth century BC, but this does not rule out its presence in Babylon earlier through contacts with merchants (Mitchell and Joyce 1965:25). "Pipes" (*sumponeyah* [TA/ZA10507, S5481]) is a difficult term. It may be a musical instrument named from the Greek word *sumphonia* [TG4858, ZG5246], or it may represent the Greek word *tumpanon* ("drum, tambourine," cf. Gen 31:27, LXX). In the first case, the evidence may favor a late date for Daniel. In the second case, it would not. In neither case is the evidence certain (Mitchell and Joyce 1965:25-27). Hence, the final word could be rendered "drum." However, Holladay (1988:414) offers "bagpipe," or taking a different perspective, it may be rendered as "in harmony," serving as a word of direction for the previous instruments. Lucas (2009:537-538) includes a listing of how six different translations render the names of these instruments.

3:7 The last word from the list of musical instruments in 3:5, *sumponeyah* [TA/ZA10507, S5481], is missing here. See also 3:10 and 3:15, where it is included. The repetition of this list four times for emphasis produces a powerful psychological effect upon the reader, driving home the self-importance and vanity of this orchestra and its useless worship celebrating the dedication of the image. The 3 + 1 pattern of comparison in Amos comes to mind: "for three sins, even for four" (Amos 1:3, 6, 9, NLT mg). This music is "too much!" The NLT omits some of the repeated lists, noting them in the margin (see 3:7, 15, NLT mg).

COMMENTARY

This chapter is tied to the preceding chapter by the presence of a gold statue, which featured a head of gold that was symbolic of King Nebuchadnezzar (2:38). By his actions it seems clear that the king wants to be more than the head of the statue; he wants to be the entire statue. He will enthrone the status quo with him as the head; he gilded the image to tie it to the head of gold. Verse 12 stresses the intimate connection between the statue, Nebuchadnezzar, and his gods; the three entities mesh here ("you" is employed four times to refer to the king, making him the focus of the discussion). He did not want to affirm a scenario of future events that excluded him, such as Daniel's interpretation of his dream asserted. He disfigured the body of the dream statue—no chest, arms, abdomen, legs, feet, or toes are present. He was satisfied to see the gold head extend itself to the base of his image. The words of the text are powerful for what is left out. They create a certain aura about the statue—Was it a god or was it Nebuchadnezzar or both? It leaves us guessing. The power of the symbolic language makes this ambience possible. The proportions of the image are odd (if not grotesque), and the lack of specificity achieves its effect well. Was it sitting on a pedestal? If so, it was even more grossly disfigured. Was it a stela? This is unlikely, as stelae were not normally referred to as "statues." There is difficulty completing the picture of the image. It is difficult to say whether worshiping the image implied worshiping Nebuchadnezzar (cf. Lucas 2009:536). Some things are clear, others are not. Finally, it should be noted that the image stands out as a colossus in chapters 2–6, and this focus suggests a relationship to the "abomination of desolation" that will be featured in chapters 8–9 and 11–12. (On the particular relationship of ch 7 to these sections, see Beasley-Murray 1983:53-55.)

This chapter also concerns the three Hebrew exiles, Shadrach, Meshach, and Abednego, who were appointed over the affairs of the province of Babylon and were mentioned in the two preceding chapters. These Jewish men become the central concern of the chapter, ultimately representing all Jews. More properly, their trust in their God (3:28) and God's amazing deliverance of them are central foci of the chapter. These three exiles from Judah defy the king's person and neurotic decree commanding them to worship his golden image.

Indications of the hubris revealed in chapter 4 (cf. 4:30 [27]) show up in Nebuchadnezzar's character in this chapter (3:1, 13-15, 19, 22) as he sets up an image (idol), shows his rage toward God's servants, and wields the power of death. He is the king; he ordered the creation of the image, and everyone will bow down to it and worship—or die (3:6, 11, 15). The king's unholy and white-hot anger against Shadrach, Meshach, and Abednego foreshadowed the anger of future persecutors of God's people, whether earthly persons or demonic agents of evil (6:5 [6]; 7:8, 11, 24-26; 8:9-11, 23-25; 9:26-27; 11:21-45). The deliverance of God's people in this chapter depicts what God can do for those who trust him (3:28), yet even death cannot ultimately deter God's deliverance of his people (12:1-3).

These seven opening verses leave no doubt about who "set up" the image. Six times the Aramaic text asserts that Nebuchadnezzar "set up" the image (3:2-3, 5, 7), and the first verse reports that he made it. So a perfect seven times in seven verses, Nebuchadnezzar's ownership of this image is noted. To drive the point home further, the king's name, Nebuchadnezzar, is used seven times by the author. Such repetition is a common literary device in ancient Semitic literature.

Reminiscent of the Tower of Babel story, this story relates an attempt to once again unite the whole world, as they would focus and worship—with one language and with one common ritual (cf. Gen 11:1)—the great gods of Babylon on the plain (the Hebrew word for "plain" in Gen 11:2 is identical to the Aramaic word for "plain" in Dan 3:1). This all foreshadows the much later attempt of Antiochus IV to force everyone in his kingdom to become "one people . . . each should give up his customs" (1 Macc 1:41-42). Then, as here, the Gentile nations accepted this move;

the wise among the Jews did not (1 Macc 1:43; cf. Dan 8:9; 11:21, 29-35, especially v. 30, 32; 12:3).

There were images of many gods in Babylonian polytheism. A "sun disk" dating to 839 BC describes the making of an image of the sun-god Shamash (COS 2.135:366b). The king was directed by a diviner to make a new image of Shamash based on an old one that had been found. Proper materials, choice of craftsmen, and purification rites were all prescribed. The king ordered that the mouth of the statue be washed, and then he had it placed in its holy place. The process of "washing its mouth" purified the new divine image, thus "turning it into a living god" (COS 2.135, note 37; cf. COS 2.141B). The image in Daniel 3 is not a mere piece of gilded wood or stone. In the worldview of the Babylonians it partook of divinity—and the king knew that. To dishonor it was to dishonor the king; to dishonor the king was to dishonor the god and his "living image."

All of the musical instruments available were used by the king to create a cosmopolitan milieu of excitement, unity, and common worship before this image. The event was important, and everyone should be present to enjoy the festivities. There was no separation of state, religion, and fine arts here. The list of instruments is given twice in these verses; the officials are listed twice as well. All of the heads of state, representing all the races, nations, and languages, also mentioned twice in these verses (3:4, 7), are there for Nebuchadnezzar's dedication of his image that he set up, evidently trying to replicate the entire human image depicted in chapter 2.

The heterogeneous mass of religious peoples were called upon to respond to the "enlightened" tyrant's instructions to fall down and worship when they hear the cacophonous sounds of the king's orchestra. But not all will be enthralled by the music; some are totally out of sync with the music and the occasion. Three present active participles in the original text indicate the continuous and ongoing nature of this confused and noisy bunch of worshipers (3:7; lit., "hearing . . . falling . . . worshiping"). There is a surrounding ambience of confusion created by the language and setting. There was confusion accompanied by "all the peoples of the earth," reminiscent of that at Babel (Gen 11:7, 9). Indeed, here as at Babel (Akkadian, *Bab-ili*, "gate of the gods"), disobedience and false worship give way to confusion. But in Daniel, an immediate contrast is presented: The gods of Babylon are to be rejected as the God of the three Jewish men is to be lifted up. There is a bit of pathetic humor in seeing the leaders of the world's kingdoms bowing before a gaunt, grotesque (cf. Longman 1999:98; Young 1949:84), slender image (90 feet high, 9 feet wide) that must have appeared like an obelisk rather than a reasonably proportioned, well-formed image.

◆ 2. The Jews Shadrach, Meshach, and Abednego defy the king (3:8-18)

8But some of the astrologers* went to the king and informed on the Jews. 9They said to King Nebuchadnezzar, "Long live the king! 10You issued a decree requiring all the people to bow down and worship the gold statue when they hear the sound of the horn, flute, zither, lyre, harp, pipes, and other musical instruments. 11That decree also states that those who refuse to obey must be thrown into a blazing furnace. 12But there are some Jews—Shadrach, Meshach, and Abednego—whom you have

put in charge of the province of Babylon. They pay no attention to you, Your Majesty. They refuse to serve your gods and do not worship the gold statue you have set up."

13 Then Nebuchadnezzar flew into a rage and ordered that Shadrach, Meshach, and Abednego be brought before him. When they were brought in, 14 Nebuchadnezzar said to them, "Is it true, Shadrach, Meshach, and Abednego, that you refuse to serve my gods or to worship the gold statue I have set up? 15 I will give you one more chance to bow down and worship the statue I have made when you hear the sound of the musical instruments.* But if you refuse, you will be thrown immediately into the blazing furnace. And then what god will be able to rescue you from my power?"

16 Shadrach, Meshach, and Abednego replied, "O Nebuchadnezzar, we do not need to defend ourselves before you. 17 If we are thrown into the blazing furnace, the God whom we serve is able to save us. He will rescue us from your power, Your Majesty. 18 But even if he doesn't, we want to make it clear to you, Your Majesty, that we will never serve your gods or worship the gold statue you have set up."

3:8 Aramaic *Chaldeans.* **3:15** Aramaic *the horn, flute, zither, lyre, harp, pipes, and other musical instruments.*

NOTES

3:8 *But.* The Aramaic text at the beginning of this verse says literally, "Because of this [situation], at that time," (cf. KJV), which shows the opportunistic character of these professional astrologers. This is essentially left untranslated in the NLT, which instead uses "but" to connect this to the preceding context.

astrologers. The word probably refers to the king's professional class of astrologers—i.e., "Chaldeans" (NLT mg; see notes on 1:4; 2:5; and Introduction).

informed on the Jews. This expresses a Semitic idiom, *wa'akalu qartsehon* [TA/ZA10030/10642, S399/7170], literally saying "and they devoured the pieces" of the Jews. It means they slandered them, accused them, denounced them.

3:9 *Long live the king!* This renders the common Semitic idiom of addressing royalty: "O king, forever may you live." It was used in 2:4 and is found over 20 times in chs 2–6.

3:10 *musical instruments.* See note on 3:5.

3:12 *in charge of.* The king appointed Shadrach, Meshach, and Abednego over the *'abidath* [TA/ZA10525, S5673] (cf. "the affairs," KJV) of the province of Babylon. The Aramaic word probably refers to the "administration" (cf. NASB) or "oversight" of this area. On the names of these men, see note on 1:7.

pay no attention. The accusers employ a wordplay using the verb *sim* and the word *te'em*. The king had "issued" (*sim* [TA/ZA10682, S7761]) "a decree" (*te'em* [TA/ZA10302, S2942]; cf. 3:10), but here they were "placing" (*sim*) no "respect" (*te'em*) on the decree of the king or the king himself.

your gods. This is probably correct; the Kethiv of MT is plural (KJV, RSV), but the Qere is the singular, "your god" (TEV, NAB, NJPS). The polytheistic setting of the story indicates that Nebuchadnezzar had no problem recognizing other gods.

3:13 *flew into a rage.* Cf. 2:12, where two stative verbs describe the king's response. Here two nouns are used preceded by *be* [TA/ZA10089], turning them practically into adverbs describing the king's action as "with rage and fury" or "in/with furious rage." They describe a unified vicious reaction. The king's character of 2:12 still overcomes him (Holladay 1988:400, 405, 420).

3:14 ***Is it true?*** This represents a word found only here in the OT. The expression is made up of the interrogative *ha* [TA/ZA10190, S871.2] and the noun *tseda'* [TA/ZA10609, S6656]. The root idea of the latter Aramaic word seems to be "firm, solid." However, some translators believe the phrase means "Is it deliberate, on purpose?" "Is forethought involved?" This idea compares favorably with the Heb. *tsadah* [TH6658, ZH7399] ("malicious intent"; NIDOTTE 3.742-743). However, "Is it true?" encompasses the idea of forethought.

3:15 ***musical instruments.*** For the list of musical instruments and descriptions, see note on 3:5.

3:16 ***need.*** This renders a participle of the verb *khashakh* [TA/ZA10287, S2818] (to need, to be obligated). The three men were not obligated to defend themselves to the king.

before you. The Aramaic text has "about this matter" *'al-denah pithgam* [TA/ZA10601, S6600] (matter, decree, issue, challenge); it refers to the king's decree, the accusations brought against them and their own response to the decree. But the implication of "before you" implies that they will deal with "the matter."

3:17-18 ***the God whom we serve is able to save us. He will rescue . . . But even if he doesn't.*** The rendering of these verses in the NLT (and NIV, NJPS) is often given, but can be challenged on the basis of context and grammar. The TEV, NAB, NRSV, and NJB render 3:17 to reflect the idea that "If God whom we serve, is able to deliver us, he will do so," and 3:18 as something like "But if he does not/will not" (Baldwin 1978a:104). This leaves open God's sovereign choice to deliver them or not. But in no case will they commit idolatry. As a third alternative, 3:17 could be rendered "If there is a God able to save us, such as our God . . ." (Hartman and Di Lella 1978:155-157). The second alternative seems preferable (cf. Lucas 2002:84-85).

from your power. This is literally "from your hand," which recalls the exodus from under Pharaoh's hand (Exod 6:8; 18:9). Ultimately, it is the king who is the enemy, not the fiery furnace, a mere instrument of the king!

your gods. See 3:12, 14 also for the plural "gods" versus "god."

you have set up. The verb here is causative; it emphasizes the king's responsibility for the golden image. The Haphel (causative) verb form of *qum* [TA/ZA10624, S6966] is used three times in these verses to emphasize the king's part in this whole affair (3:12, 14, 18).

COMMENTARY

That the presence of exiled Jews ruling over the province of Babylon did not sit well with the king's Chaldean astrologers is indicated in 3:8-12. Therefore, they seized an opportunity to remove them by discretely using the king's decree as a fulcrum. These accusers foreshadow the even more deliberate attitudes and acts of the Persian informers of chapter 6 (6:13 [14]). The fact that Daniel and the three Hebrew exiles had positions of power carried a strong message—namely, that a Jew could eventually be placed at the head of all the nations (cf. 5:7). Joseph had made it to second in authority in Egypt (Gen 41:33, 40).

The astrologers' proper court greeting, "Long live the king!" rings with irony as it addresses someone who has just threatened to cut short the lives of those who do not bow to his commands (3:6). The astrologers made Shadrach's, Meshach's, and Abednego's refusal to worship a personal affront to the king by accusing them before him: "They pay no attention to you, Your Majesty." The three Jews would have been committing idolatry if they had bowed down to the golden statue (see 3:12). The king would have to deal with these Jewish dissenters because of the position he had craftily been put in by these informers, a situation that Darius the Mede also found himself in later (6:16 [17]). Daniel would face a similar penalty when he was thrown into a den of lions (6:12 [13]).

Nebuchadnezzar's attempt to persuade these three exiles from Judah to bow down and worship his image was powerful but ineffective (3:13-15). As the previous chapter has shown, the king would not take "no" for an answer (2:5, 9, 12). The king's offer of "one more chance" is noteworthy, because he had earlier refused to give his own wise men any second chance (2:8), but had granted the Jew, Daniel, a short period of time to seek an answer (2:16). Nebuchadnezzar opened the door to a possible solution to all this when he asked Shadrach, Meshach, and Abednego a rhetorical question: "What god will be able to rescue you from my power?" His "power" translates the Aramaic word for "hand"; Daniel's God had already delivered the entire nation of Israel from the "hand" (power) of Pharaoh (Exod 6:8; 18:9)—Daniel knew this well, as did these three Judean youths.

The theme of deliverance in various circumstances is paramount in the book of Daniel (1:14-15), and this story continues to develop this theme. In both this chapter and chapter 6, the same words signifying "rescue," "deliver," and "save" are used. Both stories are referred to as models of deliverance in the New Testament (Heb 11:33-34). The three youths answered the king's rhetorical question as if it had been a real question. They used the same word twice for "rescue" that he had used when asking his questions—and they asserted that their God would, if he so chose, rescue them from the king's hand. And even if God wouldn't rescue them, they would not worship the image. Deuteronomy, the capstone book of God's law, was well known by Daniel and his friends, and their God had instructed his people to worship only him (Deut 6:13). These three Jews, as God's people, refused to be assimilated into the king's universal, syncretistic worship program. He would soon angrily pass the sentence of death upon them.

◆ 3. God's deliverance from fury and fiery furnace (3:19-27)

19 Nebuchadnezzar was so furious with Shadrach, Meshach, and Abednego that his face became distorted with rage. He commanded that the furnace be heated seven times hotter than usual. 20 Then he ordered some of the strongest men of his army to bind Shadrach, Meshach, and Abednego and throw them into the blazing furnace. 21 So they tied them up and threw them into the furnace, fully dressed in their pants, turbans, robes, and other garments. 22 And because the king, in his anger, had demanded such a hot fire in the furnace, the flames killed the soldiers as they threw the three men in. 23 So Shadrach, Meshach, and Abednego, securely tied, fell into the roaring flames.

24 But suddenly, Nebuchadnezzar jumped up in amazement and exclaimed to his advisers, "Didn't we tie up three men and throw them into the furnace?"

"Yes, Your Majesty, we certainly did," they replied.

25 "Look!" Nebuchadnezzar shouted. "I see four men, unbound, walking around in the fire unharmed! And the fourth looks like a god*!"

26 Then Nebuchadnezzar came as close

as he could to the door of the flaming furnace and shouted: "Shadrach, Meshach, and Abednego, servants of the Most High God, come out! Come here!"

So Shadrach, Meshach, and Abednego stepped out of the fire.
27 Then the high officers, officials, governors, and advisers crowded around them and saw that the fire had not touched them. Not a hair on their heads was singed, and their clothing was not scorched. They didn't even smell of smoke!

3:25 Aramaic *like a son of the gods.*

NOTES

3:19 ***face became distorted.*** This renders the Aramaic "(so that) the expression (*tselem* [TA/ZA10614, S6755]) of his face changed," as he filled with fury. There is a wordplay here, for he had set up an image (*tselem;* cf. 3:1-18), and now his facial "image" (*tselem*) changed. The "image" was an "expression" of himself!

3:21 ***fully dressed.*** This catches the essence of what the writer wants to emphasize. In 3:27 only the first article of clothing is listed. The interested reader will be impressed with the extent of which they were clothed. The items are rendered variously as follows: (1) *sarbal* [TA/ZA10517, S5622]: trousers, cloak, coat, shirt, robe, mantle; (2) *petash* [TA/ZA10582, S6361]: tunics, robes, trousers, shirts, hats; (3) *karbela'* [TA/ZA10368, S3737]: hats, turbans, shoes, headgear. See Collins (1993:188) for discussion and further sources. Montgomery (1927:211) notes that for each of these terms, every kind of clothing for head, body, and legs has been put forth.

3:24 ***advisers.*** The Aramaic word *haddabar* [TA/ZA10196, S1907] indicates some high royal class of officials (Holladay 1988:403).

3:25 ***unbound.*** This renders a Peal passive participle from *sherah* [TA/ZA10742, S8271] (to loosen). They were thrown into the fire completely bound, but they are now seen as having been loosed, unbound. They did not loose themselves, as indicated by the passive participle.

walking around. God himself had walked around (Gen 3:8-9) in the Garden of Eden with his people. The same root is used there in the Hebrew (*halak* [TH1980, ZH2143]) as is used here in the Aramaic (*halak* [TA/ZA10207, S1981]).

looks like a god. As the NLT mg observes, the Aramaic is "like a son of the gods" (*dameh lebar-'elahin* [TA/ZA10120/10033, S1247/426]). See 6:22 [23], where Daniel understands his deliverer was an angel (*mal'ak* [TA/ZA10417, S4398]). The TEV renders "looks like an angel." This is probably not a preincarnate appearance of the Son of God. In 3:28 it is indicated that Nebuchadnezzar himself understood the divine being to be an angel.

3:26 ***door.*** Lit., "opening" or "mouth" (of the furnace).

Most High God. This divine title was used by Jews in the book of Psalms; elsewhere it is found only on the lips of non-Jews (cf. Gen 14:18; Num 24:16; Deut 32:8-9; Ps 73:11; Isa 14:14). The word is found in contexts claiming universal attributes for *'el 'elyon* [TH430/5945B, ZH466/6610] (NIDOTTE 1.400-401). The Aramaic is *'elah 'illay* [TA/ZA10033/10546, S426/5943] (see 4:2, 25 [3:32; 4:22]).

3:27 ***had not touched them.*** The fire "had no power over their bodies." The verb *shelet* [TA/ZA10715, S7981] means "to have power over (something)." The experience in the furnace itself provides a contrast with other parallels. Croesus, king of Lydia, was rescued by his god, Apollo, from being burned alive by Cyrus, an event reported in both historical sources and mythical poetic creations (Herodotus *Histories* 1.82-87; Bacchylides *Odes*

3.23-62 [468 BC]), but in the biblical story the three faithful worshipers of their God are preserved within the flames of the fiery conflagration.

not scorched. This renders "not changed" or "not affected" at all.

smell of smoke. Lit., "smell of fire." No odor was attached to them, their hair, or their clothing.

COMMENTARY

This section begins with an ingenious wordplay (see note on 3:19). The image the king made and set up is referred to by the same Aramaic word that is used for the distorted facial features of the king when the three Hebrew exiles refused to bend to his command. He was so "furious" that, literally, his "image changed." The writer thus mocked the king's response and tied his visage to the face of the image (cf. 2:12). A subtle hint, perhaps, that the image did in fact reflect the king and vice versa (see commentary on 3:1-7).

The details related in 3:19-23 are there to show the enormity of the deliverance God provided for these three faithful servants. The "sevenfold" heating of the furnace is hyperbole to express the extraordinary heat directed at the destruction of these men. Surrounded and bound even by their own cumbersome clothing, there was no chance that they would escape their fate. The heat was so high even at the periphery of the fire that it was enough to kill the strongest of the king's soldiers. Fully clothed and securely bound, they fell into the midst of these flames with no chance of survival. Sealed in a fiery tomb, it would take divine intervention to save them. God had broken into the realm of the natural before to reveal a dream and its interpretation to Daniel. Could he or would he do more? Would he make his presence known by "coming down" to rescue his people?

Nebuchadnezzar witnessed the amazing deliverance of his adversaries (3:24-25). His wise men had asserted that the gods "do not live here among people" (2:11), but he now saw what he could only describe as someone who looked "like a son of the gods" (3:25, NLT mg) rescuing Shadrach, Meshach, and Abednego from their bonds, protecting them from the consuming heat, and walking about in the flame with them. No other king, according to the Bible, had such a direct encounter with the God of Israel and his delivering angel (cf. 3:28; 6:22 [23]). Unlike the distant gods of the Babylonians, this God involved himself with his people. This God had walked about in the Garden of Eden with Adam and Eve (Gen 3:8); he did not cease to walk (see notes on 3:25) with his people in the time of their greatest need, because they trusted in him (3:17, 28). He could deliver from fire as well as flood (Gen 9:18-19). Neither the hair on their heads nor their clothing was singed! All of those gathered to celebrate the dedication of the king's image witnessed a greater event—God's supernatural intervention. All of the "high officers, officials, governors, and advisers" examined the physical evidence of the deliverance surrounding these three persons who had walked out of the furnace, who would not bow down and worship the image. One can only imagine how they felt after having prostrated themselves in abject obedience to the king and before his lifeless idol, so dead compared to the living God of the Jews!

These three faithful Jews were delivered—a theme throughout the book. Daniel and his friends were "delivered" from eating the king's rich food (ch 1); the wise men of Babylon including Daniel and his friends were delivered from execution (ch 2). This will continue for Daniel and his people (chs 6, 7, 8, 9, 11–12) until they are finally granted deliverance even from the grave (12:1-4, 13; cf. Hos 13:14; 1 Cor 15:55). In the meantime, however, some will pay the ultimate price for their faithfulness. After Daniel's time, we read of seven Jewish brothers and their mother who suffered martyrdom (2 Macc 7:1-42), but who all expected to be raised up again. Although this may be a legend (Collins 1981:310-314), it was undoubtedly inspired by the deliverance of Shadrach, Meshach, and Abednego, as well as the hope of a resurrection from the dead put forth in Daniel 12:1-4. Later still, we read of a Christian saint who served Daniel's God by following his Son: In a vision, Polycarp, bishop of Smyrna, saw that he would be burned alive as a martyr for his faith in Christ. After his vision he declared, "I must be burned alive" (*Martyrdom of Polycarp* 12). At the age of 86 in the arena he was asked to revile Christ. His reply was "How can I blaspheme my King who saved me?" (*Martyrdom of Polycarp* 10.3). He gained the crown of immortality (cf. Dan. 12:13; *Martyrdom of Polycarp* 19.2).

◆ 4. Nebuchadnezzar acknowledges the God of Shadrach, Meshach, and Abednego (3:28-30)

28Then Nebuchadnezzar said, "Praise to the God of Shadrach, Meshach, and Abednego! He sent his angel to rescue his servants who trusted in him. They defied the king's command and were willing to die rather than serve or worship any god except their own God. 29Therefore, I make this decree: If any people, whatever their race or nation or language, speak a word against the God of Shadrach, Meshach, and Abednego, they will be torn limb from limb, and their houses will be turned into heaps of rubble. There is no other god who can rescue like this!"

30Then the king promoted Shadrach, Meshach, and Abednego to even higher positions in the province of Babylon.

NOTES

3:28 ***angel.*** This renders the Aramaic *mal'ak* [TA/ZA10417, S4398] and may indicate an angel or messenger. In this case, this divine being functioned as a "deliverer." Since this being was like a "son of the gods" (3:25), he is clearly more than a mere human being. He came from the heavenly realms, not from among mere men. In contrast, the "son of man" in 7:13 is "like a man," but he comes with the divine chariotry of a god—a cloud.

3:29 ***I make this decree.*** The "this" is drawn from *uminni* [TA/ZA10427, S4481] in Aramaic, "and so from me." The phrase *uminni* is placed first in the sentence for emphasis—what follows is from the king himself. The Aramaic verb *sim* [TA/ZA10682, S7761] (make, issue) indicates a formal public decree. The verb form can be parsed either as a Peal passive participle, "a decree is being issued" or a Peil perfect third-person masc. sg., "he issued a decree." The form could also be Peil imperfect (cf. Lucas 2002:82).

a word against. This renders *shalu* [TA/ZA10712, S7960], meaning "something negligent, insulting, or remiss" (also used in 6:4 [5]; NLT, "anything to criticize").

3:30 ***promoted.*** This is a translation of *tselakh* [TA/ZA10613, S6744], a verb meaning to "prosper." Its Hebrew cognate, *tsalakh* [TH6743A, ZH7503], is used to describe God's prospering of Joseph in Egypt (Gen 39:2).

COMMENTARY

It is no surprise that Nebuchadnezzar was moved to save face and issued a decree in praise of this God—rather than foolishly denying the evidence. But his inward attitude and beliefs about how great he was did not change—at least not for long (4:28-30 [25-27])—they only found another outlet. The major themes of this event are succinctly recapitulated by the king: (1) God's marvelous rescue and deliverance (3:28-29); (2) the trust of his servants (3:28); and (3) the Jews' refusal to worship any god but their God (3:28). Two further points stand out: Irony abounds in the book of Daniel. Nebuchadnezzar arrogantly commanded all people of whatever "race or nation or language" (3:29) not to speak against, mock, or blaspheme the God of these three Jewish exiles in any way—upon pain of death. The entire purpose of the king against Shadrach, Meshach, and Abednego had ended up topsy-turvy. The nations were made to recognize the true God's deliverance as it was publicized among the officials and rulers under the auspices of the royal government of Babylon.

As to the image? Nothing more is said. There is no decree praising his image or celebrating the success of the universal worship. The Jews were not obliged to worship it. We are not further informed about the other races, peoples, languages, and nations. Nebuchadnezzar let the subject drop from his decrees. The authority and force of the image was certainly greatly curtailed, to say the least. The promotion of Shadrach, Meshach, and Abednego was a clear slap in the face for those who would have demoted them (3:12). These persons could no longer dare speak in a derogatory manner against these Jews, nor their worship of their God—the God who had delivered, not only Noah from a flood, Israel from Egypt and the Assyrians, but even these three men from the furious Babylonian king's decree. Eventually, their God would deliver them from the fiery ordeals of the Exile itself. Jewish exiles now occupied some high, influential positions in the upper echelons of the governmental structures of their captors—the mighty Babylonians. The Jews' God was the God who rescues like no other god (3:29)! No greater message could have been trumpeted to the nations or to Israel in exile in Babylon, or to the individual servant of the true God who might have to give his life because of commitment to the God of Israel. Later, Daniel testifies to a remedy for even those who die trusting their God (12:1-4, 13).

In addition, Nebuchadnezzar openly declared respect and recognition for the God of Israel. Amazingly, he even praised the three Jewish exiles for trusting their God and defying his command. This praise and their subsequent promotion certainly sent a powerful message to exiled Jews, and potentially for others as well.

But where is Daniel in this narrative? It seems he was not at the dedication of this idol, perhaps having been excused by the king. Daniel knew how to handle himself at the royal court (2:16) and, undoubtedly, given his religious commitments, was excused from more than eating the king's food or wine (1:11-17), especially after his strong witness to his God before the king in chapter 2. There, the king certainly treated Daniel with amazing respect and deference, declaring his God to be God of gods (2:47). Chapters 1–2 indicate Daniel's unique place and influence at this pagan court, and chapters 4–6 bear this out. Had Daniel been at the dedication of the image, he would not have bowed and worshiped. We can be sure of that. Daniel, though, was often somewhat elusive: He never flaunted his abilities; he didn't barge arrogantly into the scene in chapter 2, but had to be sought out and brought in by Arioch (2:14, 16, 25).

He comes in "at last" (4:8 [5]) before the king in the next chapter. In chapter 5, he was extremely hard to find (5:10-13), and in chapter 6 those who wanted to destroy him had to carefully lie in wait to catch him at home before they could accuse him.

◆ C. The Exile and Restoration of a Proud Pagan (4:1-37)

1. Nebuchadnezzar's praise of the Most High God, and a terrifying dream (4:1-8)

***King Nebuchadnezzar sent this message to the people of every race and nation and language throughout the world:**

"Peace and prosperity to you!
2"I want you all to know about the
miraculous signs and wonders the Most High God has performed for me.

3 How great are his signs,
how powerful his wonders!
His kingdom will last forever,
his rule through all generations.

4*"I, Nebuchadnezzar, was living in my palace in comfort and prosperity.
5But one night I had a dream that frightened me; I saw visions that
terrified me as I lay in my bed. 6So I
issued an order calling in all the wise men of Babylon, so they could tell me
what my dream meant. 7When all the
magicians, enchanters, astrologers,* and fortune-tellers came in, I told them the dream, but they could not
tell me what it meant. 8At last Daniel
came in before me, and I told him the dream. (He was named Belteshazzar after my god, and the spirit of the holy gods is in him.)

4:1 Verses 4:1-3 are numbered 3:31-33 in Aramaic text. 4:4 Verses 4:4-37 are numbered 4:1-34 in Aramaic text. 4:7 Or *Chaldeans.*

NOTES

4:2 [3:32] ***signs and wonders.*** This is reminiscent of the signs and wonders the Lord promised to work before the nations for the sake of Israel and his glory (Exod 3:12; 13:9; 34:10). The Aramaic words are *'ath* [TA/ZA10084, S852] and *temah* [TA/ZA10763, S8540]. The equivalent Hebrew words are found in Exod 7:3; Deut 4:34; 6:22; Isa 8:18 [TH226/4159, ZH253/4603].

performed. Lit., "he was pleased to work."

4:3 [3:33] ***last forever.*** His kingdom is *'alam* [TA/ZA10550, S5957] (everlasting), a term that recalls 2:44 and the fifth kingdom mentioned there.

4:4 [1] ***my palace.*** This properly renders the parallel terms in Aramaic, "my house . . . my palace," but loses some of the emphasis of the parallel in the original text.

comfort and prosperity. The Aramaic word *ra'anan* [TA/ZA10670, S7487] means "luxuriant" or "prosperous." Its Hebrew cognate verb *ra'an* [TH7488, ZH8315] in Job 15:32 means "be luxuriant" (NLT, "be green"), and speaks of a tree "full of leaves" in 1 Kgs 14:23. Thus, there is a wordplay and a foreshadowing here of the luxuriant tree that appears in the king's dream and, in fact, represents him.

4:5 [2] ***dream.*** As the first word in this sentence, the word is emphatic. This dream suddenly interrupted the peace and prosperity of the king's life.

4:6 [3] ***issued an order.*** The phrase is the same as noted in 3:29 (cf. 2:2). Here a public summons was sent out.

4:7 [4] ***magicians, enchanters, astrologers.*** Other translations are "exorcists, liver consultants, astrologers." There is, as noted earlier, some overlap in the meanings of these words (see note on 2:2).

4:8 [5] *after my god.* This shows that even after the first dream, Nebuchadnezzar was still a polytheist, who respected Daniel's God but preferred his own god. On Belteshazzar, see note on 1:7; see also 2:26; the name is used six times in this chapter.

the spirit of the holy gods. This represents the Aramaic well: *ruakh-'elahin qaddishin* [TA/ZA10658/10620/10033, S7308/6922/426]. The holy gods lived in heaven. Now, after the dream of ch 2 and its interpretation, the king notes that their spirit is upon earth in a Jew of the Exile to whom the holy gods had revealed mysteries! Pharaoh asserted the same thing about Joseph because of his wisdom (Gen 41:37-38), as it is stated in the Hebrew phrase "spirit of the gods" (*ruakh 'elohim* [TH7307/430, ZH8120/466]). Pharaoh, also a polytheist, would have intended "gods," not "God" (cf. NLT).

COMMENTARY

This chapter continues the theme of the arrogance and hubris of a king who thought he had built the great city of Babylon and that he could disregard the warning of the Most High God through Daniel with impunity (4:24-27 [21-24]). His attempt to foster a universal worship of his image failed, so now he looked to advance his own glory through the splendor of Babylon, which he considered himself to have built. Hardly a better example of the proverb "pride goes before a fall" can be found in the Bible. The maxim to do justice, love mercy, and walk humbly with your God (Mic 6:8) went unheeded (4:27 [24]); thus, God's decree of judgment fell upon Nebuchadnezzar (4:17, 25-26 [14, 22-23]).

This chapter is a well-crafted piece, featuring literary symmetry. Poetic portions mark an *inclusio* around the chapter that also serves as a prologue and epilogue (4:1-3, 34-37 [3:31-33; 4:31-34]). Between these paeans of praise to God concerning his sovereignty and his eternity, a dream is presented (4:4-18 [1-15]), subsequently interpreted and applied (4:19-27 [16-24]), and then fulfilled (4:28-33 [25-30]). Both the presentation and interpretation of the dream feature an introduction, body, and conclusion (4:4-8, 9-17, 18, 19, 20-26, 27 [1-5, 6-14, 15, 16, 17-23, 24]; see table below). Nebuchadnezzar himself reiterates one of the main thrusts of the chapter: God "is able to humble those who are proud," thus stressing God's sovereignty over the kings and kingdoms of this world and the fleeting rulership granted to the unstable kings and kingdoms of this world.

PARALLEL STRUCTURE OF THE PRESENTATION OF THE DREAM AND ITS INTERPRETATION

Dream (4:4-18 [1-15])	Interpretation (4:19-27 [16-24])
Introduction (4:4-8 [1-5])	Introduction (4:19a [16a])
"spirit of the holy gods is in you" (4:9 [6])	Daniel's Warning (4:19b [16b])
Dream reported (4:10-17 [7-14])	Dream Interpreted (4:20-26 [17-23])
"spirit of the holy gods is in you" (4:18 [15])	Daniel's Warning (4:27 [24])

The prologue (4:1-3 [3:31-33]) and the background for the story are presented in 4:1-8 [3:31–4:5]. In 4:1a [3:31a], the author announces a statement that the king sent to everyone after the experience recounted in the chapter and presents a portion of it in 4:1b-3 [3:31b-33]. The opening is indicative of both Aramaic letters of the Persian era and of Neo-Babylonian letters. Ezra 7:12 is a biblical parallel (Lucas 2009:538, 572, notes 63-64; Longman 1999:118). The king's wish for prosperity to all the peoples and nations reflects his attitude in 4:34-37 [31-34], immediately after his humbling experience at the hand of the Most High God (4:2, 24, 32, 34 [3:32; 4:21, 29, 31]). The "original sources" for this chapter appear to a large extent to stand before us. The king himself (or his court reporter) relays much of it in the first person (4:1b-18, 34-37 [3:31b–4:15; 4:31-34]). Verses 1a [3:31a] and 19-33 [4:16-30] are from a third-person perspective of the final author who arranged the chapter in its current form.

Israel's God had performed wonders for his own people Israel (e.g., Exod 3:20; 4:21; 6:6; 7:3; 12:12; 34:10), but in these verses, the greatest Chaldean king correctly claims that the Most High God was pleased to work signs and wonders in and through him, signs and wonders that included a terrifying act of judgment upon him. (This was in agreement with Daniel's interpretation of the king's dream.) The king was glorying in the new status quo brought about by the acts of the Most High God. The Lord would remind him that time waits for no man; history will move toward the establishment of God's Kingdom (4:34b-35 [31b-32]).

The recognition of the unique, everlasting nature of the Most High's Kingdom reflects the king's enlightened understanding after he was judged (4:34 [31]), along with the revelation he had gained through Daniel in 2:44. This time, God emphasized that he rules and delegates rulership and authority.

Even though Nebuchadnezzar was as luxuriant as a green tree (that is, prospering in comfort; cf. 4:4 [1]), Daniel pointed out that there was injustice and unrighteousness in his kingdom—the poor were being neglected and oppressed (4:27 [24]). Even King Hammurabi's (1792–1750 BC) law code from the Old Babylonian Empire (1894–1595 BC) asserted in its prologue and epilogue that the king was to care for the poor, the widow, the orphan, and the weak. How much more was this humane responsibility a concern for the prophet Daniel, who knew that his God cared for the poor, the widow, the orphan—all disadvantaged or needy people (Exod 21:26-27; 22:22-24; Lev 19:9-10; Ps 10:14, 17-18; Jer 7:6—whose book Daniel studied diligently, cf. 9:2).

The inability of Babylonian wisdom to interpret the king's dream is again stressed (2:10-11, 27-28). At last, Daniel showed up. From his comments to Daniel, it seems the king had progressed in his theology and view of reality. If the gods did not dwell on earth (2:11), as his astrologers claimed, then at least their spirit was in Daniel (4:8 [5]), the Jew, for he had recounted and interpreted the king's previous dream. Pharaoh had declared the same thing about Joseph more than a millennium earlier, because he had revealed the meaning of Pharaoh's dreams. He was the wisest man in the land (Gen 41:37-39). Daniel's presence was the next best thing to having the gods present in person. Even the queen mother later asserted this (5:11) after Nebuchadnezzar had died. Daniel had shown his God's revelatory power to this pagan king. The gods could, in the king's thinking, have enabled Daniel to interpret the dream through the "spirit" of wisdom and insight that was in him. This assertion by the king forms an *inclusio* around the king's sharing of his dream with Daniel (4:8, 9, 18 [5, 6, 15]). So, three times for emphasis, the king asserted his trust in Daniel by saying "the spirit of the holy gods is in you." Daniel knew it was the Spirit of his holy God that gave him his ability—not only to reveal dreams, but to live righteously before him in a pagan country. Only the "Book of Truth" of the Most High God (a metaphor for God's omniscience; see 10:21 and comments) contained the answers to the king's dilemma, not the dream manuals of the magicians, enchanters, and astrologers. Only by God's granting of revelation to Daniel would these mysteries be unveiled.

◆ 2. Daniel interprets the dream (4:9-27)

9"I said to him, 'Belteshazzar, chief
of the magicians, I know that the spirit
of the holy gods is in you and that no
mystery is too great for you to solve.
Now tell me what my dream means.
10"'While I was lying in my bed, this
is what I dreamed. I saw a large tree
in the middle of the earth. 11The tree
grew very tall and strong, reaching
high into the heavens for all the world
to see. 12It had fresh green leaves, and
it was loaded with fruit for all to eat.
Wild animals lived in its shade, and
birds nested in its branches. All the
world was fed from this tree.
13"'Then as I lay there dreaming, I saw
a messenger,* a holy one, coming down
from heaven. 14The messenger shouted,

"Cut down the tree and lop off
its branches!
Shake off its leaves and scatter
its fruit!
Chase the wild animals from
its shade
and the birds from its branches.
15 But leave the stump and the roots
in the ground,
bound with a band of iron and
bronze
and surrounded by tender grass.
Now let him be drenched with the
dew of heaven,
and let him live with the wild
animals among the plants of
the field.
16 For seven periods of time,
let him have the mind of
a wild animal
instead of the mind of a human.
17 For this has been decreed by the
messengers*;
it is commanded by the holy ones,
so that everyone may know
that the Most High rules over
the kingdoms of the world.
He gives them to anyone he
chooses—
even to the lowliest of people."

18"'Belteshazzar, that was the dream
that I, King Nebuchadnezzar, had. Now
tell me what it means, for none of the
wise men of my kingdom can do so.
But you can tell me because the spirit
of the holy gods is in you.'

19"Upon hearing this, Daniel (also
known as Belteshazzar) was overcome
for a time, frightened by the meaning
of the dream. Then the king said to
him, 'Belteshazzar, don't be alarmed
by the dream and what it means.'
"Belteshazzar replied, 'I wish the
events foreshadowed in this dream
would happen to your enemies, my
lord, and not to you! 20The tree you
saw was growing very tall and strong,
reaching high into the heavens for
all the world to see. 21It had fresh
green leaves and was loaded with
fruit for all to eat. Wild animals lived
in its shade, and birds nested in its
branches. 22That tree, Your Majesty,
is you. For you have grown strong and
great; your greatness reaches up to
heaven, and your rule to the ends of
the earth.

23"Then you saw a messenger, a holy
one, coming down from heaven and
saying, "Cut down the tree and destroy
it. But leave the stump and the roots
in the ground, bound with a band of
iron and bronze and surrounded by
tender grass. Let him be drenched with
the dew of heaven. Let him live with
the animals of the field for seven
periods of time."
24"This is what the dream means,
Your Majesty, and what the Most
High has declared will happen to my
lord the king. 25You will be driven
from human society, and you will live
in the fields with the wild animals.
You will eat grass like a cow, and you
will be drenched with the dew of
heaven. Seven periods of time will
pass while you live this way, until
you learn that the Most High rules
over the kingdoms of the world and
gives them to anyone he chooses.
26But the stump and roots of the tree
were left in the ground. This means
that you will receive your kingdom
back again when you have learned
that heaven rules.
27"King Nebuchadnezzar, please
accept my advice. Stop sinning and
do what is right. Break from your
wicked past and be merciful to the
poor. Perhaps then you will continue
to prosper.'

4:13 Aramaic *a watcher;* also in 4:23. 4:17 Aramaic *the watchers.*

NOTES

4:9 [6] ***Belteshazzar.*** By using this name in addressing Daniel (Belteshazzar means "Bel protects the king"—Bel is Marduk, the chief Babylonian god), the king was trying to indicate that Daniel's ability to interpret dreams came from the gods (cf. note and comments on 1:7).

I know that the spirit of the holy gods is in you. This is quite an admission coming from a pagan king.

mystery. This translates *raz* [TA/ZA10661, S7328]; see note on 2:18 concerning this Persian loanword.

4:10 [7] ***what I dreamed.*** Lit., "visions of my head, which I was envisioning" (see 2:28; 4:5 [2]).

large tree. The Aramaic "large" *saggi'* [TA/ZA10678, S7690] indicates that the tree was large when he first saw it, not just after its growth in the next verse. See Coxon (1986:91-111) for a discussion of this tree symbolism.

4:11 [8] ***reaching high into the heavens.*** This is an allusion to the Tower of Babel, with its tower reaching into the sky (Gen 11:1-9).

4:12 [9] In Aramaic this verse reflects careful parallelism (A, B, C, A', B', C'): (A) Its foliage was beautiful; (B) its fruit was plenteous; (C) food for everything was in it; (A') under it the beasts of the field were sheltered; (B') in its branches feasted the birds of the sky; (C') from it all living flesh was fed.

4:13 [10] ***dreaming.*** This is better rendered "having a vision."

a messenger, a holy one. Lit., "a messenger and a holy one." This is a clear example of Waw explicative; that is, a Waw used to clarify or make something clear, rather than as the coordinating conjunction "and" (cf. 6:28 [29]; cf. Lucas 2002:145; Baker 1980:129-136 for additional examples). As the NLT mg indicates, "messenger" is often rendered as "watcher," from Aramaic *'ir* [TA/ZA10541, S5894] (watcher). These angels are especially vigilant in their assigned tasks: in this case, to watch after and protect humans (Lucas 2002:110). For a good discussion, see Collins 1993:224-226. The earliest extrabiblical references to such beings are in *1 Enoch* 1–36, a section called "The Book of the Watchers." They are also mentioned in the DSS and in other writings of the intertestamental era (see the references in Collins 1993:224-226).

4:14 [11] ***Chase the wild animals.*** This is better rendered as "Let the wild animals flee."

4:16 [13] ***seven periods of time.*** This is probably to be understood as years (also in 4:23, 25, 32 [20, 22, 29]; 7:25; 12:7; cf. Holladay 1988:415-416). However, the term *'iddan* [TA/ZA10530, S5732] may refer to a set period of time or to seven indeterminate "times" or "seasons" (cf. 2:8, a delay of time; 2:9, change in situation; 2:21, epochs in history; 3:5, 15, a set time; 7:12, a period of time. See note on 2:21).

mind of a wild animal. Lit., "let his heart be changed and the heart of a beast given to him." The terminology is not repeated in 4:25, 32 [22, 29], but is in 5:21. Josephus records the fulfillment of this event in *Antiquities* 10.10.6 [10.217]; and he cites Berossus, a Babylonian priest, saying that Nebuchadnezzar fell ill near the end of his reign (*Against Apion* 1.20 [1.146]). Many scholars suggest that it was in fact Nabonidus who went insane (see note on 5:21), but Josephus, like Daniel (4:17-21 [14-18]), clearly applies the tradition to Nebuchadnezzar, not Nabonidus. Eusebius of Caesarea, quoting Abeydenus, who depends on Megasthenes (second century BC, 300 BC, respectively), recorded a tradition of Nebuchadnezzar's strange behavior as though he were possessed by some god (*Preparation for the Gospel* 9.41). See also NBD 820-821; ISBE 3.508, where William S. LaSor holds open the possibility that rather than history, we are dealing with "apocalyptic prophecy"; that is, the imagery is not to be taken literally in this case. In my opinion, the two are not mutually exclusive (see Baldwin 1978a:108-109; Harrison 1969:1114-1115).

4:17 [14] ***decreed by.*** This is better translated as "transmitted" or "delivered," since God is the one who has issued the decree.

the Most High. Or, "the Powerful One on High."

lowliest. This is from *shepal* [TA/ZA10738, S8215]; cf. Heb., *shepelah* [TH8219, ZH9169] (lowlands). Perhaps Nebuchadnezzar's Chaldean background is part of the thought of this assertion, but within the chapter it is connected to the lowly condition in which he found himself. The theme of God exalting the lowly is common in the OT (1 Sam 2:7-8; Ps 113:7), especially in the Lord's exaltation of a shepherd boy to be king in Israel (1 Sam 16). It may also foreshadow the pedigree of Nabonidus, the last king of Babylon, who did not come from Nebuchadnezzar's family.

4:18 [15] ***because the spirit of the holy gods is in you.*** This clearly indicates that Nebuchadnezzar had learned only that the "gods" can solve certain mysteries, as opposed to believing his wise men's assertion that the gods "do not live here among people" (2:11). He had also witnessed a being protecting three exiled Jews in the furnace of fire who "look[ed] like a god" (3:25).

4:19 [16] ***your enemies.*** Lit., "those who hate you . . . those who oppose you." The NLT joins these together as "your enemies."

4:22 [19] ***That tree . . . is you.*** This recalls the same type of assertion in 2:38, "You are the head of gold." Once again, Daniel did not equivocate.

4:23 [20] ***Let him be drenched.*** "Him" is justified more clearly now as the subject of this jussive verb, since "the tree" is a symbol for "the king."

Let him live with the animals of the field. Lit., "and let his lot be with the beasts of the field."

4:25 [22] ***until you learn.*** This introduces the "recognition formula," which explains why God dealt with the king as he did. The goal was to spread the knowledge of God through the king to all the earth. This formula is also found in Exodus and Ezekiel (e.g., Exod 8:22 [18]; 9:14-16; 14:18; Ezek 6:10; 7:4; etc.).

4:26 [23] ***when you have learned.*** God's goal was not punishment but enlightenment, which would come when moral and ethical recognition was realized by the king (cf. 4:32 [29]).

heaven rules. This is the only place in the OT where "heaven" is used as a substitute for "God" (cf. 1 Macc 3:19; Luke 15:18, 21). It carries the strong connotation that God rules from heaven (see Introduction, "Theological Concerns"). God rules and he rules in and from the heavenly realms; God controls even rebellious powers in heaven and on earth, though he gives them some free reign within parameters set by him. But, in those spheres where God is recognized and worshiped and freely submitted to, there is "the Kingdom of Heaven."

4:27 [24] ***please accept my advice.*** Daniel offers a heartfelt, humble plea to the king to change his ways.

be merciful. Hammurabi, who possibly reigned 1792–1750 BC as a king in the Old Babylonian Empire, said he was charged by Marduk to care for the welfare of the people, especially the weak. He was to shepherd them and protect the orphan, the widow, and the oppressed (see especially Carpenter 2009:502-503 and notes; ANET 164, 178).

Perhaps. This introduces a conditional situation in the Aramaic text (cf. Ezra 5:17). Daniel was not promising that the Lord would lengthen the king's ease and prosperity, but he might if the king practiced the justice and mercy that the Lord expected even of the pagans (Carpenter 2009:502-503). The king's response was not favorable (4:30 [27]).

COMMENTARY

The king's confidence in Daniel and his ability to solve the mystery of his dream is impressive. Besides the fact that Nebuchadnezzar believed that the "spirit of the holy gods" was in Daniel, he had also been impressed by Daniel's God in chapter 2 (2:28, 47), as well as by Daniel himself (2:46). The fact that the king addressed Daniel last after bringing in his wise men (4:6, 8 [3, 5]), suggests that he continued to use his own Babylonian entourage as much as possible before calling upon Daniel, a Jewish exile, to help him.

Even in the king's pagan theology, the "spirit" of the holy gods was recognized as able to work through humans. In Israel, the concept of the Spirit of God inspiring the prophets was fully developed. The prophets were privy to the council and words of the Lord (1 Kgs 22:19-23; Jer 23:18, 22). In the New Testament, Peter declares that the Spirit of God was the Spirit of prophecy who moved persons to speak God's word of judgment or blessing (2 Pet 1:20-21).

Both of Nebuchadnezzar's dreams took place while he was in bed sleeping (cf. 2:1, 29). Only God knows when to reveal himself, whether in the quietness of the night (7:1), the din of a royal drinking party (5:1, 5), during a time of study and fasting (9:1-3), beside a great river or canal (10:4), or in a blazing furnace (3:25). But Daniel also found him available in his regular daily religious practices (6:10 [11]) and in special times of need (2:16-19).

The tree that the king saw in his dream was a fitting symbol for himself and his kingdom, both of whom God had blessed in order to give order and sustenance to the social structure and peoples of the earth in that day. From the second millennium BC, we have an impressive portrayal of a god as a cosmic tree that provides sustenance to all living things (Lucas 2009:540). That "all the world was fed from this tree" (4:12 [9]) makes the symbolism quite clear, as does the historical and political reality of the situation. In the Garden of Eden, it was trees that fed the first couple (Gen 2:15-17). Much like the whole world was fed through Pharaoh's Egypt in Joseph's day, and just as God had brought that about (Gen 50:19-21), so now God was caring for the whole world through the fecundity of the Babylonian Empire. Although trees were a symbol of fertility and a common subject of dreams, worship, and religious symbolism (Isa 6:13; Ezek 6:13; 17:24; 31:8), and wisdom speculation (Ps 1:3; Prov 3:18; 13:12; 15:4), this giant tree and its meaning must be understood primarily from its surrounding biblical context. The tree of Ezekiel 17:22 and God's actions toward it foreshadow God's posture toward the tree in Nebuchadnezzar's dream. Nebuchadnezzar had already adumbrated (4:4 [1]) what the subject of his dream might be, with his use of the word meaning "luxurious" or "prosperous" ("comfort and prosperity" in the NLT).

The tree's size, "reaching high into the heavens" (4:11 [8]), and its location are singled out for special attention, along with its fruitfulness (4:12 [9]). Babylon's strategic location on the eastern side of the Euphrates River placed it at the hub of human civilization during Nebuchadnezzar's reign. The tree's height, reaching to the heavens, recalls the tower of Babel in Genesis 11:4, with the tower reaching to heaven, and no doubt it also connects that tower to the temple-tower complex in Babylon in Daniel's day. The main building there bore the name "the foundation of heaven and earth" (Lucas 2009:526-527). But more than just a building, what is in view is the delegated kingship of Nebuchadnezzar that had become so extensive and extraordinary. God is interested and concerned about this great kingdom. This time he will not come down (Gen 11:5), but will send his holy watcher (angel) down to carry out his command (4:13 [10]). Unfortunately, he sees pride and confusion in Babylon repeated (4:14 [11]; Gen 11:5-7), for it had begun to seek its own autonomy again, forgetting the one who gave it sovereignty (2:28-30).

Likening himself to a god in his hubris, Nebuchadnezzar asserted that he had built this city for his own honor and splendor (4:30 [27]). The connection of these words with the tower of Babel in Genesis 11 is palpable. The people built a city to magnify their name (Gen 11:4). Here the king locates the power of rulership granted by heaven in himself, disavowing that "heaven rules" (see note on 4:26 [23]). His building activity is still evident today both in the city of Babylon and many surrounding cities and other areas (cf. Kuhrt 1995:590-597; Lucas 2009:527; Wiseman 1985:64-73). He built and restored many temples (COS 2.122) and ancient temple-tower complexes (COS 2.122B). He was pleased with the external structures he had built, but while they pleased him, they did not please God (4:27, 30-31 [24, 27-28]; cf. Gen 11:5-9).

The cutting down of the tree is spoken of in 4:13-14 [10-11], but the fact that its roots and stump are left implies that it may hopefully become healthy again and will not die. While the horticultural purpose of the band of iron and bronze (4:15 [12]) is not technically clear, with respect to the symbolism of the dream, it most probably represents God's sovereign arrangements to hold together the Babylonian government while the king passed through his time of judgment. This judgment is described as an event that will teach the king patience and humility. It allows for his renewal and for God's glorification (4:26, 34, 36 [23, 31, 33]). The fettering of the stump of the tree may also involve a subtle reference to the illness that seized the king for this period of time. God evidently provided a supportive group of persons to help keep the rulership of Nebuchadnezzar intact ("surrounded by tender grass") until he could return. In contrast, after Nebuchadnezzar's death, the empire went into a time of struggles for the throne under his successors (561–555 BC), who faced many difficulties (Kuhrt 1995:597). Finally, Nabonidus (555–539), who had no immediate family ties to the royal family in Babylon, took the throne. But under him (and his son, Belshazzar), serious political, religious, and military threats arose. The head of gold was gone, and history moved toward a new world order rather quickly after Nebuchadnezzar's 43-year reign.

The stump is more than the core rulership of the Babylonian Empire. It also represents the king himself. The original Aramaic text is shocking in its expression, for he is to take his place among the beasts, eating the grass of the field. As the grass is drenched with dew in the early morning, so he will be also. Strikingly, his own identity will be changed from being human to that of a beast. According to Genesis, humans were made in God's "image" with a heart to follow his righteous and divine ways (Gen 1:26-28). Seven "periods of time," a somewhat indeterminate amount of time, indicate that a period of time will be given for this judgment so that God's purposes can be accomplished—just as he finished his work of creation in seven days and sent Israel into exile for 70 years (7 x 10). Daniel suggested a remedy for the king that might save him from this terrifying pronouncement (4:27), though this apparently went unheeded.

The messengers who delivered the decree to the king are angels (see note on 4:13 [10]) who are vigilant to watch over God's people and do his bidding toward them. The word is often translated "watchers," signifying a group of divine beings who diligently keep watch to see that God's plans are properly and duly carried out. The term is used of the angel Raphael and the archangels discussed in *1 Enoch* 1–36 (the section traditionally entitled "The Book of the Watchers"; see further Lucas 2009:539, 573, note 71; Collins 1993:36-46).

In case there were any questions concerning what the dream was about, Daniel spelled it all out (4:19-27 [16-24]). The purpose was twofold: (1) Since the entire world could see this tree (4:11, 22 [8, 19]), it would be a clear demonstration to the nations that God alone is the truly sovereign Most High God. (2) They would see that he gives delegated authority to whomever he chooses—even to a Chaldean like Nebuchadnezzar (Kuhrt 1995:399-400), who has been humbled and made to recognize his helplessness before the Most High and that heaven rules (4:27, 34 [24, 31]).

Daniel's interpretation of the dream is reported in 4:19-27 [16-24]. The first thing Daniel realized was that the dream was aimed at the king. With tact, he informed the king of this (cf. 2:14). It is clear that the king showed great respect toward Daniel, even urging him to give the interpretation no matter what it was. So Daniel did not shrink from telling the king the truth. By contrast, Alexander the Great had augurs and soothsayers who sometimes interpreted his dreams merely to please him (Plutarch 1986:242, 250-251, 257, 295). And false prophets in Israel had prophesied smooth words instead of any true word from the Lord (Jer 28:10-11).

The tree, the king is informed, is "you" (4:22 [19]). This was both flattering and frightening at the same time. Historically, Nebuchadnezzar was the king who made the Chaldean dynasty (625–539 BC) of the Neo-Babylonian Empire famous throughout the known world. His reign lasted from 604 to 562 BC, some 43 years.

The ancient remains of Babylon even today, as well as in the time of the Greek historian Herodotus (485–425 BC), are largely the work of this unusual king. He was a statesman, a general, a politician, a religious leader, a builder, and a strategist of unusual ability. His popularity with later Babylonian generations was well deserved. He is mentioned in nine Old Testament books, over 85 times in total. Even Israel was destined by her own God to bow before him, the Lord's servant (Jer 25:9; 27:6). But for all of this, Nebuchadnezzar also fell down before Daniel, the Judean exile from Jerusalem, to honor him (2:46). His life was clearly circumscribed by the sovereign Most High God who both honored him and humbled him. It was foretold by Jeremiah that the Lord would "put everything, even the wild animals, under his control" (Jer 27:6). The splendor and genius of Babylon was tied to this man by the Most High himself. As he was the head of gold (2:38), so he was the great tree.

The decree of the Most High through his holy messenger was fixed. Nebuchadnezzar was to be judged, and the things spoken concerning him (4:13-16 [10-13]) would take place. The stump and the roots, safely bound by the band of iron and bronze and carefully fed, represented his successful restoration—after he had learned the purpose of all of this (4:17, 26 [14, 23]). Heaven rules—that is, God rules—not the Babylonian king or any other human monarch. Any human king is merely his delegated servant. This is the only place in the Old Testament where "heaven" is a circumlocution for God himself, for the king was to understand that "heaven" rules (cf. Luke 3:22; 20:4-5; John 17:1).

Verse 27 [24] is surprising but refreshing. Daniel, in his respect and concern for the king, and above all in his respect for the moral and ethical laws of his God, gave a strong but tactfully phrased admonition to the king. Although the dream would come true, God might honor the king with a longer reign if he were to abolish his sins and show mercy to the poor and oppressed (Carpenter 2009:479).

This social charge to this mighty monarch recalls the thundering prophet Amos, who called for social righteousness for the poor, the widow, the orphan, and the oppressed (Amos 4:1; 5:11-12; Carpenter 2009:479, 503). Daniel's tact in presenting his admonition reflects the wisdom of a wise man (Prov 15:1). And his mention that the king's reign might be prolonged applies the principle that God gave his people: Follow my righteous laws, and you will live long in the land I am giving you (Deut 32:47). This was a principle that was not just for Israel but for all humanity and especially all human rulers to follow (Carpenter 2009:503, 539, note 828; Exod 22:21-22; Deut 24:17). At the ancient city of Ur, kings Ur-Nammu and Shulgi had been charged to care for the widow, orphan, and poor (COS 2.153). The great Hammurabi had been told to protect the weak and the widow (COS 2.131, lines 32, 59-60). The king's peace and prosperity could have continued, but instead, within a year, a decree from heaven overtook him.

There are some hints in this chapter that all was not well with Nebuchadnezzar; these can reasonably be connected to his illness, which is often referred to as zooanthropy. A fragmentary text exists that might refer to a time during his reign when he was suffering from a mental disorder; though the conclusion is not assured, some scholars would apply it to Nebuchadnezzar (Wiseman 1985:102-103; Lucas 2009:530-561). First of all, his emotional and mental stability is open to question:

He was terrified by the dream, which was really a nightmare (4:5 [2]), he pled abjectly that Daniel help him (4:9, 18-19 [6, 15-16]), and the decree itself indicates that the king was suffering delusions of grandeur, so much so that he thought he himself was in total control of all the kingdoms of the world (4:17 [14]). Daniel's kindness to the king is addressed as if to a person in serious trouble (4:19 [16]), and his warning and admonition to the king is instructive (4:27 [24]). He had, by this time, completed his great building campaigns, including, we assume, the famous hanging gardens of Babylon. But he had done all these things while oppressing the poor (cf. Amos 3:15; 4:1). The king was loaded down with sins, was not practicing righteousness, and had not been merciful to the poor. A king with this resume would be a candidate for instability, to say the least. His seeming comfort and prosperity was shown to be false.

There remains almost no historical information about Nebuchadnezzar's last 30 years (c. 592–562 BC). Josephus (*Antiquities* 10.10.6 [10.217]) and Eusebius of Caesarea (AD 265–339) both record information about him that seems to refer to a serious possibility of insanity that may have overtaken the king for an unknown period of time (cf. Collins 1993:218-219 for Eusebius). There is also a text that records an illness that befell Nabonidus, the last king of Babylon, and his prayer for healing. He was healed from his illness by the help of a Jewish diviner (COS 1.89; Longman 1999:117; Lucas 2002:41). All these traditions are later than Daniel, and it is difficult to discern how much they reflect the illness of Nebuchadnezzar in this chapter. Longman rightly observes that it is not cogent to apply the Nabonidus text to Nebuchadnezzar on the basis of its content, and that, assuming a sixth-century date of the book of Daniel, the other texts were written with the events of the book of Daniel to inform them.

◆ 3. The king is humbled and restored to his kingdom (4:28-37)

**28"But all these things did happen
to King Nebuchadnezzar. 29Twelve
months later he was taking a walk
on the flat roof of the royal palace in
Babylon. 30As he looked out across
the city, he said, 'Look at this great
city of Babylon! By my own mighty
power, I have built this beautiful city
as my royal residence to display my
majestic splendor.'**

**31"While these words were still in
his mouth, a voice called down from
heaven, 'O King Nebuchadnezzar, this
message is for you! You are no longer
ruler of this kingdom. 32You will be
driven from human society. You will
live in the fields with the wild
animals, and you will eat grass like a
cow. Seven periods of time will pass
while you live this way, until you
learn that the Most High rules over
the kingdoms of the world and gives
them to anyone he chooses.'**

**33"That same hour the judgment
was fulfilled, and Nebuchadnezzar
was driven from human society.
He ate grass like a cow, and he was
drenched with the dew of heaven.
He lived this way until his hair was
as long as eagles' feathers and his
nails were like birds' claws.**

**34"After this time had passed, I,
Nebuchadnezzar, looked up to heaven.
My sanity returned, and I praised and
worshiped the Most High and honored
the one who lives forever.**

His rule is everlasting,
and his kingdom is eternal.
35 All the people of the earth
are nothing compared to him.
He does as he pleases
among the angels of heaven
and among the people of the earth.
No one can stop him or say to him,
'What do you mean by doing
these things?'

36"When my sanity returned to me, so did my honor and glory and kingdom. My advisers and nobles sought me out, and I was restored as head of my kingdom, with even greater honor than before.

37"Now I, Nebuchadnezzar, praise and glorify and honor the King of heaven. All his acts are just and true, and he is able to humble the proud."

NOTES

4:30 [27] ***great city of Babylon.*** For a discussion of the extent of "Nebuchadnezzar's Babylon" see ISBE 1.385-389; Kaiser 1998:414-416; Oates 1986:144-162.

this beautiful city. The famous "hanging gardens," adorned by floral contributions from many countries, would have been a part of this beauty (Abbott n.d.:170-171). The gardens were actually supported by walls and supports forming several layers of terraces.

4:31 [28] ***called down.*** Lit., "fell down." Its source is stressed by the placement of the words "from heaven" before the verb, indicating again that heaven rules (cf. 4:26 [23]).

4:35 [32] ***among the angels of heaven.*** This is better rendered as "among the host or army of heaven." Goldingay (1989:79) renders this as "forces."

4:37 [34] ***King of heaven.*** This phrase (*melek shemayya'* [TA/ZA10421/10723, S4430/8065]) is found only here and contrasts with the king of Babylon, Nebuchadnezzar.

COMMENTARY

Daniel's admonition and warning went unheeded. Within a year, disastrous things happened to the Babylonian king. He had built the famous Ishtar Gate, his royal palaces, the "hanging gardens," and much more, and he was still prospering when he laid claim to it all as a work of his "own mighty power." And he arrogantly suggested that the city had been built by him to display his own "majestic splendor" (4:30 [27]). The builders of the tower of Babel, Pharaoh, and Nebuchadnezzar are infamous Old Testament examples of "pride goes before a fall." In all cases God judged these humans and their divinelike claims at the peak of their splendor. In Nebuchadnezzar's case, God sent down a watcher who carefully observed his actions and attitudes and announced God's rejection of him and his claims (4:13, 23, 31 [10, 20, 28]; cf. Gen 11:1-9). Pharaoh Hophra (589–570 BC) nearly matched Nebuchadnezzar in his arrogant boasting (Ezek 29:3, 8-10), declaring that "The Nile River is mine; I made it for myself." Accordingly, both rulers fell. Hophra was given over to Babylon (Jer 44:29-30).

Verses 31-33 [28-30] reiterate what has already been given (4:13-16, 24-26 [10-13, 21-23]). Verse 33 [30] adds the ghastly description of the hideous judgment to which Nebuchadnezzar was subjected. The heart and mind (4:16 [13]) of an animal was accompanied by appropriate physical manifestations of animal physiognomy. This treatment of the head of gold in chapters 2–3 may signal what is coming in chapter 7 and the true vicious nature of this empire. For there, the kingdom of Babylon is represented by a beast, namely, a lion. But here the king is given the mind of a beast, and there the beast is given a human mind (7:4) and made to stand up on two legs like a human being. In both descriptions, aquiline features are a part of the symbolism. Is the human mind given to the beast (in 7:4) an indication that Nebuchadnezzar regained his sanity and lived out his reign as a humble human, ruling over his kingdom with human sensibilities, as 4:37 [34] would seem to indicate?

The paean of praise and confession closing the chapter (4:34-37 [31-34]) matches the first three verses of this chapter (4:1-3 [3:31-33]), forming an *inclusio*. The exact amount of time indicated by "seven periods of time" (4:16, 25 [13, 22]) is not made more specific even at the end of the story, but it is ironic that the king who sent Israel into exile for 7 times 10 years (= 70 years) was made to experience his own exile from humanity of "seven periods" of time until he was purified from his pride. During this time and after gaining his sanity, the king realized some things about the Most High. He undoubtedly learned much about himself in light of the God whom he encountered.

He found that God "lives forever" and rules forever over an eternal kingdom (4:36-37 [33-34]). His own immortality and the fleeting nature of his rulership and own kingdom became a reality to him, for they had been taken from him in a moment of time, at the height of his arrogance. Although all the peoples of the earth had depended upon the king and his kingdom, they were of little significance before the Most High God. The dependence of the nations upon the king did not make him a god, nor give him the right to oppress the poor, to live in sin, and to pursue iniquity. He learned that the Most High controls not only those on earth (4:35 [32]), but the angels of heaven as well, who do his bidding, serving as his messengers (4:13, 17, 23 [10, 14, 20]). He had preferred not to listen to Daniel's sage advice and admonition, insisting upon his own way (4:27-30 [24-27]) and refusing to believe that the Most High would or could stop his rulership, even though he was sinning.

Not only the destructive and disciplinary aspects of God's prophetic message were fulfilled, but God's intention to bring back the king and restore his honor and glory and kingdom was duly fulfilled (4:36 [33]). God's desired effect was reached; Nebuchadnezzar learned that God is in charge. In the end, the king confessed that God's acts are "just and true" (4:37 [34]). God could "bring low" those who live in pride: The king was given the mind of an animal, and made to eat grass like the oxen. Human pride has no place, even among great kings, before the "King of heaven."

◆ D. The Demise of the Kingdom of Babylon and the Rise of Persia (5:1-31)

1. Belshazzar's hubris and defilement of the Temple vessels (5:1-4)

Many years later King Belshazzar gave a great feast for 1,000 of his nobles, and he drank wine with them. 2While Belshazzar was drinking the wine, he gave orders to bring in the gold and silver cups that his predecessor,* Nebuchadnezzar, had taken from the Temple in Jerusalem. He wanted to drink from them with his nobles, his wives, and his concubines. 3So they brought these gold cups taken from the Temple, the house of God in Jerusalem, and the king and his nobles, his wives, and his concubines drank from them. 4While they drank from them they praised their idols made of gold, silver, bronze, iron, wood, and stone.

5:2 Aramaic *father;* also in 5:11, 13, 18.

NOTES

5:1 ***Belshazzar.*** This name means "Bel, protect the king." Its Akkadian form was *bel-sharra-usur* (cf. 5:30; 7:1; 8:1).

feast. In Aramaic *lekhem* [TA/ZA10389, S3900] usually meant bread or meal. But the context here indicates an official feast or banquet. The event was held in the banquet hall. Belshazzar's father proper was Nabonidus (see commentary and note on 4:16 [13]; see also ANET 305-315, 560-563).

5:2 ***While Belshazzar was drinking the wine.*** The Aramaic construction seems to imply "under the influence of the wine" (Holladay 1988:406; cf. Esth 1:10). The Aramaic word translated "drinking" originally meant "taste." For a succinct summary of Nabonidus's reign, see Kaiser 1998:417-419; Oates 1986:131-135; Starr 1991:139-140.

predecessor. Aramaic *'abuhi* [TA/ZA10003, S2] (his father), as per NLT mg. This term *'ab* could mean "forefather." Nebuchadnezzar was the premier king and stabilizer of the Chaldean dynasty of Babylon (cf. 5:11, 13, 18, 22). This term does not require that Nebuchadnezzar was his literal father. Belshazzar was the eldest son of the last king of the Neo-Babylonian Empire, Nabonidus. The fact that Daniel could have been made the third-highest ruler in the kingdom shows that Belshazzar took his father's de jure rulership into account, placing himself second and Daniel third (5:16). See further, Lucas 2009:542.

5:4 ***they drank.*** Herodotus notes that the dancing and enjoyment went on while the city was being conquered (*Histories* 1.191); Xenophon also records the excessive festivities and drinking, an all-night affair (*Cyropaedia* 7.5.15).

idols. Or, "gods." Either translation is acceptable, as long as the material and man-made aspect of these "gods/idols" is clear. (See Contenau 1954:278-280 for a summary of the legacy of Babylonian religion.)

COMMENTARY

Belshazzar was the son of Nabonidus (555–539 BC), the last king of Babylon (see note on 5:21 and commentary at 4:9-27). Nebuchadnezzar had died in 562 BC, and three kings had followed him. The first was his son Amel-Marduk (or as given in the OT, Evil-merodach, "servant or man of Marduk"; 2 Kgs 25:27; Jer 52:31), who reigned from 561/562 to 560 BC. He was not popular in Babylon, but he showed special favor and honor to Jehoiachin, the exiled Judean king (2 Kgs 25:27-30). Evil-merodach died a violent death. Neriglissar succeeded him (559–556 BC) and supported the restoration and upkeep of temples in both Borsippa and Babylon. He was an active military campaigner. He is mentioned in Jeremiah 39:3, 13 as Nergal-sharezer, adviser to Nebuchadnezzar. His son Labashi-Marduk reigned only three months (556 BC) and was removed from office; Nabonidus was put in his place. His reign features two especially unusual developments. First, his devotion to the great Babylonian god Marduk waned, so he devoted his energies to honoring and worshiping the moon-god Sin in Harran (ANET 305-307; 312-315; 562-563; COS 2.123A; 2.123B). This angered the people of Babylon beyond measure. Second, he placed Belshazzar his son on the throne in Babylon as regent, and he traveled to Teima, a city in northwest Arabia. He stayed there for 10 years (COS 2.123B, ii.3-31; ANET 312-315). This strange move, however, explains why Belshazzar can be called the de facto king in Babylon, even though his father was king de jure while residing in Teima. Evidently, Nabonidus returned to Babylon and fled the night it fell (5:30-31). He was eventually captured and executed in Babylon, according to Xenophon (*Cyropaedia* 7.5.33). However, according to Berossus, the Babylonian historian priest, Cyrus spared his life, and according to Cyrus, Marduk delivered Nabonidus into his hands (COS 2.124, lines 9-19; for differing views on this see Lucas 2009:543).

At any rate, this dual kingship also explains why Belshazzar offered to make Daniel third in power in the kingdom, not second (5:8, 16; cf. Gen 41:40). Nabonidus was a troubled king who experienced many dreams (see note on 5:21 and commentary on 4:9-27) that drove him to do some of the things he did. This implies that God, who certainly worked with pagan rulers through dreams, orchestrated this whole affair, setting up the downfall of the city of Babylon. Nabonidus's reasons for returning to Babylon are not recorded, but the perilous situation that Babylon faced from the Persians was certainly one reason for his return.

As chapter 5 opens, the year is 539 BC, it is the day of the New Year Festival in Babylon and the night of Babylon's fall (5:30), when Cyrus, king of Persia, received rulership of the world according to the sovereign will of Daniel's God (5:31 [6:1]). According to Daniel, as well as Herodotus (*Histories* 1.191) and Xenophon (*Cyropaedia* 7.5.15), wine flowed freely. The historical records ascribe sacrilegious acts to Nabonidus toward Marduk before and after his return that made him *persona non grata* in Babylon. Daniel reveals that the crown prince Belshazzar committed unthinkable folly by ordering that the sacred cups that had been used in the Temple ceremonies at Jerusalem be used in this debauchery. These sacred vessels were mentioned in 1:2. In the future, they would be returned to the rebuilt temple in Jerusalem by Sheshbazzar and Zerubbabel (Ezra 1:7-11), after Cyrus had ended Babylonian hegemony and turned it and the surrounding area into a province he used as an administrative center.

It is worth noting that corruption, idolatrous practices, and sacrilegious disrespect reach a new level in this scene in Daniel. Nebuchadnezzar had stored those vessels in the temple of his own God, but had not used these vessels in this way. In fact, 30 years earlier he had "worshiped the Most High and honored the one who lives forever" (4:34 [31]) and declared the righteous character of this King of heaven (4:36-37 [33-34]). He would not have thought of desecrating the vessels made to honor this God. This king had honored Daniel because the spirit of the gods was in him (4:9 [6]). But now the focus of worship had become gold, silver, bronze, iron, wood, and stone put into the form of "gods"—idols! According to Isaiah, the use and worship of idols by Israel had played a major part in sending them into exile. In similar fashion, God did not approve of the Babylonians' worship of idols. At one point in its history, there were in Babylon 53 temples to honor the major deities, 55 smaller shrines to honor the heavenly gods, 180 altars to Ishtar, consort of Marduk; 180 altars to the gods Nergal and Addad, plus altars to lesser deities. In Nabonidus's day and the time of Belshazzar, the situation was even worse.

This chapter illustrates the dangers of drinking too much wine and may give further insight as to why Daniel refused to drink the king's wine and eat his food (1:8). Daniel could not afford to be negligent or caught off guard in a culture that promoted excessive eating and drinking at its chief religious festivals. Belshazzar's drinking heightened his hubris—his audacity to defile the holy vessels of the Most High God (cf. Lev 10:8-11).

◆ 2. The handwriting on the wall (5:5-9)

[5]Suddenly, they saw the fingers of a human hand writing on the plaster wall of the king's palace, near the lampstand. The king himself saw the hand as it wrote,
[6]and his face turned pale with fright. His knees knocked together in fear and his legs gave way beneath him.

[7]The king shouted for the enchanters, astrologers,* and fortune-tellers to be brought before him. He said to these wise men of Babylon, "Whoever can read this writing and tell me what it means will be dressed in purple robes of royal honor and will have a gold chain placed around his neck. He will become the third highest ruler in the kingdom!"

[8]But when all the king's wise men had come in, none of them could read the
writing or tell him what it meant. [9]So the
king grew even more alarmed, and his face turned pale. His nobles, too, were shaken.

5:7 Or *Chaldeans;* also in 5:11.

NOTES

5:5 ***The king himself saw the hand as it wrote.*** The king saw the back of the hand or the entire hand (*pas yedah* [TA/ZA10589/10311, S6447/3028]). The word *pas* indicates the whole hand or back of the hand below the wrist. A ghostly appearance shocked the king.

5:6 ***his face turned pale.*** Lit., "the brightness of his face changed."

with fright. Lit., "his thoughts alarmed him."

his legs gave way. Or, "his hip joints shook." Cf. Felix's reaction of fear to Paul's preaching of righteousness, self-control, and judgment (Acts 24:25).

5:7 ***purple robes.*** See Esth 8:15; 1 Macc 10:20; 14:43.

gold chain. "Chain" may be better rendered as collar or necklace (Hartman and Di Lella 1978:184; Holladay 1988:403; Lucas 2002:121).

5:9 ***were shaken.*** Or "were perplexed," or "thrown into confusion."

COMMENTARY

This chapter is tied intimately to the preceding chapters of the book, as it sounds the death toll for the Babylonian Empire and its last reigning king, Belshazzar. In addition to the mention of wine, holy vessels from the Jerusalem Temple, Nebuchadnezzar's rape of the holy Temple (ch 1), idols of gold (ch 3), the king's court of astrologers and enchanters, there is a laudatory historical review of Daniel's position at the royal court of Nebuchadnezzar (5:10-12) by the queen mother and confirmation of that history by Belshazzar (5:13-14). Daniel gave a positive review of the reign of Nebuchadnezzar and his humble response to God's chastisements, including his insanity (5:17-21). So, the preceding chapters (1–4), especially chapter 4, are prologues to the tragic demise of the Babylonian king and his kingdom in this chapter.

The reasons why Belshazzar and the current sacrilegious conditions in the kingdom were to be brought to an end are spelled out in 5:22-24 (much as the fall of northern Israel is explained in 2 Kgs 17). The worship of idols and the refusal to honor the living God could not be tolerated further. There would be no extension of time for this king and his authority, as there had been for Nebuchadnezzar's reign. The first kingdom of the head of gold is passing away, a momentous event in

God's orchestration of history, and the kingdom of Persia under Cyrus is given the temporary rulership of the nations (1:21; 6:28 [29]; 10:1; 2 Chr 36:22; Ezra 1:1-7; Isa 44:28; 45:1-2, 13).

The response of Belshazzar to the handwriting on the wall shows his total emotional and physical trauma from this horrifying event. His reaction is itself shocking and puzzling. By this time, the rise of the Persians had become a dark specter haunting the Babylonian kingdom (cf. the evident references to Persia in 5:25, 28). When this blasphemous and unjust ruler was faced with the charges and claims of unrighteousness, fear and dread resulted. He was guilty; there was no way out. In the words of Cyrus the Great, Nabonidus, and by implication his son, Belshazzar, were persons of no account (COS 2.124, lines 9-19).

The panic of Belshazzar's hopeless condition shows in his pitiful offer to reward anyone of his experts who could do their job. By contrast, Nebuchadnezzar had threatened to kill all of the wise men if they did not inform him of his dream and its meaning (2:5, 8-9, 12-13). This situation reiterates the uselessness and vanity of the Babylonian enchanters, astrologers, fortune-tellers, and other advisers to the king. When the true God of heaven reveals himself, only his chosen prophets are able to interpret his actions and messages.

Daniel's special ability in the languages and literature of Babylon (1:4, 17) was observed early in the reign of Nebuchadnezzar. Now, years later, he would use that gift to honor God by announcing judgment upon Belshazzar and the passing of rulership to the Persians, as he had described to Nebuchadnezzar (2:39; cf. 7:4, 17). The nation that had destroyed his people would be judged (Isa 43–47; Jer 50–51). Although the Babylonian experts could probably read the words of this inscription (whether in Babylonian or Aramaic), they could not discern the significance of the words for the king. This was perhaps out of fear (cf. 4:19 [16]) but also because they were not attuned to spiritual realities. They needed Daniel's interpretation. From Daniel's perspective, which was already informed by God's sovereign plans for history based on the events of chapters 1–4 and 7–8, the message was a clear judgment from God: The nation of Babylon was to be destroyed because it did not measure up to God's demands of righteousness and mercy, and of the true worship of the living God (cf. 4:27 [24]; 5:22-24).

◆ 3. The queen mother remembers Daniel; Belshazzar's interview and offer (5:10-16)

**10 But when the queen mother heard what
was happening, she hurried to the ban-
quet hall. She said to Belshazzar, "Long
live the king! Don't be so pale and fright-
ened. 11 There is a man in your kingdom
who has within him the spirit of the holy
gods. During Nebuchadnezzar's reign, this
man was found to have insight, under-
standing, and wisdom like that of the
gods. Your predecessor, the king—your
predecessor King Nebuchadnezzar—made
him chief over all the magicians, enchant-
ers, astrologers, and fortune-tellers of
Babylon. 12 This man Daniel, whom the
king named Belteshazzar, has exceptional
ability and is filled with divine knowledge
and understanding. He can interpret
dreams, explain riddles, and solve difficult
problems. Call for Daniel, and he will tell
you what the writing means."**

13So Daniel was brought in before the
king. The king asked him, "Are you Daniel,
one of the exiles brought from Judah by
my predecessor, King Nebuchadnezzar? 14I
have heard that you have the spirit of the
gods within you and that you are filled
with insight, understanding, and wisdom.
15My wise men and enchanters have tried
to read the words on the wall and tell me
their meaning, but they cannot do it. 16I
am told that you can give interpretations
and solve difficult problems. If you can
read these words and tell me their meaning, you will be clothed in purple robes of
royal honor, and you will have a gold
chain placed around your neck. You will
become the third highest ruler in the
kingdom."

NOTES

5:10 ***queen mother.*** This word, *malketha'* [TA/ZA10423, S4433] (the queen), is placed first in the sentence for emphasis. Queen mothers in the OT and in the broader ancient Near East could be very influential persons (Lucas 2009:543; Anderson 1984:179-194). In some cases, they, like the kings, bore two names reflecting linguistic or ethnic diversity in the empire (Kuhrt 1995:526-527). But whose mother is in view here? Some think that she was Adad-guppi, the mother or grandmother of Nabonidus who lived to be 104 years old (COS 1.147). She claims to have fostered the worship of Sin, the moon-god, for 95 years! But, even so, she died before the events of ch 5. Nitocris, mother of Nebuchadnezzar, is therefore the better candidate and currently favored by most scholars (Collins 1993:248; Longman 1999:139; cf. Herodotus *Histories* 1.185-187). Either woman would have had a panoramic view of the historical and cultural situation.

heard what was happening. This attempts to capture the meaning of the Aramaic "because of the words of the king and his nobles."

5:11 ***the spirit of the holy gods.*** See 2:11; 4:8, 9, 18 [5, 6, 15], and notes.

insight, understanding, and wisdom. These reflect respectively the Aramaic *nahiru* [TA/ZA10467, S5094] (illumination), *soklethanu* [TA/ZA10684, S7924] (insight, understanding, perspicacity), *khokmah* [TA/ZA10266, S2452] (wisdom).

like that of the gods. Daniel's three endowments were like the wisdom of the gods.

Your predecessor, the king—your predecessor King Nebuchadnezzar. The Aramaic text encloses the second half of this sentence with "the king, Nebuchadnezzar, your father . . . your father the king," emphasizing that certainly Belshazzar should have learned from Nebuchadnezzar's experience.

5:12 ***exceptional ability.*** Lit., "extraordinary spirit."

is filled with divine knowledge. The queen's words show unwavering confidence in Daniel's divinely granted ability.

5:13 ***Are you Daniel?*** The Aramaic could possibly mean "So you are Daniel," since it can be assured that the king had been informed about Daniel before he came in. Daniel used a similar phrase addressing Nebuchadnezzar twice earlier when he told him, "You are the head of gold" and "That tree . . . is you" (2:38; 4:22 [19]).

5:14 ***the spirit of the gods.*** See notes on 4:8, 9, 18 [5, 6, 15]; 5:11. This is the proper translation of Belshazzar's point of view. From Daniel's point of view, it was most certainly "the Spirit of God" that was in him.

5:15 ***wise men and enchanters.*** For these terms, see 1:20; 2:2, 12; 5:7.

have tried to read.The NLT condenses the Aramaic text, which has the king state that the wise men and enchanters had been brought before him for the purpose of reading the text. This emphasizes the efforts the king had put forth to get the writing deciphered by his experts.

COMMENTARY

The supporting role of the queen mother to the king is impressive, as is her memory of and praise of Daniel. Queen mothers could carry great influence (see note on 5:10). The fact that the queen mother told them they needed to find Daniel shows her authority and indicates that Daniel's place at the Babylonian court was not something that he trumpeted. He was not obtrusive in the affairs of the king, but rather retiring—until called upon. The queen's address to the king, "Long live the king!" although proper court etiquette, has an ironic twist because it was addressed to a king who would be judged and killed that very night (5:26, 30)!

Her description of Daniel, now a man of perhaps 80 years of age, as one in whom "the spirit of the holy gods" resided, repeats Nebuchadnezzar's evaluation of Daniel's uniqueness in Babylonian polytheistic terms (4:8-9, 18 [5-6, 15]). From Daniel's perspective, it was the Spirit of the living God who was in him, imparting wisdom, skill, and understanding to him just as the Spirit had to Bezalel, Moses, and the prophets. His possession of wisdom like that belonging to the gods made some think that "a godlike" man might be among them (cf. 2:11). But in the world of Daniel, to be "like God" meant living a righteous, holy, loving, and wise life.

The interpretation of the writing on the wall, which evidently remained there for all to see and examine, and which the king sought so diligently, was a devastating announcement and revelation that confirmed the worst fears of Belshazzar's anxiety attack. Knowing the significance of the writing would prove far more disconcerting than the angst of not knowing what it meant. Daniel, as a true prophet, would tell them what it meant. His prophetic word would, like Jeremiah's message, bring down a nation (Jer 1:9-10).

The king recalled the exile of Daniel by Nebuchadnezzar (1:1-3; 5:13). Literarily, this connects this section to the preceding chapters centering on Nebuchadnezzar. Belshazzar's mention of Nebuchadnezzar enabled Daniel to present him as the model the current crown prince should have followed (5:17-21).

The king's proposition to Daniel was the same he offered to all of the other wise men. But Daniel did not work for the crown prince; he served the King of heaven (4:37 [34]), who revealed his secrets to his servant (2:22-23, 27-29) and gave him all of his abilities (1:17). Daniel was ready to speak the message of God to the king because he had been positioned by God to do his will.

◆ 4. Interpretation, application, and fulfillment of the handwriting (5:17-31)

17 Daniel answered the king, "Keep your gifts or give them to someone else, but I will tell you what the writing means.
18 Your Majesty, the Most High God gave sovereignty, majesty, glory, and honor to your predecessor, Nebuchadnezzar. 19 He made him so great that people of all races and nations and languages trembled before him in fear. He killed those he wanted to kill and spared those he wanted to spare. He honored those he wanted to honor and disgraced those he wanted to disgrace. 20 But when his heart and mind were puffed up with arrogance, he was brought down from his royal throne and stripped of his glory. 21 He was driven from human society. He was given the mind of a wild animal, and he lived among the

wild donkeys. He ate grass like a cow, and he was drenched with the dew of heaven, until he learned that the Most High God rules over the kingdoms of the world and appoints anyone he desires to rule over them.

22"You are his successor,* O Belshazzar, and you knew all this, yet you have not humbled yourself. 23For you have proudly defied the Lord of heaven and have had these cups from his Temple brought before you. You and your nobles and your wives and concubines have been drinking wine from them while praising gods of silver, gold, bronze, iron, wood, and stone—gods that neither see nor hear nor know anything at all. But you have not honored the God who gives you the breath of life and controls your destiny! 24So God has sent this hand to write this message.

25"This is the message that was written: MENE, MENE, TEKEL, and PARSIN. 26This is what these words mean:

Mene means 'numbered'—God has
numbered the days of your reign
and has brought it to an end.
27 *Tekel* means 'weighed'—you have been
weighed on the balances and have
not measured up.
28 *Parsin** means 'divided'—your kingdom
has been divided and given to the
Medes and Persians."

29Then at Belshazzar's command, Daniel was dressed in purple robes, a gold chain was hung around his neck, and he was proclaimed the third highest ruler in the kingdom.

30That very night Belshazzar, the Babylonian* king, was killed.*

31*And Darius the Mede took over the kingdom at the age of sixty-two.

5:22 Aramaic *son.* 5:28 Aramaic *Peres,* the singular of *Parsin.* 5:30a Or *Chaldean.* 5:30b The Persians and Medes conquered Babylon in October 539 B.C. 5:31 Verse 5:31 is numbered 6:1 in Aramaic text.

NOTES

5:17 ***Keep your gifts.*** Lit., "Your gifts to you let them be." Daniel would translate the writing without pay.

5:18 ***your predecessor.*** Lit., "your father" (see 5:11, 13).

5:19 ***races.*** See 3:29; 4:1 [3:33].

spared. Lit., "he kept alive"; a delegated power from the living God.

disgraced. Lit., "he brought down"; this power to bring down peoples was granted by the God of Daniel.

5:20 ***puffed up with arrogance.*** The Aramaic is "to act insolently," indicating that Nebuchadnezzar's heart was raised up and his spirit strengthened. These characteristics also marked the arrogance of some of Egypt's pharaohs (cf. the pharaoh of the Exodus [Exod 9:13-14; 10:3-4] and Pharaoh Hophrah [Ezek 29:3]) and the hardened hearts of the Canaanite kings whom the Lord destroyed (Josh 11:20).

5:21 ***He was driven from human society.*** Nebuchadnezzar is in view here in the text, but because no satisfactory explanation has yet been put forth concerning Nabonidus's move to Teima in Arabia for 10 years, some scholars believe the insanity of Nebuchadnezzar really happened to Nabonidus and that the author of Daniel has mistakenly transferred the event to Nebuchadnezzar. Joan Oates reports this as certain (1986:132-133). So also Milik (1956:408). But anyone who reads the text of Daniel along with "The Prayer of Nabonidus" (aka 4QprNab; cf. COS 1.89; García-Martinez 1996:289) will be struck by the major differences between them. This all remains a mere hypothesis, for the difference between The Prayer of Nabonidus and the biblical text remains unsatisfactorily explained. Furthermore, the diseases each king suffered are quite different (see commentary on 4:9-27; Baldwin 1978a:116-118; ISBE 3.468-470). In fact, the lives and deaths of the kings of the Chaldean dynasty after Nebuchadnezzar are all tragic: Evil-merodach (561–560 BC) was assassinated in a revolution as a hated king at the hands of Neriglissar; Neriglissar (Nergal-sharezer, 559–556) died under strange circumstances; Labashi-Marduk was deposed in nine months and murdered; then Nabonidus became king (Thomas 1961:89-91). For Herodotus's confused mention of Nabonidus and Nebuchadnezzar each as Labynetos of Babylon see his *Histories* 1.74.3; 1.77.2; 1.188.1.

like a cow. This may be rendered as "ox" or "cattle" as well (NIV, NJPS, RSV, TEV).

until he learned. This shows the redemptive purpose of God's judgment (cf. 4:25, 32 [22, 29]).

5:22 ***successor.*** Lit., "his son" (see NLT mg).

5:23 ***his Temple.*** Lit., "his house."

gives you the breath of life. Lit., "your breath is in his hand."

5:25 ***MENE, MENE, TEKEL, and PARSIN.*** This represents the Aramaic *mene' mene' teqel uparsin* [TA/ZA10428/10770/10593, S4484/8625/6537]. Literally these words are "mina, mina, shekel, half-mina" (or "half-shekel"). Minas were units of weight measurement for gold and silver. A mina weighed about 50 shekels or 500 grams. Shekels were units of weight, a shekel weighing about 10 grams. But there is a wordplay here because *mene'* also functions as a Peal passive participle of *menah* [TA/ZA10431, S4483] (to number). As a passive participle, *mene'* means "numbered." Likewise, *teqel* functions as a passive participle of *teqal* [TA/ZA10769, S8625] (to weigh). As a passive participle *teqel* means "weighed." The word *parsin* can be taken as a Peal passive participle of *peras* [TA/ZA10592, S6537] (to divide). In this context, "divided" = "halved" (or two half minas or half shekels), thereby indicating that the Babylonian Empire had been evaluated and was to be given to two peoples, the Medes and the Persians (see Brewer 1991:311-316). In an excellent article, Wolters (1991:176-177) has shown the ingenious aspects of Daniel's interpretation that involve both meaning and literary symmetry. He identifies three levels of the response that are unified and feature three assertions in each level. In addition, there may be a polemical dimension to Daniel's response that is "anti-astrological" in significance, specifically a disclaimer that Libra is not a great god of heaven as was thought in Babylonian astrology. For a description of weights and scales, see COS 2.136; 2.146; Lucas 2009:544.

5:29 ***proclaimed the third highest ruler.*** Daniel's status was recognized through the official channels of the kingdom.

5:30 ***Babylonian king.*** Lit., the "Chaldean king" (so NLT mg). This brought the Chaldean dynasty to its end, de facto and de jure, for Belshazzar's father, Nabonidus, was probably in Babylon at this time (see comments on 5:1-4 and especially 4:9-27). Nabonidus (an absentee king) was defeated and died in 539 BC. See comments on Belshazzar in the Introduction for historical and genealogical issues concerning him, Nebuchadnezzar, and Nabonidus. The amazing Chaldean Neo-Babylonian Empire lasted from 625 to 539 BC, a total of 65 years. The Persians conquered Babylon in October of 539 BC.

COMMENTARY

Since Daniel had studied Jeremiah diligently, he undoubtedly also knew the other prophecies concerning the demise of Babylon (Isa 47) and the rise of Cyrus the Persian (Isa 44:28; 45:1-3). It is highly unlikely that an exile of Daniel's background and ability was ignorant of the traditions of his own people; he evidences extensive knowledge of Israel's past (cf. 1:4; 9:4-19). Isaiah had also declared that the astrologers and stargazers would not be able to deliver Babylon from her fateful destiny (Isa 47:12-15). This most certainly was general information that Daniel was aware of from his own traditions. He spoke the truth now, however, based upon the immediate revelation that God had produced for the king: The end had come (5:26; on the fall of Babylon, see Lucas 2009:543). But this mantic interpretive skill and wisdom imparted to Daniel by his God would have been subordinate and servant to the knowledge he had of his own traditions, written and oral. His God had prepared him for this task from the time of his youth (1:1-4).

Daniel summarized the moral, ethical, and religious high points of chapter 4, highlighting the fact that Nebuchadnezzar was "teachable" and that he did learn to be humble before the God of heaven. He learned especially that the Most High rules and appoints whom he chooses to rule the kingdoms of the earth. The flow of history is in his hand. And, undoubtedly, Nebuchadnezzar's 43-year reign gave force to Daniel's words. Nebuchadnezzar had learned that wickedness and oppression of the poor, as well as megalomaniacal pride, could lead to self-destruction (4:27, 30, 37 [24, 27, 34]).

The genre of the book of Daniel, didactic theological history reported in the form of court tales (with apocalyptic elements skillfully crafted in), is well illustrated by Daniel's own words here. The lessons that Belshazzar should have learned by God's historical treatment of Nebuchadnezzar should have become powerful shapers of his own character and reign. God intended Nebuchadnezzar's history to be didactic, but Belshazzar had missed the lessons entirely—not because he did not have them, but because he did not seek after righteousness.

Many scholars today apply the moral lessons that God brought into Nebuchadnezzar's life to the last king of Babylon, Nabonidus. Or they argue that the author has inaccurately identified Nebuchadnezzar as the king to whom these things happened (see note on 5:21). Daniel, however, applied them unequivocally to Nebuchadnezzar. Belshazzar had a model in Nabonidus to follow, but it was not one that Daniel or the Most High God would have approved. To take Daniel's words as ignorantly or falsely applied to Nebuchadnezzar and apply them to Nabonidus, a later king whose character and action and sacrilegious nature are diametrically opposed to Nebuchadnezzar's, is to drain this theological lesson of its didactic power.

Nebuchadnezzar had learned humility (4:37 [34]). But Belshazzar did not know the word (5:22), although he had the lessons of revelation and history to instruct him along the way. The golden cups that Nebuchadnezzar had kept under lock and key in his god's temple stayed there during that king's reign. He was respectful of the Most High God from whose Temple he had taken these objects. One can be sure that Daniel, Shadrach, Meshach, and Abednego had made it clear that they did not worship idols, but the living God, who sees, hears, and knows everything (5:23). Daniel knew from the dreams and visions he had already dealt with (chs 2, 7–8), that the destiny of kings lay in God's hand—along with the destiny of their peoples and nations.

Daniel appropriately applied the writing on the wall to the world situation of his day (5:24-28). He believed that this conjunction of national events was going to usher in a new world order. He was present at the passing of the first great kingdom (according to the dream and vision of chapters 2 and 7). Within the next one to three years, he would be granted visions that would give him an even more detailed panoramic view of the flow of human history toward its consummation (9:2; 10:1). These visions are unequaled in any ancient literature. Daniel would undoubtedly continue to observe "current events," study his own historical and oral traditions, and consider his divinely orchestrated placement in them, although his role would soon come to an end (12:13).

That God held Belshazzar's "breath of life" in his hand, as well as his personal destiny, is demonstrated in 5:25-30. God had numbered the days of his reign because he was arrogant and corrupt, as well as morally depraved (Lucas 2009:543). Xenophon depicts Belshazzar (in Goldingay's words [2002:127/1989:107]) as "a riotous, indulgent, cruel, and godless young man" (see Xenophon *Cyropaedia* 4-7). Another major theme of the book is emphasized in 5:28: God tears down nations, builds up nations, and gives rulership to whomever he will (see 2:21; 4:17, 34-35 [14, 31-32]). The God who gave Belshazzar his breath of life took it back that very night (5:30), as well as the golden vessels that he had profaned.

Daniel's own expectations must have been high at this point, wondering what would happen to him and his people. He knew the prophets (9:1-2), and he understood that God had something in store for his people at this momentous juncture in history. In less than a year he would know for sure what to expect.

Daniel's position in Babylon at its demise is nothing short of astonishing. He, a Jewish exile, was "third . . . in the kingdom." He had functioned as a kingdom adviser for 43 years under Nebuchadnezzar. He had witnessed the creation of the city under this great king, along with its splendor. He remained unimpressed and faithful to his God. He was, in a significant sense, a symbol of the rising power of the Kingdom of God to rule over all the nations in the future (chs 2, 7). He represented his people well. His righteousness not only exalted him before God, but also exalted his people. He was enabled by God's Spirit!

In 5:29 it is indicated that an official herald (see note) made Daniel's installation complete. At the end of the Babylonian kingdom, and for one evening only, he was third in power. While two kings lost their authority (one dies and one flees the city or is captured), Daniel got promoted! But he was not likely too impressed with his new position. Like Jeremiah, the winning side favored him (cf. Jer 40:1-6). He was received with great respect into Darius the Mede's upper echelons of government (6:3 [4]). Darius would soon seek to advance him further.

◆ E. Daniel's Deliverance from Destruction (6:1-28)

1. Daniel's ability and success against religious opposition (6:1-5)

1*Darius the Mede decided to divide the kingdom into 120 provinces, and he appointed a high officer to rule over each province. 2The king also chose Daniel and two others as administrators to supervise the high officers and protect the king's interests. 3Daniel soon proved himself more capable than all the other administrators and high officers. Because of Daniel's great ability, the king made plans to place him over the entire empire.

4Then the other administrators and high officers began searching for some fault in the way Daniel was handling government affairs, but they couldn't find anything to criticize or condemn. He was faithful, always responsible, and completely trustworthy. 5So they concluded, "Our only chance of finding grounds for accusing Daniel will be in connection with the rules of his religion."

6:1 Verses 6:1-28 are numbered 6:2-29 in Aramaic text.

NOTES

6:1 [2] *Darius the Mede.* For the historical issues concerning Darius the Mede, see the Introduction, "Historical Accuracy." The versification of the Aramaic in this chapter is one number higher than the English versification because 6:1 is 5:31 in the Aramaic text.

120 provinces. Cf. Esth 1:1; 8:9 regarding the time of Xerxes (485–465 BC). The size of these satrapies may have been smaller districts than the 20 satrapies mentioned by Herodotus (*Histories* 3.89) in the time of Darius I (522–486 BC); cf. Lucas 2002:148; Collins 1993:264.

high officer. Lit., "satraps," a word that comes from Old Persian through Greek into English and can be translated "princes," "presidents," or "governors." A province, area, or administrative unit of the empire was placed under each satrap (see 3:2). For the historical reality of these political and administrative divisions in the empire, see Yamauchi (1990:179).

6:2 [3] *protect the king's interest.* Rebel "satraps," Olmstead (1948:397) observes, threatened to destroy the empire of Persia. The kings needed dependable men to rule for them.

6:3 [4] *Daniel.* The Aramaic has "This man Daniel," but the wording is merely stylistic, not emphatic.

more capable. This represents the Aramaic "excellent spirit" (*ruakh yattira'* [TA/ZA10658/10339, S7308/3493]).

made plans. More literally, the king was "in the process of planning" to raise up Daniel.

6:4 [5] *some fault.* The Aramaic (*'illah* [TA/ZA10544, S5931]) means "a ground or basis" or even "pretext" for doing something.

always responsible, and completely trustworthy. This gives the thought of the Aramaic, "no remissness or lax practices were found against him."

6:5 [6] *rules of his religion.* Lit., "the requirements (*dath* [TA/ZA10186, S1882]) of his God" (see 6:8, 12, 15 [9, 13, 16] and Ezra 7:12, 14, 25).

COMMENTARY

This chapter relates another court narrative of internal conflict. It focuses on one main theme: the rescue and deliverance of God's servant (6:19-22 [20-23]). The first 13 verses describe Daniel's entrapment by false charges of sacrilege and disrespect toward King Darius. According to the "law of the Medes and Persians," he was found to be guilty. The last 14 verses record the rescue operation by a God who is not at all bound by the immutable laws of the Medes and Persians (6:8, 12, 15 [9, 13, 16]). Human laws that do not reflect the laws of the Most High God will eventually be broken. God does not condemn the innocent. Though Daniel's fate was "sealed" (6:17 [18]), his God rescued him because he trusted him and was innocent (6:22-23 [23-24]; cf. Heb 11:33).

The fact that the first half of the chapter is used to describe Daniel's ensnarement emphasizes the magnitude of the rescue that delivered him. The words for "rescue" and "deliver" are together used seven times—symbolic of completeness—to describe the divine deliverance of Daniel (see note on 6:14 [15]). The writer used the legal phrase the "laws of the Medes and Persians" three times to assert the seeming impossibility of Daniel's deliverance. Not even Cyrus (or his appointed administrator over Babylon; see Introduction, "Historical Accuracy"), the newly proclaimed ruler of the Babylonian Empire and the new head of the Persian nation and new world order, could rescue him (6:14-15 [15-16]).

The structure of the chapter serves its theme and plot: the foiling of the conspiracy to destroy Daniel and thus remove him from office.

- I. The Entrapment of Daniel (6:1-13 [2-14])
  - A. Introduction and background (6:1-2 [2-3])
  - B. Daniel's success (6:3 [4])
  - C. Plot to destroy Daniel (6:4a [5a])
  - D. His perfect life and service (6:4b [5b])
  - E. His vulnerable spot—his religion (6:5 [6])
  - F. The execution of the plot to entrap him (6:6-13 [7-14])
    1. The plot conceived (6:6-9 [7-10])
    2. Ensnarement of Daniel (6:10-13 [11-14])
- II. The Rescue and Deliverance of Daniel (6:14-27 [15-28])
  - A. The king's futile response (6:14-15 [15-16])
  - B. Daniel sentenced but rescued (6:16-22 [17-23])
    1. Daniel cast into the den of lions (6:16-18 [17-19])
    2. The king's anxiety (6:19-20 [20-21])
    3. Daniel's response concerning his rescue (6:21-22 [22-23])
  - C. The king's joyous response (6:23 [24])
  - D. His judgment against Daniel's accusers (6:24 [25])
  - E. His paean of praise (6:25-27 [26-28])
- III. Daniel's Prosperity Continues (6:28 [29]; cf. 6:3 [4])

The amazing stability and durability of Daniel is further revealed in 6:1-3 [2-4]. His allegiance was to a kingdom and a king that must ultimately supersede all earthly kingdoms. His court influence is striking, and he stands out in his allegiance to his God. Others, including both the king and some who were hostile toward him, had become aware of his daily worship practices, although he did not make them conspicuous. And so he continued to prosper, even under a new foreign power, with no perceivable identity crisis. Nebuchadnezzar's original attempt to assimilate him into the Babylonian culture failed. In contrast, Nebuchadnezzar and Belshazzar had suffered identity crises and trauma when they encountered Daniel (chs 2, 4, and 5), and the Babylonian culture was now in decline—discredited to a great extent. Daniel continued and would continue to interpret reality for kings when called upon, a view of reality informed by both his practical Jewish wisdom (9:1-19) and the mantic knowledge that had been given to him (cf. 1:4, 17). They would have to face what this man, in whom was the "spirit of the holy gods," said to them. Daniel's continued unwavering identity with his God, his people, and the law of his God provided a worldview that stabilized him even through the changing of empires. Earlier in the biblical narratives, Joseph is put in prison because of false accusations (Gen 39). God rescued him and then prospered him. God would do the same for his faithful servant Daniel.

The Neo-Babylonian Empire was the final flowering of the great Mesopotamian civilizations that went all the way back to Sumer. Daniel and the exiles faced the coming of a new age in the Medo-Persian Empire. This was a major breaking point in this age of antiquity. From splendor to eventual dissolution, this last great golden age of Mesopotamian civilization had risen swiftly and had fallen quickly

(625–539 BC). Its ongoing dissolution would, however, continue for some time (cf. 7:12). While the buildings of Babylon were not destroyed, under Cyrus the city and its wealth were under new hegemony. World authority had been taken from the Babylonians and placed into the hands of the Persians with a certain finality. Isaiah the prophet had said, "O beautiful Babylon, sit now in darkness and silence. Never again will you be known as the queen of kingdoms" (Isa 47:5). But Daniel handled this "rite of passage" to a new era well, for he had never bought into the legacy of Babylon. He, in fact, was looking for a new era of deliverance for his people (Isa 44:28; 45:1-7, 13; Jer 25:12; 29:10-14; cf. Dan 9:2).

Darius the Mede (most likely Cyrus; see Introduction, "Historical Accuracy") was a magnanimous administrative genius, as illustrated by his expedient incipient organization of the greatest and most complex nation that had yet arisen on earth (cf. Esth 1:1; 8:9, which depict the empire about 55 years later), encompassing more than 25 separate nations or peoples, plus groups not officially recognized (cf. Solomon's reorganization of Israel into 12 administrative units, 1 Kgs 4:7-19). A person of such qualities certainly knew genius and character and appreciated it when he saw it; Daniel would be made the first-ranking administrative officer of the empire, exceeding even Joseph's position in Egypt.

Daniel, however, was an exile from Judah, a Jew, and a captive from Babylon, which the Medes and the Persians had just conquered. Could he be trusted? Darius the Mede apparently thought so, but Daniel's peers could not endure the honor he was about to receive; they wanted it for themselves. Daniel's character was impeccable, and his quality of work could not be criticized. Only a trumped-up charge against him would catch him, and it would need to be carefully crafted to succeed. The religious devotion that he showed to his God, his detractors thought, was his Achilles' heel. They did not, however, take into account that he actually served a living God (6:20 [21]) who would act on behalf of his servant, if he so chose (3:16-18). What they thought was his weakness turned out to be his strength and their downfall.

Through Daniel his servant, the living God would reveal himself before yet another of the mighty nations and monarchs of the world. God would deliver Daniel from the jealousy and hatred of his enemies, who stood against him because he was faithful to his God, the king, and his work.

◆ 2. The entrapment of Daniel (6:6-13)

**6So the administrators and high officers
went to the king and said, "Long live King
Darius! 7We are all in agreement—we ad-
ministrators, officials, high officers, advis-
ers, and governors—that the king should
make a law that will be strictly enforced.
Give orders that for the next thirty days
any person who prays to anyone, divine or
human—except to you, Your Majesty—will
be thrown into the den of lions. 8And now,
Your Majesty, issue and sign this law so it
cannot be changed, an official law of the
Medes and Persians that cannot be re-
voked." 9So King Darius signed the law.**

**10But when Daniel learned that the law
had been signed, he went home and knelt
down as usual in his upstairs room, with
its windows open toward Jerusalem. He
prayed three times a day, just as he had
always done, giving thanks to his God.
11Then the officials went together to
Daniel's house and found him praying and**

asking for God's help. 12So they went straight to the king and reminded him about his law. "Did you not sign a law that for the next thirty days any person who prays to anyone, divine or human—except to you, Your Majesty—will be thrown into the den of lions?"

"Yes," the king replied, "that decision stands; it is an official law of the Medes and Persians that cannot be revoked."

13Then they told the king, "That man Daniel, one of the captives from Judah, is ignoring you and your law. He still prays to his God three times a day."

NOTES

6:6 [7] *went.* The verb *regash* [TA/ZA10656, S7284] in this context seems to mean "hustled in," "thronged," or "stormed in."

6:7 [8] *should make a law that will be strictly enforced.* The Aramaic indicates the forceful planning and action of the officials to establish a royal decree and an accompanying interdict to enforce it. This story, therefore, presents a contest between Daniel's "law" (the Torah) and the law of the Medes and Persians. The advisers and counselors of the king were supposed to be righteous and just men. If they were caught taking bribes or committing unjust actions, they were executed (Olmstead 1948:128-130).

6:8 [9] *cannot be revoked.* Lit., "will not pass away," a rather arrogant claim, for all human laws had passed away until the Persians and Medes came along. In any event, the laws of the Medes and Persians were supposed to foster law and justice, not lawlessness and injustice (Esth 1:13-14; Herodotus *Histories* 3.31). Esther 1:19; 8:8 also asserts that a law sealed by the Persian king could not be revoked (cf. Montgomery 1927:270; Lucas 2009:547).

6:9 [10] *So.* Or, "Thereupon." No resistance or questioning by the king is recorded. In 6:12 [13] he parrots the words of his advisers in 6:8 [9]. The king was not aware of the full extent of Daniel's commitment. He may have hoped to deal with a religious split that was present and worsening in his kingdom, a split between Zoroastrianism, which was more narrow and demanding (and which the decree sought to support), and the more ancient traditional religion that allowed for syncretism (Walton 1988:283-286). It is perhaps better simply to understand that he did not fathom the radical monotheistic faith of Daniel (cf. Lucas 2009:546).

6:10 [11] *as usual.* This rendering may rest on repointing the Aramaic of MT from *hu'* [TA/ZA10200, S1932] to *hawa'* so that an alternate spelling of the verb *hawah* [TA/ZA10201, S1934] (he was) is read. Together with the participle for "kneeling," this verb would describe a habitual past action—literally, "he used to kneel down upon his knees." Or the NLT rendering may anticipate the clause "just as he had always done," found at the end of the verse.

6:11 [12] *asking.* Lit., "imploring mercy."

6:12 [13] *that decision stands.* Lit., it was "fixed, reliable, and established" (cf. 2:8, 45; 3:24).

COMMENTARY

In 6:6-9 [7-10], a host of various officials plot against Daniel and dupe an unsuspecting king. The text indicates that they "thronged in forcefully" to present their flattering conclusions to a flustered King Darius (6:6 [7]; see note). Their greeting, "Long live King Darius," carries irony, for within a month's time they would be summarily executed (6:6, 23-24 [7, 24-25]; cf. 5:10). The "law" that they had decided upon was rather a prohibition aimed squarely at Daniel's religious practices. They knew that Daniel (at the age of 80 to 83) would not stop praying, petitioning his God—not even for a temporary period of 30 days (cf. 3:16-18). Their desire was to see him not only removed, but killed by lions. The famous statement asserting the unchanging nature of the law of the Medes and Persians is well established (cf. Esth 1:19; 8:8; see note on 6:8 [9]). But these laws were merely laws of frail humans. Moreover, these pushers of the laws of the Medes and Persians, which were supposed to provide justice, were ironically using their legal system to achieve the greatest injustice—a premeditated destruction of an innocent person!

This chapter suggests what Daniel would have done if he had been required to bow to Nebuchadnezzar's golden image in chapter 3: There would have been five men walking about in the fiery furnace (3:25). Both chapter 3 and chapter 6 recount God's servants in the Exile putting their lives on the line. Shadrach, Meshach, and Abednego had been commanded to do something they would not do. Daniel was required to stop something he could not stop. His enemies knew his faithfulness to his God. In the Old Testament and the ancient Near East in general, lions were considered especially voracious animals, ready to tear off the head or limbs of persons (Deut 33:20; Hos 13:8; cf. 1 Pet 5:8) and never satiated (COS 1.86:264).

Lions were abundant in Persia and were hunted by kings in antiquity as an especially significant animal to slay in the hunt. The Assyrian, the Babylonian, the Persian, and the Egyptian kings proudly pursued this sport. An ample supply of lions was at hand for the contests. Some of the most famous Babylonian buildings, processional ways and monuments, featured lions in relief. Lions and dragons adorned the deep royal blue glazed brick of the Babylonian walls. The brick background was glazed deep blue with white or yellow lions in relief with yellow or red manes. In the court story of Daniel 6, these beasts were being kept in confinement for use in destroying enemies of the king and state. Those who accused Daniel are thrown to them and immediately devoured. Only a special rescue by God delivers Daniel (cf. Ps 57:1-5; cf. Collins 1993:267).

Darius had hastily signed an inviolable decree, and the king was the backbone of the laws (Ahlström et al. 1993:842). He deeply regretted it later (6:14 [15]), even becoming odious to himself. It was too late; Daniel had been set up for entrapment. His God would have to deliver him from the hatred of his enemies, from the laws of the Medes and Persians, and from the executioners, the lions.

The execution of the plot to ensnare Daniel is recounted in 6:10-13 [11-14]. Daniel again calmly "handled the situation with wisdom and discretion" (2:14); his focus remained on his God who could deliver him (cf. 3:28). Daniel had the previous lesson of his three friends to encourage and sustain him. Though he prayed alone in his upstairs room, he opened his windows toward Jerusalem (6:10 [11]), which made his worship publicly known. But the text indicates that the accusers of Daniel impinged upon his privacy somehow in order to gather their incriminating evidence. The prohibition of the Medes and Persians evidently encompassed private as well as public worship, but Daniel would not forget Jerusalem, for Jerusalem was the city of his God: "If I forget you, O Jerusalem, let my right hand forget how to play the harp. May my tongue stick to the roof of my mouth if I fail to remember you, if I don't make Jerusalem my greatest joy" (Ps 137:5-6).

The language and grammar of 6:10-11 [11-12] indicate that Daniel carried out his worship as usual. Daniel will reveal in chapter 9 what much of his prayers were concerned with—namely, his God, his city, his law, and the present devastation and confusion of his people in exile. He prayed toward Jerusalem as Solomon had envisaged (1 Kgs 8:41-43). He realized he had passed through the Exile; now he wanted to see his people restored.

It remained only for the enemies of Daniel to present their evidence to Darius. His chief administrator, whom he knew to be faithful to him in all that he did, was now entrapped. He could not escape the "law of the Medes and Persians." His accusers reported what they had seen: Daniel prayed three times a day to his God. Because of the new prohibition, Daniel was disrespecting the king. Both Daniel and the king were ensnared by the "law of the Medes and Persians." The king had to uphold the law (cf. Esth 1:19), and Daniel had to receive its stated punishment. The only hope for both was some miraculous intervention by Daniel's God.

◆ 3. "May your God rescue you!" (6:14-24)

**14Hearing this, the king was deeply trou-
bled, and he tried to think of a way to
save Daniel. He spent the rest of the day
looking for a way to get Daniel out of this
predicament.**

**15In the evening the men went togeth-
er to the king and said, "Your Majesty, you
know that according to the law of the
Medes and the Persians, no law that the
king signs can be changed."**

**16So at last the king gave orders for
Daniel to be arrested and thrown into the
den of lions. The king said to him, "May
your God, whom you serve so faithfully,
rescue you."**

**17A stone was brought and placed over
the mouth of the den. The king sealed the
stone with his own royal seal and the
seals of his nobles, so that no one could
rescue Daniel. 18Then the king returned to
his palace and spent the night fasting. He
refused his usual entertainment and
couldn't sleep at all that night.**

**19Very early the next morning, the king
got up and hurried out to the lions' den.
20When he got there, he called out in an-
guish, "Daniel, servant of the living God!
Was your God, whom you serve so faith-
fully, able to rescue you from the lions?"**

**21Daniel answered, "Long live the king!
22My God sent his angel to shut the lions'
mouths so that they would not hurt me,
for I have been found innocent in his
sight. And I have not wronged you, Your
Majesty."**

**23The king was overjoyed and ordered
that Daniel be lifted from the den. Not a
scratch was found on him, for he had
trusted in his God.**

**24Then the king gave orders to arrest
the men who had maliciously accused
Daniel. He had them thrown into the
lions' den, along with their wives and
children. The lions leaped on them and
tore them apart before they even hit the
floor of the den.**

NOTES

6:14 [15] ***deeply troubled.*** This renders *saggi' be'esh* [TH10678/10091, S7690/888], "very displeased" with himself.

save. Words for "save" (*shezib* [TA/ZA10706, S7804], 5 times) and "deliver" (*netsal* [TA/ZA10489, S5338], 2 times) are found 7 times in 6:14, 16, 20, 27 [15, 17, 21, 28]. The Hebrew cognate for "deliver" (*natsal* [TH5337, ZH5911]) was important particularly in describing God's deliverance of his people from Egypt (Exod 3:8; 5:23; 6:6; 18:4, 8-10).

6:15 [16] ***signs.*** Lit., "establishes."

6:16 [17] ***May your God . . . rescue you.*** Goldingay (1989:121) suggests "he must deliver you." A jussive seems possible here, but we have so little biblical Aramaic to draw on that it is difficult to be completely certain (cf. Hartman and Di Lella 1978:195).

serve so faithfully. Or, "worship continually," the participle of *pelakh* [TA/ZA10586, S6399] (to worship), thereby stressing Daniel's continued faithful worship of his God.

6:17 [18] ***so that no one could rescue Daniel.*** The idea in Aramaic is that nothing could change the king's decree concerning Daniel.

6:18 [19] ***fasting.*** The king was not fasting for religious purposes, but because of his troubled mind and spirit. The Aramaic word is *tewath* [TA/ZA10297, S2908], which is not etymologically related to the Hebrew word for religious fasting (*tsom* [TH6685, ZH7427]). Cf. Holladay 1988:406.

6:19 [20] ***Very early.*** Lit., "He arose at dawn."

6:21 [22] ***Long live the king!*** In addition to being proper court etiquette (cf. 6:6 [7]), Daniel's response plays off of the king's use of "living God" (*'elaha' khayya'* [TA/ZA10033/10261, S426/2417], cf. 6:20 [21]), with "[Long] live (*kheyi* [TA/ZA10262, S2418]) the king."

6:23 [24] ***lifted from the den.*** This indicates that he had been in some sort of pit, the literal meaning of the word rendered "den."

6:24 [25] ***who had maliciously accused Daniel.*** This renders the figurative Aramaic idiom, "who had devoured his bones."

COMMENTARY

This section (6:14-24 [15-25]) records God's granting of Darius's wish that Daniel's God rescue him. Two different words that can mean "save, rescue, deliver" are used a total of seven times in this section (see note on 6:14 [15]). (The NLT uses "get Daniel out of this predicament" once in 6:14 to translate one of these words; see 6:14 [twice], 16, 20, 27 [three times].) The same words are used in chapter 3 to describe the rescue of the three Hebrew young men from the fire. In both cases, the New Testament stresses the act of faith and trust as the moral functional element that led to their deliverance (Heb 11:33-34).

The king literally "became odious" to himself for what he had allowed to happen (6:14 [15]), but he was entrapped; he could not change the laws of the Medes and Persians. This point has historical value, for Nebuchadnezzar, during his reign, could have acted on his own (2:6; 3:1-6, 15; 4:30-31 [27-28]). It is a historical fact that Darius the Mede could not do so, just as Xerxes could not do so in Esther's day (Esth 1:19). Evidently, Daniel's enemies were worried, because for a third time they thronged the king to reinforce the inviolability of the prohibition the king had signed (6:15 [16]).

Darius's attitude toward Daniel is noteworthy; for it highlights even more the stature and respect of Daniel before this great king. This situation also shows the failure of governmental rule through law because it shows that a righteous person can be falsely accused, no matter how blameless they are. Daniel, by a senseless technical point of law, was condemned as guilty—but not before God. The king was bound by his own decree (6:9, 15 [10, 16]). There was no hope left for a rescue operation other than through Daniel's God. Darius the Mede and Cyrus (if the two were different men; see Introduction, "Historical Accuracy") were both tolerant of other religions in their day; they showed great respect toward the Jews and their God, as well as toward the gods of other nations. In a formal procedure, a stone placed on the opening of the den crushed all hope for Daniel (cf. 2:34, 45). To this natural seal the king added the official seal of his rulership and those of his high-ranking officers. They could not open his seal and he could not open theirs without either party knowing about it.

While Nebuchadnezzar had lost sleep over the dreams he had, Darius could not sleep because he knew that he had been forced into condemning an innocent man. His refusal to eat and carry on as usual witnesses to the magnanimity of his heart and conscience. That he rose at dawn indicates that there had been a time limit set on Daniel's peril. If the lions had not devoured him by now, then he was considered innocent and free. At the appearance of the fiery sun (since fire was holy to the Persians), the period of jeopardy was over.

Darius's use of the phrase "servant of the living God" (6:20 [21]) recalls Daniel's description of the dead, senseless gods that Belshazzar had chosen to serve (5:23). Daniel had no doubt made the point often that he served a living God. Jeremiah used this phrase concerning God (Jer 10:10; 23:36), and Daniel knew Jeremiah's writings well. Daniel had probably informed Darius the Mede of his living God. Now, Darius knew that Daniel's God was the God who "rescues and saves" his people (6:27 [28]). God's rescue of Daniel moved him to poetry, wherein he addressed the nations about Daniel's God.

Daniel's answer to Darius was superb. Jeremiah (the prophet whose writings Daniel studied diligently) had been delivered from a cistern, a pit (Jer 38:6-12). Daniel was delivered from a pit of lions (6:19-23), but God had shut the lions' mouths—"so that" they did not harm him. Daniel's words, "Long live the king," were not mere court etiquette; he meant it (cf. 6:6 [7]). And the king did live on (see Introduction, "Historical Accuracy"). Daniel furthermore noted that he was innocent in God's sight (6:22 [23]).

Verses 23-24 [24-25] record the king's joy as he rescued Daniel—that is, he let him out of the den. (God granted Darius a small part in the rescue.) At the same time, these verses record the king's anger as he vented his wrath against his enemies, who had made a fool of him and sought to kill Daniel. Vengeance by ancient Persian kings could be unspeakably horrible and inhumane; sons or whole families could be executed with a guilty person who threatened the king or his royal line in any way. Astyages, king of the Medes (594–559 BC), sought to have the son of his own daughter clandestinely killed so that he could not supplant him in the kingdom (Herodotus *Histories* 1.108-120). Perhaps similarly, Joshua 7:25 records the execution of Achan's entire family along with him because Achan had betrayed the covenant and his God. Darius the Mede had to rid his court of the conspirators whom he could no longer trust and who might seek to overthrow him. As these men and their wives and children were thrown into the lions' pit, the lions leaped up to devour them before they reached the ground. The lions in this case devoured the guilty. But in the New Jerusalem, on the new earth, God's children will be at peace with the wild beasts (see Isa 11:1-9). The Branch, the stump of Jesse's line, "will not judge by appearance nor make a decision based on hearsay."

Daniel's standing was enhanced before this pagan king and his court. A Jew, awaiting the restoration of his people and his city, was poised to be placed "over the entire empire" (6:3 [4]), for he was a man of impeccable integrity, approved of and rescued by his God. Moreover, he was greatly loved by God (9:23; 10:11, 19). The same cannot be said for Daniel's enemies.

◆ 4. Darius's praise of God for Daniel's rescue (6:25-28)

25 Then King Darius sent this message to the people of every race and nation and language throughout the world:

"Peace and prosperity to you!
26 "I decree that everyone throughout my kingdom should tremble with fear before the God of Daniel.

For he is the living God,
and he will endure forever.
His kingdom will never be destroyed,
and his rule will never end.
27 He rescues and saves his people;
he performs miraculous signs
and wonders
in the heavens and on earth.
He has rescued Daniel
from the power of the lions."

28 So Daniel prospered during the reign of Darius and the reign of Cyrus the Persian.*

6:28 Or *of Darius, that is, the reign of Cyrus the Persian.*

NOTES

6:25 [26] ***race.*** This is more often translated as "peoples."

Peace and prosperity. The Aramaic verb indicates a "great abundance" of these things.

6:26 [27] ***living God.*** See note on 6:21 [22].

he will endure forever. He will continue without end, while all merely earthly kingdoms will disappear.

6:27 [28] ***rescues . . . saves . . . performs.*** Three active participles (*shezib* [TA/ZA10706, S7804], *netsal* [TA/ZA10489, S5338], and *'abad* [TA/ZA10522, S5648]) used here show God's continuing activity on behalf of his people (cf. 2:21, 22; 3:15, 28; 4:35 [32]; 5:25-28), saving, delivering, working wonders—just as he did at the exodus from Egypt (Exod 14–15). The author moved from the general to the specific—Daniel was a specific example of God's deliverance, a representative of God's people.

6:28 [29] ***the reign of Darius and the reign of Cyrus the Persian.*** Cf. NLT mg: "[the reign] of Darius, that is, the reign of Cyrus the Persian." The NLT mg expresses correctly the Waw explicative; that is, a Waw used to introduce a clarifying phrase (see note on 4:13 [10]; cf. Lucas 2002:145; Baker 1980:129-136). On the identification of Darius the Mede with Cyrus, see Introduction, "Historical Accuracy."

COMMENTARY

Darius's message would have made an impact upon the people of his day. The Persian Empire, even at this early stage, was well organized, having subjects from most of the nations of the known world. Persepolis, one of the capitals of the later kings Darius I (522–486 BC) and Xerxes (486–465 BC), included the famous "Gate of all Nations" on which some 23 or more "nations" or peoples within the Persian Empire were listed. Even in the days of Darius the Mede, the huge dimensions of the budding empire were evident, being dominated by two peoples, the Medes and Persians.

God had not left himself without a witness (Acts 17:27-28; Rom 1:18-23). His historical, natural revelation and acts of salvation throughout history have revealed him to all the nations of the earth. In Daniel he trumpeted himself before the nations using the mouths and pens of pagan kings. Darius went beyond Nebuchadnezzar's decree (3:29-30) by instructing the people to fear and tremble before Daniel's God, rather than merely to refrain from "speak[ing] a word against" the God of the three young Hebrew men (3:29).

Two things are emphasized by Darius in his announcement: (1) the living God and his kingdom will go on forever (2:44; 4:3 [3:33], 34 [31]; Ps 99:1-3); (2) the living God delivers his people and keeps on delivering them. Daniel is the particular example. So as to lift up Daniel and put down the memory of his enemies, Darius noted that Daniel's God delivers, not just from political enemies, but from the king of the animal kingdom as well. Throughout this book, we see the God of Daniel rescuing his people: (1) from having to eat the king's food and drink his wine (ch 1), (2) from the decree of death at the hand of Nebuchadnezzar (ch 1), (3) from Nebuchadnezzar's furnace of blazing fire (ch 3), (4) from the possible displeasure of Nebuchadnezzar when Daniel delivered a prophetic word of warning to him (ch 4), (5) from the danger of death before Belshazzar and the overthrow of the Babylonian Empire (ch 5), and (6) from enemies and lions (ch 6). Soon, the people of God would be delivered from their Babylonian captivity. The greatest deliverance for all God's people, however, is yet to come—deliverance from death through resurrection (12:1-4, 13).

With his enemies removed, Daniel prospered into the third year of Cyrus the Persian (10:1) and continued to receive revelations from his God and visits from heavenly beings.

◆ III. Visions and Interpretations for the Present and Future: Daniel's Faithfulness and Wisdom Demonstrated on Behalf of His People, Israel (7:1–12:7)

A. Daniel's Divine Wisdom concerning Israel and the Nations in World History: The Establishment of God's Kingdom (7:1-28)

1. Daniel's vision of the four beasts (7:1-14)

Earlier, during the first year of King Belshazzar's reign in Babylon,* Daniel had a dream and saw visions as he lay in his bed. He wrote down the dream, and this is what he saw.

2In my vision that night, I, Daniel, saw a great storm churning the surface of a great sea, with strong winds blowing from every direction. 3Then four huge beasts came up out of the water, each different from the others.

4The first beast was like a lion with eagles' wings. As I watched, its wings were pulled off, and it was left standing with its two hind feet on the ground, like a human being. And it was given a human mind.

5Then I saw a second beast, and it looked like a bear. It was rearing up on one side, and it had three ribs in its mouth between its teeth. And I heard a voice saying to it, "Get up! Devour the flesh of many people!"

6 Then the third of these strange beasts
appeared, and it looked like a leopard. It
had four bird's wings on its back, and it
had four heads. Great authority was given
to this beast.
7 Then in my vision that night, I saw a
fourth beast—terrifying, dreadful, and
very strong. It devoured and crushed its
victims with huge iron teeth and trampled
their remains beneath its feet. It was dif-
ferent from any of the other beasts, and
it had ten horns.
8 As I was looking at the horns, sud-
denly another small horn appeared among
them. Three of the first horns were torn
out by the roots to make room for it. This
little horn had eyes like human eyes and
a mouth that was boasting arrogantly.

9 I watched as thrones were put in place
  and the Ancient One* sat down
    to judge.
His clothing was as white as snow,
  his hair like purest wool.
He sat on a fiery throne
  with wheels of blazing fire,
10 and a river of fire was pouring out,
  flowing from his presence.
Millions of angels ministered to him;
  many millions stood to attend him.
Then the court began its session,
  and the books were opened.

11 I continued to watch because I could
hear the little horn's boastful speech. I
kept watching until the fourth beast was
killed and its body was destroyed by fire.
12 The other three beasts had their author-
ity taken from them, but they were al-
lowed to live a while longer.*
13 As my vision continued that night, I
saw someone like a son of man* coming
with the clouds of heaven. He approached
the Ancient One and was led into his
presence. 14 He was given authority, honor,
and sovereignty over all the nations of the
world, so that people of every race and
nation and language would obey him. His
rule is eternal—it will never end. His king-
dom will never be destroyed.

7:1 The first year of Belshazzar's reign (who was co-regent with his father, Nabonidus) was 556 B.C. (or perhaps as late as 553 B.C.). 7:9 Aramaic *an Ancient of Days;* also in 7:13, 22. 7:12 Aramaic *for a season and a time.* 7:13 Or *like a Son of Man.*

NOTES

7:1 ***Earlier.*** This word is not in the MT; it is supplied by the translators to make the reader aware of the fact that this vision took place before the events of chs 5 and 6. For a demonstration of the structural and thematic unity of this magnificent chapter, see Ferch 1979:136-145.

the first year of King Belshazzar's reign. This was somewhere between 553–551, probably 552–551. Although G. Hasel (1976:153-168) argues for a date of 550–549 BC in 7:1 and 548–547 in 8:1, his argument is not cogent. The events recorded in chs 1–4 were part of Daniel's past experience by the time this vision occurred, but the events of chs 5–6 had not yet happened. This chapter goes back several years and starts a new chronological sequence—chapters 7–12 proceed chronologically. The repeated and more developed themes of the dreams and visions of chs 7–12 drive the literary and narrative arrangement of the book (see "Literary Style" and "Literary Unity" in the Introduction).

this is what he saw. This renders a difficult phrase in Aramaic *re'sh millin 'amar* [TA/ZA10646/10418/10042, S7217/4406/560]. It could be translated, "the sum of the matter [words] he reported," or "he reported (*'amar*) the beginning (*re'sh*) of the matter (*millin*)." Appropriately, 7:28 records "the end (*sopa'* [TA/ZA10509, S5491]) of the matter."

7:2 ***a great sea.*** Lit., "*the* Great Sea," the standard designation in the Bible for the Mediterranean Sea, which gave rise to the many nations surrounding it (e.g., Ezek 47:10, 15, 19, 20). Later it was called the "Roman Lake." A number of scholars see here an allusion to the primordial ocean of chaos (Gen 1:2; 7:11; Isa 51:10; Amos 7:4; cf. Seow 2003:97, 101).

strong winds blowing from every direction. The Aramaic reads "the four winds of heaven." This phrase occurs also in 8:8; Zech 2:6 (cf. Jer 49:36; Ezek 37:9, which contain the phrase "the four winds"). This imagery is connected to Babylonian culture, and the references in Daniel, Ezekiel, and Zechariah can be connected to Babylon. The expression "the four winds" is found in the *Enuma Elish* creation epic (COS 1.111, line 42), where the winds were to capture or contain Tiamat (the primordial Babylonian sea-goddess representing chaos). That epic is datable to the Old Babylonian period. The same phrase is also found in an Egyptian coffin text describing the "creator of the four winds" (COS 1.17:26). Lucas has shown that the overall ambience of the imagery in this chapter is best considered as arising from the imagery of the OT, although a polemical note is sounded here, for Daniel's God overcomes, controls, and destroys the beasts produced by the great sea (Tiamat?) and the winds that created them (cf. Lucas 1990:164-183). Lucas concludes that the implication for the origin of ch 7 is that the images likely arose from a Jew in the eastern dispersion of Mesopotamia (see COS 2.122A:309), rather than in the Hellenistic culture of Palestine. Whatever extrabiblical sources may have been drawn on were made to serve the purposes of the author (cf. Collins 1989:20; Walton 2001:69-89 gives more potential ancient parallels for ch 7). The Mischwesen (composite beings in art and architecture and misshapen births depicted in the Summa Izbu omen texts) present another ancient parallel to the images in ch 7. Through this powerful, culturally relevant imagery of the ancient Near East, God communicated through Daniel, tying his new revelation to the unfolding revelation of the OT (cf. also Lucas 2009:548-549).

7:3 ***four huge beasts.*** See previous note. For a presentation of the view of the ancient Greek writer Hesiod (c. 700 BC) about the four/five ages of the world, see Boardman, Griffin, and Oswyn 1986:96. See further J. W. Swain 1940, who does not accept an early date of Daniel. See also the discussion in Baldwin 1978a:55, 96 (cf. Lucas 2009:534-535; Schlegel and Weinfeld 2006:60-62, lines 110-195).

out of the water. That is, out of the Mediterranean Sea. The Mediterranean basin gave birth to many great ancient civilizations. The sea was also a source of imagery concerning evil in the ancient Near East.

7:4 ***like a human being . . . a human mind.*** These expressions recall the humanlike image in chapter 2 and Nebuchadnezzar's reception of the "mind" of a beast in 4:16 [13]. The close thematic connections between chs 2, 4, 7 are evident in this verse. (For a sampling of the use of lions in Babylonian art and architecture, with pictures, see Oates 1986:150-156.)

7:7 ***It was different.*** The Aramaic lays added stress on the discontinuity between this beast and the preceding ones by use of an adversative Waw [TA/ZA10221, S2050.3] (but, however) before the phrase "it was different." This beast is hardly human or animal—it is partly impersonal, sullen, lifeless metal, even in its teeth, though it does have animal horns.

7:8 ***torn out.*** Lit., "plucked" or "rooted out."

eyes like human eyes. Human eyes are surprising in this strange horn, which arises from and is of the nature of the beast. These eyes are, however, a product of the beast and work in tandem with it.

7:9 ***the Ancient One.*** Lit., "the Ancient of Days" (*'attiq yomin* [TA/ZA10578/10317, S6268/3118]), a circumlocution for God also found in 7:13, 22.

7:10 ***many millions.*** This translates the idiom "myriads of myriads," a numberless amount.

court. This translates *dina'* [TA/ZA10170, S1780] (the judge). Chapter 7 is the center of the book in many ways, and Daniel's name, "God is my judge," certainly finds an echo here. The past judgment that sent the people into the Exile is far surpassed by the judgment portrayed in this chapter. Israel's breaking of her covenant sent her into exile (Deut 28:58-62, 64-68).

the books were opened. In the Babylonian creation story, at an assembly of the gods (cf. 7:9), the destinies of everything are decreed and written on tablets (the Tablets of Destiny; COS 1.111, II.43, 160-163). Some helpful parallels to this scene are found in *1 Enoch* 14:18-23 (Collins 1993:299-301). In Daniel, books are opened before the "Ancient One," surrounded by his holy angels.

7:11 *I could hear.* It is because of the voice of the little horn that Daniel's attention remained focused upon it.

7:12 *while longer.* The Aramaic *zeman we'iddan* [TA/ZA10232/10530, S2166/5732] indicates a set duration of time.

7:13 *like a son of man.* The Aramaic *kebar 'enash* [TA/ZA10120/10050, S1247/606] indicates that Daniel did not see a human being (lit., a "son of man"), but a being "like" a human being. The imagery leaves the identity and function of this being open. The literature concerning this being is voluminous. See especially TDNT 8.400-477 and Carpenter 1978:180-204 for discussions of the Son of Man figure. See also Collins 1993:304-311 and the commentary below.

was led. The word *qereb* [TA/ZA10638, S7127] is used here in the Haphel stem to describe the presentation of a person. Although the form is an active third-person pl., its meaning is passive; its Hebrew cognate (*qarab* [TH7126, ZH7928]) was used to describe the bringing of sacrificial offerings to the holy altar before God (Exod 29:3; Lev 1:2; cf. 1 Sam 10:20).

7:14 *all the nations of the world.* This is added by NLT to clarify the extent of the Ancient One's royal authority.

race and nation and language. These words have been used often before (see 3:4, 7; 4:1 [3:31]; 5:19; 6:25 [26]). Now all people will serve the eternal Kingdom.

would obey. Lit., "serve" or "worship" (*yiplekhun* [TA/ZA10586, S6399]). See Kaiser 1995:201 regarding the messianic implications of 7:13-14.

His rule is eternal. Marduk, king of the Babylonian gods, is similarly given "Lordship [forever] of heaven and earth" in *Enuma Elish* (COS 1.111:401, VI.99-100).

COMMENTARY

This chapter is a literary masterpiece whose meaning is expressed in its skillful composition as well as its majestic but at times ominous content. It has traditionally been divided into two major sections: the vision (7:1-14) and the interpretation (7:15-28). This is a helpful division of the chapter, though it is clear it is encompassed by a prologue (7:1-2a) and an epilogue (7:28). Verses 15-16 serve as a pivot and introduction to the second half. In general, the chiasm in the second half corresponds to the chiasm in the first half and develops it. This is biblical apocalyptic literature at its best, presenting divinely originated messages that speak concomitantly of both heavenly and earthly realities.

The language of this chapter (Aramaic) ties it to the court stories of chapters 2–5, as does its date, which is the first year of Belshazzar (c. 552–551 BC). Thus, this vision preceded the events in chapters 5–6, as well as the visions described in chapters 8–12. So this unique chapter is securely anchored to what precedes and what follows in various ways: Its close parallel to chapter 2 has been noted often (see especially 2:36-45), ever since the time of the church fathers (e.g., Hippolytus and

Eusebius; see commentary on ch 2 and Introduction, "Literary Style" and "Literary Unity"). The Son of Man figure in this chapter (vv. 13-14) and the rock in chapter 2 are often considered parallels (Jerome, as cited in Archer 1958:80; Tertullian, as cited in Evans 2001:509). It demonstrates God's gift to Daniel to interpret visions and dreams (1:17). This chapter provides the first glimpse of the "little horn," and a similar horn is adumbrated in following chapters.

This chapter develops the thought of the Kingdom of God (chs 2, 4) and foreshadows chapters 8–12. It became a key chapter for the writers of the New Testament.

A brief sketch of the chapter may be helpful:

- Prologue (7:1-2a)
- Vision (7:2b-14, direct speech)
  - Four Beasts, Little Horn, and the Ancient One arise (7:2b-10)
  - Little Horn, Fourth Beast, and other nations judged (7:11-12)
  - A being "like a son of man" appears (7:13-14)
- Introduction to interpretation (7:15-16)
- Interpretation of vision (7:17-27)
  - A divine being gives an overall interpretation (7:17-18)
  - Daniel seeks specific detail about the Fourth Beast, Little Horn, the Ancient One, and the Holy People (7:19-22)
  - A divine being gives details on the Fourth Beast, Little Horn, the Ancient One, and the Holy People (7:23-27)
- Epilogue (7:28)

From this sketch of the chapter, it is clear that both the heavenly interpreter (7:18, 22, 27) and Daniel (since Daniel accepts the application of the "one like a son of man" vision to the saints—7:18, 27) understand the "one like a son of man" to embody the "people of God" as well as being a separate personage. If Daniel had not accepted this understanding of the figure of 7:13-14, he certainly would have asked for further specificity about the one like a son of man; however, he did not do so.

The first overview of what Daniel saw is given in 7:2b-10. There is no reference to "the holy people," who are mentioned six times in the rest of the chapter (7:18, 21, 22 [twice], 25, 27). They are noted for the first time in the summary interpretation (7:17-18).

The march of history depicted by these four kingdoms emphasizes God's sovereignty over human kingdoms. Again, Daniel shows history moving toward a final goal. After these "beastly" kingdoms of the fallen nations of this age, a figure "like a son of man" appears and is approved by the Ancient One (7:13-14). Subsequently, the saints or holy people of the Most High are given the Kingdom that lasts forever (7:14, 21-22, 25-27). Thus ends history as we know it. And, in a real sense, history finds its ultimate fulfillment, according to the judgments rendered by the Ancient One, the Most High.

The ancient Near East had seen the rise and fall of kingdoms, but it was not clear what the end or goal of history was, or if there even was a goal or purpose to history. Both Daniel 2 and 7 answer this question. The earlier Greek writer, Hesiod

(c. 700 BC), had depicted history as four basic ages: the Golden Age (paradise), the Silver and Bronze ages, and finally, the corrupt and degenerate Iron Age of his own day. In both chapters 2 and 7 iron is part of the imagery of the fourth kingdoms. Like a good Greek, however, Hesiod placed a Greek heroic age into his scheme between the Bronze and Iron ages, spoiling its logical pattern of decline and giving five, rather than four, ages of human history. Hesiod offers no goal for history—no fifth (or sixth) crowning age as a regenerative rebirth of history. Hesiod could only look backward with nostalgia to better times. Daniel was shown a *future fifth* kingdom that would be the best kingdom, a kingdom he could long for much as Hesiod longed for the Heroic Age of Greek history (*Works and Days,* lines 154-173). Hesiod could never enter into the age he longed for, but Daniel would one day enter into the fifth kingdom he saw and live there with the "holy saints" (7:18, 27; cf. 12:13). There he would dwell with the heroes of faith who trusted their God (Heb 11:39). In the dream of chapter 2, the conclusion of history was reached in this fifth, eternal kingdom. In the scheme of chapter 2, Daniel himself was living in the tottering golden age of the statue in Nebuchadnezzar's dream. Hesiod, on the other hand, found himself trapped in the iron age of disintegration, with the heroic age of the Greek heroes and the golden age of antiquity gone.

The symbolism in chapter 7 recalls the lions of chapter 6, the head of gold in chapter 2, and the illness of Nebuchadnezzar in chapter 4. The lion was a prominent part of the decorative art and architecture of Babylonian walls, gates, palaces, and monuments. The most famous landmark of Babylon was a huge statue of a lion trampling a man. Nebuchadnezzar's throne room featured a facade with lions on it. The famous processional way had walls decorated with 120 lions in relief. Lions were connected with the goddess Ishtar. Nebuchadnezzar was described as a lion and an eagle when he attacked Edom (Jer 49:19, 22). Daniel remained unharmed not only in the den of lions, but also in the den of the Babylonian exile. The eagles' wings (7:4) recall that Nebuchadnezzar's hair had grown as eagles' feathers (4:33 [30]). But the animal features of the lion and beast give way to human features in this symbolism: The beast becomes a human, standing on two legs and two feet with a heart changed from the heart of an animal to the heart or mind of a human being (7:4). Similarly, the head of gold in chapter 2 implies a mind and stands atop a human figure. Daniel had told Nebuchadnezzar, "You are the head of gold" (2:38). Nebuchadnezzar's "conversion" after his illness changed him into a human being with a human mind and heart once again (4:34 [31]). This kingdom was dominated by King Nebuchadnezzar, and the metamorphosis of this kingdom, represented in chapter 2 by the head of gold, is shown in the shedding of his animal characteristics to become humanlike. This picture keeps intact the basically positive portrait of Nebuchadnezzar that is presented in chapters 1–4, as he gradually becomes more humane, even recognizing Daniel's God and shedding his pride for humility (4:34-35 [31-32]). While the beast's loss of wings represents the demise of the political and military power of this kingdom, this also represents the humbling of Babylon's greatest king (4:37 [34]). This symbolism indicates that a king can represent a kingdom. One is, in fact, unthinkable without the other. It is impossible to imagine Babylon without thinking of its most important king.

The second beast, which resembled a bear, is clearly characterized in direct speech, following the sovereign God's command, as voraciously hungry (cf. 2 Kgs 2:24; Hos 13:8; Amos 5:19). That it devoured many peoples signifies that this bearlike animal is most likely a representation of the Persian Empire, for it did encompass more peoples, languages, and territories than any before it—even the coming Roman Empire would not match it in this respect. The author of Daniel understood the kingdom that followed Babylon, the head of gold (2:38), to be the Medes and Persians (2:34-40; 6:8, 12, 15 [9, 13, 16]; 8:20). The fact that the bear is raised on one side points to the dominance of Persia over Media; at the same time, it indicates the intricate relationship between these two ancient peoples. Cyrus, who was of both Median and Persian blood (Herodotus *Histories* 1.107-108; Lucas 2009:556), the head of this nation, was summoned by God to do his bidding (Isa 44:28; 45:1, 13; 46:11). The fact that the author recorded a divine command to this beast (7:5; "Get up! Devour the flesh of many people!") corresponds to the stress the prophets laid upon the Lord's declaration that this kingdom would conquer many nations (e.g., Isa 41:2-3). Again, the kingdom and its representative king cannot be separated. Through this king, the kingdom is realized. Not only this beast but each beast operates only according to the divine directives and permissions of the sovereign God.

This empire overtook so many nations that one of its kings, Darius the Great (522–486 BC), set up the famous "Gate of All Nations" to enumerate the host of peoples and nations that were incorporated within the boundaries of Persia. Isaiah 41:2-3 foretells that God would enable Cyrus to conquer "many nations and . . . kings." Proverbs 28:15 describes the furious charge or attack of a bear to destroy its prey. The three ribs in the bear's mouth most likely represent the kingdoms of Babylon, Media, and Lydia, all conquered swiftly by Cyrus. If these three kingdoms are not intended, perhaps the three should be Media, Lydia, and the countries east of Cyrus's empire (since he conquered these before he sacked Babylon). Chapters 6, 9, and 10 also record that in all of this conquering of the nations by Darius the Mede (i.e., Cyrus; see Introduction, "Historical Accuracy") and his successors, God witnessed powerfully to these kings and to his servant Daniel (1:21; 5:31 [6:1]; 6:1 [2]; 9:1; 10:1). God did not merely watch the historical, political, and military process; he was in the process, creating and governing it.

The third beast (7:6) possessed speed, as indicated by its wings and leopardlike appearance. Habakkuk used the leopard as a symbol of speed and swiftness (Hab 1:8, NLT mg). The wings on its back emphasize its great speed and mobility. This type of imagery indicates the nature of the kings and armies involved; Alexander was still planning further conquests and organizing an empire just before he died; he had forced his army on endless marches eastward. He had desired a positive oracle for his Persian crusade and had forced one out of the Pythia (high priestess) at Delphi. She proclaimed that he was "invincible," and he used this word as one of his regular titles for himself (Green 2007:7, 14). Speedy army marches were the pride of ancient kings and generals. The Assyrian King Sargon II (722–705 BC) had bragged about how he made all of the contingents of his military move with great speed over the land (ANET 286). V. Hanson says of Alexander's army, "No army before or after was so finely organized and so independent of lengthy support trains and camp followers. Yet to support Alexander's army for a single day—infantry, cavalry, support troops, baggage and pack animals—over 250 tons of grain and forage alone were required, and over 70,000 gallons of water" (1999:177). The number four is significant in the identification of this beast; chapter 8 helps to narrow down the possibilities (8:5, 21). Based on history and the symbolic fourfold features of this beast, it appears to represent the Greek kingdom under its first and most famous king, Alexander the Great, and his four successors (he is mentioned more clearly in 11:3).

In a brief life span of 33 years, Alexander traveled and conquered the world from Macedonia to the Indus River in India and back to Babylon, where he died. He left no capable offspring to inherit his throne; thus, his relatives, officials, generals, and others all vied for position, eventually engaging in the "wars of the *diadochi* (successors)" (V. Hanson 1999:323-381). By 305 BC, and after numerous political and military intrigues and battles, four divisions of Alexander's kingdom emerged, each with its own "head": Cassander in the west, Lysimachus in the east, Seleucus in the north, and Ptolemy in the south (cf. Green 2007:34-38; V. Hanson 1999:323-381; Lucas 2009:557; Shipley 2000:33-59). The imagery regarding this kingdom will be more fully developed in chapters 8 and 11 (see commentary there).

The fourth beast (7:7, 11) was not only a different beast from each of the others, but it had characteristics that put it in a different category of being from the other three. It was different in kind, not just degree. This aspect of the beast recalls the legs, thighs, and toes consisting of iron and clay in the statue of chapter 2. That part of the statue, composed of two elements, set it off from the other parts, each of which was made of only one metal. The iron teeth of this beast relate it to the iron symbolism of the fourth kingdom in chapter 2. Iron was known for its strength and power; it was used for weapons and especially chariot wheels (King and Stager 2001:167-176). It is not difficult to understand this beast as symbolizing violence and sinister forces of evil.

The significance of the 10 horns will be revealed later in the chapter (7:24). There is dissension and fighting among the elements of this beast, thereby recalling the inability of the iron and clay to mix (as in the image of ch 2). An infamous little horn causes strife. The horn is characterized as having eyes "like human eyes" and as boasting greatly, using a human mouth—something Nebuchadnezzar had learned not to do (4:30-31 [27-28]). The great classicist J. B. Bury spoke of history coming under the "pernicious influence of rhetoric," and that could be said of politics in both Greece and Rome (2006:97; see Lewis 2003:479-516 to read Cicero's second Philippic, in which he assassinates Mark Antony with words). To what extent is this figure "animal" and to what extent "human"? It is powered by the superhuman forces as well (10:13, 20-21; cf. Rev 13:1-2).

Verses 9-10 clearly portray the Most High under the imagery of the Ancient One. God is portrayed as a human to a degree not encountered yet in the Old Testament (Niehaus 1995:322-325). Into the midst of this seemingly godless march of history, the Judge, the Most High, enters. He is ultimately the judge and executor. This vision is one of several throne visions in the Old Testament (1 Kgs 22:19; Isa 6; Ezek 1:3, 22-24; 10:1). God will serve as judge just as he served as creator. The white clothes (not black) of the judge represent purity, while his wool-like hair emphasizes his antiquity. His throne recalls that in Ezekiel's visions (Ezek 1:15-28; 10:1, 15-18). The river of fire indicates the purifying fire of God. The scene is of the great heavenly courtroom, a scene that is repeated in Revelation 1. The books are not legal textbooks, but books of truth recording every word and deed of each person (10:21; 12:1; Exod 32:32; Pss 69:28; 139:16; Eccl 12:14; Phil 4:3; Rev 20:12, 15; 21:27).

Amazingly, amid all these sights, it was the boasting of the little horn that arose from the beast that caught Daniel's attention. The fourth beast actually becomes, in the end, the kingdom that generates the little horn but is totally under its dominance (7:11-12). Surprisingly, the execution of the fourth beast is recorded first—by fire, no doubt drawn from the river of fire from the Ancient One's throne. When it dies, the little horn dies as well. Again, unexpectedly, the other beasts are permitted to live longer, but with no authority. They will bow and serve another king in a fifth kingdom to come (7:27). The visible monstrous empire is cut off with an amazing finality (7:26).

The identity of the fourth beast is puzzling. Traditionally, it has been identified with the Roman Empire, less often with the Greek Empire. Ancient historians emphasized the ways that the Roman Empire surpassed all other kingdoms in dominion, splendor of achievements, length of reign, and brutality (Ward-Perkins 2006:176). The successful Greek army with its phalanxes and its strategies was effective in its day, but when the disciplined and highly equipped Roman legions appeared, all enemies succumbed to them (Rodgers 2008:128-178). Rome ruled every country in the civilized world; on land and sea, Rome was supreme. Even though the Romans conquered the other kingdoms, especially Greece, the Greeks reciprocated by conquering the Romans culturally and philosophically—even religiously, to a great extent, a process that was aided by the Romans' avid accommodation to the influential Greeks in the time of Augustus (Bowersock 1965:1-149, especially 140-149). The Roman Empire arose farther west than the other empires, making it significantly "different."[1] Greece has been shown to have had significant contact with the eastern kingdoms (especially Egypt), resulting in reciprocal lines of influence. The culture, religion, and philosophy of the Babylonian and Persian Empires similarly infiltrated the Roman Empire, influencing the remaining civilizations even after the "eternal city's" empire was defunct. But this symbolic kingdom suggests further a final kingdom beyond Rome; yet, much like Rome, it comes under the dominance of the last little horn (cf. 8:9-14; 9:25-27; 11:21-45; 12:1-7).

The symbol of the little horn of 7:8 appears at the end of the fourth kingdom—that is, at the end of the apocalyptic eschatological historical process. Although in the book it is presented first, it has forerunners that precede it historically. The little horn of chapter 8, symbolizing Antiochus Epiphanes (175–163 BC), is one such forerunner (see commentary on ch 8; cf. 11:40-45; 12:11-12). Daniel 9:26-27 describes a powerful person of evil who ushers in horrible devastation; he seems to come after Antiochus and yet also serves as a forerunner to the little horn of 7:8. This will be examined in greater detail in the commentary on 11:21-35, 36-45; it should be noted that the figure of 9:26-27 and 11:36-45 is opposed by Michael, the archangel, who ushers in the end (12:1; cf. 10:13) with an unprecedented time of violence that concludes with the resurrection of the dead. So the little horn of 7:8 is foreshadowed in historical circumstances in the person described in 8:9-14 and in 11:21-35 (and possibly in the person described in 9:26-27, but this person seems further to foreshadow an event in the future). There seem to be historical events and persons of the Roman Empire who also foreshadow the little horn of 7:8 but do not exhaust the realities behind its image; these, too, qualify as forerunners of the final appearance of the abominable "little horn" (7:8; see commentary on 7:19-28). The historical empire of Rome was archetypal, pointing to something beyond itself. The Roman poet Virgil has the chief god Jupiter declare regarding Rome, "I set no bounds in space or time; but have given empire without end" (*Aeneid* 1.278-279). Cicero had hoped that the Roman republic would "live forever and our empire to be without end" (quoted in Everitt 2003:98).

The book of Revelation appropriates and develops the imagery concerning the beasts. Indeed, the beast introduced in Revelation 13:1 is a composite of the beasts of Daniel 7 and more, for it asserts that the beast was empowered by the dragon (Rev 12:9; 13:2, 4; 20:10). The beast in Revelation 13 embodies all of the pagan and evil spiritual forces that energized the horrific beasts and arrogant little horn of Daniel 7.

Finally, 7:13-14 records Daniel's vision of a being that looked "like a son of man." Amazingly, this son of man came with the clouds of heaven up to the Ancient One, a scenario indicating the movement of a divine being (see Matt 25:31; Mark 13:26; Luke 21:27; John 12:34; Rev 1:13; 14:14; 2 Esdr 13; *1 Enoch* 37–71 for additional canonical and noncanonical references to this enigmatic figure). The Lord, as king, was often pictured as surrounded by clouds and as one who rides upon the clouds (Pss 68:4; 97:2; Carpenter 2009:428-429). Clouds are the dust of his feet (Nah 1:3). He was in the cloud that guided his people at the Exodus, and he descended upon Sinai in a cloud (Exod 13:21-22; 19:9). Clouds will accompany the second coming of the Son of Man, as stated in the New Testament (Matt 24:30; 26:64; Acts 1:9-11; Rev 1:7), and at that time, God's holy people will be caught up into a cloud with the Lord (1 Thess 4:17). When Daniel's son of man was ushered into the presence of the Ancient One, he was given an eternal kingdom (7:14). Nebuchadnezzar and Darius the Mede had recognized that only the Most High, the living God, had this kind of kingdom and authority (2:44-45, 47; 4:3, 34-35 [3:33; 4:31-32]; 5:21; 6:26-27 [27-28]), and he delegated it to whomsoever he desired. Here the Ancient One, the Most High, passes an eternal kingdom and eternal authority on to one like a son of man, who becomes an eternal king. The fourth beast, the kingdom of the little horn, is gone; the kingdom of this one like a son of man takes the place of the fourth kingdom, while the other kingdoms continue to exist for a while to serve and obey this king.

The two figures, the son of man and the little horn, are diametrical opposites in this scenario; they have kingdoms, one takes a kingdom by force and violence, one is given a kingdom by divine decree from the Ancient of Days (cf. 1 Cor 15:24-28). While the little horn with humanlike eyes and mouth is clearly opposed to God, the one like a son of man is approved by God. This figure seems to be a messiah, an anointed person for the kingship. The way in which he receives his dominion seems to indicate a humble, obedient messianic figure who receives his eternal kingdom without doing violence.

All of this is indeed difficult to grasp. Some further authoritative interpreter is needed—even for Daniel (7:15). Thereupon enters a heavenly being to help him (7:16), assuring Daniel (and us, the readers) that the interpretation is correct and comes from God himself.

ENDNOTE

1. For an ancient description and analysis of the Roman Empire, see Dionysius of Halicarnassus *Roman Antiquities* 1.2-5. Rome was, in his opinion, the greatest empire and military machine the world had ever experienced. Few, if any, would challenge this assessment (Rodgers 2008:1-250; Lewis 2003:1-523).

2. The four beasts are four kingdoms (7:15-18)

15I, Daniel, was troubled by all I had seen, and my visions terrified me. 16So I approached one of those standing beside the throne and asked him what it all meant. He explained it to me like this: 17"These four huge beasts represent four kingdoms that will arise from the earth. 18But in the end, the holy people of the Most High will be given the kingdom, and they will rule forever and ever."

NOTES

7:15 ***I . . . was troubled by all I had seen.*** Lit., "My spirit was troubled . . . in the midst of the sheath" (*nidneh* [TA/ZA10464, S5085]). Hartman and Di Lella (1978:206-207) assert that the concept of the spirit in the sheath of the body is late (cf. the word's use in the Genesis Apocryphon from Qumran, 1QapGen ar 2.10; and its occurrence in 1 Chr 21:27). But this Persian word need not be considered late, as Baldwin has noted (1978a:144-145). The rendering "by all I had seen" follows the LXX attempt to render the idiom as "in these things."

7:16 ***beside the throne.*** This phrase is not in the Aramaic text but seeks to clarify the scene (cf. NIV, RSV).

what it all meant. Lit., the "truth" or "essence" or "certainty" of all this. Daniel, using this same word, described his earlier interpretation of Nebuchadnezzar's dream as being "certain" or "firm" (2:45).

7:17 ***kingdoms.*** Lit., "kings," but kings here stand for kingdoms.

7:18 ***in the end.*** This is not in the Aramaic and may confuse the complicated sequencing of these kingdoms reported in 7:11-12.

the holy people. The phrase *qaddishe 'elyonin* [TA/ZA10620/10548, S6922/5946] (lit., "the holy ones of the Most High") refers to the people of the Most High (used 6 times in this chapter—7:18, 21, 22 [twice], 25, 27). The same word (*qaddish*) [TA/ZA10620, S6922] (holy) refers in ch 4 to "holy ones" = watchers = divine messengers (angels) (4:13, 17, 23 [10, 14, 20]) and in chs 4–5 to the "holy gods" (4:8, 9, 18 [5, 6, 15]; 5:11). Daniel qualifies as a part of the "holy people"; indeed, he is a model for them.

rule. Or, "take over," "possess."

COMMENTARY

As might be expected, based upon the meaning of the dream about a statue in chapter 2 (2:36-43), these beasts represent kingdoms, according to the heavenly interpreter. Here, as in chapter 2, the fluidity of speaking of kings as kingdoms and vice versa is evident (2:37-39). The heavenly interpreter says, literally, "These are four kings" (7:17). That these kingdoms arise from the earth and the Mediterranean Sea basin demonstrates their origins from the power structures of the world, not heaven, although the Most High grants them their authority and sovereignty, as well as setting the parameters for each kingdom (cf. Deut 32:8-9; Dan 4:26, 35 [23, 32]).

Some ancient Akkadian prophetic texts assert that consecutive kingdoms will arise in history (cf. Longman 1991:188; cf. Dan 2:36-38).

Verse 18 introduces "the holy people" (7:21, 22, 25, 27), who clearly correspond to the one "like a son of man" in the last part of Daniel's vision (7:13-14). They will inherit the fifth kingdom seen by Daniel. Just like the figure there, the holy people are given the kingdom and rule forever and ever. As kings could represent their kingdoms and kingdoms could represent kings, the holy people and the one like a man, but coming from heaven (from the clouds—not the sea or the earth) can stand for each other. In the Old Testament, Israel's king was to be humble and one with his people (Deut 17:15, 20). If the king was perfect before God, he would rule for a long time (Deut 17:20). He was not to be arrogant or prideful. In the literary pattern and structural presentation of the dream and its interpretation, the son of man figure and the holy people (saints of the Most High) occupy the same place (7:13-14, 18, 21-22, 27).

Daniel could not think straight, let alone interpret all of this. His reaction of being "troubled," "terrified," and stumped recalls the reactions of the Babylonian kings, Nebuchadnezzar and Belshazzar, to their respective visions (2:1-3; 4:4-5 [1-2]; 5:6). To be God's conduit for his revelation in this case was enervating, for the revelation itself needed an explanation. But Daniel knew that help was available and where to find it. His question asked for the significance and certainty of it all (7:16). He had rendered the same himself concerning Nebuchadnezzar's dream (2:45). The heavenly interpreter obliged him.

◆ 3. Interpretation of the fourth beast, little horn, Ancient One, and holy people (7:19-28)

19Then I wanted to know the true meaning of the fourth beast, the one so different from the others and so terrifying. It had devoured and crushed its victims with iron teeth and bronze claws, trampling their remains beneath its feet. 20I also asked about the ten horns on the fourth beast's head and the little horn that came up afterward and destroyed three of the other horns. This horn had seemed greater than the others, and it had human eyes and a mouth that was boasting arrogantly. 21As I watched, this horn was waging war against God's holy people and was defeating them, 22until the Ancient One—the Most High—came and judged in favor of his holy people. Then the time arrived for the holy people to take over the kingdom.

23Then he said to me, "This fourth beast is the fourth world power that will rule the earth. It will be different from all the others. It will devour the whole world, trampling and crushing everything in its path. 24Its ten horns are ten kings who will rule that empire. Then another king will arise, different from the other ten, who will subdue three of them. 25He will defy the Most High and oppress the holy people of the Most High. He will try to change their sacred festivals and laws, and they will be placed under his control for a time, times, and half a time.

26"But then the court will pass judgment, and all his power will be taken away and completely destroyed. 27Then the sovereignty, power, and greatness of all the kingdoms under heaven will be given to the holy people of the Most High. His kingdom will last forever, and all rulers will serve and obey him."

28That was the end of the vision. I, Daniel, was terrified by my thoughts and my face was pale with fear, but I kept these things to myself.

NOTES

7:19 ***its victims.*** These words, not in the Aramaic, clarify the text.

bronze claws. These were not noted in the earlier description of the vision, but this fills in the picture (cf. 2:32, 41).

7:20 ***human.*** See note on 7:8.

7:21 ***holy people.*** Lit., "holy ones" (*qaddishin* [TA/ZA10620, S6922]; cf. 7:18, 22, 25, 27); the word can also refer to gods (4:8, 9, 18 [5, 6, 15]), and holy watchers = angels (4:13, 17, 23 [10, 14, 20]). The "holy people" in ch 7 are the faithful Israelites, God's people.

7:24 ***will rule.*** The Aramaic indicates that these kings will arise (*qum* [TA/ZA10624, S6966]) from this kingdom.

7:25 ***oppress.*** Lit., "to wear out." The Hebrew cognate of this verb is used to describe the clothes of Israel that did not wear out during the time in the wilderness (Deut 8:4; 29:5; cf. Isa 50:9).

sacred festivals and laws. Lit., "times and law." These are closely connected but not a hendiadys as per Goldingay (1989:143, 146).

time. Aramaic, *'iddan* [TA/ZA10530, S5732] (cf. 2:8, 9, 21; 3:5, 15; 4:16, 23, 25, 32 [13, 20, 22, 29]; 7:12); the word can mean "time" (duration of or specific) or "year," depending upon context. It is used 13 times in Daniel.

7:26 ***completely destroyed.*** This translates two infinitives that indicate the purpose of removing the rebellious king's power—"to utterly bring it to an end."

7:27 ***will be given.*** Possibly render "will have been given" (cf. 11:36; Goldingay 1989:143).

7:28 ***terrified . . . pale with fear.*** Words earlier used to describe Nebuchadnezzar's and Belshazzar's fear and dread are applied to Daniel (see 2:1; 4:5 [2]; especially 5:6 and notes).

I kept these things to myself. That is, he kept them in his heart, even though he wrote them down (7:1). He may have shared his experience with others later, but his written summary was at least the first record of these visions.

COMMENTARY

Daniel requested and received more detailed information about the fourth beast, 10 horns, little horn, and holy people. As such, he received greater understanding of the vision he had, especially concerning the little horn and the holy people (7:20-22). He adds a new detail that the beast had bronze claws (7:19), which emphasizes the power and strength of this empire to destroy its adversaries. He then relates that the object of the arrogant and violent activity of the little horn was primarily the holy people. The horn was overcoming them until the Ancient One arrived and acted on behalf of the holy people. Only then would there be a new world era with the holy people in control (7:22), the fifth kingdom of Daniel's vision and the dream of Nebuchadnezzar (ch 2).

Both Daniel and the interpreter stress the difference of this fourth beast from the others (7:19, 23). The second kingdom had "devoured many people," but this beast trampled the "whole world" or the entire earth. This fourth beast is different from the other three because its 10 horns are 10 kings that will rule the empire. The number 10 is probably to be taken as symbolic for completeness. Then another king will arise, who is the "little horn" (7:20). This enigmatic king is symbolized by an animal's horn (a common symbol for persons, kings, and strength in apocalyptic writing), but it has some humanlike features (mouth, eyes). This king attacks the holy people violently. He certainly is not like Nebuchadnezzar or Cyrus, except as regards Nebuchadnezzar's excessive hubris and pride (4:30, 37 [27, 34]). Nor is he like the other kings who do not focus their efforts against the holy people. He is an enemy to men in general (three kings are overthrown), as well as to God (7:25). This violence among the horns of this beast also makes its presentation different from the other symbolic beings. Haman, who tried to destroy the Jews throughout the Persian Empire, was of his ilk (Esth 3:8-9), as was Pharaoh (Exod 1:22; 14:5-7).

The little horn's ultimate objects of hatred and blasphemy are the Most High (7:25) and the holy people of the Most High (cf. Isa 14:13-17; Ezek 28:2-24). In the third kingdom, Antiochus Epiphanes (8:9-14) prefigured the little horn of 7:8. In the context of the fourth kingdom of Daniel's vision, several Roman emperors have been suggested as having that function: Gaius ("Caligula"; AD 37–41), Claudius (AD 41–54), Nero (AD 54–68), Vespasian (AD 69–79), and Domitian (AD 81–96). Of these, Caligula threatened to set up an image of himself in the Temple at Jerusalem, but he was assassinated by his own soldiers before he could do so. Vespasian came to power (AD 69) in the same year that three emperors (Galba, Otho, and Vitellius) had taken the throne and then been dethroned in their attempts to succeed Nero (cf. 7:8). Vespasian earlier began the siege of Jerusalem, but once made emperor he assigned the demolition of Jerusalem and the Temple to his son Titus (AD 79–81). In this possible scenario, the abomination of desolation would have been the acts of the Romans who destroyed the holy Temple (cf. Luke 21). This scenario is impressive and certainly reflects some fulfillment of Daniel's vision, but these historical occurrences did not exhaust Daniel's vision. Shortly after these events, the book of Revelation paints a scenario that presents an even larger universal climax to the visions of the little horn.

It is noteworthy that the little horn will try to destroy the identifying history of the holy people as preserved in their festivals, feasts, and laws—their religion (7:25). These were times of celebration and remembrance established by God for his people; these celebrations served to further confirm them as God's people. Only God can change times and seasons, as Nebuchadnezzar had declared (2:21). If the worship and sacred history of this people could be removed, they would lose their identity and become like all of the other peoples. They are "different" in a way approved by God, for he established this difference (Exod 8:22; 9:4; 19:5-6; Deut 4:5-8; 26:18-19). Destroying the roots of the holy people could be even more insidious and threatening than any violent attempts to exterminate this holy people (cf. 8:9-14). God, in his sovereign will, gives his people over to this little horn for a period of time, but he remains in control, just as when he allowed Satan to afflict Job, his blameless servant (Job 1:12; 2:6). The period of oppression for the people of the Most High will be limited as will its accomplishments. The expression "time, times, and half a time" indicates an approximate duration of time; it is short, roughly three and one-half years (cf. 7:12; 12:7). Its symbolic function is to designate the set parameters of time during which God's purposes will be worked out.

Verses 26-27 are comforting; they tell us that God will remain in control of this whole flow of world history, for all four kingdoms were granted their authority by him (cf. 7:4-6, 11). Now the power of the Most High and his sovereign will for the consummation of history is stressed. Sometime after the end of the "time, times, and half a time" (7:25), the Ancient One holds court (cf. Rev 20). With the demise of the little horn, the fourth beast is also gone (7:11-12). The kingdom of the little horn, which is the final expression of the fourth beast, passes away. A new kingdom from the Most High, evidently set up on earth, but whose origin and authority is from heaven, takes the place of the fourth beastly kingdom, the kingdom of the little horn. As 7:12 indicates, however, the other nations are allowed to remain, but all kings and authority are subsumed under the kingdom of the holy people and the one like a son of man. This will be no resurrected Nebuchadnezzar with his native Chaldeans forming a unified kingdom, but the kingdom of one who is divine (see note on 3:28), and yet like a son of man (7:13), with a people who share his holiness.

Who rules the kingdom and is served is ambiguous (7:27b), for the original text may be asserting that it is the "one like a son of man," the "holy people," or God Most High, or a combination of all of these possibilities. The inspired, ingenious biblical writer probably had all three possibilities in mind. This kingdom will cling together (cf. 2:42-43), unlike the fourth kingdom, with a leader who has been placed on the throne by the Most High (7:14).

The different nature of the fourth beast and little horn results in their total demise (7:11, 26). That nature and character can only be described, as focused in the little horn, as fiercely hostile toward the Most High and his holy people. This beast's imagery approaches that of a dragon, a symbol of rage and rebellion against God in the Old and New Testaments alike. The explicit violence against the saints recalls the ancient goal of the serpent in the garden to destroy God's people (Gen 3:15; Rev 12:9; 20:2), and his work through Pharaoh (Exod 1–15) to cut them off. The fourth kingdom is one that God removes (cf. Rev 20:2-3, 7-9) and burns by fire (7:11; cf. Rev. 13:5-6; 19:20; 20:10). This kind of opposition to the saints of the Kingdom of God will not be allowed to remain. The three other empires, however, are permitted in some fashion to live on, but in subservience to the one like a son of man and the holy people. Three is a number of symbolic significance, representing completeness (ABD 4.1145), and these three nations represent all of the other nations of the world. For all other known nations, except the fourth empire, were in essence historically encompassed in these three kingdoms (chs 4–8), and their paramount purpose was not to oppose Israel's God or the saints of the Most High, as displayed in the little horn of the fourth beast.

Interestingly, Rome, the greatest political, historical, military empire of antiquity, fell in AD 476 (see Ward-Perkins 2006 for a cogent argument and demonstration that Rome did in fact "fall" in about AD 476). By then Christianity had been recognized as the official religion, and within the time of that empire, a Kingdom of God had been born. A King reigning from heaven was receiving allegiance; within the borders of this empire, pagan institutions and evil forces had begun to be destroyed in a deep spiritual sense (even the oracle of Delphi was dismantled in AD 395; cf. comments in Broad 2006:70-71). Even Julian the Apostate (AD 361–363) could not reverse the process. Various people groups lived within the skeleton of the Roman Empire and had begun to hear about a new Kingdom and a new potential for life. But Rome fell, and it remains a symbol that is recalled when nations fall or begin to crumble today. Similarly, but in a positive mode, its former glory remains a symbol for rising nations. Could a new Rome take shape that would embody the imagery of Daniel in the ways depicted in Revelation (e.g., Rev 12, 13, 18, 20)?

Daniel's encounter with the revelation from the Most High recorded in chapter 7 understandably terrified him and sapped his strength. In the presence of divinity, humans can only tremble in both praise and fear (10:8, 15; Exod 34:8).

◆ B. The Israelite Nation Divinely Delivered from a Furious King (8:1-27)

1. Daniel's vision of the ram, he-goat, and small horn (8:1-14)

**1*During the third year of King Belshaz-
zar's reign, I, Daniel, saw another vision,
following the one that had already ap-
peared to me. 2In this vision I was at the
fortress of Susa, in the province of Elam,
standing beside the Ulai River.***

**3As I looked up, I saw a ram with two
long horns standing beside the river.*
One of the horns was longer than the
other, even though it had grown later
than the other one. 4The ram butted
everything out of his way to the west, to
the north, and to the south, and no one
could stand against him or help his vic-
tims. He did as he pleased and became
very great.**

**5While I was watching, suddenly a male
goat appeared from the west, crossing
the land so swiftly that he didn't even
touch the ground. This goat, which had
one very large horn between its eyes,
6headed toward the two-horned ram that
I had seen standing beside the river, rush-
ing at him in a rage. 7The goat charged
furiously at the ram and struck him,
breaking off both his horns. Now the ram
was helpless, and the goat knocked him
down and trampled him. No one could
rescue the ram from the goat's power.**

**8The goat became very powerful. But at
the height of his power, his large horn
was broken off. In the large horn's place
grew four prominent horns pointing in
the four directions of the earth. 9Then
from one of the prominent horns came a
small horn whose power grew very great.
It extended toward the south and the
east and toward the glorious land of Is-
rael. 10Its power reached to the heavens,
where it attacked the heavenly army,
throwing some of the heavenly beings
and some of the stars to the ground and
trampling them. 11It even challenged the
Commander of heaven's army by cancel-
ing the daily sacrifices offered to him and
by destroying his Temple. 12The army of
heaven was restrained from responding
to this rebellion. So the daily sacrifice
was halted, and truth was overthrown.
The horn succeeded in everything it did.***

**13Then I heard two holy ones talking to
each other. One of them asked, "How long
will the events of this vision last? How
long will the rebellion that causes dese-
cration stop the daily sacrifices? How long
will the Temple and heaven's army be
trampled on?"**

**14The other replied, "It will take 2,300
evenings and mornings; then the Temple
will be made right again."**

8:1 The original text from this point through chapter 12 is in Hebrew. See note at 2:4. **8:2** Or *the Ulai Gate;* also in 8:16. **8:3** Or *the gate;* also in 8:6. **8:11-12** The meaning of the Hebrew for these verses is uncertain.

NOTES

8:1 The language of the text switches back from Aramaic to Hebrew beginning with this verse; cf. note on 2:4, where the Aramaic section began. The text of Daniel continues in Hebrew from here until the end of the book.

third year of King Belshazzar's reign. This would have been about 550/549 BC, so this vision, like that of ch 7, preceded the events in chs 5–6, as well as chs 9–12. At this point, there were 9 to 13 years remaining before Babylon fell (5:31 [6:1]). (We do not know exactly when the king's reign began; cf. Lucas 2009:548; ANET 313.)

following. This word (*'akhare* [TH310, ZH339]) in context seems to indicate a relationship of this vision with the previous one (Goldingay 1989:195).

8:2 ***In this vision I was.*** The text states this twice. The repetition is evidently emphatic, stressing the intensity with which Daniel was caught up in the vision (cf. Lucas 2002:202).

Susa. For information on this place, see ISBE 4.667-668; Yamauchi 1990:279-303.

Ulai River. This is probably better rendered as "Ulai Canal," since it was man-made and connected two small rivers. Goldingay (1989:196) with some cogency prefers to translate it as "gate" (see also NLT mg).

8:3 ***two long horns.*** See Yamauchi 1990:69, for an example of a Persian metalwork of a ram's head with two horns.

8:4 ***no one.*** Rather, "no animal."

became very great. Lit., "he made himself great" (Holladay 1988:56), stressing the determination of Cyrus to conquer (cf. Isa 44:28).

8:5 ***watching.*** Lit., "considering" or "pondering."

large horn. This renders *qeren khazuth* [TH7161/2380, ZH7967/2607], "a visible/prominent horn." Daniel 8:21 makes it clear that this horn was Alexander the Great.

8:8 ***at the height of his power.*** Lit., "just as it had become mighty."

8:9 ***toward the glorious land of Israel.*** Lit., "toward the beautifulness" (*hatsebi* [TH6643, ZH7382]). It is clear from the use of this word in 11:16, 41 that the land of Israel is meant. The goal of the horn's action was the Jerusalem Temple and the city itself (Collins 1993:331).

8:11 ***offered to him.*** This could plausibly be rendered "on account of him" (either the horn or the leader).

destroying his Temple. Lit., "the place of his sanctuary was cast down." This does not have to mean the entire Temple edifice was physically destroyed; it means that the Temple's function was disrupted and corrupted for a time (cf. 8:14). Antiochus IV installed pagan priests to serve in the Temple, which contributed to its corruption (Josephus *Antiquities* 12.5.1 [12.237-239]). We have no historical record that the second Temple was ever demolished by Antiochus IV. Herod the Great used some aspects of it to develop the Temple of his day (4 BC–AD 37)—see Josephus *Antiquities* 15.11.2-7 [15.388-425].

8:12 ***The army of heaven was restrained.*** The MT is very difficult to decipher. According to the context, it seems that the earthly Israelite army was not granted success (during this period of rebellion) with respect to maintaining the daily offerings, but this occurred only because God permitted it by holding back the heavenly forces (cf. Longman 1999:202). So, in effect, both heavenly and earthly armies are in view in this apocalyptic report.

truth was overthrown. Truth was cast to the ground, along with the sanctuary (Temple; see note on 8:11), so that this little horn prospered as it acted.

8:13 ***rebellion that causes desecration.*** In Hebrew this is *pesha' shomem* [TH6588/8074, ZH7322/9037]. The rebellion is said to cause the desecration or desolation (cf. 9:27; 11:31; see Ford 1979:111-131).

8:14 ***2,300 evenings and mornings.*** This equals 1,150 days; the evening (*'ereb* [TH6153, ZH6847]) and morning (*boqer* [TH1242, ZH1332]) refer to the continual sacrifices (*tamid* [TH8548,

ZH9458]) offered each evening and morning. Some scholars, however, understand the statement as 2,300 days, and others believe that these days are symbolic, indicating that God has set chronological parameters during which he allows evil to work.

COMMENTARY

This vision takes place in 550/549 BC. The events of chapters 1–4 and 7 preceded this event. By now, Daniel had accumulated a significant amount of revelatory information in the form of dreams, visions, and their interpretations. This chapter develops by means of expanded Hebrew synthetic parallelism, bringing forward the kings and kingdoms of chapter 7 (7:5-6) with additional symbolism. It further reports a vision of a little horn arising from one of the four horns of the goat (8:8-11), which is to be correlated with the third kingdom of chapter 7, and also foreshadows the rise of the little horn of the fourth beast (7:7-8) and the desolater of 9:27. It parallels the abomination in 11:31.

This chapter divides according to structure and content into two parts with a brief, one-verse epilogue (8:27). It is helpful to arrange the two parts side by side:

I. VISION (8:1-14)	II. INTERPRETATION (8:15-26)
A. Introduction (8:1-2) and setting of vision; saw vision at Susa	A. Introduction and setting of the interpretation (8:15), related to end times under God's wrath (8:19)
B. Vision (8:3-14)	B. Interpretation (8:20-26)
1. Ram with two horns, one larger than the other (8:3-4)	1. Ram symbolizes the kings of Media and Persia (8:20)
2. Male goat with one long horn (8:5-14)	2. Male goat symbolizes Greece; large horn, first king (8:21-26)
a. Defeats the ram and becomes very powerful (8:6-8a)	a. Assumed
b. Long horn broken; replaced by four prominent horns (8:8b)	b. Symbolizes breakup of Greek Empire into four parts, after first king (8:21-22)
c. A small horn develops from one of the four horns (8:8-14)	c. A fierce king, master of intrigue (8:23-26)
(1) Developed great power (8:9-14a)	(1) Developed great power, not by human means (8:24-26)
(2) Restoration of Temple (8:14b)	(2) Restoration of Temple announced (8:14b) after 2,300 mornings and evenings kept silent (8:26)

Verses 1-2 locate Daniel in Susa in Elam. Susa is located 130 to 150 miles north of the Persian Gulf and 200 miles east of Babylon. Today that would put him in the Iranian province of Khuzistan. Darius I turned it into his administrative capital (c. 521 BC). It is evident that we need to picture Daniel as a person who moved about in the empire to do his administrative jobs; he was not stuck at any one royal court all the time. The Ulai was a canal (see note on 8:2) east of the city. The setting of the book of Esther was also in Susa, and the fortress of Susa is mentioned 10 times in that book (see, e.g., Esth 1:2, 5; 2:3). Nehemiah reported that he was in the fortress at Susa when he received a report about the poor condition of the returned exiles and the deteriorated condition of Jerusalem (Neh 1:1-4). Susa is mentioned in several classical sources (e.g., Herodotus *Histories* 5.32). In Belshazzar's reign, the city was ruled by Babylon in the province of Elam. The Persians made it one of their capitals and developed its splendor and beauty. Alexander the Great captured the city in 331 BC. The entire city was highly fortified (Lucas 2009:552-553) and was simply called "the fortress" or "the citadel." The palace or fortress in Susa was famous and was decorated with glazed griffins, winged bulls, and a lion, so animal symbolism (as in the vision) was not as surprising a symbol as we might think. Both goats and rams were indicative of strength and power in the Old Testament (Jer 50:8; Ezek 34:17; 39:18; Zech 10:3), and these may be the source of the choice of imagery here (rather than astrological geography, Lucas 2009:553-554 and 1990:161-185).

As the vision opens, Daniel sees a ram with two different-sized horns (8:3-4). There is a kingdom in antiquity that reflects the symbolism of two different-sized horns quite well—namely, Medo-Persia (cf. 8:20). The fact that the horns were of unequal size (making for a strange-looking ram) points to a certain conjunction of peoples. A key to the vision is the fact that the larger horn started to grow after the smaller horn. Though Cyrus and the Persians built up their power later than the Medes, they soon outstripped them, defeating King Astyages (546 BC) and the Babylonians (539 BC; cf. Yamauchi 1990:80-90). The ram's path of conquest lay in three directions: north, south, and west. The expression "did as he pleased" is a common phrase in Daniel; it indicates that a person or kingdom is victorious in all of its maneuvers while God permits it free reign (8:4; 11:3, 16, 36). King Cyrus was invincible in his military exploits, defeating the smaller "horn," the Medes in 559 BC, although the Medes had been united since at least 670 BC. Finally, only Persia remained as a mighty kingdom. Persia continued to expand in all directions, conquering Lydia, suppressing Greeks in Ionia (even attempting to subjugate the Greek homeland), conquering Babylon and Egypt, and spreading east as far as India and north to the Black Sea. The author of Daniel was mainly interested in the geographical directions of expansion that would play a large part in the history of the holy people Israel. This kingdom seems to correspond to the second beast of chapter 7 (7:5).

The male goat from the west is described in 8:5-14 (cf. 8:21). Its swift movement is symbolized by its traversing the land without even touching the ground (8:5). This recalls the speed of the leopard in 7:6. Both sets of imagery stress the swiftness with which this empire completed its conquests. Greece was the first great Western power to invade and conquer the Middle East; the single large horn represents Alexander the Great, who united the Greeks in this conquest, and whose tutor was Aristotle. Alexander was perhaps even more influenced by his chosen book of books, the *Iliad*, which he learned as a boy and carried with him. Probably the Heroic Age of the Greeks had influenced him as it had Hesiod. Green notes that as a boy Alexander was encouraged to think of himself as a new Achilles, and his Homeric desire was to be a great king, an excellent spear fighter, and to strive to excel all others (Green 2007:5; cf. Homer *Iliad* 3.179).

The wrath and fury with which the goat charged the ram is astounding. The Persians had tried to conquer the Greeks under Darius the Great (522–486 BC) at the battle of Marathon (490 BC) and again under Xerxes (486–465 BC) at Salamis and Thermopylae (480 BC). Xerxes succeeded in looting and burning Athens and destroying many Greek temples. Under Darius, the Persians had taken a bronze statue of Apollo to Ecbatana. It is therefore no surprise that Alexander the Great mercilessly burned Persepolis to avenge the Greeks. The last Persian king literally had no significant power to help him stand against Alexander and pleaded for peace. Alexander, nevertheless, hunted Darius III down, even after he fled from his armies' defeat at Gaugamela. Alexander eventually found Darius III stabbed to death by his own countrymen. By 331 BC, Alexander had taken over as the premier world power of his day. The great authority (cf. 7:6) Alexander had attained was unequaled in the ancient world. A leader with threatening delusions of grandeur reminiscent of Nebuchadnezzar, he declared himself a god before he died at Babylon (323 BC) at the age of 33 (cf. 8:8). He had conquered the known world in 13 years. In 1 Maccabees 1:1 he is described as conqueror of the Persian Empire and the founder of the Greek Empire.[1] Most significantly for our purposes, in Daniel he is described as part of God's work in history, as God made himself known to the nations. Josephus (*Antiquities* 11.8.5 [11.336-339]) records a tradition that the Jews showed Alexander Daniel's prophecies concerning him .

The division of the Greek Empire into four parts is described in 8:8-12 in the image of the large horn being broken and four horns growing in its place. Alexander was ultimately succeeded by four of his generals: Antipater Cassander received Macedonia and Greece; Lysimachus received Thrace and Asia Minor; Syria went to Seleucus I; and Palestine and Egypt went to Ptolemy (see commentary on 7:1-14). The lines of the Seleucids and Ptolemies produced the kings of the north and south that appear in the vision of chapter 11.

Ptolemy I Soter
(323–285 BC) [11:5]

Ptolemy II Philadelphus
(284–246 BC) [11:6]

Ptolemy III Euergetes
(246–221 BC) [11:7-9]

Berenice Syra
(m. Antiochus II)
(250 BC) [11:6]

Ptolemy IV Philopator
(221–203 BC) [11:10-12]

Ptolemy V Epiphanes
(203–181 BC) [11:14-17]

Ptolemy VI Philometor
(181–146 BC) [11:25-28]

The Ptolemies, 323–146 BC.
After Alexander's death (323 BC), his general Ptolemy became Egypt's king; his dynasty continued until the death of Cleopatra VII in 30 BC. The diagram shows those Ptolemies who correspond to the king of the south in 11:5-28.

Verses 9-12 describe the exploits of Antiochus IV, the "small horn whose power grew" (8:9). He arose from the line of the Seleucids, who ruled in Syria. He most likely appears again in 11:21-35 (and possibly in 11:36-39; see comments on these verses). He ruled from 175 to 164/163 BC. The author of 1 Maccabees said that "a sinful root, Antiochus Epiphanes, came from Alexander's successors" (1 Macc 1:10).

Though there is much symbolic language in the text of Daniel, the underlying reality to its enigmatic assertions is that to attack God's holy people is to attack God and his forces. The holy people of God have such a close connection with "heaven" that to talk of Israel's armies is to talk also of God's heavenly armies (cf. Judg 5:3-15). From an apocalyptic perspective, divine actions govern earthly history. Spiritual forces are part of "biblical realism" and a holistic view of God's total creation (cf. 9:23; 10:12-14; 10:20–11:1). The small horn of this vision (Antiochus IV) arises from the third empire of Daniel 7, so it is not the same as that mentioned in 7:8. But this horn foreshadows that little horn of the fourth empire—it is a preliminary fulfillment of the image. And both will come to a similar end (7:26; 8:14; 9:27; 11:40-45). The small horn's actions in chapter 8 are carefully monitored and limited by God. This horn grew large and succeeded, but only because the "army of heaven" was restrained from victory. Literarily, the horn of 7:8 foreshadows this horn and establishes its archetype. Antiochus was the first but not the last manifestation of the little horn of Daniel 7:8. One could say that there are already several "little horns" that have come and gone in history, but the full reality of the evil pointed to by 7:8 had not yet been manifested (cf. 9:26-27; 2 Thess 2; 1 John 2:18).

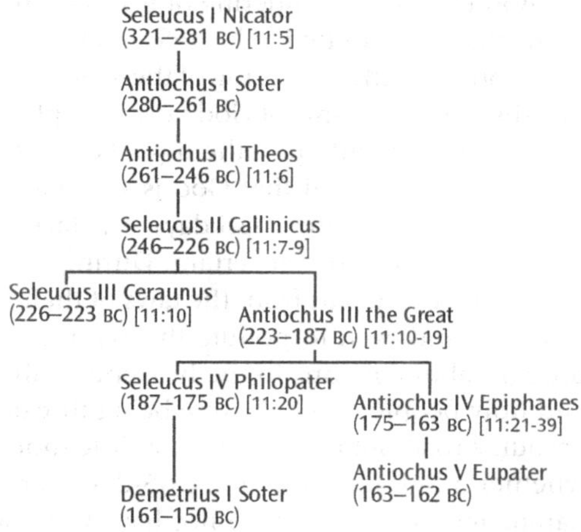

The Seleucids, 321–150 BC. Seleucus I, a Macedonian commander in Alexander's army, took control of the province of Babylon in 321 BC; his dynasty ruled until 60 BC. The diagram includes those Seleucids who correspond to the king of the north in 11:5-39.

This horn progressed to such an extent that it affected heaven, much as the influence and power of Nebuchadnezzar had reached a point where it touched heaven (4:22 [19]) with its great arrogance. God decided to respond at that point and become involved. The heavenly armies, the heavenly beings, and the stars (8:10) refer to fierce opponents engaged in conflict both on earth and in heaven. Both earthly and heavenly realms suffer at the hands of this "small horn." This is the genius of apocalyptic language and narrative. It reveals and ties together (earthly) history and (heavenly, spiritual) metahistory. "The glorious land" is none other than Israel (cf. 11:16, 41), God's place of beauty reflecting the beauty of heaven. This small horn challenged God, the Commander of heaven's army (8:11) by attacking the commanders and armies of his holy people on earth and by taking away their place of worship and daily expression of praise and worship of their God. Defeat for God's people on earth is defeat for God's forces in heaven. In all of this, the small horn (8:9) is like the little horn of chapter 7.

The Temple was not destroyed but cast down—that is, its function was interrupted (8:11) for a period of time. Antiochus IV did all of this (according to 1 Macc 1:41-64; 2 Macc 6:1-17; 9:1–10:9) to try to unify his kingdom as one people, with one religion, a Hellenistic cult. He saw a chance to combine the Seleucid (Syria) and Ptolemaic (Egypt) realms; others in the fourth empire of Daniel would have schemes even more grandiose (Green 2007:128). The actions of Antiochus IV parallel the themes of chapter 3 of Daniel in many ways, for there, an abominable idol was set up by the king, and everyone was forced to worship it. It is difficult to decipher 8:12; the NLT has a viable rendering (see note). Accepting this rendering, the army that was restrained is to be understood as both the earthly forces of the holy people Israel and their supportive cast in heaven. The small horn's sin is specifically the removal of the daily sacrifice (8:11). Since the small horn succeeded, the truth of God's law, true worship, and the proper expression of praise to God were under vicious attack, to the extent that the holy Scriptures were torn up and burned when they could be found (1 Macc 1:56-57).

Another possible rendering of 8:12 (see note) indicates that "an army was given over," that is, permitted to be defeated for the time being during this rebellion. The rebellion, not only consisting of the actions of the small horn, would then also indicate the failure of some of God's own people to keep his covenant. Subsequently, his wrath is poured out upon them (cf. Longman 1999:204; Collins 1993:335).

Verses 13-14 reveal that God is sovereign over all. The answer to the question of 8:13 translates into 1,115 days. The fact that two heavenly beings do the calculating makes the answer certain. During this time the Jews, the holy people, were compelled to "depart from the laws of their fathers, and to cease living by the laws of God," and even to pollute the Temple (2 Macc 6:1-6). These events on earth brought about actions in the heavenly realm and vice versa, for God's holy place and holy people on earth were being threatened and defiled. This period of time amounts to about three years or a little more (see note on 8:14), depending upon whether a 360-day year or a 365-day year is in mind. Apocalyptic timing gives parameters of time that do not have to be worked out with mathematical precision. The times set by God to complete his goals are real, but are not intended to be worked out in detail so that his people can arrogantly predict the timing and events of history. They are markers of assurance and to be observed from the perspective of faith. God's sovereignty orchestrates his plans according to his purposes. Accordingly, history records that Antiochus polluted the Temple in December (15th of Kislev), 167 BC, offering unclean sacrifices on it on the 25th of Kislev. It was cleansed and rededicated in December (25th of Kislev) three years later (cf. 1 Macc 1:54; 4:52-53; 2 Macc 10:5). (Hanukkah continues to commemorate this event; cf. John 10:22.) God had set a time when he would rescue and bring an end to the evil machinations of Antiochus IV. The word used to describe the restoration of the Temple in Daniel indicates not that it was to be rebuilt, but "set right"—i.e., made functional again. (Exactly why it must be set right will yet be revealed in 11:31; cf. 9:27.) Hence, the Temple was not physically destroyed (see note on 8:11). It is also significant to note that God's people were not delivered *en masse* from this time of oppression until the end; that is, the end that extends far beyond the time of Antiochus IV.

ENDNOTE

1. More recent evaluations of Alexander are not flattering: Grainger (2007:188) describes him as "a failed empire builder" whose work was superficial and whose hubristic dream of world conquest caused him to neglect the empire he ruled briefly.

◆ 2. Gabriel interprets the vision (8:15-27)

15As I, Daniel, was trying to understand the meaning of this vision, someone who looked like a man stood in front of me.

16And I heard a human voice calling out from the Ulai River, "Gabriel, tell this man the meaning of his vision."

[17]As Gabriel approached the place where
I was standing, I became so terrified that
I fell with my face to the ground. "Son of
man," he said, "you must understand that
the events you have seen in your vision
relate to the time of the end."
[18]While he was speaking, I fainted and
lay there with my face to the ground. But
Gabriel roused me with a touch and
helped me to my feet.
[19]Then he said, "I am here to tell you
what will happen later in the time of wrath.
What you have seen pertains to the very
end of time. [20]The two-horned ram repre-
sents the kings of Media and Persia. [21]The
shaggy male goat represents the king of
Greece,* and the large horn between his
eyes represents the first king of the Greek
Empire. [22]The four prominent horns that
replaced the one large horn show that the
Greek Empire will break into four king-
doms, but none as great as the first.
[23]"At the end of their rule, when their
sin is at its height, a fierce king, a master
of intrigue, will rise to power. [24]He will
become very strong, but not by his own
power. He will cause a shocking amount
of destruction and succeed in everything
he does. He will destroy powerful leaders
and devastate the holy people. [25]He will
be a master of deception and will become
arrogant; he will destroy many without
warning. He will even take on the Prince
of princes in battle, but he will be broken,
though not by human power.
[26]"This vision about the 2,300 evenings
and mornings* is true. But none of these
things will happen for a long time, so
keep this vision a secret."
[27]Then I, Daniel, was overcome and lay
sick for several days. Afterward I got up
and performed my duties for the king, but
I was greatly troubled by the vision and
could not understand it.

8:21 Hebrew *of Javan.* 8:26 Hebrew *about the evenings and mornings;* compare 8:14.

NOTES

8:15 ***looked like a man.*** Lit., "like the appearance of a man" (*geber* [TH1397, ZH1505]). The word *geber* often refers to a strong man (BDB 149-150), but also can simply mean "man."

8:16 ***Gabriel.*** This angel is also mentioned in 9:21 and in Luke 1:19, 26. The name means "man of God"; this is the first instance of a named angel in the OT.

8:17 ***Son of man.*** Heb., *ben-'adam* [TH1121/120, ZH1201/132]; the phrase emphasizes the idea of a human being, as opposed to heavenly beings, such as Gabriel.

8:18 ***I fainted.*** Heb., *nirdamti* [TH7290, ZH8101]. The exact meaning is difficult. Some prefer "fell into a trance" or "fell into a deep sleep." See note on 10:9 (cf. Collins 1993:338).

8:19 ***very end of time.*** The Hebrew refers to an "appointed time for the end."

8:21 ***of Greece.*** This represents *yawan* [TH3120, ZH3430] ("of Javan"; see NLT mg).

8:23 ***when their sin is at its height.*** Lit., "when the rebels have completed [their rebellion]."

master of intrigue. This literally describes a person who understands riddles, but here is being used of a person who uses this skill deceptively (Collins 1993:339).

8:24 ***devastate the holy people.*** The word "devastate" is not in the MT; the NLT properly carries it over from "destroy."

8:25 ***master of deception.*** Lit., "with respect to his cunning" (cf. the king of Tyre in Ezek 28).

8:26 ***2,300 evenings and mornings.*** See note on 8:14.

keep this vision a secret. Lit., "seal the vision"; Daniel was to seal the written account of the vision (cf. 7:1).

COMMENTARY

The interpretation of the vision for Daniel sometimes states the obvious for us who live after the time of the empires spoken of here. They have risen and fallen—as God had revealed to Daniel before it happened. The interpretation is made certain through the first named angel in the Bible (8:16), Gabriel ("strong man of God" or, possibly "God has been strong"). Gabriel was presumably the being asking questions in 8:13. Now, the other holy one directs him to give the significance of the vision to Daniel. Gabriel was the one whose appearance was like a human being (8:15). Even though Gabriel looked like a man, his heavenly status was clear to Daniel; thus, his response of terror and prostration was appropriate. Gabriel placed Daniel in the category of human being. As a "son of Adam" (8:17), he was a mere frail person of the human race. Gabriel then gave Daniel a needed orientation about the visions—all of these relate to the time of the end (8:19), that is, a long time from now, for Daniel was told that he would die and be resurrected "at the end of the days" (12:1, 13). These things were to happen within the historical horizon of the small horn, which represented Antiochus IV (175–164 BC). Daniel should not expect these things to occur in his lifetime; he was already around 73! During his lifetime under Babylonian and Persian kings, he did not need to share this experience with anyone (8:26). This may indicate why the use of the book of Daniel did not become prevalent until the times of the Greek Empire, Qumran, and the New Testament. Based on 7:1, we understand that Daniel wrote all this down. He was probably the author of nearly all of chapters 7–12. If a later inspired editor put all this together, he had these written materials based on eyewitnesses and divine interpreters to use (see Introduction).

The sovereignty of God is evident in orchestrating the consummation of all of the events up until the appointed end of time. This is not history gone wild, history without purpose or controls. God has established a set time for the end of even the particular historical events that would last from approximately 559 BC to 164 BC, and symbolically point to an even more devastating time and desolating sacrilege at the end of time (7:8, 23-25; 9:27; 12:7). That the period is known as a "time of wrath" (8:19) indicates God's displeasure. From Daniel and the books of Maccabees (1 Macc 1:10–6:16; 2 Macc 1–10; 4 Macc 4:15–18:22), it is clear that the wrath and rebellion spoken of in 8:12 is God's wrath engendered by the actions of the small horn against the glorious land and by the rebellious actions of some of the people of Israel (8:10-12).

In the interpretation of 8:20-22, the only new information is that the four horns (8:8) represent kings or power (Zech 1:18-21 [2:1-4]; *1 Enoch* 90:9), which is pretty standard apocalyptic symbolism in Daniel, elsewhere in Scripture, and outside of Scripture, being "common in Babylonian art, mythology, and birth omens" (Lucas 1990:175-185; Collins 1993:299). As mentioned above, this came to pass in the division of Alexander's empire at his death. That these kings would not become as great as the large horn (Alexander) was suspected already (8:5-8).

Verses 23-24 focus on the small horn (8:9) and provide significant theological comment. This violent, boastful, deceptive, destructive horn will focus his activity against the holy people (8:24), their leaders, and even God. Through intrigue and deception, the small horn will seek to destroy the people of the covenant, using means already noted above. His power and success is, however, not really his own; eventually, the divine power will break him.

As noted above, these activities reflect the career of Antiochus IV. Antiochus died, according to 1 Maccabees, with these words of confession: "Now I remember the evils I did in Jerusalem. I seized all her vessels of silver and gold; and I went to destroy the inhabitants of Judah without good reason. . . . I am perishing of deep grief in a strange land" (1 Macc 6:12-13). He died in Persia, partly for thinking he could "command the waves of the sea" and "touch the stars of heaven" (2 Macc 9:8, 10). Reminiscent of Nebuchadnezzar (4:30, 37 [27, 34]), he confessed that "no mortal should think that he is equal to God" (2 Macc 9:12). The God of Israel had "struck him with an incurable and unseen blow" (2 Macc 9:5, 28). Daniel foresaw his death as one "broken, though not by human power" (8:25). Thus ends the life of the one who foreshadowed the anti-God, anti-son of man, "little horn" of the fourth beast (7:8, 11; 9:27; 11:40-45). This will be reviewed in greater detail in 11:21-35, 36-45. The symbol of the little horn of chapter 7 gradually unfolds using Antiochus as a type of it. (It was good Hebrew narrative style to mention something once and then develop it to its fullness in subsequent narratives and stories; this is a common feature of Daniel.) Like the small horn in this chapter, the final "little horn" will likewise center all of its destructive energies against the holy people and their God. In the end, there will be a battle solely between the heavenly forces of God and the rebellious armies of the final little horn (cf. 12:1-4).

According to 8:26, it would have been unwise for Daniel to have shared this vision and interpretation with anyone at that time. Ancient kings discussed the perplexing rise and fall of kingdoms, fate, and the will of the gods, as when Cyrus and Croesus discussed the turn of events that had led to the destruction of Lydia (in the west) by Cyrus (Herodotus *Histories* 1.87-91; cf. *Histories* 1.33, 46-56). In Belshazzar's day, how would the vision have been received, if not as a book of insurrection? Babylon under Belshazzar had 11 or 12 years left before it fell. Later, Cyrus would not likely have appreciated the destiny of the ram in the story. And others might have disregarded his message because it referred to the distant future, as Israel did with Ezekiel (Ezek 12:27). So this revelation was kept secret. Nevertheless, with the Medes and Persians threatening Babylon from the east, the anticipation and anxiety of Daniel in this scenario made it an ideal time for God to give more revelation to Daniel.

That Daniel could not understand it all is due partly to his struggles to fully understand the years of exile he and his people were experiencing. In the first year of Darius the Mede, this puzzle finally became clear to him (9:1-2). He was undoubtedly shocked to think of a time in the future when his holy people would suffer such devastation again. What would this "little horn" be?

◆ C. The Exile and Restoration of a Rebellious Nation (9:1-27)

1. Daniel's prayer for his people in exile (9:1-19)

It was the first year of the reign of Darius the Mede, the son of Ahasuerus, who became king of the Babylonians.* [2]During the first year of his reign, I, Daniel, learned from reading the word of the LORD, as revealed to Jeremiah the prophet, that Jerusalem must lie desolate for seventy years.* [3]So I turned to the Lord God and

pleaded with him in prayer and fasting. I also wore rough burlap and sprinkled myself with ashes.

[4]I prayed to the LORD my God and confessed:

**"O Lord, you are a great and awesome God! You always fulfill your covenant and keep your promises of unfailing love to those who love you and obey
your commands. [5]But we have sinned and done wrong. We have rebelled against you and scorned your
commands and regulations. [6]We have refused to listen to your servants the prophets, who spoke on your authority to our kings and princes and ancestors and to all the people of the land.**

**[7]"Lord, you are in the right; but as you see, our faces are covered with shame. This is true of all of us, including the people of Judah and Jerusalem and all Israel, scattered near and far, wherever you have driven us because of our disloyalty
to you. [8]O LORD, we and our kings, princes, and ancestors are covered with shame because we have sinned
against you. [9]But the Lord our God is merciful and forgiving, even though we have rebelled against him.
[10]We have not obeyed the LORD our God, for we have not followed the instructions he gave us through his
servants the prophets. [11]All Israel has disobeyed your instruction and turned away, refusing to listen to your voice.**

**"So now the solemn curses and judgments written in the Law of Moses, the servant of God, have been poured down on us because of our sin.
[12]You have kept your word and done to us and our rulers exactly as you warned. Never has there been such a disaster as happened in Jerusalem.
[13]Every curse written against us in the Law of Moses has come true. Yet we have refused to seek mercy from the LORD our God by turning from our sins
and recognizing his truth. [14]Therefore, the LORD has brought upon us the disaster he prepared. The LORD our God was right to do all of these things, for we did not obey him.**

**[15]"O Lord our God, you brought lasting honor to your name by rescuing your people from Egypt in a great display of power. But we have sinned and are full of wickedness.
[16]In view of all your faithful mercies, Lord, please turn your furious anger away from your city Jerusalem, your holy mountain. All the neighboring nations mock Jerusalem and your people because of our sins and the sins of our ancestors.**

[17]"O our God, hear your servant's prayer! Listen as I plead. For your own sake, Lord, smile again on your desolate sanctuary.

[18]"O my God, lean down and listen to me. Open your eyes and see our despair. See how your city—the city that bears your name—lies in ruins. We make this plea, not because we deserve help, but because of your mercy.

[19]"O Lord, hear. O Lord, forgive. O Lord, listen and act! For your own sake, do not delay, O my God, for your people and your city bear your name."

9:1 Or *the Chaldeans.* **9:2** See Jer 25:11-12; 29:10.

NOTES

9:1 ***Darius the Mede.*** This designation distinguishes this Darius (c. 539 BC) from Darius I (also known as Darius the Great, or Darius Hystaspes), who reigned 522–486 BC (cf. Ezra 4:24; Hag 1:1; Zech 1:1), and is another name used in Daniel for Cyrus the Great (see Introduction, "Historical Accuracy," and notes on 6:1, 28 [2, 29]). Cyrus was born to the daughter of Astyages, king of the Medes, and to Cambyses, a Persian. The Persians were, at the time of Cyrus's birth, dominated by the Medes. Hence, the ancient Delphic Oracle had declared him, figuratively, a mule (Herodotus *Histories* 1.53-58, 91), an oracle that was completely misunderstood by Croesus, king of Lydia.

son of Ahasuerus. This is a Hebrew rendering of a Persian word, which was taken into Greek as Xerxes (cf. NIV). This name is found in Ezra 4:6, where it refers to Xerxes I (486–465 BC). Baldwin (1978a:163) cites Wiseman and Frye, however, who argue cogently that the term Ahasuerus may be an ancient royal title of the Achaemenid Dynasty, to which all Persian kings belonged. Hence, Daniel can be considered historically accurate on this point. The time of this vision was 539 BC (cf. Ezra 1:1), the same year of the events in chs 5 and 6. Darius's Median connections (lit., "from the seed of Media") are mentioned so as to relate him to both the Medes and the Persians, thus fulfilling the writing on the wall (5:28). Another less likely possibility is that this "Xerxes" (Ahasuerus) designated Cyaxares, maternal great-grandfather of Cyrus (cf. Lucas 2009:556; Shea 1991:252-253).

Babylonians. Lit., "Chaldeans" (see NLT mg), as in 1:4; 2:2, 5, 10; 3:8; 4:7 [4]; 5:30.

9:2 ***the word.*** Lit., "the books," properly, "scrolls."

9:3 ***sprinkled myself with ashes.*** Cf. Num 19:9; 2 Sam 13:19; Esth 4:1; Ezek 28:18. This action indicates Daniel's grief and mourning for the condition of his people.

9:4 ***a great and awesome God.*** In Hebrew these adjectives have the definite article, "the great, the awesome God," thus setting this God apart from all other gods.

You . . . keep your promises . . . to those who love you and obey your commands. This emphasizes the reciprocal, bilateral aspects of the Sinai covenant, and is a clear expression of the fact that liberation from exile was tied to the prayers and worship of God's people within the parameters of God's sovereign will.

9:5 Daniel employs four key words describing "sin" in the OT: (1) *khata'* [TH2398, ZH2627] (sin by missing the mark; that is, failing to meet the expectations set on someone; cf. Judg 20:16); (2) *'awah* [TH5753, ZH6390] (commit iniquity, wrong); (3) *rasha'* [TH7561, ZH8399] (do wrong, act wickedly, be wrong); (4) *marad* [TH4775, ZH5277] (to rebel)—see NIDOTTE 2.87-93, 1098-1099; 3.351, 1201-1204.

9:6 ***your servants the prophets.*** This was a special class of the Lord's servants, the prophets (cf. Ezra 9:11; also "my servants the prophets"; 2 Kgs 9:7; Jer 7:25; Ezek 38:17; and "his servants the prophets," 9:10; 2 Kgs 17:23; 21:10; Jer 25:4). See Robinson (1979) and Young (1955).

9:10 ***the instructions.*** This is *torah* [TH8451, ZH9368] in its broad sense, which was delivered by Moses and by those who came after him as well, who expounded on and delivered teaching to Israel. The Torah was the fountainhead of prophecy and prophets in Israel (Deut 34:10-12).

he gave us through his servants the prophets. Moses was considered the greatest prophet (Deut 34:10-12), and this phrase is inclusive of all of God's prophets who spoke to Israel. Daniel explicitly mentions Jeremiah (9:2), but the phrase "my servants the prophets" is found often, especially in Jeremiah (cf. 2 Kgs 9:7; 17:13, 23; 21:10; 24:2; Jer 7:25; 26:5; 44:4; Ezek 38:17; Amos 3:7; Zech 1:6; Rev 10:7).

9:11 ***because of our sin.*** Lit., "because we have sinned against him [God]."

9:13 ***seek mercy from the LORD.*** Lit., "we have not sought to make pleasant the face of the LORD."

9:16 ***your faithful mercies.*** This represents the MT's *tsidqotheka* [TH6666, ZH7407] (your righteous acts).

our sins and the sins of our ancestors. Two different words are used here: *khet'* [TH2399, ZH2628] and *'awon* [TH5771, ZH6411]. See note on 9:5; these two words correspond to the verbal roots of points (1) and (2), respectively.

9:17 ***your servant's.*** Interestingly, Daniel uses the term *'ebed* [TH5650, ZH6269] to refer to himself (cf. 9:6), which echoes the idiom "your servants the prophets." See note on 9:10.

prayer . . . plead. These are two different words for prayer: *tepillah* [TH8605, ZH9525] (prayer), and *takhanun* [TH8469, ZH9384] (plea, supplication).

smile. Lit., "cause your face to shine upon."

9:18 ***your mercy.*** Lit., "your manifold mercies."

9:19 ***Lord.*** The word *'adonay* [TH136, ZH151] occurs three times in this verse, along with "God" (*'elohim* [TH430, ZH466]). The terms "Lord" (*'adonay*), "God" (*'elohim* and *'el* [TH410A, ZH446]), and "Yahweh" (*yhwh* [TH3068, ZH3378], 6 times) occur 26 times in Daniel's prayer! References to "his name" and pronominal suffixes referring to the Lord increase the references to divinity greatly within these verses (9:4-19). Yahweh, the covenant name and personal name of God, is used only in this chapter of Daniel.

COMMENTARY

The experiences of Daniel in this chapter follow the events of chapters 1–5 and 7–8 chronologically. Daniel's deliverance from the lions and from his Persian detractors (6:1-3 [2-4]) may have occurred before this event or after it. Daniel's prayer in this chapter reflects the character and religious practices of a man who prayed three times a day as a regular act of humility and honor to his God (cf. 6:10 [11]), a picture of Daniel that is consonant with his pious attitudes and actions as a young man (1:3-14). Through a diligent study of Jeremiah (Jer 25:7-12; 29:10), Daniel learned that the 70-year exile of his people was over, though he does not record any chronological scheme by which he assessed this. He then realized that the Lord had promised to take his people back to Judah and Jerusalem to fulfill his plans to do good to them, to prosper and restore them. The Lord would be found by his people again, as he returned them to their homeland (Jer 29:11-14; cf. Deut 4:29).

Cyrus would soon issue his famous, magnanimous decree. This decree, which is recorded twice in Scripture, permitted the Jews and all other subjugated people to return home to rebuild their temples and to worship (2 Chr 36:22-23; Ezra 1:1-4; cf. Ezra 6:1-12). Thus in Cyrus's first year, in accord with the word of Jeremiah, Cyrus was moved by the Lord to issue his decree and let the Jews return home. We learn in this chapter that Cyrus's decree was also issued in answer to Daniel's passionate and informed prayer. Only in this prayer is the intimate covenant name of God, "the LORD" (Yahweh), used in Daniel. The fulfillment of Jeremiah's prophecy was not an automatic performance by God; it was done in response to the pleas of his people to deliver them from exile and return them to the land. God's workings involve his peoples' prayers. Not long after Daniel's model prayer, he received an answer, for he had indeed prayed according to the will of his God. (Similar to Daniel's prayer, the prayers of God's people in Ezra 9 and Nehemiah 9 offer some of the high points of prayer in the OT, prayers that rival those recorded in the book of Psalms.) Daniel, like Moses, prayed for his people, identifying with them in their need and their sin (9:15-16; Exod 32:30-32). Their destiny was his destiny, and it all depended upon the character of their God—a God of mercy (9:18) who would act for the honor and glory of his great name (9:18-19). A God whose character had been spelled out in Exodus 34:6-7 as one of love, compassion, and mercy—to this God Daniel appealed.

This prayer was a momentous occasion for Daniel, because he prayed for and expected the restoration of the holy city Jerusalem and the holy people. But he got more than he expected; God presented to him a vision of a future 70 weeks of years (or 70 sets of seven) that would replace the 70 years of the Babylonian captivity. God, in his sovereignty, had much more to tell Daniel than he could have imagined. The things he revealed to Daniel stretched far beyond 539 BC.

In the introduction to this chapter (9:1-3), Daniel tells his readers that the word of God gave him the key to understanding the historical devastation of his people. Since the 70 years predicted by Jeremiah (Jer 25:12) were now completed, Daniel turned to the Lord in prayer and began seeking the restoration of his people. His use of sackcloth (rough burlap) and ashes was traditional ancient Near Eastern garb for people in mourning (Neh 9:1; Esth 4:1; Lam 2:10; Luke 10:13). His fasting emphasized that his spiritual concerns were more important than his physical comfort. The Lord had declared that his people would find him when they sought him with all their heart—even in a foreign land where he would scatter them (Deut 4:25-31; 30:5; Jer 29:13). Chapter 6 shows that daily worship was a regular practice of Daniel; he prayed three times a day with his window open facing Jerusalem (6:10 [11]), the holy city.

Daniel's prayer of confession is recorded in 9:4-11a, a confession of the sins of Daniel's people, as well as his own. He confessed, "We have sinned and done wrong" (9:5). He used four key Hebrew words to describe what he and his people had done: They had missed the mark (sinned), they had committed iniquities, they had brought guilt upon themselves, and they had rebelled against the Lord, turning away from his commandments (9:5; Deut 27–28). Daniel mentioned the leaders, as well as the common people of the land, for all were guilty (9:6). God, however, had been true to his character, faithfully keeping the covenant, showing kindness to those faithful to him (9:4; Exod 34:6-7; Deut 5:10; Ps 136). Daniel's prayer is permeated with quotes and echoes of the Torah and the Prophets, as well as the Psalms. He was not only a student of Jeremiah but of all of the prophets and the books of Moses. He read history from a theological and covenantal perspective. History was God's interaction with his people, not a mere process of events following upon events.

He realized, through his study of the Torah and the prophets, that the scattering of his people in exile was the work of the Lord, not merely a result of the realpolitik of the current world order. His continued assertion of the love and mercies of God was the basis of his appeal for forgiveness (9:4, 9, 13, 16, 18). Only the special group the Lord had called, "his servants the prophets," had kept their faith in the Lord. Daniel echoed Jeremiah here (2 Kgs 9:7; 17:13; Jer 7:25; 25:4-5; 35:15; 44:4). The great commandment of the Lord, the Shema ("to listen"; Deut 6:4), had not been obeyed (9:11).

The warning of both the Torah of the Lord's servant Moses and the prophets had come to pass—the curses and judgments had arrived (Lev 26; Deut 27–28).

According to Daniel, this exile of a whole people by their God specifically because of their refusal to keep their God's holy laws was unique in history (9:12), not in the mere physical movement of the people, but in the goal, purpose, and objective God had for this people (cf. Amos 3:1-2; 9:7). This fact remains true today. Even after the return in our day of many Jews to Israel since 1948, there are still more Jews outside of Israel than reside in the nation. Just as the purpose and goal of the exodus out of Egypt remains unparalleled in the history of any nation, so also the goal and purpose of the exile into and the exodus out of Babylon is unprecedented (Isa 43:14-21; Jer 29:10). Seeking mercy from the Lord could only be effective if his people would turn from their sins and become wise in his truth. Words alone would not do.

Daniel's cry for God to rescue his people (9:15-18) is based upon four observations he made. First, the Lord had rescued his people from Egypt; so he could rescue them now by acting on their behalf (9:15, 18). Second, the honor of the Lord's name is connected with what happens to his people. The Lord should rescue them for the honor of his name (9:15, 17, 19). The pivot of these five verses is 9:17. It mentions the third point that Daniel made—God's sanctuary was desolate; therefore, he and his name were being mocked (9:16, 18). His fourth point is the key, for he implores God to act on behalf of his people because he is the merciful God (9:16, 18). This prayer is, as might be expected, much like the prayer of Moses (Exod 32:12-14), whom Daniel had been studying in addition to Jeremiah (9:2). As Daniel pled for the Lord to act on behalf of his people and his city, he echoed Moses's words (Exod 5:22-23; 6:1; 32:11-13). It was, according to Daniel's understanding of Scripture, time for God to act, but he knew that it was still up to the God of mercy. In the end, this prayer by this servant of God was heard (9:17, 23), and it became an integral part of the fabric of God's sovereign actions.

Daniel's prayer was much like a high priestly prayer that the high priest would offer up for his people and himself, during which the he bore the 12 tribes of Israel before the Lord over his heart (Exod 28:15-21, 29-30). There was no Temple at that time, but God was still hearing and answering prayer. Daniel's prayer also reveals his personal relationship with his Lord and God (cf. 6:10-11 [11-12]). In 9:19 alone he addresses God as Lord three times and then indicates that the Lord is his God. In all, Daniel references God 26 times in his prayer (see note on 9:19). Addressing the Lord, he mentions "your name" three times (9:15, 18, 19). The personal address of God by Daniel makes this prayer one of the most intimate prayers in the Old Testament (cf. Ezra 9:6-15; Neh 1:5-11; 9:6-37).

◆ 2. Daniel's prayer answered (9:20-23)

**20I went on praying and confessing my sin
and the sin of my people, pleading with
the LORD my God for Jerusalem, his holy
mountain. 21As I was praying, Gabriel,
whom I had seen in the earlier vision,
came swiftly to me at the time of the
evening sacrifice. 22He explained to me,
"Daniel, I have come here to give you in-
sight and understanding. 23The moment
you began praying, a command was given.
And now I am here to tell you what it was,
for you are very precious to God. Listen
carefully so that you can understand the
meaning of your vision.**

NOTES

9:20 ***my people.*** Lit., "my people Israel."

9:21 ***swiftly.*** The MT has *mu'ap bi'ap* [TH3286/3288, ZH3615/3618], which most likely means "wearied with weariness, exhausted" and refers to Daniel, not Gabriel. The first form is a Hophal participle (cf. Goldingay 1989:228, and BDB 419, 733). But most versions, ancient and modern, assume that the word is connected to *'up* [TH5774, ZH6414] (to fly). Isaiah 6:2 lends some credence to this, but seraphs are in mind there, not angels in human form as here. The NJPS version translates this phrase as "was sent forth in flight," a possible rendering, if *ye'ap* [TH3288, ZH3618], meaning "flight," is a legitimate homonym of *ye'ap,* meaning "weariness" (Hartman and Di Lella 1978:243).

9:22 ***insight and understanding.*** This renders the Hiphil infinitive construct of *sakal* [TH7919, ZH8505] followed by the noun *binah* [TH998, ZH1069]. Cf. 1:4; 9:13, 25; 11:33, 35 for important functions of the root of *sakal.* The NLT translates *sakal* in these verses as "train," "recognize," "understand," and "wise."

COMMENTARY

These introductory verses to Gabriel's message to Daniel impart some important truths. Daniel's prayer was more than what was recorded in 9:1-19, inasmuch as he continued his prayer of confession and pleading for mercy (9:20). The words in 9:20 and the use of the covenant name of God (Yahweh = "the LORD") tie this section to the recorded prayer. Daniel was praying at the time of the evening sacrifice, but there was no sacrifice being offered because the Jerusalem altar had been destroyed. Daniel filled the void with prayer, and Gabriel returned to Daniel with answers (cf. 8:15, 17).

Proverbs 1:5, a part of the superb preface to the book of Proverbs, says that a wise man will add to his understanding. Prayer is one way to acquire wisdom from God, just as James taught (Jas 1:5). God listens to the cries of his servants. At the beginning of Daniel's supplication, a word went forth in answer to Daniel's request (cf. 4:31 [28]). This "word" may have been the word to Cyrus to restore and build Jerusalem, as well as "a word" that explained the revelation Daniel was going to receive. The messenger's announcement that Daniel was highly valued by God reveals as much about the character of God as it does about Daniel. Consider also God's high estimation of Job (Job 1:8; 2:3). He, too, was righteous and blameless before God. And he, too, had his prayers heard by the Lord (Job 1:5; 42:9). He prayed for the sins of his own family and friends (Job 1:5). The prayer of Elijah was likewise effective (Jas 5:16-17). Daniel's heavenly interpreter would again give him an interpretation (9:25). God would act on behalf of Jerusalem, the Lord's holy mountain (9:20).

Gabriel did not promise Daniel all the "answers," but rather "insight and understanding" about what was really occurring. Daniel would realize that the Lord is in charge. The Lord would demonstrate the honor of his name, by rescuing Jerusalem and his people according to his appointed time (9:27).

◆ 3. Seventy weeks decreed and described (9:24-27)

24"A period of seventy sets of seven* has been decreed for your people and your holy city to finish their rebellion, to put an end to their sin, to atone for their guilt, to bring in everlasting righteousness, to confirm the prophetic vision, and

to anoint the Most Holy Place.* 25 Now listen and understand! Seven sets of seven plus sixty-two sets of seven* will pass from the time the command is given to rebuild Jerusalem until a ruler—the Anointed One*—comes. Jerusalem will be rebuilt with streets and strong defenses,* despite the perilous times.

26 "After this period of sixty-two sets of seven,* the Anointed One will be killed, appearing to have accomplished nothing, and a ruler will arise whose armies will destroy the city and the Temple. The end will come with a flood, and war and its miseries are decreed from that time to the very end. 27 The ruler will make a treaty with the people for a period of one set of seven,* but after half this time, he will put an end to the sacrifices and offerings. And as a climax to all his terrible deeds,* he will set up a sacrilegious object that causes desecration,* until the fate decreed for this defiler is finally poured out on him."

9:24a Hebrew *seventy sevens.* **9:24b** Or *the Most Holy One.* **9:25a** Hebrew *Seven sevens plus sixty-two sevens.* **9:25b** Or *an anointed one;* similarly in 9:26. Hebrew reads *a messiah.* **9:25c** Or *and a moat,* or *and trenches.* **9:26** Hebrew *After sixty-two sevens.* **9:27a** Hebrew *for one seven.* **9:27b** Hebrew *And on the wing of abominations;* the meaning of the Hebrew is uncertain. **9:27c** Hebrew *an abomination of desolation.*

NOTES

9:24 *seventy sets of seven.* This attempts to render the Hebrew "seventy weeks" (*shabu'im shib'im* [TH7620/7651, ZH8651/8679]; see remarks in commentary). Compare 9:27 ("one week") and 10:2-3 ("three weeks of days"). Normally in Hebrew the plural of "week" ends with *-oth* (the fem. pattern) as in the "Festival of Weeks" (*khag shabu'oth* [TH2282/7620, ZH2504/8651]; see Exod 34:22; Deut 16:9, 10; Jer 25:8-14), but in Dan 9 it ends with *-im* (the masc. pattern). The masc. form is present in Dan 10:2-3 and in some Qumran documents (1QS 10.7-8, with suffix; 4Q320 4.iii.5). See especially Lucas (2002:244-245) for further discussion. Konkel argues that *shabu'im* should be translated only as "weeks," with a masc. pl. indicating a unified stretch of time; "an uninterrupted chronological period that cannot be made indefinite in historical time" (NIDOTTE 4.21). This would rule out separating the last, 70th week, from the preceding 69 weeks. Most interpreters have not been convinced by his argument. These 70 sets of seven are usually taken to refer to 70 weeks of years (490 years), or 70 jubilees of 49 years. These weeks are understood by many interpreters to be symbolic of periods of meaningful time (time that is not just slipping by, but that encompasses the accomplishment of set goals and purposes), rather than chronological markers (cf. especially Collins 1993:352-353).

rebellion. Or, "transgression" (cf. NIV, NJPS).

guilt. Or, "wickedness" (NIV).

Most Holy Place. Heb., *qodesh qadashim* [TH6944, ZH7731] (holy of holies); this is a Hebrew superlative expression.

9:25 *Seven sets of seven.* The pointing of the MT with an *athnach* after "seven sets of seven" may indicate the time during which the city is rebuilt. But the accents and vowels of the MT were added later.

sixty-two sets of seven. The next 62 sets of seven may also indicate the duration of time during which the city would continue to be rebuilt. It is best to place the appearing of the "anointed one, a prince" at the end of the total of 69 weeks. For a messianic interpretation of 9:25-26, see Kaiser (1995:202-204).

a ruler—the Anointed One. MT reads in order "an anointed one, a ruler" (*nagid* [TH5057, ZH5592], "prince"). An "anointed one" in Israel could refer to an anointed king, priest, or prophet, or anyone chosen by God for a task.

9:26 ***will be killed.*** Lit., "will be cut off." Elsewhere the verb *karath* [TH3772, ZH4162] (cut) was used regularly with *berith* [TH1285, ZH1382] to indicate the cutting of a covenant in which the death of a living being was involved to seal the covenant (NIDOTTE 2.729-731). Here the living being is "an anointed" person and appears simply to be cut off from his community and his holy function (e.g., Exod 12:15; 30:33; Lev 7:21, 25; Num 4:18; 19:20).

appearing to have accomplished nothing. This would be surprising for an anointed figure in ancient Israel.

ruler. This renders *nagid* [TH5057, ZH5592], the same term used to describe the Anointed One in 9:25 above. Here, however, it refers to a ruler who comes after the Anointed One is cut off.

armies. The very difficult syntax of this verse does not include this specific word, though "armies" is a plausible rendering of *'am* [TH5971A, ZH6639] (people).

Temple. Lit., "the Holy Place."

The end. Or, "His end," "Its end." The end of the city and Temple is in view.

flood. This is figurative for swift, devastating destruction (11:10, 22, 40; Prov 27:4; Nah 1:8).

9:27 ***make a treaty.*** It is difficult to discern the nuance of this expression; other suggested renderings are: "a covenant will prevail" (Goldingay 1989:226); "impose a covenant" (Lacocque 1979:187); "make a strong alliance" (Hartman and Di Lella 1978:240); and "make a firm covenant" (NJPS).

the people. Lit., "the many."

one set of seven. Or, "one week."

And as a climax to all his terrible deeds. Lit., "And on a wing of abominations" (see NLT mg). This is probably to be understood as an overspreading or all-encompassing sacrilegious object causing desolation. The word for wing (*kanap* [TH3671, ZH4053]) is also used of the presence of the Lord. The Lord spread his wings to take in Israel (Deut 32:11); he rescued them from Egypt on eagles' wings (Exod 19:4). The psalmist takes refuge under the wing of the Lord (Pss 17:8; 36:7; 57:1; 61:4; 63:7). Rather than the familiar symbol of strength and protection, the wing here becomes a symbol of this all-encompassing, enshrouding expression of evil. (Cf. 9:27, KJV, and see ISBE 1.930-931, where Kaiser also notes the connecting or overspreading meaning of the root of this verb.)

a sacrilegious object that causes desecration. Lit., "an abomination of desolation." This is referred to by Jesus in Matt 24:15; Mark 13:14, and probably by Paul in 2 Thess 2:4. Scholars have suggested the following identifications for the abomination of desolation (see Ford 1979:158-172): (1) A statue of Titus supposedly erected beside the desolated Temple (AD 70). It is now thought that this was a mere patristic legend. (2) Statues supposedly set up by Pilate (AD 26) in the Temple and later by Hadrian (AD 117), where the Temple had stood. Ford (1979:158-172) notes that the historical accuracy of some of these items is suspect. (3) The atrocities of the Zealots during the siege of Jerusalem (Josephus *War* 4.3.9, 13-14 [4.158-161, 215-223]; 4.4.5-7; 4.5.1, 5 [4.283-313, 345-352]; c. AD 70). (4) The threat of Caligula to set up his image in the Temple (AD 37–41). (5) The future and final Antichrist himself will be the overspreading desolating abomination; the Greek masc. sg. participle (*hestēkota* [TG2476, ZG2705]) used in Mark 13:14 suggests this view. (6) The Roman army that invaded and destroyed the city and the Temple (AD 70; cf. especially Luke 21). (7) Antiochus IV Epiphanes' desolating sacrilege (1 Macc 1:54; cf. Josephus *Antiquities* 12.5.4 [12.248-256]). (8) The erection of an altar to Olympian Zeus/Jupiter (often identified in that region with Baal Shamen; cf. Lucas 2002:245; 2 Macc 6:2). It is clear that the solution to this question is difficult, and the ambiguity of the text is a feature of apocalyptic literature. See commentary for further suggestions. As the little horn announced in 7:8 finds Antiochus (8:9-14) as a forerunner of its fulfillment, so this figure seems to find a preliminary fulfillment in the NT era in the time of the Roman Empire, but its intent is not exhausted by the events that occurred then.

decreed. This indicates that this time of utter destruction and confusion is under God's control, for it and the end of the desolater have been decreed (Gurney 1981:29-36).

COMMENTARY

These verses set out succinctly what was to be accomplished by a period of 70 sevens (or weeks). This period of 70 sevens or 70 weeks challenged even the earliest interpreters of Daniel. If it means 70 weeks of years or 70 jubilees, then it equals 490 chronological years. However, it has also been understood to represent an indefinite period of chronological time, but definite with respect to what must be accomplished during this time. Hence, 70 sets of seven (or weeks) indicates a sufficient amount of time to fulfill God's goals and purposes for his people and the nations. All opposition to God, his people, and his anointed one will be destroyed (9:24-27). No person, certainly not Daniel (12:8-9; cf. Mark 13:32-36; Acts 1:6-7) knows the time when all these things will be consummated. God's people must trust that the assured goals of God's counsel will be worked out in his own time.

All that Daniel had asked God to do (9:1-19) would be accomplished beyond his expectations in the six things listed in 9:24. Then God's desolate sanctuary would be restored (9:17), and Jerusalem and his people would be rescued and restored (9:18-19). God would reveal even more of his plans for his people and future history, using multiples of 7, 10, 70, as well as one-half of seven (cf. 7:25; 9:27; 12:7). Daniel and his people would have been familiar with dividing time into sevens, for the Jubilee year was based upon 7 x 7 years = 49 years (Lev 25; 26:40-45). One reason Israel had gone into exile for 70 years was because she had not kept her Jubilees or her Sabbath rests every seventh year to let the land lie fallow (2 Chr 36:21). Daniel stated that he fasted for "three weeks of days" in the time of Cyrus (10:2), clearly identifying those weeks as weeks of seven days. In 9:24 it simply says that "seventy sets" are determined upon the people. The NLT rendering of "seventy sets of seven" is excellent. This phrase probably means "seventy weeks (of years)," or 490 years, but, as noted above, it is also speaking of an indefinite period of time during which God accomplishes his purposes.

During the period of the 70 sets of seven, Daniel's people and city would be delivered. Much is to be accomplished during this time: Rebellion and sin are brought to an end; iniquity is covered; eternal righteousness is brought in. All this will confirm the truthfulness of the prophetic vision (9:24). Then a new Most Holy Place (or possibly Person) will be anointed. These goals will be reached partially or preliminarily in historical events throughout this 70-week period as envisioned in the dreams and visions of Daniel (2:44-45; 7:1-14, 17-27; 8:10-12). The course of history is driven, not by some evolutionary force, but by God's divine directive toward his Kingdom. God's goals and purposes for his eternal city and people pierce the centuries, unerringly achieving his aims. While the nations may be in total ignorance of what it is that drives the movement of history, God's people know the moral, ethical, and religious character of history and the contours of the road and the ultimate goal. These verses must refer to quelling the rebellion, not only that of chapter 8 under Antiochus (8:13-14), but ultimately of the final rebellion and sin under the little horn of chapters 7 (7:8, 22, 25-26) and 12 (12:7, 11). Chapters 11 and 12 (11:21-45; 12:1-7, 11) deal with these same issues. At the end of these accomplishments, Daniel's people and holy city will be secure and reestablished.

The historical unfolding of the 70 sets of seven is recorded in 9:25-27. They are divided as follows:

1. The beginning of these sets of seven commences with a decree to restore and rebuild Jerusalem (9:25)—this could be 587 BC (Jer 30:18-22; 31:38-40), or 539 BC (Ezra 1:1-4; cf. Isa 44:28), or 458 BC (Ezra 7:12-26), or 445 BC (Neh 2:7-8). Lucas favors the dates 587 and 445 BC as the most probable for the decree or "word" going forth concerning the restoration of Jerusalem (2002:242-243). Using the date 539 as the starting date, the date of the Cyrus decree (Ezra 1:1-2), the 70 weeks would end about 49 BC. If 458 is used, the time when Ezra was permitted to travel to Jerusalem to rebuild the Temple and restore worship, the 70 weeks would end around AD 32. (Jesus Christ died c. AD 30–33.) If 445 is used (the date that Nehemiah was permitted to return to Jerusalem so as to rebuild the walls of the city), then the 70 weeks would end around AD 45, which is near to the time when Caligula (Gaius) threatened to set up a statue of himself in the Temple. Those who argue that these weeks were fulfilled in the time of Antiochus IV use 587 BC as their starting date and get these results: Seven sevens (7 x 7 = 49 years) reach to about 539 BC; the next 62 weeks of years (62 x 7 = 434) come to about 105 BC. But the high priest Onias III, who served from 190 BC until he was replaced by his brother, Jason, in 175 BC when Jason bought the office of high priest, was deposed during the years 175–c. 171 BC. Onias was eventually murdered, even though he was still considered the legitimate high priest, and in our text is the anointed one usually referred to in this interpretive approach. He died in 172 or 171 BC. Onias's death at that time indicates that half of the last week that remains would end in c. 167 BC, which is a fair fit with Daniel, since the Temple was cleansed in 164 BC, and Antiochus died in that year. It is also usually claimed by those who hold this view that Antiochus destroyed the city and Temple, but there is no record of this occurring. He did, however, set up a sacrilegious object in the Temple (1 Macc 1). However, the following is significant: As noted above, it is clear that from 539 BC, the 62 weeks of years leads to about 105 BC—not close to 171 BC—thus giving a date that is much too late. This approach generally solves the discrepancy by saying that the author was simply incorrect. It seems rather that Antiochus IV fits in reasonably well in 8:9-14, but does not do so in this passage (Lucas 2002:244-247). Each of these options offers both advantages and disadvantages for properly interpreting the passage. None of them are exact, nor, given the symbolic use of numbers in Daniel and its literary genre, should we expect them to be.

2. After 69 sets of seven, an anointed one, a prince, appears (9:25-26). During this time Jerusalem will be built under stressful conditions (9:25). The stressful conditions during the first set of sevens for the rebuilding of Jerusalem and the walls could refer to the period (7 x 7 = 49 years) when Israel returned in 539 BC or to 445 BC (Nehemiah). If these dates are used, the 62 sevens lead to the dates

490 and 396 BC, respectively. After this, an anointed one will be cut off and the holy city will be destroyed by the people of a coming ruler (9:26). According to 9:26, its end will come like a flood, wars will continue to the end, and desolation is decreed for the city and sanctuary. Subtracting 434 years from 490 and 396 BC takes us, respectively, to 56 BC and AD 37. In the second case (AD 37) the 62 sevens finish around the death of Christ, and the final week of seven years ends near the time of Caligula, who threatened to set up an image of himself in the Temple. If the final week is held to be figurative, it could stretch on to the fall of the city and the Temple in AD 70 (cf. Luke 21).

3. During the 70th week (9:27) an unspecified "he" (the logical antecedent is "the ruler" mentioned in 9:26) will enforce a covenant with the majority for one week; for half the week he will stop the sacrifice and offerings; and he will set up an all-encompassing (overspreading) sacrilegious object (abomination) that causes desolation until the decreed end is poured out on the defiler (desolater).

As noted, during the 70 weeks, the six goals of 9:24 will be realized. God's sovereignty is evident in the whole process, not least because he reveals all of it to Daniel through Gabriel beforehand. Discussions about these verses fill volumes.

The interpretation now considered the standard "critical" position understands these 70 sets of seven as being fulfilled as pseudo-prophecy (*vaticinium ex eventu* = a prophecy after the event) in the life and times of Antiochus IV Epiphanes (175–163 BC). Almost all scholars who maintain this position date the final composition of the book around 164 BC. This is often called a historical interpretation of the book. Most evangelical scholars do not favor this view; some excellent scholars do, however (Goldingay, Lucas, Bruce). While this commentary maintains that Antiochus IV Epiphanes was in the thought of the inspired text in chapters 8 and 11:21-39 and that he foreshadowed the little horn spoken of in chapter 7 as well as the mysterious figures in 9:27 and 11:36-39, 40-45; 12:1-7, 8-13, it also asserts that the book of Daniel does not find its ultimate culmination in this historical figure. The figure portrayed in these latter passages far surpasses the diabolical deeds of Antiochus. Moreover, it is practically impossible to fit the 70 "weeks" sufficiently into the chronology that results when Antiochus is made the goal to which everything is related in the book of Daniel. Even a symbolic interpretation of the 70 weeks is hard-pressed to coincide in any cogent way with the pattern of dates and events leading up to 167–164 BC. Furthermore, it is clear that the New Testament writers saw a greater overspreading abomination of desolation to occur than had appeared under Antiochus during 167–164 BC, or in the much later fall of the Temple and the city to Rome in AD 70. Although these latter events fulfilled aspects of 9:26-27 (e.g., Christ as the Anointed One was cut off and the city and Temple were razed), there was more to come according to the writers of the New Testament. At the same time, much is learned from an examination of the critical position.

The challenges of interpreting 9:24-27 are many, and throughout the history of evangelical interpretations of Daniel, two amazingly different conclusions generally have been reached about the content of these verses. First, many (e.g., Young) conclude that these verses are a magnificent prophecy about the coming of the Messiah. After 69 sets of seven, the Anointed Prince, the Messiah, will come. Before he comes,

Jerusalem will continue to be rebuilt, whether for seven sets of seven or during the entire 69 sets of seven. Either period could indicate the duration of time the building of Jerusalem took place. The development of the city and Temple was still going on during Jesus' day. In 164 BC the Temple had to be renovated by the Maccabees. Beginning from 539 BC, alien forces erected fortresses and other defiling structures in Jerusalem that were torn down. In any case, the Anointed One, Christ, was killed after 69 sets of seven (died AD 30–33) and seemingly had accomplished nothing. The coming prince (or "ruler," v. 26) was often considered to be the Roman general Titus, who destroyed Jerusalem in AD 70 (some suggest that Hadrian [AD 134] is in mind here). His armies surrounding and razing Jerusalem were the desolating sacrilege of 9:27, according to some interpreters. The "he" of 9:27 is again the Messiah (the anointed one of v. 26, not the ruler mentioned in that verse), who caused a covenant to prevail for one week, but he put an end to sacrifices and offering by his death in the middle of the week. The last part of 9:27 returns to the topic of the ruler-prince of 9:26 and the destruction of the Temple and Jerusalem in AD 70. Some of the church fathers saw in these verses the greatest Old Testament prediction of the coming of the Messiah, Jesus Christ. This view generally maintains that the 70 weeks are to be interpreted as a continuous whole, without any gap separating the last week from the preceding 69 weeks.

However, many interpreters (Longman 1999; Miller 1994) hold the second position today, arguing that this passage leads up to a presentation of both the Messiah and the final "antichrist" (in Daniel this is better termed "anti-God") figure (7:8; 11:36-39, 40-45). According to this view, the 62 sets of seven lead up to the Messiah, the Anointed Prince (9:25) who is killed, appearing to have accomplished nothing (9:26). The ruler to come would then be the Roman general Titus, who destroyed Jerusalem and the Temple in AD 70 (9:26). Verse 26b depicts the destruction of Jerusalem in AD 70 or the continuing conditions of great conflict until the final end (12:1-4), or both. But in this view, 9:27 is separated from the preceding 62 (or 69) sets of seven by a large, undefined chronological gap, and the major abominable object or actor becomes the final anti-God, antichrist figure, a nondescript "he" who causes a covenant to stand with the people of Israel for half of a set of seven, committing all-encompassing sacrilege, until he is destroyed as decreed.

A major challenge to this position is the separation of the 70th week from the preceding 69 weeks. It appears, however, that the presentation of the little horn in chapter 7, its development in chapter 11, and implications in chapter 12 warrant the approach of this interpretation. Verse 26b seems to imply a continuation of conditions of strife for some time "until the end" that is coming (sometime) and is described in verse 27. It seems that the author would have indicated who enforced the covenant (9:27) if he, in fact, were the Messiah, the Anointed One. It is not likely that "he" would be used to refer to the anointed one in such a nondescript way. Instead, just as the little horn (7:8; 11:36-45; 12:1-7) remains a mysterious final figure, so does the "he" who enforces a covenant in 9:27a and is echoed in 11:40-45; 12:7, 11. The ruler and forces described in verse 26 can easily be applied to Rome (though not in a final sense), but the "he" of verse 27 remains mysterious beyond identification.

It is not uncommon for prophecy to have "gaps" between the topics or times discussed in consecutive verses (Isa 61:1-2; Joel 2:29-30; Luke 4:18-19). Daniel himself skips over about 150 years in 11:2-3, as he passes from the Persian King Xerxes (486–465 BC) to Alexander the Great (died 323 BC).

It is also difficult to see how 9:27 could refer to the Messiah on other grounds. The natural antecedent for the subject of this verse would be the nearest one, the ruler-prince who will arise (9:26), not the more distant anointed one of 26a. The Hebrew verb used to describe the "enforcement" (see note on 9:27) of a covenant already in place is difficult to apply to Christ's establishment of the new covenant by his blood, as described elsewhere (Jer 31:31-34; cf. Matt 26:28; Mark 14:24; Luke 22:20; 1 Cor 11:25; 2 Cor 3:6; Heb 9; 11:8-12).

Finally, the second half of 9:27 is difficult to decipher. The NLT notes that its meaning is uncertain; the NIV renders the puzzling word *kanap* (see note on 9:27) as "on a wing of the temple." The Septuagint and the Vulgate read "Temple" here. The Theodotionic Greek text reads "pinnacle," with "of the Temple" implied. (Some would emend this to read "in this place [of sacrifice]"; however, there is no textual support for this [Lucas 2002:230].) It seems best to render the significance of *kanap* as "all-encompassing" or "overspreading" (so KJV). Then the translation of the last part of the verse refers to "an overspreading or all-encompassing sacrilegious object causing desolation" (see note on 9:27). Total desolation will mark the most cherished place of worship, where the Lord's care, strength, and protection had encompassed his holy people with the shadow of his presence (cf. Exod 19:4; Deut 32:11; Pss 17:8; 61:4; 91:4). As such, the picture is of the sinister overshadowing effect of this final symbol of a defiling, sacrilegious object, whose fate finally arrives (cf. Isa 10:23; 28:22 where the same statement is found). The desolater suffers desolation (cf. 8:25; 11:45).

This all-encompassing, desolating sacrilegious object is noted in the New Testament by Jesus and Paul, who each point to events beyond their own day (Matt 24:15; Mark 13:14; Luke 21:20; cf. 2 Thess 2:3; Rev 13). John notes that the antichrist is coming and that forerunners of him are present, for the *last hour* has arrived (1 John 2:18-19). Whatever adumbrating historical fulfillment there was of this abominable object in the time of Antiochus IV or in the New Testament era and Rome, it will yet have its apocalyptic eschatological appointed time at the end.

◆ D. The Fall of the Kingdom of Persia and the Rise of Greece (10:1–11:1)

1. Daniel's vision by the Tigris River in Cyrus's reign (10:1–9)

In the third year of the reign of King Cyrus of Persia,* Daniel (also known as Belteshazzar) had another vision. He understood that the vision concerned events certain to happen in the future—times of war and great hardship.

2When this vision came to me, I, Daniel, had been in mourning for three whole weeks. 3All that time I had eaten no rich food. No meat or wine crossed my lips, and I used no fragrant lotions until those three weeks had passed.

4On April 23,* as I was standing on the bank of the great Tigris River, 5I looked up and saw a man dressed in linen clothing, with a belt of pure gold around his waist.

6His body looked like a precious gem. His face flashed like lightning, and his eyes flamed like torches. His arms and feet shone like polished bronze, and his voice roared like a vast multitude of people.

7Only I, Daniel, saw this vision. The men with me saw nothing, but they were suddenly terrified and ran away to hide. 8So
I was left there all alone to see this amazing vision. My strength left me, my face grew deathly pale, and I felt very weak.
9Then I heard the man speak, and when I heard the sound of his voice, I fainted and lay there with my face to the ground.

10:1 The third year of Cyrus's reign was 536 B.C. **10:4** Hebrew *On the twenty-fourth day of the first month,* of the ancient Hebrew lunar calendar. This date in the book of Daniel can be cross-checked with dates in surviving Persian records and can be related accurately to our modern calendar. This event occurred on April 23, 536 B.C.

NOTES

10:1 ***King . . . of Persia.*** This term (*melek paras* [TH4428/6539, ZH4889/7273]) is not anachronistic (also found in 2 Chr 36:22; Ezra 1:1), as some have supposed; the argument that Cyrus never used the term of himself (Collins 1993:372; Baldwin 1978a:26; R. D. Wilson 1917:90-145) is true but not convincing. The title "king of Babylon" appears at 7:1, and Nabonidus is also called "king of Babylon" in the Nabonidus Chronicle 2.15 (ANET 306a).

Belteshazzar. This name is found 10 times in Daniel. This reminds the reader that this is the same Daniel whom Nebuchadnezzar renamed (1:7; 2:26; 4:8, 9, 18, 19 [5, 6, 15, 16]; 5:12) earlier in the book, in the time of the Babylonian Empire under Nebuchadnezzar.

had another vision. Lit., "something was revealed." The Hebrew word here, *dabar* [TH1697, ZH1821], is rendered variously as "oracle, revelation, message, word." In the Hebrew text it parallels *mar'eh* [TH4758, ZH5260], "vision," which is the last word in the MT of this verse. A powerful interplay of "word" (*dabar*) and "vision" (*mar'eh*) is used in this chapter.

concerned events certain to happen in the future. Lit., "was true." The NLT attempts to clarify by expanding upon the MT (cf. Lucas 2002:254).

war and great hardship. Lit., "great conflict." This translation fits the context best because most of the vision involves conflict (10:12–12:4). But this could also be rendered "with great effort he understood the vision."

10:3 ***wine . . . lotions.*** These were available only to the wealthy, especially the perfumed oils for the body (Olmstead 1948:79). Daniel's statement that in his mourning he had not used any fragrant lotions has a helpful parallel in Adad-guppi, mother (or grandmother?) of Nabonidus, the last king of Babylon. She states that she was mourning for the return of her god Sin (moon-god) to Hurran, and notes that "I did not allow perfumes (or) fine oil to touch my body" (COS 1.147:478a). In a later text, some Jewish mourners (c. 407 BC) at Elephantine, Egypt, wore sackcloth, fasted, stopped using body oils, drank no wine, and abstained from their wives (COS 3.51:128a, lines 20-21; cf. 2 Sam 14:2; Isa 61:3).

10:4 ***April 23.*** To this can be added 536 BC (see 10:1, NLT mg). It was the first month, 24th day of Abib (Nisan), by Israel's calendar.

Tigris River. Heb., *khiddeqel* [TH2313, ZH2538]. This name is also mentioned in Gen 2:14 as a river in the Garden of Eden, from which humankind was exiled.

10:5 ***saw.*** This word is followed by *hinneh* [TH2009, ZH2180], a particle indicating surprise and suddenness.

10:6 ***precious gem.*** The word *tarshish* [TH8658, ZH9577] refers to a brilliant jewel or precious stone. Its exact identity is unknown; it could be chrysolite, beryl, or topaz (cf. Exod 28:20 and Rev 21:20).

10:7 ***to hide.*** This verb is also found in the Garden of Eden story describing Adam and Eve's flight and fright when God approached them (Gen 3:10).

10:8 *I was left . . . alone.* The "I" in Hebrew is emphatic, "I myself." This together with the word "alone" further stresses Daniel's unique experience and the hidden nature of the message to Daniel.

10:9 *fainted.* Lit., "I myself fell into a deep sleep" (cf. 8:18; Judg 4:21; Jonah 1:5). Before God made Eve from Adam, a deep sleep fell upon Adam (Gen 2:21). Daniel did more than faint from the terror and fear of divinity before him; this response shows the weakness of humanity in the presence of a heavenly being. Cf. also Abraham's "deep sleep" where the same root is used (Gen 15:12; Collins 1993:338).

COMMENTARY

Daniel's final vision occurred in 536 BC, the third year of King Cyrus, and possibly 2 or 3 years after the decree of Cyrus to restore and rebuild Jerusalem had gone forth. Daniel informs us that he was in mourning for 21 days (see note on 10:3). Just as the Lord had revealed information during Belshazzar's reign, the last king of Babylon, so he would share more knowledge about future events during the reign of the Persians (the second kingdom of ch 2, and the ram of ch 8). This vision regards events that will take place during the hegemony of the next kingdom to come, Greece (the third kingdom of ch 2, and the goat of ch 8). But just as God had revealed the coming of the final kingdom of his holy people and his holy king, so this vision has both the end of earthly kingdoms in view and the rise of the eternal kingdom of Daniel's people (2:34-35, 44; 7:9-10, 18, 21, 26-27; 12:1-4), even envisioning their final rescue (cf. chs 3, 6) from the ultimate enemy—death. This vision continues to the last chapter of the book (12:1-7), with an epilogue and *inclusio* concluding the book (12:8-13).

The events of the vision describe a tangled, drawn-out, monotonous historical display of the incurable bent of mankind toward war and kings toward megalomania, focusing especially on the hostile efforts of God's enemies to destroy his people. The seed of the serpent is discernible (Gen 3:15), but the opposition will be defeated at the appointed time. This warfare in the spiritual and heavenly realm is tied intrinsically to war among the earthly armies of pagan nations and Daniel's people on earth (10:13, 20). The earthly armies of Persia and Greece, and the kings of the north (Syria) and the south (Egypt), which Greece spawned, were to become trapped in an imbroglio that only God could bring to an end. The spirit princes of Greece and Persia, along with Gabriel, Michael (Israel's spirit prince), and the dazzling humanlike being that speaks with Daniel would also be entangled in the conflict. His appearance has features that recall the throne figure who resembled a man in Ezekiel 1:26-28 (cf. Ezek 9:2-3, 11; 10:2, 6-7). His identity is not given, but he may be Gabriel as in chapters 8 and 9. These beings were the leaders of the spirit hosts of God for Israel. God is exceedingly interested in the fortunes of his holy people; he will see that they are victorious in the end—even over death (12:1-4). In chapters 3 and 6, he showed himself to be the God who rescues his people (3:28; 6:27 [28]; 12:1-4). He defeated the Egyptian pharaohs who had imprisoned his people as their slaves when he rescued his nation from Egypt (Exod 14–15). He brought judgment upon arrogant oppressors of his people in every age (cf. Jer 46:1–51:64; Nah 3:18-19). He would also bring an end to the little horns of the earth and heaven who would destroy his people.

Chapter 10 serves to introduce the heavenly informants and sources of Daniel's vision, to explain how it was possible for Daniel to receive this divine message, to give the basic orientation of the vision (for the future, 10:14; 10:21–11:1), and to locate its occurrence in history. God's revelation meets and penetrates Daniel's human existence because God takes the initiative and makes it possible for Daniel to receive the divine vision. As Daniel and Nebuchadnezzar had learned, God is a God who reveals future things and their significance (2:22, 28-30).

This great conflict in heaven and on earth and between heaven and earth (11:36) covers the period from 536 BC to the end of time (11:40; 12:1-4), highlighting key episodes where God intervenes to move history to its appointed conclusion. The time perspective of the vision looks beyond the third kingdom (Greece) in chapters 2, 7, 8, although chapter 8 foreshadows this end. It extends to the end appointed for the little horn and the fourth kingdom of chapters 2 and 7. It has the encompassing abomination of 9:27 in view and the figure of 11:40-45. Historically, the fourth kingdom was almost certainly Rome (as noted above), but the bestial and demonic spiritual characteristics of the fourth kingdom and little horn ("king") extend its identity beyond Rome, for Rome and Babylon became apocalyptic code names for the final hostile nations that would arrogantly challenge God and his people.

The reception of this vision is again related to Daniel's persistent and consistent life of seeking the face of his God through humbling ascetic practices (10:2-3). He constantly denied himself and sought to know God and his ways more closely. He practiced spiritual disciplines (1:8-14; 9:2; 10:2-3). He had no doubt been seeking further understanding concerning the plight of his people, for previous visions had left him puzzled (7:28), and he had discovered that his God was gracious toward him (9:20-23), both on his behalf and on behalf of his people. He also recognized his part as a member of a previously rebellious people (9:4-19). He would be given more wisdom and understanding about his people, even though some of them were freed and on the way to Jerusalem according to Cyrus's edict (Ezra 1–2).

Daniel evidently drank wine in his new cultural setting, since it was no longer part of a cultural indoctrination program and tied to the king's rich food (1:8), but for a period he was abstaining from it (10:2-3). He was also living in the time of the liberation of his people from Babylon and could indeed celebrate this new era with wine and food. Yet he desired to know even more about the future of his people (10:12-14). The "man" whom Daniel saw was another unnamed heavenly being. It was not God, for Michael came to help him against the spirit prince of Persia (10:13; 12:1). As apocalyptic literature, the book of Daniel looks behind the human prince of Persia to see a spiritual prince of Persia. War, hostility, and violence are more than human—they are satanic and demonic!

The fact that only Daniel saw the vision of this man (10:7) is quite amazing. His friends were somehow terrified and fled (10:7). At Sinai the people had trembled at the theophany of their God and had heard his voice but discerned no form (Exod 20:18; Deut 4:12; cf. Collins 1993:374; Longman 1999:248). It is similar to the apostle Paul's encounter with the risen Christ—only he saw the vision of the Lord (Acts 9:4-7; cf. Acts 22:6-9). Daniel states emphatically in Hebrew that he was left alone, which accounts for the "secret" nature of his apocalyptic visions (cf. 7:28; 8:26).

◆ 2. Daniel's encounter with a manlike being (10:10-19)

10 Just then a hand touched me and lifted
me, still trembling, to my hands and knees.
11 And the man said to me, "Daniel, you are
very precious to God, so listen carefully to
what I have to say to you. Stand up, for I
have been sent to you." When he said this
to me, I stood up, still trembling.
12 Then he said, "Don't be afraid, Daniel.
Since the first day you began to pray for
understanding and to humble yourself be-
fore your God, your request has been heard
in heaven. I have come in answer to your
prayer. 13 But for twenty-one days the spir-
it prince* of the kingdom of Persia blocked
my way. Then Michael, one of the arch-
angels,* came to help me, and I left him
there with the spirit prince of the kingdom
of Persia.* 14 Now I am here to explain what
will happen to your people in the future, for
this vision concerns a time yet to come."
15 While he was speaking to me, I looked
down at the ground, unable to say a word.
16 Then the one who looked like a man*
touched my lips, and I opened my mouth
and began to speak. I said to the one
standing in front of me, "I am filled with
anguish because of the vision I have seen,
my lord, and I am very weak. 17 How can
someone like me, your servant, talk to
you, my lord? My strength is gone, and I
can hardly breathe."
18 Then the one who looked like a man
touched me again, and I felt my strength
returning. 19 "Don't be afraid," he said,
"for you are very precious to God. Peace!
Be encouraged! Be strong!"
As he spoke these words to me, I sud-
denly felt stronger and said to him,
"Please speak to me, my lord, for you
have strengthened me."

10:13a Hebrew *the prince;* also in 10:13c, 20. **10:13b** Hebrew *the chief princes.* **10:13c** As in one Greek version; Hebrew reads *and I was left there with the kings of Persia.* The meaning of the Hebrew is uncertain. **10:16** As in most manuscripts of the Masoretic Text; one manuscript of the Masoretic Text and one Greek version read *Then something that looked like a human hand.*

NOTES

10:10 ***a hand.*** The text does not make it clear whose hand this was, but it was probably the hand of the man described in 10:5ff (see commentary).

lifted me. This would be better rendered "shook me" or "roused me." It translates a Hiphil form of *nua'* [TH5128, ZH5675], "to swing, move back and forth, wave."

10:11 ***you are very precious to God.*** See 9:23; 10:19 for this expression, which indicates that Daniel was pleasing to the Lord. (Cf. Gen 3:6, where the Niphal stem of this verb describes the desirable aspects of the tree of the knowledge of good and evil.)

listen carefully. Lit., "Understand!"

10:12 ***in heaven.*** These words are not in the MT, but are reasonably implied by the text.

your prayer. Lit., "your words." God heard Daniel's "words" and responded by sending Daniel "words" and a vision.

10:13 ***spirit prince.*** This rendering is demanded by the context. The Hebrew is simply "prince," but no earthly figure is in view. Deuteronomy 32:8-9 seems to imply such spirit princes over nations. That text in MT reads, "when the Most High gave the nations their inheritance, when he divided all mankind, he set up boundaries for the peoples *according to the sons of Israel.*" But texts found at Qumran (4QDeut[j, q], supported by LXX; cf. Collins 1993:374) state the final phrase as "*according to the number of the sons of God.*" The reading with "sons of God" is preferable (see Carpenter 2009:516 and Heiser 2001:54-74).

archangels. Lit., "chief angels" or "chief princes" (*hassarim hari'shonim* [TH8269/7223, ZH8569/8037]).

I left him. This follows the LXX reading. The MT is difficult, but probably should be rendered, "since I was left [detained] there by the king of Persia."

10:14 ***in the future.*** Lit., "in the latter days" (cf. 2:28).

10:17 ***my lord.*** This renders the word *'adoni* [TH113, ZH123], which was used of human beings as well as of God or his divine messengers.

10:19 ***you are very precious to God.*** Cf. 9:23; 10:11.

Peace. This renders the word *shalom* [TH7965, ZH8934], which here functions as a greeting, wishing "well-being, health" to the recipient.

COMMENTARY

This section begins with the statement, "Just then a hand touched me and lifted me" (10:10), an action also recorded of the angelic being in *4 Ezra* 5:14-15. The hand that touched Daniel belonged to the man whom Daniel had described with words that do not entirely fit a mortal man (10:5-6). This man touched Daniel two more times to give him strength to speak (10:15-16, 18). Until his lips were touched, Daniel stood before the man trembling. God is the one who gives people the ability to speak. He had done so for Moses (Exod 4:11-12), and he had enabled his prophet Isaiah to speak with purged lips (Isa 6:5-7). Daniel's ability to speak was restored, and his whole being was strengthened by the divine touch (10:18).

In the book of Daniel, the descriptions of how human beings react to divine beings are instructive—whether they react to the presence of divine messengers from the Lord or are confronted with his amazing revelations through dreams, visions, or interpretations of these. Nebuchadnezzar's reaction to Daniel, in whom was the spirit of the "gods," stands in a similar vein (2:46). They tremble, fear, fall prostrate, weaken, cannot talk, cannot breathe, lay sick, are overcome, are terrified, lose color, their legs and knees give way; but they also often end up praising the Most High, humbling themselves, confessing the true living God, and composing poetry in praise of this God!

Daniel is described as being loved or highly esteemed three times in this book (9:23; 10:11, 19). A careful study of his life makes the reason for this clear: He loves God supremely and loves and respects his fellow human beings, be they king or friend, Jew (his three Hebrew companions) or Gentile (the Babylonian wise men, 2:15-16), rich or poor (4:27 [24]). He acted justly, loved mercy, and walked humbly before his God (Mic 6:8).

This manlike heavenly being makes clear the value of prayer for Daniel, even in exile in a foreign land, for God's sovereignty does not obviate the prayers of his people but rather works in and through them. From the first day—three weeks before—Daniel's prayer had been heard. Prayer and scripture study (9:2-3) were Daniel's key to not only survival but success before God. This inspiring being had been sent by the heavenly King of all that is at the request of a mere human being. This being was to serve Daniel, not enslave him. Even Michael, one of the chief princes of the nations, ministered to Daniel by answering his prayer (10:12).

Michael had come to aid the unnamed man after that being had engaged in some kind of battle with the spirit prince of Persia for 21 days. We are not told what the conflict was about, but it probably involved the holy people and probably concerned the continued return of Daniel's people from the Babylonian exile. God is the one who appoints and removes world rulers and dominions (2:37-38; 4:25 [22]; 7:27; 2 Chr 36:22-23; Ezra 1:1-2; Isa 45:1-4). This was a momentous time of empire demolition and building; we are given an apocalyptic glimpse behind the scenes. Daniel may have expected the eternal Kingdom of the Rock (2:34-35, 44-45a) to come and the "one like a son of man," belonging to "the holy people" to appear soon (7:13, 18). Similarly, after Christ's ascension from earth, the apostles still expected the kingdom of Israel to be established in their day (Acts 1:6-7). Daniel knew how things would end, but not the time. He was informed here that it would be in "a time yet to come" (10:14).

◆ 3. The manlike being explains his visitation (10:20–11:1)

20 He replied, "Do you know why I have come? Soon I must return to fight against the spirit prince of the kingdom of Persia, and after that the spirit prince of the kingdom of Greece* will come. 21 Meanwhile, I will tell you what is written in the Book of Truth. (No one helps me against these spirit princes except Michael, your spirit prince.* 11:1 I have been standing beside Michael* to support and strengthen him since the first year of the reign of Darius the Mede.)

10:20 Hebrew *of Javan.* **10:21** Hebrew *against these except Michael, your prince.* **11:1** Hebrew *him.*

NOTES

10:20 ***Do you know?*** Or, "Do you understand?"

after that the spirit prince of the kingdom of Greece will come. Possibly to war against Israel, as is illustrated in 11:3-35.

10:21 ***the Book of Truth.*** Lit., "the writing of truth." This book contains the heavenly and historical course of history. It resembles the heavenly tablets of Enoch (*1 Enoch* 93:2). Extrabiblical literature refers to the Tablets of Destiny (Carpenter 2009:517; Lucas 2009:552-553). The Greeks and even their gods were bound by "the dictates of fate," which they could not change (Balme and Lawall 2003:166, 221). This "book" is a metaphor for God's omniscience.

11:1 ***Michael.*** This is added for clarity; the Hebrew is "him" (so NLT mg).

Darius the Mede. See discussion in the Introduction, "Historical Accuracy," and the notes on 6:1, 28 [2, 29].

COMMENTARY

Daniel was anxious to know exactly why his heavenly visitor had come. He had learned that there were surprises awaiting him from God's messengers, as well as headaches and sickness (7:28; 8:27). The messenger revealed that a battle in the spiritual realm awaited him. He and Michael would finish their battle with the spirit prince of Persia. Then a ferocious new conflict would begin with the spirit prince of Greece, for this would be the nation from which the historical forerunner of the anti-God, anti-Israel figure would arise—Antiochus Epiphanes, whose career is outlined in 11:21-35. But even in these verses the language indicates that more than

Antiochus's historical and bellicose rampages were driving the course of events. Divine forces, good and bad, were involved. In all of this, God's sovereignty over the process is clear.

The fourth kingdom (chs 2 and 7), which symbolizes historical Rome and other nations that will oppose God and his people (including the kingdom of the Antichrist in Revelation), is not mentioned here. The remaining chapters of Daniel are primarily devoted to the theologically significant historical events that occurred in the time of the successors of the Greek Empire. The fourth kingdom, the kingdom that gives rise to the final ferocious "king" who blasphemes God, does appear in 11:40-45 and stands largely behind the account of Antiochus in 11:36-39, 40-45. Although God reveals the fourth kingdom per se only in chapters 2 and 7, he reveals the "little horn" king who is the last king of that monstrous empire several times (7:8, 20-22, 24-26; 9:26-27). This "little horn" is also foreshadowed numerous times in Daniel in other historical figures (8:9-14; 9:26-27; 11:31-39).

The divine messenger mentions the Book of Truth (10:21). God's truth is the foundation of all things. Daniel had seen truth overthrown, cast to the ground (8:12); he recognized God's truth as the guide for his people (9:11b-13). Moses knew of a book that God kept that contained the names of those approved of the Lord (Exod 32:32-33); those who sinned against God were blotted out of that book by the divine Judge (7:9-10, 18, 22, 26-27). Evil persons are blotted out of the book of life, but the righteous have their names in it (Ps 69:28). Daniel knew of the book of life. Those whose names are found in it will experience resurrection, if necessary (12:1-2).

This messenger, however, was speaking of a book that recorded not names, primarily, but the events that would come to pass "soon"—as presented in 11:2–12:7. The psalmist also knew of a book that contained all his days before they had even begun (Ps 139:16). Thus, the messenger would tell the truth (11:2) based on the Book of Truth. God does not, of course, keep a literal set of books. This is figurative speech. But the truth implied is real. God is in control and knows the course of all things, without overtaking the free will and responsibility of persons made in his image—witness Nebuchadnezzar, Belshazzar, and Shadrach, Meshach, and Abednego as examples (3:16-18; 4:27 [24]; 5:22-24).

Michael, the great prince of Daniel's people, appears at the end of this vision to rescue those who are righteous and wise (12:1). He is accompanied by this messenger angel (10:13; 11:1) and by their heavenly armies. Since the time of Darius the Mede, Michael and this angel fought to procure, most likely, the liberation of the holy people from Babylon—against the wishes of the spirit prince of Persia. God's Spirit stirred the heart of Cyrus to return the Jews, and many other dispersed peoples in his empire, to their homelands (2 Chr 36:22-23; Ezra 1:1-4; cf. the Cyrus Cylinder, ANET 315-316). The realpolitik of the day was secondary, a tool used by Daniel's God. It would be even a more daunting task to deliver them from the spirit prince of the time of the end (7:22, 26; 9:27; 11:40; 12:1).

The mention of "spirit princes" associated with Persia and Greece implies that there was one for Babylon and would be one for the fourth kingdom of chapters 2 and 7. The most likely candidate will be the "spirit prince" behind the "little horn" of chapter 7 (cf. 9:26-27; 11:36-39, 40-45). In the book of Revelation, the final demonic prince behind the demonic kingdom and the rise of the beast is Satan himself, a dragon, the prince of evil (Rev 13:1-2; cf. Rev 12:9; 20:1-2), who inspires even a second beast (Rev 13:11).

In his sovereignty, the Lord divided the world among the human race and assigned portions to the nations. He assigned the people's boundaries according to the extent (number) of the sons of Israel (Deut 32:8, MT), or more probably, according to the number of the "sons of God" (see note on 10:13; Carpenter 2009:516; cf. Heiser 2001). God is over Israel, and Michael is its spirit prince. Hence, the geographical extent and authority of the nations was ordained by God, as reflected by Daniel's answers to Nebuchadnezzar (2:36-37; 4:19-27 [16-24]) and affirmed by the apostle Paul (Acts 17:26-28). The other nations will hold their boundaries and authority, and they will have their spirit princes as assigned to them, for in the end God's goal is to bless all nations through the descendants of Abraham (Gen 12:1-3).

◆ E. The Deliverance of Israel from Destruction, Resulting in the Triumph of God's People (11:2–12:7)

1. The truth concerning the kingdoms of Persia and Greece (11:2-4)

2"Now then, I will reveal the truth to you. Three more Persian kings will reign, to be succeeded by a fourth, far richer than the others. He will use his wealth to stir up everyone to fight against the kingdom of Greece.*

3"Then a mighty king will rise to power who will rule with great authority and accomplish everything he sets out to do.
4But at the height of his power, his kingdom will be broken apart and divided into four parts. It will not be ruled by the king's descendants, nor will the kingdom hold the authority it once had. For his empire will be uprooted and given to others.

11:2 Hebrew *of Javan.*

NOTES

11:2 ***reveal.*** This is better rendered as "tell" (cf. NJPS, NIV), since it is from the verb *nagad* [TH5046, ZH5583] (tell), not *galah* [TH1540, ZH1655] (reveal).

succeeded by a fourth. The fourth king has been identified as Xerxes (Ahasuerus) most often, but also as Darius II or III (cf. Hartman and Di Lella 1978:87-88; but Yamauchi [1990:188] favors Xerxes). The previous kings (after Cyrus) were Cambyses, Gaumata (a usurper), and Darius I, the Great.

11:3 ***accomplish everything he sets out to do.*** Lit., "he will act according to his own will."

11:4 ***four parts.*** Lit., "divided up to the four winds of heaven."

king's descendants. Lit., "his posterity."

his empire. This refers to Alexander's empire. For a brief summary of Alexander's career, see Starr 1991:394-403. See further V. Hanson's (1999:173-207) especially penetrating treatment of Alexander as the cruel, vicious, murdering general that he was.

COMMENTARY

This chapter views the history of Persia, and then Greece, and then the successors of Alexander the Great from a theological perspective in which they are always under the control and watchful eye of the God of heaven. Metahistory is ultimately more important than mere history on the human level of existence. It eventually (11:36-45) purports to speak of events both spiritual and earthly that have not yet happened and that are determined more and more by forces outside of earthly history. The apocalyptic history (Goldingay calls the genre "quasi-prophecy" [1989:310-312]) of this final vision is real, as it presents the forces of God working for his people and against their opponents until the appointed time arrives and God's goals for history are realized (11:40; 12:1-4). It is properly designated apocalyptic because it presents future historical events that are to take place within the confines of God's sovereign plan to bring history to its proper end with the destruction of evil on earth and in heaven, and the establishment of God's rule, his Kingdom on earth and in heaven (see Introduction, "Literary Style" and "Literary Unity").

As might be expected, a "history" book written from a heavenly perspective and inspired by God will have a historiographical methodology that breaks the mold of modern secular accounts of history, which axiomatically rule out any divine involvement or divine purpose to the flow of history. This chapter is not a mere presentation of the brute facts, informed only by human theories that do not rise above the horizontal level of reality and explanation. The divine origin and perspective of the Book of Truth (10:21) is the key to its content and presentation.

See the Outline in the Introduction for a brief look at the structure and content of this section, which encompasses 11:2–12:7. In this section, we encounter the divine messenger's report from the Book of Truth. The end goal of this is God's ultimate and eternal rescue of his people (12:1-4), when he will establish an everlasting Kingdom from those who are resurrected (12:2, 13), as well as from the wise and the righteous who are rescued alive at the time of the end. They will all receive their inheritance along with Daniel (12:13). The course of world events and God's everlasting Kingdom has been described previously in language referring to the fifth, everlasting Kingdom of God, which encompasses both heaven and earth (2:21; 4:3, 34-35 [3:33; 4:31-32]; 6:26, 27 [27, 28]; 7:14, 18, 22, 27; 9:24; 12:1-2, 13). Daniel's previous assertion that his God "controls the course of world events; he removes kings and sets up other kings" (2:21; 6:28 [29]) is demonstrated powerfully in this final vision. The end as well as the beginning belongs to God, the Most High. As Daniel had told Nebuchadnezzar, the Lord had revealed what would happen in the future (2:28).

These chapters (and perhaps 8:23-25) report on the course of future history. They share some features of basic literary style, form, and content with the Akkadian Prophecies (c. 1200–300 BC), which purport to describe the reigns of historical rulers and then conclude with a prophecy about future history (see Longman 1991:131-195; cf. Grayson and Lambert 1964:7-30; for a brief excerpt of a text see Lucas 2009:569, who also shows probable connections between these texts and Daniel). Both list kings and reigns connected by "(after him) a king will arise," and use figurative, enigmatic language. The Akkadian Prophecies are closely connected to omen texts that Daniel may have studied in Babylon (1:4). The eschatological aspects of these texts, however, do not extend to the final end as they do in Daniel (for more comparisons and contrasts see Longman 1991:187-189). Nor do they speak of God's control and appointed times for the final events as Daniel does (11:27, 35, 40, 45; 12:1, 7; see Walton 1992:224-225). Daniel could have been influenced by this genre of literature, but he would have adapted it to his goals and purposes.

Regarding the contrast between the extent of these chapters' apocalyptic and eschatological elements and those found in the Akkadian Prophecies, several things can be noted: The literature in Daniel is not used to legitimate any king, but rather pushes forward to the last enigmatic king (11:21-35, 36-45) to discredit him, recording his rise and destruction by God (11:45). The inspired author of Daniel is giving an actual prophetic announcement about the future throughout the entire chapter. His presentation encompasses history that is future to the author, even the early years of Antiochus's rise to power (11:21-35). Verses 36-39 begin to assert things about Antiochus that are more difficult to identify and apply based on extant historical documents, and, finally, aspects of 11:36-39 and all of 11:40-45 must be assigned to a figure beyond Antiochus IV's career. These verses recall the little horn of 7:8, 21b-22, 24b-25, and underline the fact that Daniel's apocalyptic eschatological perspective extends to the consummation of God's goals and purposes.

In 11:2-4, the messenger begins his revelatory report of truth. The exact persons and events that the author refers to in 11:2-45 are sometimes difficult to identify. In the following commentary, an attempt is made to identify historical figures, but these are made with some reserve. The fourth king of Persia is most likely Xerxes, also called Ahasuerus (Esth 1:1, 485–465 BC), but this second "name" may be a title rather than a proper name (cf. 9:1-2). Xerxes amassed the largest army that had yet been mustered in the ancient world to fight against Greece. His father, Darius (522–486 BC), had tried to conquer the Greeks but had failed, losing one of the most significant battles of antiquity at Marathon (490 BC). Some 20,000 Persians were killed by 6,000 Greeks at Thermopylae. In 480 BC, Xerxes suffered an even more staggering loss in one of the most famous battles in antiquity—the Persian naval fleet was annihilated at Salamis (V. Hanson 1999:95-96). Aeschylus, in his tragedy, *Persians* (472 BC), presents Xerxes as the supreme example of *hubris* (human arrogance and pride), a man who was punished by divine vengeance. Xerxes had burnt the acropolis of Athens—a godless act that shocked the Greeks—but lost the war, and this sent a tremor through the Persian kingdom. Herodotus (*Histories* 7.184-186) records that 5,283,220 (this impossible number has been estimated to have been closer to 360,000) soldiers and attendants marched with Xerxes, and his huge force should have demolished the Greeks. Hence, a messenger in Aeschylus's play is made to say that it was not the Greeks that crushed Persia, "but some spirit crushed the host" (*Persians* line 345).

The career of Alexander the Great is described in 11:3-4. His own sons did not inherit his kingdom. His incompetent brother Philip, another brother Heracles, and Alexander IV (born after his death to Roxanne, his Persian wife) were swept aside. Then, rival generals forcefully split the empire into four smaller kingdoms (see comments on 8:8-12). His kingdom was rooted out and given to those not having his stature or his vision. Alexander died on June 10, 323 BC at the age of

33. His conquests were unequaled. His success was an enigma even to himself! Plutarch (1986:242, 256, 259, 269) recorded a legend that a spring near the city of Xanthus washed up a bronze tablet that foretold the destruction of the Persians by the Greeks. This is not a reliable historical source, but nonetheless, Alexander's destruction of Persia was considered a divine work even among pagans. Signs, dreams, and oracles were part and parcel of the third empire depicted in chapters 2 and 7 (Balme and Lawall 2003:190-192).

There were, of course, more than five kings that ruled the Persian Empire; there were in fact 13 (J. M. Cook 1983:206). Daniel's vision did not include an exhaustive list of these kings, but stopped and highlighted Xerxes, whose actions would be tied to the eastward expansion of the empire. After Xerxes, eight more kings would reign; the last one was assassinated in 330 BC, Darius III. But the vicious and arrogant attempts of Darius I and Xerxes to conquer the Greeks and their ignominious defeats were enough to assure that the Greeks would seek vengeance and have their day. The fury and speed of the male goat (8:7) would come in the person of Alexander "the Great," whom V. Hanson has compared to Hitler rather than Hannibal or Napoleon. He observes that "Under thirteen years of generalship of Alexander the Great, more people were killed through his use of western warfare than had died in all the Greek battles in the century and a half from Marathon to Chaeronea. And his successors were eager to continue" (1999:197). The author's use of the pattern of 3 + 1 ("three more . . . a fourth"; 11:2), a common literary device in Hebrew literature (cf. Prov 30:15, 18, 21, 29; Amos 1:3, 6, 9; 2:1, 4, NLT mg) probably indicates that these 3 + 1 kings stand for the entire Achaemenid line of Persian kings. Both the wisdom tradition and the prophetic tradition in Israel used this device.

◆ 2. The kings of the south triumph (11:5-12)

**5"The king of the south will increase in
power, but one of his own officials will
become more powerful than he and will
rule his kingdom with great strength.**

**6"Some years later an alliance will be
formed between the king of the north and
the king of the south. The daughter of the
king of the south will be given in mar-
riage to the king of the north to secure
the alliance, but she will lose her influ-
ence over him, and so will her father. She
will be abandoned along with her sup-
porters. 7But when one of her relatives*
becomes king of the south, he will raise
an army and enter the fortress of the king
of the north and defeat him. 8When he
returns to Egypt, he will carry back their
idols with him, along with priceless arti-
cles of gold and silver. For some years
afterward he will leave the king of the
north alone.**

**9"Later the king of the north will invade
the realm of the king of the south but will
soon return to his own land. 10However,
the sons of the king of the north will as-
semble a mighty army that will advance
like a flood and carry the battle as far as
the enemy's fortress.**

**11"Then, in a rage, the king of the south
will rally against the vast forces assembled
by the king of the north and will defeat
them. 12After the enemy army is swept
away, the king of the south will be filled
with pride and will execute many thou-
sands of his enemies. But his success will
be short lived.**

11:7 Hebrew *a branch from her roots.*

NOTES

11:5 ***with great strength.*** This should possibly be rendered "an extensive dominion." For an excellent, succinct presentation of the Ptolemies, Antiochids, and the Seleucids, see ISBE 1.143-147; 3.1048-1050; and 4.385-386. For primary literature, see 1–4 Maccabees as cited in the commentary. Josephus, Herodotus, Livy, and other ancient historians also record some of this material.

11:6 ***and so will her father.*** Lit., "and his arm (power) will not stand." Some translations prefer to read "seed" or "offspring" (*zera'* [TH2233, ZH2446]) for "arm" (power) (*zeroa'* [TH2220, ZH2432]) as do the LXX, Theodotion, and Vulgate. The consonants are the same, but the pointing is different. The verse, however, remains nuanced and difficult to translate, since "seed" in the sense of offspring and "arm" can both be understood in the sense of political force/power. "Power" (arm) fits the context well, and it would fit with Daniel's tendency toward repetition (the same word is used earlier in the verse, translated "influence" in NLT). But "seed," offspring, was an accepted way for kings and royalty to develop and maintain both political and military power. The NLT correctly follows the MT.

supporters. The NLT oversimplifies the difficulties of the text. Three groups, at least, are mentioned: "her attendants" (or, those who brought her), "the one who bore her" (i.e., "her father"), and the one who strengthened her ("supported her"). Each of these groups of "supporters" are noted separately in the MT.

11:7 ***raise an army.*** Or, "come against the army."

11:8 ***idols.*** Lit., "their gods."

11:11 ***will defeat them.*** Rather, "the horde will be given into his [the king of the south's] hand." The passive verb of the Hebrew emphasizes God's sovereign involvement (cf. 1:1-2).

11:12 ***his success will be short lived.*** Lit., "he will not prevail."

COMMENTARY

In 11:5-45 the kings of the south and the north are depicted as constantly fighting for the hegemony over the coastal lands of Syria and Palestine. The horns of the fourth kingdom (ch 7) and the third kingdom (chs 7–8) stood for kings. Now the horn imagery is dropped and kings are referenced directly. By their violence and ruthless rule, these kings still display the character of the horns used to represent them earlier. These historical kings were the Ptolemies, kings of Egypt, and the Seleucids, kings of Syria. Egypt and Syria battled to achieve victory in the realpolitik of the day, both attempting to position themselves to achieve their goals. By 301 BC, the Seleucids were entrenched in Syria and the Ptolemies in Egypt, under their victorious rulers Seleucus I and Ptolemy I Soter, respectively. The ambience of these narratives, however, suggests that "between the lines" lurk political envy, maneuvering, conspiracies, and intrigues.

The listing of names and rulers and selected events in this chapter is not a detailed history that leaves no questions unanswered about why and when who did what. Events that would help us understand the successions of persons are sometimes obscure or not referred to. The author does not dwell on historical detail. He is writing to give us a broad sweep of the events that lead up to "the end," and to introduce the figure and events of 11:36-39 and 40-45. These final verses paint a picture of a figure who exalts himself against God, peoples, and a holy people, and who will be destroyed (11:45). Then "the final" end comes (12:1-7) with cataclysmic events.

The events in 12:1-7 overlap with those in 11:36-39 and 40-45 to some extent, but go beyond them. Our goal will be to follow the theological purpose of the text, but giving some historical information where possible (on ch 11, see especially Green 2007; Shipley 2000; Tcherikover 1959).

The successful rule of the Ptolemies of Egypt is described in 11:5-12; they were kings of the south. The king of the south mentioned in 11:5 is most likely Ptolemy I Soter (323–285 BC), the founder of the dynasty. The official under him was Seleucus I Nicator (312–280 BC). Both had been outstanding generals under Alexander the Great. Seleucus I had received the area from Palestine to Babylon to rule initially, but had been ousted by Antigonus. He made his capital Babylon and appears to have imagined himself as being a second Alexander (cf. 11:4). He eventually received the largest portion of Alexander's empire, including Palestine and Syria (see comments on 8:8 regarding the division of Alexander's empire). Ptolemy I Soter, however, seized Palestine, and the Ptolemies (as Daniel's kings of the south) controlled this strategic area until 198 BC. This strip of Palestine and southern Syria was a bone of contention for many years after this. Most important to the reader of Daniel is the fact that the holy city, Jerusalem, and the holy people were located in this corridor of contention. Though Israel, the holy city, and the people of Daniel lay between these two warring factions, God remained in control and had appointed a time of closure for these events (11:27, 35, 40, 45; 12:1, 7). The drama achieves its major focus later in the chapter when the people of the holy covenant (11:28, 30), the Temple and sanctuary, and the sacrifices are attacked and endangered. The heavenly narrator is concerned about those who violate the holy covenant (11:32) and about an object set up in the Temple or on the altar of burnt offering that causes desecration and sacrilege (11:31). He is especially concerned to note that the wise and those who know their God will escape all of this (11:32), but some will have to die (11:33), and many will be refined and cleansed by this time of wrath (11:35-36). God will bring it all to an end, including the destruction of the king of the north who arrogantly blasphemes God (11:36). His hubris reaches the heavens (cf. 4:22 [19]). This is what the writer wants us to see and hear and learn. This is didactic—theological—history, history reported in a way that is subservient to moral, spiritual, religious, and ethical teachings for God's people. The author is more concerned about the motivation and character of the historical participants than he is of the external "facts." But by reporting a good amount of historical detail, he makes these historical depictions applicable to real life, for motivation and character must be worked out in the arena of historical existence by God's people.

The report of a great struggle and hardship (10:1) continues in 11:6. The king of the south (now Ptolemy II Philadelphus) gave his daughter Bernice to be the new wife of the king of the north (now Antiochus II Theos). Bernice had a child who was to be Antiochus's heir, but then Ptolemy II died, and Antiochus returned to his earlier, divorced wife, Laodice, and made her eldest son, Seleucus II (246–226 BC), king. (Thus, the influence of the king of the south and his daughter was lost.) After Seleucus became king, Laodice poisoned Antiochus and murdered Bernice and her infant son. The typical court intrigues of the day were demonstrated in all their evil—they sound familiar even today. But time moves on toward the appointed end, for God's presence is active behind the externals (cf. the book of Esther).

In 11:7-8, Bernice's brother, Ptolemy III Euergetes (246–221 BC; the new king of the south), takes vengeance upon the king of the north, Seleucus II (246–226 BC), who was involved in the murder of Bernice. Ptolemy III was able to bring back some spoils from this vengeful expedition into Syria. Seleucus II was having his own problems at this time and died early. Ptolemy III extended the Ptolemaic kingdom to its greatest geographical area. The "fortress" mentioned in 11:7 was the city of Antioch with its port Seleucia. An attempted reprisal in response to Ptolemy III's expansion occurred years later under the next two kings of the north (11:10), Seleucus III Ceraunus (226–223 BC) and his brother Antiochus III (223–187 BC), who succeeded him at his death. This continued against the next king of the south, Ptolemy IV Philopater (221–203 BC). As Antiochus III won substantial victories (11:10), he refused peace agreements and pressed the war even farther into the south, and in this time Ptolemy IV was able to gather strength (11:11). Ptolemy IV finally defeated Antiochus III at Raphia in 217 BC (cf. 11:12). This triumph of the king of the south, however, would be short lived (11:12), for all this paved the way for the coming king of the north, the "despicable man" (11:21), the "sinful root" (1 Macc 1:10), who was the son of Antiochus III. With him the kings of the north became dominant.

◆ 3. The rise of the king of the north (11:13-20)

13"A few years later the king of the north will return with a fully equipped army far greater than before. 14At that time there will be a general uprising against the king of the south. Violent men among your own people will join them in fulfillment of this vision, but they will not succeed. 15Then the king of the north will come and lay siege to a fortified city and capture it. The best troops of the south will not be able to stand in the face of the onslaught.

16"The king of the north will march onward unopposed; none will be able to stop him. He will pause in the glorious land of Israel,* intent on destroying it. 17He will make plans to come with the might of his entire kingdom and will form an alliance with the king of the south. He will give him a daughter in marriage in order to overthrow the kingdom from within, but his plan will fail.

18"After this, he will turn his attention to the coastland and conquer many cities. But a commander from another land will put an end to his insolence and cause him to retreat in shame. 19He will take refuge in his own fortresses but will stumble and fall and be seen no more.

20"His successor will send out a tax collector to maintain the royal splendor. But after a very brief reign, he will die, though not from anger or in battle.

11:16 Hebrew *the glorious land.*

NOTES

11:14 *general uprising.* Lit., "many will arise."

fulfillment of this vision. The word "vision" is not definite in the MT (i.e., "a vision," not "this/the vision"), and it is unclear what it refers to.

11:16 *glorious land of Israel.* Lit., "the glorious land" (so NLT mg); here it refers to Israel; cf. 8:9; 11:41.

11:17 *from within.* This is not in the MT but is implied in the words of the text, hence it is added by the NLT to further describe the overthrow in the context.

his plan will fail. Lit., "but there will be nothing to (for) him" (cf. 9:26).

11:18 ***retreat in shame.*** The idea in Hebrew is that "he [the king of the north] will not return his insolence against him [the commander]."

11:19 ***take refuge.*** This may be in order "to attack and loot them," not to use the fortresses as a refuge (cf. Goldingay 1989:273).

be seen no more. Lit., "will not be found."

11:20 ***tax collector.*** The Hebrew is less clear; it indicates "an oppressor/exactor (for) the splendor of the kingdom"—probably referring to Heliodorus (2 Macc 3:1-40).

COMMENTARY

The line of northern kings again takes the upper hand later in the reign of Antiochus III (the Great), the father of Antiochus IV (Epiphanes). Enraged by the defeats he had suffered (11:9-12), Antiochus came with renewed and expanded forces and met with success (11:13-19). Some Jews supported an uprising against the king of Egypt (Ptolemy IV), evidently favoring Antiochus III (11:14), but this was put down by an Egyptian military leader, Scopas. At the battle of Panias, Ptolemaic rule in Palestine was permanently replaced by Antiochus III (11:15). This Seleucid ruler was intent on destroying Israel (11:16) because of their refusal to join him or to become Hellenized, but some of the Jews approved of him and won his favor, evidently deterring him by flattery (Josephus *Antiquities* 12.3.3-4 [12.129-153]). These Jews were, according to Josephus, part of the "lawless ones" among Daniel's people.

Antiochus III then set his heart on the entire Near East. His goal was empire, and he gave protection to the great Carthaginian general, Hannibal, and also attempted to support Greece against Rome. He gave his daughter Cleopatra to be the wife of the king of the south (Ptolemy V, 203–181 BC) to strengthen his influence there (11:17). His plans to employ Egypt to help him gain territory and influence failed (Green 2007:89-91), because although the union of his daughter Cleopatra I to Ptolemy V succeeded with Egypt at first (Josephus *Antiquities* 12.4.1), it angered Rome. (Yet, after Ptolemy V's death, Cleopatra did serve as co-regent with her son, Ptolemy VI Philometer.) Antiochus also undertook numerous military campaigns, but his attempt to become a world conqueror was thwarted by the Romans, who defeated him in several key battles, including the battle of Magnesia (190 BC). He was later killed while plundering a temple in Elymais (187 BC; 11:19) to get money to meet his obligations to Rome (Green 2007:90).

A key issue is raised in the text—namely, the involvement of lawless persons from among Daniel's people who join the forces of Antiochus and/or support him (11:14, 16). The writer notes the reason for this—to fulfill the vision of rebellion that was depicted in 8:13 and in Gabriel's answer (9:24). This did not succeed because the appointed end had not arrived—that would occur under Antiochus IV, his younger son. Unfortunately, Daniel's people would rebel in lawlessness (cf. 11:32), but God would defeat them (11:14). It is not clear exactly who these persons were (Lucas 2002:281). Then the king of the north will be in control (11:16).

Antiochus III's humiliating defeat in Magnesia at the hands of a famous Roman general, Cornelius Scipio Asiaticus (cf. 11:18), would be surpassed by the humiliation of his arrogant son by the Romans. That son, Seleucus IV Philopator (187–175 BC), was under heavy tribute from Rome throughout his reign and eventually surrendered his own heir as a hostage to Rome (cf. Appian *Roman History: Syrian Wars* 8.45) in exchange for the freedom of his brother (Antiochus IV Epiphanes [175–164 BC]). Seleucus IV became known as the infamous one who sent out a tax collector, Heliodorus, especially to oppress the people of Israel. Heliodorus was sent to exact a large sum of money from the Temple treasury in Jerusalem to meet the Seleucus's government expenses and obligations to Rome, but he was miraculously thwarted from doing so (2 Macc 3:1-40). Heliodorus murdered Seleucus IV, whose death is foretold in 11:20 (see Shipley 2000:292).

◆ 4. The rise of Antiochus IV Epiphanes (11:21-24)

21"The next to come to power will be a despicable man who is not in line for royal succession. He will slip in when least expected and take over the kingdom by flattery and intrigue. 22Before him great armies will be swept away, including a covenant prince. 23With deceitful promises, he will make various alliances. He will become strong despite having only a handful of followers. 24Without warning he will enter the richest areas of the land. Then he will distribute among his followers the plunder and wealth of the rich—something his predecessors had never done. He will plot the overthrow of strongholds, but this will last for only a short while.

NOTES

11:21 ***despicable.*** Goldingay (1989:279) makes the cogent suggestion that this person was "despised" because of his lack of a proper pedigree and because he usurped the throne from his brother's son.

man. This is Antiochus IV. An account of his life is given in the commentary. First Maccabees (c. 104 BC) is basically a reliable historical source. Second Maccabees (first century BC) differs from 1 Maccabees usually in the order of events, and it is not always clear which source is to be preferred. First Maccabees is usually considered more accurate historically. Both books see the hand of God operative in Antiochus IV's life, but only 2 Maccabees records miraculous interventions in his narratives. 4 Maccabees (c. AD 20–50) is untrustworthy historically. Antiochus is described in several places in Josephus (e.g., *Antiquities* 12.5.3 [12.246-247]). For helpful accounts see Shipley 2000:292; Green 2007:93-103.

flattery and intrigue. Lit., "smooth words" (cf. Holladay 1988:107; cf. 11:34).

11:23 Rather opposite the logic of the NLT's translation, the first sentence of this verse seems to mean that "By means of alliances contracted with him, he will effect deception."

11:24 ***for only a short while.*** Lit., "for a certain time" or "only for a time" (NJPS).

COMMENTARY

Antiochus IV Epiphanes (meaning "God manifest" or "Illustrious"), later scornfully named Epimanes ("madman") by the Jews, is the historical person toward whom this chapter has been moving. He is the "little horn" of 8:9, but can hardly be the little horn of the fourth beast seen in 7:8 or the desolater of 9:27, although he foreshadows these enemies of God. He is similarly transcended by the figure in

11:40-45. Antiochus was the brother of the murdered Seleucus IV (187–175 BC; 2 Macc 4:7) and the younger son of Antiochus III. He arose as a sinful root from the line of Seleucus I, Alexander's general (1 Macc 1:10; see commentary on ch 8 for complete references). He reigned 175–163 BC. He usurped the throne (cf. 11:21) from Demetrius Soter I (162–150 BC), the son of Seleucus IV (1 Macc 7:1, 4). He established himself on the throne through flattery and intrigues with the Romans (Shipley 2000:292). A summary of his evil and vicious actions are given in the books of the Maccabees (1 Macc 1:7–6:16; 2 Macc 1:1–10:5; 4 Macc 4:15–18:5). (See also the comments on 8:9-14, 23-26.) What was presented briefly earlier is now expanded by the heavenly messenger in his words to Daniel. The presentation of Antiochus IV uses ominous descriptions, such as despicable, unworthy of the kingship, slipped in, take over, flattery, and intrigue (cf. 11:21). An atmosphere is skillfully created that leaves no doubt that this person is someone who forebodes evil. Although God could have prevented these events, they are clearly within the permissible plan of him who controls the flow of history to the end. The description of the evil figure and his deeds echo aspects of 7:8, 21, 24b-25; 8:9-12; 9:26-27.

Graham Shipley's evaluation of Antiochus IV is that "he may be accounted one of the more successful Seleukid [*sic*] kings." Shipley notes that "controversy rages about his treatment of the Jews in the 160s" (2000:292-293). In 166/165 BC, he displayed his military in a procession before undertaking military campaigns in the east. The Greek historian Polybius describes the procession:

> *The mass of statues is impossible to describe; for images of all the gods and guardian spirits who are named or honoured by men were carried, some gilded, others clothed in gold-embroidered garments. All of these were accompanied by the appropriate legends, executed according to the traditional narratives in expensive materials. Following these were an image of Night and one of Day, of Earth and Heaven, of Dawn and Midday. One may comprehend how great was the mass of gold and silver objects in the following way: one thousand slaves belonging to Dionysios, the king's secretary, walked in procession bearing silver vessels, none of which had a weight less than 1,000 drachmas. There were royal slaves numbering six hundred, bearing golden vessels; then came about two hundred women sprinkling (the spectators) with perfumes from golden urns. Behind these processed eighty women in golden-footed litters, and five hundred in silver-footed, richly dressed. And these were (only) the most spectacular things in the procession. (Polybius Histories 30.25-26 [31.3 = Athenaeus Deipnosophists 5.194 (5.23)], as quoted in Shipley 2000:293)*

It is the wickedness of Antiochus's reign and his furious attack against the holy people that catches the eye of the biblical author. The covenant prince that was slain (171 BC; 11:22) was probably Onias III, a righteous high priest who lived before 175 BC (cf. 8:10; 9:25-26). He had been removed from office and replaced with Jason, his brother, by Antiochus (2 Macc 4:7-20), but was then slain (171 BC) at the instigation of Menelaus, who then outbid Jason for the office of priest and served as high priest (172–162 BC). Jason and Menelaus were Hellenizers. Antiochus avenged Onias's death, but then was won over by Menelaus (2 Macc 3:1; 4:1-38; cf. 4 Macc 4:1-16). Antiochus strove to destroy the sacred traditions of the Jews by setting them aside. In their place, he tried to foster Greek religion, culture, and philosophy. He flattered and rewarded all of those in Israel who would support him by doing these things; these were the "lawless men" from Israel (1 Macc 1:11; cf. Dan 11:29, 32, 34). He even seized the valuable utensils from the sanctuary, reminiscent of Nebuchadnezzar's acts (1:1-2; 1 Macc 1:20-23). He took tribute from Jerusalem, plundered it, and set up a military presence there. He made the city a citadel for his forces (1 Macc 1:29-40). In an attempt to unify his kingdom (see commentary on 8:9), he forced the people of Israel to follow alien customs. His goal was to cause Israel to abandon the Mosaic law and to change the ordinances, feasts, and festivals (1 Macc 1:44-50) that the Most High had given them. On the 15th of Kislev, 167 BC, he desecrated the Temple area, setting up an abomination that caused desolation on the altar of burnt offering. He searched out books of the Torah and burned them (1 Macc 1:54-58). The first desecrating offerings were offered on the 25th of Kislev, 167 BC. But some of the faithful (cf. 11:32-35) held firm when great oppression came upon Israel (1 Macc 1:59-63; cf. Dan 11:30-31). The early actions of the king are reflected in 11:21-24 in a sweeping overview. More specific actions that increasingly affect the holy people, Israel, are related in 11:25-35. Some in Israel turned against their traditions and adopted Greek ways and religion. However, the writer comforts his reader by declaring that the success of this king will be short (11:24), the appointed end will come no matter what (11:27), and those who know their God will stand firm and resist the king (11:32).

◆ 5. Antiochus Epiphanes opposes the holy covenant (11:25-35)

**25"Then he will stir up his courage and
raise a great army against the king of the
south. The king of the south will go to
battle with a mighty army, but to no avail,
for there will be plots against him. 26His
own household will cause his downfall.
His army will be swept away, and many
will be killed. 27Seeking nothing but each
other's harm, these kings will plot against
each other at the conference table, attempting to deceive each other. But it will
make no difference, for the end will come
at the appointed time.**

**28"The king of the north will then return
home with great riches. On the way he
will set himself against the people of the
holy covenant, doing much damage before continuing his journey.**

**29"Then at the appointed time he will
once again invade the south, but this time
the result will be different. 30For warships
from western coastlands* will scare him
off, and he will withdraw and return
home. But he will vent his anger against
the people of the holy covenant and reward those who forsake the covenant.**

**31"His army will take over the Temple
fortress, pollute the sanctuary, put a stop
to the daily sacrifices, and set up the sacrilegious object that causes desecration.*
32He will flatter and win over those who
have violated the covenant. But the people
who know their God will be strong and
will resist him.**

**33"Wise leaders will give instruction to
many, but these teachers will die by fire
and sword, or they will be jailed and
robbed. 34During these persecutions, little
help will arrive, and many who join them
will not be sincere. 35And some of the wise
will fall victim to persecution. In this way,
they will be refined and cleansed and
made pure until the time of the end, for
the appointed time is still to come.**

11:30 Hebrew *from Kittim.* 11:31 Hebrew *the abomination of desolation.*

NOTES

11:25 ***great army.*** Lit., "with an exceedingly large and mighty army."

11:26 ***His own household.*** This renders the phrase "those who eat his fine food" (cf. 1:5, 8, 13, 15, 16). This was food of the "inner circle" of the royal household and government. Daniel refused to eat it with Nebuchadnezzar (1:8).

11:27 ***each other's harm.*** Lit., "their heart to [i.e., set on] evil" (Holladay 1988:216).

plot against. Lit., "they will speak lies."

make no difference. Lit., this plotting "will not succeed."

the end will come at the appointed time. God in his sovereignty has determined an appointed time for the end.

11:30 ***from western coastlands.*** This renders "from Kittim" (see NLT mg). Kittim was originally the name for a Phoenician colony on the island of Cyprus (cf. several of the Arad Ostraca, COS 3.43A-H:82-84). Then it was used to refer to islands and coastal lands of the Great (i.e., Mediterranean) Sea. It most likely refers here to the Romans, as it does in the Qumran documents (cf. 1QpHab 2:12; 1QpIsa 3:7, 9, 12; Collins 1993:384; Charlesworth 2002:23, 33, 113). In 1 Macc 1:1; 8:5 it refers to Greece and Macedonia, and the term can refer to Assyria as well (Schultz 2007:63-77).

reward. This is preceded by *shab* [TH7725, ZH8740], which may mean "and again" or "he will return," possibly with the idea of returning "to reward" the apostates or "returning" after victory.

11:31 ***the sacrilegious object.*** Heb., *hashiqquts meshomem* [TH8251/8074, ZH9199/9037], "the abominable/detestable thing that desolates"; see 8:13; 9:27; and notes.

11:32 ***flatter.*** This could also be rendered "cause to apostatize."

resist him. Or, "take action," not only defensive but offensive action.

11:33 ***jailed and robbed.*** This catches the idea of "captivity" (*shebi* [TH7628, ZH8660]) and "plunder" (*bizzah* [TH961, ZH1023]).

11:34 ***not be sincere.*** Here the idea is hypocrisy (Holladay 1988:207).

11:35 ***will fall victim to persecution.*** Lit., "will stumble," meaning they will be deceived by Greek ways of thought and life, not just subject to physical persecution.

the appointed time is still to come. Cf. 11:27. Great stress is laid upon the determined time that sets the parameters for this tyrant's activities, thus indicating that God is in charge.

COMMENTARY

Antiochus IV Epiphanes' attempt to expand his kingdom by conquering Egypt (1 Macc 1:16-24) is described in 11:25-27. Ptolemy VI Philometor was king of Egypt at this time. Antiochus attacked Egypt twice during 170–168 BC. The deceitfulness of both kings is highlighted (11:27), a regular feature of international relations in this time of wrath. The author, however, assures his reader that God is in control of all the events. These times of intrigue and wrath will be fulfilled, and the appointed end will come (11:27), indicating also that the king under whom all of this will happen is on the throne by God's will and power (cf. 11:14). In late 170 BC, Antiochus won a definitive battle at Pelousion and took all of Egypt except Alexandria, in addition to Cyprus. On his return home (late 170 BC or early 168 BC), he plundered and devastated Jerusalem and the Temple area (highlighted in 11:28; cf. Tcherikover

1959:186-189, 473-474). He killed thousands and sold some into slavery. He carried off wealth from the Temple (1 Macc 1:20-42; 2 Macc 5:1-23). He committed murder and spoke with great arrogance (1 Macc 1:24-25). This first abuse of the city created much opposition for Antiochus there (cf. Tcherikover 1959:186-187).

A further encounter with Egypt (later in 168 BC) is recorded in 11:29-35. This may be a second invasion during the time of the Maccabees, or it may merely be a second phase of the invasion recorded earlier (11:25-27; 1 Macc 1:16-19; cf. Shipley 2000:208). Antiochus was determined to gain control of Alexandria. This time Rome appeared ominously in the east, in Egypt, its major source of grain, and prevented Antiochus from annexing Egypt to his kingdom. Antiochus was also forced to give up Cyprus. Upon arriving at Alexandria ready to attack it with his army, he was met by a Roman delegation. He was humiliated by the Romans, led by Popilius Laenas, who challenged him in front of his own soldiers. He drew a circle in the sand, ordered Antiochus to step into it, and gave him an ultimatum to either return home or prepare for war before exiting the circle. His departure from Egypt was "prophesied" (after the fact) in two demotic ostraca in the archive of Hor (see Shipley 2000:209 for a translation of the ostraca). Antiochus was forced to defer to the Romans, and his consequent anger was taken out on the Jews in Jerusalem, who had evidently, as the king perceived, begun to revolt against his authority (Tcherikover 1959:187-188). In 167 BC, he set up decrees that led to the Maccabean uprising (167 BC). He rewarded those who came over to him from the holy covenant, a group that accepted Greek religion, language, and culture (11:32). He polluted the altar as noted above. It is not clear what the desolating sacrilege was that he set up, but it probably included an altar to Olympian Zeus, the Greek equivalent of Syrian Baal Shamen; this presumably included a statue of Zeus, the Greek god, a foreshadowing of the all-encompassing, overspreading sacrilege that causes desolation (9:27; cf. 11:31). Antiochus had regularly given gifts to the sanctuary of Olympian Zeus in Athens for diplomatic purposes (Shipley 2000:292).

Good and bad events are recorded in 11:33-35. Some of the faithful of Israel, who do not bow to the oppression and the appeals of Antiochus to give up their own customs and worship (cf. 1 Macc 1:41-42) will die or be persecuted. The "little help" that arrives (11:34) possibly refers to the Maccabean uprising, a group that arose from the Jewish family of Mattathias (the Hasmoneans). The Maccabees shared a common ancestor named Hashmonia according to Josephus (*Antiquities* 12.6.1 [12.265]). The name Maccabees was adopted to refer to them and came from the name of Judas, called Maccabeus, one of the five sons of Mattathias. Mattathias was a priest from the family of Joarib who had moved from Jerusalem to Modein (1 Macc 2:1-6). He and his sons refused to submit to the king's syncretistic Hellenistic reforms and would not offer a pagan sacrifice and become enrolled as "friends of the king." When they witnessed other Jews succumbing to these policies in the countryside and in the city of Jerusalem, they rebelled and offered some powerful opposition against the king and all subsequent Hellenizers.

As their strength grew, this family led a revolt that saw the demolition of the abomination that Antiochus had set up; they also saw the altar of burnt offering restored and sacrifices presented again in three years (1 Macc 6:42-61). The sacrilegious altar was dismantled, and a new one of unhewn stones was set up in its place. Renovation and restoration were completed on and in the Temple, and it was made ready for worship. On 25 Kislev, 164 BC (i.e., November/December, 164 BC), sacrifices and offerings were offered again on this altar, exactly three years to the day after it had been defiled (8:14, 26; 1 Macc 1:59). Antiochus died in this year (1 Macc 6:14-16). This fulfilled the vision of chapter 8; the Temple was again made functional (8:11, 14). This event is celebrated today by Jews in the Hanukkah festival, which falls in December, although it can sometimes start in November and in other years it ends in January.

As an alternative to the idea that 11:34 refers to the Maccabean uprising, it may be that very little relief and help will appear during the times foreseen here, and even some of that help will be insincere or wrong (cf. Lucas 2002:287; Collins 1993:386). The wise in 11:35 will in fact die because they do not receive sufficient help, but their sufferings and oppression will only refine, cleanse, and purify them.

Whether the "little help" of 11:34 refers to the Maccabees or not, some who know their God would endure and not be overcome by all of the deception, deceit, and political and religious intrigues (11:32). In this time of wrath and rebellion, many would be refined and cleansed. Serving God was still possible during this time of persecution. Many chose it; and some died because of it (2 Macc 6–7; cf. 1 Macc 7:19; 4 Macc 1:10-11; 16:25; 17:21; 18:4). The situation would be bleak and get worse (12:1), but the appointed end would finally come (cf. 11:35-36, 40, 45; 12:4, 7-8, 13).

◆ 6. The despicable king who does as he pleases (11:36-45)

**36"The king will do as he pleases, exalting
himself and claiming to be greater than
every god, even blaspheming the God of
gods. He will succeed, but only until the
time of wrath is completed. For what has
been determined will surely take place.
37He will have no respect for the gods of
his ancestors, or for the god loved by
women, or for any other god, for he will
boast that he is greater than them all.
38Instead of these, he will worship the
god of fortresses—a god his ancestors
never knew—and lavish on him gold, sil-
ver, precious stones, and expensive gifts.
39Claiming this foreign god's help, he will
attack the strongest fortresses. He will
honor those who submit to him, appoint-
ing them to positions of authority and
dividing the land among them as their
reward.***

**40"Then at the time of the end, the king
of the south will attack the king of the
north. The king of the north will storm out
with chariots, charioteers, and a vast navy.
He will invade various lands and sweep
through them like a flood. 41He will enter
the glorious land of Israel,* and many na-
tions will fall, but Moab, Edom, and the
best part of Ammon will escape. 42He will
conquer many countries, and even Egypt
will not escape. 43He will gain control over
the gold, silver, and treasures of Egypt,
and the Libyans and Ethiopians* will be
his servants.**

**44"But then news from the east and the
north will alarm him, and he will set out
in great anger to destroy and obliterate
many. 45He will stop between the glorious
holy mountain and the sea and will pitch
his royal tents. But while he is there, his
time will suddenly run out, and no one
will help him.**

11:39 Or *at a price.* 11:41 Hebrew *the glorious land.* 11:43 Hebrew *Cushites.*

NOTES

11:36 *blaspheming.* This renders "speaking extraordinary or unsuitable things."

11:37 *the god loved by women.* This is usually understood to refer to Tammuz or Damuzi, a relatively unimportant god of the Babylonians and Assyrians (cf. Ezek 8:14). The reference may, however, be to Dionysius, god of wine and the vine who was popular in both Egypt and Syria. Whichever god is in view would be rejected by Antiochus Epiphanes in his hubris, an unexpected action for a publicly religious man.

he will boast that he is greater. Lit., "he will magnify himself."

11:38 *god of fortresses.* Antiochus Epiphanes, foreshadowing a future anti-God figure, built fortresses and engines of war, and pursued various kinds of military issues. His major military threat to Daniel's people was the Acra, the citadel that he had constructed in Jerusalem and which he used to suppress and control the inhabitants. He recognized various gods who fostered military might: Jupiter Capitolinas (Antioch), Zeus Akraios (per inscription found at Sythopolis), and Olympian Zeus (2 Macc 6:2). Cf. Lucas 2002:290; Collins 1993:387-388.

11:39 *those who submit to him.* Or, "those whom he recognizes."

appointing them to positions of authority. Or, "setting them up to rule over multitudes."

dividing the land . . . as their reward. This is probably better understood as "distributing land at a price."

11:41 *glorious land.* Heb., *'erets hatsebi* [TH776/6643, ZH824/7382] (cf. 8:9; 11:16).

best part. This is possibly "the leaders" (*re'shith* [TH7225, ZH8040]).

11:43 *Ethiopians.* Heb., "Cushites" (so NLT mg); cf. Ezek 38:5. These names, while referring to a group of ancient distant peoples living south of Egypt, point just as importantly to the threatening entourage of God in Ezek 38:5. The modern African nation of Ethiopia is not referred to in the historical reference here.

be his servants. Lit., "will be in his train" or "will be at his heels" (*bemits'adayw* [TH4703, ZH5202]).

11:40-45 As Lucas (2002:291) notes in a convenient summary, these verses do not correspond to the events reported about the demise and death of Antiochus Epiphanes as he closed out his blasphemous career. His final days are reported in 1 Macc 6:1-17; 2 Macc 1:11-17; 9:1-29; Polybius *Histories* 31.11. These verses depict what will happen to any figure he anticipates.

11:45 *his time will suddenly run out.* Lit., "he will come to his end" (*uba' 'ad-qitso* [TH7093, ZH7891]).

COMMENTARY

This section refers, to some extent, to Antiochus IV. However, it is the Epimanes ("Madman") aspect of the king that becomes dominant. The person in these verses is less clearly reflected in the mere historical man Antiochus IV. Echoes of Nebuchadnezzar's overweening hubris (4:30 [27]) are here; but the Madman far surpasses the delusions of the Babylonian king and the historical Antiochus IV. Verse 36 would seem to reflect what is recorded of Antiochus in Maccabees (2 Macc 9:1–10:5), where he admits he had thought himself to be equal to God (2 Macc 9:12). But the king (according to these verses) was to continue having success until the time of wrath was completed, and that includes the resurrection of the dead and the rise of heavenly and earthly warfare in which Michael would fight for Daniel's people (12:1). Antiochus, however, was forced to leave the fight in Judea to one of his generals while he traveled east to defend his empire against the Parthians. He died in 163 BC in the mountains of Persia, while returning to Jerusalem intending to make it a "cemetery of Jews" (2 Macc 9:4, 28; 10:5). In the vision of 8:9-14 the altar was cleansed after the allotted time; that occurred in the time of Antiochus. Here, however, the vision continues to describe this king's career without reference to any cleansing of the altar. The heavenly messenger, after describing Antiochus's historical career (which made him a threatening figure of evil), now goes beyond him, for the little horn of 7:8 comes into view. These verses make a gradual transition from the earthly Antiochus, who adumbrated the "little horn," "coming ruler (prince)," and "desolater," to a person larger than history and still more abominable than Antiochus (9:27). There is a subtle "seam" in the text (cf. 9:26-27) as the author moves from the historical and suggestive figure of Antiochus to a rebellious madman of huge proportions.

This king will succeed until the time of wrath has been completed—until the determined end comes (11:36). The cleansing of the altar afterwards will be an act of God (9:27), and resurrection follows (12:1-4). But until then, the lawless ones among Daniel's people will not cease, and many more trials and desolations await the holy people. According to 11:37, this king becomes the center of religion, for he claims to exceed all gods. But he worships power (the god of fortresses, 11:38). His will is permitted free reign in almost all matters (11:36). Antiochus IV, a forerunner of this figure, in the throes of death, stricken by God, grieved over and attempted to repent of the things he had done to the Jews, their Temple, their traditions, Jerusalem, and their God (1 Macc 6:8-16; 2 Macc 9:1-29). God refused to have mercy upon him (2 Macc 9:13). There is no hint of this attempted repentance concerning the king spoken of in 11:36-45. He is blasphemous to the appointed end. No past or religious traditions suit him. They all stop and start with him. He goes beyond "I am the state" (*L'etat, c'est moi*) to "I am everything!"

The heavenly messenger refers to a king that fits the mold of both the "little horn" of the fourth kingdom of chapter 7 and the mysterious "he" of chapter 9 (7:8, 11; 9:27), a rebellious king who destroys others and exalts himself, even against God and his holy people. Antiochus IV foreshadowed him, but he was not him. In the end, he will be destroyed by God, along with the mysterious fourth beast (7:11). Those who hold the view that these verses continue to describe Antiochus IV's career are forced to admit that if such is the case, the text of 11:40-45 is a failed prophetic attempt to prognosticate Antiochus's end. The events described are not reflected in the records found in any other literature of the time. If this is the case, the divine messenger did not truly speak from the Book of Truth (10:21; 11:2).

In 11:40-45 the titles "king of the south" and "king of the north" are used to describe the activities of opposing forces of the time of the end; no longer are the Ptolemies and Seleucids in view. They are now only a backdrop for the final apocalyptic eschatological events that will occur. The events of "the time of the end" (cf. 12:1), mentioned often, are announced again in 11:40. This time, human history will come to its consummation, and the evil powers of this age will be dealt with and defeated by the help of heavenly beings, with God delivering his people even from death (12:1-4). This occurs after a time of ongoing warfare that carries on to the end. The final transition from the ephemeral and unstable kingdoms of the world into the Kingdom of God, the Son of Man, and his holy ones, takes place at last (2:34-35, 44-45; 4:34-35 [31-32]; 5:31 [6:1]; 6:28 [29]; 7:11, 13-14, 22, 26-27; 9:27).

The king described here will have realized unparalleled success by the end, as stated in the text. The boundaries of his empire will be beyond anything Antiochus IV or Antiochus III ever controlled (11:40b-43), and they had aspired to universal empires in their own time (Green 2007:128)—even Egypt, Libya, and Ethiopia would be included. The apocalyptic, figurative language stresses the extent of his success. Yet some peoples do not succumb to him (11:41). His time runs out (11:45), and the end comes (12:1-4).

These events must, of course, remain ambiguous until they occur. No dates and no modern names can be given. However, as always, the glorious land of Israel gets special mention (11:41). It is the apple of God's eye (Deut 32:10). In this catastrophic setting of violence and war, the impression is given that the holy people will be destroyed unless God acts on their behalf. This evil king will also attack and conquer many nations. The mention of the ancient lands of Moab, Edom, and Ammon as escaping his domination uses biblical nomenclature known to the people of antiquity. It does not update these names. This king is set on conquering the Middle East and more, from which he would control most of the world. He is an enemy of all peoples, not just Israel. His end finally comes between the Holy Mount (Jerusalem's Temple) and the Mediterranean Sea (11:45). His battles with his political and military enemies will lead to his defeat, just as God has orchestrated it. God has set a time limit on the rampages of this diabolical king and will bring about his defeat. No one can help him because his defeat is an act of God (11:45). Finally, the decreed end will be poured out (9:27) upon this monstrous desolater of Israel and many surrounding nations. During that time of conflict and extending beyond it, Michael will be active and ultimately rescue Daniel's people and nation, both those alive and dead (12:13)—all those whose names are written in the book (12:1).

This king's actions have reflected those of the "little horn" of chapter 7. Eventually, his kingdom will end, just as the fourth kingdoms of chapters 2 and 7 were broken. God's goal has always been the realization of his fifth Kingdom, prepared for his holy ones, beings both heavenly and human. This arrogant king has a relationship to his kingdom reminiscent of the relationship of the little horn of 7:8 that grew from the beast yet remained part of it. The little horn represented the spirit and mind of the beast and vice versa. The fourth kingdom and the final little horn (king) rise or fall because of a common origin and purpose. They feed on each other, but can also devour each other. Some of the nations outside of this king's rulership will continue (cf. 7:12) to serve the Kingdom to be set up after the final deliverance of Israel.

This visible barrage of political and military intrigues, however, is being and will be matched by an even more fierce battle behind the scenes: An apocalyptic, eschatological ending to the book of Daniel now reports that Michael, a chief messenger of God, will step into the fray. Daniel's people will be rescued (12:1-4).

Even those who have died for their faith during this time of earthly and heavenly war will be brought back to life at the end of this "time of the end" (11:40; 12:4). The final deliverance defeats the enemy of not only the Jews and Israel, but of all humanity—death.

◆ 7. The deliverance of God's people (12:1-7)

"At that time Michael, the archangel*
who stands guard over your nation, will
arise. Then there will be a time of an-
guish greater than any since nations first
came into existence. But at that time ev-
ery one of your people whose name is
written in the book will be rescued.
2 Many of those whose bodies lie dead
and buried will rise up, some to everlast-
ing life and some to shame and everlast-
ing disgrace. 3 Those who are wise will
shine as bright as the sky, and those who
lead many to righteousness will shine
like the stars forever. 4 But you, Daniel,
keep this prophecy a secret; seal up the
book until the time of the end, when
many will rush here and there, and
knowledge will increase."
5 Then I, Daniel, looked and saw two
others standing on opposite banks of the
river. 6 One of them asked the man dressed
in linen, who was now standing above the
river, "How long will it be until these
shocking events are over?"
7 The man dressed in linen, who was
standing above the river, raised both his
hands toward heaven and took a solemn
oath by the One who lives forever, saying,
"It will go on for a time, times, and half a
time. When the shattering of the holy
people has finally come to an end, all
these things will have happened."

12:1 Hebrew *the great prince.*

NOTES

12:1 ***At that time.*** This equals the end of the "time of the end" (12:4). This Hebrew expression (*uba'et* [TH6256, ZH6961] *hahi'*) occurs three times in this verse.

the archangel. Lit., "the great prince" (*hassar haggadol* [TH8269/1419, ZH8569/1524]). Michael is traditionally referred to as "the great prince" or "the archangel." He is also mentioned in Dan 10:13, 21; Jude 1:9; Rev 12:7.

will arise. In the book of Enoch, Michael is the patron and intercessor for Israel (*1 Enoch* 20:5). In 1QWar Scroll (1QM) and 4QWords of Michael (4Q259), Michael takes his stand as commander of the armies of the sons of light who engage the sons of darkness led by Belial (see commentary).

written in the book. This is not the Book of Truth, mentioned in 10:21, but the book of life. See the commentary on 10:21 for further discussion (cf. Rev 20:12, 15).

12:2 ***Many of those whose bodies lie dead and buried will rise up.*** Lit., "Many of those who sleep in the dust will awaken" (cf. Gen 3:19; Eccl 12:7). The NLT makes it clear that they will arise from the grave/ground, which is implied in the MT.

12:3 ***Those who are wise.*** These are the people mentioned in 11:33, 35 (cf. 1:4, 17; 8:25; 9:22, 25; 12:10). The wise know their God and keep his ways (11:32).

12:4 ***keep this prophecy a secret.*** Lit., "keep the words secret."

seal up the book. Thus, the secrecy of the vision is maintained, per the statement of 10:7-8 (cf. 7:28; 8:26). Only Daniel knew the content of the vision until, in God's appointed time, it would be revealed. The prophetic visions that were sealed up most likely include chs 7–12. Colophons demanding secrecy are pressed in certain Akkadian prophecy texts (Lucas 2002:271). For a translation of the colophon, see Longman 1991:240. The words could be shared only with the initiated (cf. *4 Ezra* 14:26, 45-47; regarding the initial audience, see Introduction, "Occasion of Writing," and "Audience"). Some argue that the secrecy colophons in Daniel were a device used by the author to conceal the fact that the book was written after or during the time of some of the events described in the book (especially ch 11), but the canonical book of Daniel certainly records these statements in accord with their *prima facie* purpose: The visions were to be sealed and would primarily become known in due time as God's plan in history unfolded.

rush here and there. This renders *yeshotetu* [TH7751, ZH8763] accurately. The apparatus of BHS suggests moving a diacritical dot (changing Shin to Sin), so that the meaning would be "will apostatize" (*yesotetu* [TH7750, ZH8454]). The emendation is not necessary; cf. Amos 8:12, where the same expression is found (Collins 1993:399).

knowledge. The apparatus in BHS offers the conjecture that the text reads "evil" here (*ra'oth* [TH7451/7451B, ZH8273/8288], or a similar form), rather than MT's *da'ath* [TH1847, ZH1981] (knowledge). This would be attributable to a scribal confusion of the similar letters Resh (ר) and Daleth (ד). The MT, which is followed by the NLT, seems preferable. The general trustworthiness of the MT is to be preferred here and contains the more difficult reading.

12:5 *the river.* This is the Tigris River, as in 10:4.

12:7 *raised both his hands.* Lit., "he raised his right hand and his left hand." The gesture indicates a doubly solemn oath, but is also an expression of worship (Pss 28:2; 63:4). See further Deut 32:40; Rev 10:5-6.

time, times, and half a time. This is a rendering of *mo'ed mo'adim wakhetsi* [TH4150/2677, ZH4595/2942]. These terms indicate set, appointed times, and may suggest a division of the 70 weeks of years into three parts (9:24-27). The terms also point back to 7:25, tying them to the little horn of 7:8, 20-22, 25.

COMMENTARY

The final deliverance (12:1) of Daniel's people occurs at the time of the end (11:40; 12:4) and provides God's people a permanent escape from defilement, fire, lions, exile, and—through resurrection—even from *death.* The literature of the ancient Near East does not witness to a hope of life through resurrection, but rather to a murky, shadowy existence somewhere. Even in the Old Testament outside of Daniel this assertion is present (cf. Pss 16:9-11; 49:15; 73:23-26), though there are passages that hold forth a brighter hope. Ezekiel's reference to a resurrection (Ezek 37) is metaphorical for Israel's return from exile, as is probably also the case with Isaiah 26:19 (cf. Hos 6:2). In the New Testament era, the Greeks rejected the idea of a resurrection (Acts 17). But in Daniel's vision, the great and powerful prince, a heavenly being, will take charge. Every person whose name is found written in the book (see note on 12:1) will be rescued, whether they are alive or have died. While some would restrict this unprecedented event to the Jews alone, Daniel's nation, this does not seem to fit sufficiently the universal perspective of the book. A resurrection of universal proportions is envisioned in keeping with the all-encompassing sovereign power of God's actions throughout the book. God has left a witness of himself, not just to the Jews, but to Gentile kings and peoples (chs 2–6). The full number of God's people will be delivered (cf. Matt 24:21-22), and that number will include all languages, nations, peoples, tongues (Gen 12:3; 14:18-20; Exod 18:10-20; Josh 2:11; 1 Kgs 17:8-9, 24; 2 Kgs 5). The decrees and confessions of Nebuchadnezzar (2:46-47; 3:28-29; 4:34-37 [31-34]) and Darius (Cyrus; 6:25-27 [26-28]) are not trivial assertions, but clearly create an ambience in which the witness of and about Daniel's God—Israel's God—is being disseminated among the nations. Certainly some Gentiles responded and recognized this God. Esther 8:17 indicates that because of Xerxes' decree, many non-Jews became Jews. The declarations of these kings accomplished their purpose according to God's plan; that is, to proclaim his name before the nations.

When Michael arises to deliver his people, a time of unprecedented struggle will take place. Like the Lord who arises to deliver those who call upon him (Pss 3:7; 7:6; 12:5; 68:1; Isa 33:10), Michael will deliver Israel. This prediction is echoed in the Dead Sea Scrolls (see note on 12:1), which picture Michael in command of the armies of light as they engage the armies of darkness headed by Belial. Michael had earlier helped the divine messenger (10:13) who was being detained forcefully by the spirit prince of Persia. He was the leader of God's forces against the Persian forces. When Greece succeeded Persia, Michael and the divine messenger led their forces against the spirit prince of Greece (10:20-21)—and undoubtedly they also did so against Antiochus IV (8:9-14, 23-26; 11:21-35). Now it is said that Michael will arise to defeat the final king of the north, an anti-God, and therefore, an anti-Messiah figure. In the New Testament, this blasphemous figure is the Antichrist, who will oppose God and the Kingdom of the Messiah (7:13-14) at the time of Christ's return (Mark 13:14; 1 Thess 4:13-18; 2 Thess 2:3-12). Ultimately, this Antichrist will be destroyed by fire, along with his beastly comrade (Rev 19:19-21; cf. Dan 7:11, 26). Michael is probably the one, under the direction of Jesus Christ, who captures the Beast (the Antichrist) and False Prophet and then casts them into the lake of fire (Rev 19:19-21).

In 2 Thessalonians 2, Paul identifies this era as the time of a great rebellion against God when the man of lawlessness will be revealed, exalting himself above God, even proclaiming himself to be God. Lawlessness implies the forsaking of God's laws and his worship, as well as open rebellion against God. Paul's prophetic words are based on those found in Daniel 11:36-45. Since Paul applied these words to an Antichrist yet to come, centuries after Antiochus IV was gone, the apostle saw the fulfillment of these words as being in the future (i.e., after the time he wrote the Thessalonian letters). Paul did not, however, set a date on the time of their fulfillment.

The divine messenger, speaking to Daniel the truth from the Book of Truth (10:21; 11:2), depicts a resurrection of the dead of those who remained faithful and had their names written in the book (12:1-3). The martyrs of the time of the Maccabees hoped for a resurrection to physical life, but those who died were not resurrected when Antiochus IV died or when the altar in Jerusalem was cleansed from the desolating abomination that he set up. Daniel himself hoped for resurrection at the time of the end (11:40; 12:1, 13), but he has not experienced it—even to this day.

This resurrection awaits the end of time (12:1, 4) and leads to two differing results—some will be resurrected to experience eternal life, and some will be resurrected to experience everlasting disgrace. The resurrection in Daniel, by implication, is a general resurrection—the Hebrew word for "many" (in 12:2) means "multitudes without number" in this context. Those who are resurrected involve the all-inclusive two groups of persons, the righteous and the wicked. Those who are asleep (i.e., dead) in the grave (Gen 3:19; Eccl 12:7) will be rescued (12:1-2). Their names would also be found in "the book" (12:1; cf. 7:10; 10:21).

This judgment scene echoes the universal judgment scene in chapter 7 (7:9-10, 13-14, 18, 22, 26-27) where the Ancient One, the Judge, sits with the books open. After the fourth beastly kingdom is cut off and the little horn's boastful talk is destroyed, a universal court is convened—and this one is final, not a historical foreshadowing. It is within this framework that 11:35-45 and 12:1-7 are to be read; the Judge will not rule over persons who remain dead. The judgement is thus a time of moral, ethical, and spiritual accounting to the Most High. Human conscience will be on trial and on display before God. It is a time of reckoning for every human being before the Supreme Court and the Supreme Judge of the nations (7:9-10, 22, 26-27; cf. Eccl 12:14).

These passages clearly lie behind the New Testament presentation of the resurrection, but there it is further refined temporally. There will be not only two groups resurrected, but their resurrections will be separated in time (Rev 20:1-15). The first group will be resurrected to life and reign with Christ; the second group will consist of those whose names are found (1) in the books and (2) the book of life; thus the latter group consists of two groups. Daniel 12:1-3 supplies the foundational revelational event for the New Testament's further development of the resurrection awaiting all of God's people.

The blessed will experience everlasting and eternal life. This is significant because it is the only time the phrase "eternal life" is found in the Old Testament. In the Gospel of John, we discover that Jesus gave the believers eternal life, which is a life that guarantees resurrection unto eternal life, a blessed resurrection (John 11:25-26). "Eternal life" flows from a relationship with God that brings God's approval and presence—true spiritual life is not mere length of life, it is life essentially in the Spirit. The "length" of life (i.e., everlasting life) is a function of the quality of life. Those who receive everlasting life have already shown themselves wise and righteous before God—eternal life follows "naturally," as God's gift. The opposite of eternal life is a state of eternal shame and everlasting contempt (12:2; cf. Gen 2:25; 3:7), that lacks a life-giving spiritual relationship with God. In light of the qualities of eternal life, the implication is that "eternal death" is a condition of being separated from God that can be described as "shame and everlasting disgrace" (12:2).

There are hints that those who are rescued at this time and the group raised to everlasting life will see the nations of those who escaped the ravages of the anti-God figure (11:41-43; Isa 19:21-23). In other words, these nations will still remain. The kingdom of the "one like a son of man" will be established after the little horn and fourth beast are destroyed by fire so that their evil influence is removed (Rev 20:3; cf. Dan 2:44; 7:11-12, 26); the nations that are not destroyed with the fourth kingdom and the little horn will serve and obey him (7:12, 14). Those who are resurrected to eternal life (12:2) become part of the holy people of the Most High who receive the kingdom from the hands of the Ancient One, according to chapter 7 (7:22, 27). In the similar scenario depicted by John in the book of Revelation, we see the holy people of God resurrected from the dead to reign with Christ, and we see many nations serving God (Rev 20:4-6; 21:24). The throne scene in Daniel (7:9-10) provides the background for the judgment in Revelation 20:11-15. Those who are resurrected into everlasting shame are not further described in the book of Daniel, but the book of Revelation makes it clear that they will face the "Great White Throne" judgment of God (Rev 20:4, 11).

The encouraging words about the reward of those who are wise (12:3) refer to those who shared the wisdom of Daniel—a wisdom of God that kept them faithful to God through the rise and fall of Babylon and on into the time of the Persian Empire. Their wisdom was both practical and mantic, enabling them to live wisely and to understand the apocalyptic dreams and visions revealed to them. The word describing those who are wise in 12:3 (*maskilim* [TH7919, ZH8505]) also describes Daniel and the young men chosen to be trained in all the language and literature of Babylon in 1:4; the two verses thus form an *inclusio* around the book's main contents. Daniel did not rebel; he was faithful and wise. "Those who lead many to righteousness" (*matsdiqim* [TH6663, ZH7405]) is a designation parallel to the "wise" mentioned in the first half of 12:3, and Daniel will therefore also be one of those who will "shine like stars" forever. By his words and life, kings were taught righteousness throughout the book (4:27 [24]). Those who have walked in Daniel's steps have shown that they know their God and have true wisdom. As with Daniel, they have also taught others righteousness and true wisdom (11:33). The wisdom that Daniel (and Shadrach, Meshach, and Abednego) possessed was what caused them to come out "purified, cleansed, and refined" when they passed through persecution (12:10). The point of the metaphorical language is that these persons, hated and despised by the world, were loved and esteemed by God, just as Daniel had been (9:23; 10:11, 18-19).

Unlike Isaiah or Amos or Jeremiah, Daniel was told to keep his vision a secret until the end, for this vision was for the future and was not to be proclaimed openly to everyone immediately (but see Introduction, "Audience"). At the time of the fulfillment of certain of the prophetic visions (early Persian period, Cyrus; Greek period, Alexander), the vision would be made available to the community, but it was to remain sealed in Daniel's day. This means that there would be a late availability of an apocalyptic and prophetic word that had been spoken earlier. This assertion does not imply a late date for the final form of the book, and the material is presented as something revealed secretly to Daniel long before it would be revealed publicly. This also does not mean that all parts of the book were sealed; some were made public to kings (chs 2–6) and through decrees of kings to many people (cf. Esth 8:13-17). In the case of this vision, however, at the time of the end it would be unsealed (9:24). It was, indeed, during the time of Antiochus IV Epiphanes (175–167 BC) that the book of Daniel became a book of encouragement, especially because it had God's promise of an appointed end for all of Israel's tribulation. It was used by the Qumran community as Holy Scripture, equal with the Torah and the Prophets. In the New Testament, it is used by Jesus, Paul, Peter, and John (the author of Revelation) to interpret reality in their day, and some parts of Daniel are projected into the future as seen through the lens of the Christ event.

This section of Daniel indicates that people will pursue an increase of knowledge that will be in vain, for through the revelation of the Book of Truth a divine messenger has shared what will certainly to come to pass. Other philosophies or theories about where history is going or how it will end might arise, but this word is firm (cf. 2:45b). "Rush here and there" (see note on 12:4) uses a word that is also found in Amos 8:12. Amos asserts that people will run to and fro to find a word from the Lord, but will not be able to find it. Daniel's vision is sealed, and it is and will be sufficient for God's people when the time comes (cf. Collins 1993:399).

Two men appear now in addition to the first being (10:4-5), and the ensuing conversation is reminiscent of the conversation in 8:13-14 between two holy beings. One of them addresses the figure of 10:5. Evidently heavenly beings also ask questions about the course of events (8:13-14; cf. 1 Pet 1:12), for they are not omniscient, and some are more fully informed than others.

Daniel asks the perennial question: When will the time of wrath take place? In a gesture indicating a doubly solemn oath (by raising both hands), the messenger gave a helpful but cryptic answer: "a time, times, and half a time" (12:7). Thus, the divine messenger informed Daniel that the wrath will be for a set time, which is controlled and limited by God. More specifically, when the time of wrath and rebellion during which Israel is subject to persecution is over and the holy people are broken, then the end would come. If God had not provided for her rescue (12:1), Israel would be utterly annihilated. This period of time matches the phrase given in 7:25 (see also 7:8, 20-22; see note on 7:25), which records the time the holy people would be under the power of the little horn of the fourth kingdom, and (roughly) the time under the little horn of the third kingdom (8:9), which was a historical forerunner of the horn of 7:8. It agrees with the three and one-half years of Daniel's 70th week (9:27), which also has the appointed end time as its chronological marker. The final blasphemous figure of 11:36-45 goes beyond Antiochus IV (8:9) and represents the one whom Michael the chief prince will overcome. But the end for the little horn and his kingdom (7:11, 22, 25-26) is the beginning for the eternal kingdom ruled by the "one like a son of man" (7:13-14, 18, 22, 27), and for the holy people, even the resurrected faithful written in the book—including Daniel (12:13).

◆ IV. Conclusion: The Lord's Sovereignty and Rewards (12:8-13)

8I heard what he said, but I did not understand what he meant. So I asked, "How will all this finally end, my lord?"

9But he said, "Go now, Daniel, for what I have said is kept secret and sealed until the time of the end. 10Many will be purified, cleansed, and refined by these trials. But the wicked will continue in their wickedness, and none of them will understand. Only those who are wise will know what it means.

11"From the time the daily sacrifice is stopped and the sacrilegious object that causes desecration* is set up to be worshiped, there will be 1,290 days. 12And blessed are those who wait and remain until the end of the 1,335 days!

13"As for you, go your way until the end. You will rest, and then at the end of the days, you will rise again to receive the inheritance set aside for you."

12:11 Hebrew *the abomination of desolation.*

NOTES

12:10 ***purified, cleansed, and refined.*** These reflect the same three verbs used in 11:35 but with the order of the first and third words reversed.

those who are wise will know. Lit., "the insightful ones (*hammaskilim* [TH7919, ZH8505]) will understand (*yabinu* [TH995, ZH1067])" when these further events occur.

12:11 ***sacrilegious object.*** Cf. 11:31 and note.

12:13 ***until the end.*** "The end" is not to be dropped as Goldingay does (1989:281; Collins 1993:402; Lucas 2002:263). The word *laqqets* [TH7093, ZH7891] (end) refers back to and echoes the end or that time when even the dead will rise (11:40; 12:1) and is not a mere dittography of the second occurrence of the word in this verse.

the inheritance set aside for you. Heb. *goral* [TH1486/1632, ZH1598] is used to designate that which was appointed by God as a person's "lot," his divinely appointed inheritance. It is found, for example, in Ps 125:3; Jer 13:25; 1QS 3.24; and 11QMelch 1.8. In relation to this verse and its concept of inheritance, Collins (1993:402) notes that the most pertinent biblical reference may be Col 1:12, "the lot of the saints in light." Daniel's destiny is indeed to be that of the wise who rise to eternal life and light (12:3).

COMMENTARY

Daniel's final question (12:8) is politely unanswered. Fortunately for us, the New Testament provides revelation about "how it will finally end"—still without timetables, however, but with contours and frameworks within which God's sovereign plan will be completed (cf. Eph 1:4), and a plan that will perfect the Old Testament saints along with the New Testament people of God (Heb 11:39-40). The heavenly messenger had cut off the presentation from the Book of Truth at 12:4 (cf. 10:21), but he repeated a message that needs to be trumpeted always.

Above all, the message is that God's goal for his people is that they be purified, cleansed, and refined, even in the midst of wrath and rebellion, a statement repeated from 11:35 because of its importance. These will be the characteristics of the wise and those who seek righteousness. By contrast, the wicked will stay entrenched in their wickedness (12:10; cf. Rev 22:10-11). Their spiritual blindness makes it impossible for them to understand God's actions in history.

The cryptic comments about certain time periods in 12:11-13 are given to encourage God's people to realize that God has placed a limitation on the desolation caused by the overspreading sacrilege. Blessed are those who endure this time, for they will see that sacrilegious object removed by God's actions and the desolater destroyed. The violence done in this apocalyptic eschatological time will be extensive (lasting 1,290 and 1,335 days), but it will end.

The 1,290 days equals about three and one-half years, so it can be correlated with the statement the divine messenger previously made (12:7) and, therefore, with the actions of the little horn of chapter 7. But the mention of two separate numbers of days that are separated and differ by 45 days possibly indicates a beginning and an end to the worship of some sacrilegious object that causes desolation (cf. 7:21, 26; 8:11-14; 9:27; 11:40-45). So by implication and analogy, this scenario refers to the actions of the king of the north in 11:36-45, as well as to the desolater and desolations of the last week of Daniel's 70 sets of seven (9:27). Those who can endure the 1,290 days and then some (another 45 days) will see God's actions on behalf of his people (12:12). During the period of the 45 days, God's people are called upon to endure. They will be rescued, and the abomination will be removed. But God alone knows the exact time, and that is enough for those who live by faith, for "Faith is the confidence that what we hope for will actually happen; it gives us assurance about things we cannot see" (Heb 11:1). These days are markers of assurance for our faith, not exact dates to be figured out in mathematical detail; nor are these assertions to be taken as evidence of failed past calculations of the end (cf. Collins 1993:401). To do the former is to disregard the apocalyptic eschatological genre of the material being presented, and to accept the latter is to bring doubt into the author's message of hope.

In 12:13 the heavenly messenger foretells a beautiful ending to the life of this prophet, a prophet in a new mold, who was a wise, faithful servant of the Lord who had fought the good fight and kept the faith. He had not only delivered sealed dreams in written form that spoke of the future, but had spoken words of rebuke and warning to the kings (4:26-27 [23-24]; 5:22-28) and announced the rise and fall of empires as Jeremiah had (ch 2; cf. Jer 1:9-10). (See further the Introduction, endnote 15.)

In this last vision, Daniel delivers a written message for the people of God, a sealed message declaring the final solution to the retribution principle, for the judgment of the righteous and the wicked will be completed at the resurrection, not in this fallen age. The resurrection of the dead became the foundation upon which the entire hope of the New Testament faith was established. Without it, everything else is in vain. As Paul said, "If our hope in Christ is only for this life, we are more to be pitied than anyone in the world" (1 Cor 15:12-20). Paul asserts that "Death is swallowed up in victory" (1 Cor 15:54-55; a citation of Hos 13:14), and Daniel is assured (12:13) that the Old Testament saints will also be raised. Though he would die, Daniel could now rest, certain that one day he would rise to everlasting life and his own decreed inheritance. No doubt Daniel was glad to hear that God had decreed an inheritance for him. He had learned that what God has determined will happen in its appointed time.

BIBLIOGRAPHY

Abbott, Jacob

n.d. *Cyrus the Great.* Akron, OH: Werner.

Adler, W.

1996 The Apocalyptic Survey of History Adapted by Christians: Daniel's Prophecy of 70 Weeks. Pp. 201-238 in *The Jewish Apocalyptic Heritage in Early Christianity.* Editors, J. C. VanderKam and W. Adler. Assen / Minneapolis: Van Gorcum / Fortress.

Ahlström, G. W., G. O. Rollefson, and D. V. Edelman

1993 *The History of Ancient Palestine from the Palaeolithic Period to Alexander's Conquest.* Journal for the Study of the Old Testament Supplement 146. Sheffield: Sheffield Academic.

Albertz, Rainer

2001 The Social Setting of the Aramaic and Hebrew Book of Daniel. Pp. 171-204 in *The Book of Daniel: Composition and Reception*, vol. 1. Editors, J. J. Collins and P. Flint. Boston: Brill.

Alter, R. A.

1981 *The Art of Biblical Narrative.* New York: Basic.

Anderson, R. A.

1984 *Signs and Wonders: A Commentary on the Book of Daniel.* International Theological Commentary. Grand Rapids: Eerdmans.

Archer, Gleason L., Jr.

1958 *Jerome's Commentary on Daniel.* Grand Rapids: Baker.

1985 Daniel. Pp. 1-158 in *The Expositor's Bible Commentary*, vol. 7. Grand Rapids: Zondervan.

Arnold, Bill T., and Bryan E. Beyer

2002 *Readings from the Ancient Near East.* Grand Rapids: Baker Academic.

Baker, D. W.

1980 Further Examples of the *Waw Explicativum. Vetus Testamentum* 30:129-136.

Baldwin, Joyce

1978a *Daniel: An Introduction and Commentary.* Downers Grove, IL: InterVarsity.

1978b Is There Pseudonymity in the Old Testament? *Themelios* 4:6-12.

Balme, Maurice, and Gilbert Lawall

2003 *Athenaze: An Introduction to Ancient Greek*, books I-II. New York: Oxford University Press.

Barton, John

2001 Theological Ethics in Daniel. Pp. 661-670 in *The Book of Daniel: Composition and Reception*, vol. 2. Editors, J. J. Collins and P. Flint. Boston: Brill.

Beale, G. K.

1984 *The Use of Daniel in Jewish Apocalyptic Literature and in the Revelation of St. John.* Lanham, MD: University Press of America.

1986 A Reconsideration of the Texts of Daniel in the Apocalypse. *Biblica* 67:539-543.

Beale, G. K., and D. A. Carson, editors

2007 *Commentary on the New Testament Use of the Old Testament.* Grand Rapids: Baker Academic.

Beasley-Murray, G. R.

1983 The Interpretation of Daniel 7. *Catholic Biblical Quarterly* 45:44-58.

Beckwith, Roger T.

1985 *The Old Testament Canon of the New Testament Church.* Grand Rapids: Eerdmans.

Bertman, S.

2003 *Handbook to Life in Ancient Mesopotamia.* New York: Facts on File.

Boardman, John, Jasper Griffin, and Murray Oswyn

1986 *The Oxford History of the Classical World.* New York: Oxford.

Bowersock, G. W.

1965 *Augustus and the Greek World.* Oxford: Clarendon.

Brewer, D. I.
1991 Mene Mene Teqel Uparsin: Daniel 5:25 in Cuneiform. *Tyndale Bulletin* 42:311-316.

Broad, William J.
2006 *The Oracle: The Lost Secrets and Hidden Message of Ancient Delphi.* New York: Penguin.

Brown, Harold
1995 *Mesopotamia: The Mighty Kings.* New York: Time Life.

Bruce, F. F.
1988 *The Canon of Scripture.* Downers Grove, IL: InterVarsity.

Buchanan, George Wesley
1999 *The Book of Daniel.* The Mellen Biblical Commentary 25. Editor, G. W. Buchanan. Lewiston, NY: Edwin Mellen.

Bury, J. B.
2006 *The Ancient Greek Historians.* New York: Barnes & Noble. (Orig. pub. 1909.)

Cantor, Norman F.
2003 *Antiquity: From the Birth of Sumerian Civilization to the Fall of the Roman Empire.* New York: HarperCollins.

Caragounis, C. C.
1993 History and Supra-history: Daniel and the Four Empires. Pp. 387-397 in *The Book of Daniel in the Light of New Findings.* Editor, A. S. van der Woude. Leuven: University Press.

Carpenter, Eugene E.
1978 The Eschatology of Daniel Compared with the Eschatology of Selected Intertestamental Documents. Ph.D. diss., Fuller Theological Seminary.

2009 *Deuteronomy.* Pp. 418-547 in *Zondervan Illustrated Bible Backgrounds Commentary,* vol. 1. Editor, J. Walton. Grand Rapids: Zondervan.

Charlesworth, James H.
1983 *The Old Testament Pseudepigrapha,* vol. 1. New York: Doubleday.

1985 *The Old Testament Pseudepigrapha,* vol. 2. New York: Doubleday.

2002 *The Pesharim and Qumran History.* Grand Rapids: Eerdmans.

Chavalas, M.
2006 *The Ancient Near East.* Oxford: Blackwell.

Collins, John J.
1975 The Court Tales in Daniel and the Development of Apocalyptic. *Journal of Biblical Literature* 94:218-234.

1981 *Daniel, First Maccabees, Second Maccabees: With an Excursus on the Apocalyptic Genre.* Wilmington, DE: Michael Glazier.

1984 *Daniel: With an Introduction to Apocalyptic Literature.* The Forms of the Old Testament Literature 20. Editors, R. P. Knierim and G. M. Tucker. Grand Rapids: Eerdmans.

1989 *The Apocalyptic Imagination: An Introduction to the Jewish Matrix of Christianity.* New York: Crossroad.

1991 Genre, Ideology and Social Movements in Jewish Apocalypticism. Pp. 11-32 in *Mysteries and Revelations: Apocalyptic Studies since the Uppsala Colloquium.* Journal for the Study of the Pseudepigrapha Supplement 9. Editors, J. J. Collins and J. H. Charlesworth. Sheffield: Journal for the Study of the Old Testament Press.

1993 *Daniel.* Hermeneia. Minneapolis: Fortress.

1998a *The Apocalyptic Imagination: An Introduction to Jewish Apocalyptic Literature.* 2nd ed. Grand Rapids: Eerdmans.

1998b From Prophecy to Apocalypticism: The Expectation of the End. Pp. 129-161 in *The Encyclopedia of Apocalypticism, vol. 1: The Origins of Apocalypticism in Judaism and Christianity.* New York: Continuum.

2001 Current Issues in the Study of Daniel. Pp. 1-15 in *The Book of Daniel: Composition and Reception,* vol. 2. Editors, J. J. Collins and P. Flint. Boston: Brill.

Contenau, George
1954 *Everyday Life in Babylon and Assyria.* London: Arnold.

Cook, E. M.
1989 In the Plain of the Wall (Dan. 3:1). *Journal of Biblical Literature* 108:115-116.

Cook, J. M.
1983 *The Persian Empire*. London: Dent.

Cook, S. L.
1995 *Prophecy and Apocalypticism: The Postexilic Social Setting*. Minneapolis: Augsburg Fortress.

Coxon, Peter W.
1986 The Great Tree of Daniel 4. Pp. 91-111 in *A Word in Season*. Editors, James D. Martin and Philip R. Davies. Journal for the Study of the Old Testament Supplement 42. Sheffield: Journal for the Study of the Old Testament Press.

Currid, John D.
1997 *Ancient Egypt and the Old Testament*. Grand Rapids: Baker.

Davies, P. R.
1985 *Daniel*. Sheffield: Journal for the Study of the Old Testament Press.

Delcor, M.
1971 *Le Livre de Daniel*. Paris: Librairie Lecoffre.

Di Lella, A.
2001 The Textual History of Septuagint-Daniel and Theodotion-Daniel. Pp. 586-598 in *The Book of Daniel: Composition and Reception*, vol. 2. Editors, J. J. Collins and P. Flint. Boston: Brill.

Dillard, Raymond, and Tremper Longman III
2006 *An Introduction to the Old Testament*. Grand Rapids: Zondervan.

Doukhan, Jacques
1987 *Daniel: The Vision of the End*. Berrien Springs, MI: Andrews University Press.

Dougherty, R. P.
1929 Nabonidus and Belshazzar. *Yale Oriental Series* 15:61-79.

Dressler, H. H.
1979 The Identification of the Ugaritic Dnil with the Daniel of Ezekiel. *Vetus Testamentum* 29:153-161.

Driver, S. R.
1925 *An Introduction to the Literature of the Old Testament*. New York: Scribner's.

Dunn, James D. G.
2001 The Danielic Son of Man in the New Testament. Pp. 528-549 in *The Book of Daniel: Composition and Reception*, vol. 2. Editors, J. J. Collins and P. Flint. Boston: Brill.

Ellis, E. Earle
1988 The Old Testament Canon in the Early Church. Pp. 653-690 in *Mikra: Text, Translation, Reading, and Interpretation of the Hebrew Bible in Ancient Judaism and Early Christianity*. Editors, M. Mulder and H. Sysling. Philadelphia: Fortress.

Evans, Craig A.
2001 Daniel in the New Testament: Visions of God's Kingdom. Pp. 490-527 in *The Book of Daniel: Composition and Reception*, vol. 2. Editors, J. J. Collins and P. Flint. Boston: Brill.

Everitt, Anthony
2003 *Cicero*. New York: Random House.

Farber, W.
1995 Witchcraft, Magic, and Divination in Ancient Mesopotamia. Pp. 1895-1909 in *Civilizations of the Ancient Near East*. Editor, T. M. Sasson. New York: Scribner's.

Ferch, Arthur J.
1979 *The Son of Man in Daniel Seven*. Andrews University Seminary Doctoral Dissertation Series 6. Berrien Springs, MI: Andrews University Press.

1983 The Book of Daniel and the "Maccabean Thesis." *Andrews University Seminary Studies* 21:134-136.

Flint, Peter W.
2001 The Daniel Tradition at Qumran. Pp. 329-367 in *The Book of Daniel: Composition and Reception*, vol. 2. Editors, J. J. Collins and P. Flint. Boston: Brill.

Flint, Peter W., and Craig A. Evans
1997 *Eschatology, Messianism, and the Dead Sea Scrolls*. Grand Rapids: Eerdmans.

Flusser, David

1972 The Four Empires in the Fourth Sibyl and in the Book of Daniel. *Israel Oriental Society* 2:148-175.

Ford, Desmond

1978 *Daniel.* Nashville: Southern Publishing Association.

1979 *The Abomination of Desolation in Biblical Eschatology.* Washington, DC: University Press of America.

Gammie, John G.

1976 The Classification, Stages of Growth, and Changing Intentions in the Book of Daniel. *Journal of Biblical Literature* 95:191-204.

García-Martinez, Florentino

1996 *The Dead Sea Scrolls Translated.* Grand Rapids: Eerdmans.

Goldingay, John E.

1989 *Daniel.* Word Biblical Commentary 30. Waco: Word.

2001 Daniel in the Context of Old Testament Theology. Pp. 639-660 in *The Book of Daniel: Composition and Reception,* vol. 2. Editors, J. J. Collins and P. Flint. Boston: Brill.

Grabbe, L. L.

1988 Another Look at the Gestalt of "Darius the Mede." *Catholic Biblical Quarterly* 50:198-213.

1989 The Social Setting of Early Jewish Apocalypticism. *Journal for the Study of the Pseudepigrapha* 4:27-47.

2001 A Dan(iel) for All Seasons: For Whom Was Daniel Important? Pp. 229-246 in *The Book of Daniel: Composition and Reception,* vol. 1. Editors, J. J. Collins and P. Flint. Boston: Brill.

Grainger, J. D.

2007 *Alexander the Great Failure: The Collapse of the Macedonian Empire.* London: Hambledon Continuum.

Grant, Michael

1970 *The Ancient Historians.* New York: Charles Scribner's Sons.

1992 *Readings in the Classical Historians.* New York: Charles Scribner's Sons.

Grayson, A. K., and W. G. Lambert

1964 Akkadian Prophecies. *Journal of Cuneiform Studies* 18:7-30.

Green, Peter

2007 *The Hellenistic Age.* New York: Modern Library.

Gurney, R. M.

1981 The Seventy Weeks of Daniel 9:24-27. *Evangelical Quarterly* 53:29-36.

Hallo, W. W.

1966 Akkadian Apocalypses. *Israel Exploration Journal* 16:231-242.

Hallo, William W., and William K. Simpson

1971 *The Ancient Near East: A History.* New York: Harcourt Brace Jovanovich.

Hanson, Paul D.

1979 *The Dawn of Apocalyptic: The Historical and Sociological Roots of Jewish Apocalyptic Eschatology.* Rev. ed. Philadelphia: Fortress.

Hanson, V. D.

1999 *The Wars of the Ancient Greeks: And Their Invention of Western Military Culture.* London: Cassell.

Harrison, R. K.

1969 *Introduction to the Old Testament.* Grand Rapids: Eerdmans.

Hartman, Louis F., and Alexander Di Lella

1978 *The Book of Daniel.* Anchor Bible 23. New York: Doubleday.

Hasel, Gerard

1976 The First and Third Years of Belshazzar (Dan. 7:1; 8:1). *Andrews University Seminary Studies* 15:153-168.

Heiser, Michael S.

2001 Deuteronomy 32:8 and the Sons of God. *Bibliotheca Sacra* 158:54-74.

Hess, Richard S.

2007 *Israelite Religions.* Grand Rapids: Baker Academic.

Holladay, William Lee

1988 *A Concise Hebrew and Aramaic Lexicon of the Old Testament: Based upon the Lexical Work of Ludwig Koehler and Walter Baumgartner.* Grand Rapids: Eerdmans.

Josephus, Flavius
1960 *Josephus: The Complete Works.* Translator, William Whiston. Grand Rapids: Kregel.

Kaiser, Walter C.
1995 *The Messiah in the Old Testament.* Grand Rapids: Zondervan.
1998 *A History of Israel.* Nashville: Broadman & Holman.

Kalafian, Michael
1991 *The Prophecy of the Seventy Weeks of the Book of Daniel.* New York: University Press of America.

King, Philip J., and Lawrence E. Stager
2001 *Life in Biblical Israel.* Louisville: Westminster John Knox.

Kitchen, K. A.
1965 *Notes on Some Problems in the Book of Daniel.* London: Tyndale Press.
2003 *On the Reliability of the Old Testament.* Grand Rapids: Eerdmans.

Klein, Ralph W.
1979 *Israel in Exile.* Philadelphia: Fortress.

Knibb, Michael
2001 The Book of Daniel in Its Context. Pp. 16-35 in *The Book of Daniel: Composition and Reception,* vol. 1. Editors, J. J. Collins and P. Flint. Boston: Brill.

Koch, Klaus
1985 Is Daniel Also among the Prophets? *Interpretation* 39:117-130.

Kraft, Robert A., and George W. E. Nickelsburg
1986 *Early Judaism and Its Modern Interpreters.* Philadelphia: Fortress.

Kuhrt, A.
1995 *The Ancient Near East: ca. 3000–330 BC.* London: Routledge.

Lacocque, André
1979 *The Book of Daniel.* Translator, David Pellaver. Atlanta: John Knox.

LaSor, William S., Frederic Bush, and David Hubbard
1996 *Survey of the Old Testament.* 2nd ed. Grand Rapids: Eerdmans.

Lawson, Jack N.
1997 "The God Who Reveals Secrets": The Mesopotamian Background to Daniel 2.47. *Journal for the Study of the Old Testament* 22:61-76.

Leupold, H. C.
1969 *Exposition of Daniel.* Grand Rapids: Baker.

Lewis, Jon E., editor
2003 *The Mammoth Book of Eyewitness Ancient Egypt.* New York: Caroll & Graf.
2007 *The Mammoth Book of Eyewitness Ancient Rome.* Philadelphia: Running.

Longman, Tremper, III
1991 *Fictional Akkadian Autobiography: A Generic and Comparative Study.* Winona Lake, IN: Eisenbrauns.
1999 *Daniel.* The NIV Application Commentary. Grand Rapids: Zondervan.

Lucas, E. C.
1990 The Sources of Daniel's Animal Imagery. *Tyndale Bulletin* 41:161-185.
2000 Daniel: Resolving the Enigma. *Vetus Testamentum* 50:66-80.
2002 *Daniel.* Tyndale Old Testament Commentary. Downers Grove, IL: InterVarsity.
2009 Daniel. Pp. 518-575 in *Zondervan Illustrated Bible Backgrounds Commentary,* vol. 4. Editor, John Walton. Grand Rapids: Zondervan.

McComiskey, T. E.
1985 The Seventy "Weeks" of Daniel against the Background of Ancient Near Eastern Literature. *Westminster Theological Journal* 47:18-45.

Meadowcroft, T. J.
1995 *Aramaic Daniel and Greek Daniel: A Literary Comparison.* Journal for the Study of the Old Testament Supplement 198. Editors, D. A. Clines and P. R. Davies. Sheffield: Sheffield Academic Press.

Merrill, Eugene H.
1986 Daniel as a Contribution to Kingdom Theology. Pp. 211-225 in *Essays in Honor of J. Dwight Pentecost.* Editors, Stanley D. Touissant and Charles H. Dyer. Chicago: Moody.

1991 A Theology of Ezekiel and Daniel. Pp. 365-395 in *A Biblical Theology of the Old Testament*. Editor, Roy B. Zuck. Chicago: Moody.

Milik, J. T.
1956 Piére de Nabonide et autres écrite d'un Cycle de Daniel. *Revue Biblique* 63:407-415.

Millard, A. R.
1977 Daniel 1-6 and History. *Evangelical Quarterly* 49:67-73.

Miller, Stephen R.
1994 *Daniel*. New American Commentary. Nashville: Broadman & Holman.

Mitchell, T. C.
1992 The Music of the Old Testament Reconsidered. *Palestine Exploration Quarterly* 124:124-143.

Mitchell, T. C., and R. Joyce
1965 The Musical Instruments in Nebuchadnezzar's Orchestra. Pp. 19-27 in *Notes on Some Problems in the Book of Daniel*. Editor, D. J. Wiseman. London: Tyndale.

Montgomery, James A.
1927 *The Book of Daniel*. New York: Scribner's Sons.

Mulder, Martin, and Henry Sysling, editors
1988 *Mikra: Text, Translation, Reading, and Interpretation of the Hebrew Bible in Ancient Judaism and Early Christianity*. Philadelphia: Fortress.

Niditch, S., and R. Doran
1977 The Success Story of the Wise Courtier: A Formal Approach. *Journal of Biblical Literature* 96:179-193.

Niehaus, J. J.
1995 *God at Sinai: Covenant and Theophany in the Bible and Ancient Near East*. Grand Rapids: Zondervan.

Oates, Joan
1986 *Babylon*. New York: Thames & Hudson.

Olmstead, A. T.
1948 *History of the Persian Empire*. Chicago: University of Chicago Press.

Oppenheim, A. Leo
1956 The Interpretation of Dreams in the Ancient Near East. *Transactions of the American Philosophical Society* 46:179-373.

1977 *Ancient Mesopotamia: Portrait of a Dead Civilization*. Chicago: University of Chicago Press.

Patterson, Richard
1993 Holding on to Daniel's Court Tales. *Journal of Evangelical Theological Society* 36:445-454.

Paul, S. M.
2001 The Mesopotamian Babylonian Background of Daniel 1-6. Pp. 55-68 in *The Book of Daniel: Composition and Reception*, vol. 1. Editors, J. J. Collins and P. Flint. Boston: Brill.

Péter-Contesse, René, and John Ellington
1993 *A Handbook on the Book of Daniel*. UBS Handbook Series. New York: United Bible Societies.

Pfeiffer, Robert H.
1952 *Introduction to the Old Testament*. London: Black.

Plutarch
1986 *The Age of Alexander*. Translator, Ian Scott-Kilvert. New York: Viking Penguin.

Polak, F.
1993 The Daniel Tales in Their Aramaic Literary Milieu. Pp. 249-265 in *The Book of Daniel in the Light of New Findings*. Editor, A. S. van der Woude. Leuven: University Press.

Porteous, Norman
1965 *Daniel*. Philadelphia: Westminster.

Price, Randall
1996 *Secrets of the Dead Sea Scrolls*. Eugene, OR: Harvest.

Provan, I., V. P. Long, and T. Longman III
2003 *A Biblical History of Israel*. Louisville: Westminster John Knox.

Robinson, Theodore H.
1979 *Prophecy and the Prophets*. 3rd ed. London: Duckworth.

Rodgers, Nigel

2008 *The Rise and Fall of Ancient Rome.* London: Hermes House.

Rowley, H. H.

1949 The Unity of the Book of Daniel. Pp. 247-280 in *The Servant of the Lord and Other Essays in the Old Testament.* 2nd ed. Oxford: Blackwell.

Saggs, H. W. F.

1962 *The Greatness That Was Babylon.* New York: Hawthorne.

Sailhamer, John

1990 Genesis. Pp. 1-284 in *The Expositor's Bible Commentary*, vol. 2. Editor, Frank E. Gaebelein. Grand Rapids: Zondervan.

Sandy, D. Brent, and Daniel M. O'Hare

2007 *Prophecy and Apocalyptic.* Grand Rapids: Baker Academic.

Santoso, Agus

2007 *Die Apokalyptik als jüdische Denkbewegung: Eine literarkritische Untersuchung zum Buch Daniel.* Marburg: Tectum-Verlag.

Schiffman, Lawrence

1995 *Reclaiming the Dead Sea Scrolls.* New York: Doubleday.

Schlegel, Catherine M., and Henry Weinfeld, editors

2006 *Theogony; and, Works and Days. Hesiod; Translated and with Introductions by Catherine M. Schlegel and Henry Weinfield.* Ann Arbor: University of Michigan Press.

Schultz, Brian

2007 The Kittim of Assyria. *Revue de Qumran* 23/1:63-77.

Seow., C. L.

2003 *Daniel.* Louisville: Westminster John Knox.

2004 The Rule of God in the Book of Daniel. Pp. 219-246 in *David and Zion: Biblical Studies in Honor of J. J. M. Roberts.* Winona Lake, IN: Eisenbrauns.

Shea, W. H.

1971 An Unrecognized Vassal King of Babylon in the Early Achaemenid Period. *Andrews University Seminary Studies* 9:51-57.

1972 Darius the Mede. *Andrews University Seminary Studies* 10:177.

1982 Darius the Mede. *Andrews University Seminary Studies* 20:229-247.

1991 Darius the Mede in His Persian-Babylonian Setting. *Andrews University Seminary Studies* 29:235-257.

Shipley, Graham

2000 *The Greek World after Alexander, 323–30 B.C.* New York: Routledge.

Sim, D. C.

1995 The Social Setting of Ancient Apocalypticism: A Question of Method. *Journal for the Study of the Pseudepigrapha* 13:5-16.

Soden, Wolfram von

1992 *The Ancient Orient.* Translator, Donald G. Schley. Grand Rapids: Eerdmans.

Soggin, Albert O.

1980 *Introduction to the Old Testament.* Philadelphia: Westminster.

Starr, Chester

1991 *A History of the Ancient World.* New York: Oxford.

Stefanovic, Zdravko

1992 *The Aramaic of Daniel in the Light of Old Aramaic.* Journal for the Study of the Old Testament Supplement 129. Sheffield: Journal for the Study of the Old Testament Press.

Stuckenbruck, Loren T.

2001 Daniel and Early Enoch Traditions in the Dead Sea Scrolls. Pp. 368-386 in *The Book of Daniel: Composition and Reception*, vol. 2. Editors, J. J. Collins and P. Flint. Boston: Brill.

Swain, J. W.

1940 The Theory of Four Monarchies: Opposition History under the Roman Empire. *Classical Philology* 35:1-21.

Tcherikover, Victor
1959 *Hellenistic Civilization of the Jews.* New York: Atheneum.

Thomas, D. Winston
1961 *Documents from Old Testament Times.* New York: Harper & Row.

Ulrich, Eugene
2001 The Text of Daniel in the Qumran Scrolls. Pp. 573-585 in *The Book of Daniel: Composition and Reception,* vol. 2. Editors, J. J. Collins and P. Flint. Boston: Brill.

Wallace, Ronald S.
1979 *The Message of Daniel.* Downers Grove, IL: InterVarsity.

Waltke, Bruce K., and M. O'Connor
1990 *An Introduction to Biblical Hebrew Syntax.* Winona Lake, IN: Eisenbrauns.

Walton, John H.
1986 The Four Kingdoms of Daniel. *Journal of the Evangelical Theological Society* 29:25-36.
1988 The Decree of Darius the Mede in Daniel 6. *Journal of the Evangelical Theological Society* 31:279-286.
1992 *Ancient Israelite Literature in Its Cultural Context.* Grand Rapids: Zondervan.
2001 The Anzu Myth as Relevant Background for Daniel 7. Pp. 69-89 in *The Book of Daniel: Composition and Reception,* vol. 2. Editors, J. J. Collins and P. Flint. Boston: Brill.

Ward-Perkins, Bryan
2006 *The Fall of Rome and the End of Civilization.* Oxford: Oxford University Press.

Wenham, David
1987 The Kingdom of God and Daniel. *Expository Times* 98:132-134.

Wenham, Gordon J.
1977 Daniel: The Basic Issues. *Themelios* 2:49-52.

Whitcomb, John C.
1959 *Darius the Mede.* Grand Rapids: Eerdmans.

Wilson, Gerald H.
1985 Wisdom in Daniel and in the Origin of Apocalyptic. *Hebrew Annual Review* 9:373-381.

Wilson, R. D.
1917 The Title "King of Persia" in the Scriptures. *Princeton Theological Review* 15:90-145.

Wiseman, D. J.
1961 *Chronicles of Chaldean Kings (626–556 BC).* London: The Trustees of the British Museum.
1965 *Notes on Some Problems in the Book of Daniel.* London: Tyndale Press.
1985 *Nebuchadnezzar and Babylon.* Oxford: Oxford University Press.

Wolters, Al
1991 The Riddle of the Scales in Daniel 5. *Hebrew Union College Annual* 62:155-177.

Wood, Leon
1973 *A Commentary on Daniel.* Grand Rapids: Zondervan.

Yamauchi, Edwin C.
1980 Hermeneutical Issues in the Book of Daniel. *Journal of the Evangelical Theological Society* 23:14-22.
1981 Daniel and Contacts between the Aegean and the Near East before Alexander. *Evangelical Quarterly* 53:37-47.
1990 *Persia and the Bible.* Grand Rapids: Baker.

Young, E. J.
1949 *The Prophecy of Daniel.* Grand Rapids: Eerdmans.
1955 *My Servants the Prophets.* Grand Rapids: Eerdmans.

Zadok, R.
1984 The Origin of the Name Shinar. *Zeitschrift für die alttestamentliche Wissenschaft* 74:240-244.